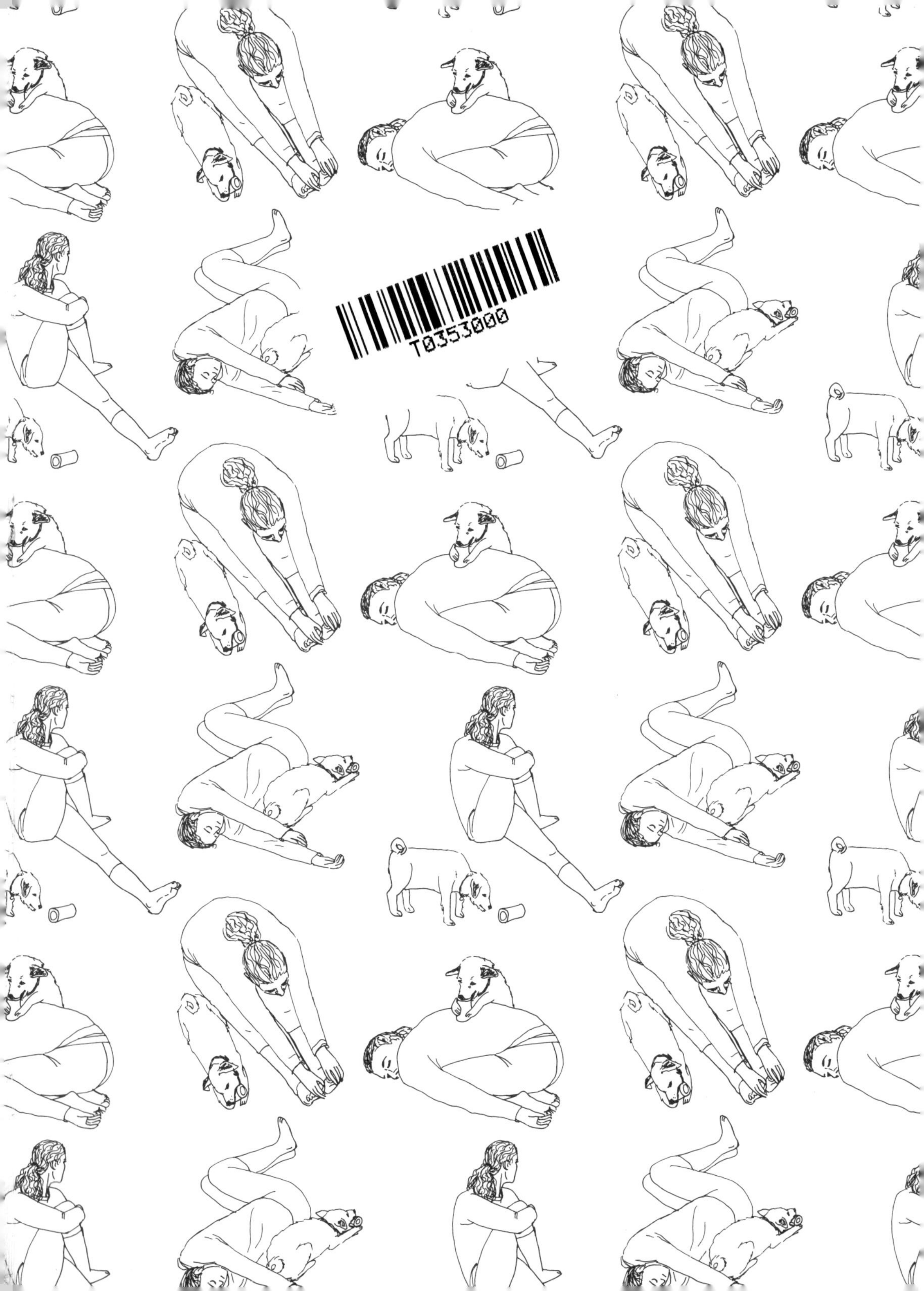

Dedicated to Scott, Xia, Mom, Dad, and Amie.

Thank you to everyone at Drawn & Quarterly!

Thank you to my family and friends!

Keiler Roberts has also written *My Begging Chart,* and is co-author of *Creepy* together with Lee Sensenbrenner.

This book is a collection of previously published work and includes material from *Powdered Milk* (2012), *Miseryland* (2015), *Sunburning* (2017), *Chlorine Gardens* (2018), and *Rat Time* (2019).

drawnandquarterly.com
keilerroberts.com

MIX Paper from responsible sources FSC® C104723

ISBN 978-1-77046-622-7 | First edition: October 2022
Printed in China | 10 9 8 7 6 5 4 3 2 1

Cataloguing data available from Library and Archives Canada.

Published in the USA by Drawn & Quarterly, a client publisher of Farrar, Straus and Giroux. Published in Canada by Drawn & Quarterly, a client publisher of Raincoast Books. Published in the United Kingdom by Drawn & Quarterly, a client publisher of Publishers Group UK.

THE JOY OF QUITTING

KEILER ROBERTS

Drawn & Quarterly

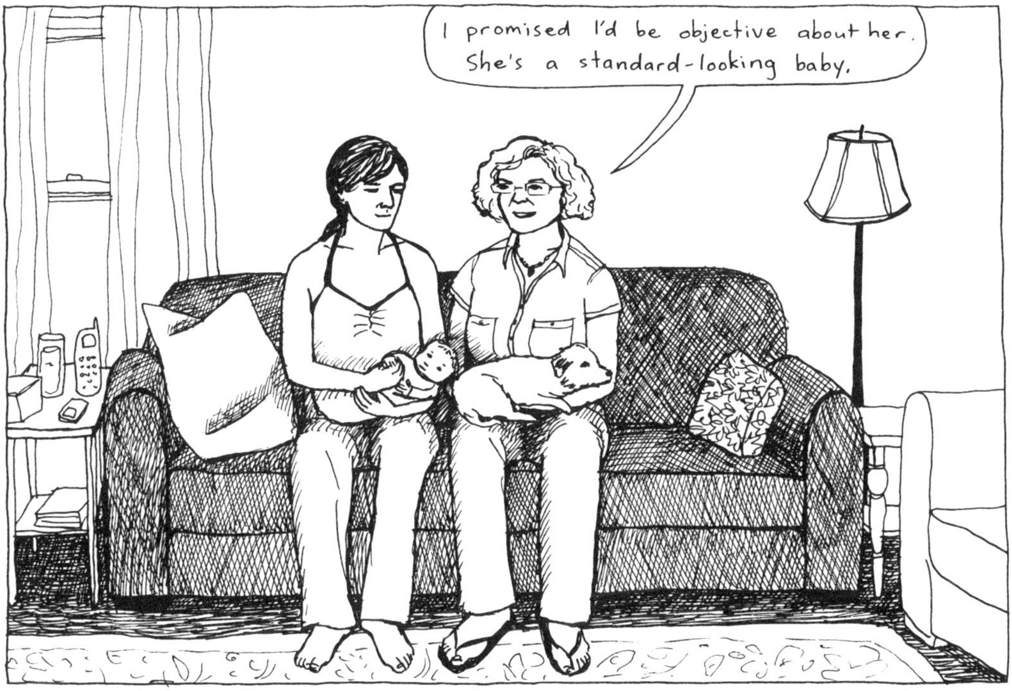
I promised I'd be objective about her. She's a standard-looking baby.

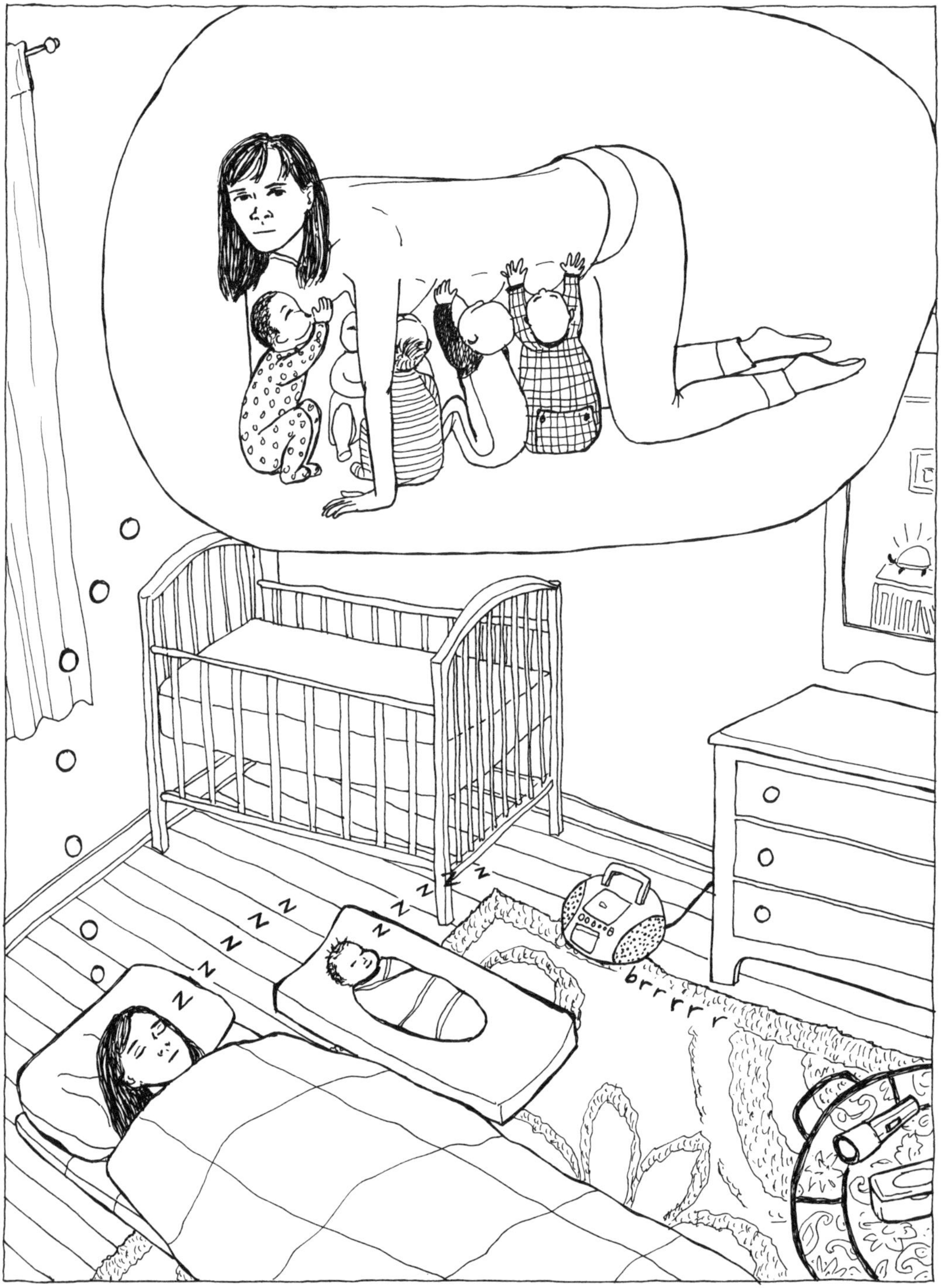
Z Z Z Z Z Z Z Z
Z Z Z Z
brrrrr

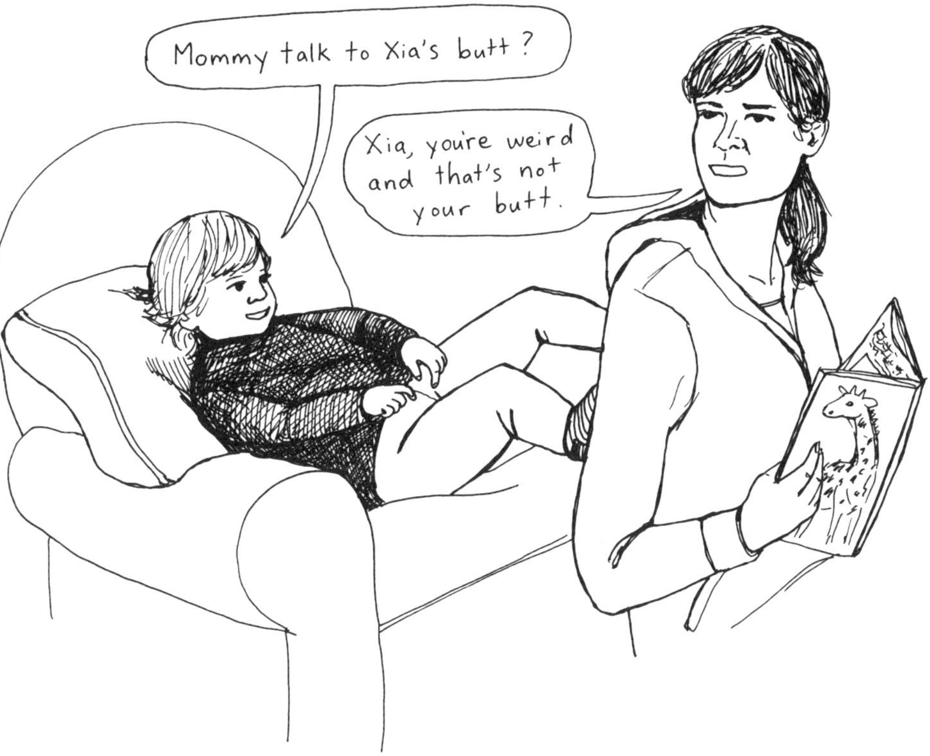
Mommy talk to Xia's butt?
Xia, you're weird and that's not your butt.

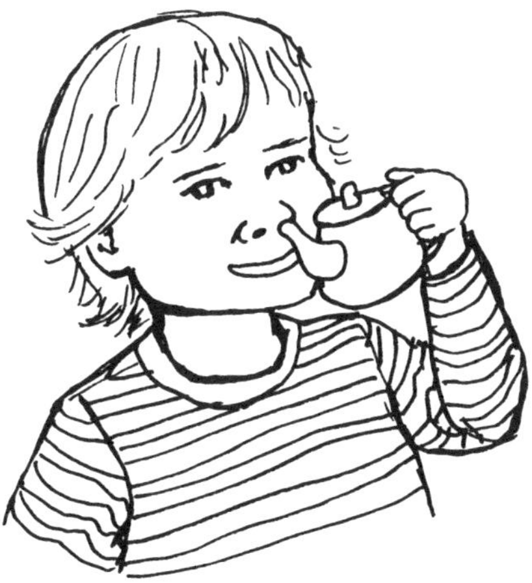

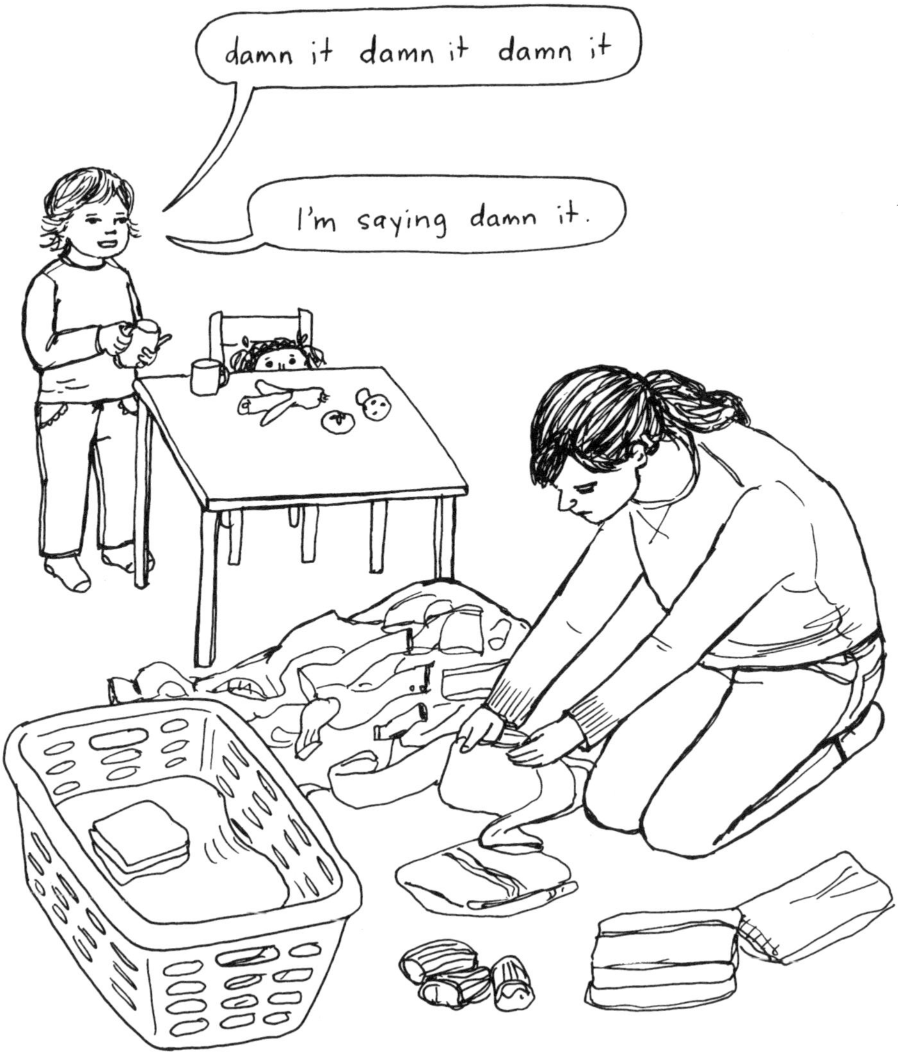
damn it damn it damn it
I'm saying damn it.

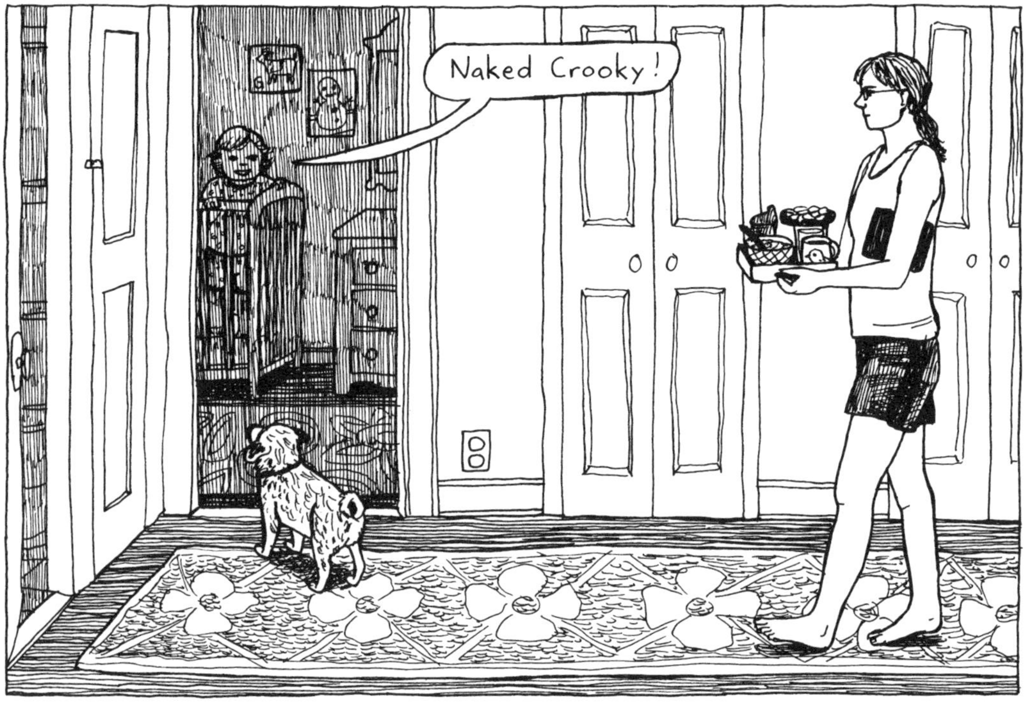
Naked Crooky!

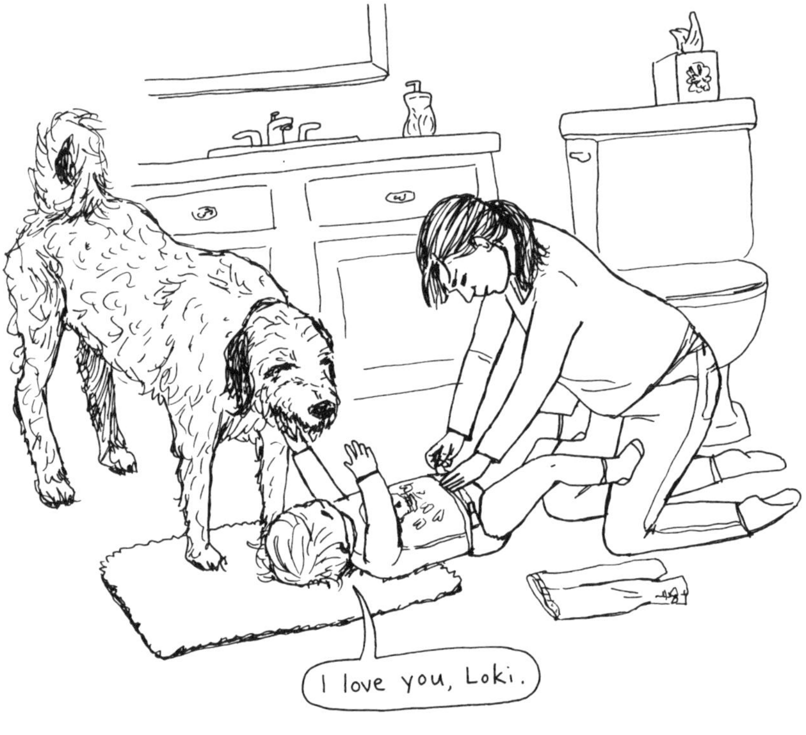
I love you, Loki.

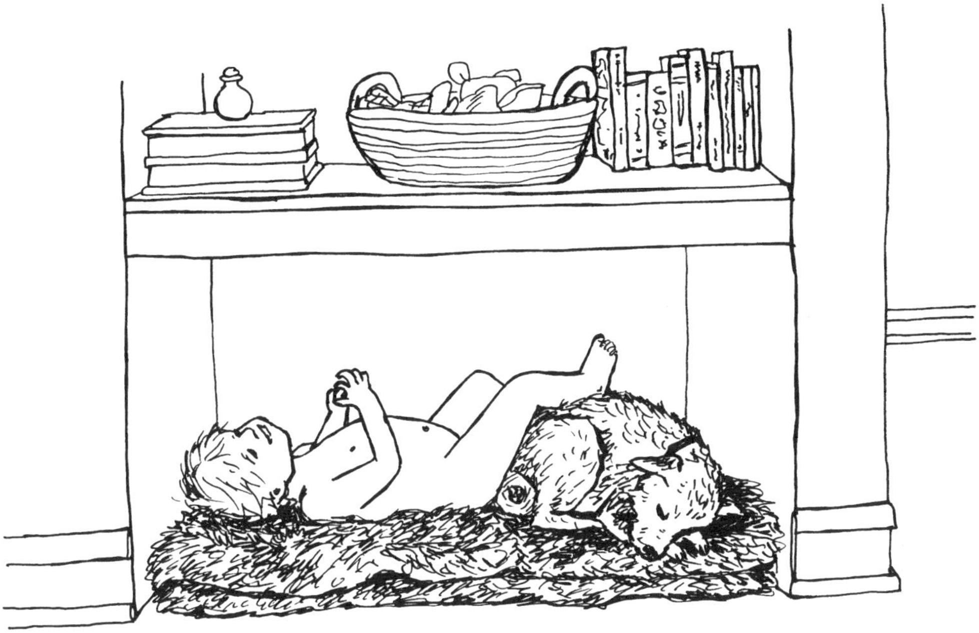

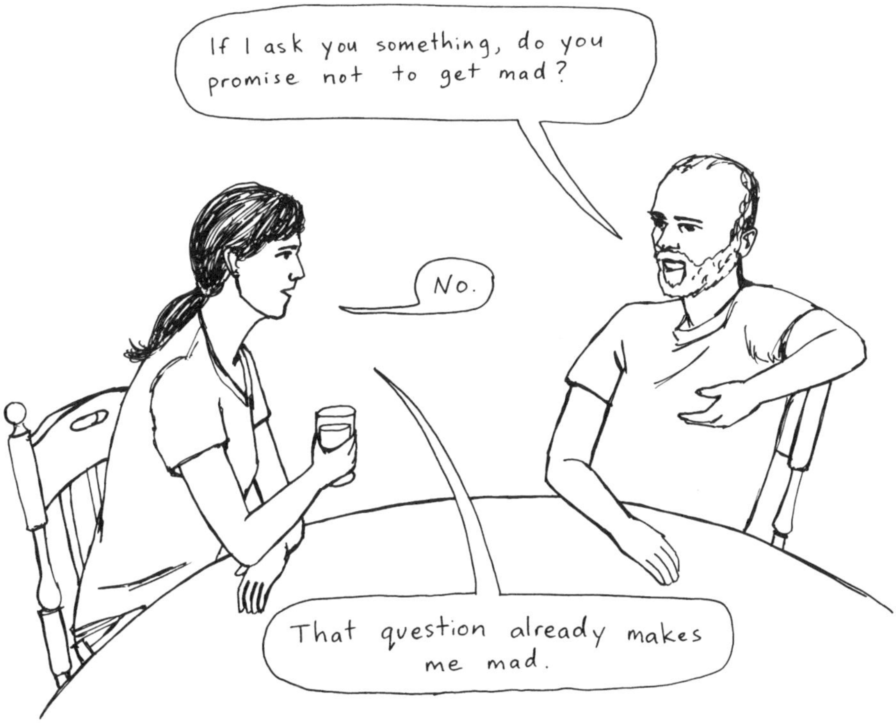
If I ask you something, do you promise not to get mad?
No.
That question already makes me mad.

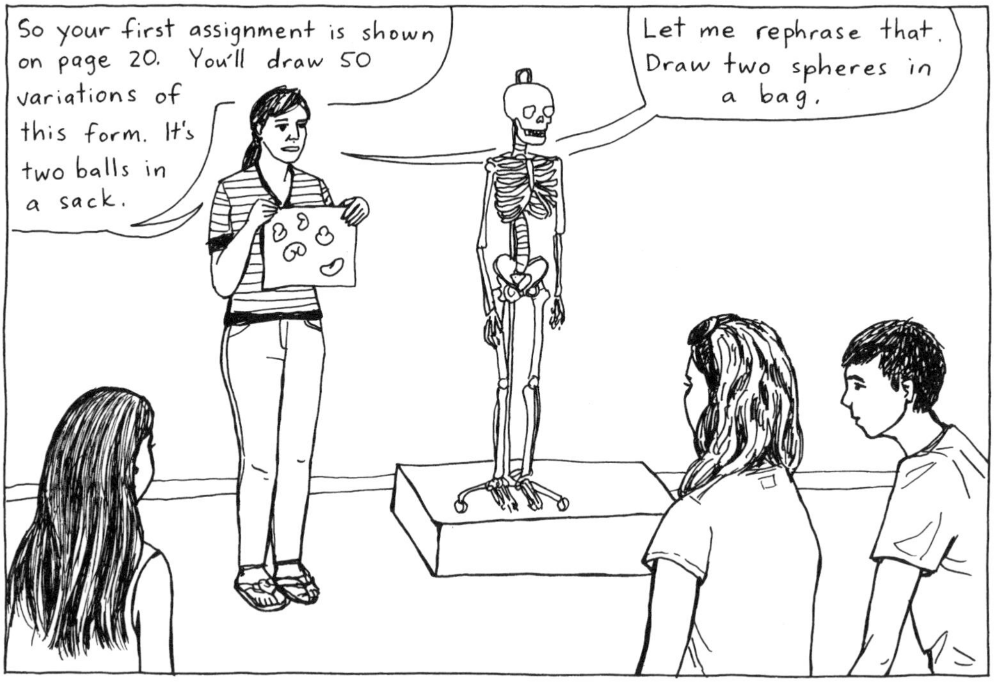
So your first assignment is shown on page 20. You'll draw 50 variations of this form. It's two balls in a sack.
Let me rephrase that. Draw two spheres in a bag.

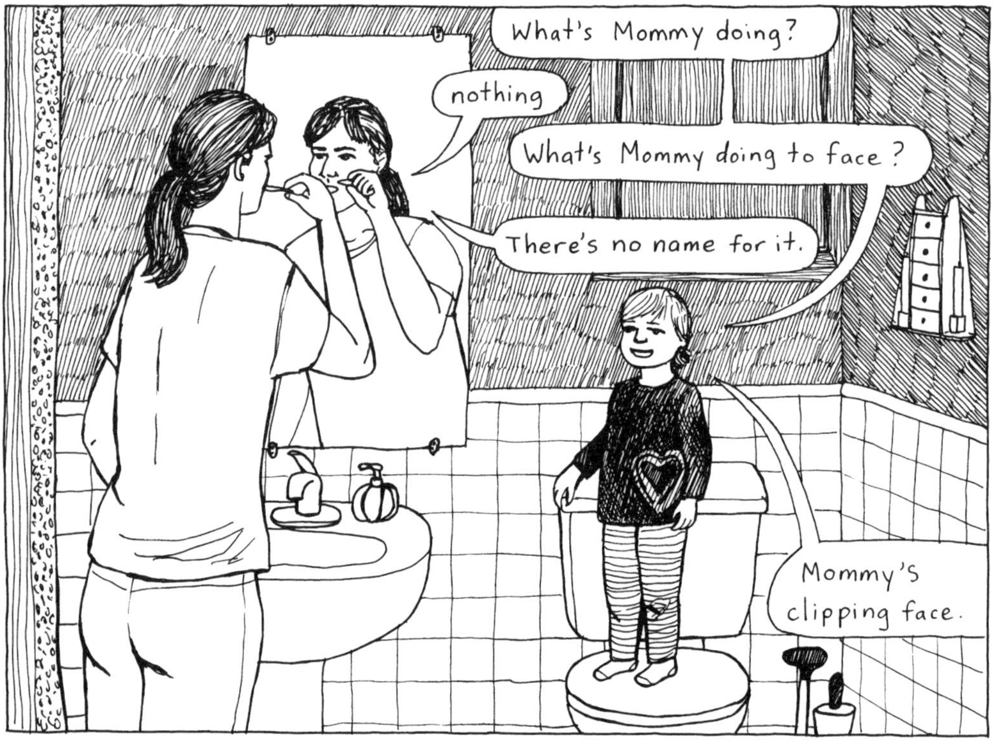
What's Mommy doing?
nothing
What's Mommy doing to face?
There's no name for it.
Mommy's clipping face.

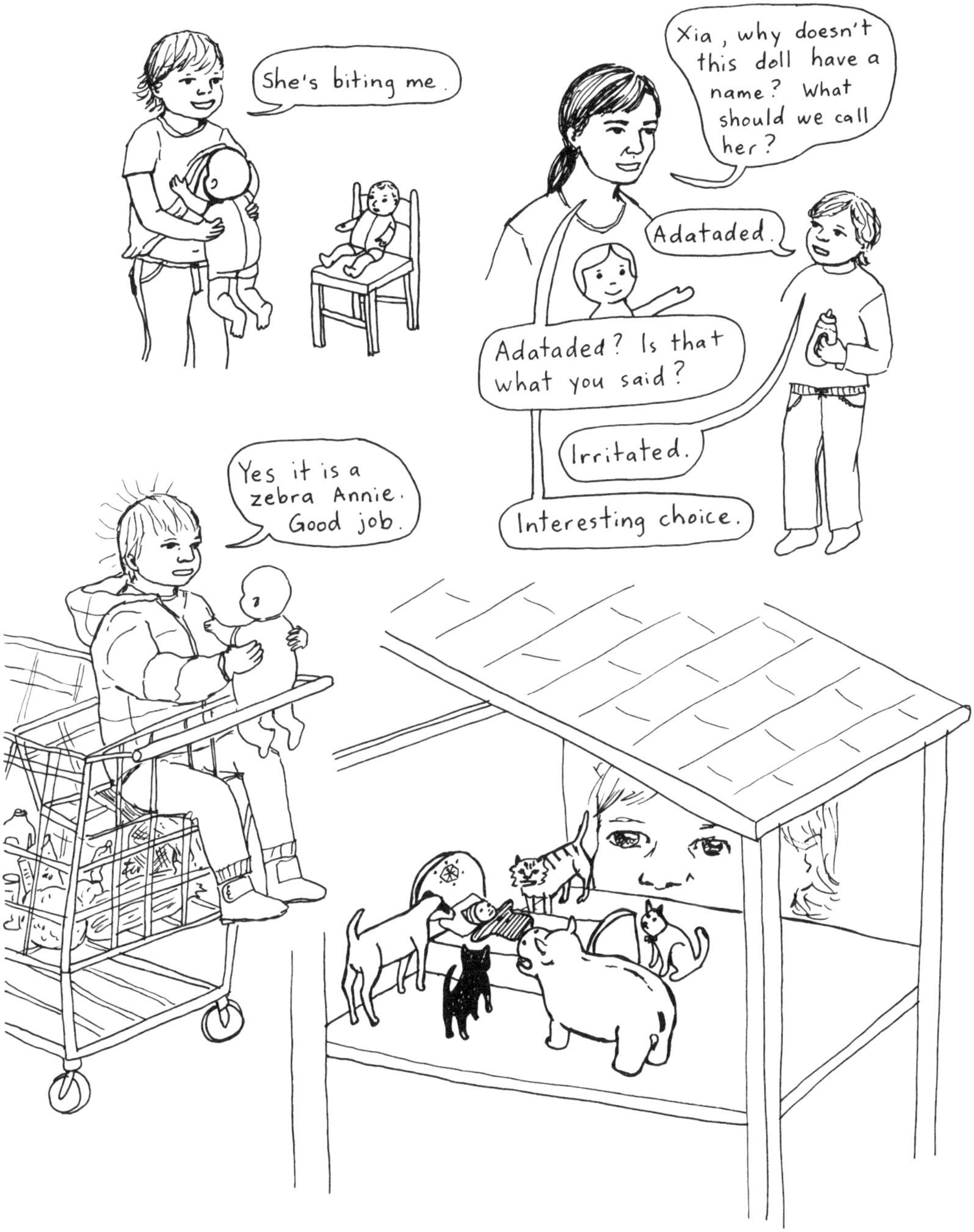
She's biting me.
Xia, why doesn't this doll have a name? What should we call her?
Adataded.
Adataded? Is that what you said?
Irritated.
Interesting choice.
Yes it is a zebra Annie. Good job.

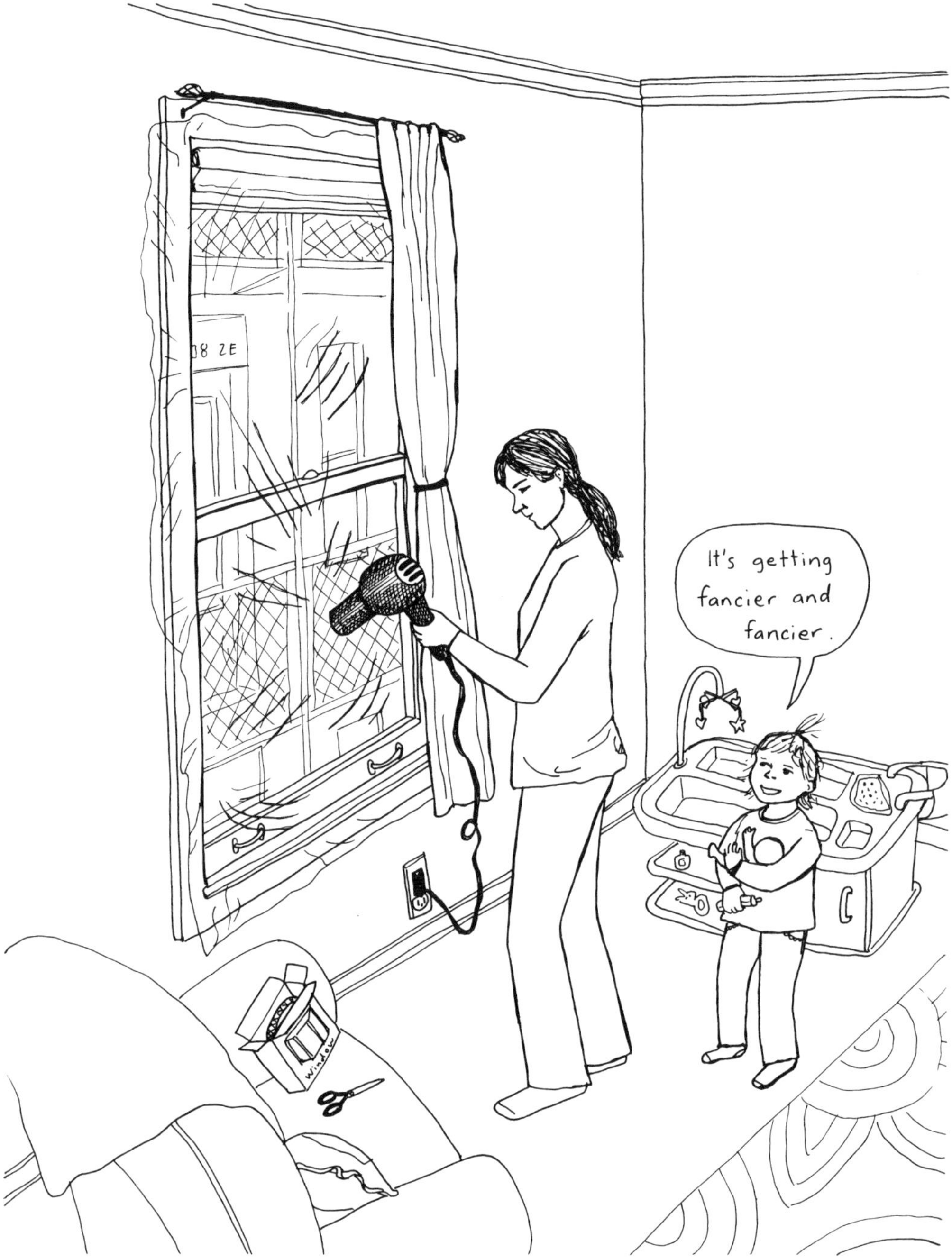
It's getting fancier and fancier.
Window

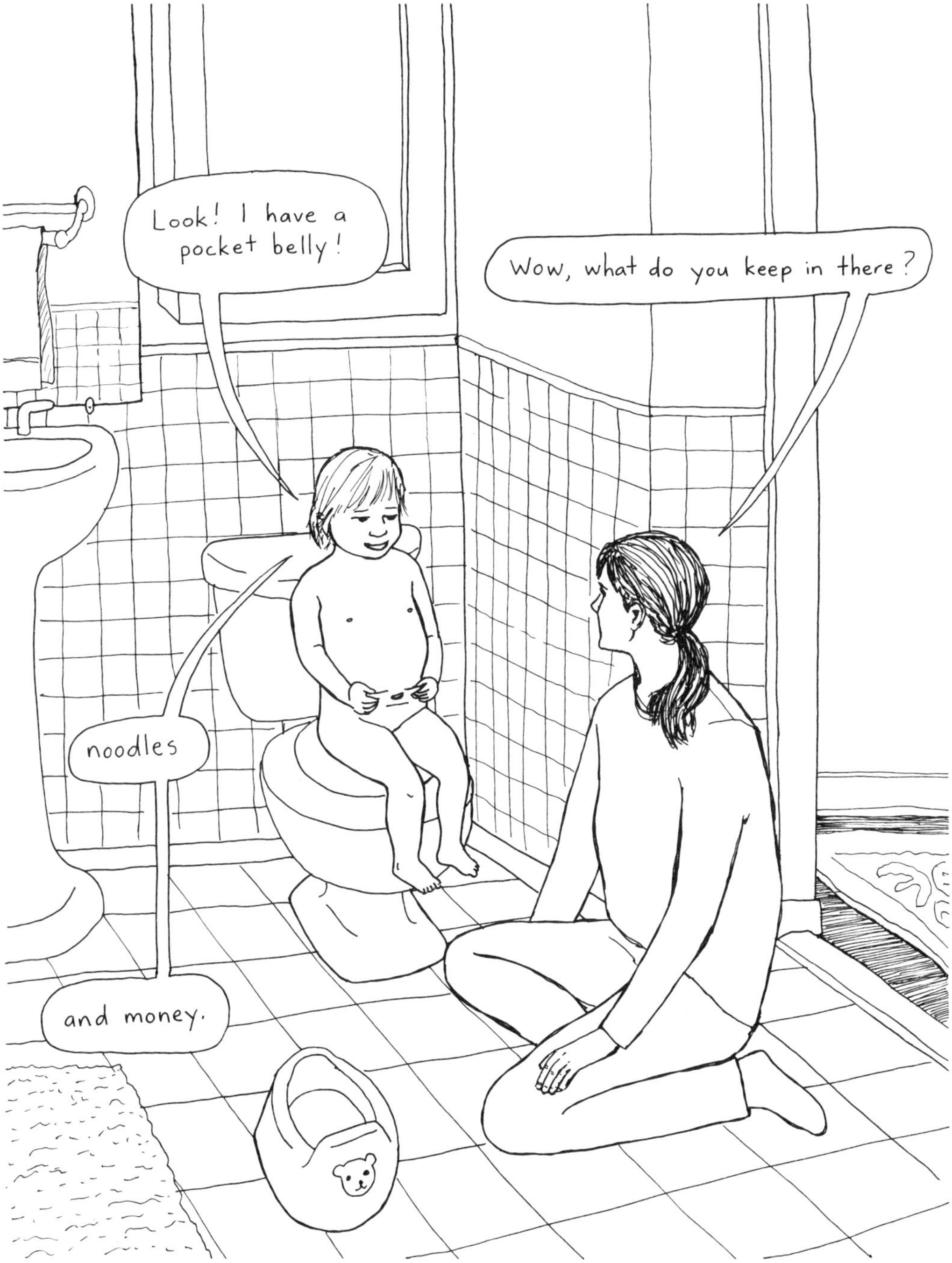
Look! I have a pocket belly!
Wow, what do you keep in there?
noodles
and money.

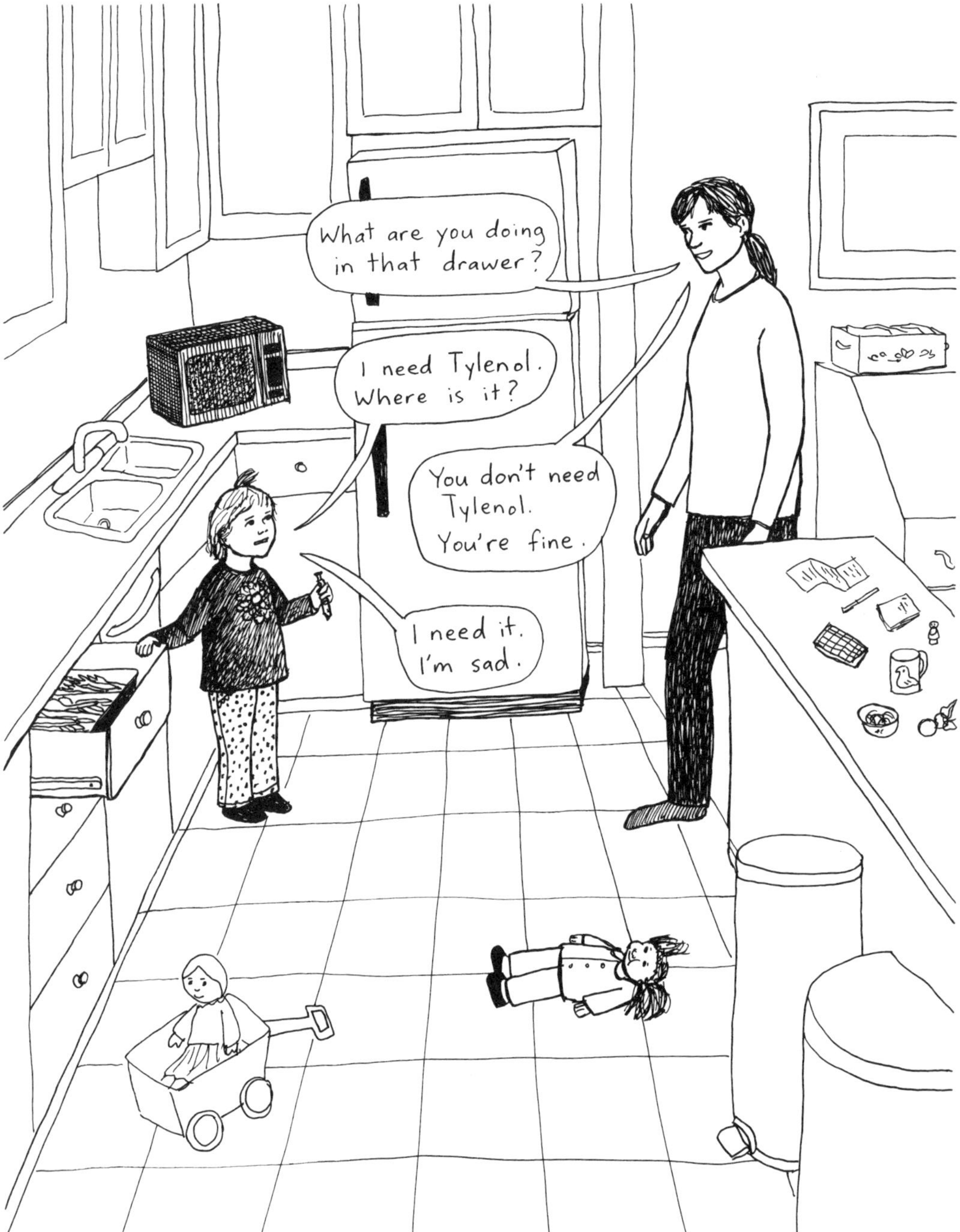
What are you doing in that drawer?
I need Tylenol. Where is it?
You don't need Tylenol. You're fine.
I need it. I'm sad.

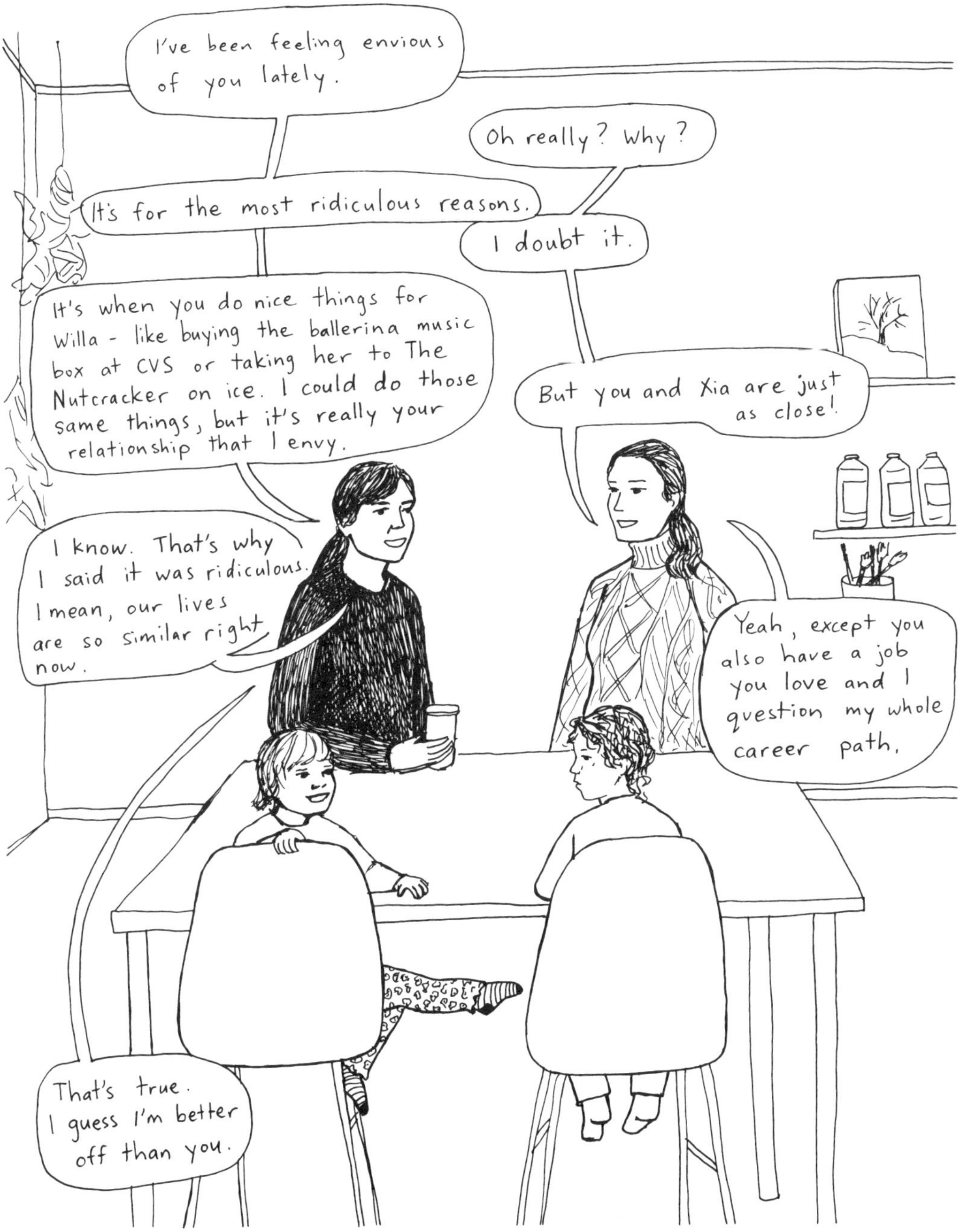
I've been feeling envious of you lately.
Oh really? Why?
It's for the most ridiculous reasons.
I doubt it.
It's when you do nice things for Willa - like buying the ballerina music box at CVS or taking her to The Nutcracker on ice. I could do those same things, but it's really your relationship that I envy.
But you and Xia are just as close!
I know. That's why I said it was ridiculous. I mean, our lives are so similar right now.
Yeah, except you also have a job you love and I question my whole career path.
That's true. I guess I'm better off than you.

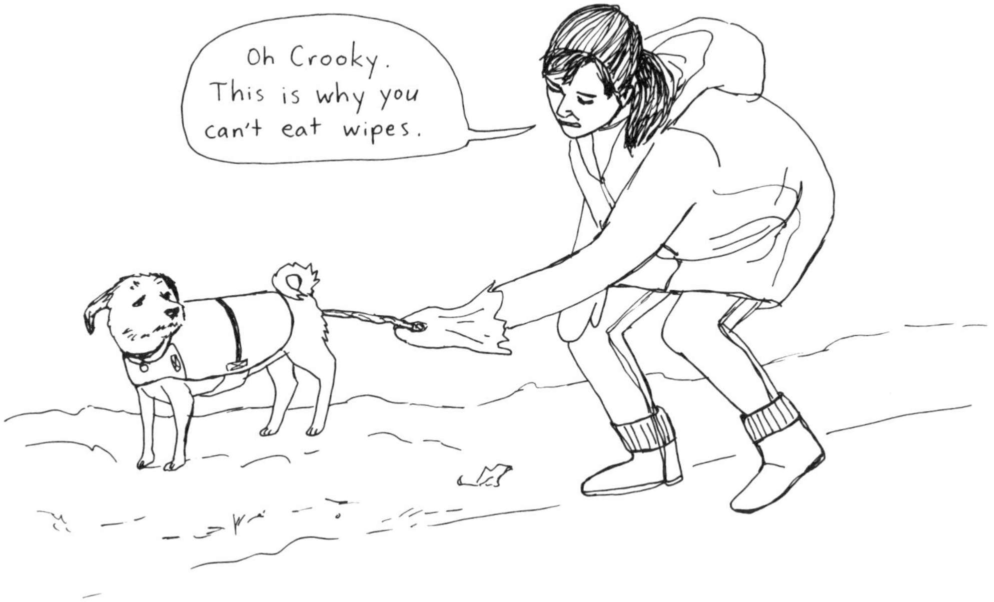
Oh Crooky. This is why you can't eat wipes.

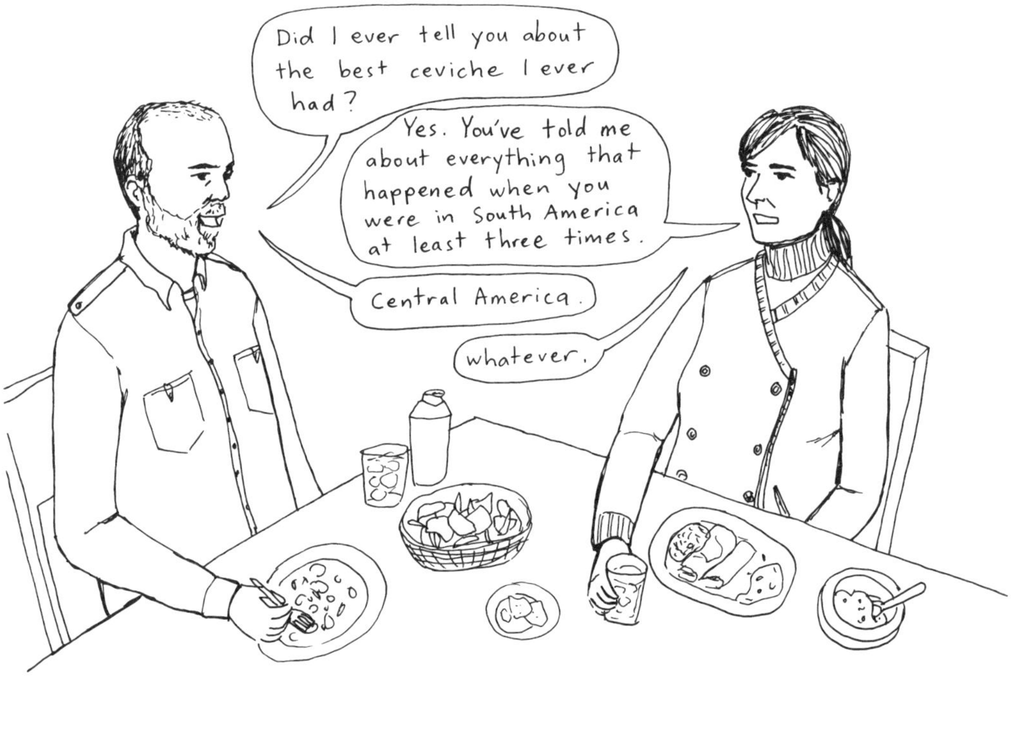
Did I ever tell you about the best ceviche I ever had?
Yes. You've told me about everything that happened when you were in South America at least three times.
Central America.
whatever.

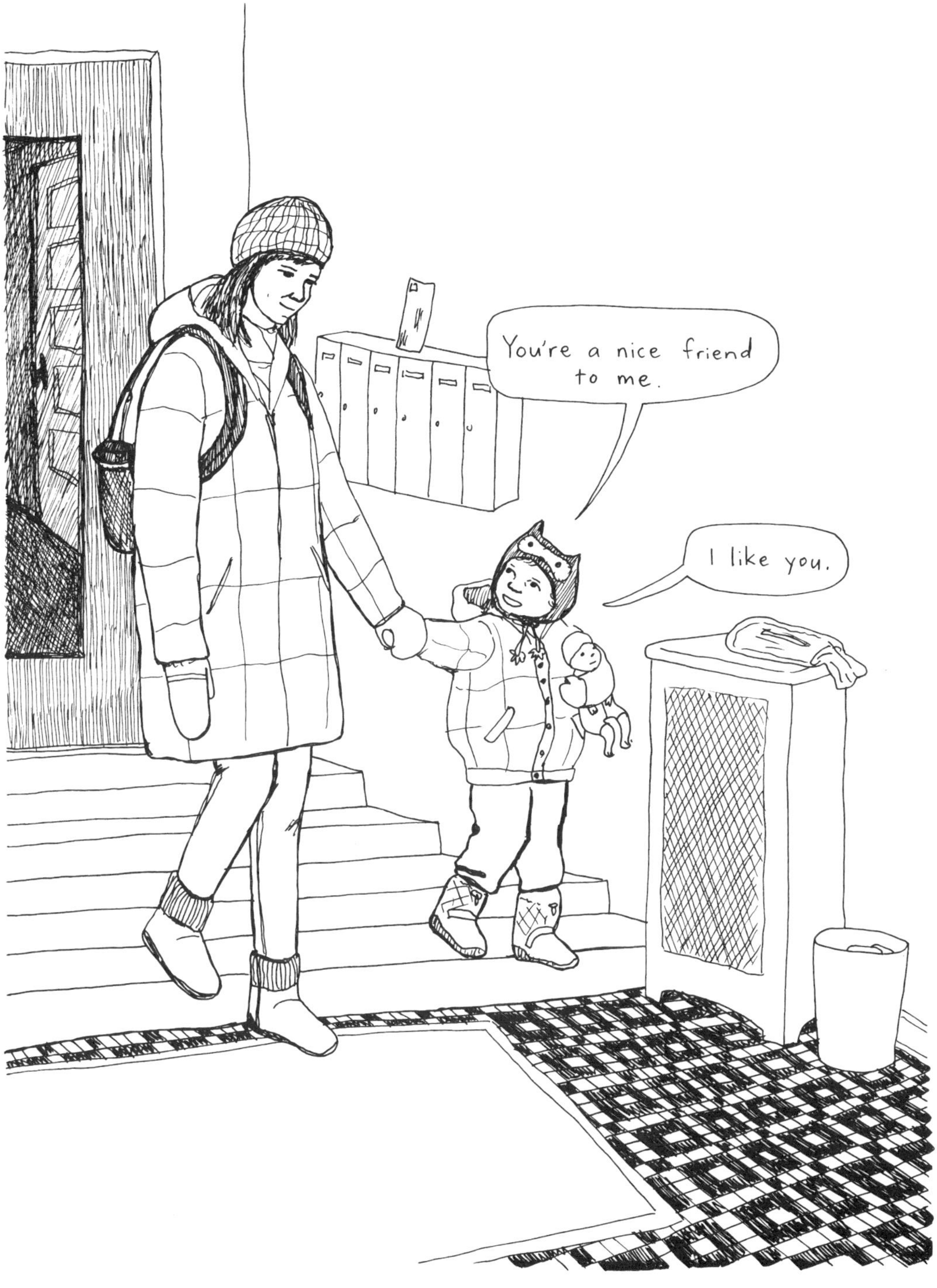
You're a nice friend to me.
I like you.

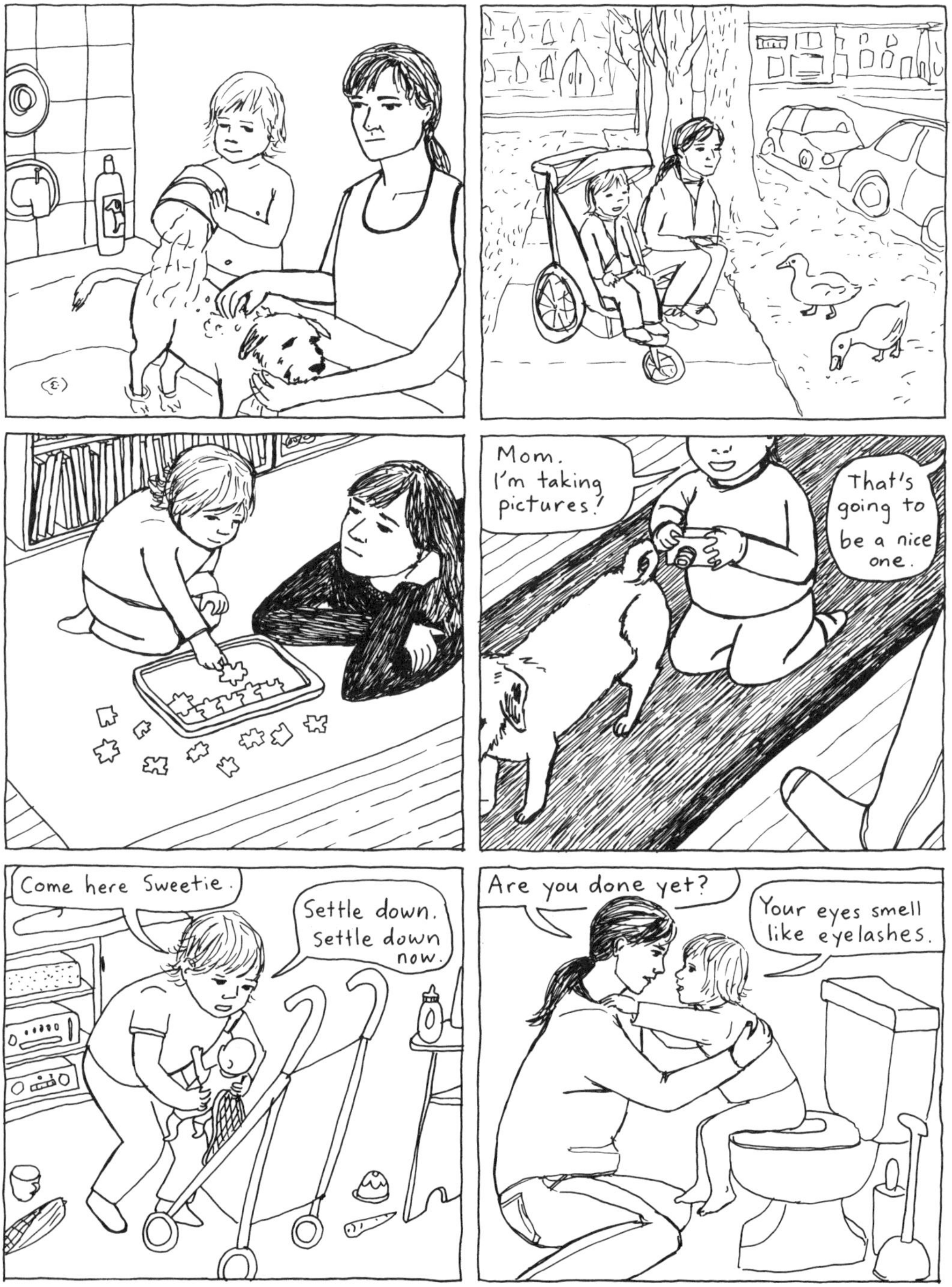

Mom. I'm taking pictures!
That's going to be a nice one.
Come here Sweetie.
Settle down. settle down now.
Are you done yet?
Your eyes smell like eyelashes.

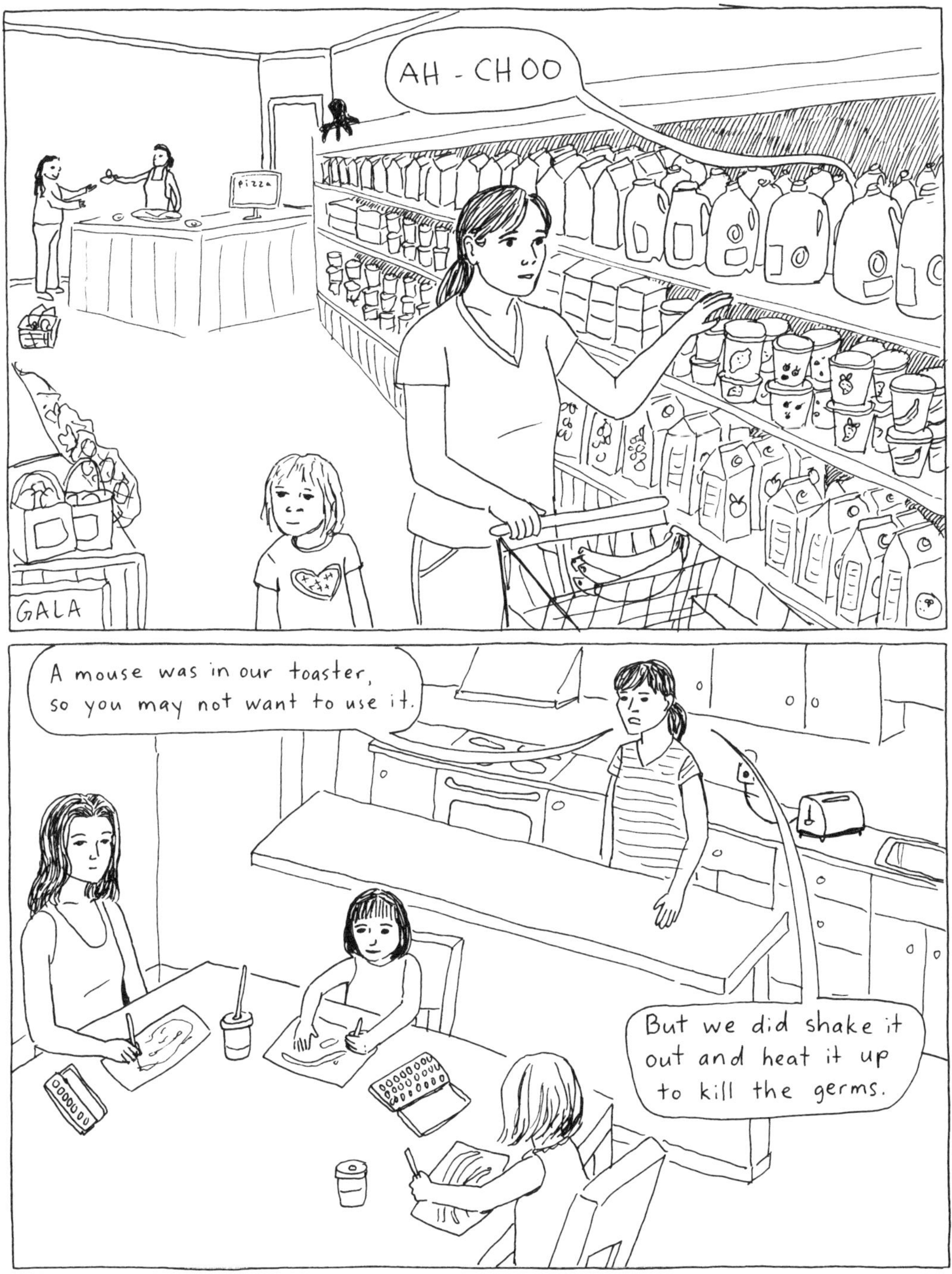
pizza
AH - CHOO
GALA
A mouse was in our toaster, so you may not want to use it.
But we did shake it out and heat it up to kill the germs.

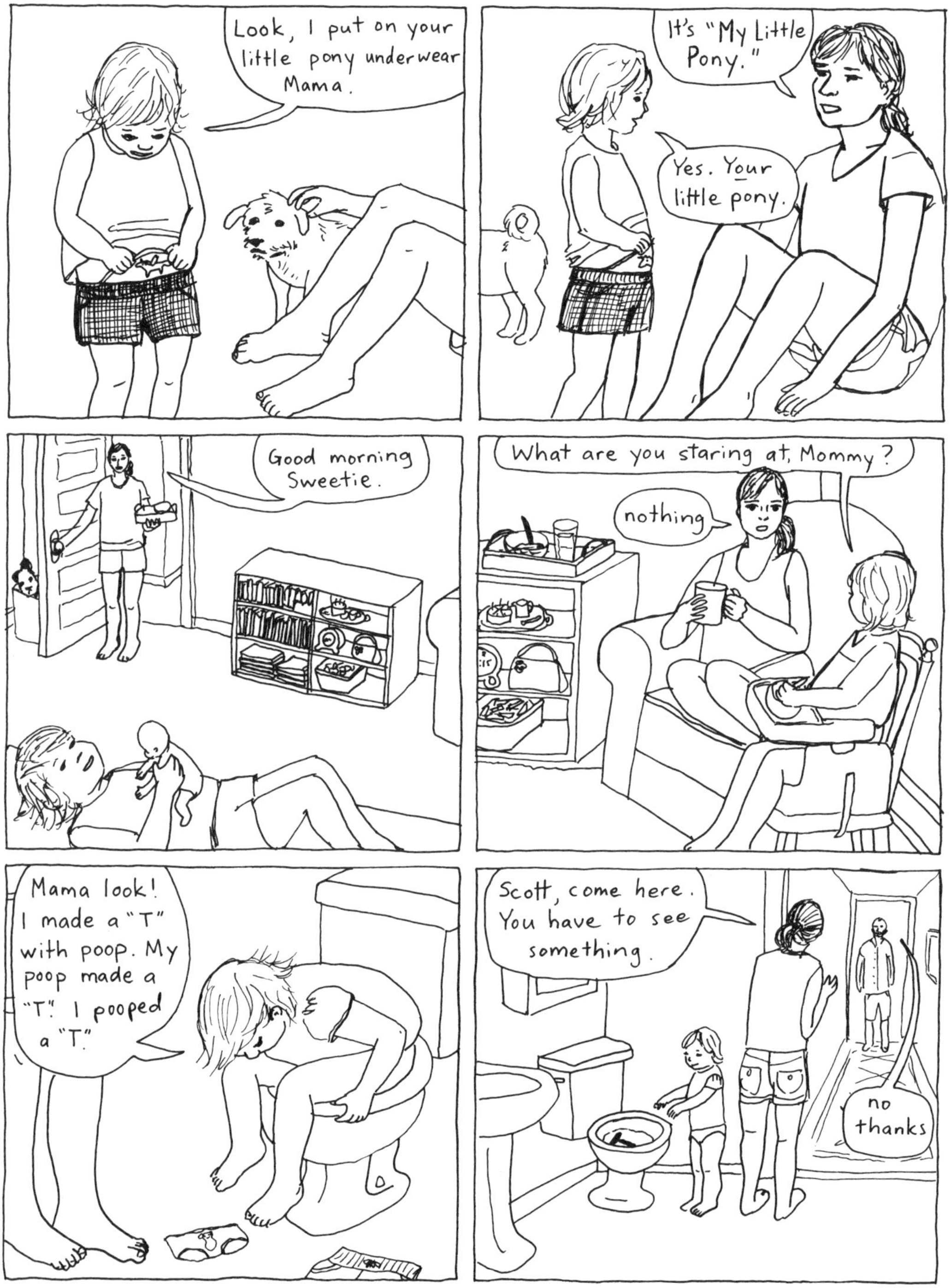
Look, I put on your little pony underwear Mama.
It's "My Little Pony."
Yes. Your little pony.
Good morning Sweetie.
What are you staring at, Mommy?
nothing
Mama look! I made a "T" with poop. My poop made a "T." I pooped a "T."
Scott, come here. You have to see something.
no thanks

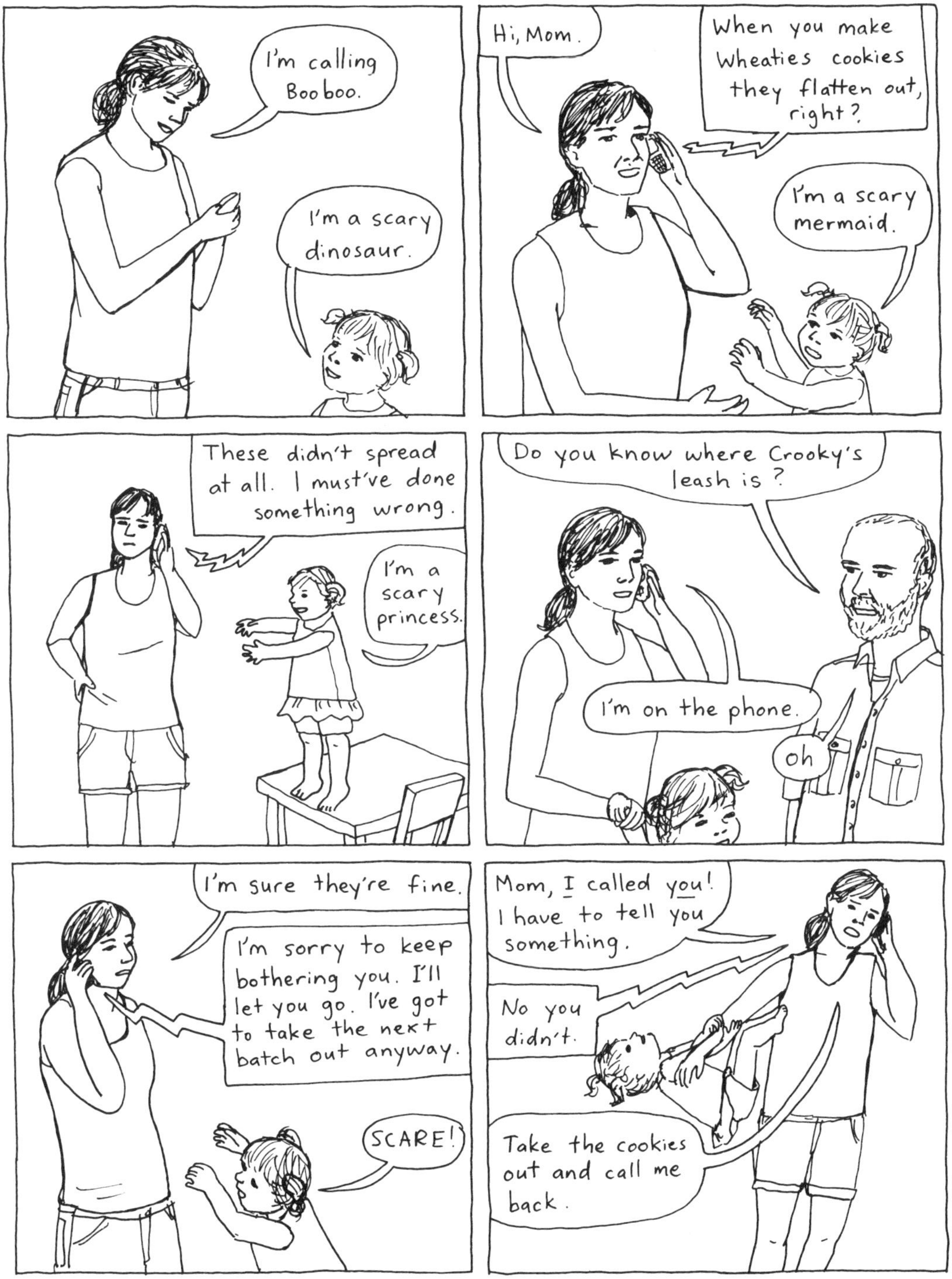
I'm calling Booboo.
I'm a scary dinosaur.
Hi, Mom.
When you make Wheaties cookies they flatten out, right?
I'm a scary mermaid.
These didn't spread at all. I must've done something wrong.
I'm a scary princess.
Do you know where Crooky's leash is?
I'm on the phone.
oh
I'm sure they're fine.
I'm sorry to keep bothering you. I'll let you go. I've got to take the next batch out anyway.
SCARE!
Mom, I called you! I have to tell you something.
No you didn't.
Take the cookies out and call me back.

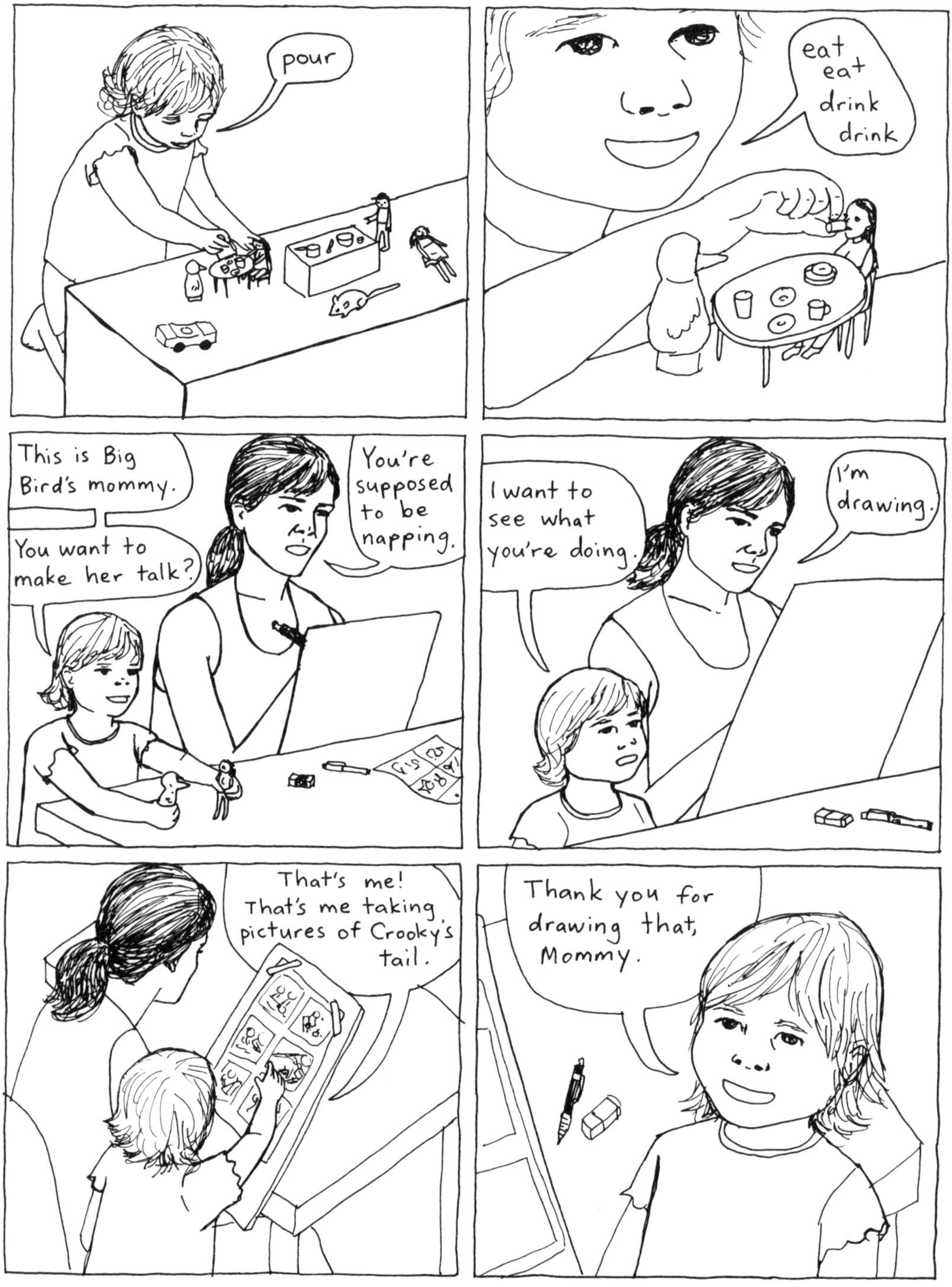
pour
eat eat drink drink
This is Big Bird's mommy.
You want to make her talk?
You're supposed to be napping.
I want to see what you're doing.
I'm drawing.
That's me! That's me taking pictures of Crooky's tail.
Thank you for drawing that, Mommy.

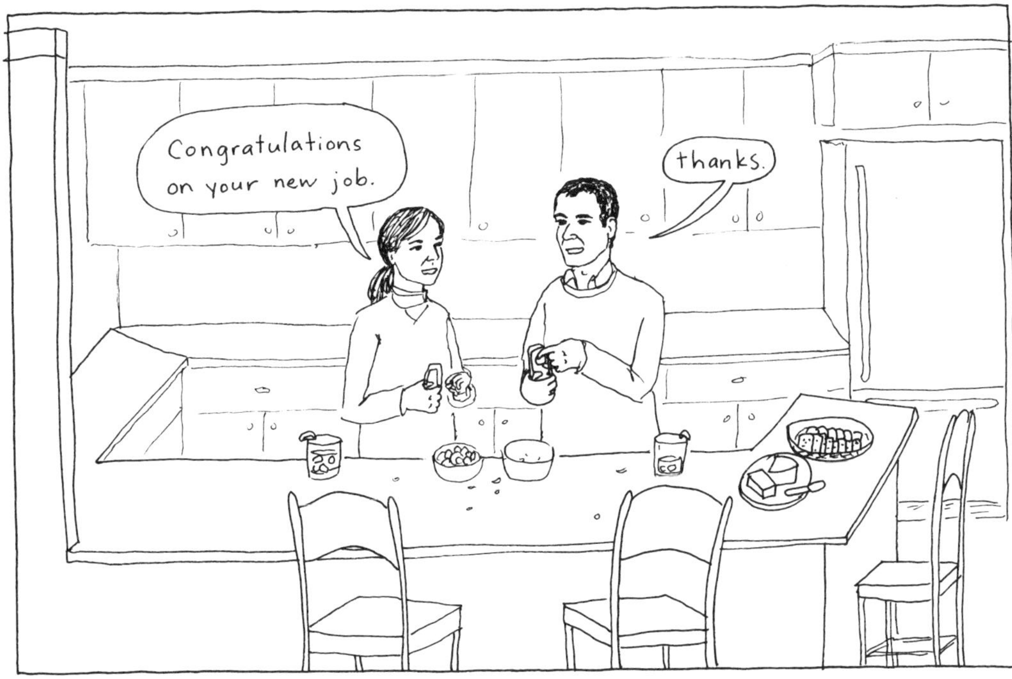
Congratulations on your new job.
thanks.

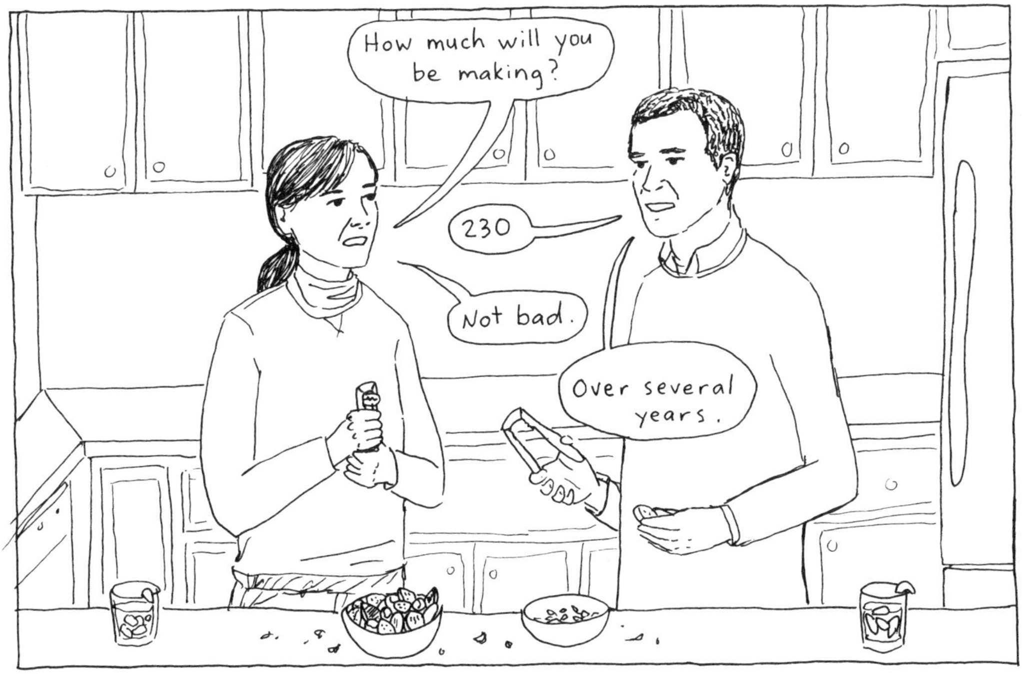
How much will you be making?
230
Not bad.
Over several years.

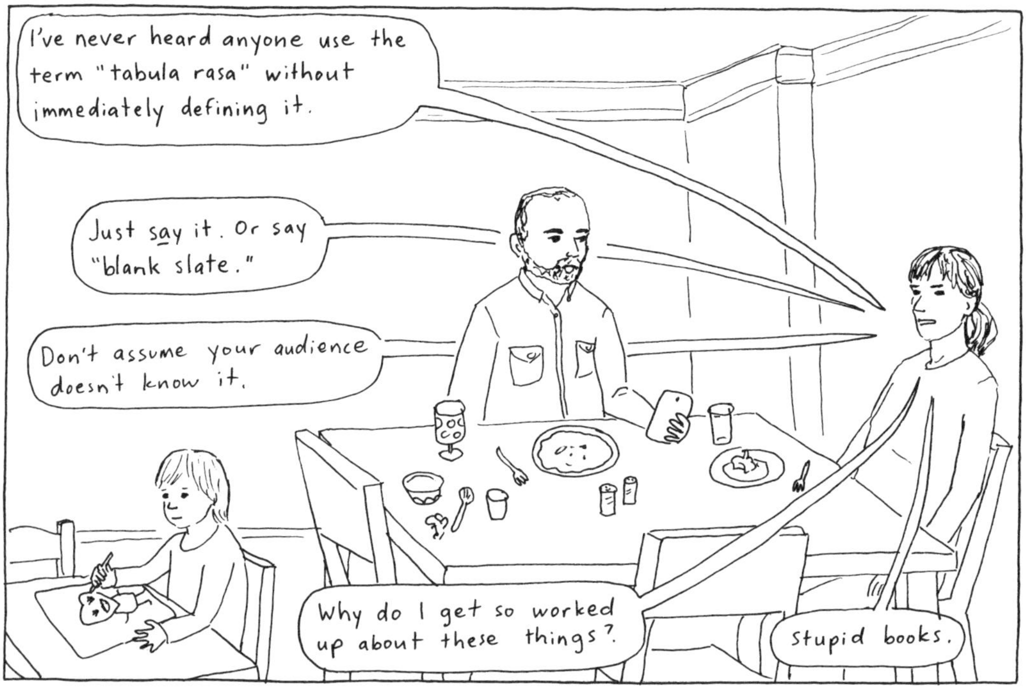
I've never heard anyone use the term "tabula rasa" without immediately defining it.
Just say it. Or say "blank slate."
Don't assume your audience doesn't know it.
Why do I get so worked up about these things?
Stupid books.

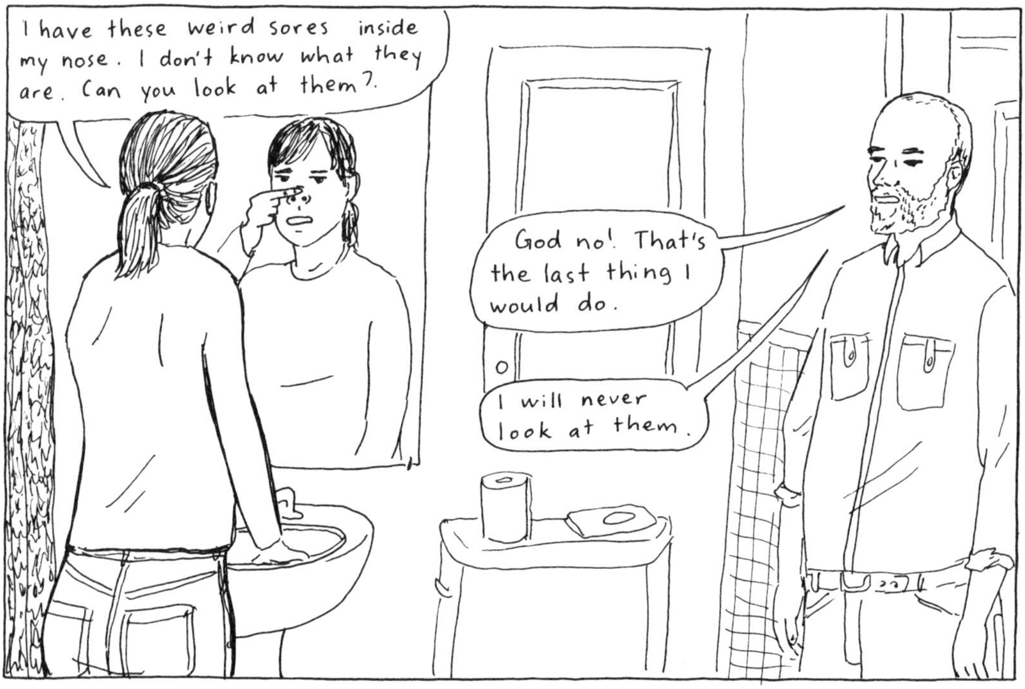
I have these weird sores inside my nose. I don't know what they are. Can you look at them?
God no! That's the last thing I would do.
I will never look at them.

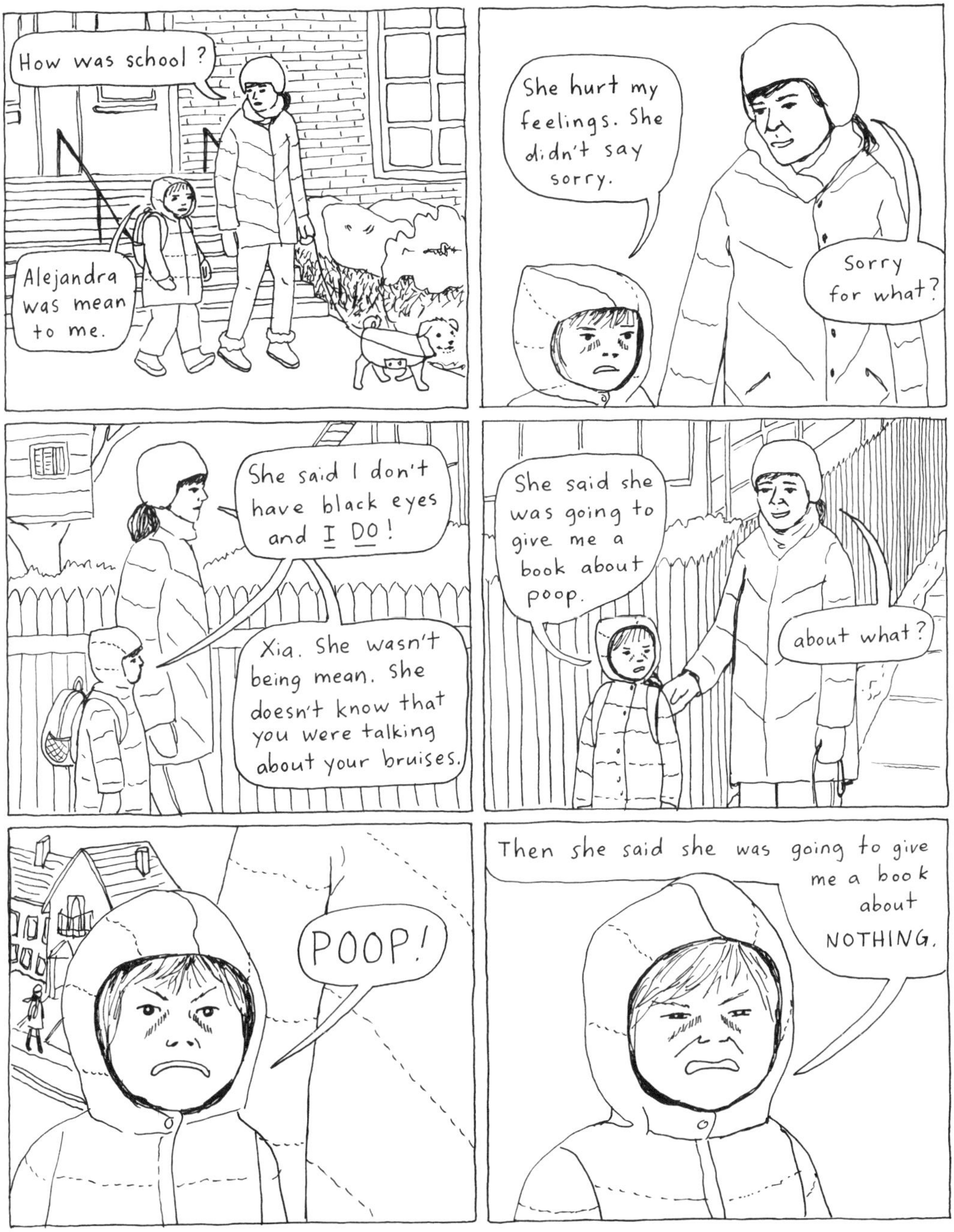
How was school?
Alejandra was mean to me.
She hurt my feelings. She didn't say sorry.
Sorry for what?
She said I don't have black eyes and I DO!
Xia. She wasn't being mean. She doesn't know that you were talking about your bruises.
She said she was going to give me a book about poop.
about what?
POOP!
Then she said she was going to give me a book about NOTHING.

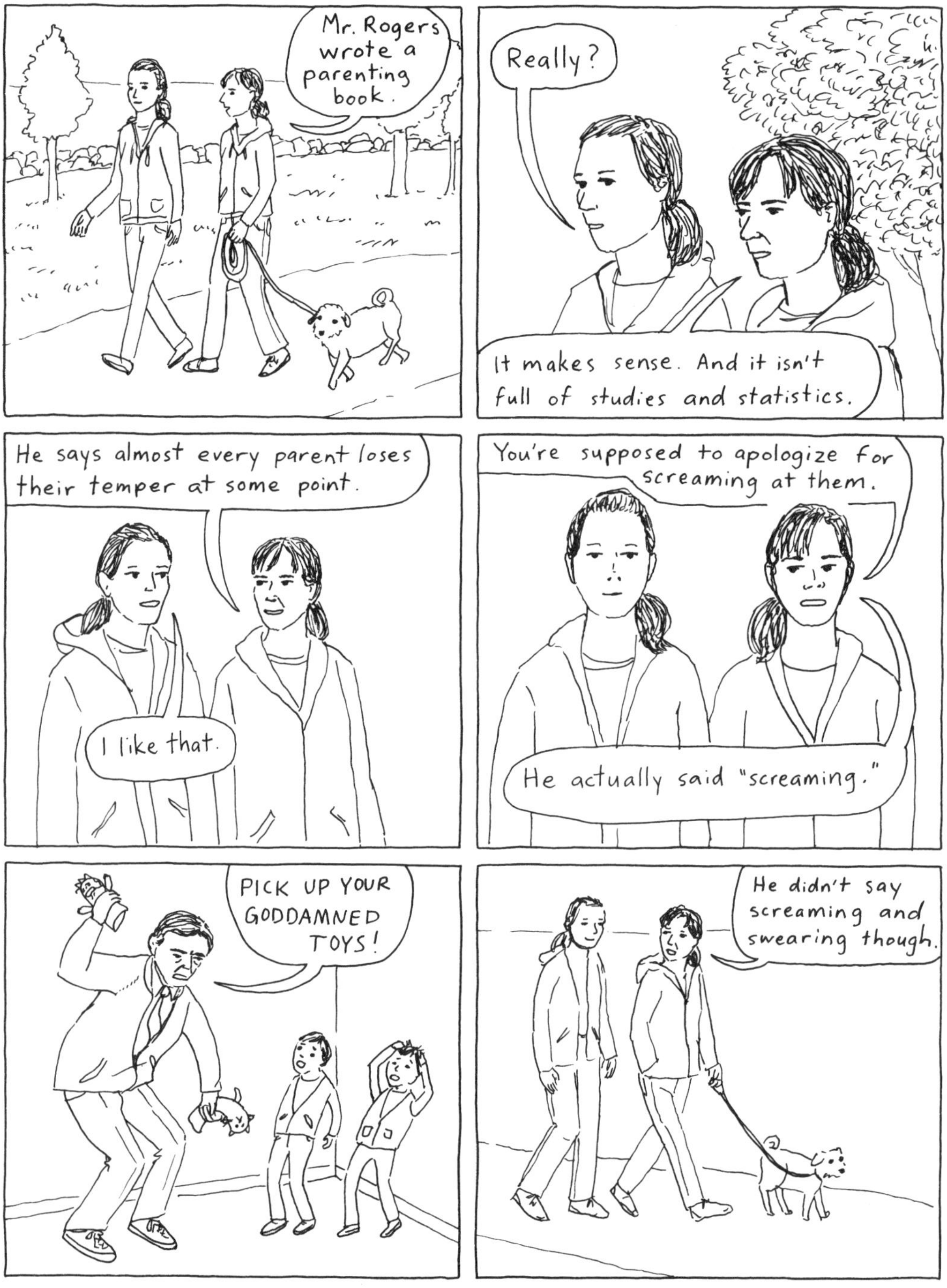
Mr. Rogers wrote a parenting book.
Really?
It makes sense. And it isn't full of studies and statistics.
He says almost every parent loses their temper at some point.
I like that.
You're supposed to apologize for screaming at them.
He actually said "screaming."
PICK UP YOUR GODDAMNED TOYS!
He didn't say screaming and swearing though.

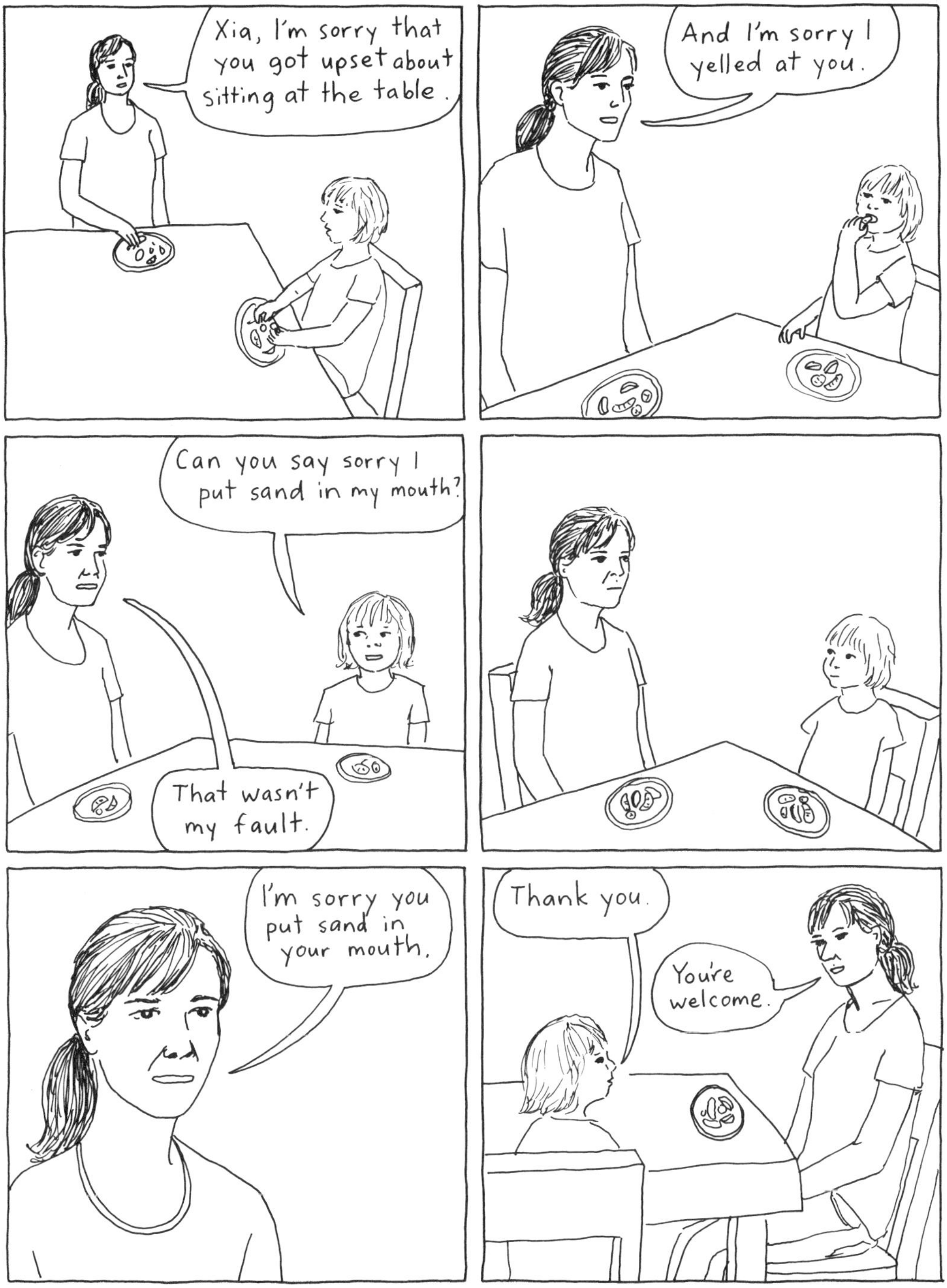
Xia, I'm sorry that you got upset about sitting at the table.
And I'm sorry I yelled at you.
Can you say sorry I put sand in my mouth?
That wasn't my fault.
I'm sorry you put sand in your mouth.
Thank you.
You're welcome.

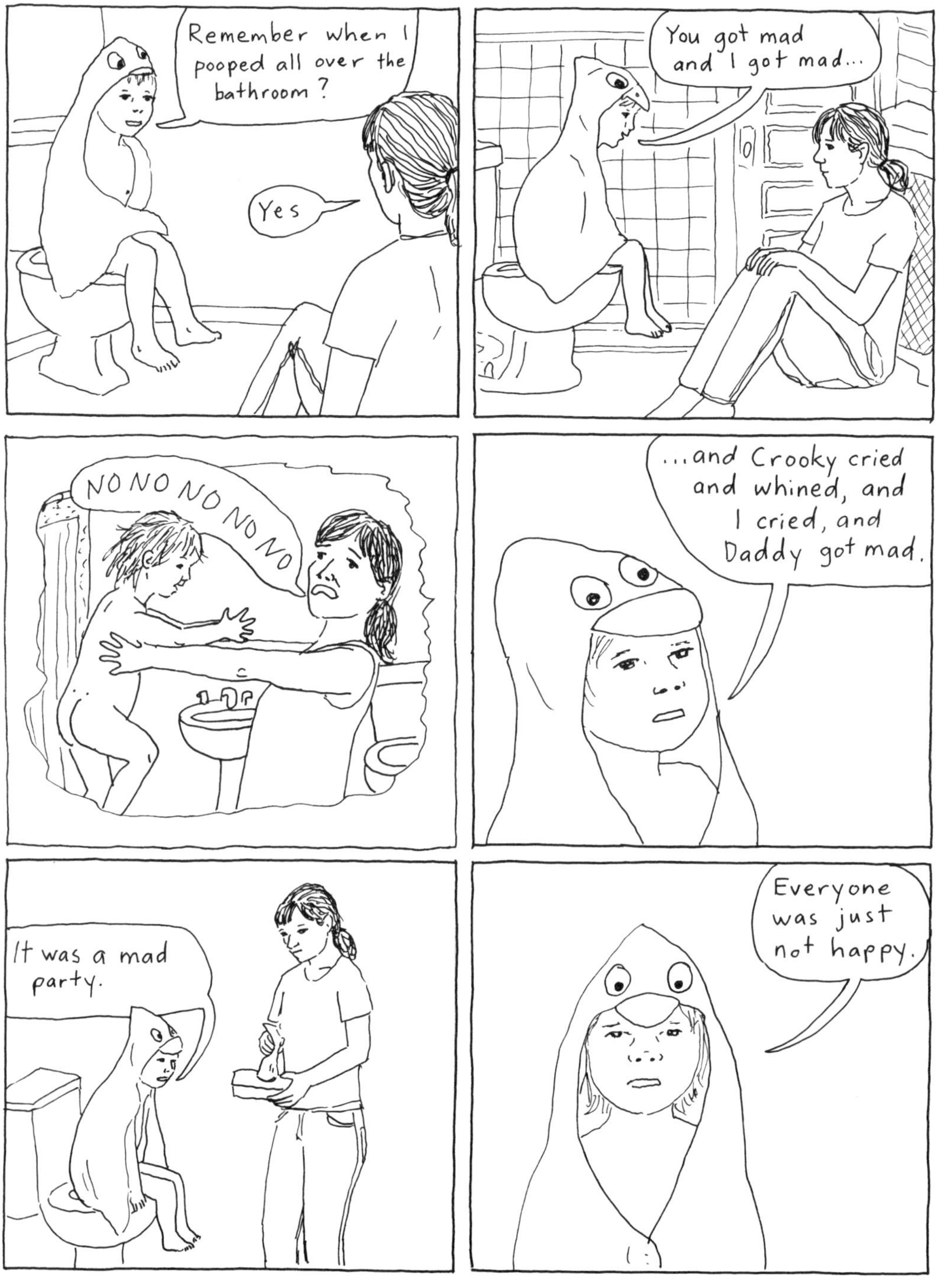

Remember when I pooped all over the bathroom?
Yes
You got mad and I got mad...
NO NO NO NO NO NO
...and Crooky cried and whined, and I cried, and Daddy got mad.
It was a mad party.
Everyone was just not happy.

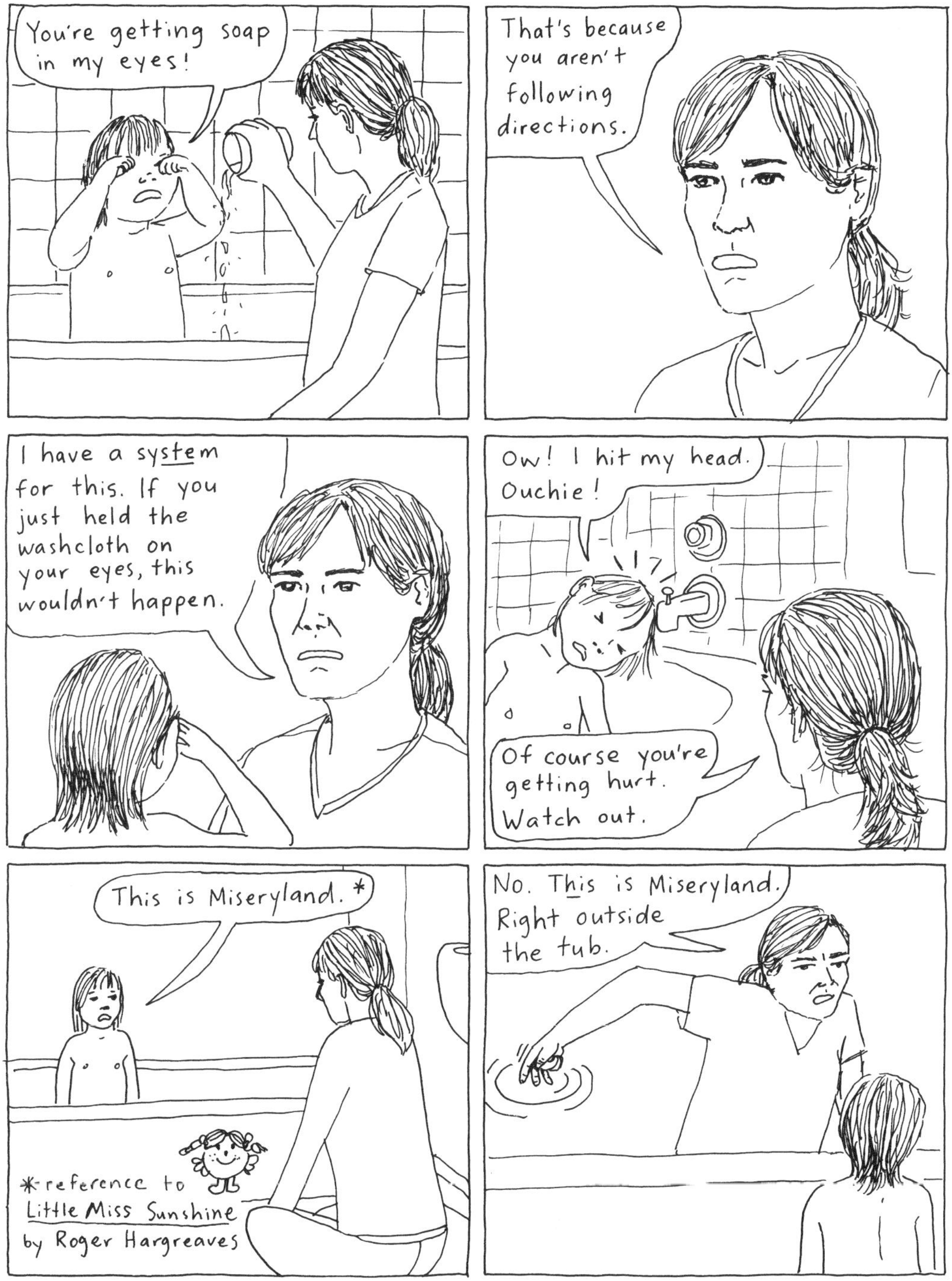
You're getting soap in my eyes!
That's because you aren't following directions.
I have a system for this. If you just held the washcloth on your eyes, this wouldn't happen.
Ow! I hit my head. Ouchie!
Of course you're getting hurt. Watch out.
This is Miseryland.*
*reference to Little Miss Sunshine by Roger Hargreaves
No. This is Miseryland. Right outside the tub.

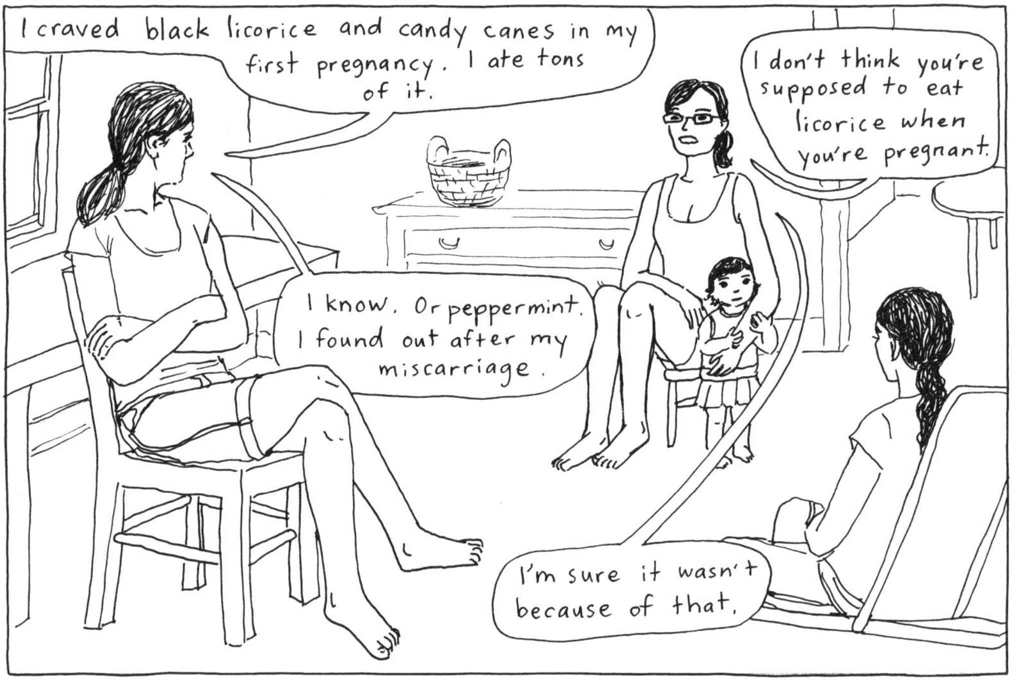
I craved black licorice and candy canes in my first pregnancy. I ate tons of it.
I don't think you're supposed to eat licorice when you're pregnant.
I know. Or peppermint. I found out after my miscarriage.
I'm sure it wasn't because of that.

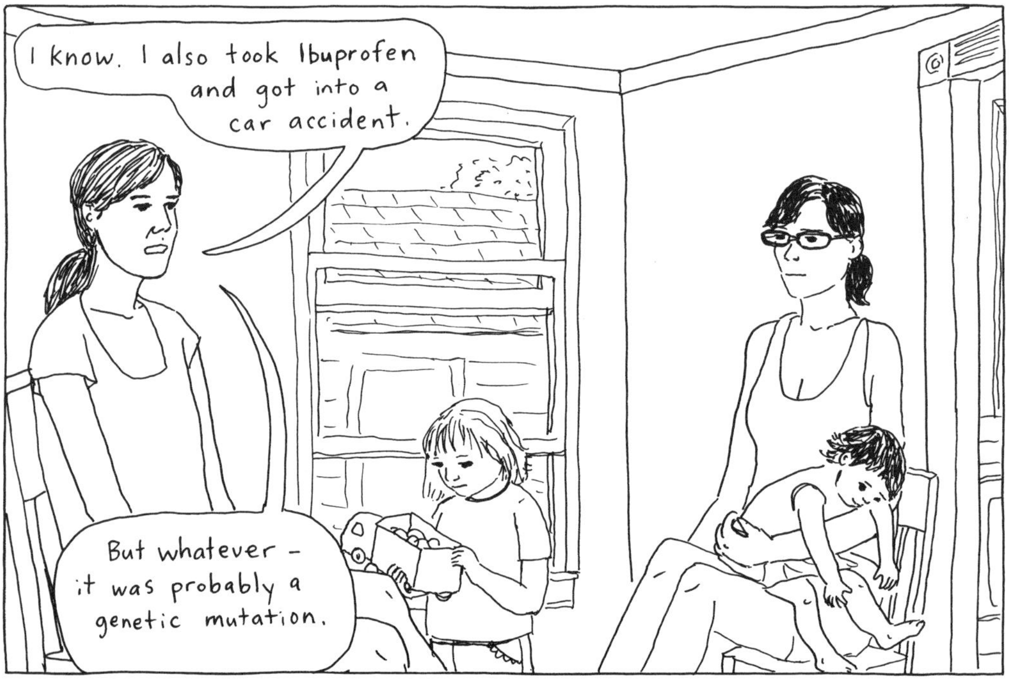
I know. I also took Ibuprofen and got into a car accident.
But whatever - it was probably a genetic mutation.

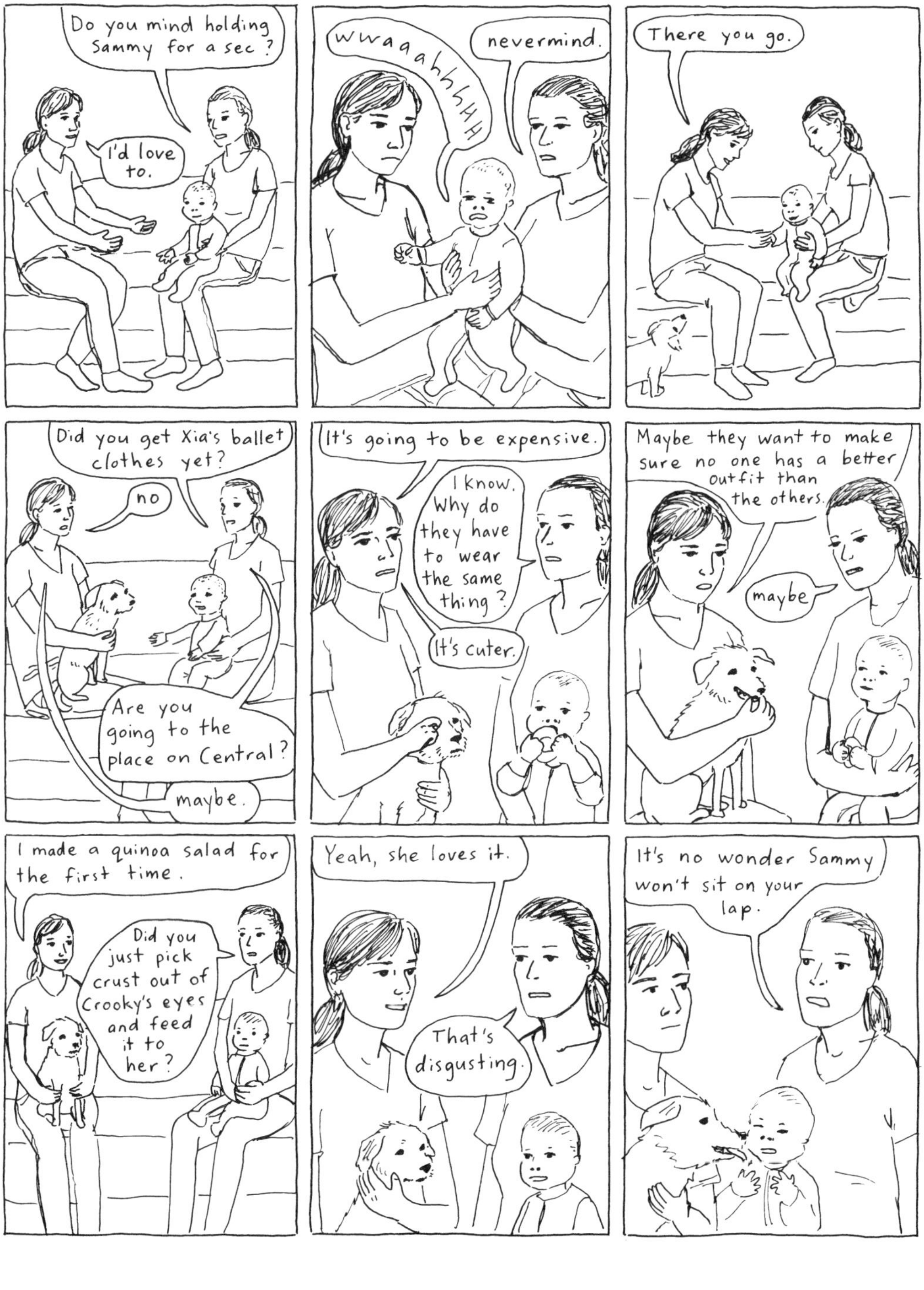

Do you mind holding Sammy for a sec?
I'd love to.
WWaaahhhHHH
nevermind.
There you go.
Did you get Xia's ballet clothes yet?
no
Are you going to the place on Central?
maybe.
It's going to be expensive.
I know. Why do they have to wear the same thing?
It's cuter.
Maybe they want to make sure no one has a better outfit than the others.
maybe
I made a quinoa salad for the first time.
Did you just pick crust out of Crooky's eyes and feed it to her?
Yeah, she loves it.
That's disgusting.
It's no wonder Sammy won't sit on your lap.

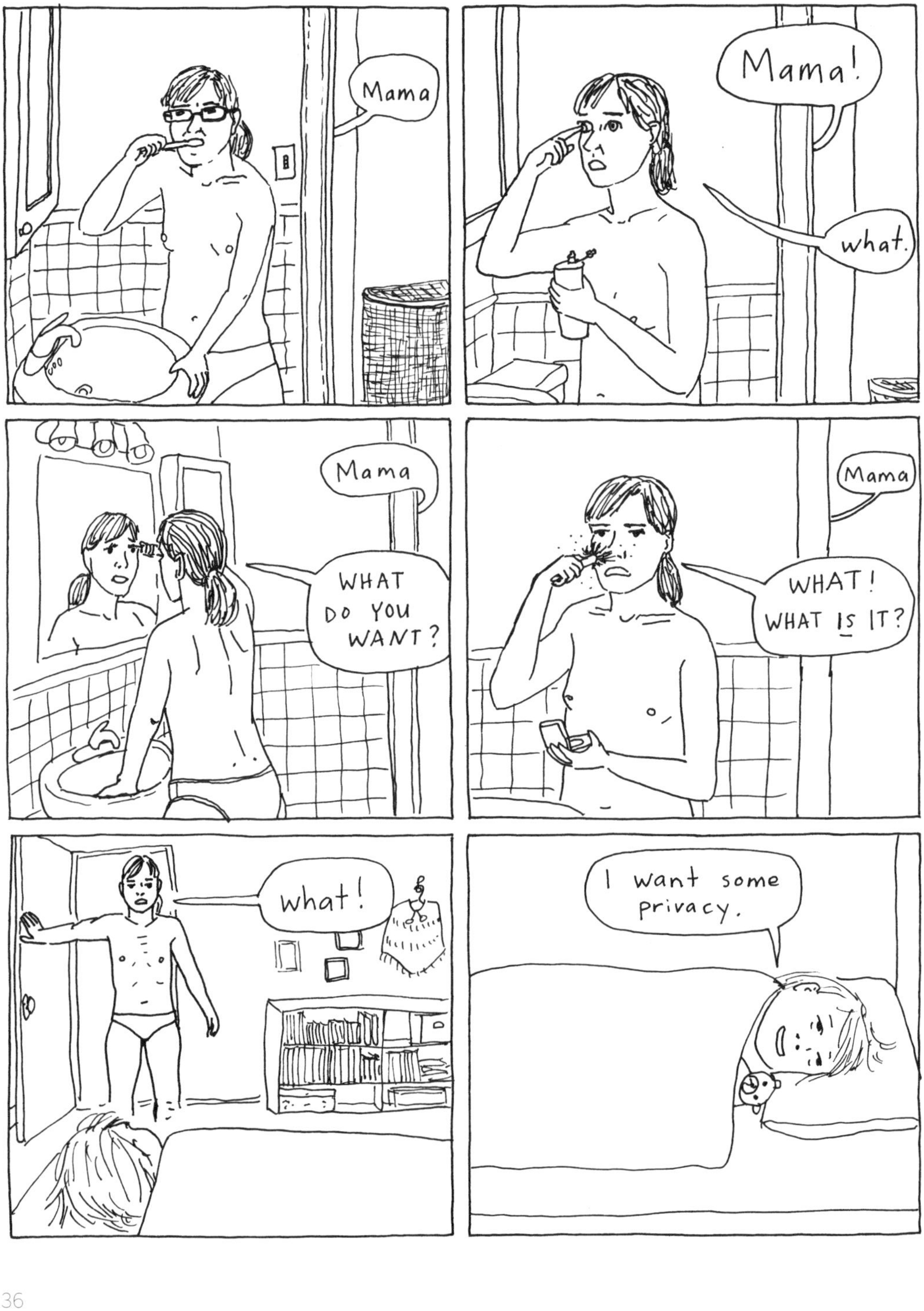
Mama
Mama!
what.
Mama
WHAT DO YOU WANT?
Mama
WHAT! WHAT IS IT?
what!
I want some privacy.

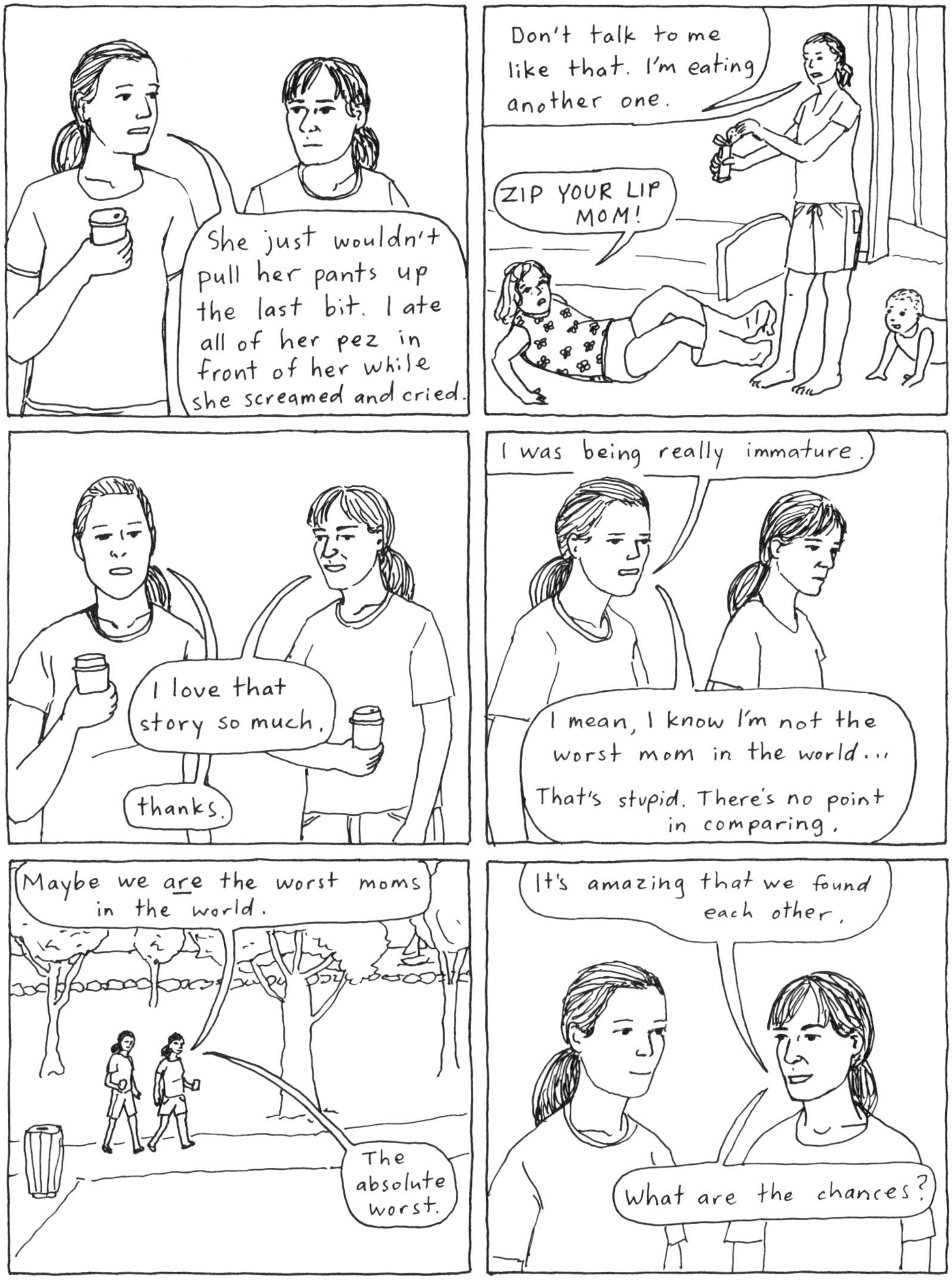
She just wouldn't pull her pants up the last bit. I ate all of her pez in front of her while she screamed and cried.
Don't talk to me like that. I'm eating another one.
ZIP YOUR LIP MOM!
I love that story so much.
thanks.
I was being really immature.
I mean, I know I'm not the worst mom in the world...
That's stupid. There's no point in comparing.
Maybe we are the worst moms in the world.
The absolute worst.
It's amazing that we found each other.
What are the chances?

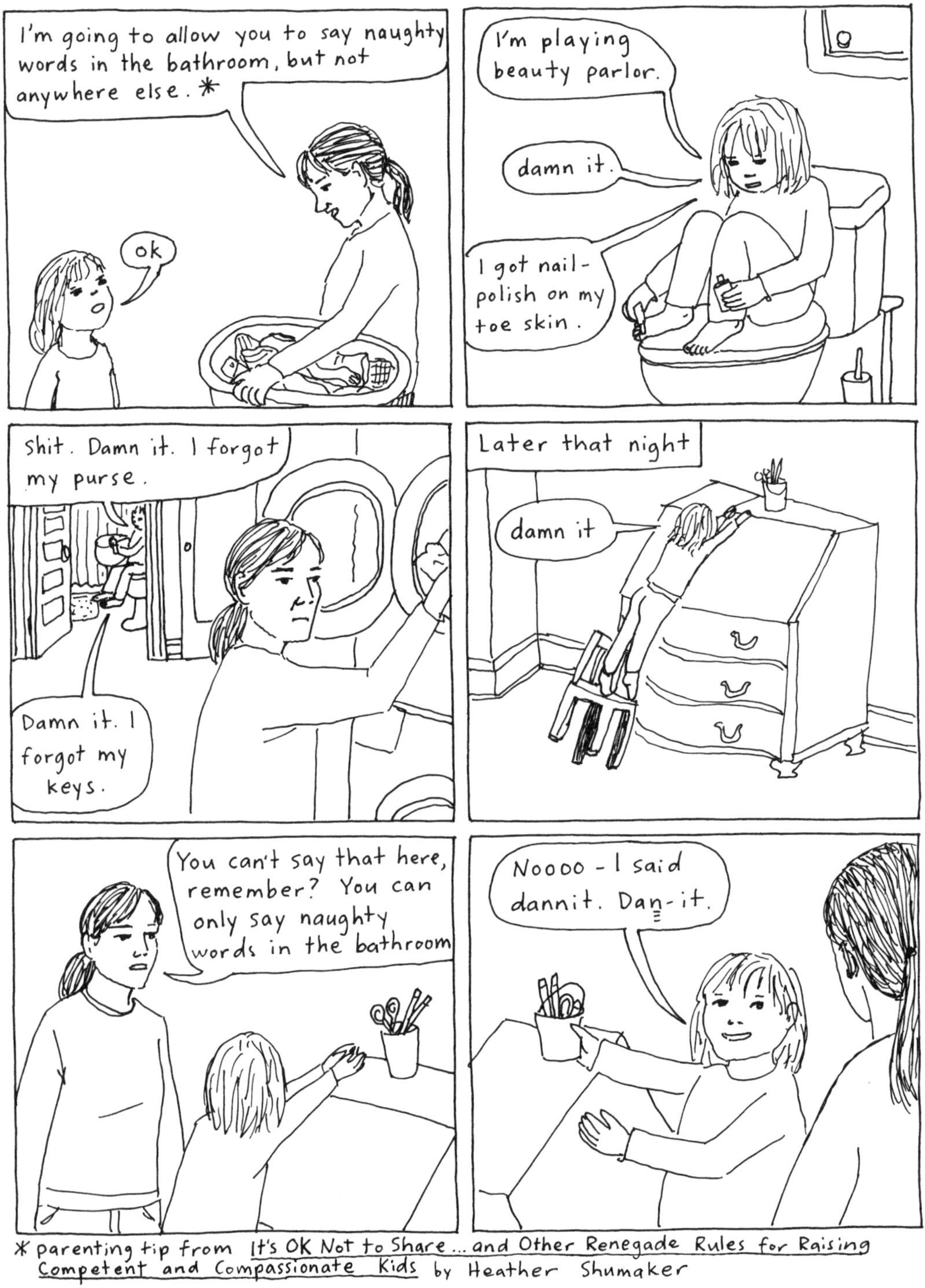
I'm going to allow you to say naughty words in the bathroom, but not anywhere else. *
ok
I'm playing beauty parlor.
damn it.
I got nail-polish on my toe skin.
Shit. Damn it. I forgot my purse.
Damn it. I forgot my keys.
Later that night
damn it
You can't say that here, remember? You can only say naughty words in the bathroom
Noooo - I said dannit. Dan-it.

* parenting tip from It's OK Not to Share ... and Other Renegade Rules for Raising Competent and Compassionate Kids by Heather Shumaker

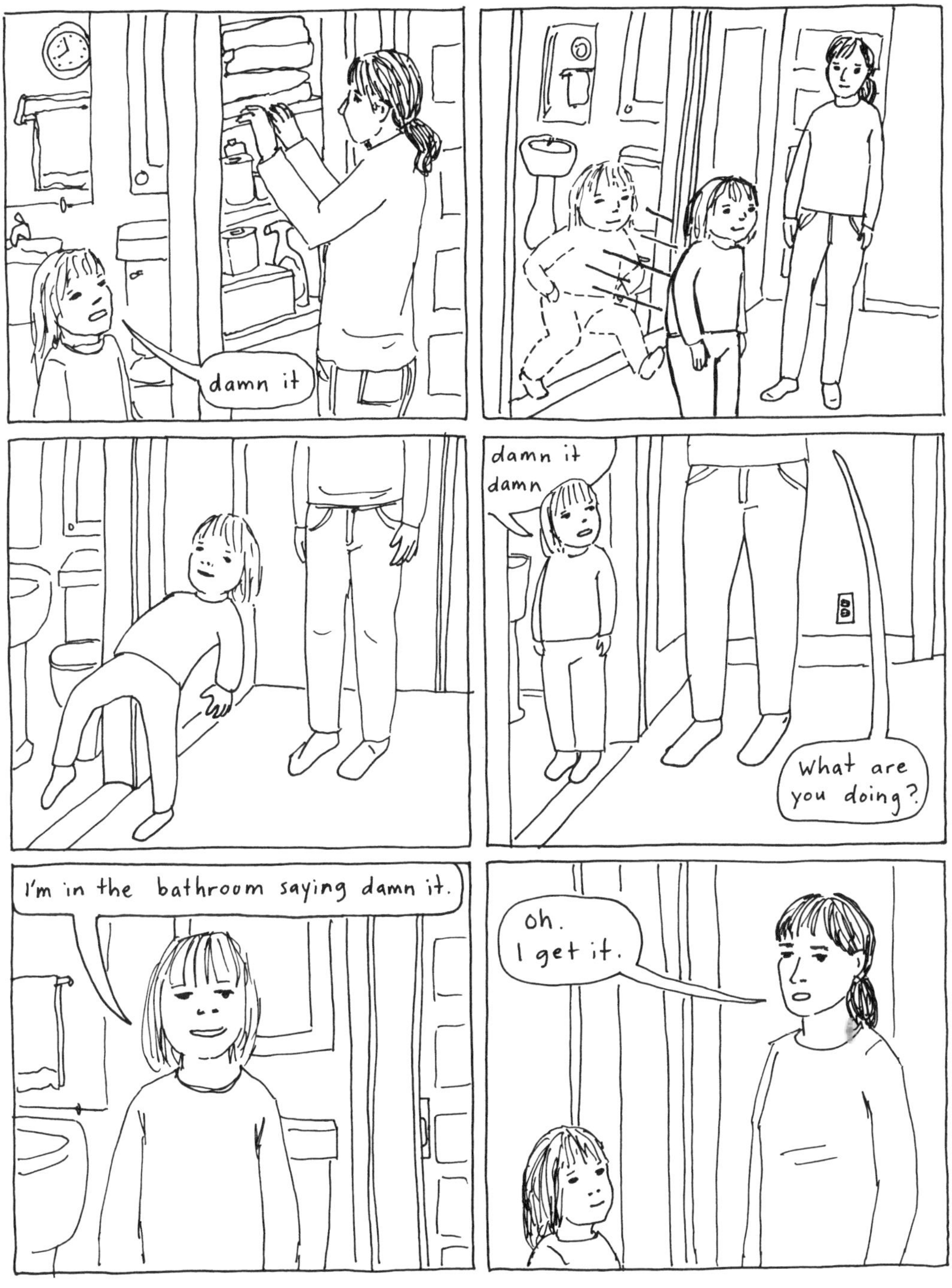
damn it
damn it
damn
What are you doing?
I'm in the bathroom saying damn it.
Oh.
I get it.

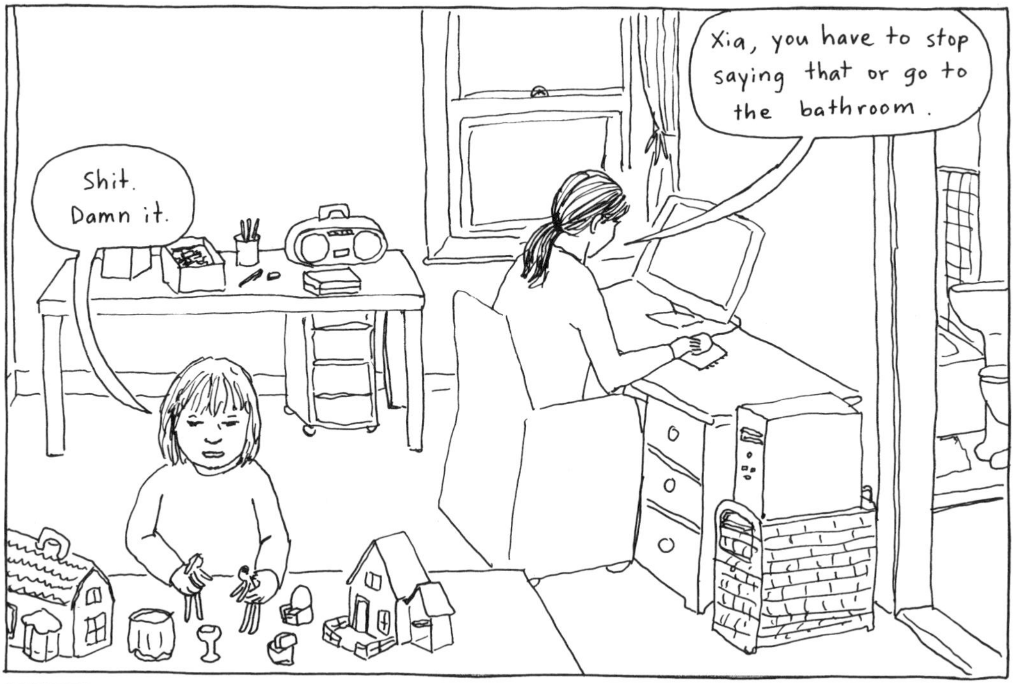
Shit.
Damn it.
Xia, you have to stop saying that or go to the bathroom.

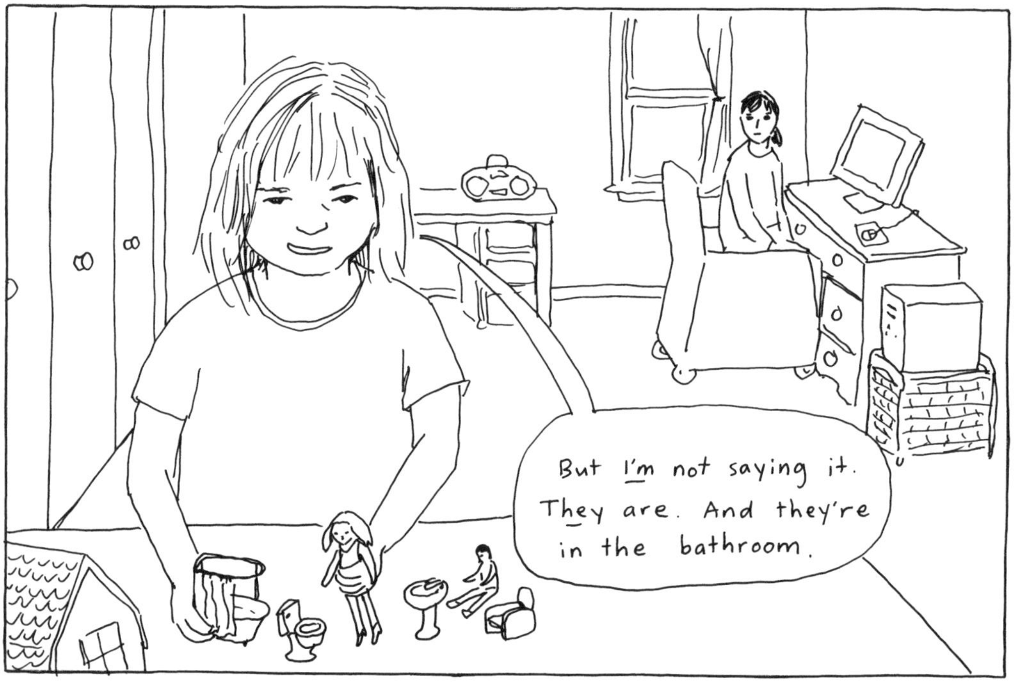
But I'm not saying it. They are. And they're in the bathroom.

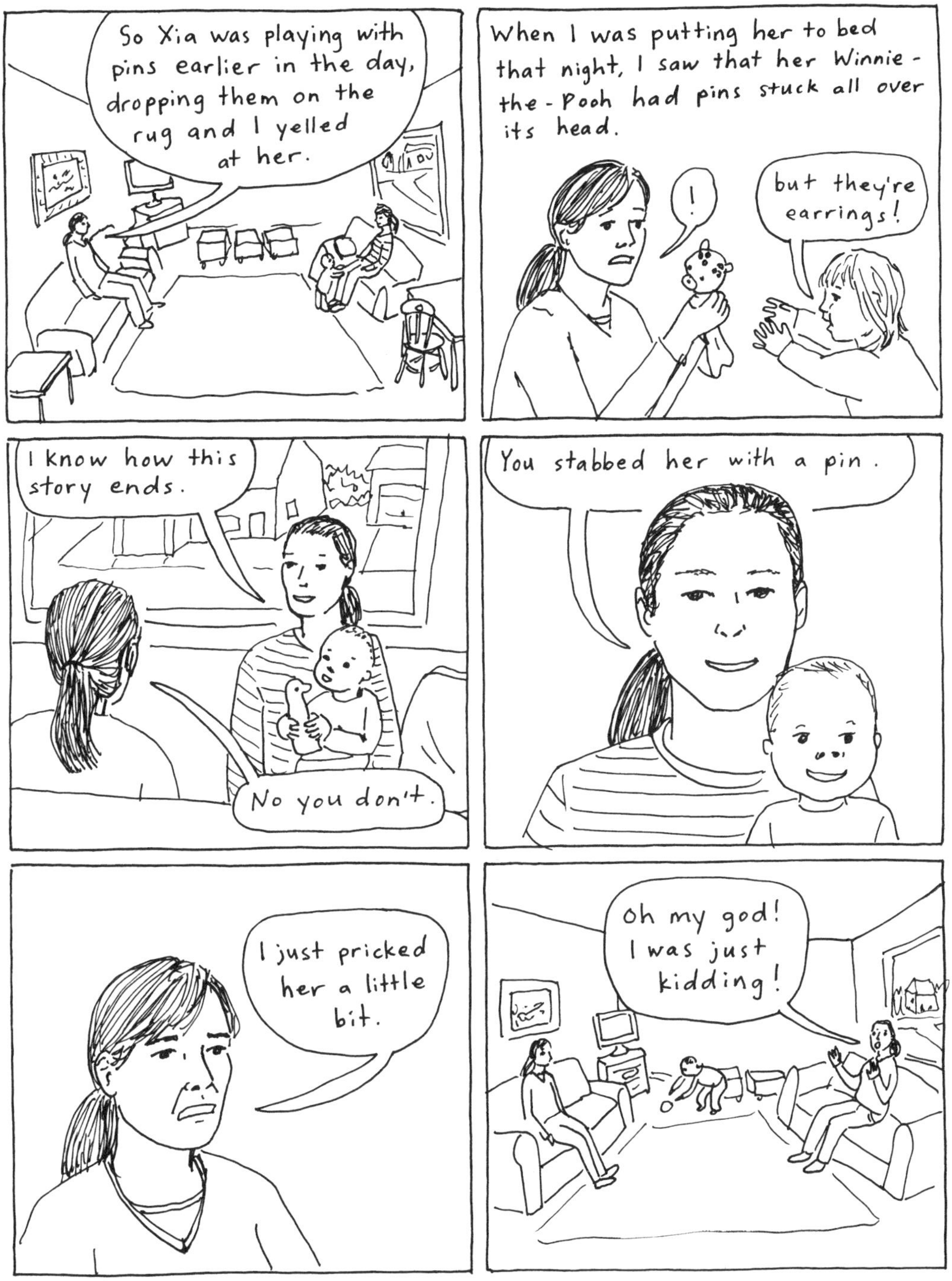
So Xia was playing with pins earlier in the day, dropping them on the rug and I yelled at her.
When I was putting her to bed that night, I saw that her Winnie-the-Pooh had pins stuck all over its head.
!
but they're earrings!
I know how this story ends.
No you don't.
You stabbed her with a pin.
I just pricked her a little bit.
Oh my god! I was just kidding!

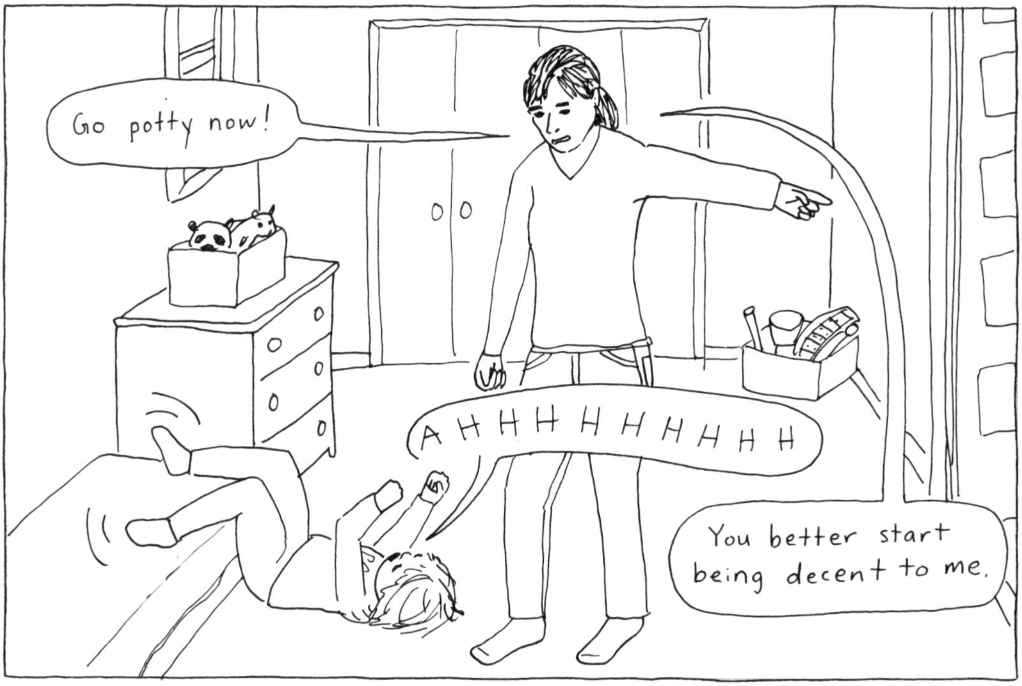
Go potty now!
AHHHHHHHHHH
You better start being decent to me.

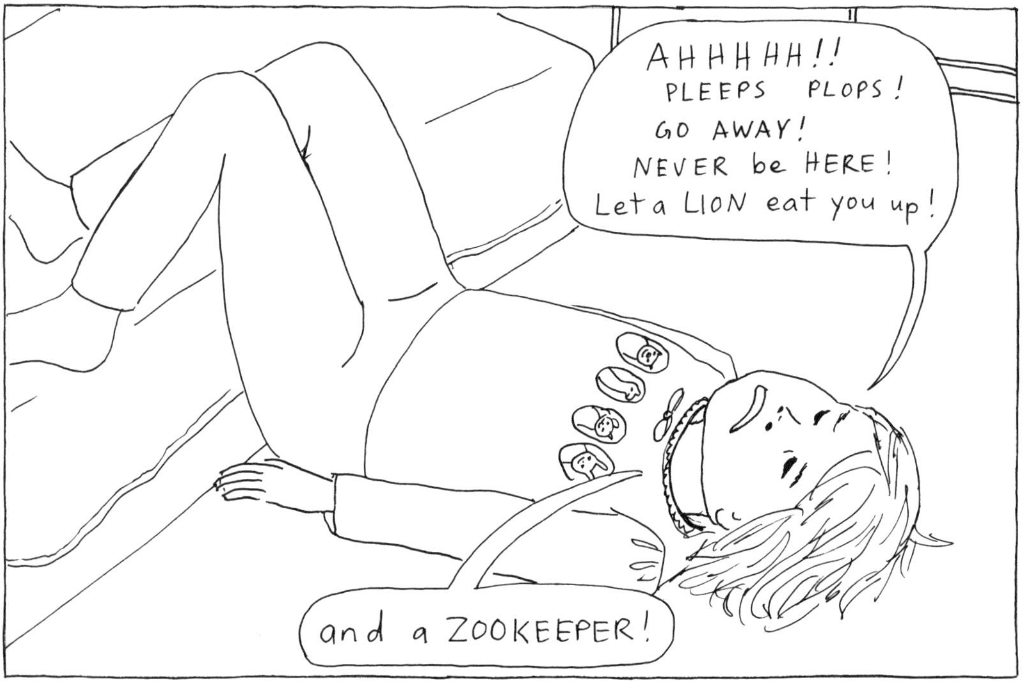
AHHHHH!! PLEEPS PLOPS! GO AWAY! NEVER be HERE! Let a LION eat you up!
and a ZOOKEEPER!

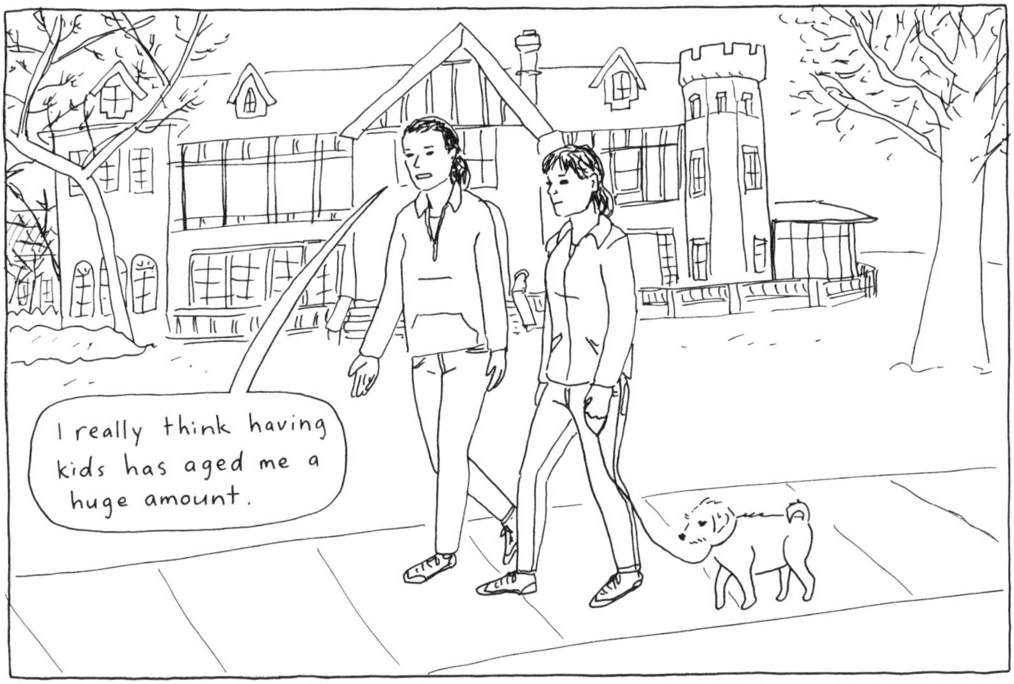
I really think having kids has aged me a huge amount.

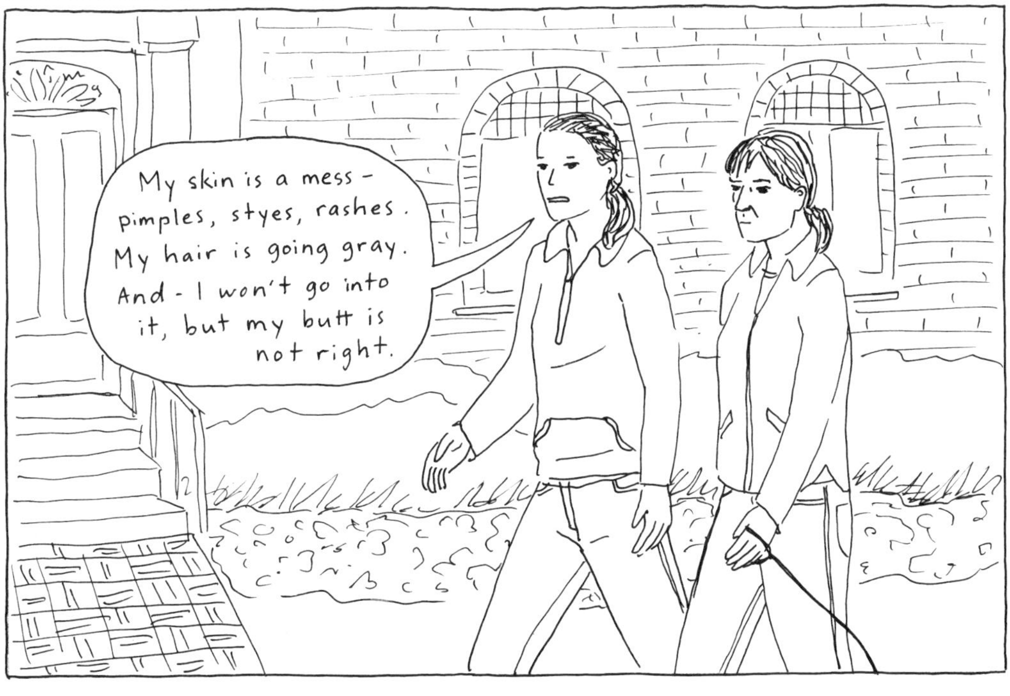
My skin is a mess - pimples, styes, rashes. My hair is going gray. And - I won't go into it, but my butt is not right.

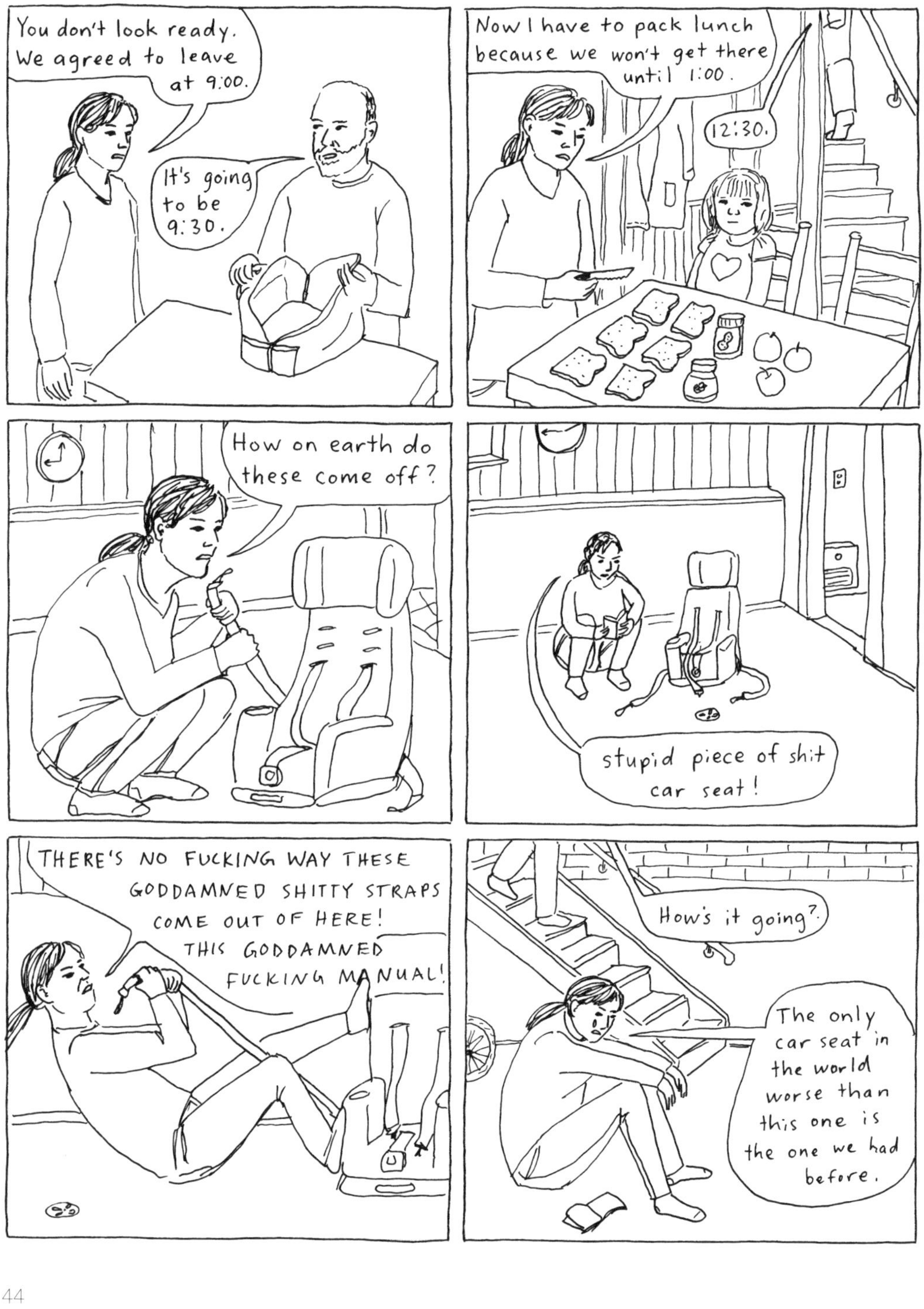
You don't look ready. We agreed to leave at 9:00.
It's going to be 9:30.
Now I have to pack lunch because we won't get there until 1:00.
12:30.
How on earth do these come off?
stupid piece of shit car seat!
THERE'S NO FUCKING WAY THESE GODDAMNED SHITTY STRAPS COME OUT OF HERE! THIS GODDAMNED FUCKING MANUAL!
How's it going?
The only car seat in the world worse than this one is the one we had before.

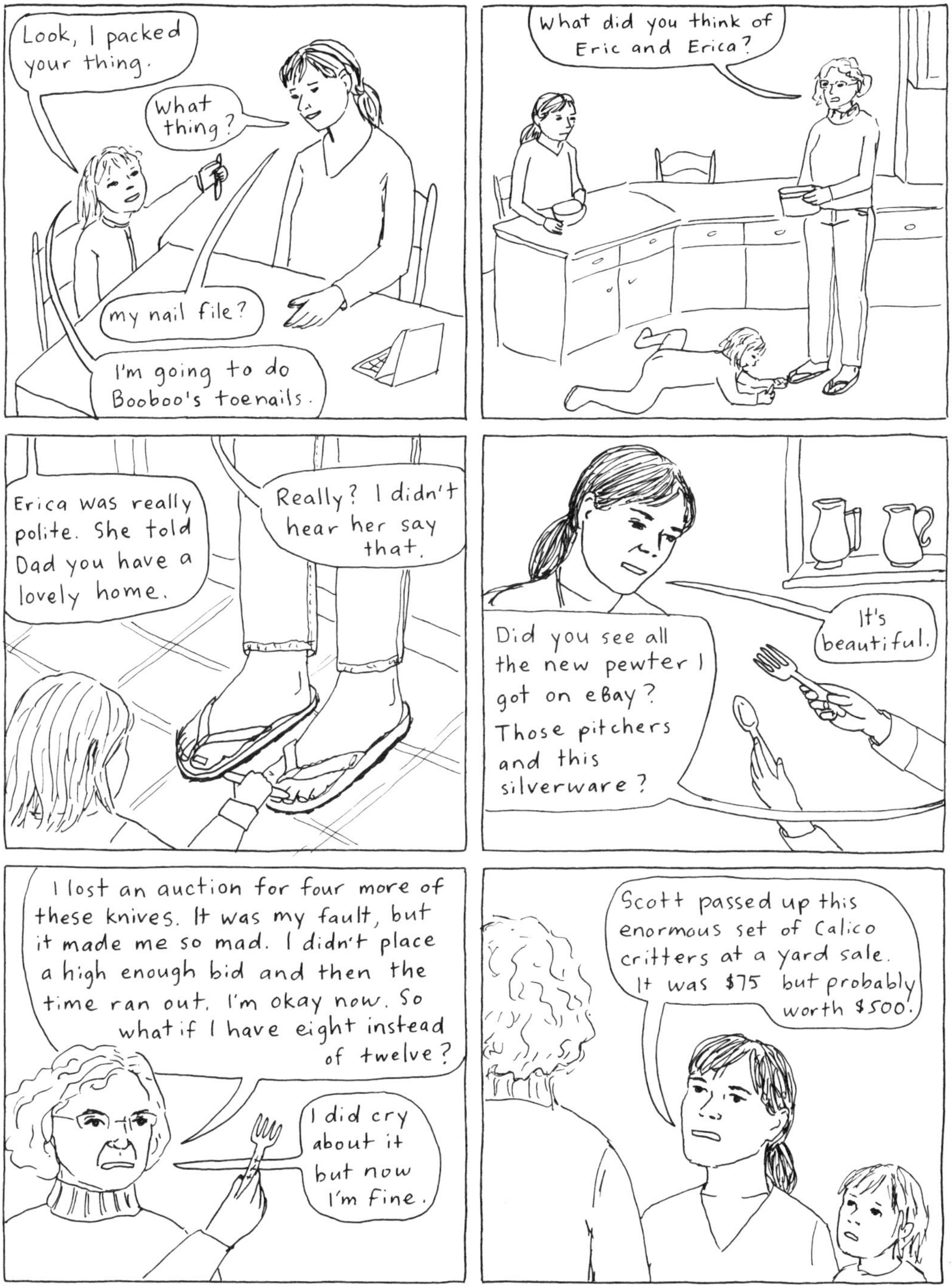
Look, I packed your thing.
What thing?
my nail file?
I'm going to do Booboo's toenails.
What did you think of Eric and Erica?
Erica was really polite. She told Dad you have a lovely home.
Really? I didn't hear her say that.
Did you see all the new pewter I got on eBay? Those pitchers and this silverware?
It's beautiful.
I lost an auction for four more of these knives. It was my fault, but it made me so mad. I didn't place a high enough bid and then the time ran out. I'm okay now. So what if I have eight instead of twelve?
I did cry about it but now I'm fine.
Scott passed up this enormous set of Calico critters at a yard sale. It was $75 but probably worth $500.

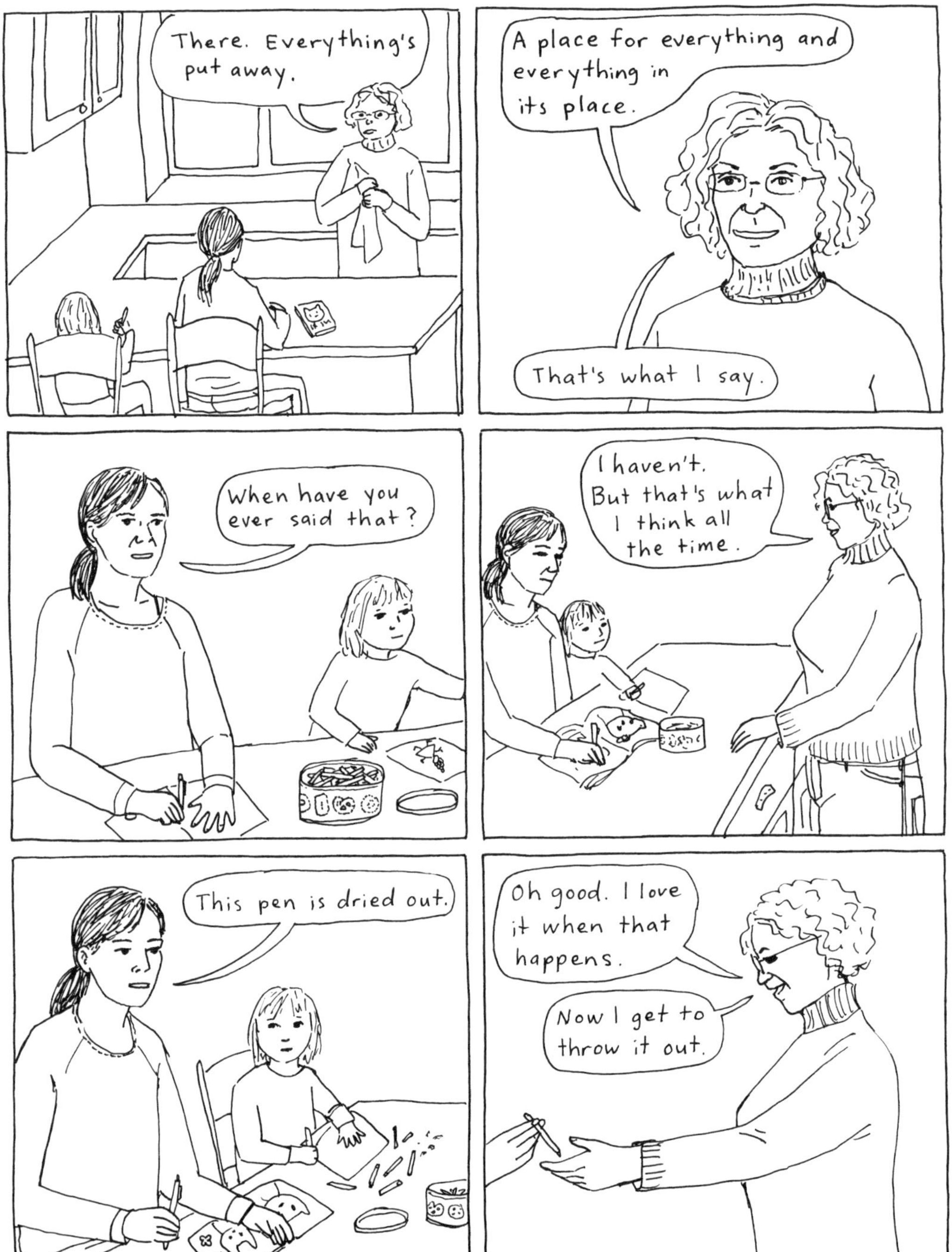
There. Everything's put away.
A place for everything and everything in its place.
That's what I say.
When have you ever said that?
I haven't. But that's what I think all the time.
This pen is dried out.
Oh good. I love it when that happens.
Now I get to throw it out.

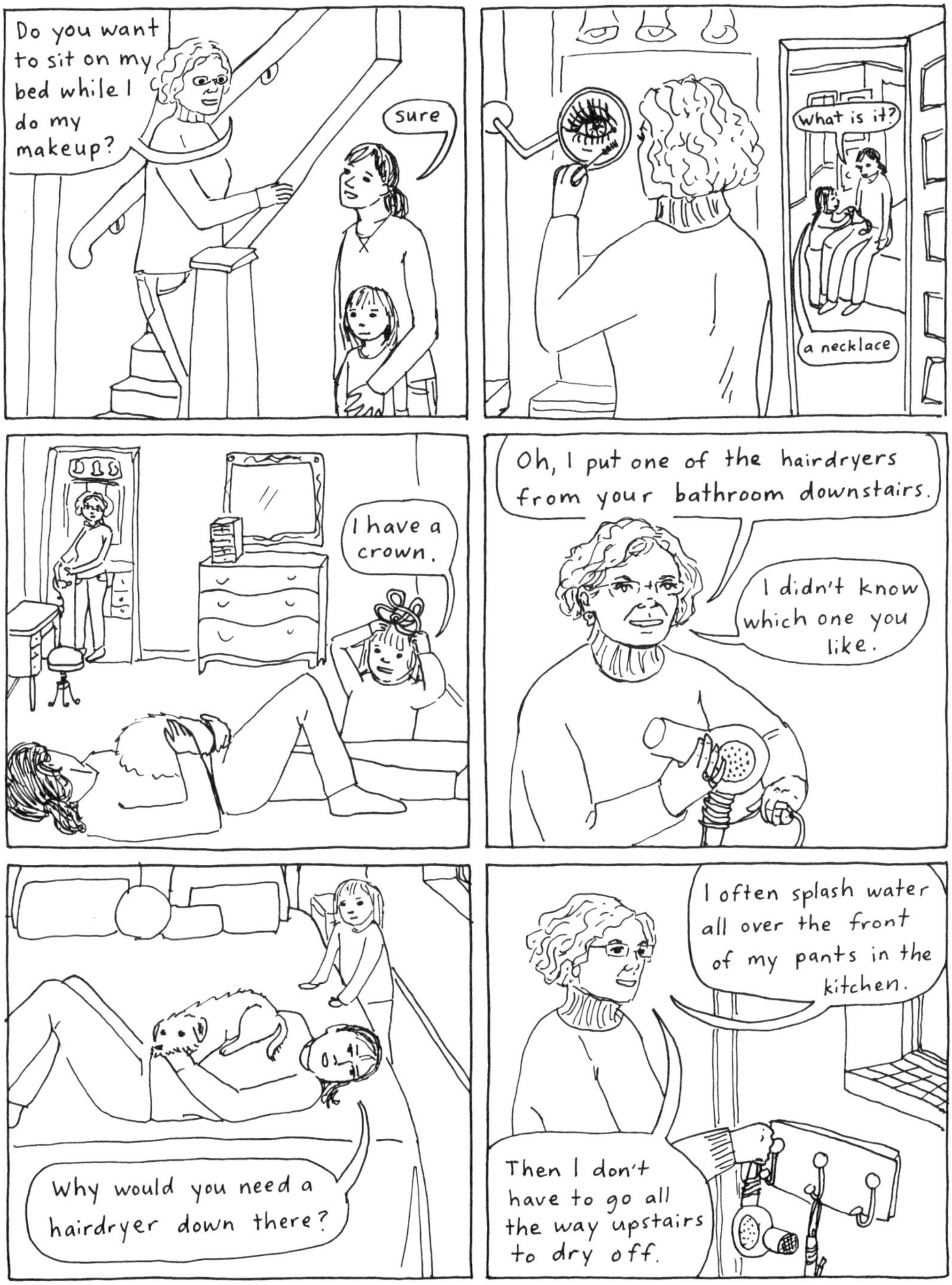

Do you want to sit on my bed while I do my makeup?
sure
What is it?
a necklace
I have a crown.
Oh, I put one of the hairdryers from your bathroom downstairs.
I didn't know which one you like.
Why would you need a hairdryer down there?
I often splash water all over the front of my pants in the kitchen.
Then I don't have to go all the way upstairs to dry off.

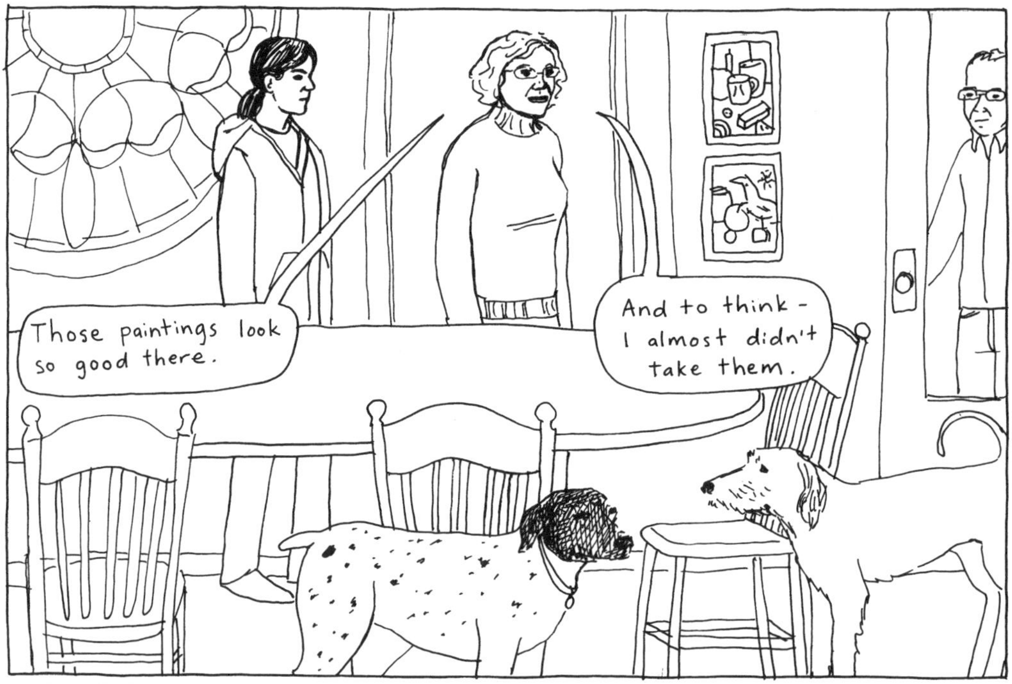
Those paintings look so good there.
And to think - I almost didn't take them.

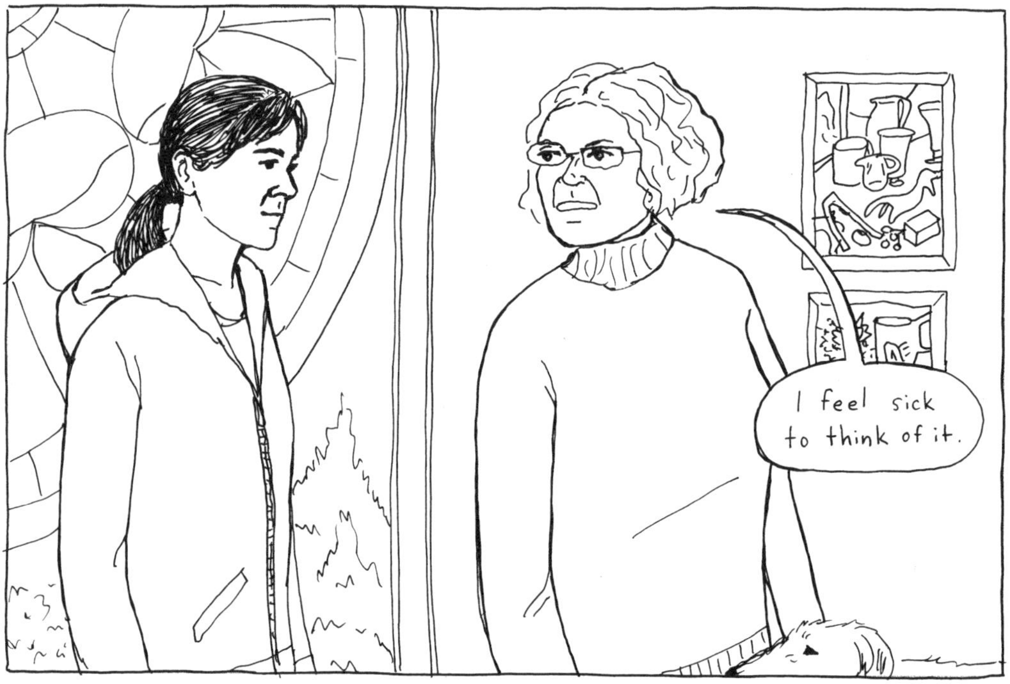
I feel sick to think of it.

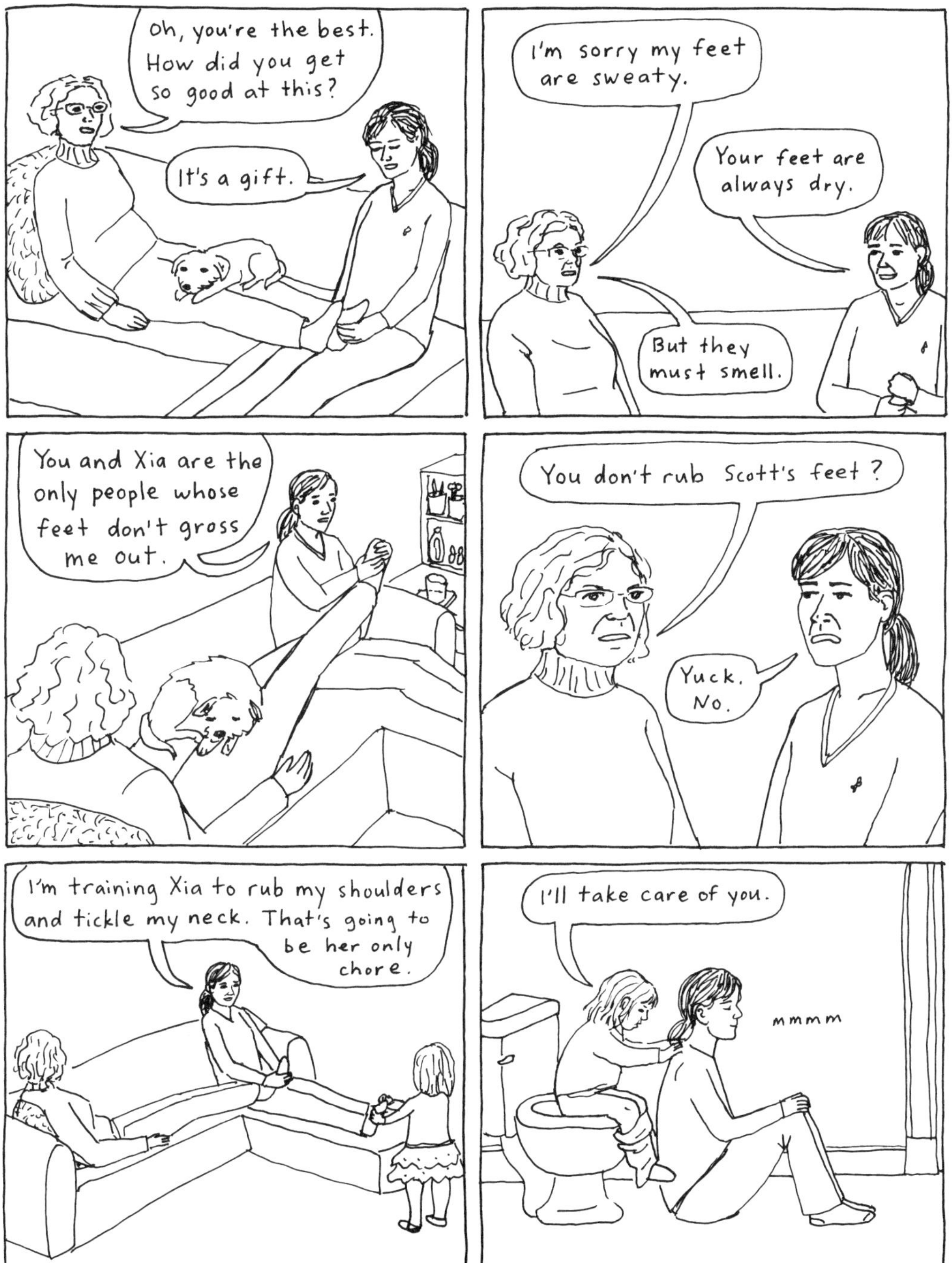
Oh, you're the best. How did you get so good at this?
It's a gift.
I'm sorry my feet are sweaty.
Your feet are always dry.
But they must smell.
You and Xia are the only people whose feet don't gross me out.
You don't rub Scott's feet?
Yuck. No.
I'm training Xia to rub my shoulders and tickle my neck. That's going to be her only chore.
I'll take care of you.
mmmm

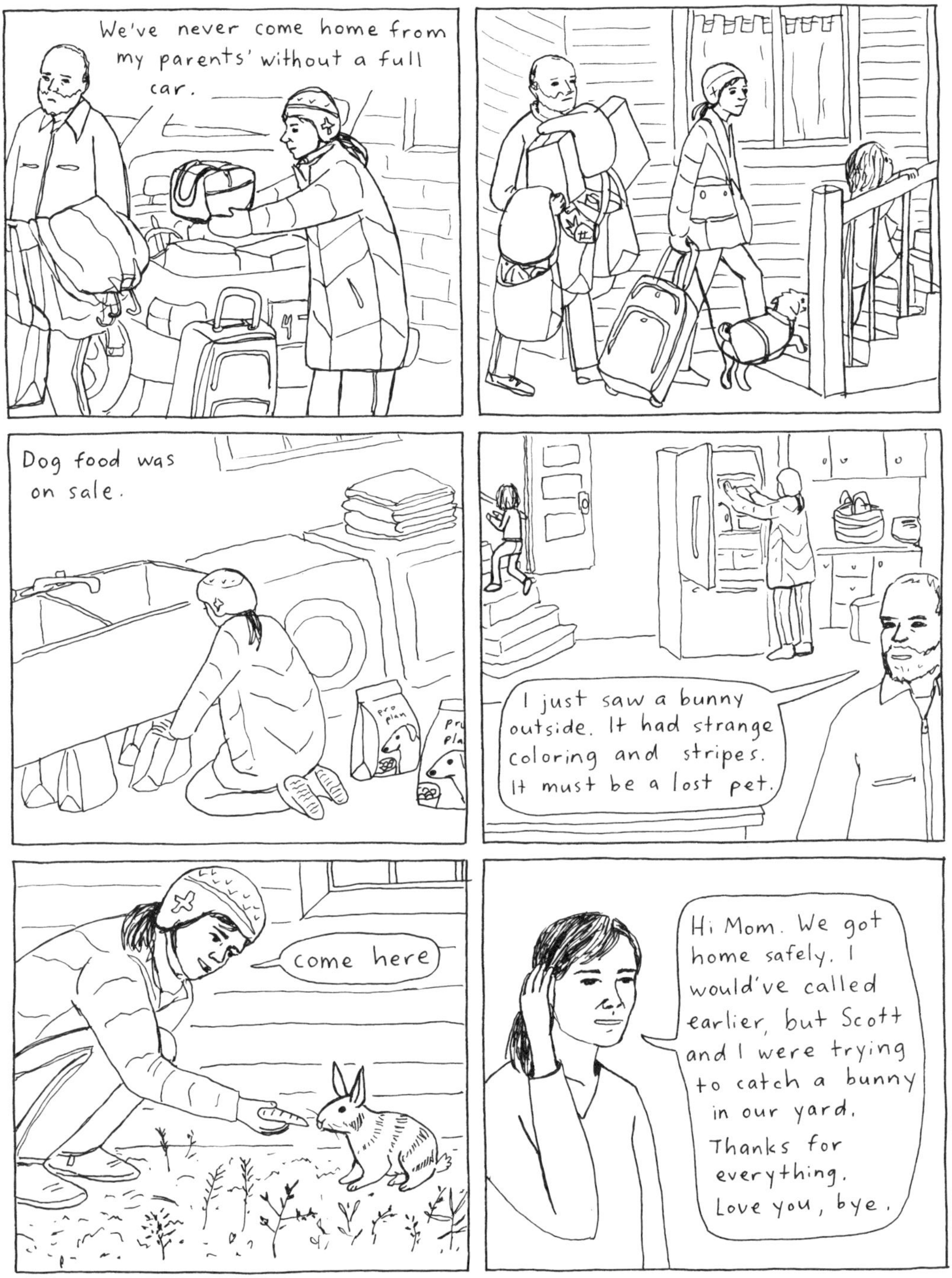
We've never come home from my parents' without a full car.
Dog food was on sale.
pro plan
I just saw a bunny outside. It had strange coloring and stripes. It must be a lost pet.
come here
Hi Mom. We got home safely. I would've called earlier, but Scott and I were trying to catch a bunny in our yard. Thanks for everything. Love you, bye.

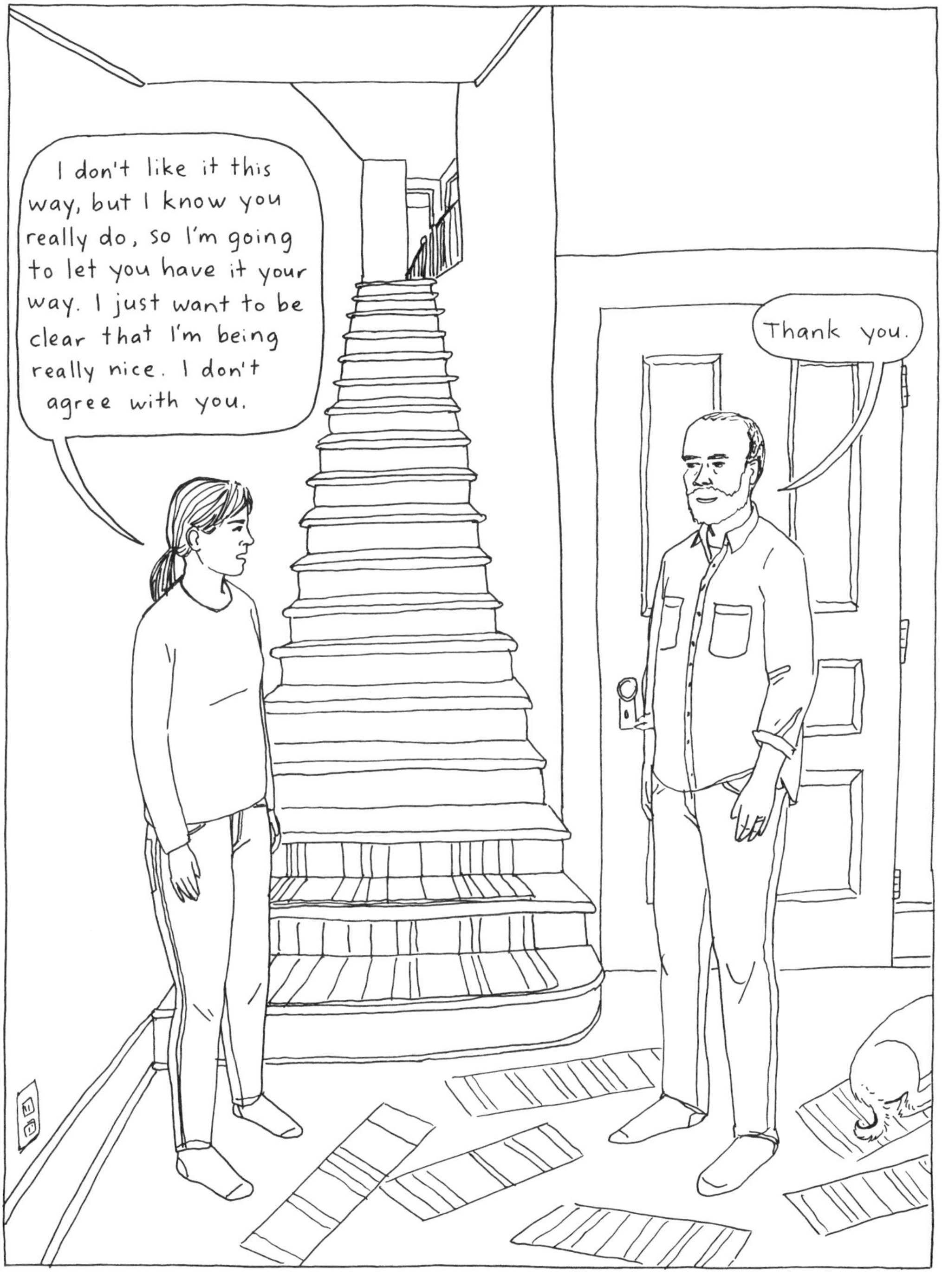
I don't like it this way, but I know you really do, so I'm going to let you have it your way. I just want to be clear that I'm being really nice. I don't agree with you.
Thank you.

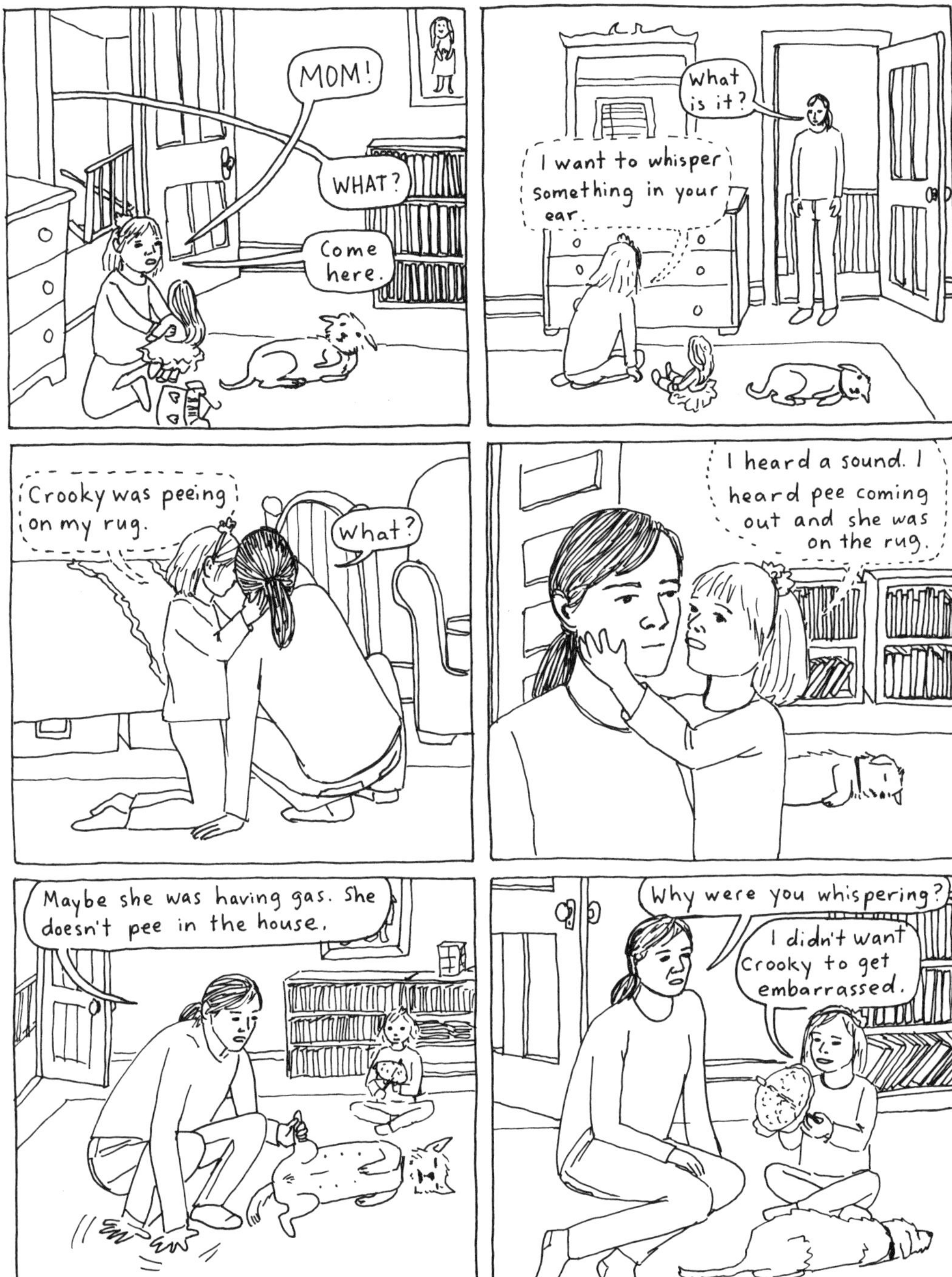
MOM!
WHAT?
Come here.
What is it?
I want to whisper something in your ear.
Crooky was peeing on my rug.
What?
I heard a sound. I heard pee coming out and she was on the rug.
Maybe she was having gas. She doesn't pee in the house.
Why were you whispering?
I didn't want Crooky to get embarrassed.

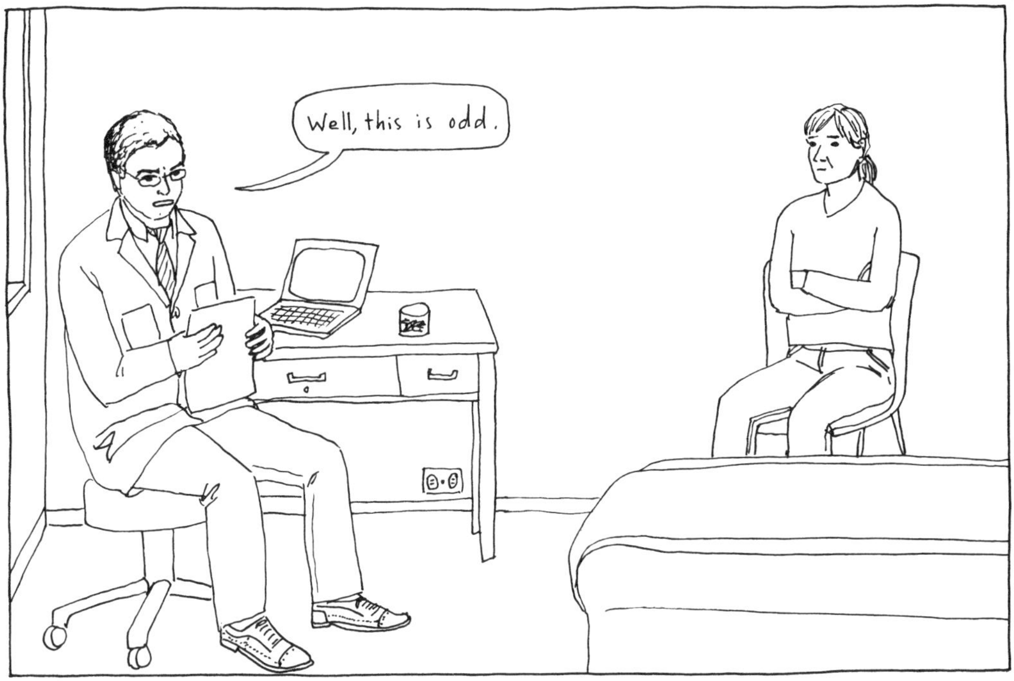
Well, this is odd.

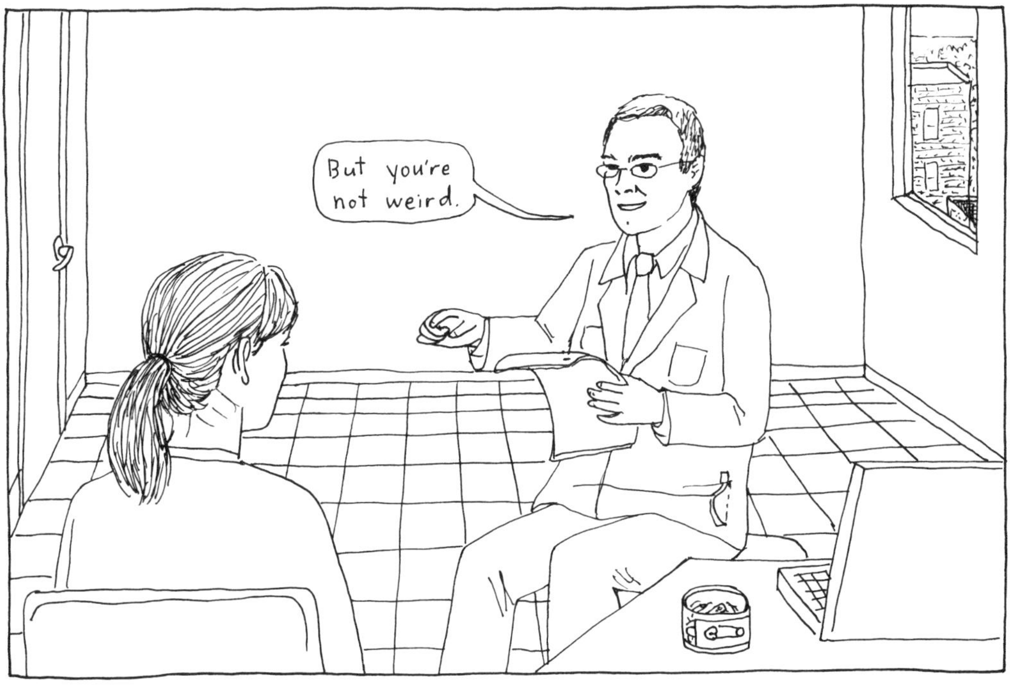
But you're not weird.

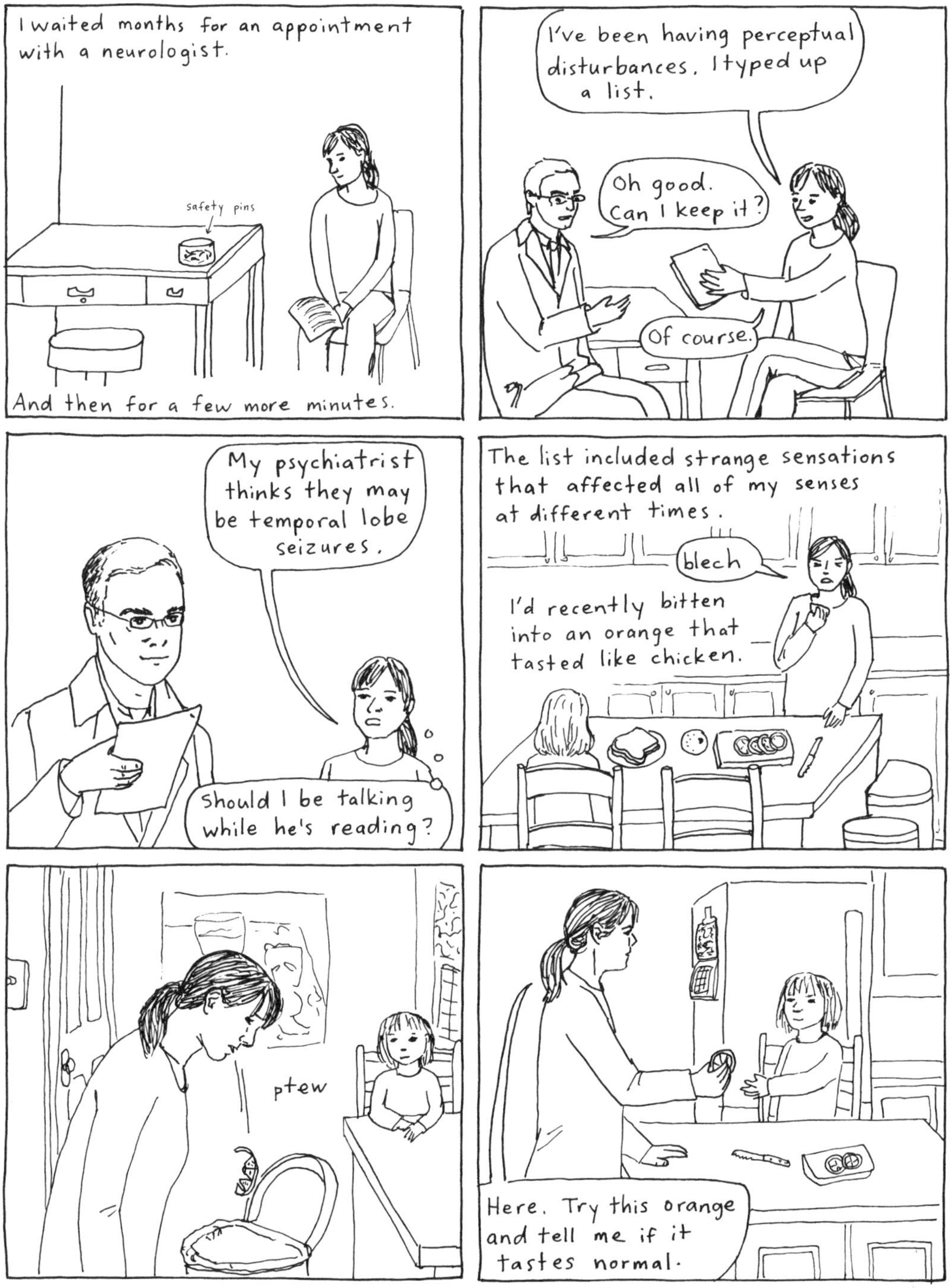

I waited months for an appointment with a neurologist.
safety pins
And then for a few more minutes.
I've been having perceptual disturbances. I typed up a list.
Oh good. Can I keep it?
Of course.
My psychiatrist thinks they may be temporal lobe seizures.
Should I be talking while he's reading?
The list included strange sensations that affected all of my senses at different times.
blech
I'd recently bitten into an orange that tasted like chicken.
ptew
Here. Try this orange and tell me if it tastes normal.

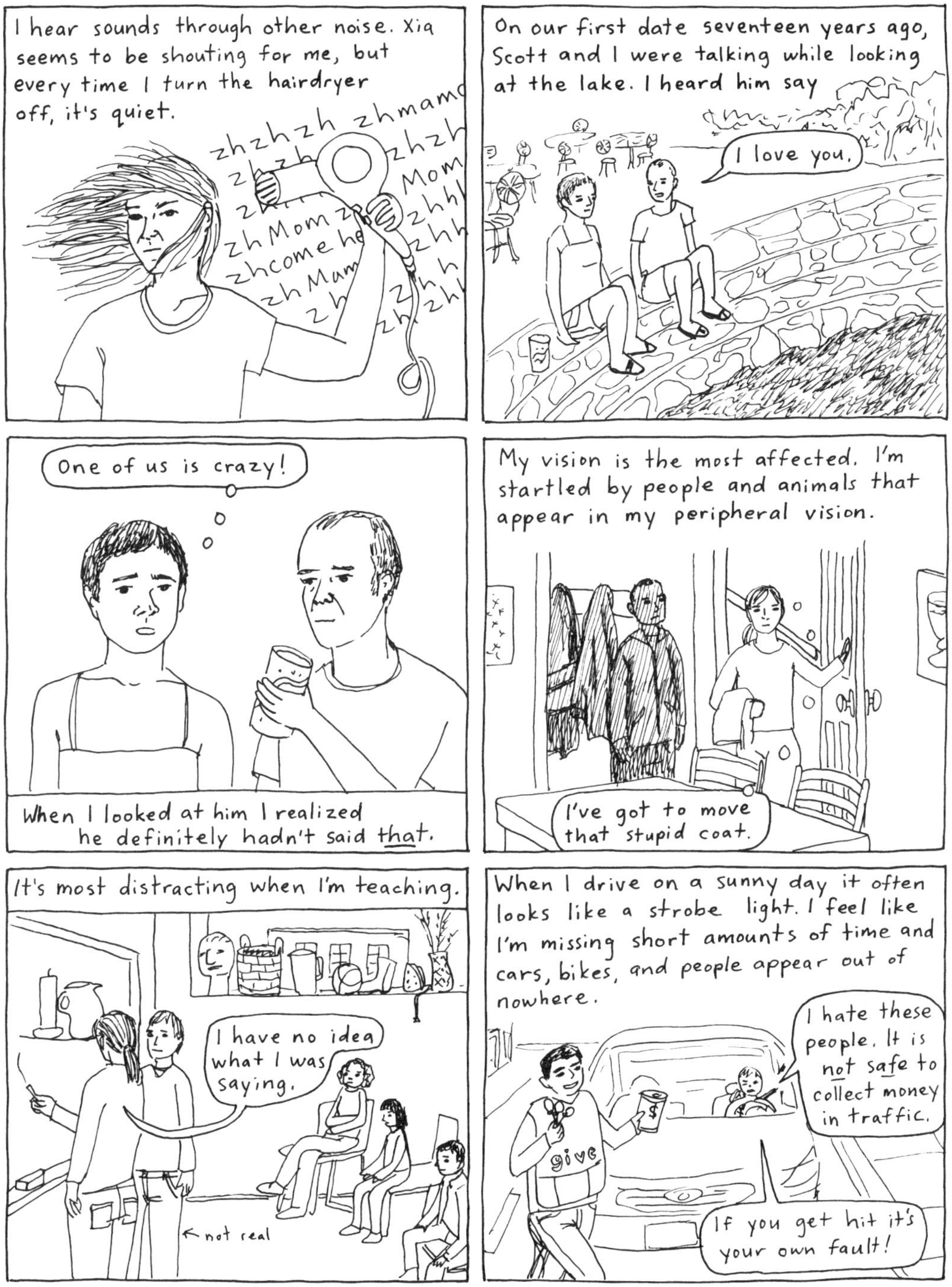
I hear sounds through other noise. Xia seems to be shouting for me, but every time I turn the hairdryer off, it's quiet.
On our first date seventeen years ago, Scott and I were talking while looking at the lake. I heard him say
I love you.
One of us is crazy!
When I looked at him I realized he definitely hadn't said that.
My vision is the most affected. I'm startled by people and animals that appear in my peripheral vision.
I've got to move that stupid coat.
It's most distracting when I'm teaching.
I have no idea what I was saying.
← not real
When I drive on a sunny day it often looks like a strobe light. I feel like I'm missing short amounts of time and cars, bikes, and people appear out of nowhere.
give
I hate these people. It is not safe to collect money in traffic.
If you get hit it's your own fault!

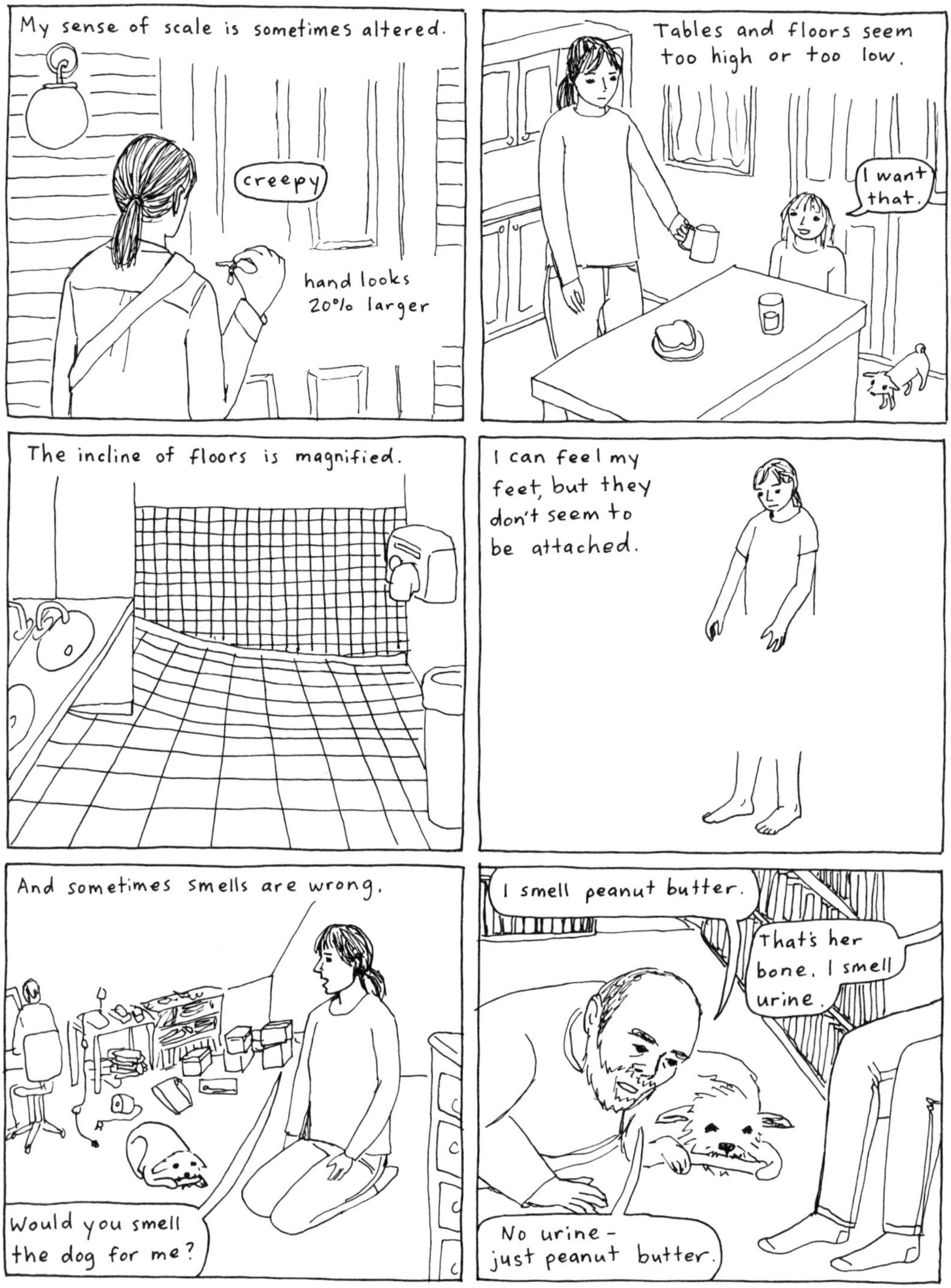

My sense of scale is sometimes altered.
creepy
hand looks 20% larger
Tables and floors seem too high or too low.
I want that.
The incline of floors is magnified.
I can feel my feet, but they don't seem to be attached.
And sometimes smells are wrong.
Would you smell the dog for me?
I smell peanut butter.
That's her bone. I smell urine.
No urine - just peanut butter.

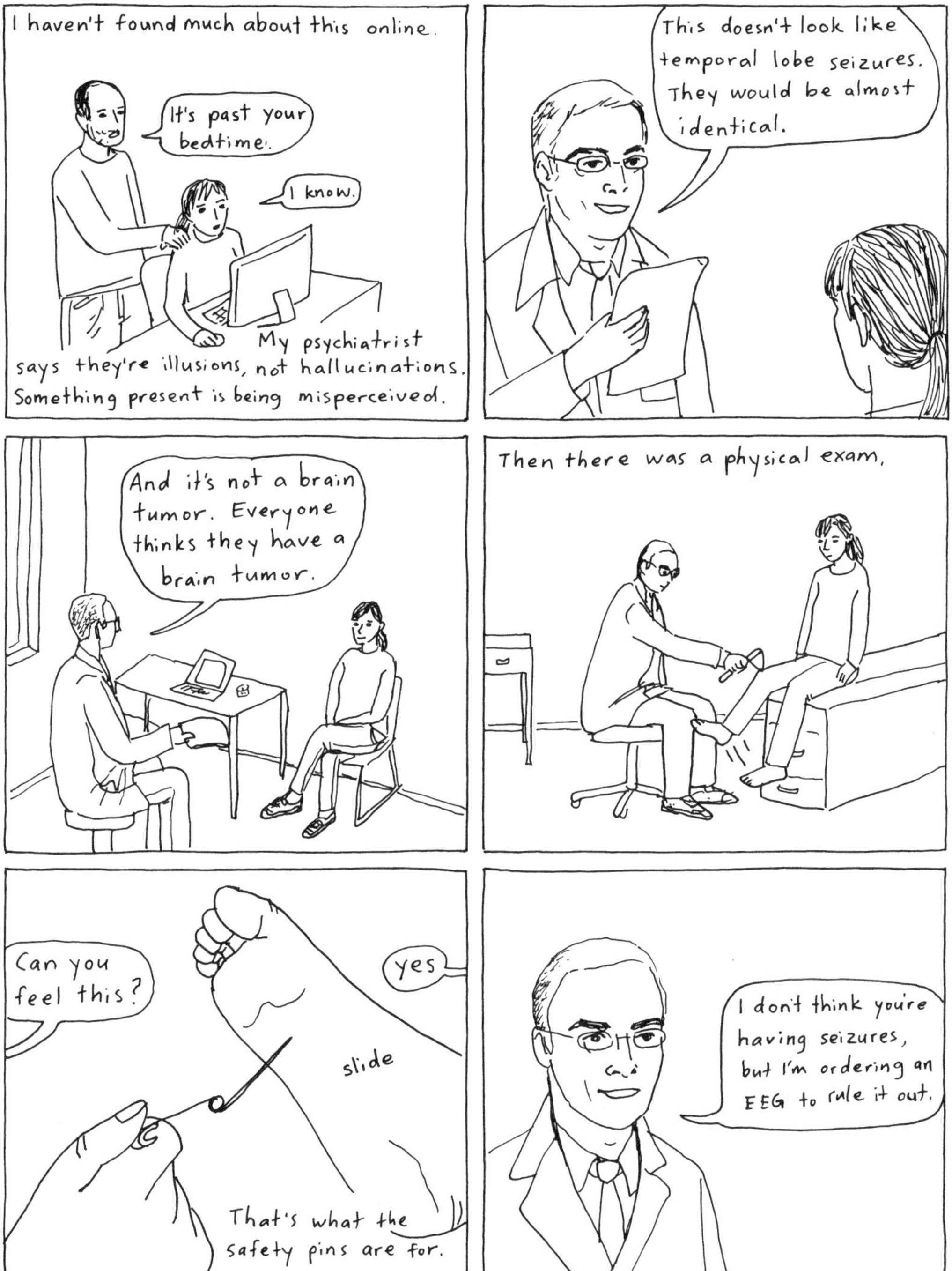
I haven't found much about this online.
It's past your bedtime.
I know.
My psychiatrist says they're illusions, not hallucinations. Something present is being misperceived.
This doesn't look like temporal lobe seizures. They would be almost identical.
And it's not a brain tumor. Everyone thinks they have a brain tumor.
Then there was a physical exam,
Can you feel this?
yes
slide
That's what the safety pins are for.
I don't think you're having seizures, but I'm ordering an EEG to rule it out.

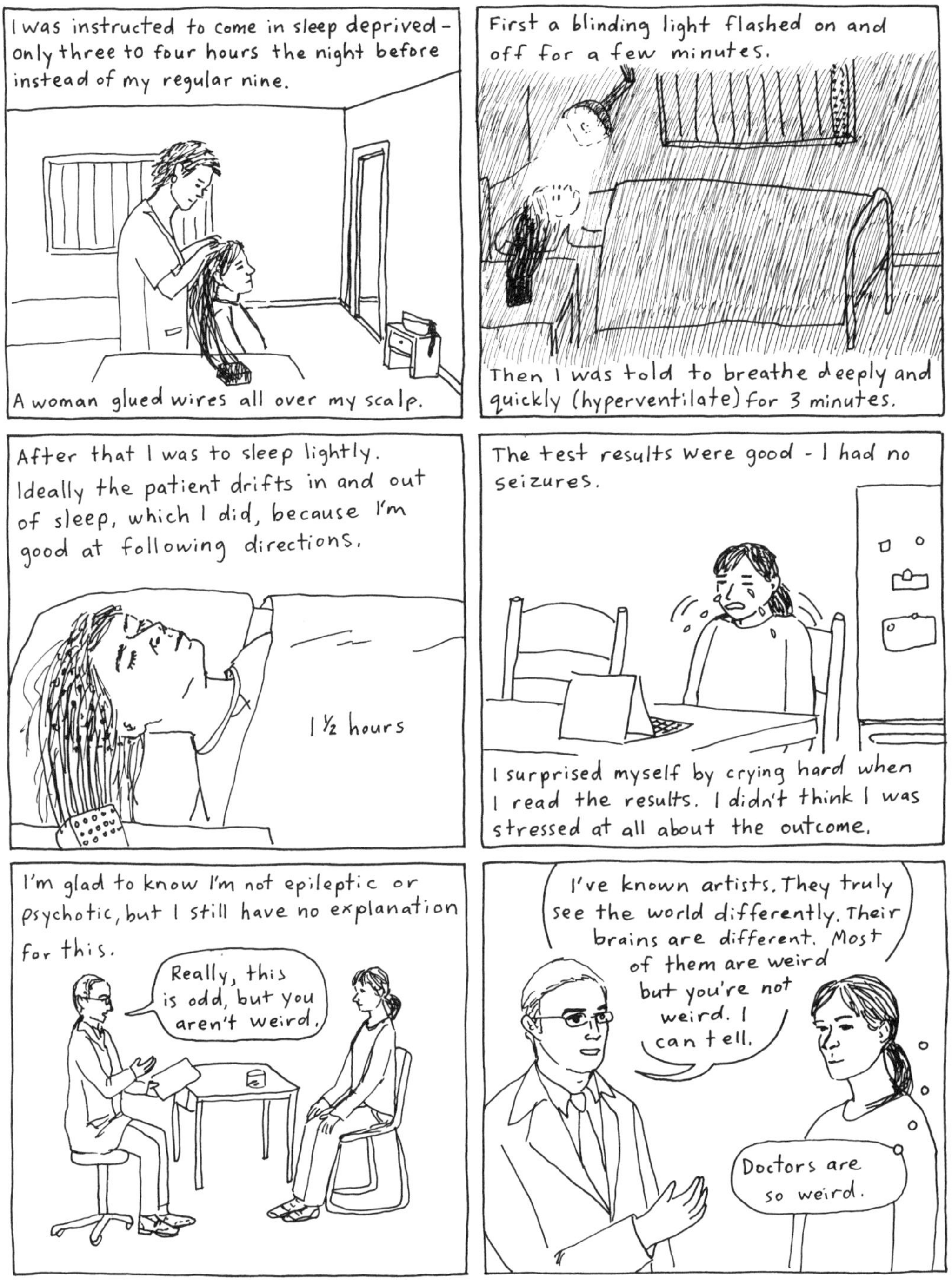

I was instructed to come in sleep deprived - only three to four hours the night before instead of my regular nine.
A woman glued wires all over my scalp.
First a blinding light flashed on and off for a few minutes.
Then I was told to breathe deeply and quickly (hyperventilate) for 3 minutes.
After that I was to sleep lightly. Ideally the patient drifts in and out of sleep, which I did, because I'm good at following directions.
1 ½ hours
The test results were good - I had no seizures.
I surprised myself by crying hard when I read the results. I didn't think I was stressed at all about the outcome.
I'm glad to know I'm not epileptic or psychotic, but I still have no explanation for this.
Really, this is odd, but you aren't weird.
I've known artists. They truly see the world differently. Their brains are different. Most of them are weird but you're not weird. I can tell.
Doctors are so weird.

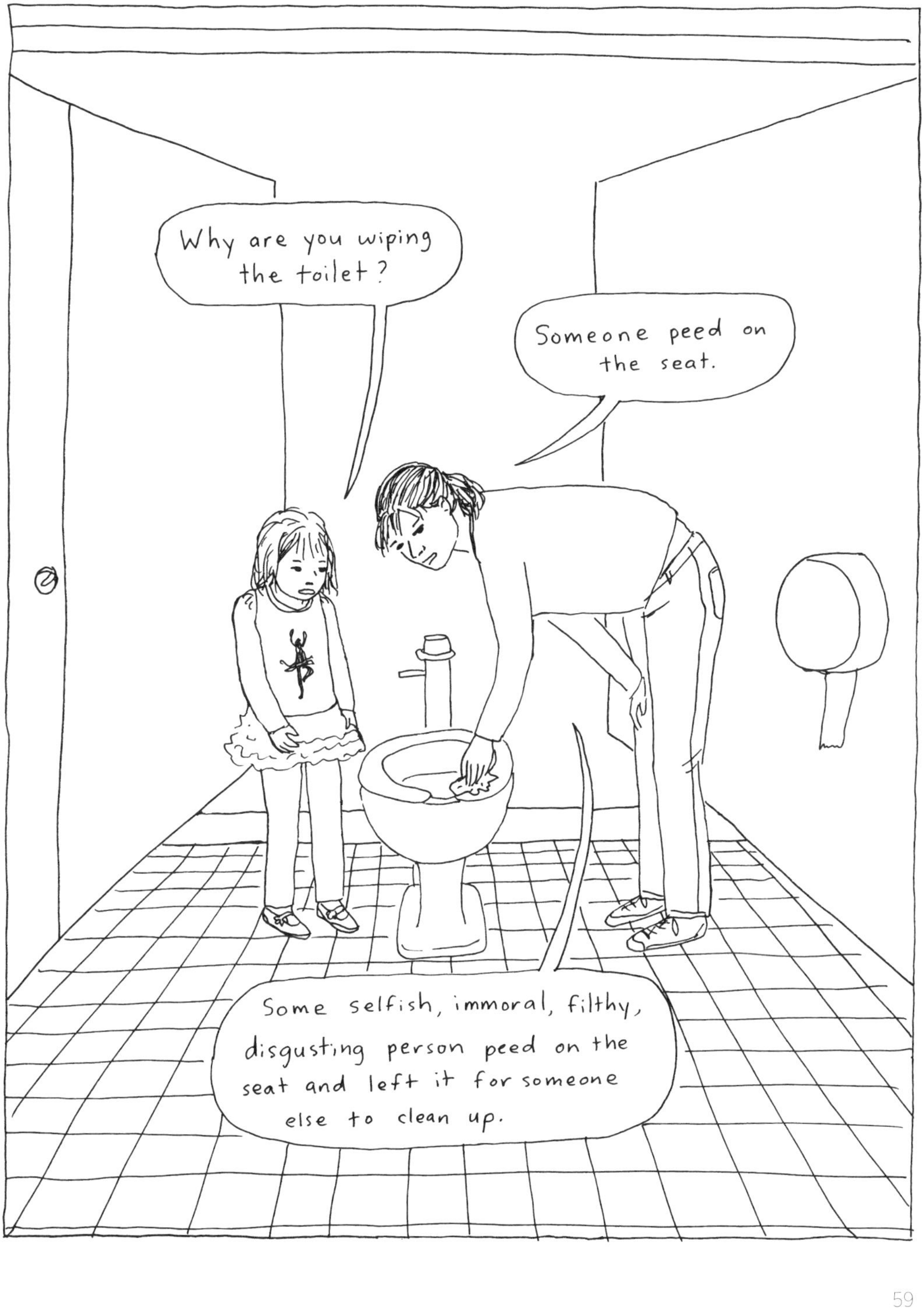
Why are you wiping the toilet?
Someone peed on the seat.
Some selfish, immoral, filthy, disgusting person peed on the seat and left it for someone else to clean up.

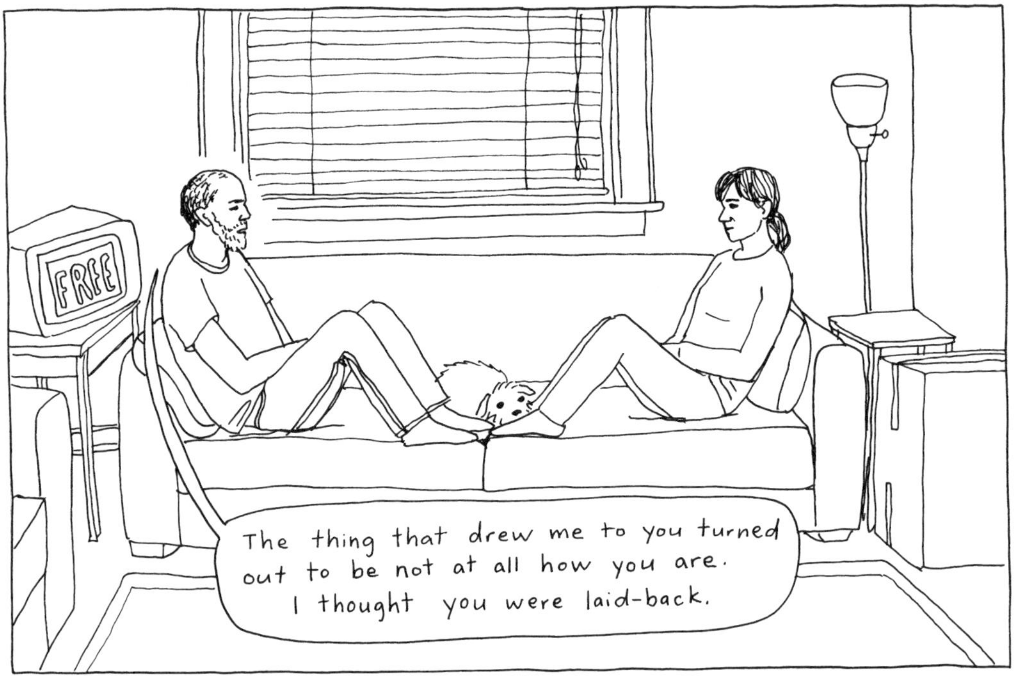
FREE
The thing that drew me to you turned out to be not at all how you are. I thought you were laid-back.

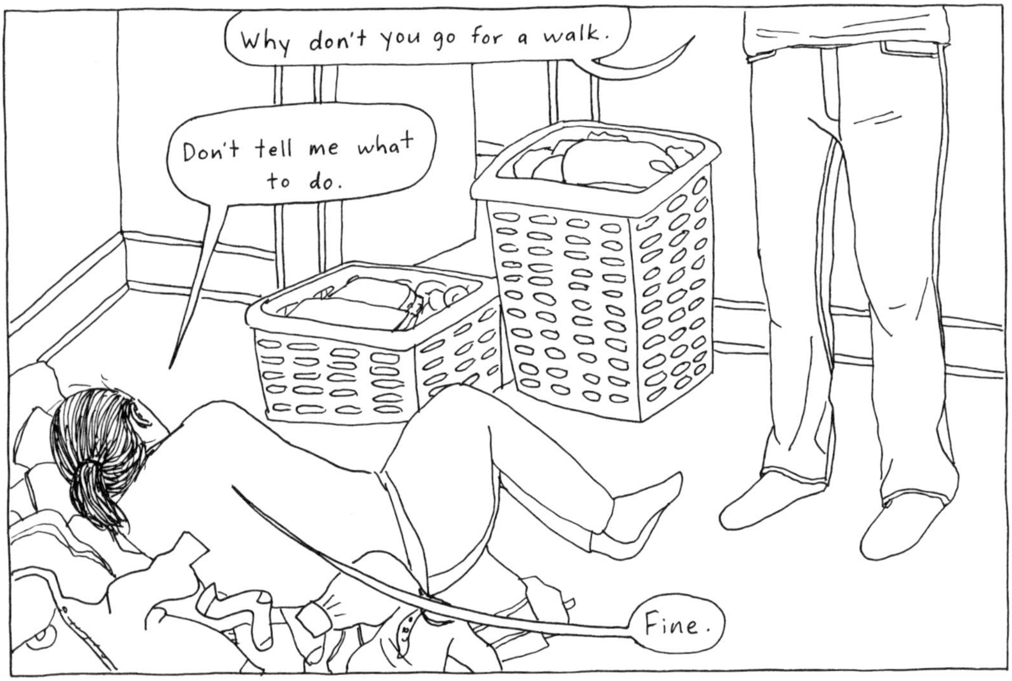
Why don't you go for a walk.
Don't tell me what to do.
Fine.

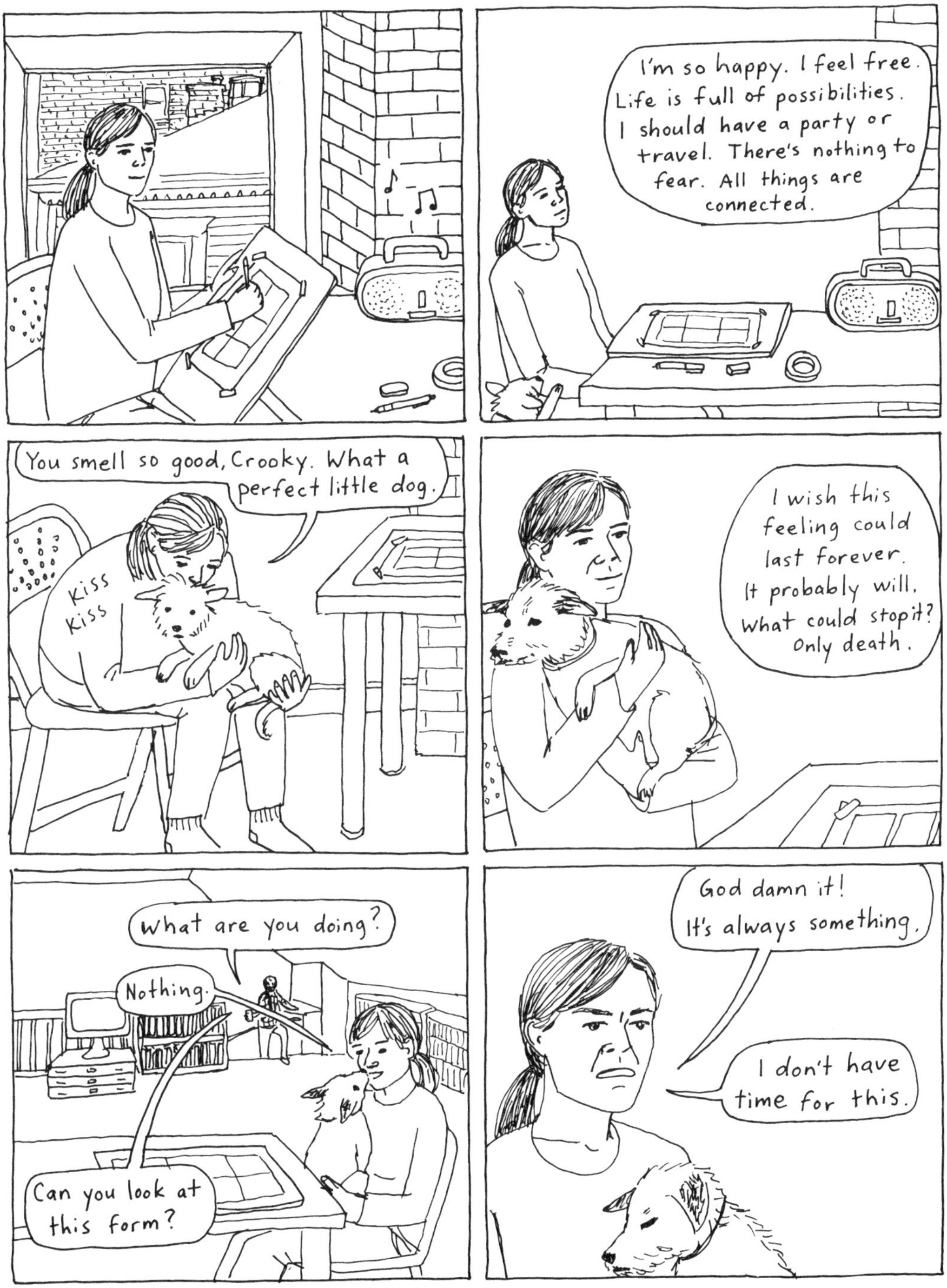
I'm so happy. I feel free. Life is full of possibilities. I should have a party or travel. There's nothing to fear. All things are connected.
You smell so good, Crooky. What a perfect little dog.
KISS KISS
I wish this feeling could last forever. It probably will. What could stop it? Only death.
What are you doing?
Nothing.
Can you look at this form?
God damn it! It's always something.
I don't have time for this.

A couple years ago my psychiatrist recommended I try the partial hospitalization program.
Linden
hospital
Centra
The lobby of the Evanston Hospital looks like a nice hotel.
welcome
two-story water fountain wall
bloodtakers hidden away
player piano
concierge
fireplaces not shown
There was a lot of paperwork.
State your goals:
I want to get rid of the extremes and live in the middle. I want to be in control.
Every morning we had to rate our mood and describe our sleep and appetite. We also rated our hopefulness on a scale from 1-10.
5
My mood went up several points during my first morning there.
One day we were asked, "What makes you happy?" This is a tough question for a room of depressed people to answer. I probably said:
art
or
comics
or
making things

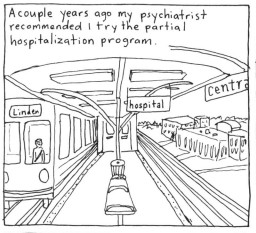

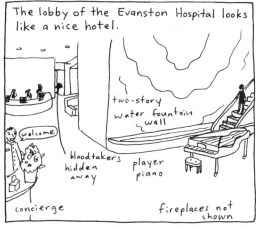

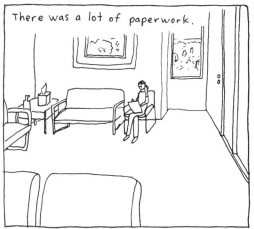

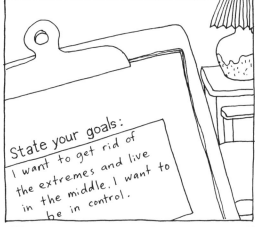

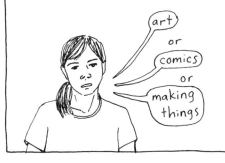

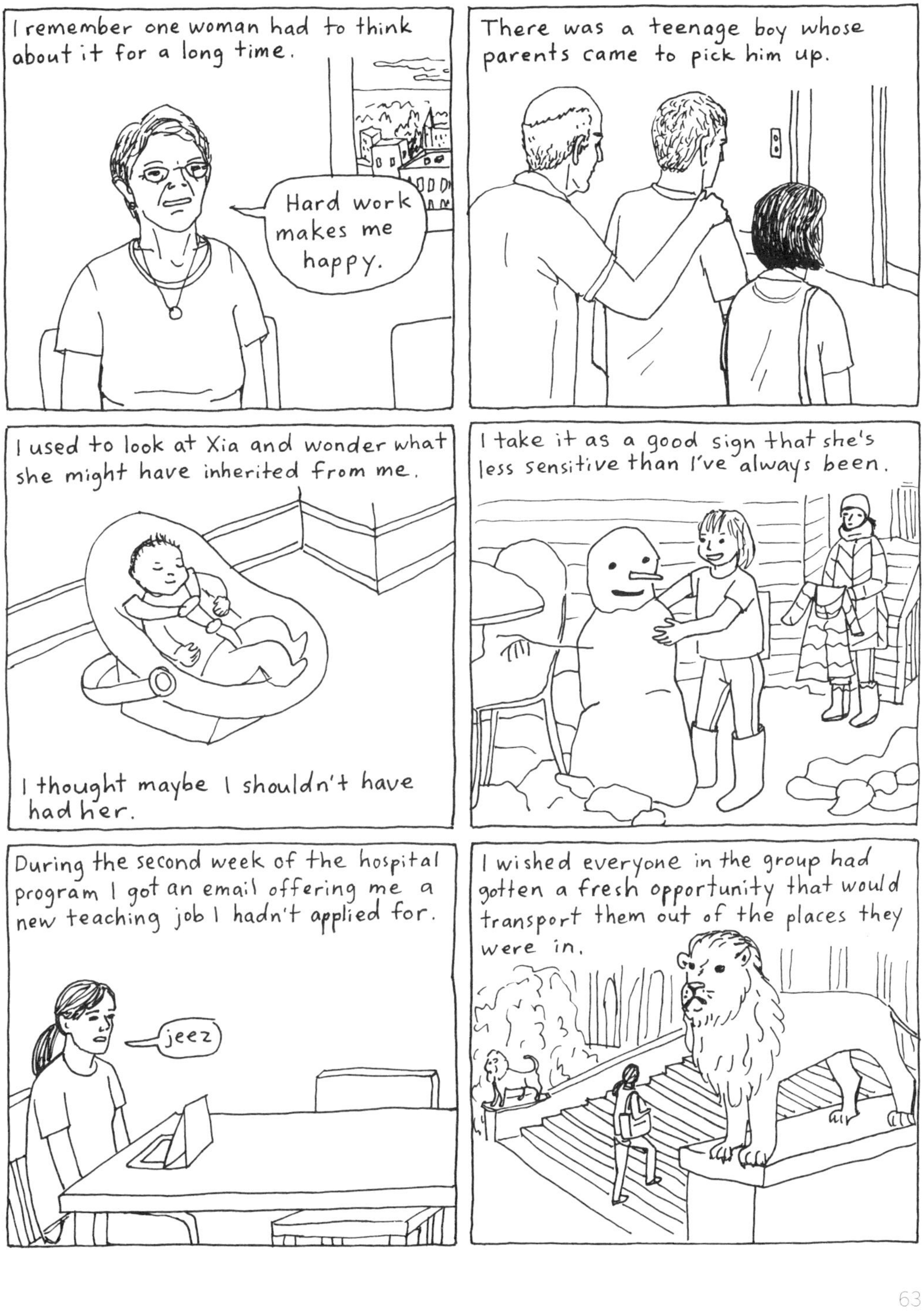
I remember one woman had to think about it for a long time.
Hard work makes me happy.
There was a teenage boy whose parents came to pick him up.
I used to look at Xia and wonder what she might have inherited from me.
I thought maybe I shouldn't have had her.
I take it as a good sign that she's less sensitive than I've always been.
During the second week of the hospital program I got an email offering me a new teaching job I hadn't applied for.
jeez
I wished everyone in the group had gotten a fresh opportunity that would transport them out of the places they were in.

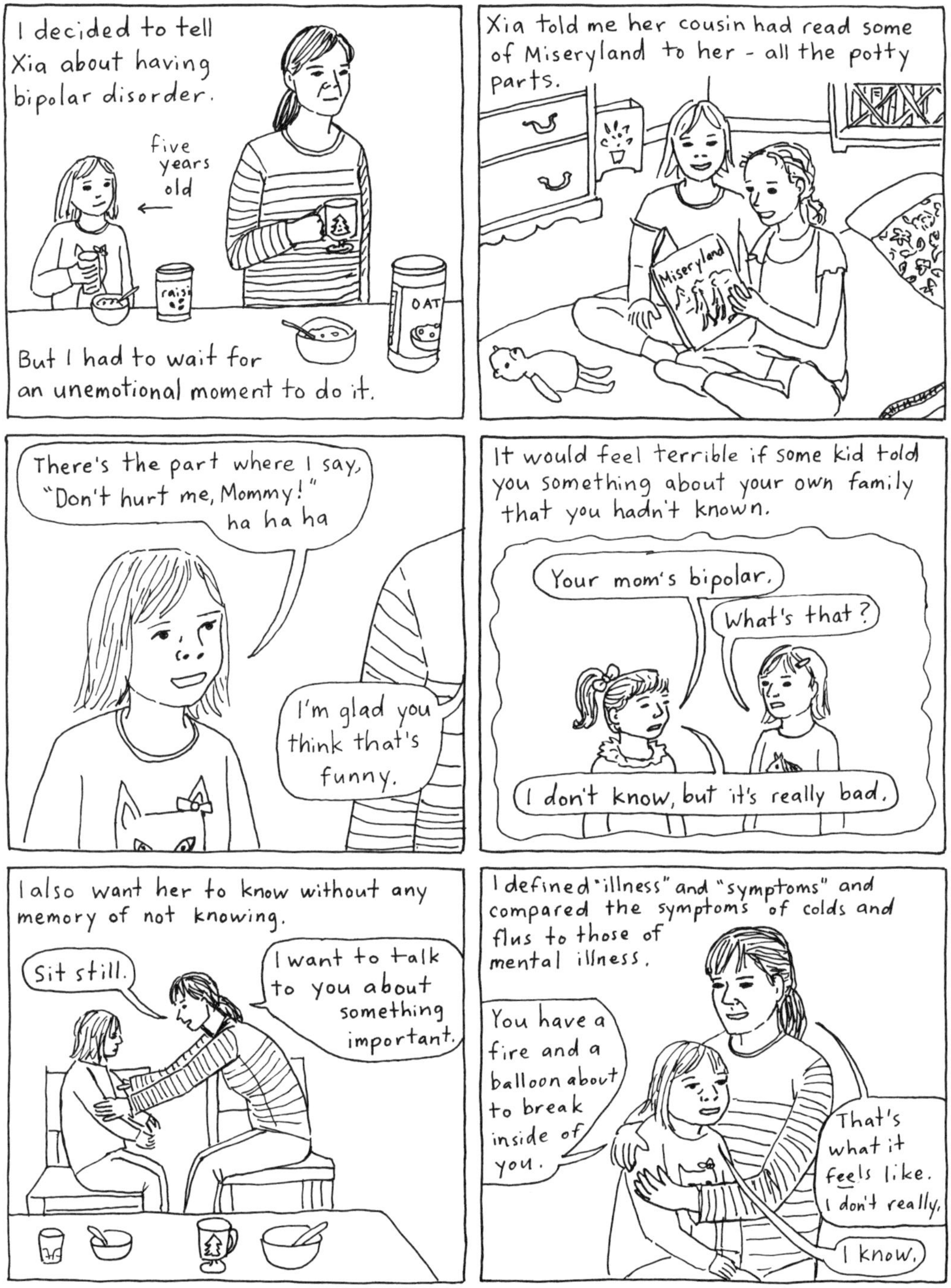
I decided to tell Xia about having bipolar disorder.
five years old
raisi
OAT
But I had to wait for an unemotional moment to do it.
Xia told me her cousin had read some of Miseryland to her - all the potty parts.
Miseryland
There's the part where I say, "Don't hurt me, Mommy!" ha ha ha
I'm glad you think that's funny.
It would feel terrible if some kid told you something about your own family that you hadn't known.
Your mom's bipolar.
What's that?
I don't know, but it's really bad.
I also want her to know without any memory of not knowing.
Sit still.
I want to talk to you about something important.
I defined "illness" and "symptoms" and compared the symptoms of colds and flus to those of mental illness.
You have a fire and a balloon about to break inside of you.
That's what it feels like. I don't really.
I know.

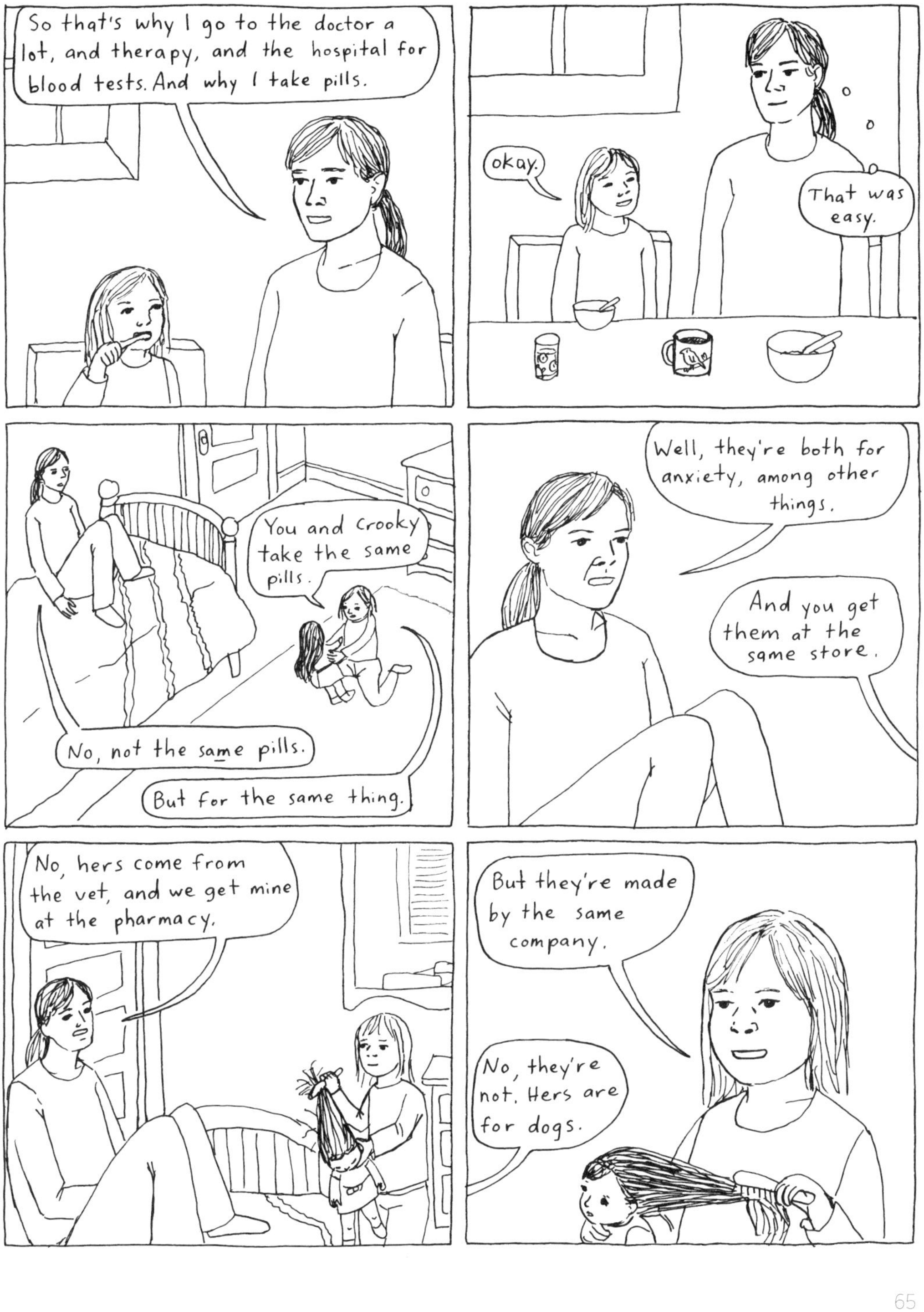
So that's why I go to the doctor a lot, and therapy, and the hospital for blood tests. And why I take pills.
okay.
That was easy.
You and Crooky take the same pills.
No, not the same pills.
But for the same thing.
Well, they're both for anxiety, among other things.
And you get them at the same store.
No, hers come from the vet, and we get mine at the pharmacy.
But they're made by the same company.
No, they're not. Hers are for dogs.

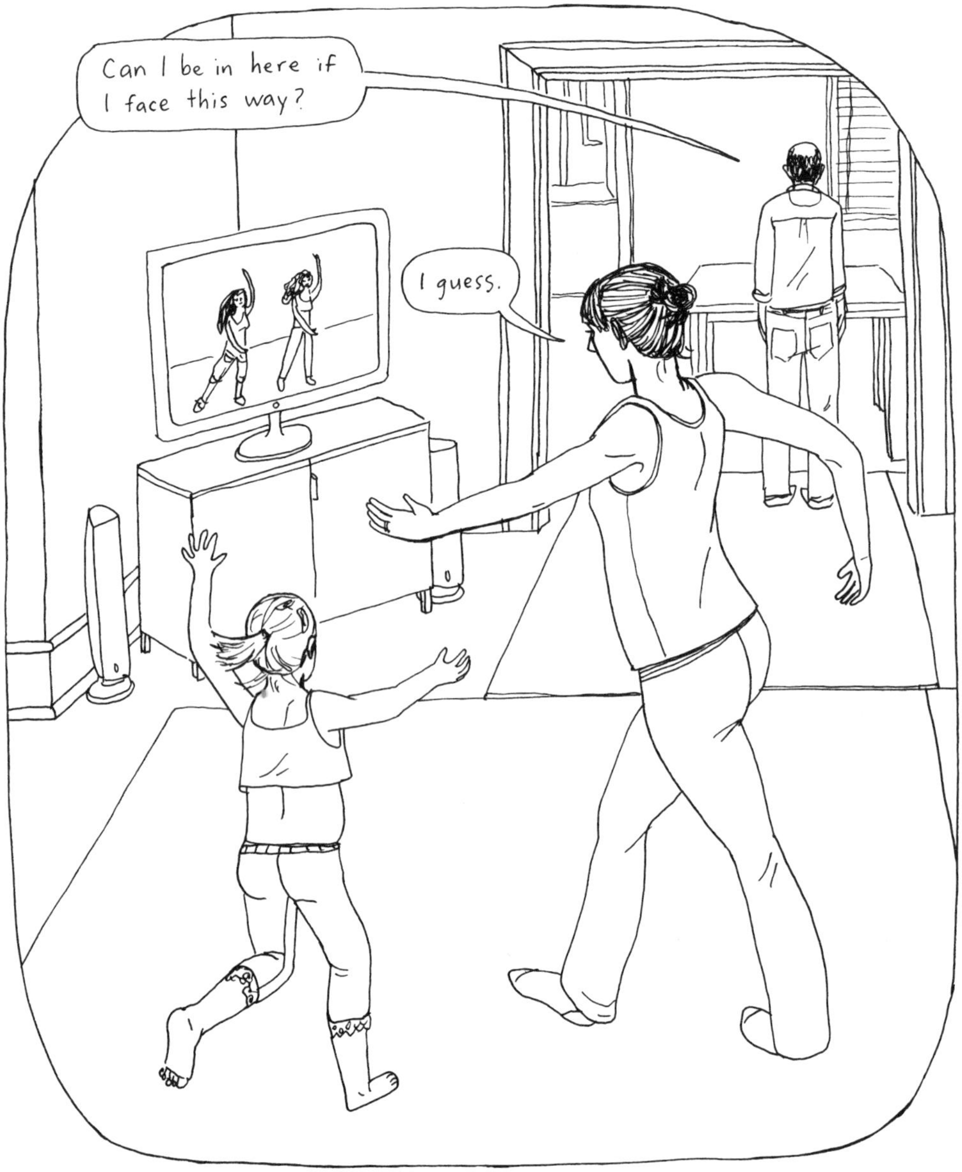
Can I be in here if I face this way?
I guess.

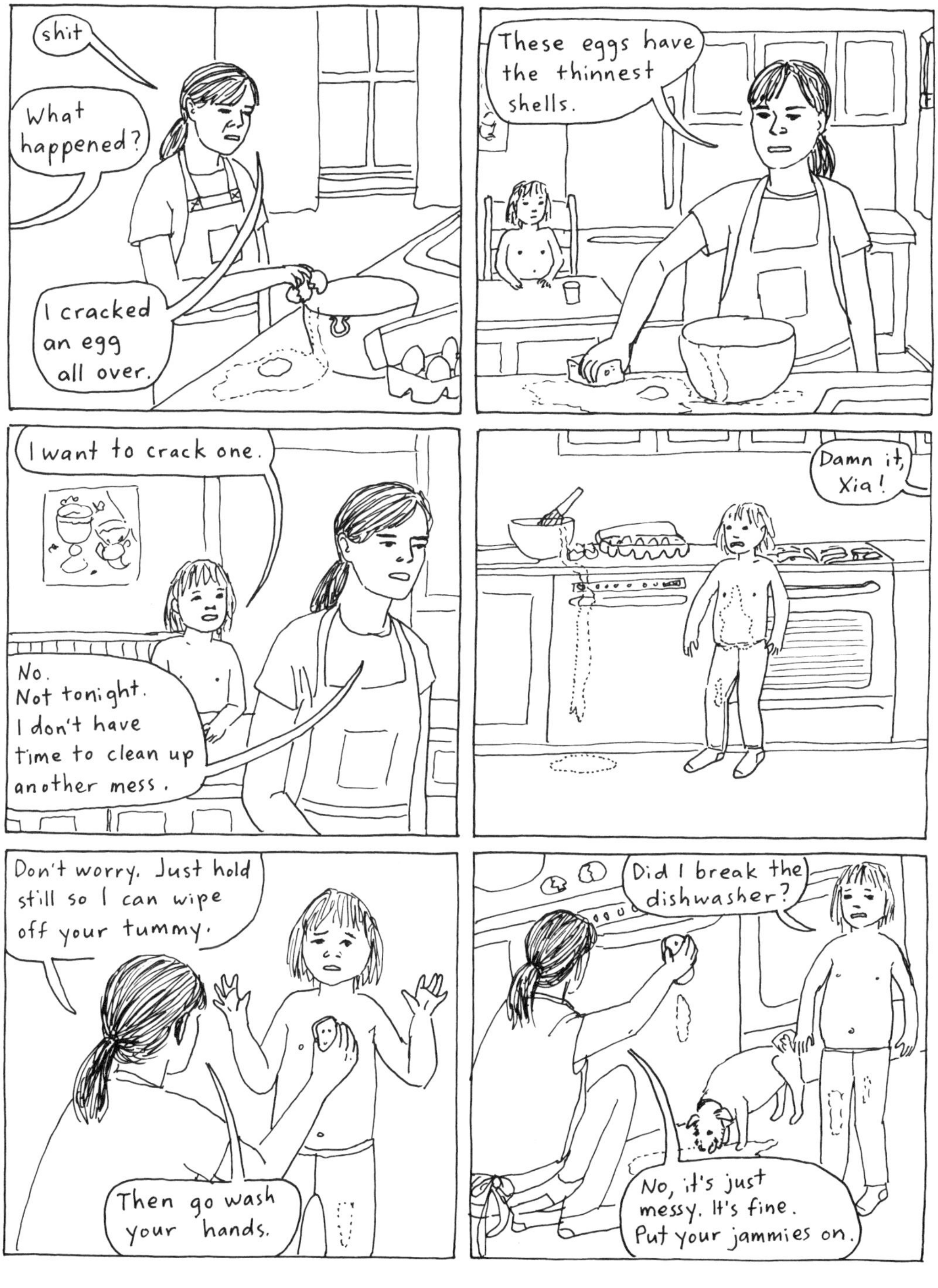
shit
What happened?
I cracked an egg all over.
These eggs have the thinnest shells.
I want to crack one.
No. Not tonight. I don't have time to clean up another mess.
Damn it, Xia!
Don't worry. Just hold still so I can wipe off your tummy.
Then go wash your hands.
Did I break the dishwasher?
No, it's just messy. It's fine. Put your jammies on.

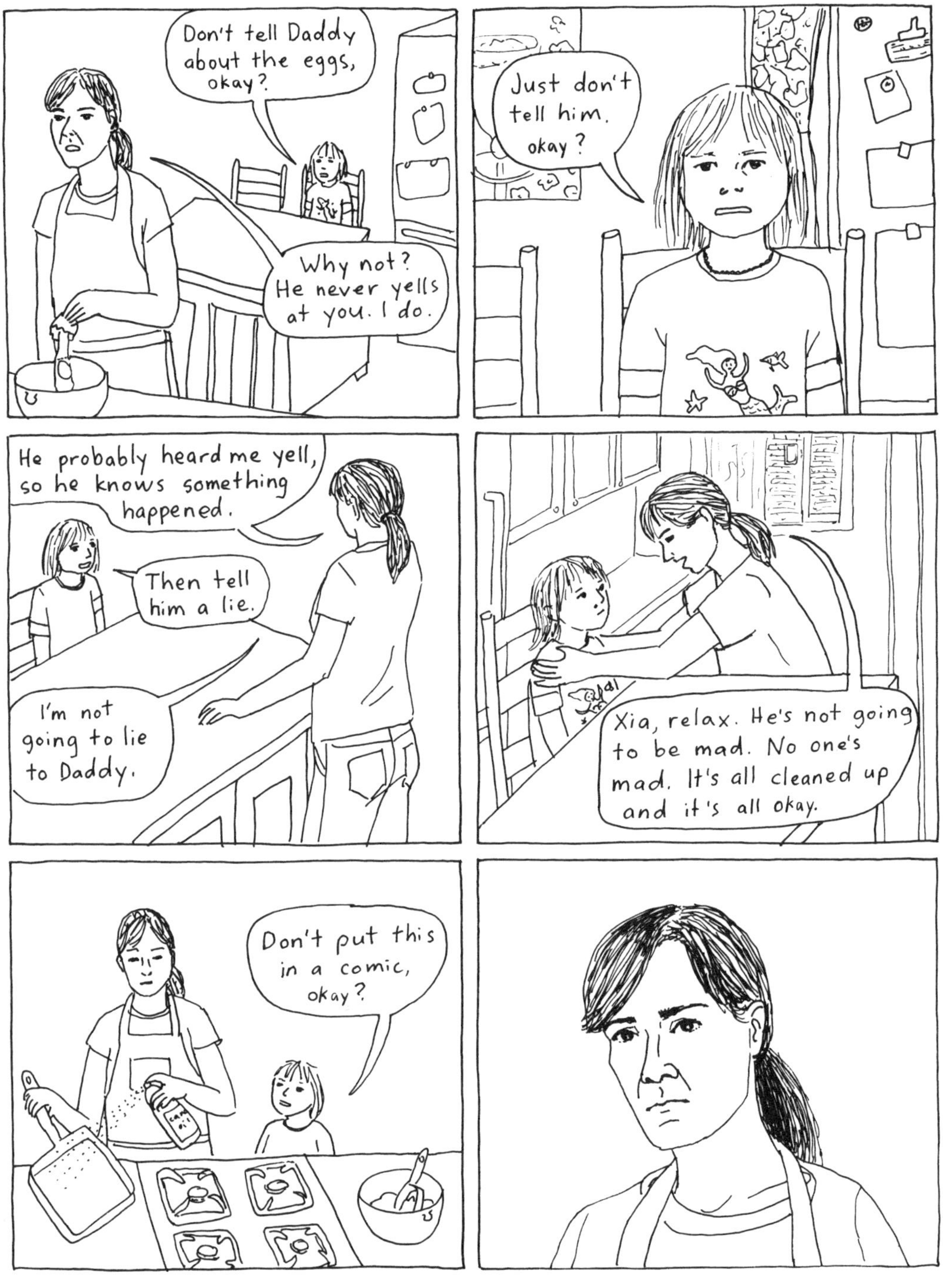
Don't tell Daddy about the eggs, okay?
Why not? He never yells at you. I do.
Just don't tell him, okay?
He probably heard me yell, so he knows something happened.
Then tell him a lie.
I'm not going to lie to Daddy.
Xia, relax. He's not going to be mad. No one's mad. It's all cleaned up and it's all okay.
Don't put this in a comic, okay?

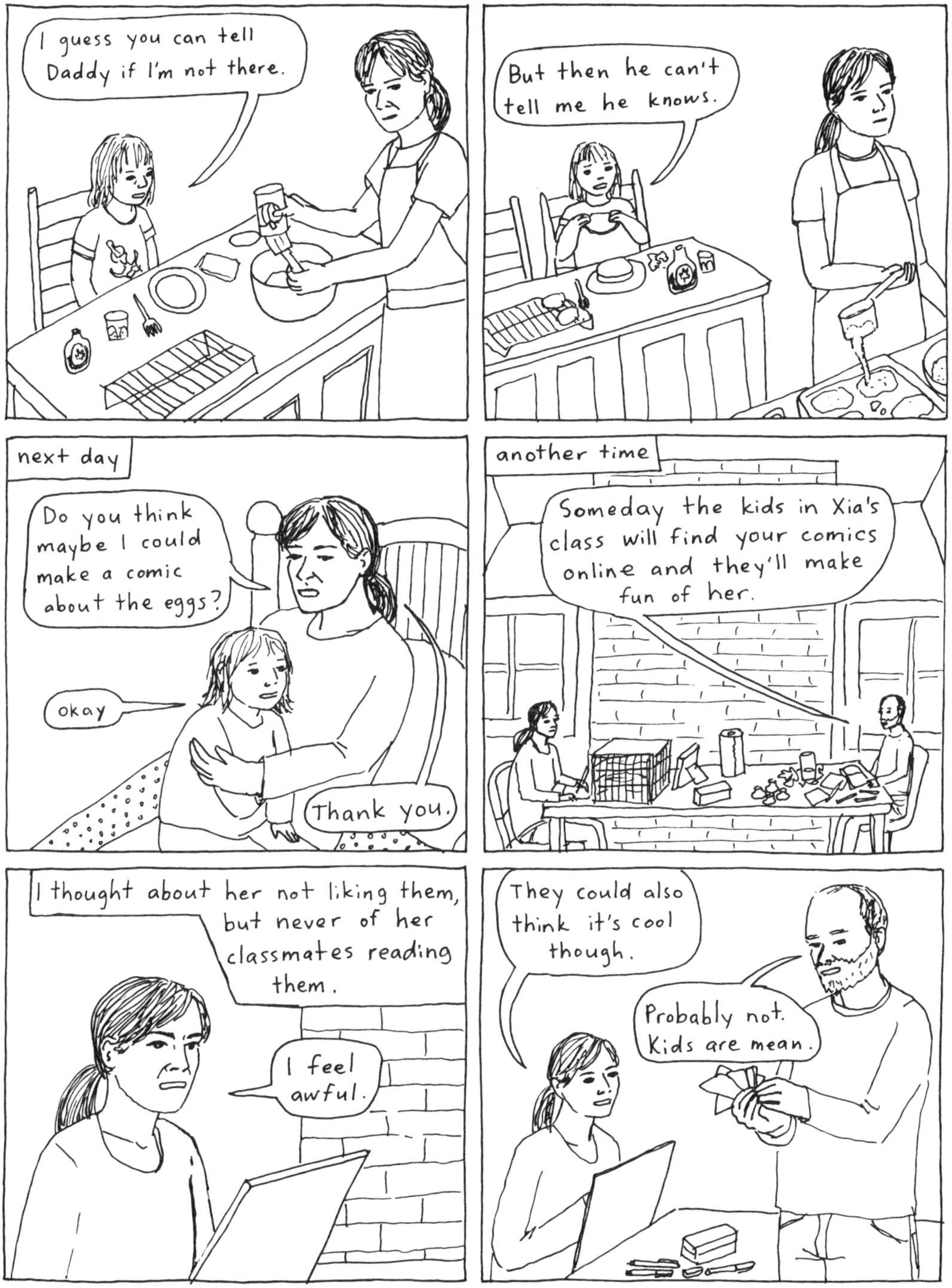
I guess you can tell Daddy if I'm not there.
But then he can't tell me he knows.
next day
Do you think maybe I could make a comic about the eggs?
okay
Thank you.
another time
Someday the kids in Xia's class will find your comics online and they'll make fun of her.
I thought about her not liking them, but never of her classmates reading them.
I feel awful.
They could also think it's cool though.
Probably not. Kids are mean.

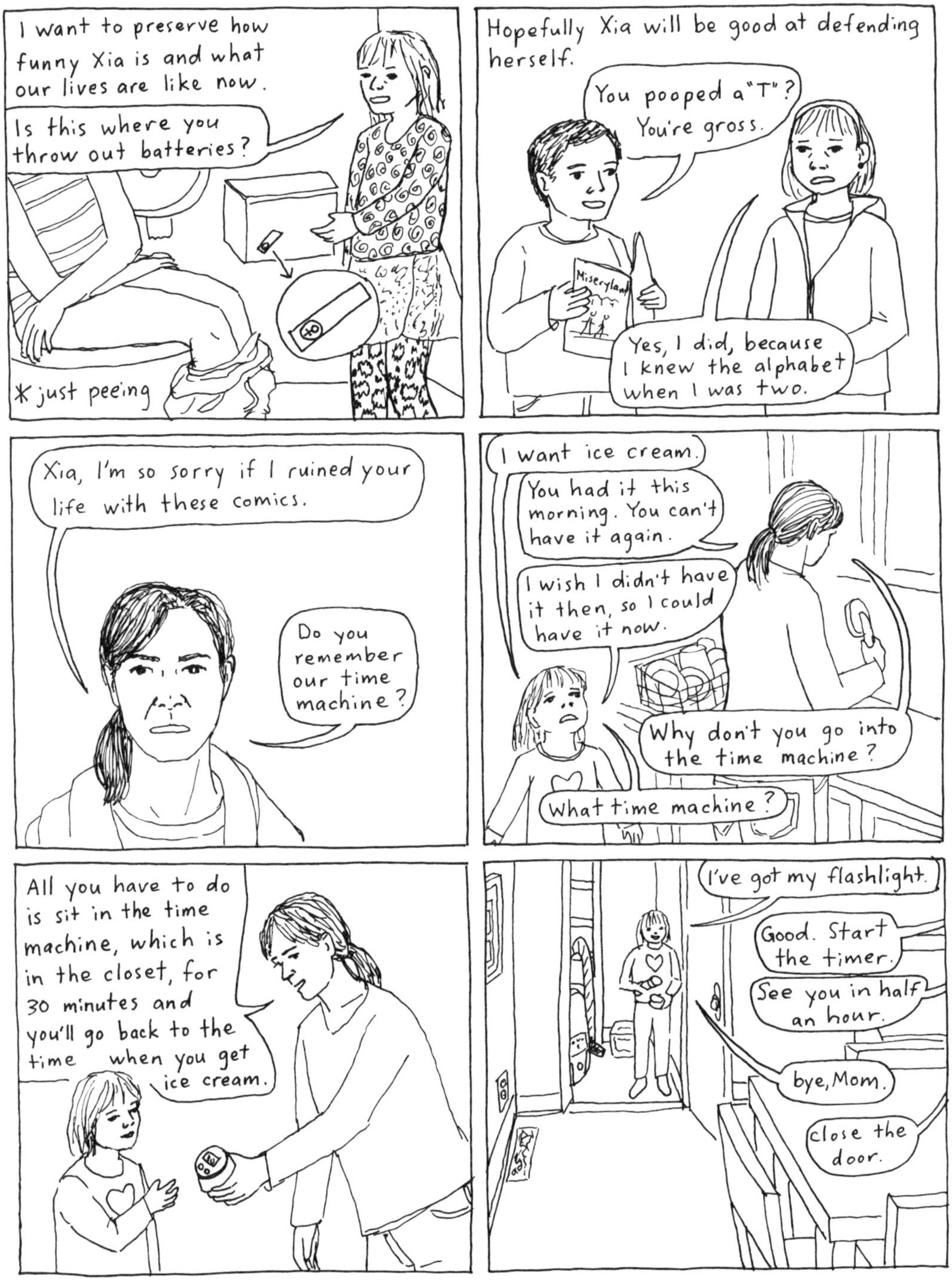
I want to preserve how funny Xia is and what our lives are like now.
Is this where you throw out batteries?
* just peeing
Hopefully Xia will be good at defending herself.
You pooped a "T"? You're gross.
Miseryland
Yes, I did, because I knew the alphabet when I was two.
Xia, I'm so sorry if I ruined your life with these comics.
Do you remember our time machine?
I want ice cream.
You had it this morning. You can't have it again.
I wish I didn't have it then, so I could have it now.
Why don't you go into the time machine?
What time machine?
All you have to do is sit in the time machine, which is in the closet, for 30 minutes and you'll go back to the time when you get ice cream.
I've got my flashlight.
Good. Start the timer.
See you in half an hour.
bye, Mom.
close the door.

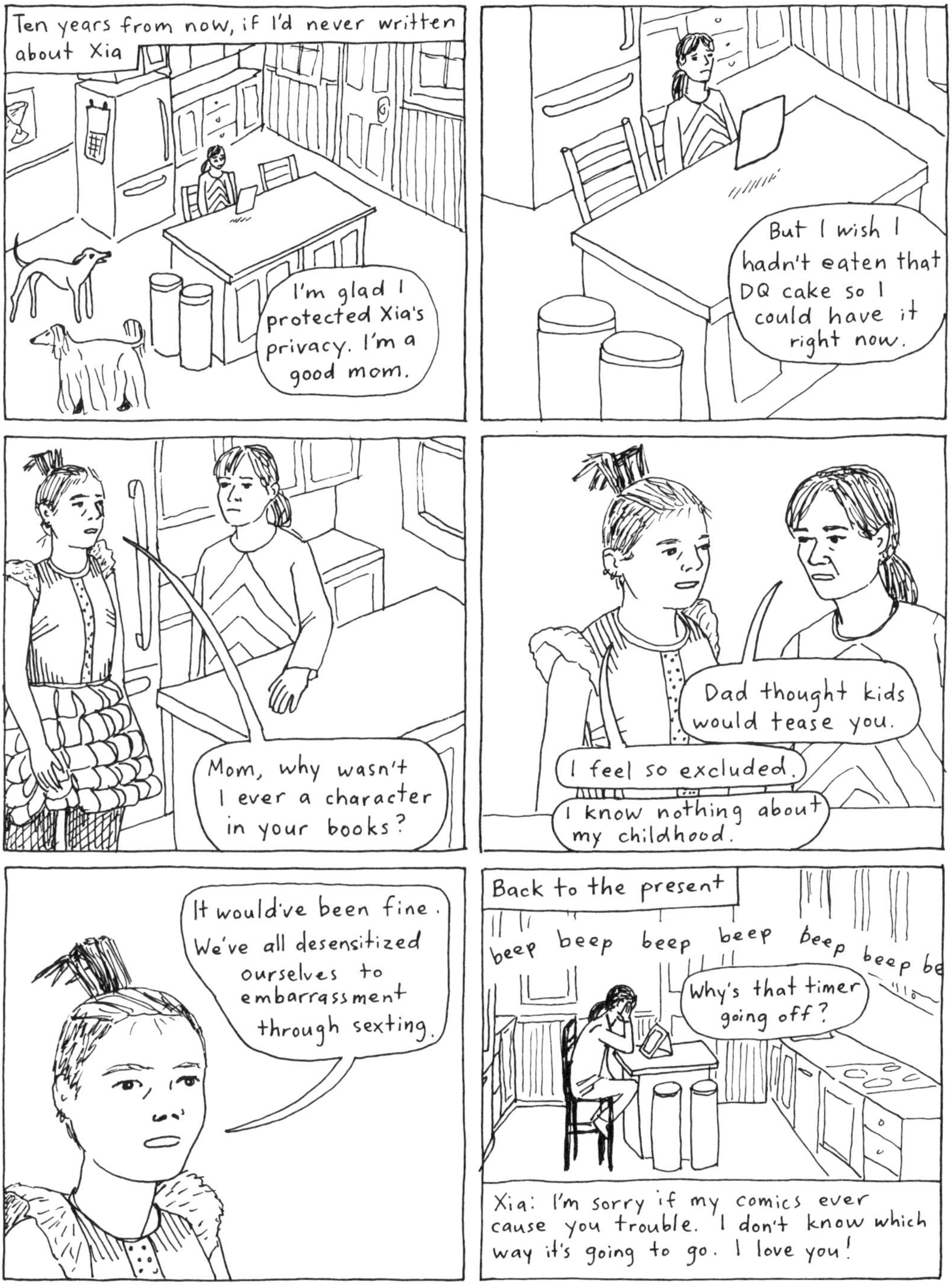

Ten years from now, if I'd never written about Xia
I'm glad I protected Xia's privacy. I'm a good mom.
But I wish I hadn't eaten that DQ cake so I could have it right now.
Mom, why wasn't I ever a character in your books?
Dad thought kids would tease you.
I feel so excluded.
I know nothing about my childhood.
It would've been fine. We've all desensitized ourselves to embarrassment through sexting.
Back to the present
beep beep beep beep beep beep be
Why's that timer going off?
Xia: I'm sorry if my comics ever cause you trouble. I don't know which way it's going to go. I love you!

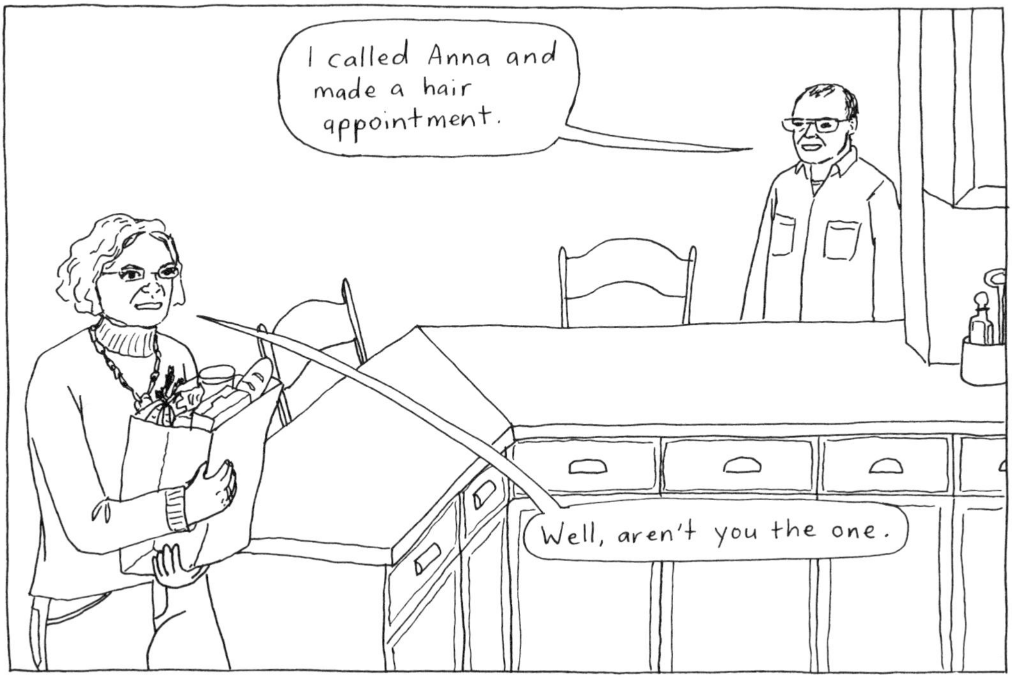
I called Anna and made a hair appointment.
Well, aren't you the one.

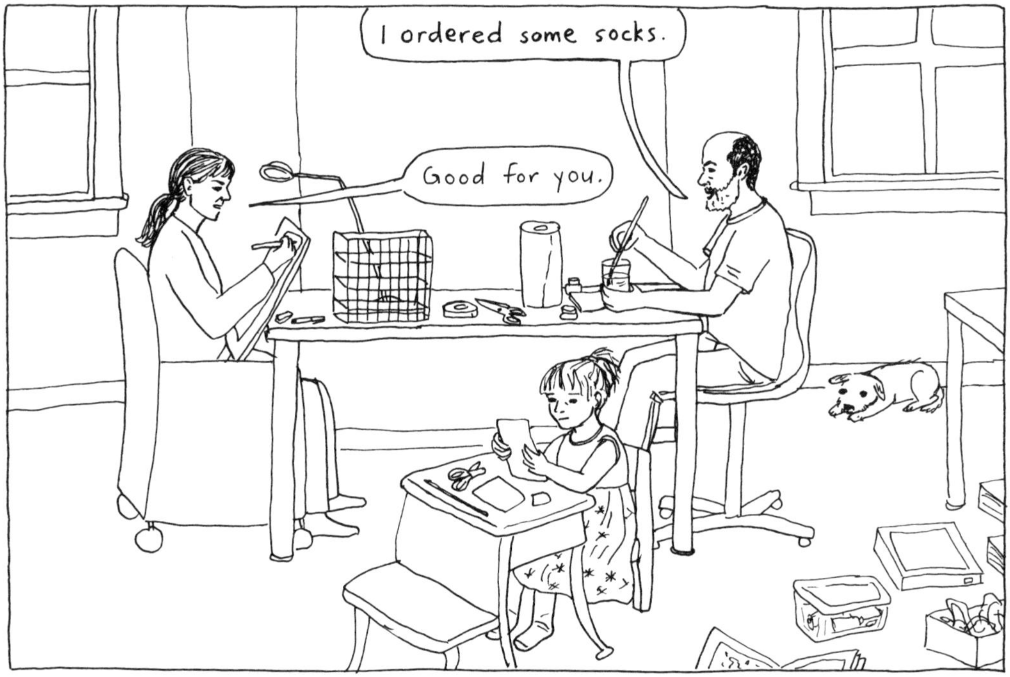
I ordered some socks.
Good for you.

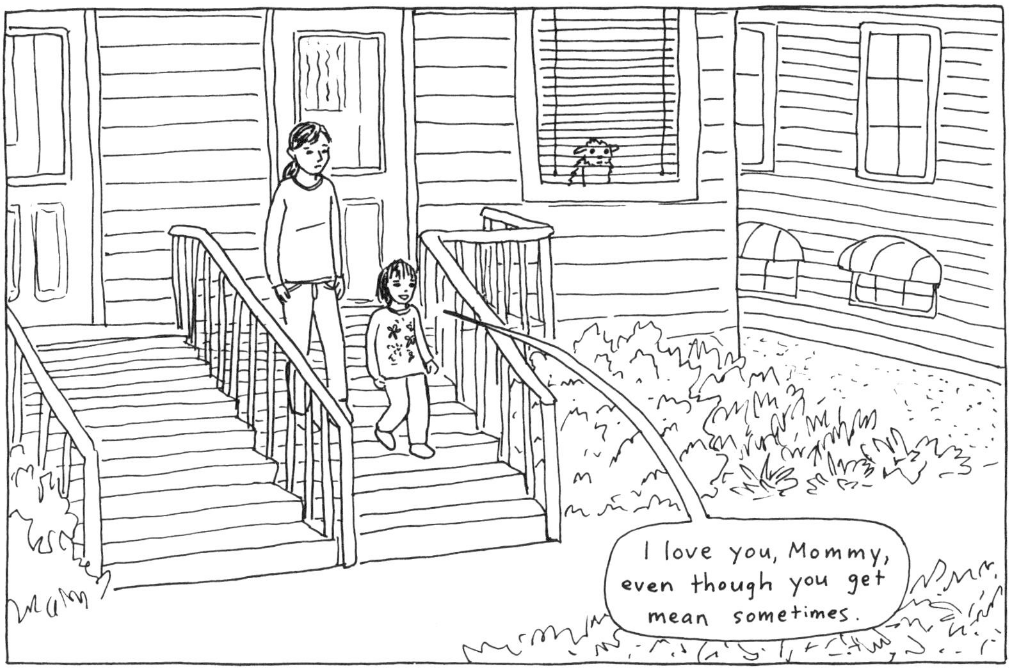
I love you, Mommy, even though you get mean sometimes.

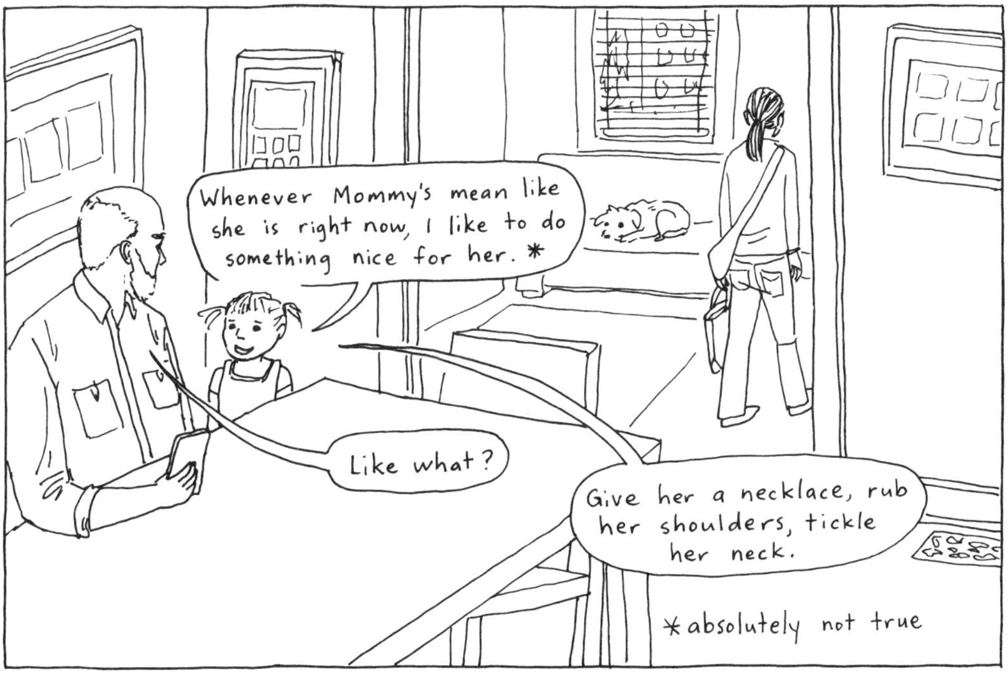
Whenever Mommy's mean like she is right now, I like to do something nice for her. *
Like what?
Give her a necklace, rub her shoulders, tickle her neck.
*absolutely not true

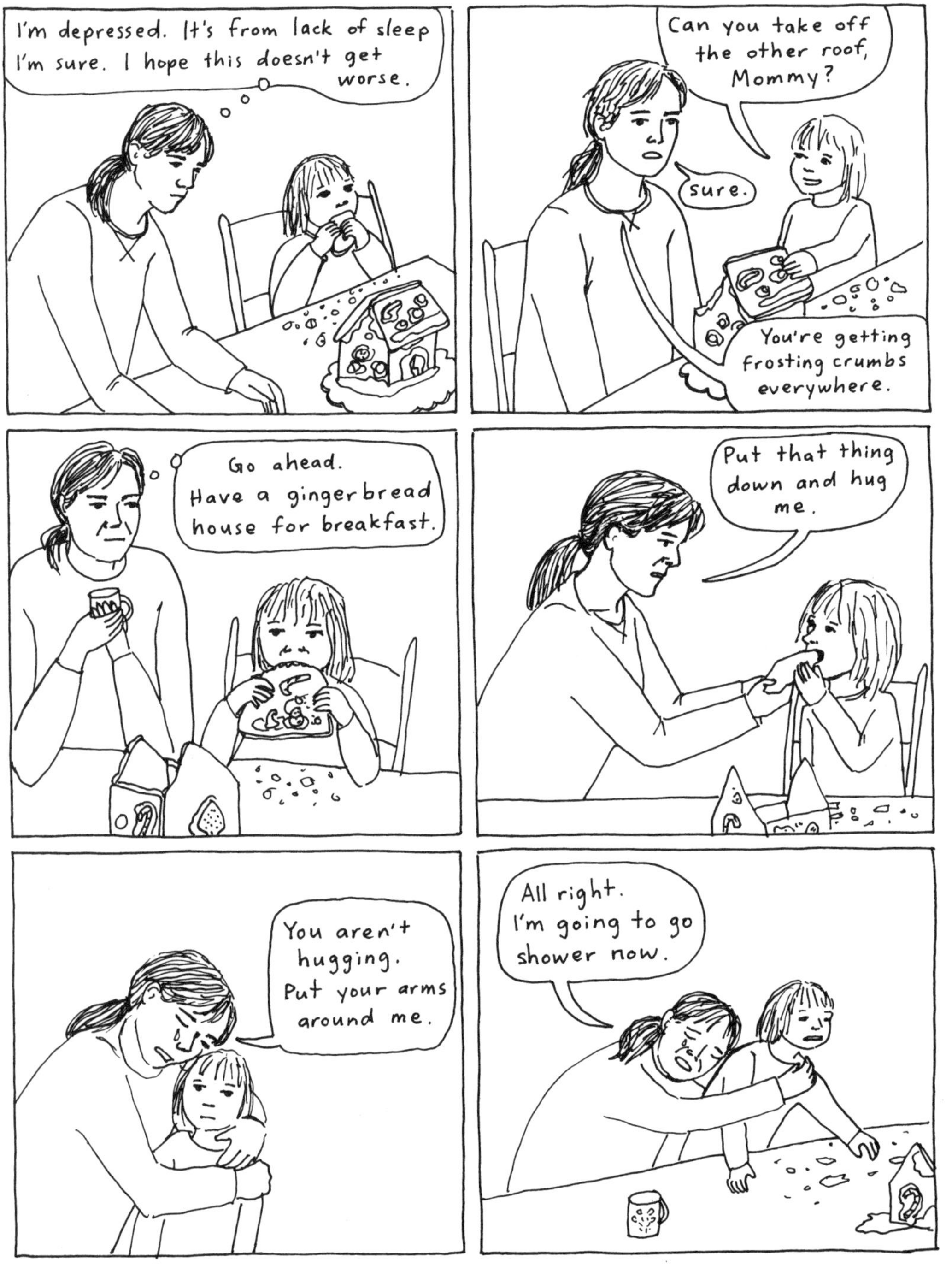

I'm depressed. It's from lack of sleep I'm sure. I hope this doesn't get worse.
Can you take off the other roof, Mommy?
sure.
You're getting frosting crumbs everywhere.
Go ahead. Have a gingerbread house for breakfast.
Put that thing down and hug me.
You aren't hugging. Put your arms around me.
All right. I'm going to go shower now.

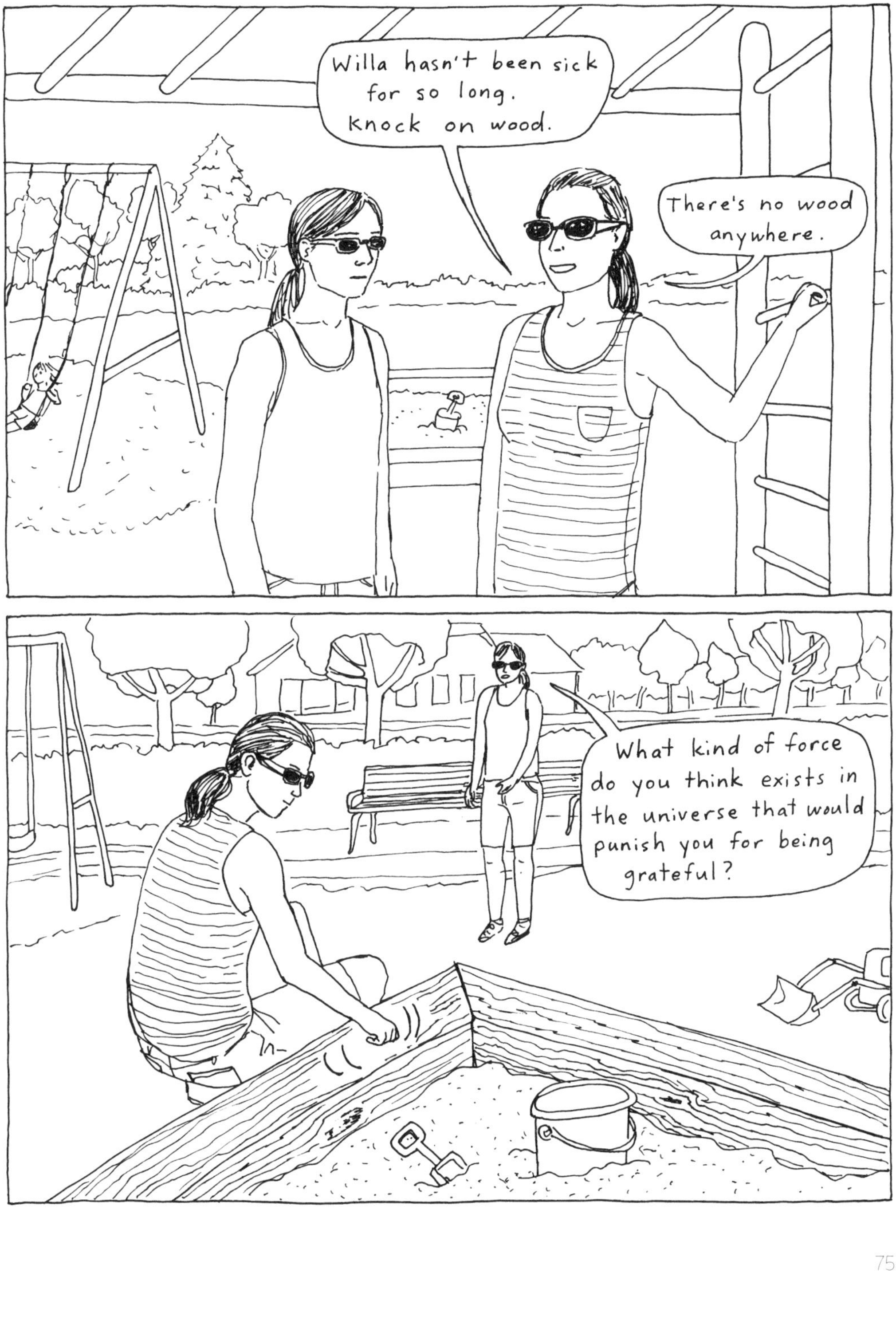
Willa hasn't been sick for so long. Knock on wood.
There's no wood anywhere.
What kind of force do you think exists in the universe that would punish you for being grateful?

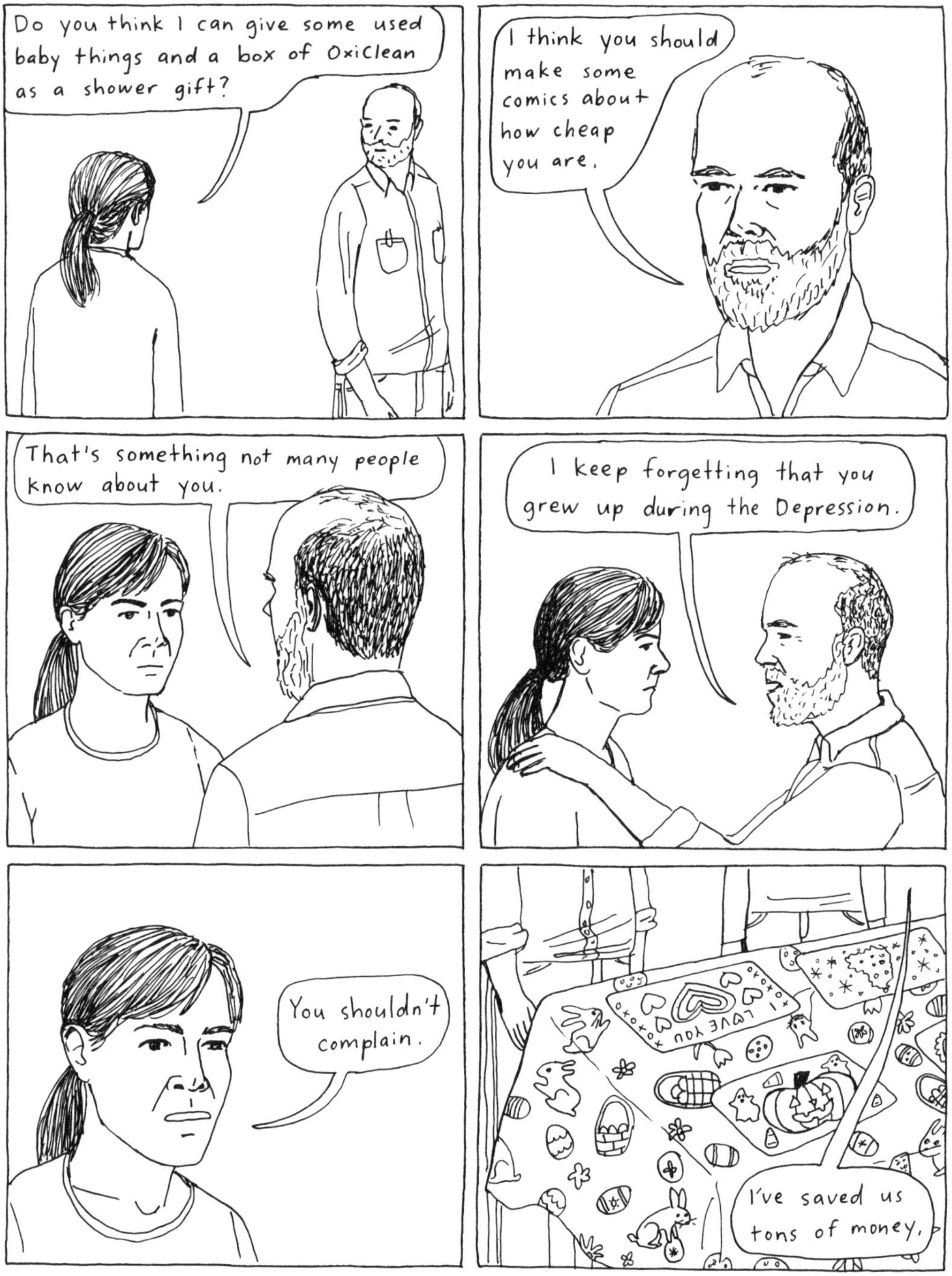
Do you think I can give some used baby things and a box of OxiClean as a shower gift?
I think you should make some comics about how cheap you are.
That's something not many people know about you.
I keep forgetting that you grew up during the Depression.
You shouldn't complain.
I LOVE YOU
I've saved us tons of money.

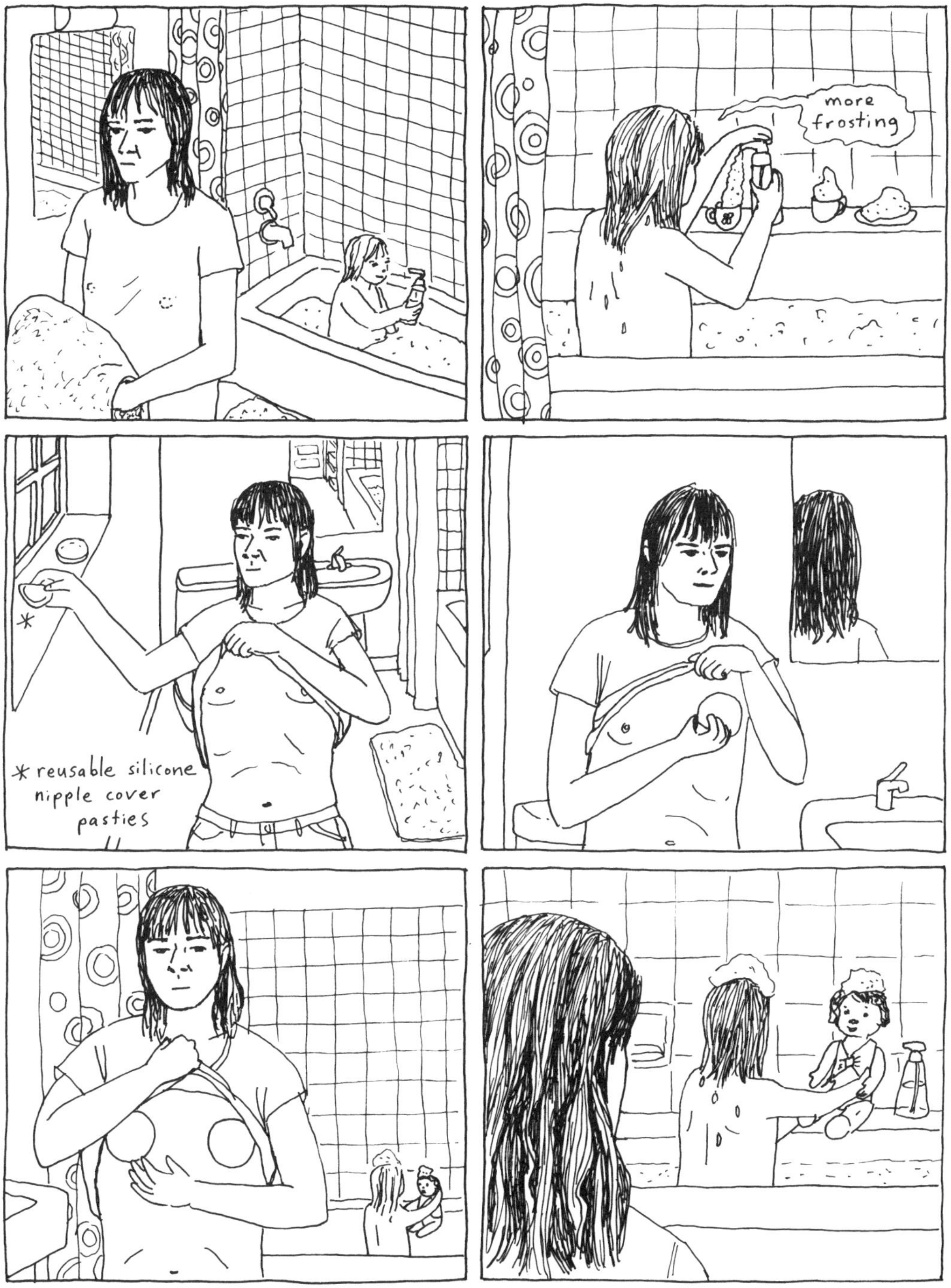
more frosting
*
* reusable silicone nipple cover pasties

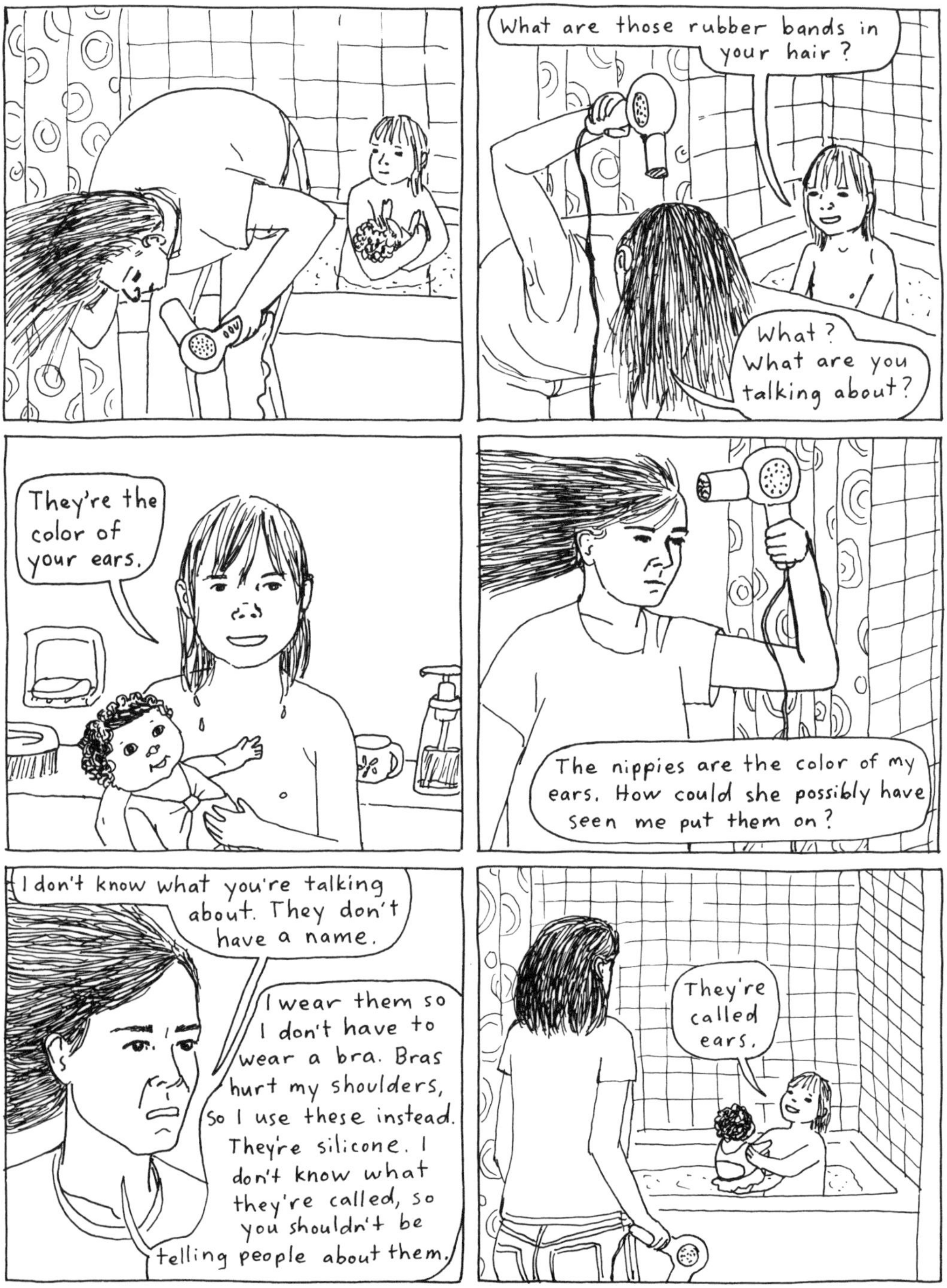
What are those rubber bands in your hair?
What? What are you talking about?
They're the color of your ears.
The nippies are the color of my ears. How could she possibly have seen me put them on?
I don't know what you're talking about. They don't have a name.
I wear them so I don't have to wear a bra. Bras hurt my shoulders, so I use these instead. They're silicone. I don't know what they're called, so you shouldn't be telling people about them.
They're called ears.

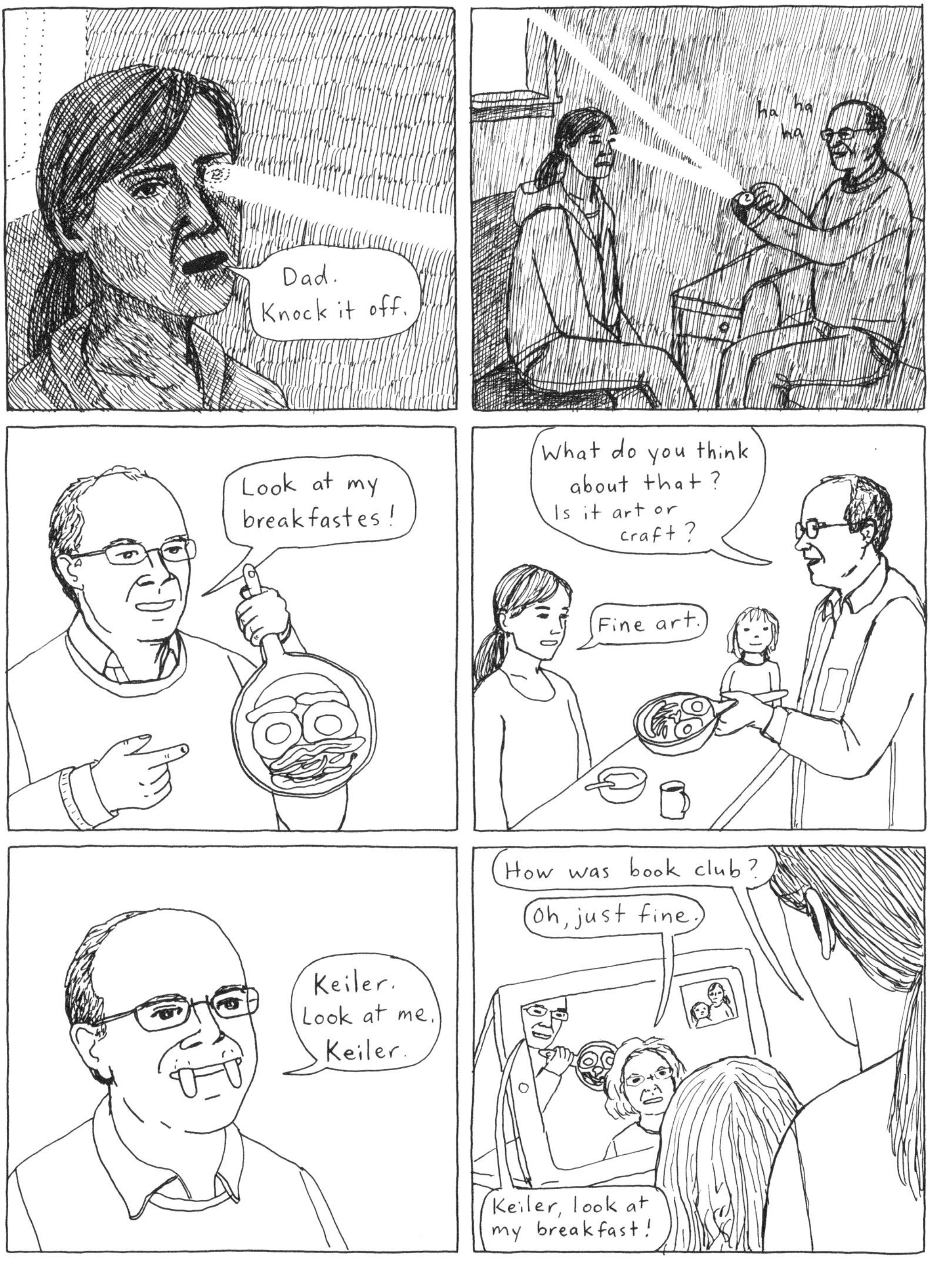
Dad.
Knock it off.
ha ha ha
Look at my breakfastes!
What do you think about that? Is it art or craft?
Fine art.
Keiler. Look at me. Keiler.
How was book club?
Oh, just fine.
Keiler, look at my breakfast!

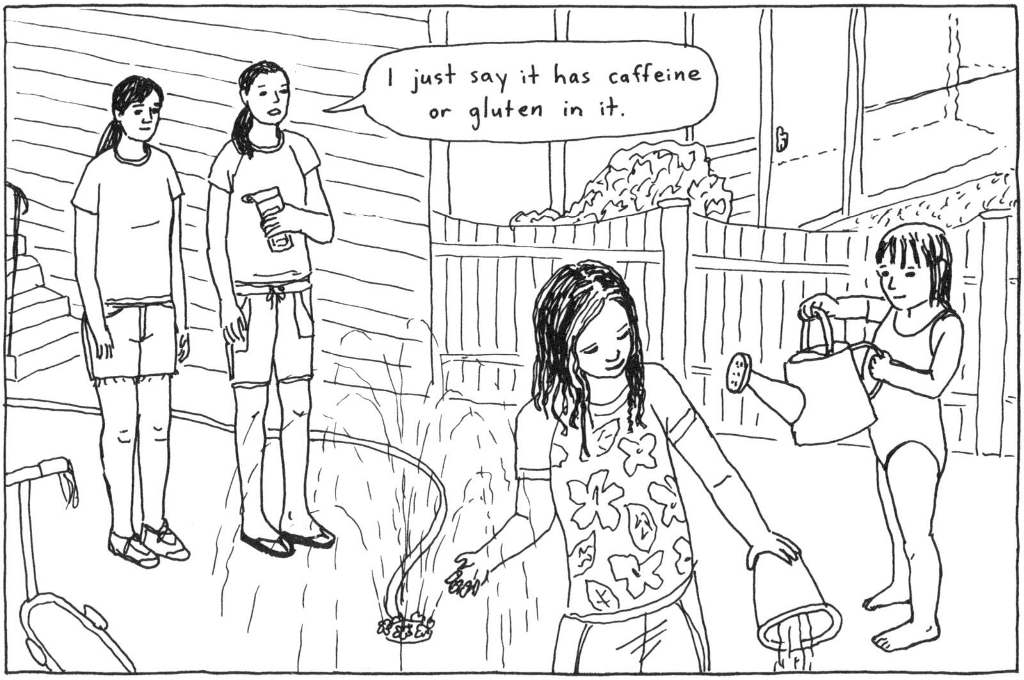
I just say it has caffeine or gluten in it.

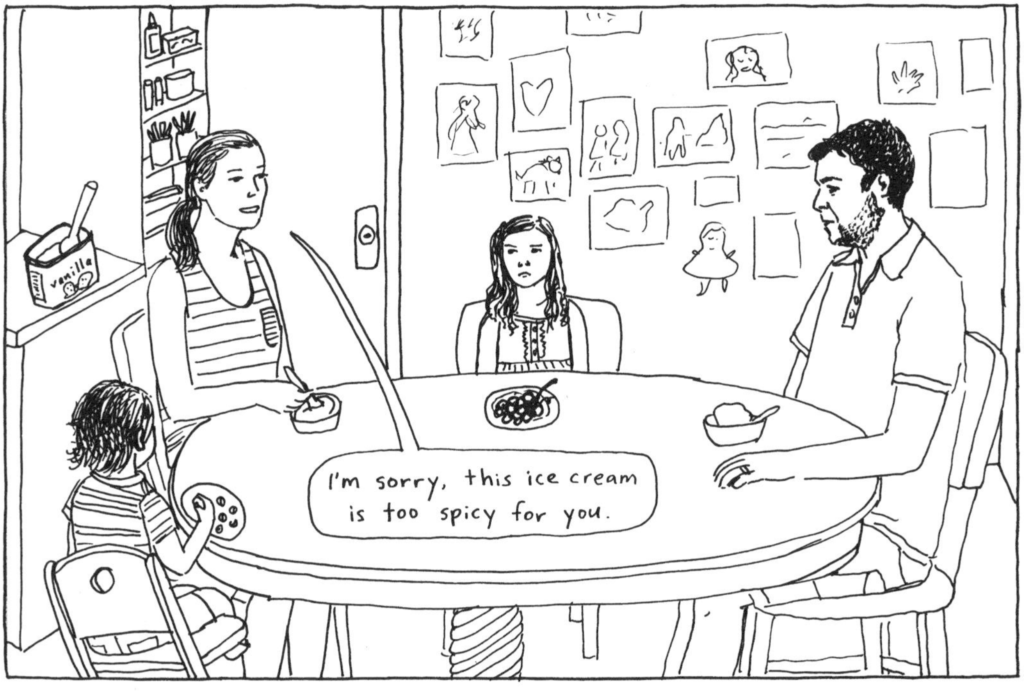
vanilla
I'm sorry, this ice cream is too spicy for you.

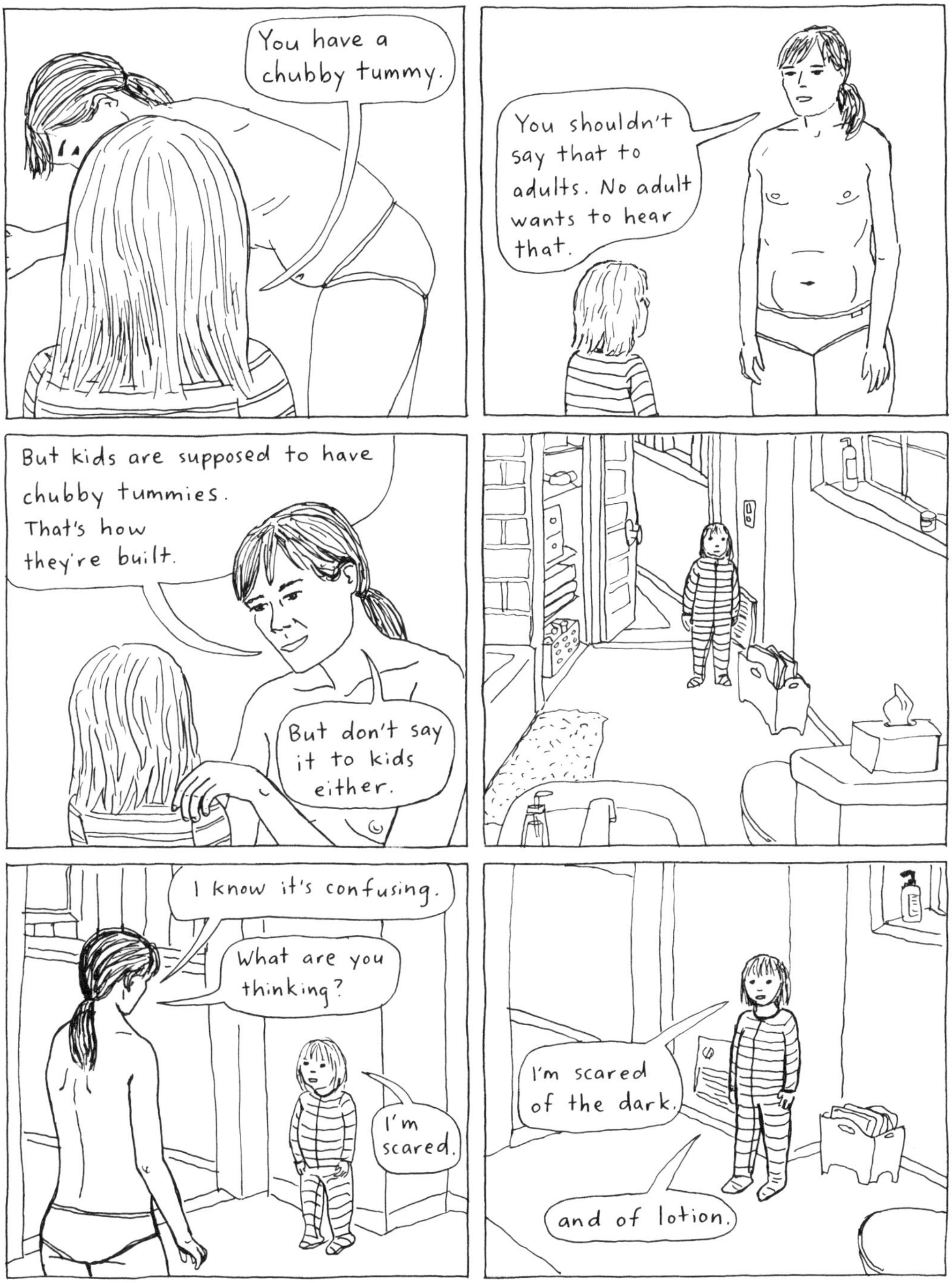
You have a chubby tummy.
You shouldn't say that to adults. No adult wants to hear that.
But kids are supposed to have chubby tummies. That's how they're built.
But don't say it to kids either.
I know it's confusing.
What are you thinking?
I'm scared.
I'm scared of the dark.
and of lotion.

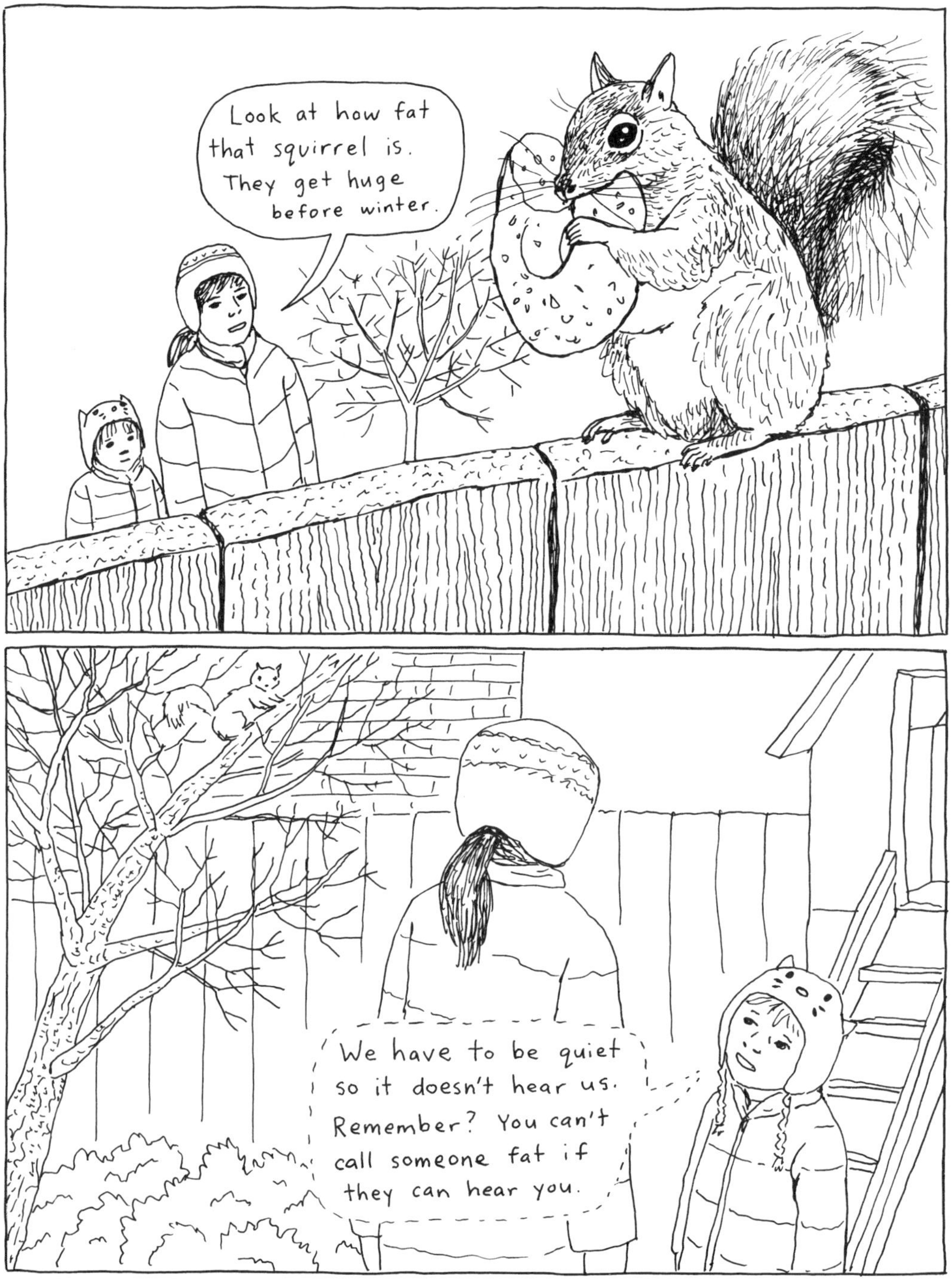
Look at how fat that squirrel is. They get huge before winter.
We have to be quiet so it doesn't hear us. Remember? You can't call someone fat if they can hear you.

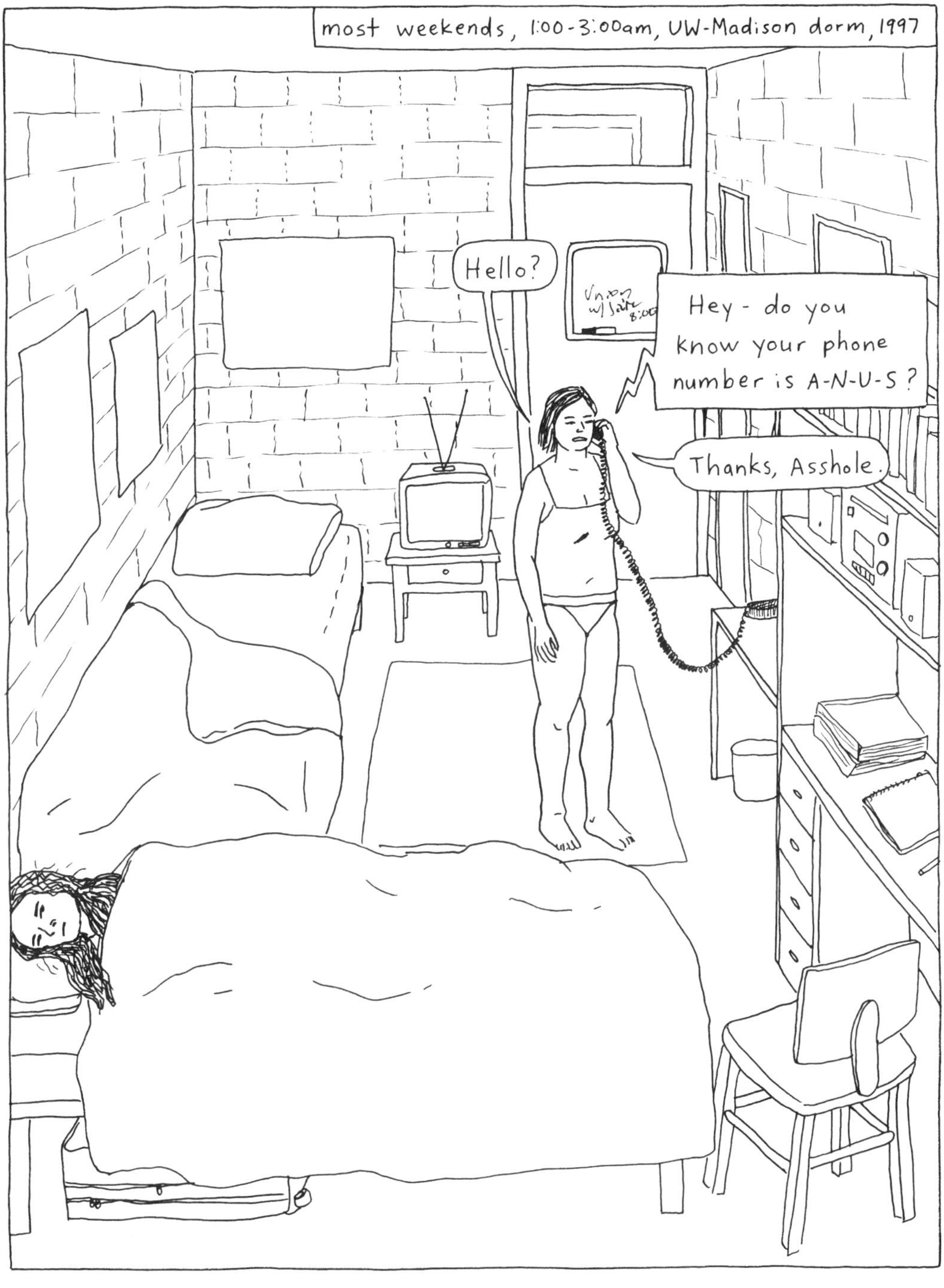
most weekends, 1:00-3:00am, UW-Madison dorm, 1997
Hello?
Hey - do you know your phone number is A-N-U-S?
Thanks, Asshole.

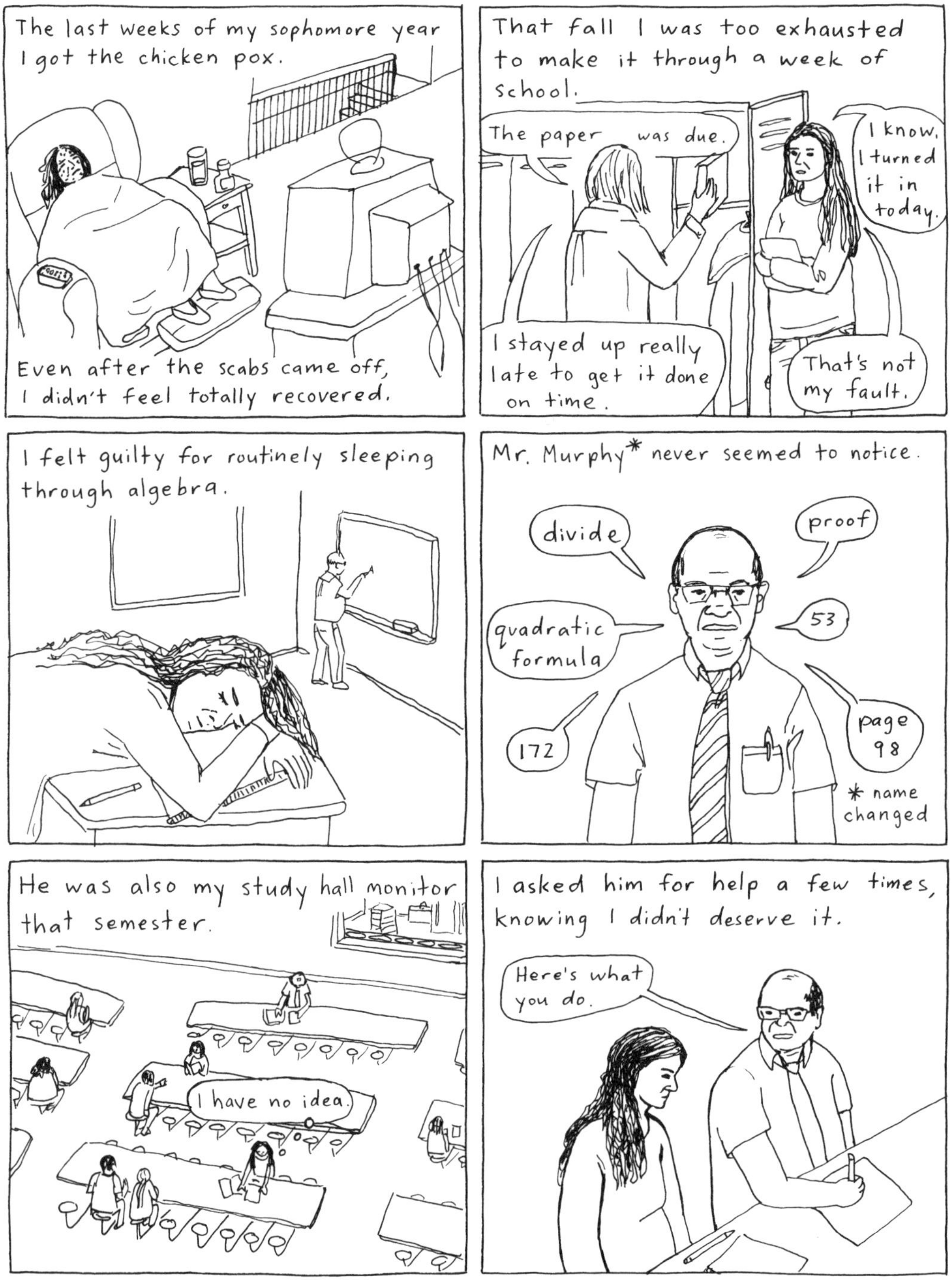
The last weeks of my sophomore year I got the chicken pox.
Even after the scabs came off, I didn't feel totally recovered.
That fall I was too exhausted to make it through a week of school.
The paper was due.
I know, I turned it in today.
I stayed up really late to get it done on time.
That's not my fault.
I felt guilty for routinely sleeping through algebra.
Mr. Murphy* never seemed to notice.
divide
proof
quadratic formula
53
172
page 98
* name changed
He was also my study hall monitor that semester.
I have no idea.
I asked him for help a few times, knowing I didn't deserve it.
Here's what you do.

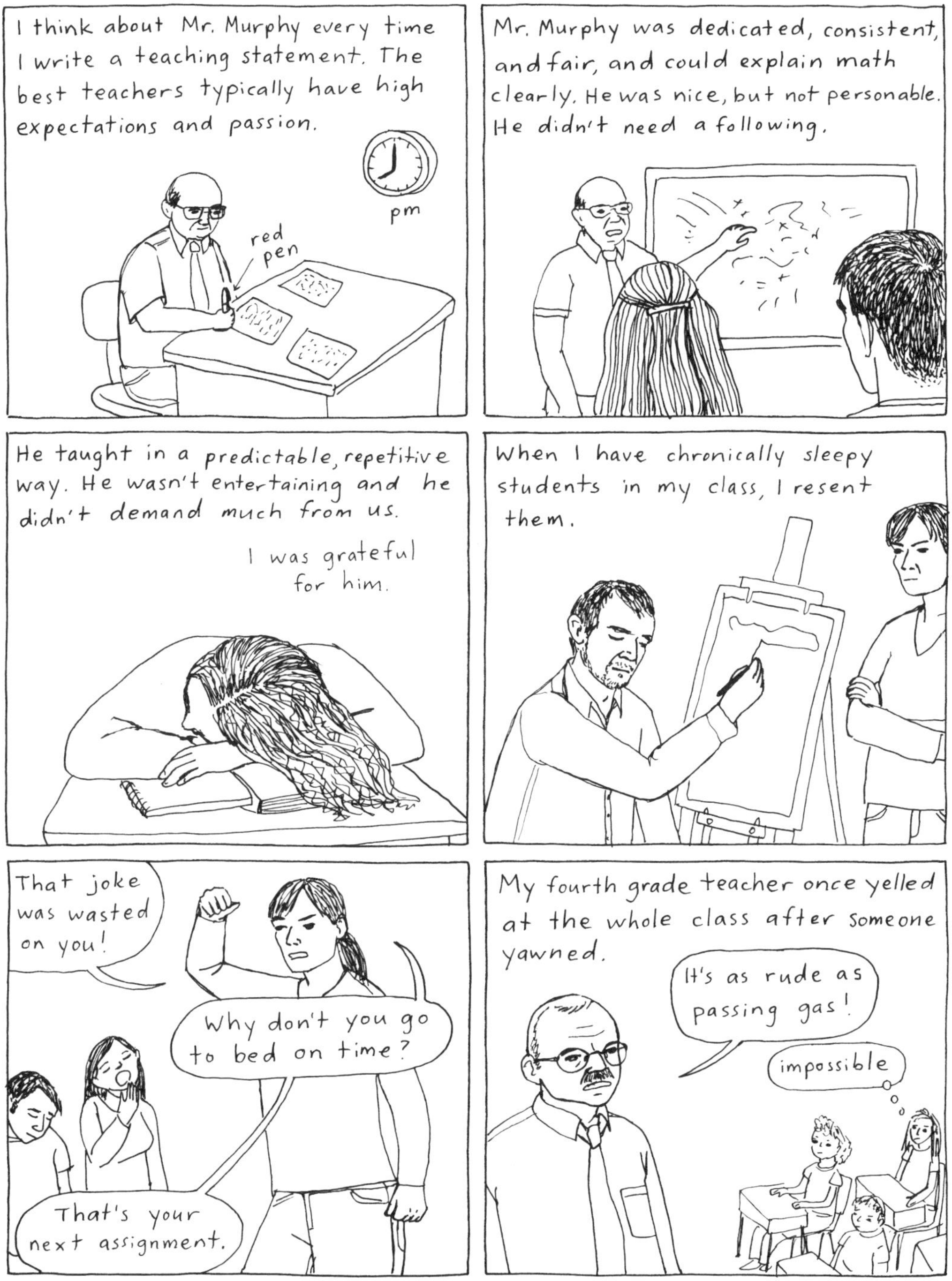
I think about Mr. Murphy every time I write a teaching statement. The best teachers typically have high expectations and passion.
pm
red pen
Mr. Murphy was dedicated, consistent, and fair, and could explain math clearly. He was nice, but not personable. He didn't need a following.
He taught in a predictable, repetitive way. He wasn't entertaining and he didn't demand much from us.
I was grateful for him.
When I have chronically sleepy students in my class, I resent them.
That joke was wasted on you!
Why don't you go to bed on time?
That's your next assignment.
My fourth grade teacher once yelled at the whole class after someone yawned.
It's as rude as passing gas!
impossible

I had unbearable fatigue— it was like wearing a pile of lead aprons—

or watching a swim meet.

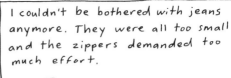

I couldn't be bothered with jeans anymore. They were all too small and the zippers demanded too much effort.

The sweatpants I bought were beyond ugly,

An adorable small child couldn't have pulled them off.

What's the story over there?

no clue.

You might have chronic fatigue syndrome.

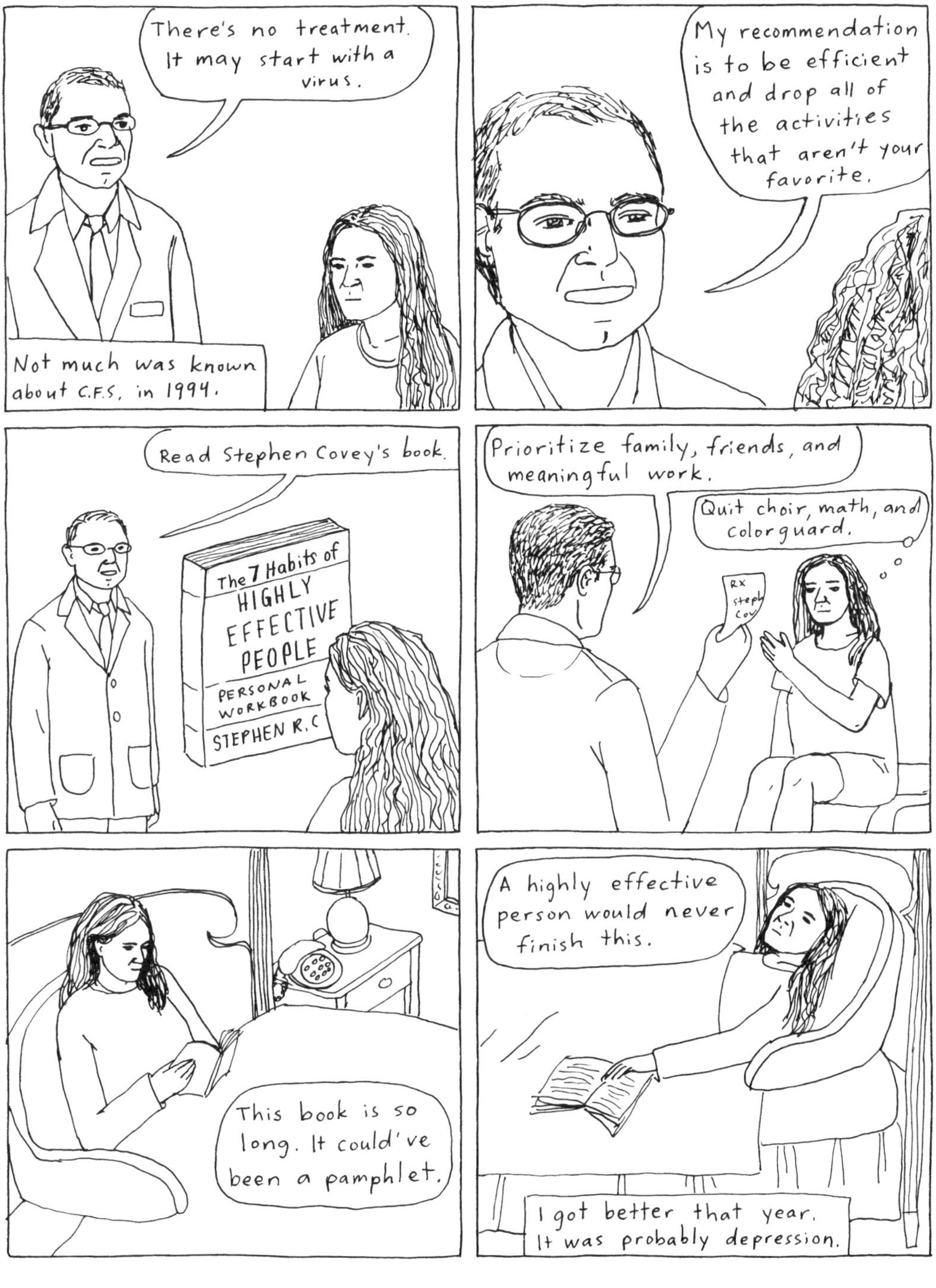
There's no treatment. It may start with a virus.
Not much was known about C.F.S. in 1994.
My recommendation is to be efficient and drop all of the activities that aren't your favorite.
Read Stephen Covey's book.
The 7 Habits of HIGHLY EFFECTIVE PEOPLE PERSONAL WORKBOOK STEPHEN R. C
Prioritize family, friends, and meaningful work.
Quit choir, math, and colorguard.
RX steph Cov
This book is so long. It could've been a pamphlet.
A highly effective person would never finish this.
I got better that year. It was probably depression.

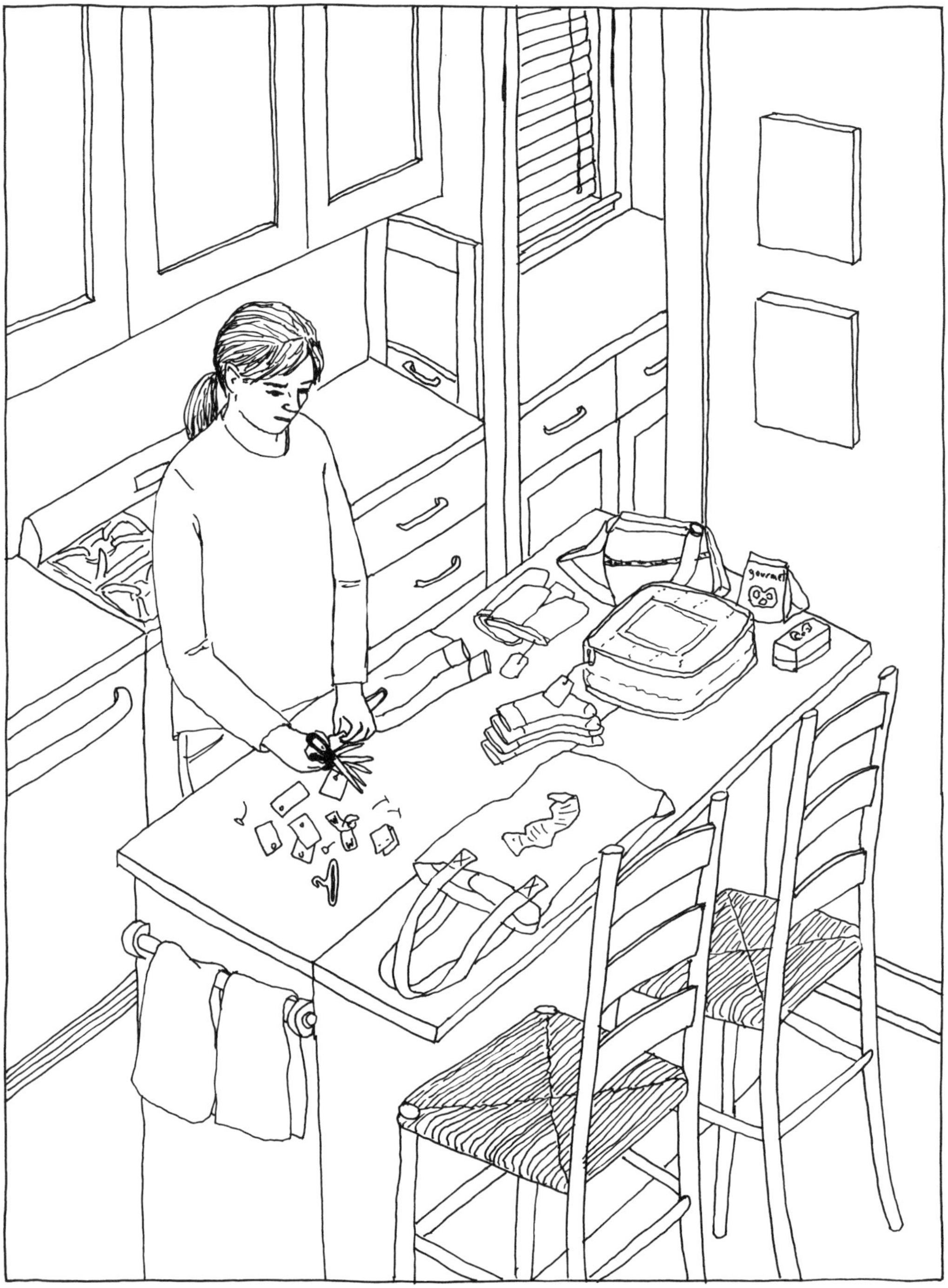
gourmet

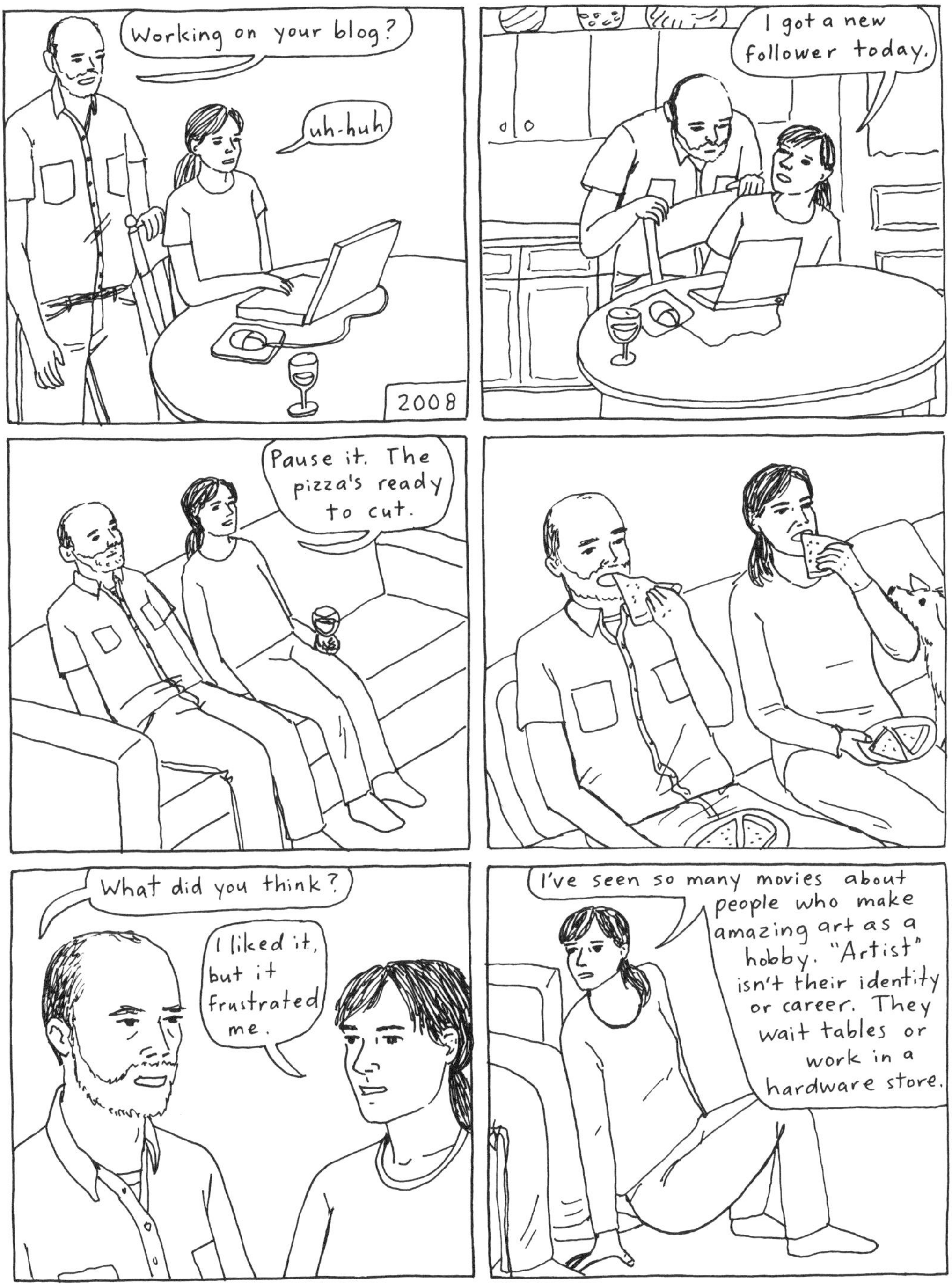
Working on your blog?
uh-huh
2008
I got a new follower today.
Pause it. The pizza's ready to cut.
What did you think?
I liked it, but it frustrated me.
I've seen so many movies about people who make amazing art as a hobby. "Artist" isn't their identity or career. They wait tables or work in a hardware store.

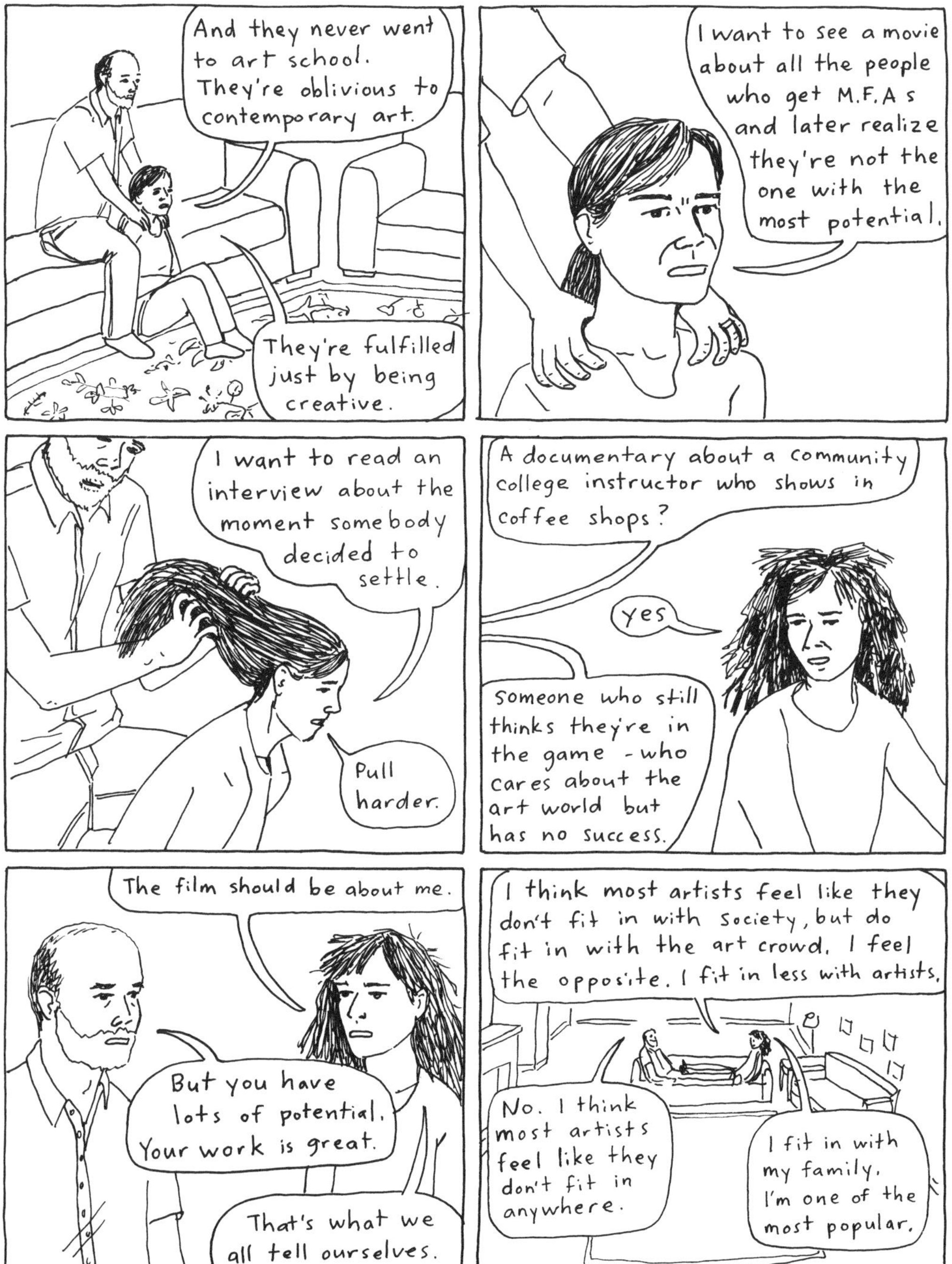
And they never went to art school. They're oblivious to contemporary art.
They're fulfilled just by being creative.
I want to see a movie about all the people who get M.F.A s and later realize they're not the one with the most potential.
I want to read an interview about the moment somebody decided to settle.
Pull harder.
A documentary about a community college instructor who shows in coffee shops?
yes
Someone who still thinks they're in the game - who cares about the art world but has no success.
The film should be about me.
But you have lots of potential. Your work is great.
That's what we all tell ourselves.
I think most artists feel like they don't fit in with society, but do fit in with the art crowd. I feel the opposite. I fit in less with artists.
No. I think most artists feel like they don't fit in anywhere.
I fit in with my family. I'm one of the most popular.

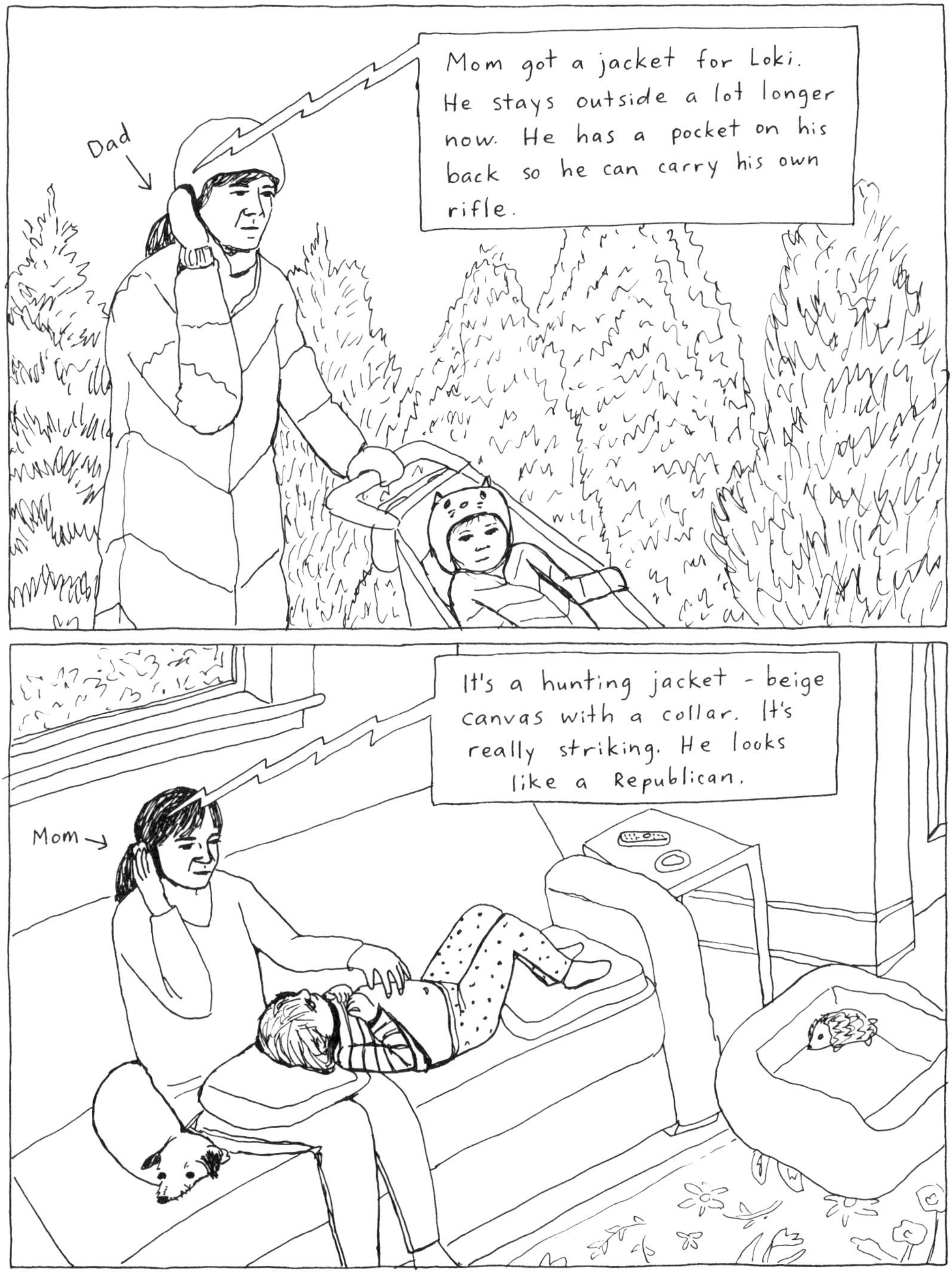
Mom got a jacket for Loki. He stays outside a lot longer now. He has a pocket on his back so he can carry his own rifle.
Dad
It's a hunting jacket - beige canvas with a collar. It's really striking. He looks like a Republican.
Mom

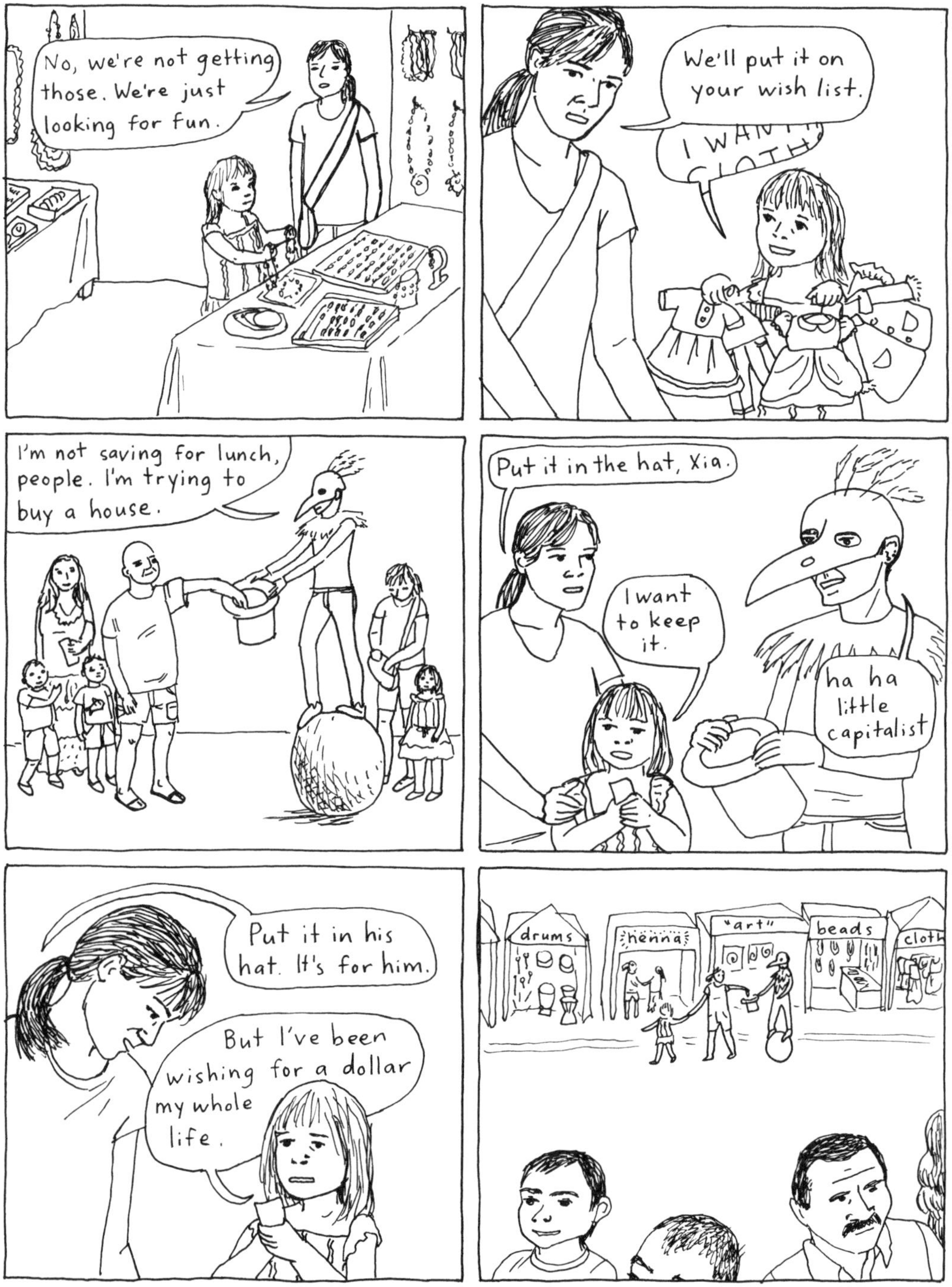
No, we're not getting those. We're just looking for fun.
We'll put it on your wish list.
I'm not saving for lunch, people. I'm trying to buy a house.
Put it in the hat, Xia.
I want to keep it.
ha ha little capitalist
Put it in his hat. It's for him.
But I've been wishing for a dollar my whole life.
drums
henna
"art"
beads

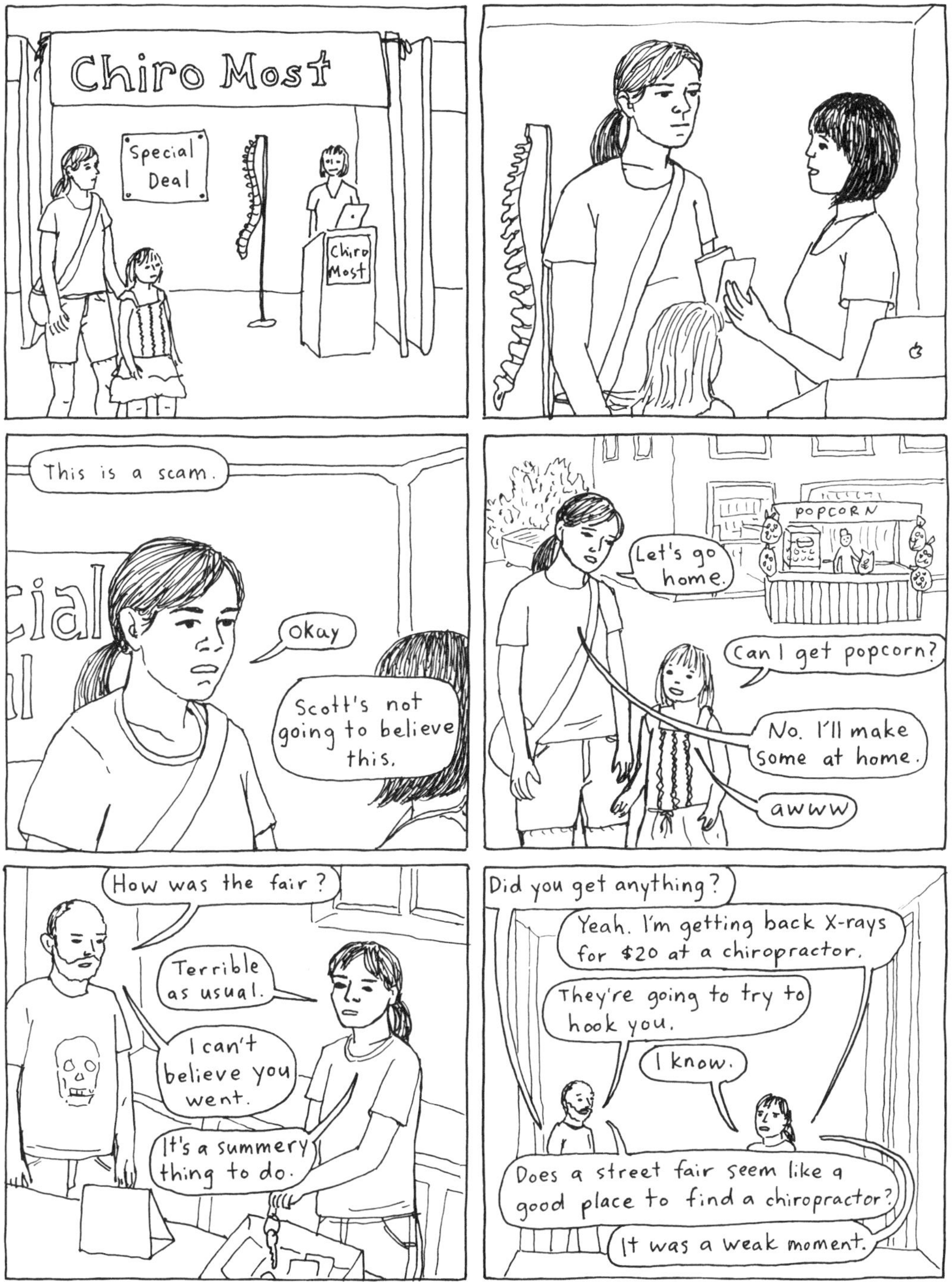

Chiro Most
Special Deal
Chiro Most
This is a scam.
Okay
Scott's not going to believe this.
Let's go home.
POPCORN
Can I get popcorn?
No. I'll make some at home.
awww
How was the fair?
Terrible as usual.
I can't believe you went.
It's a summery thing to do.
Did you get anything?
Yeah. I'm getting back X-rays for $20 at a chiropractor.
They're going to try to hook you.
I know.
Does a street fair seem like a good place to find a chiropractor?
It was a weak moment.

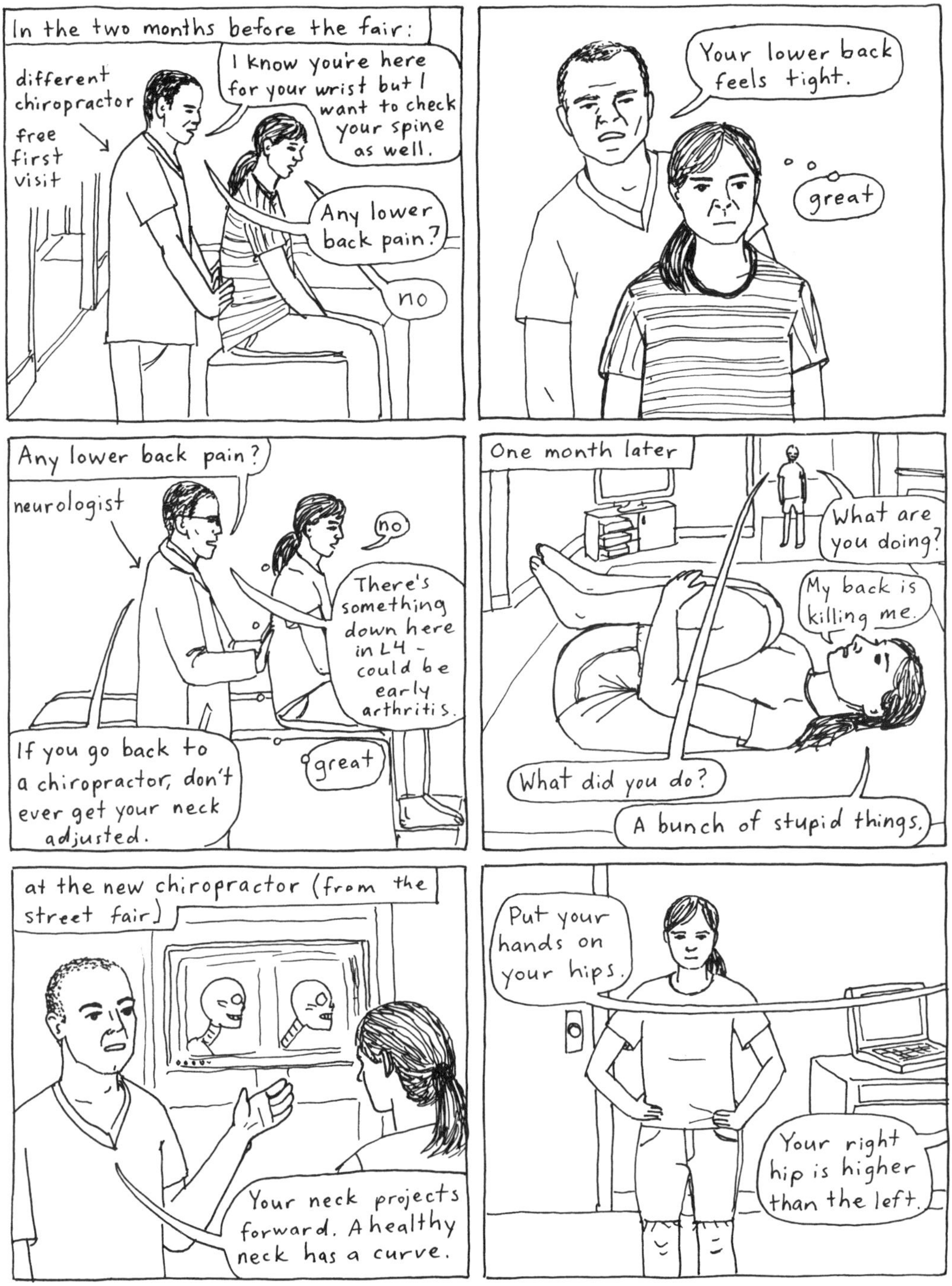

In the two months before the fair:
different chiropractor
free first visit
I know you're here for your wrist but I want to check your spine as well.
Any lower back pain?
no
Your lower back feels tight.
great
Any lower back pain?
neurologist
no
There's something down here in L4 - could be early arthritis.
If you go back to a chiropractor, don't ever get your neck adjusted.
great
One month later
What are you doing?
My back is killing me.
What did you do?
A bunch of stupid things.
at the new chiropractor (from the street fair)
Your neck projects forward. A healthy neck has a curve.
Put your hands on your hips.
Your right hip is higher than the left.

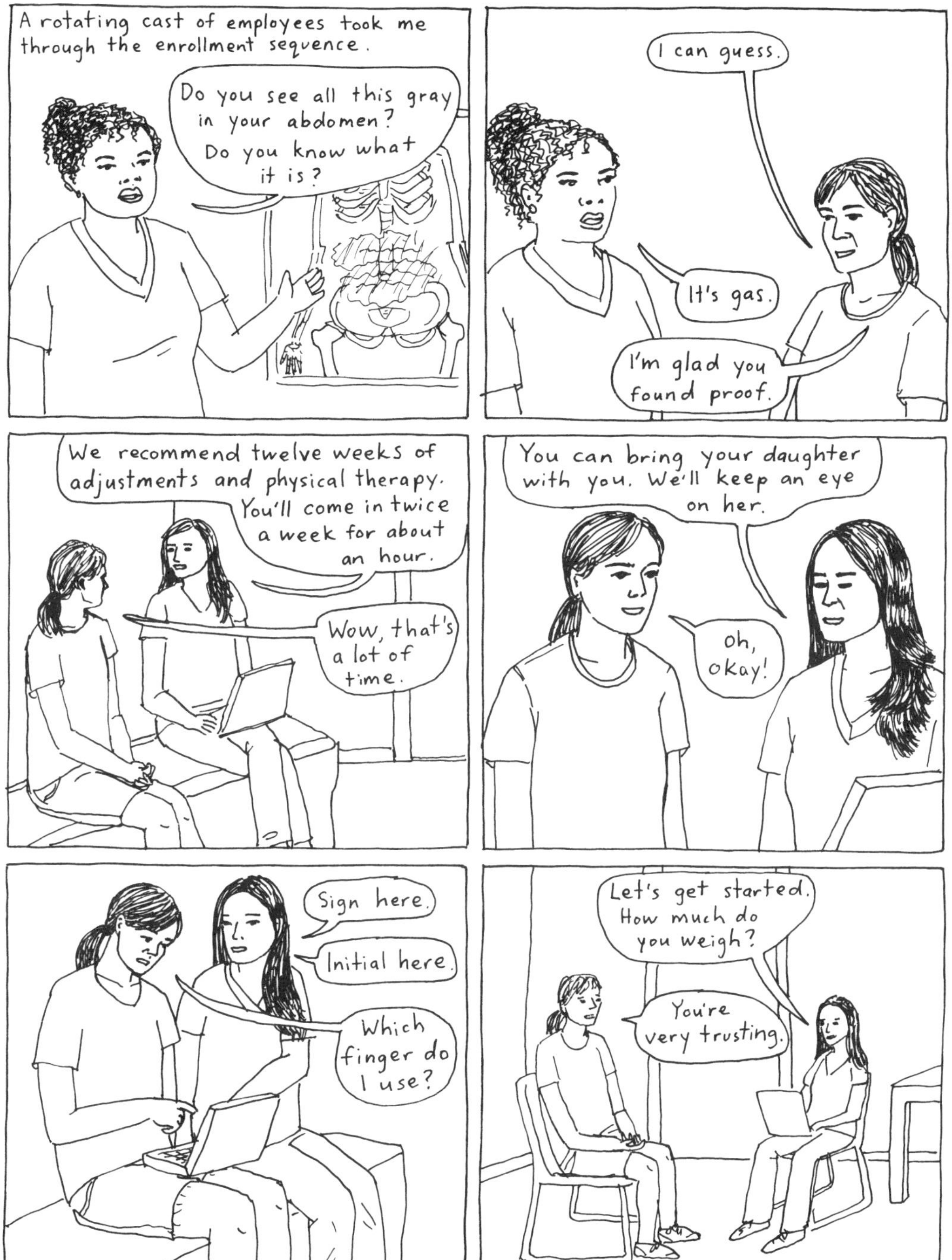
A rotating cast of employees took me through the enrollment sequence.
Do you see all this gray in your abdomen? Do you know what it is?
I can guess.
It's gas.
I'm glad you found proof.
We recommend twelve weeks of adjustments and physical therapy. You'll come in twice a week for about an hour.
Wow, that's a lot of time.
You can bring your daughter with you. We'll keep an eye on her.
Oh, okay!
Sign here.
Initial here.
Which finger do I use?
Let's get started. How much do you weigh?
You're very trusting.

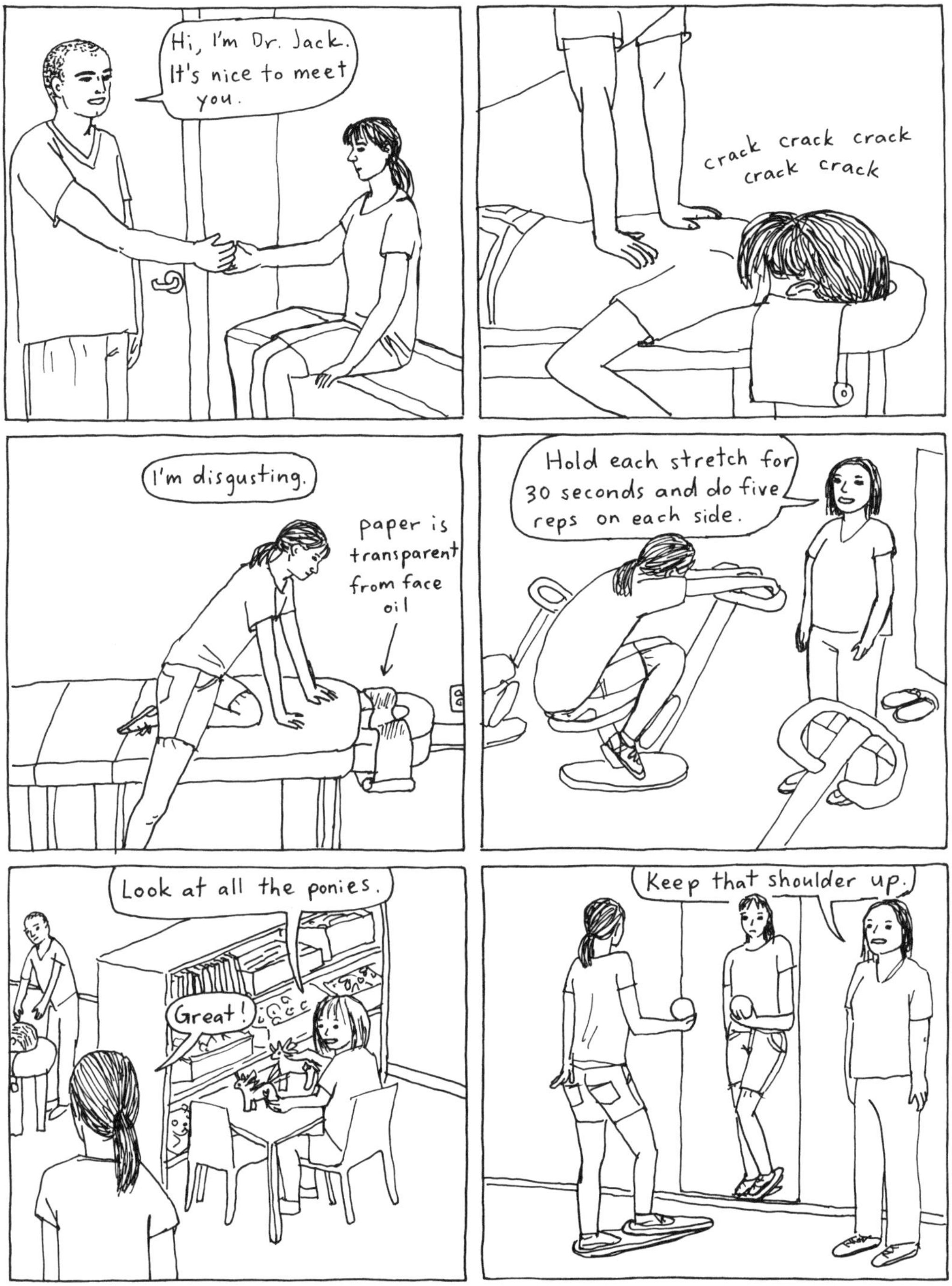
Hi, I'm Dr. Jack. It's nice to meet you.
crack crack crack crack crack
I'm disgusting.
paper is transparent from face oil
Hold each stretch for 30 seconds and do five reps on each side.
Look at all the ponies.
Great!
Keep that shoulder up.

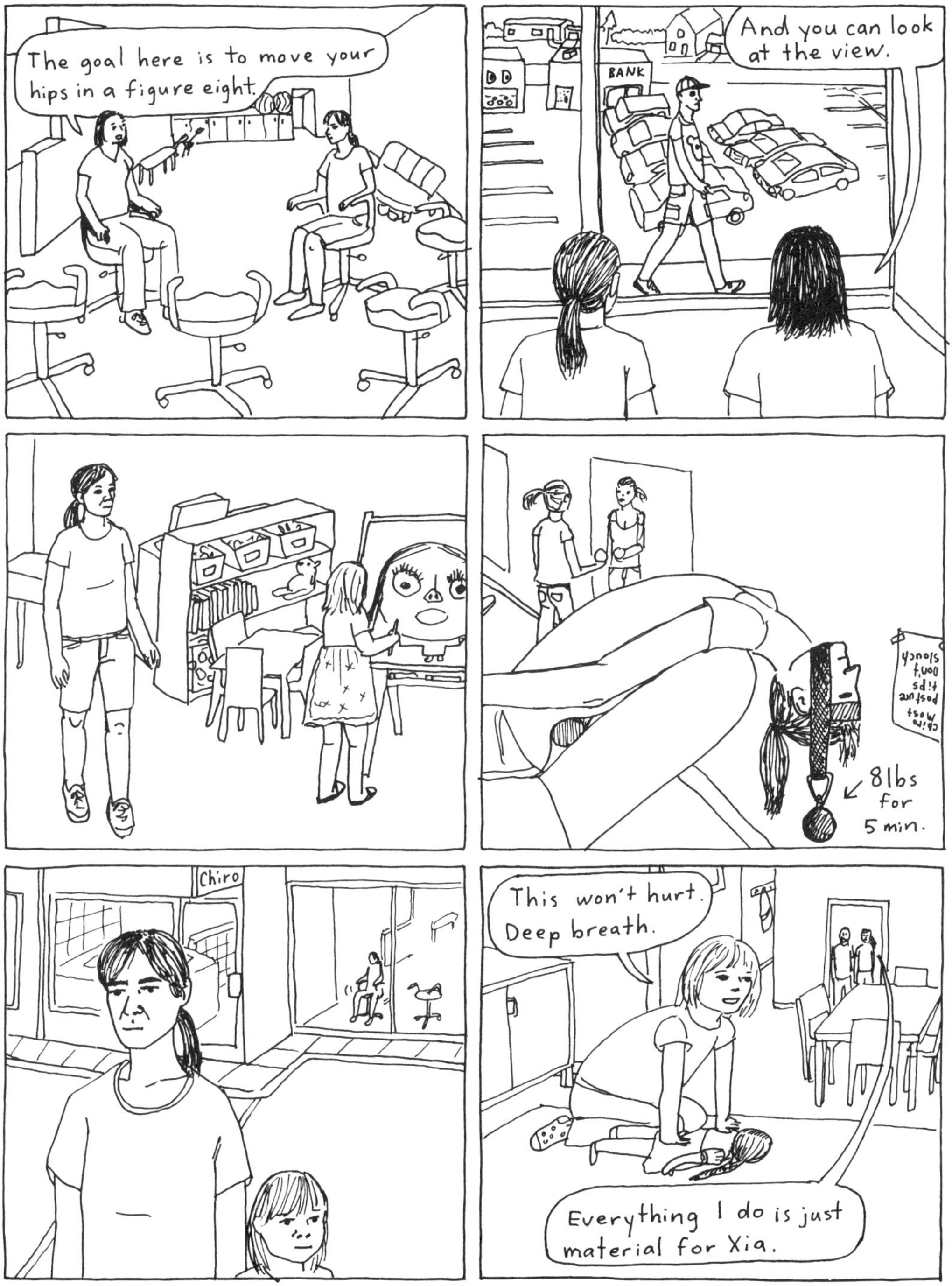
The goal here is to move your hips in a figure eight.
BANK
And you can look at the view.
8lbs for 5 min.
Chiro
This won't hurt. Deep breath.
Everything I do is just material for Xia.

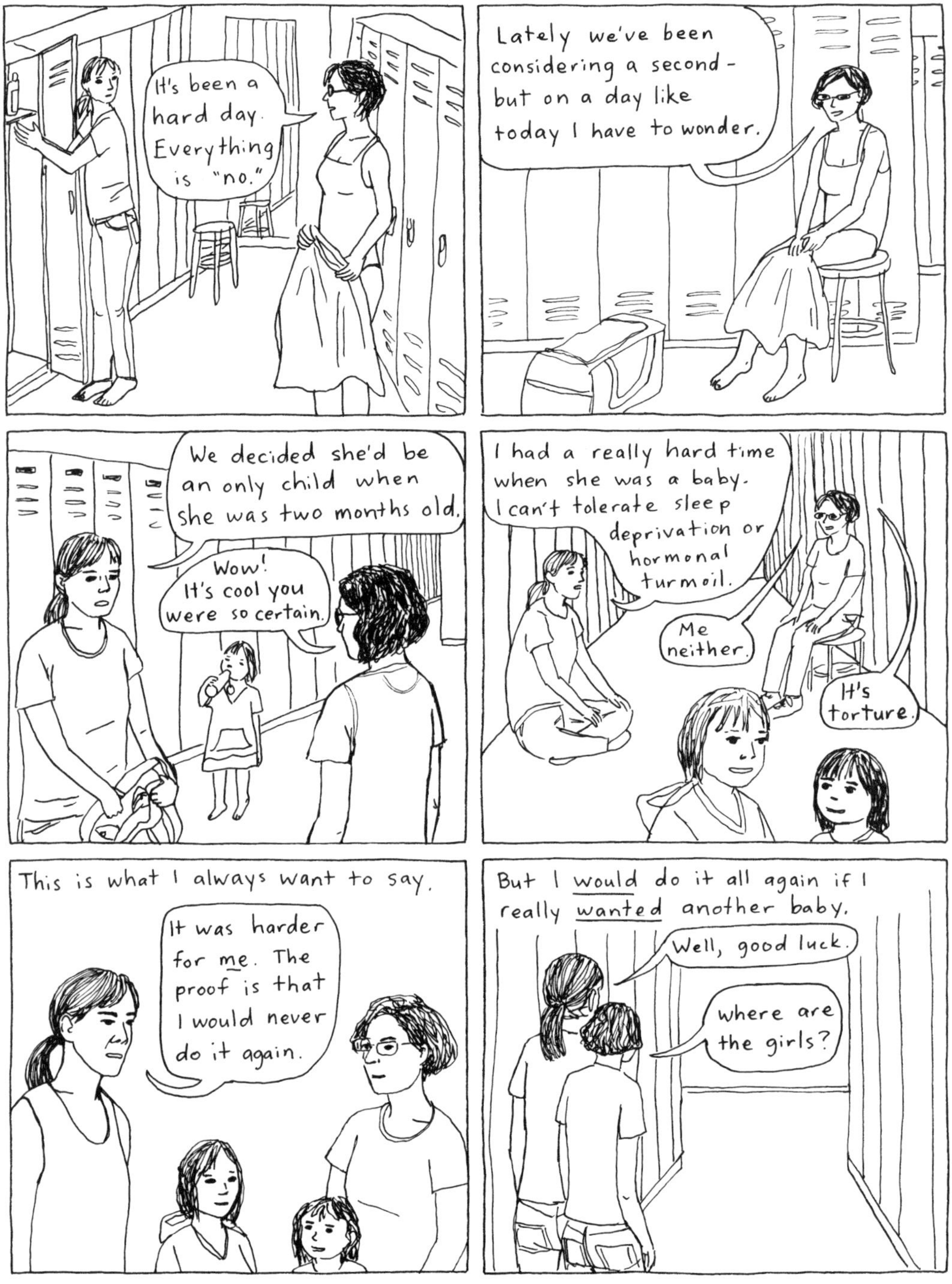
It's been a hard day. Everything is "no."
Lately we've been considering a second - but on a day like today I have to wonder.
We decided she'd be an only child when she was two months old.
Wow! It's cool you were so certain.
I had a really hard time when she was a baby. I can't tolerate sleep deprivation or hormonal turmoil.
Me neither.
It's torture.
This is what I always want to say.
It was harder for me. The proof is that I would never do it again.
But I would do it all again if I really wanted another baby.
Well, good luck.
Where are the girls?

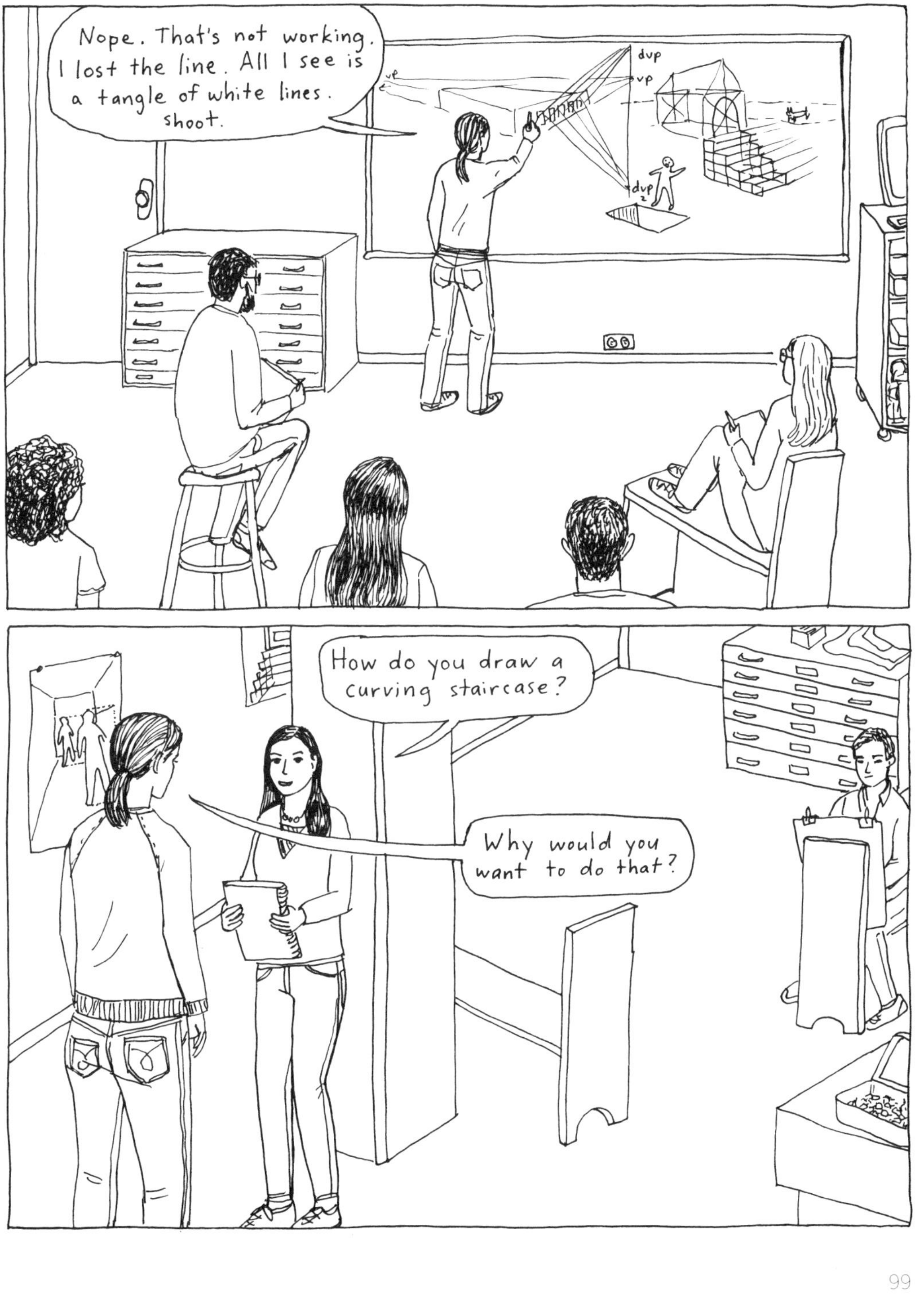
Nope. That's not working. I lost the line. All I see is a tangle of white lines. shoot.
dvp
vp
vp
dvp
How do you draw a curving staircase?
Why would you want to do that?

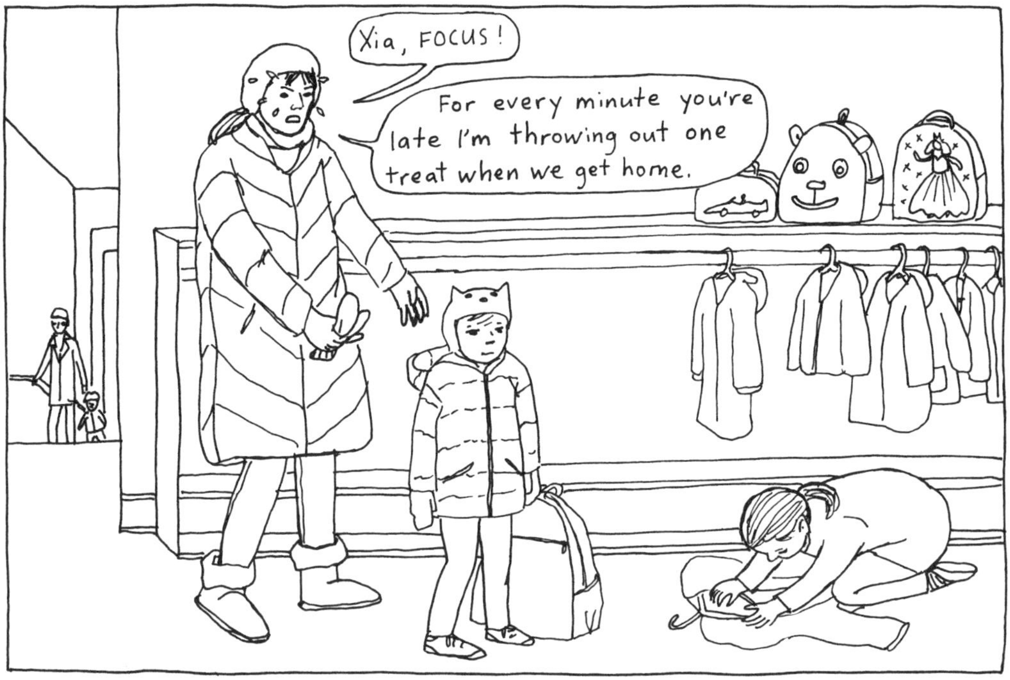
Xia, FOCUS!
For every minute you're late I'm throwing out one treat when we get home.

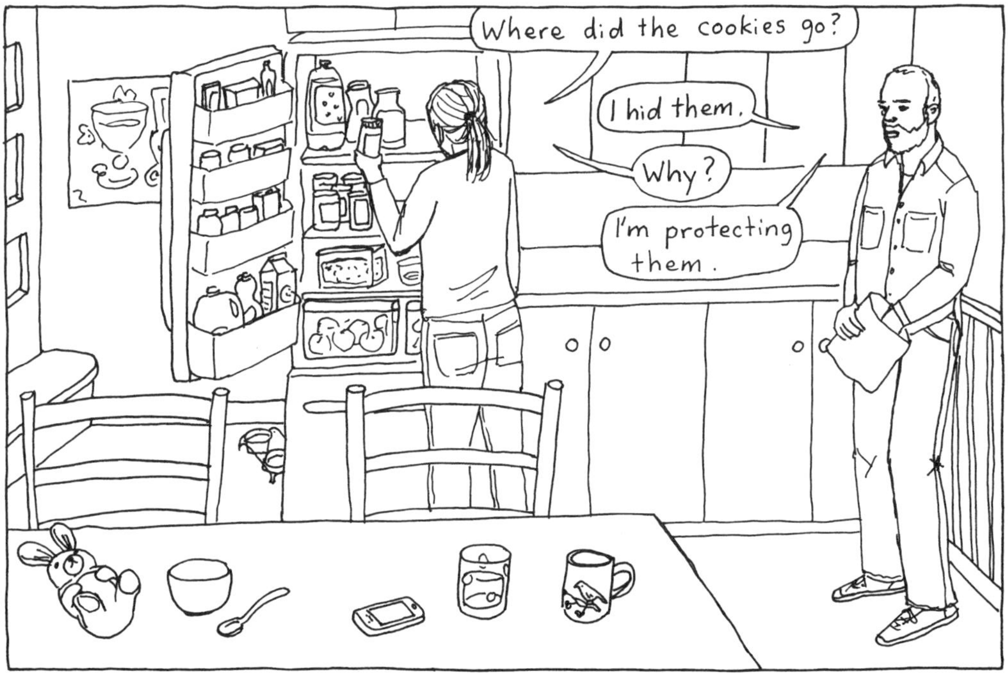
Where did the cookies go?
I hid them.
Why?
I'm protecting them.

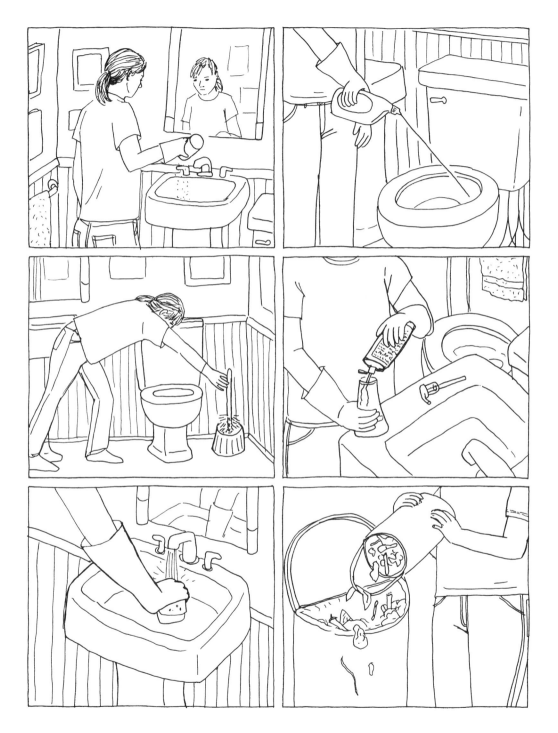

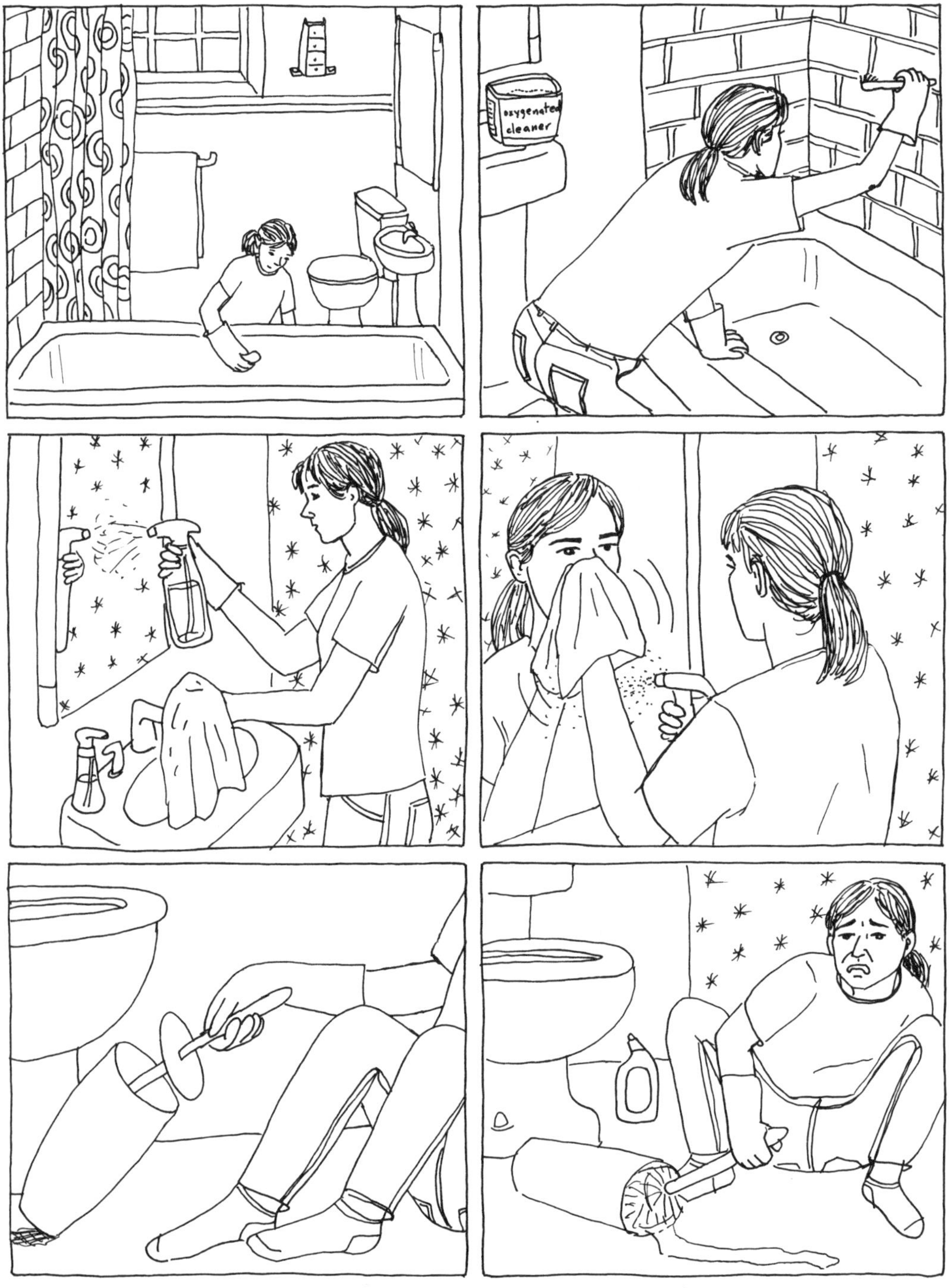
oxygenated
cleaner

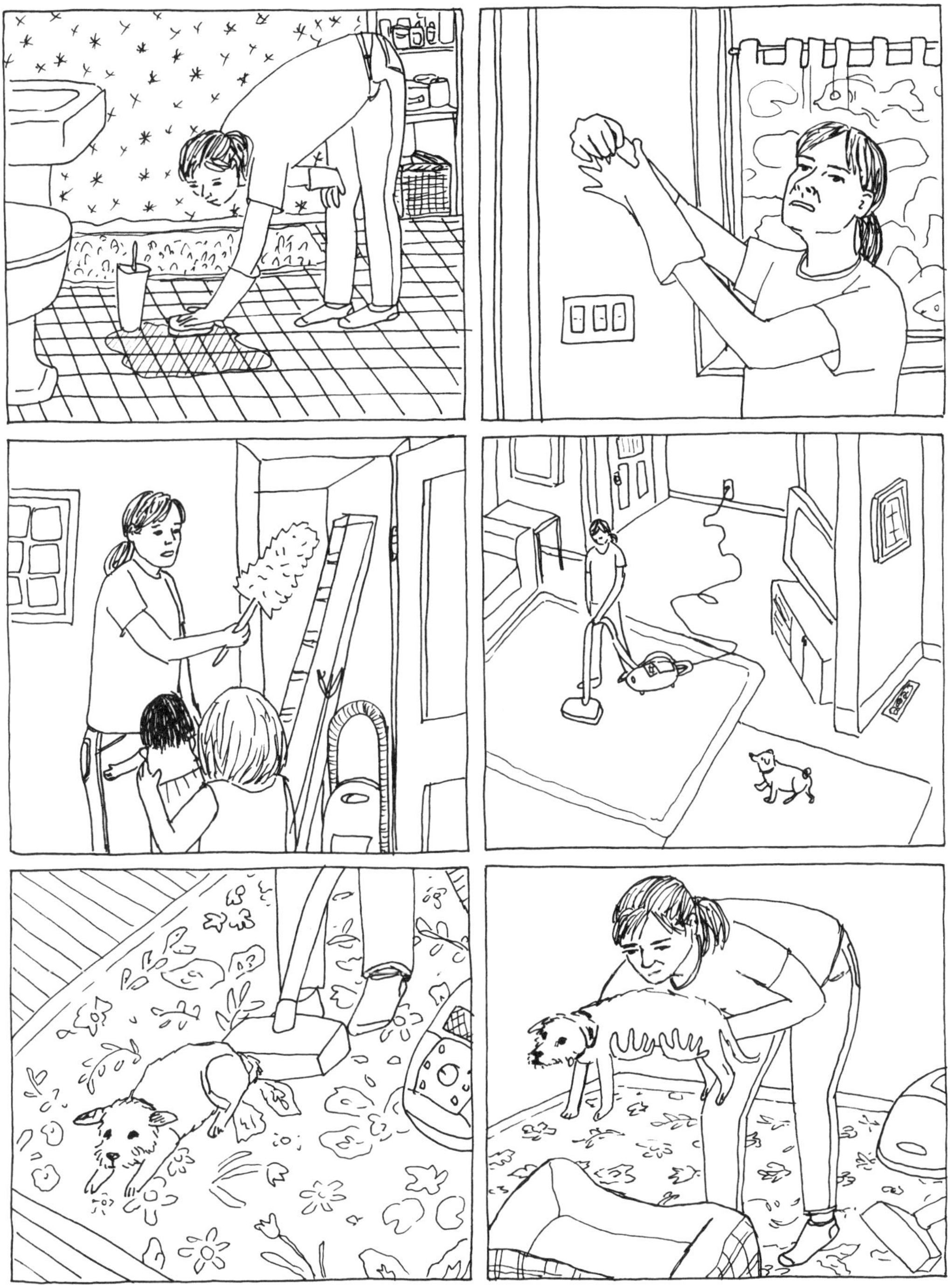

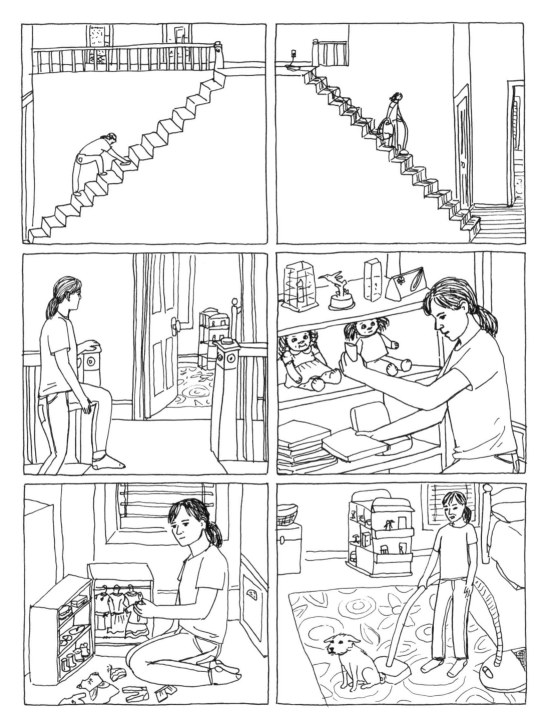

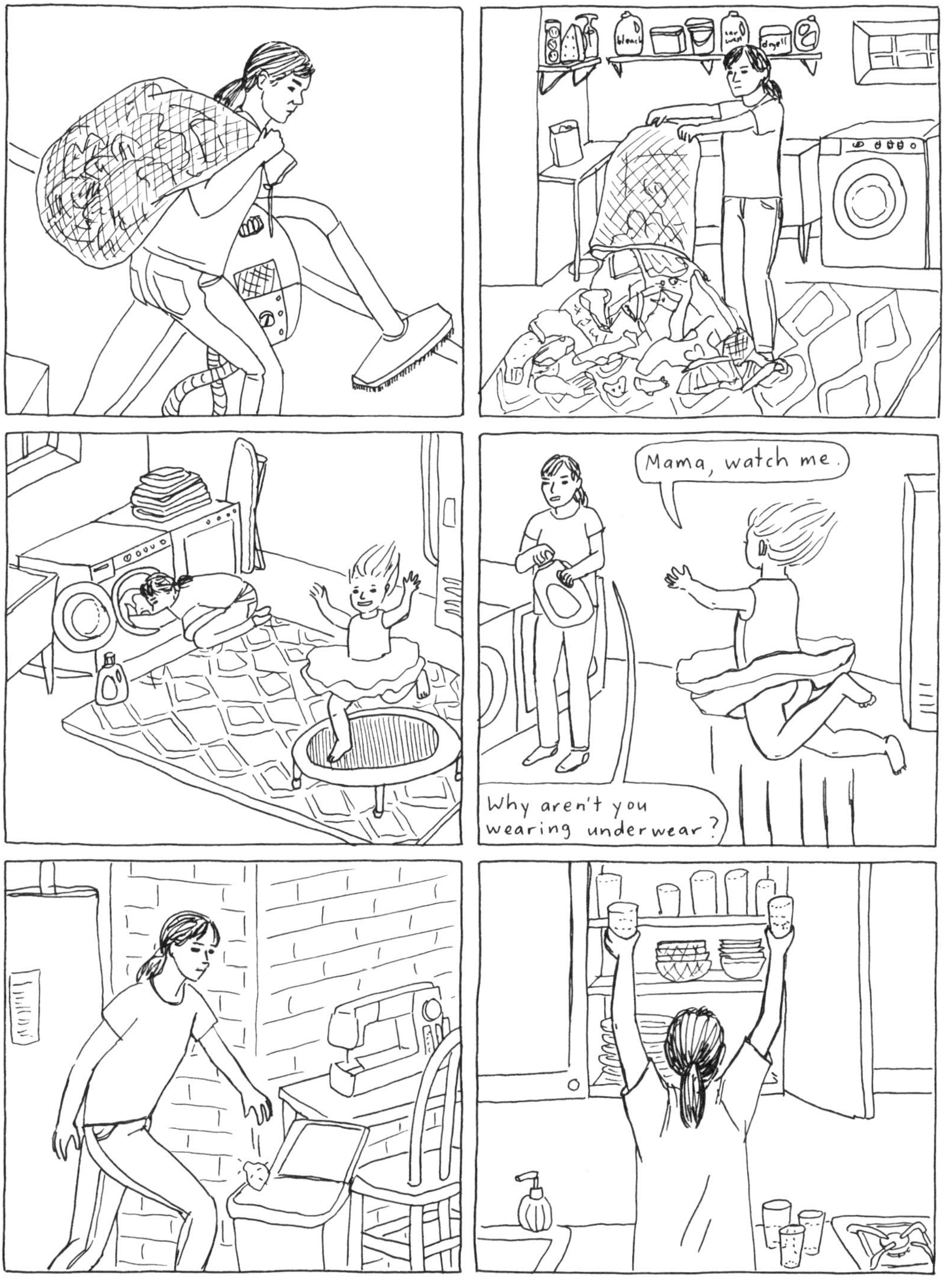
bleach
Mama, watch me.
Why aren't you wearing underwear?

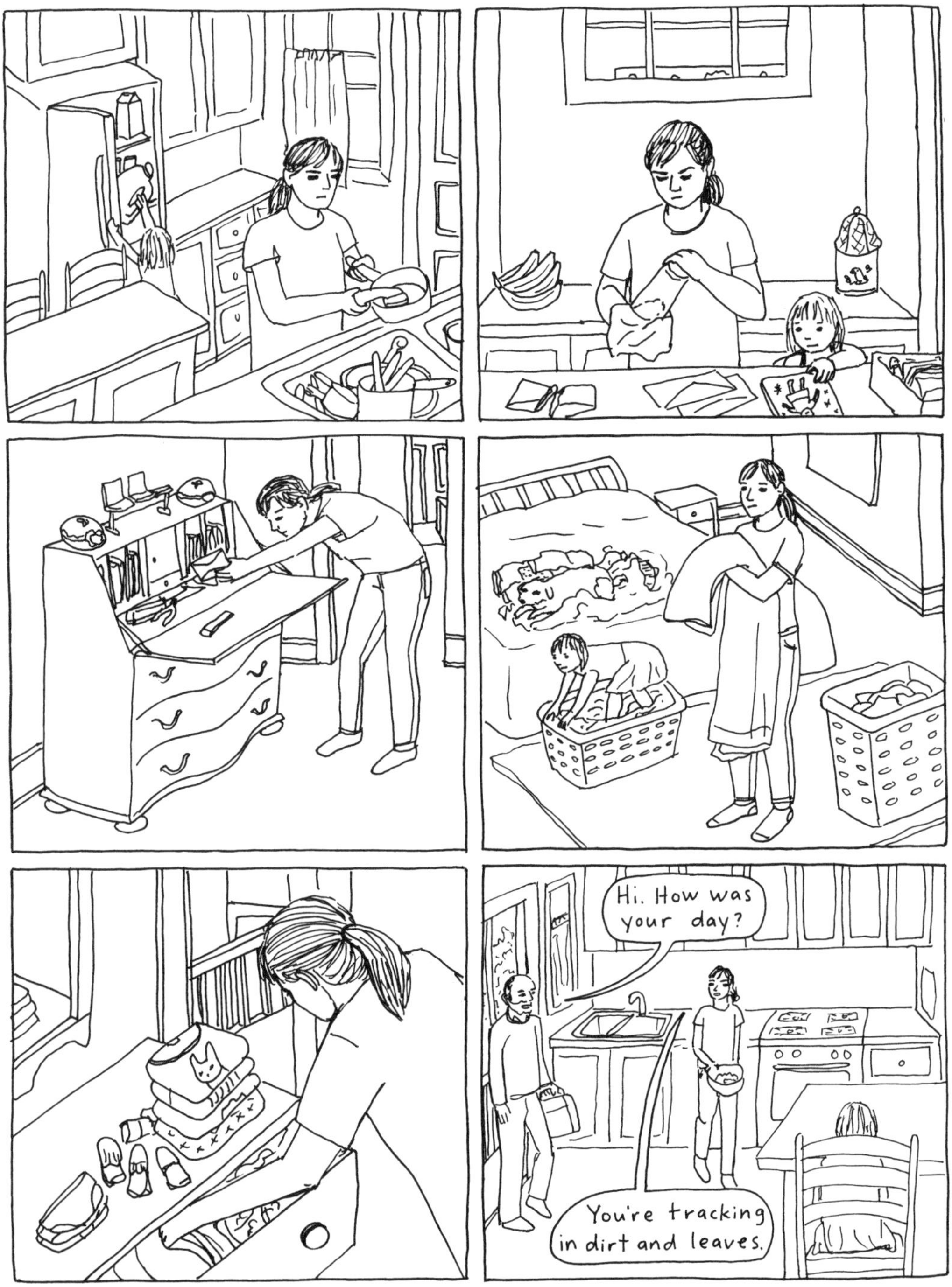
Hi. How was your day?
You're tracking in dirt and leaves.

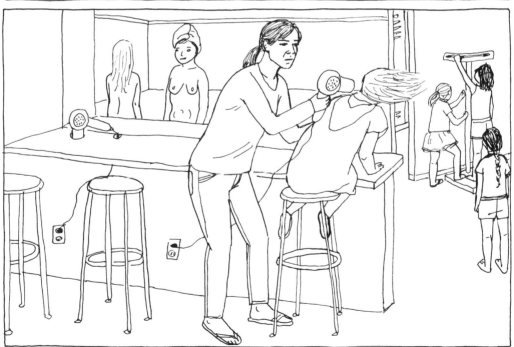

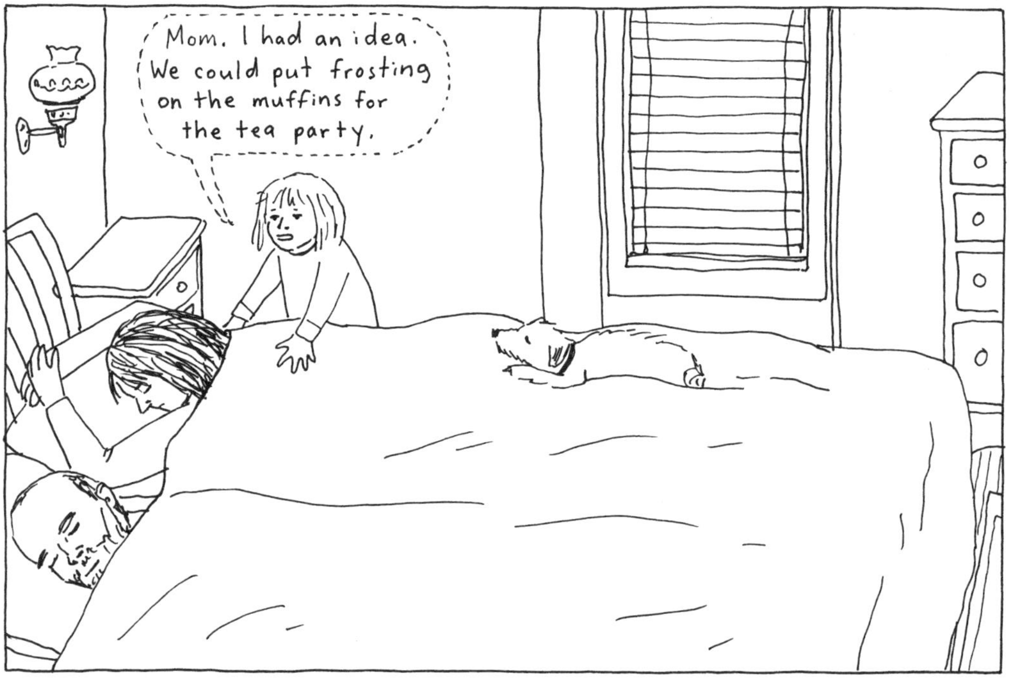
Mom. I had an idea. We could put frosting on the muffins for the tea party.

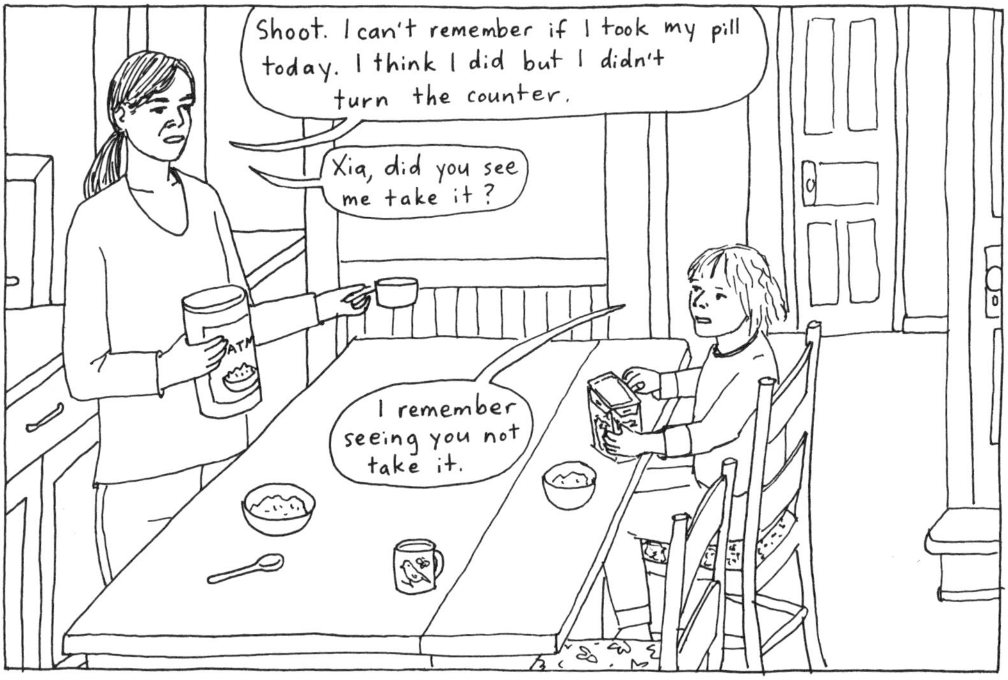
Shoot. I can't remember if I took my pill today. I think I did but I didn't turn the counter.
Xia, did you see me take it?
I remember seeing you not take it.

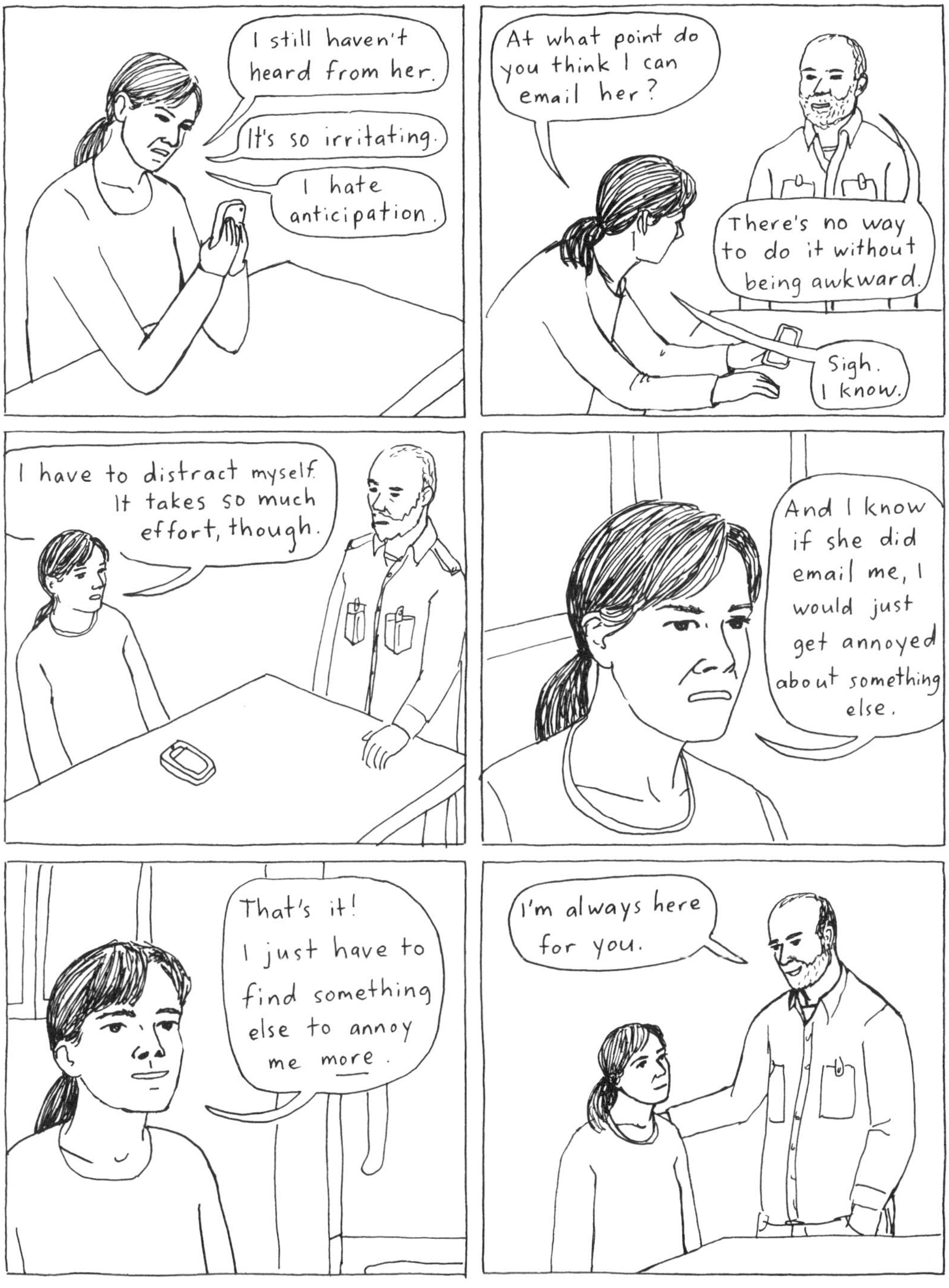
I still haven't heard from her.
It's so irritating.
I hate anticipation.
At what point do you think I can email her?
There's no way to do it without being awkward.
Sigh. I know.
I have to distract myself. It takes so much effort, though.
And I know if she did email me, I would just get annoyed about something else.
That's it! I just have to find something else to annoy me more.
I'm always here for you.

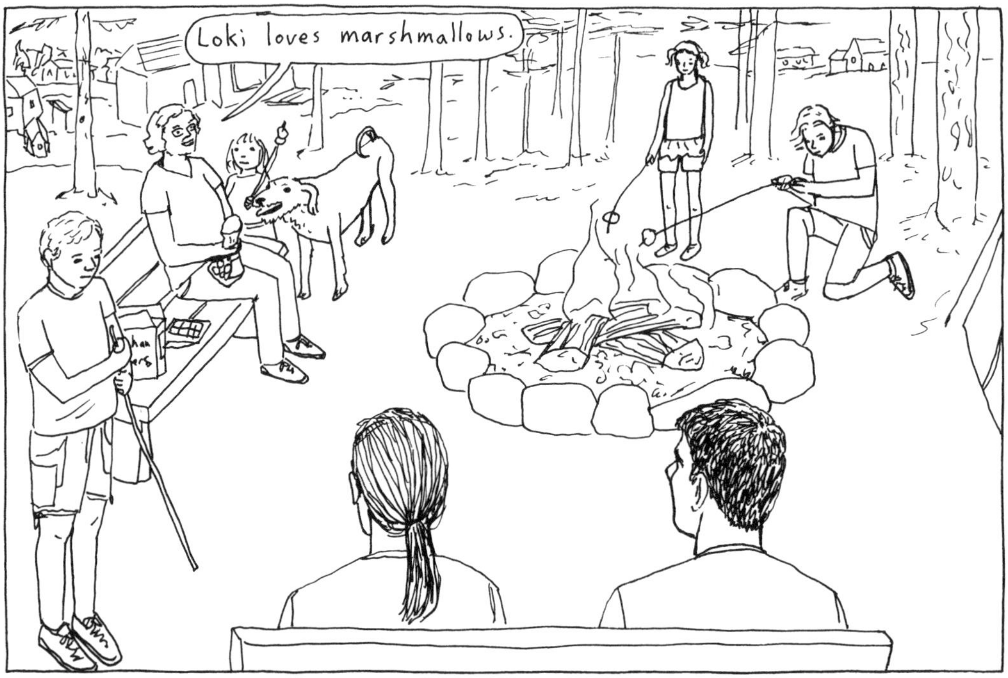
Loki loves marshmallows.

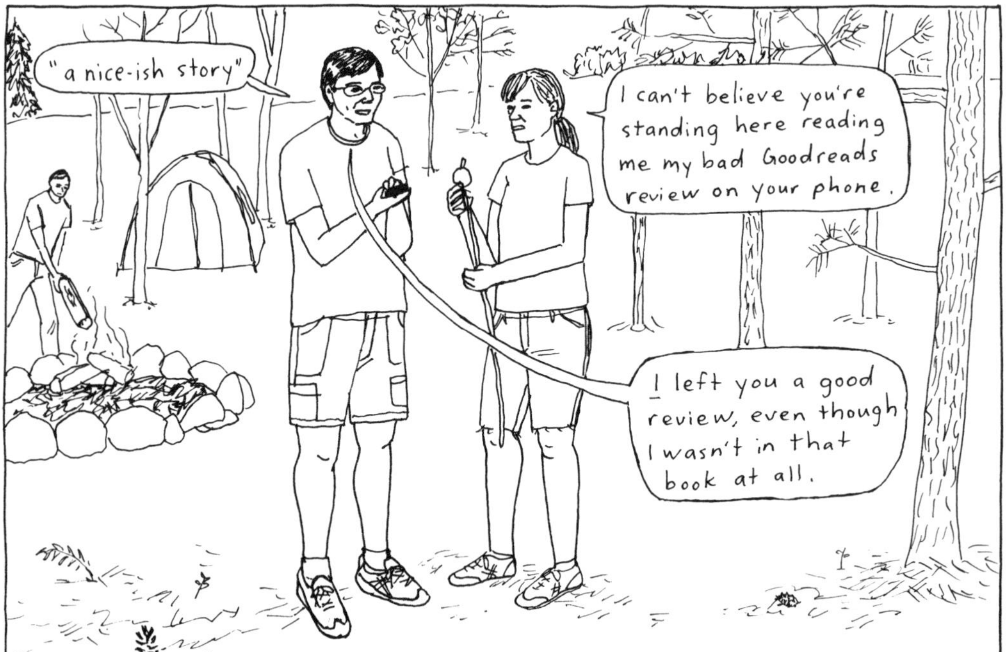
"a nice-ish story"
I can't believe you're standing here reading me my bad Goodreads review on your phone.
I left you a good review, even though I wasn't in that book at all.

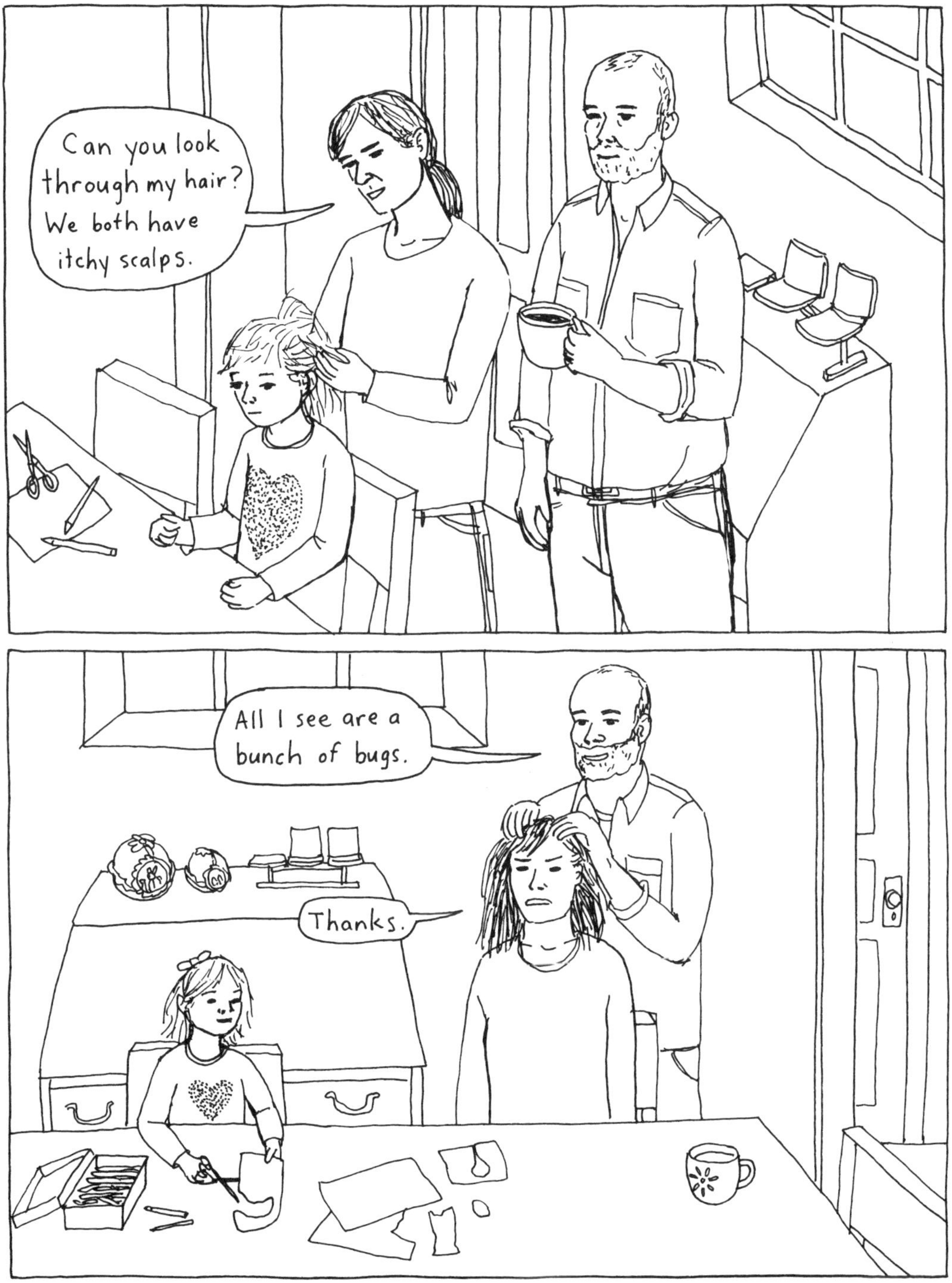
Can you look through my hair? We both have itchy scalps.
All I see are a bunch of bugs.
Thanks.

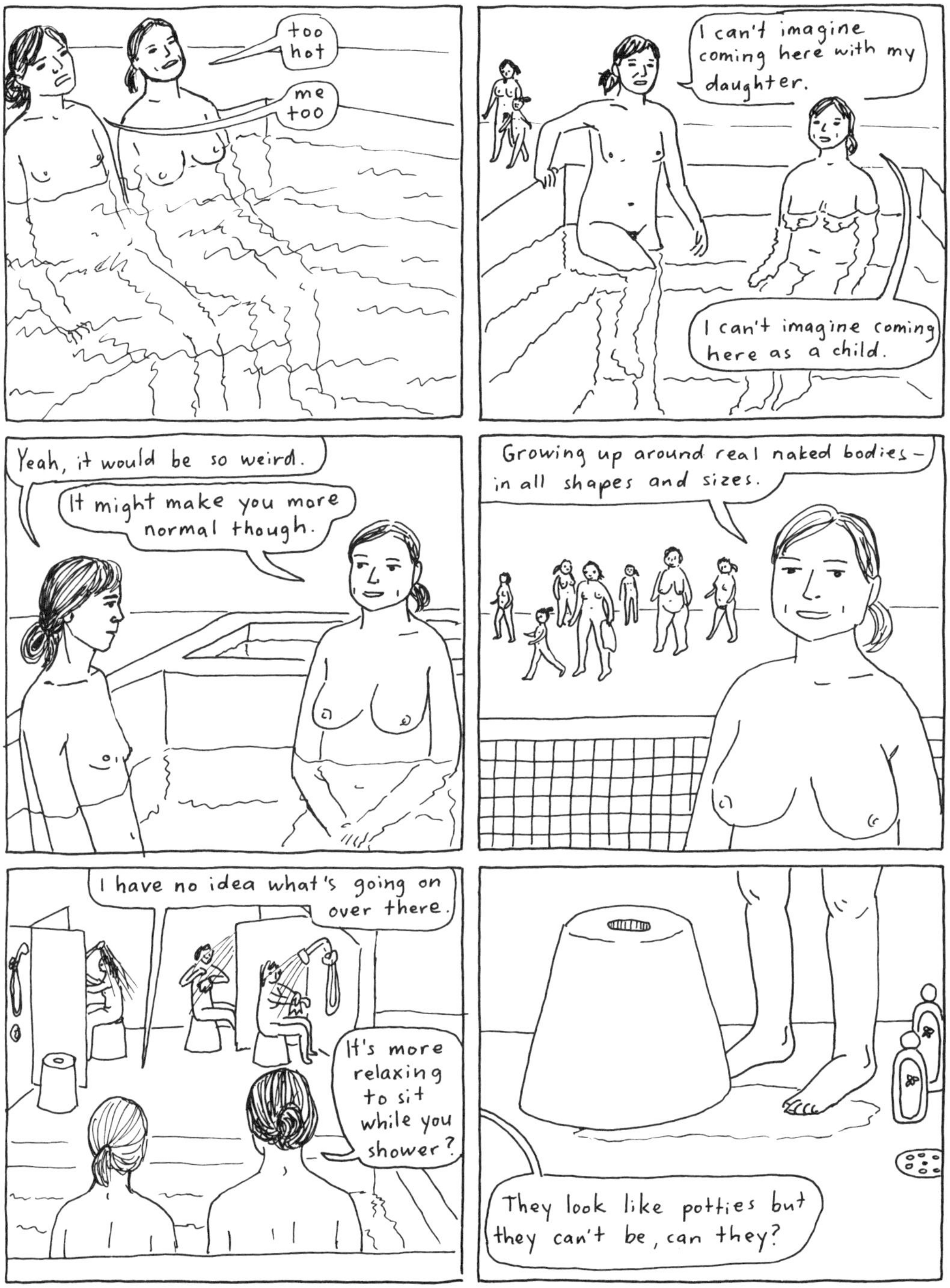
too hot
me too
I can't imagine coming here with my daughter.
I can't imagine coming here as a child.
Yeah, it would be so weird.
It might make you more normal though.
Growing up around real naked bodies - in all shapes and sizes.
I have no idea what's going on over there.
It's more relaxing to sit while you shower?
They look like potties but they can't be, can they?

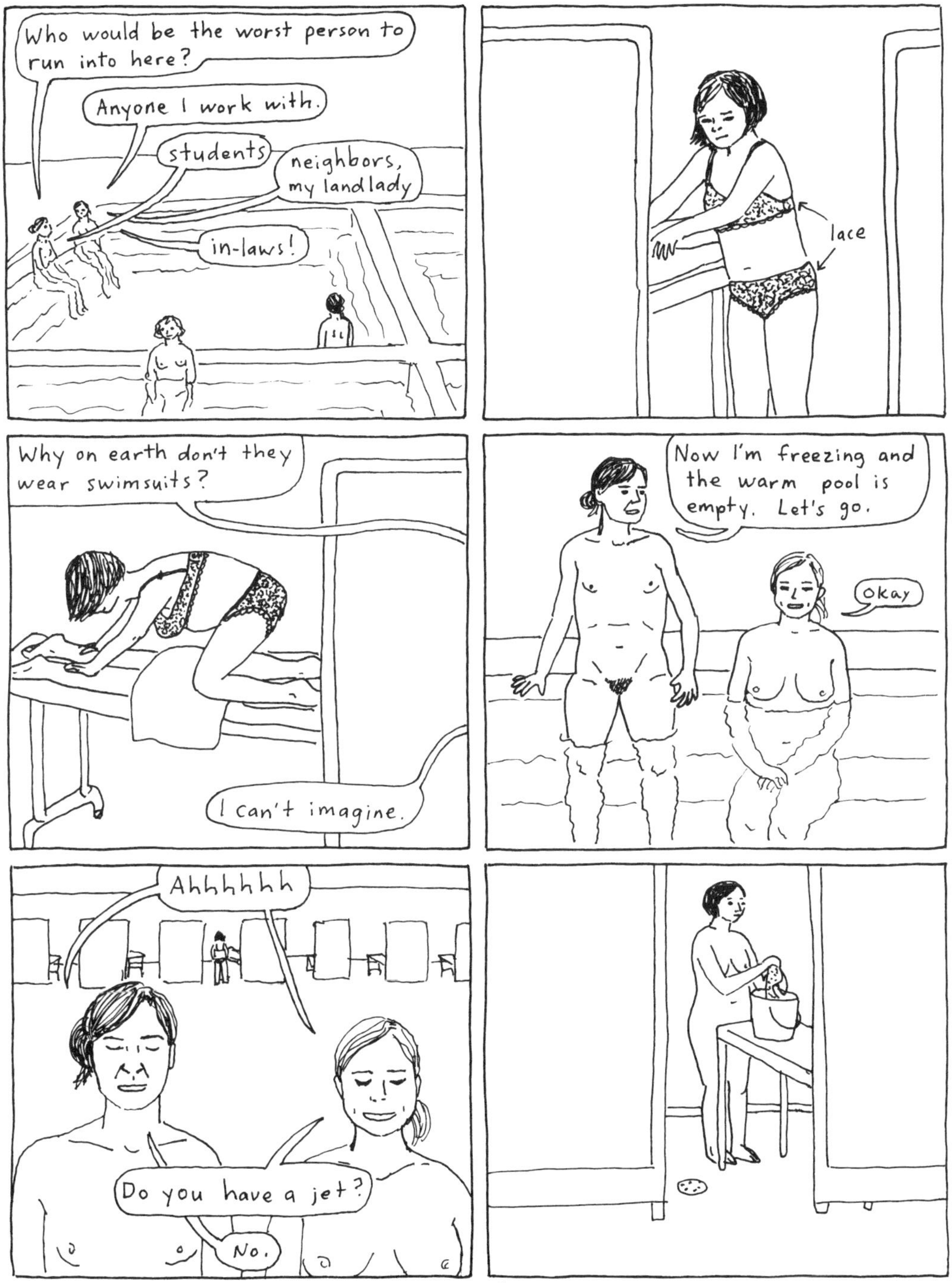
Who would be the worst person to run into here?
Anyone I work with.
students
neighbors, my landlady
in-laws!
lace
Why on earth don't they wear swimsuits?
I can't imagine.
Now I'm freezing and the warm pool is empty. Let's go.
Okay
Ahhhhhh
Do you have a jet?
No.

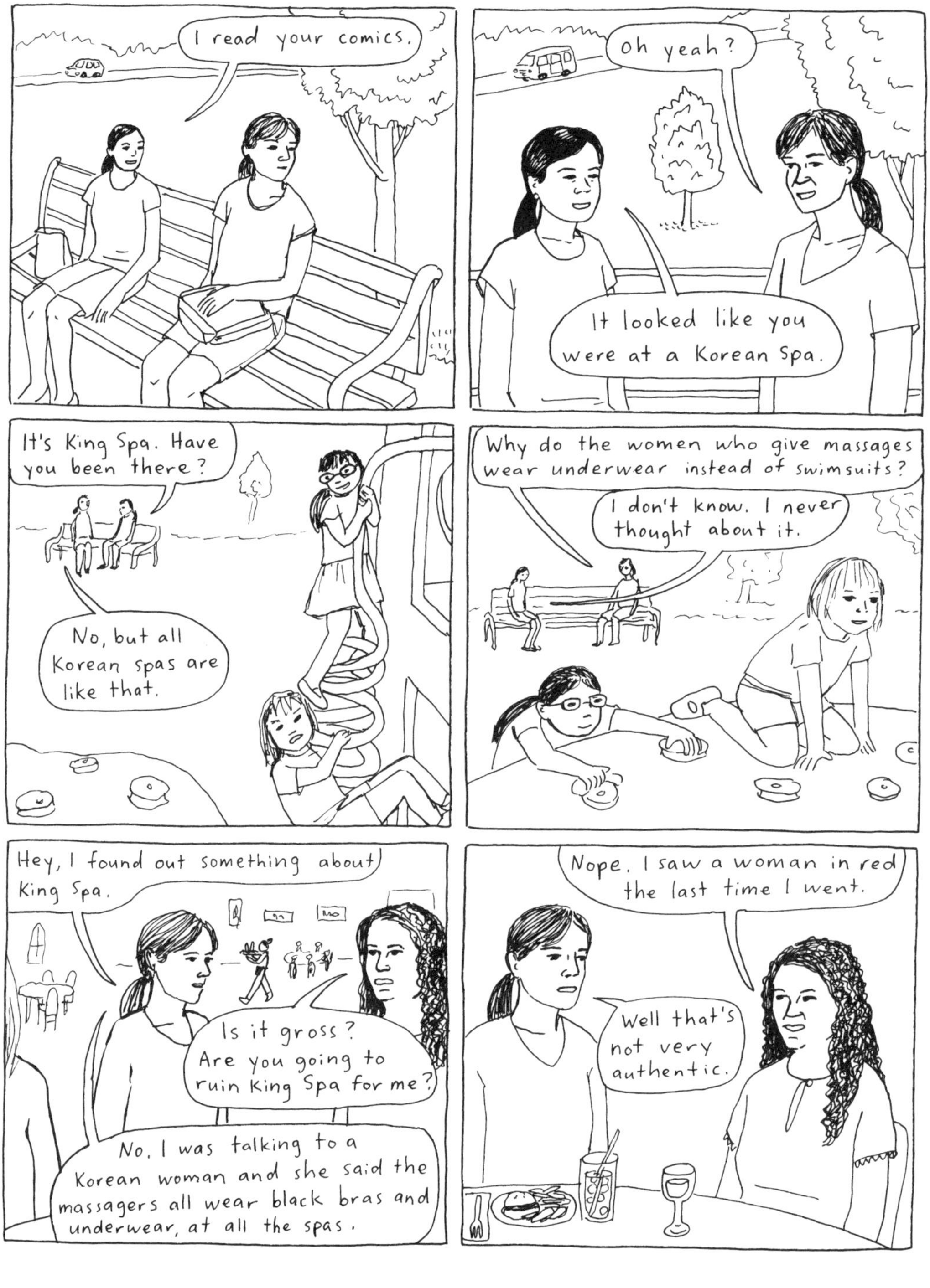
I read your comics.
Oh yeah?
It looked like you were at a Korean Spa.
It's King Spa. Have you been there?
No, but all Korean spas are like that.
Why do the women who give massages wear underwear instead of swimsuits?
I don't know. I never thought about it.
Hey, I found out something about King Spa.
Is it gross? Are you going to ruin King Spa for me?
No. I was talking to a Korean woman and she said the massagers all wear black bras and underwear, at all the spas.
Nope. I saw a woman in red the last time I went.
Well that's not very authentic.

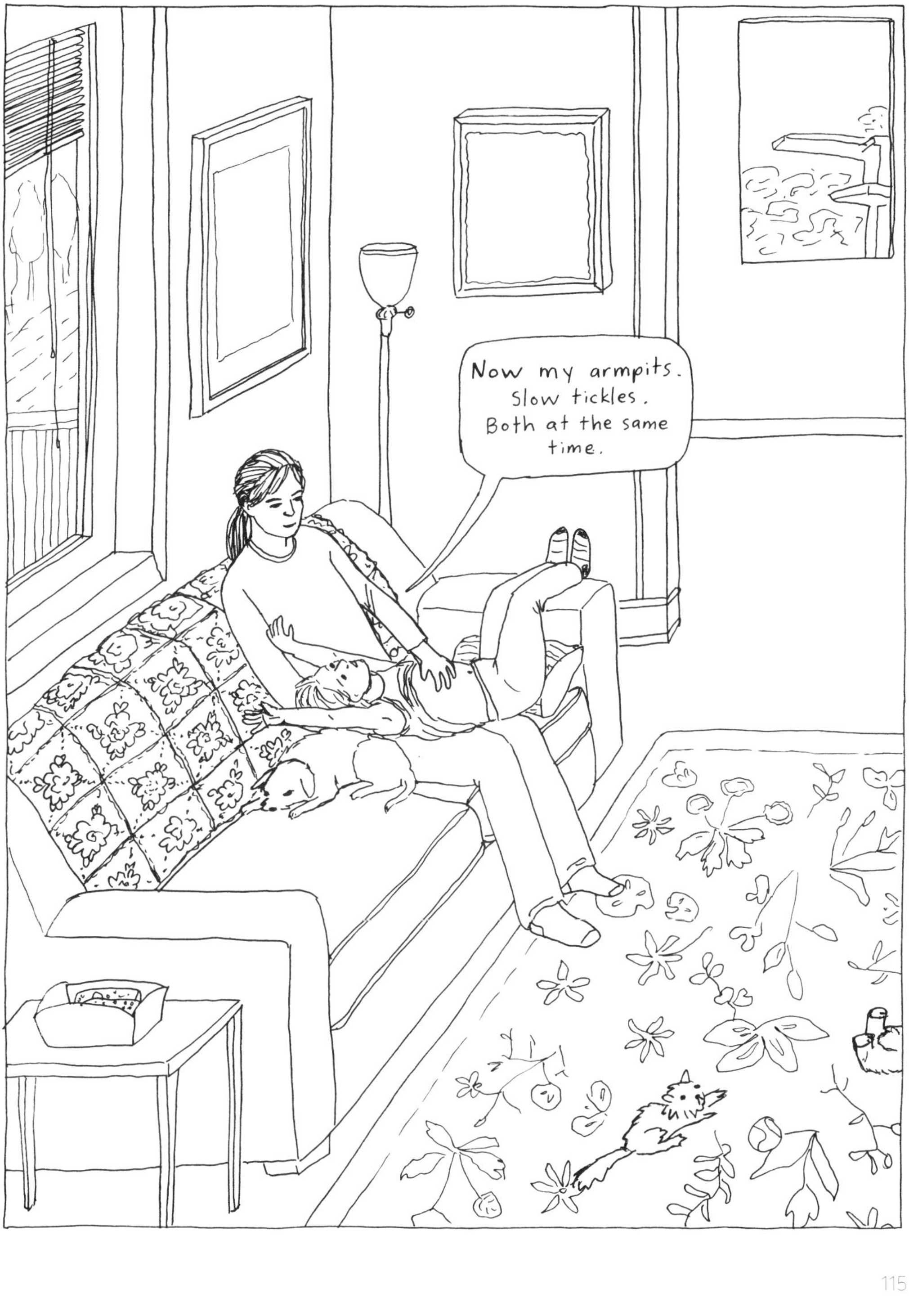
Now my armpits. Slow tickles. Both at the same time.

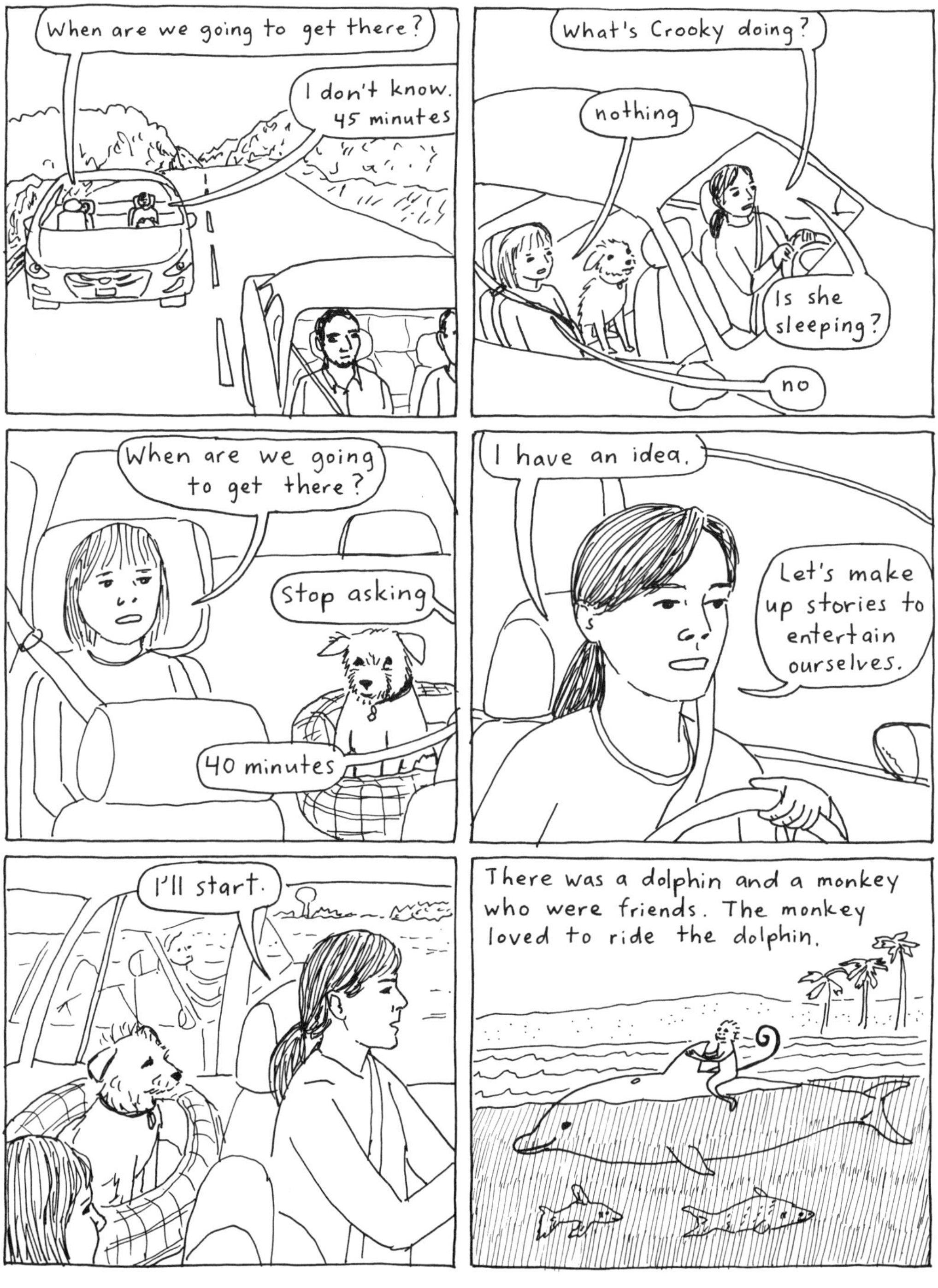
When are we going to get there?
I don't know. 45 minutes
What's Crooky doing?
nothing
Is she sleeping?
no
When are we going to get there?
Stop asking
40 minutes
I have an idea.
Let's make up stories to entertain ourselves.
I'll start.
There was a dolphin and a monkey who were friends. The monkey loved to ride the dolphin.

Sometimes the dolphin would forget about the monkey.

She would dive deep down...

and do flips underwater.

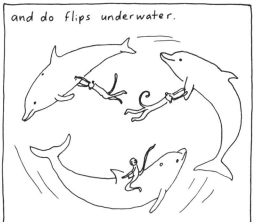

The monkey would dig her claws into the dolphin's sides and pinch as hard as she could.

But dolphins have thick, rubbery skin, and to him it felt like being tickled.

Okay, now you finish the story.

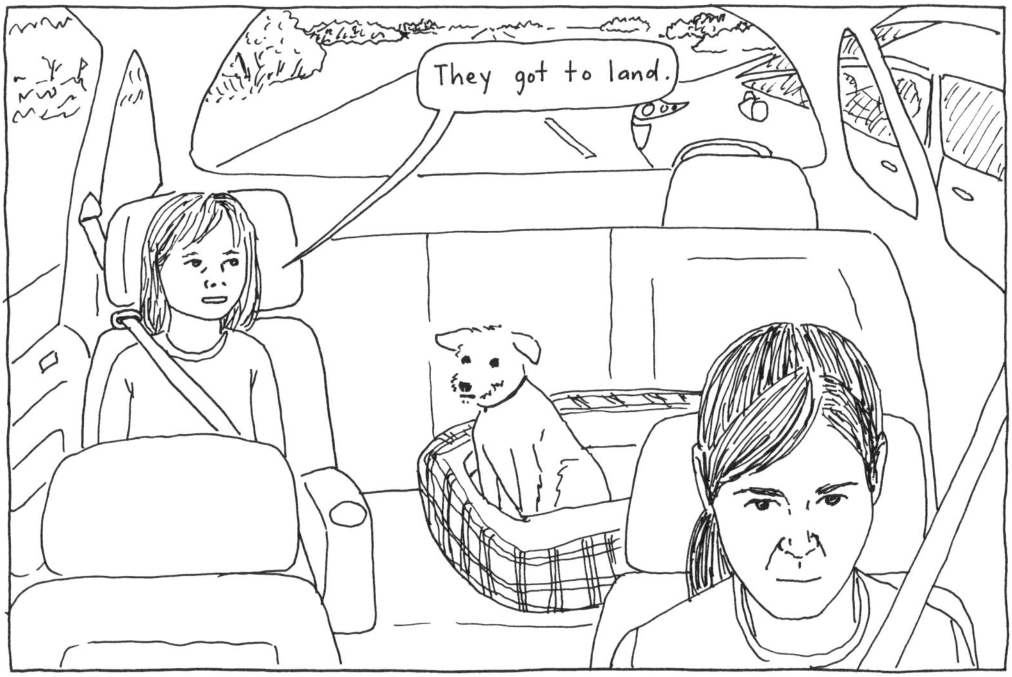
They got to land.

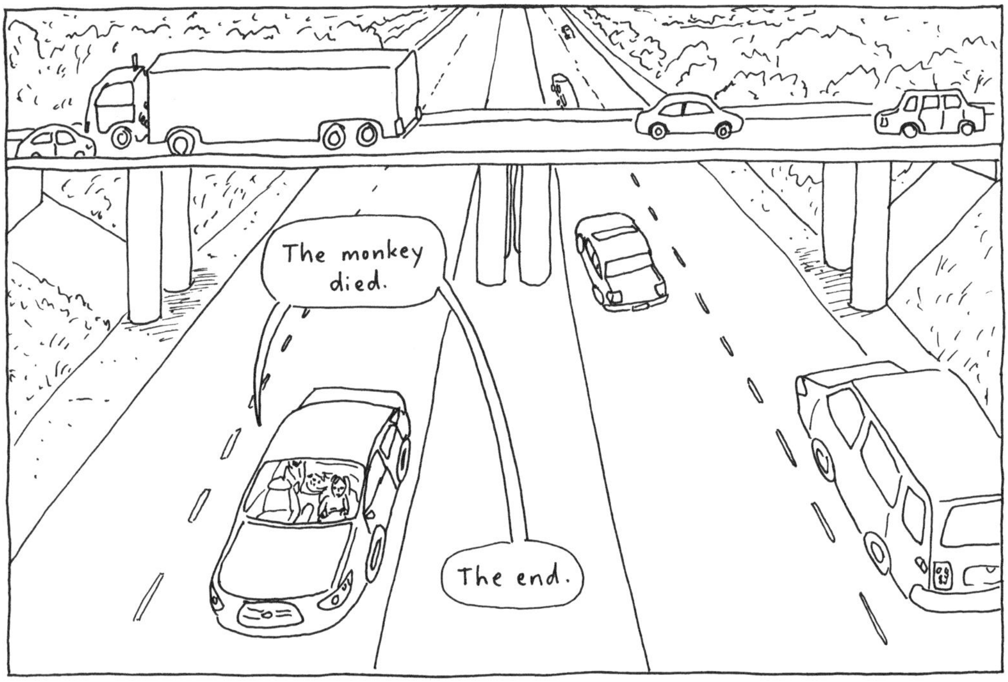
The monkey died.
The end.

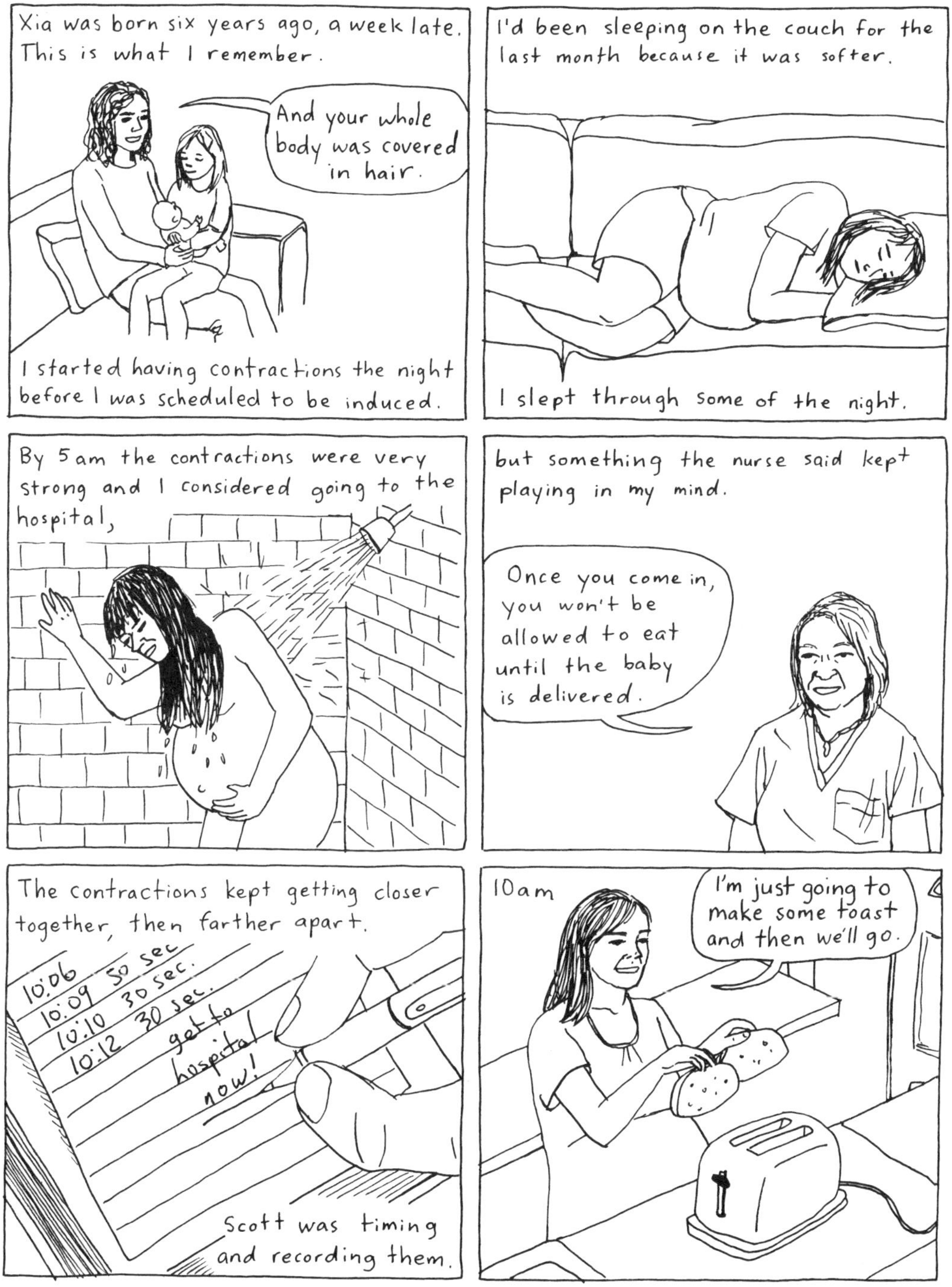
Xia was born six years ago, a week late. This is what I remember.
And your whole body was covered in hair.
I started having contractions the night before I was scheduled to be induced.
I'd been sleeping on the couch for the last month because it was softer.
I slept through some of the night.
By 5am the contractions were very strong and I considered going to the hospital,
but something the nurse said kept playing in my mind.
Once you come in, you won't be allowed to eat until the baby is delivered.
The contractions kept getting closer together, then farther apart.
10:06 50 sec
10:09 30 sec.
10:10 30 sec.
10:12
get to hospital now!
Scott was timing and recording them.
10am
I'm just going to make some toast and then we'll go.

Ten seconds later:

We're going RIGHT NOW!

The hospital was nearby, but by the time I got a bed, I was in constant pain.

The nurse had misled me.

Between contractions you'll rest. You can meditate through them. The pain increases, decreases, then pauses. It helps if you can visualize it.

There was never a pause.

It got worse. The IV of antibiotics they gave me (because I tested positive for strep B) hurt as much as the labor pain.

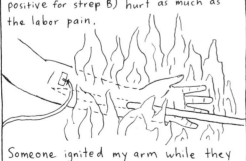

Someone ignited my arm while they skewered it with a metal stake.

I couldn't handle it. I wasn't going to get a gold star.

Can I have an epidural?

Can she have an epidural?

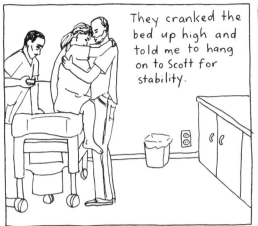

They cranked the bed up high and told me to hang on to Scott for stability.

Every pregnant woman learns if you move during an epidural you'll be paralyzed forever and probably go to hell.

Isn't there something I can hang on to that can't move?

It worked. Everything was bright and glorious.

There may have been angels singing.

Now I just had to wait until 4:00, the established pushing time.

I didn't mind not eating.

My parents had gotten into town and stopped by our place to take the dog out. They were looking at a photo album I'd made for labor.

This was another of the nurse's suggestions at the hospital's birth class.

Bring soothing pictures.

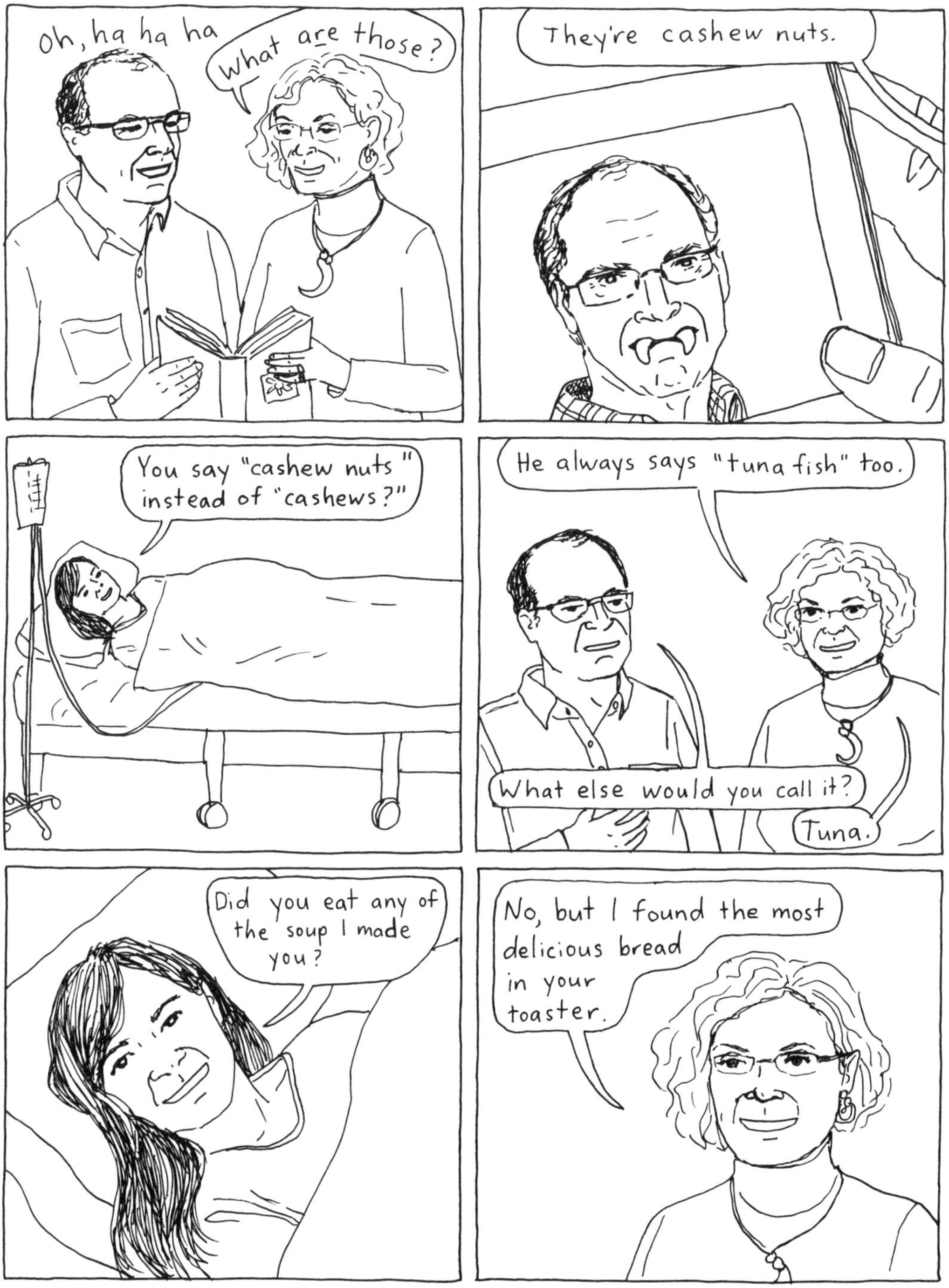
Oh, ha ha ha
What are those?
They're cashew nuts.
You say "cashew nuts" instead of "cashews?"
He always says "tuna fish" too.
What else would you call it?
Tuna.
Did you eat any of the soup I made you?
No, but I found the most delicious bread in your toaster.

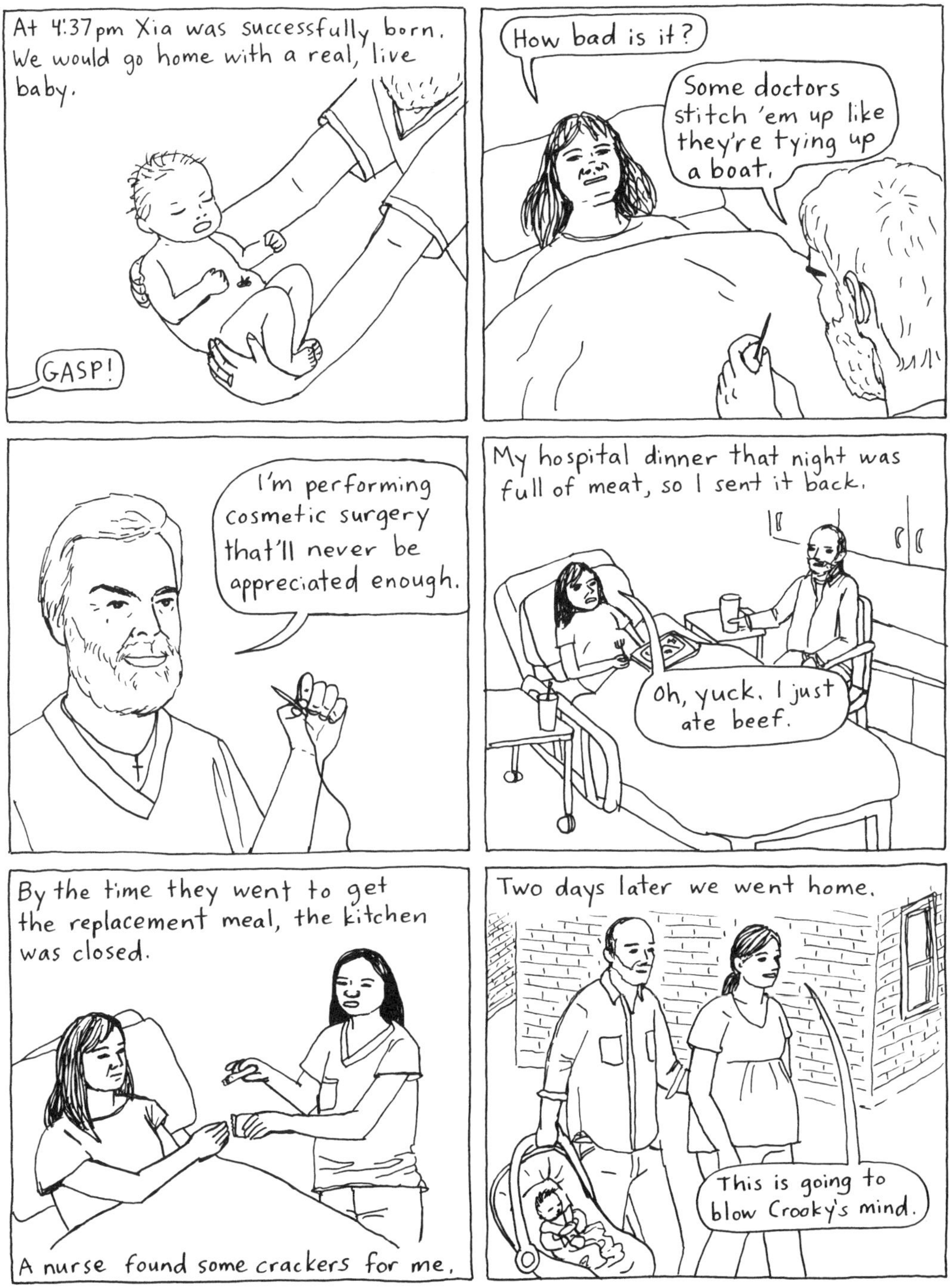
At 4:37 pm Xia was successfully born. We would go home with a real, live baby.
GASP!
How bad is it?
Some doctors stitch 'em up like they're tying up a boat.
I'm performing cosmetic surgery that'll never be appreciated enough.
My hospital dinner that night was full of meat, so I sent it back.
Oh, yuck. I just ate beef.
By the time they went to get the replacement meal, the kitchen was closed.
A nurse found some crackers for me.
Two days later we went home.
This is going to blow Crooky's mind.

When I became pregnant, my doctor recommended an OB-GYN who wasn't available, so I booked an appointment with her partner in practice.

Old, white man

I never imagined I'd see a male gynecologist, but pregnancy made me lazy. I never sought out other options.

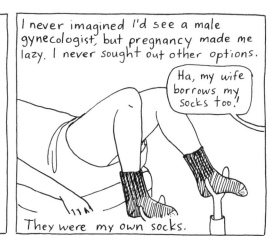

Ha, my wife borrows my socks too!

They were my own socks.

The Hispanic ladies shout, "Ay ay ay!" when they give birth.

And the Jewish ones yell "Oy oy oy!"

White women just scream, "Oh, FUCK!"

Oh.

heh heh

I stayed. Even after my miscarriage, I went back to him.

This 350 lb. woman gave birth while crossing the street. The baby just fell out. The guy at the pizza place saw it and rushed out to wrap the baby in tinfoil.

Why wasn't she wearing underwear?! Ha!

He told me a story every time I saw him.

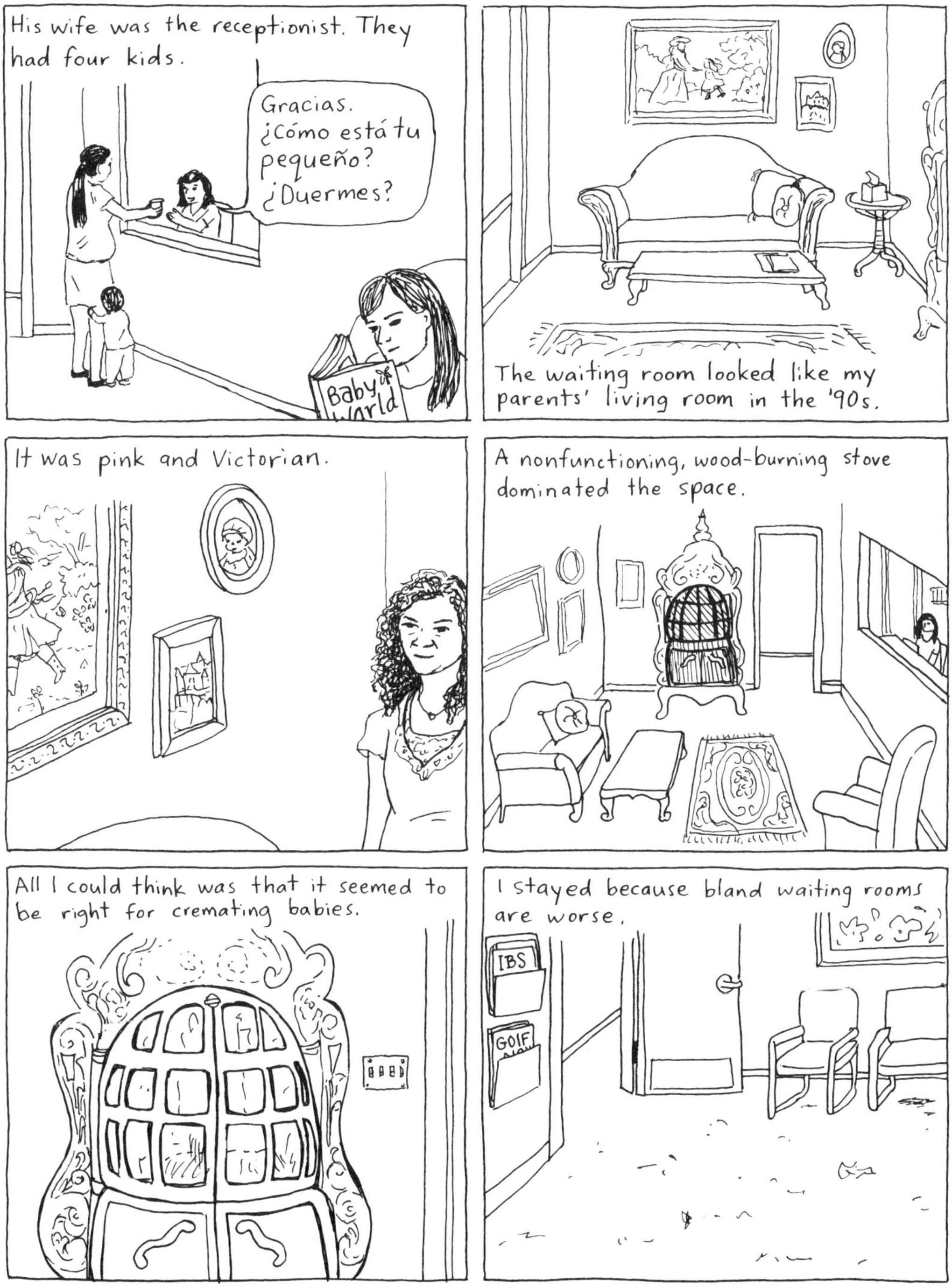
His wife was the receptionist. They had four kids.
Gracias. ¿Cómo está tu pequeño? ¿Duermes?
Baby World
The waiting room looked like my parents' living room in the '90s.
It was pink and Victorian.
A nonfunctioning, wood-burning stove dominated the space.
All I could think was that it seemed to be right for cremating babies.
I stayed because bland waiting rooms are worse.
IBS
GOIF

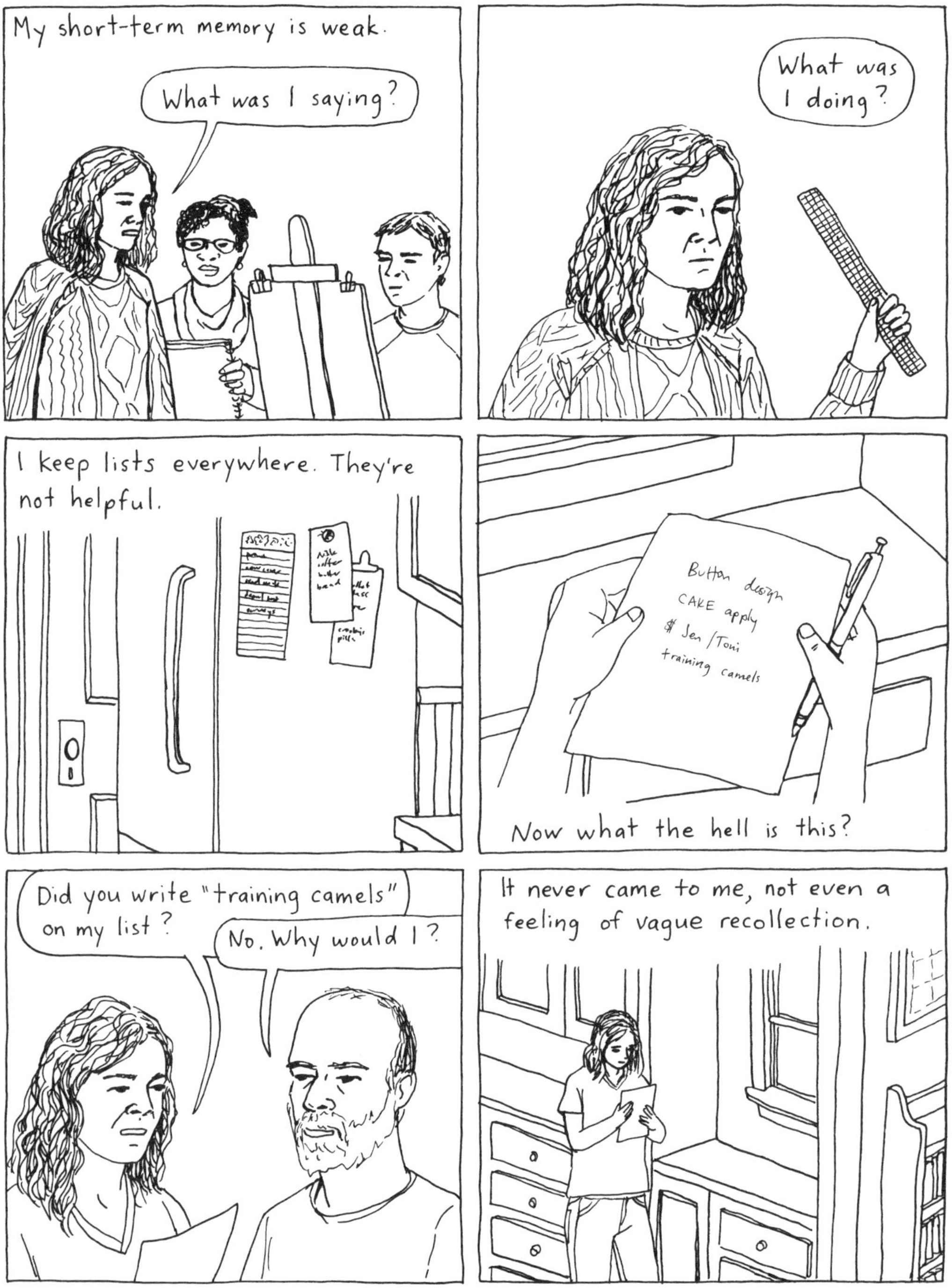
My short-term memory is weak.
What was I saying?
What was I doing?
I keep lists everywhere. They're not helpful.
Button design
CAKE apply
$ Jen/Toni
training camels
Now what the hell is this?
Did you write "training camels" on my list?
No. Why would I?
It never came to me, not even a feeling of vague recollection.

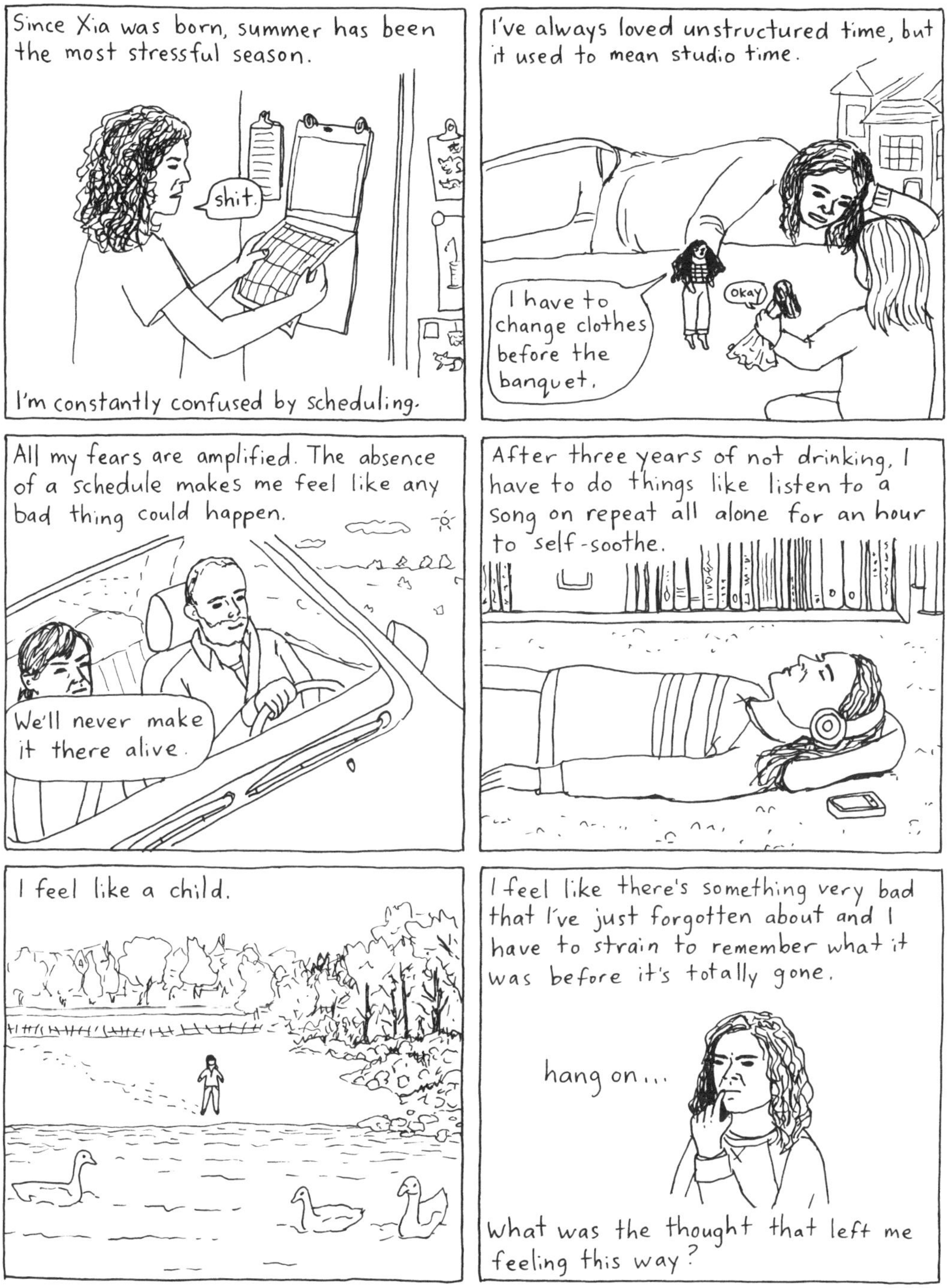
Since Xia was born, summer has been the most stressful season.
shit.
I'm constantly confused by scheduling.
I've always loved unstructured time, but it used to mean studio time.
I have to change clothes before the banquet.
okay
All my fears are amplified. The absence of a schedule makes me feel like any bad thing could happen.
We'll never make it there alive.
After three years of not drinking, I have to do things like listen to a song on repeat all alone for an hour to self-soothe.
I feel like a child.
I feel like there's something very bad that I've just forgotten about and I have to strain to remember what it was before it's totally gone.
hang on...
What was the thought that left me feeling this way?

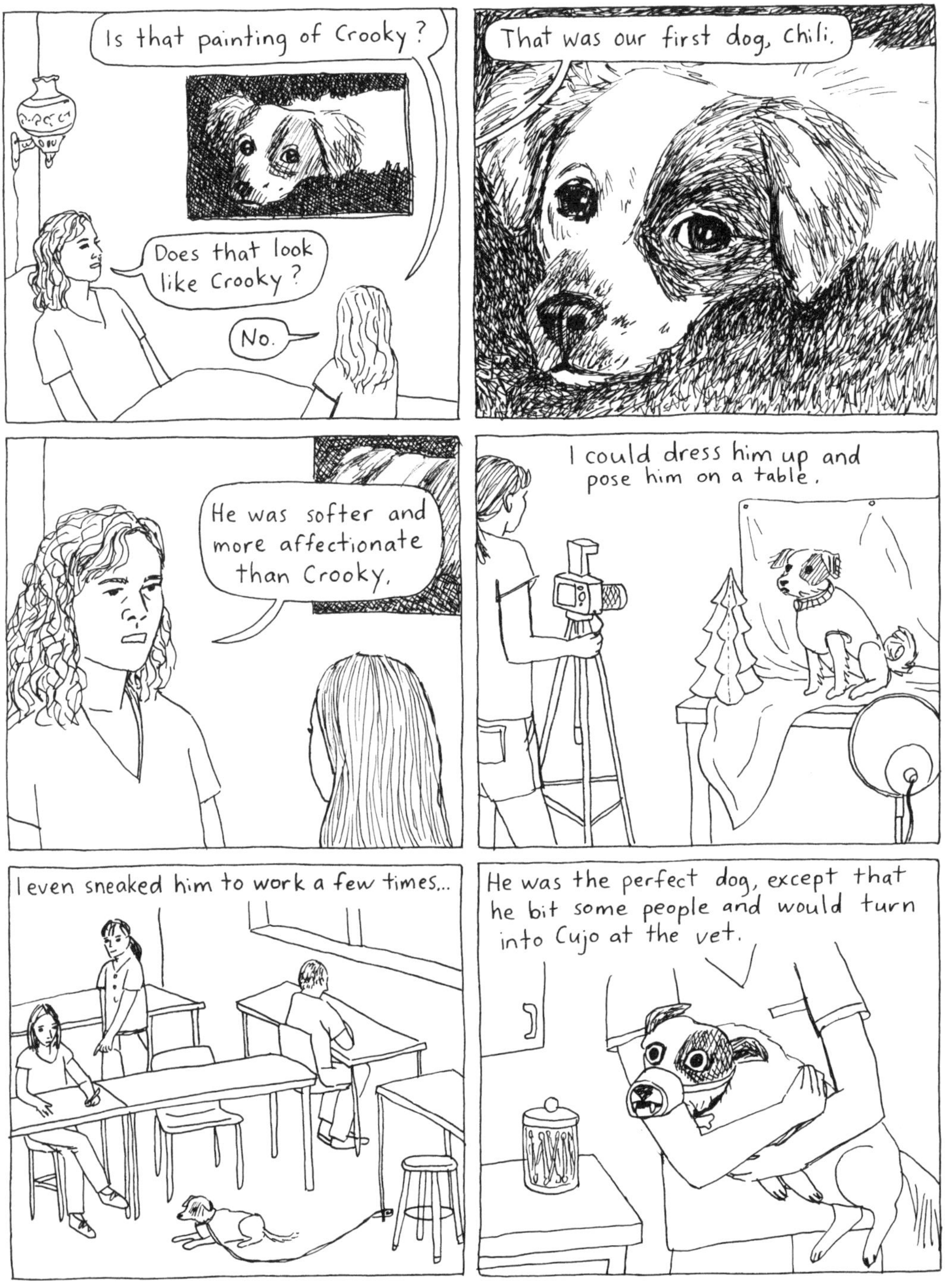

Is that painting of Crooky?
Does that look like Crooky?
No.
That was our first dog, Chili.
He was softer and more affectionate than Crooky.
I could dress him up and pose him on a table.
I even sneaked him to work a few times...
He was the perfect dog, except that he bit some people and would turn into Cujo at the vet.

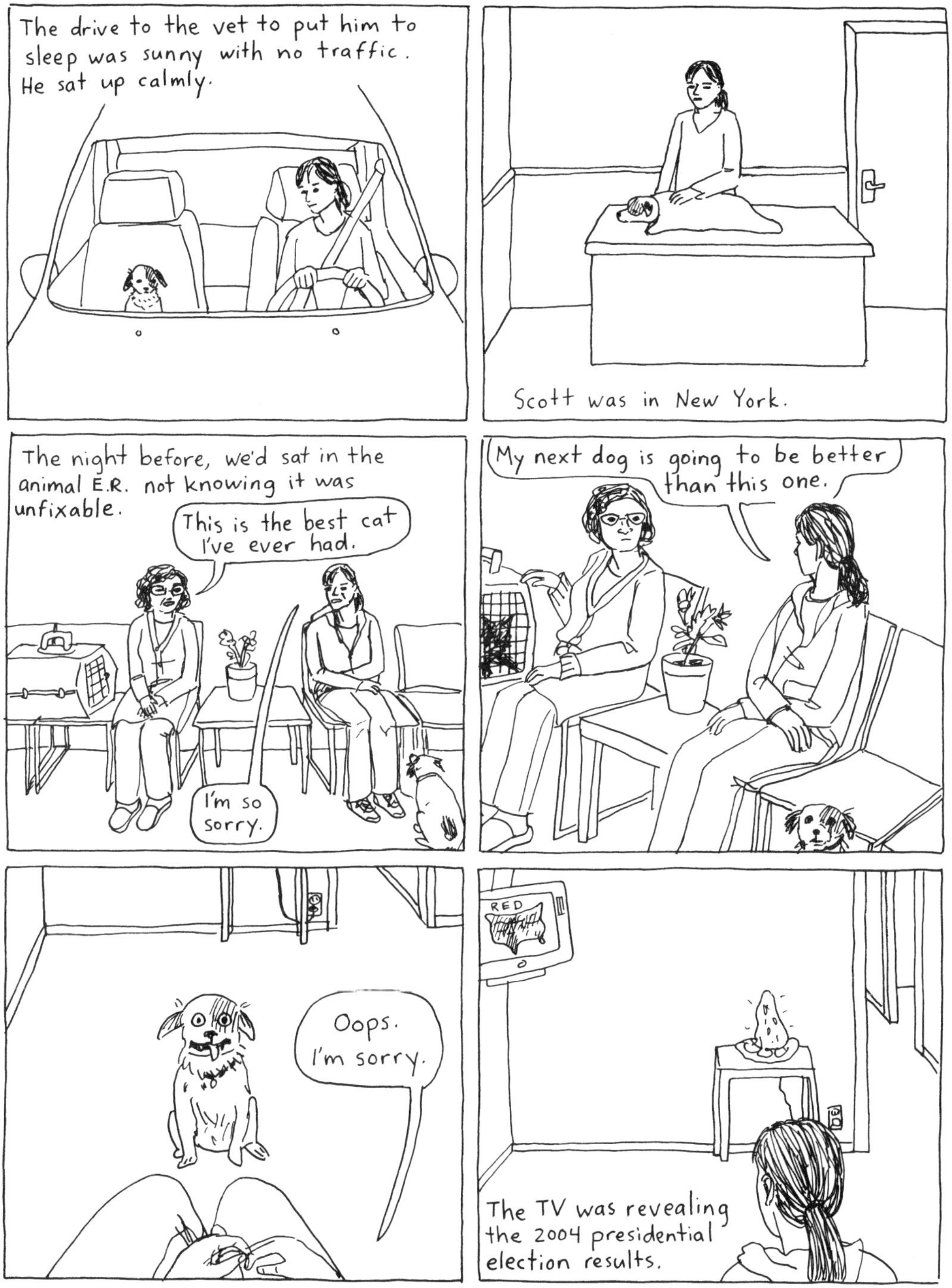
The drive to the vet to put him to sleep was sunny with no traffic. He sat up calmly.
Scott was in New York.
The night before, we'd sat in the animal E.R. not knowing it was unfixable.
This is the best cat I've ever had.
I'm so sorry.
My next dog is going to be better than this one.
Oops. I'm sorry.
RED
The TV was revealing the 2004 presidential election results.

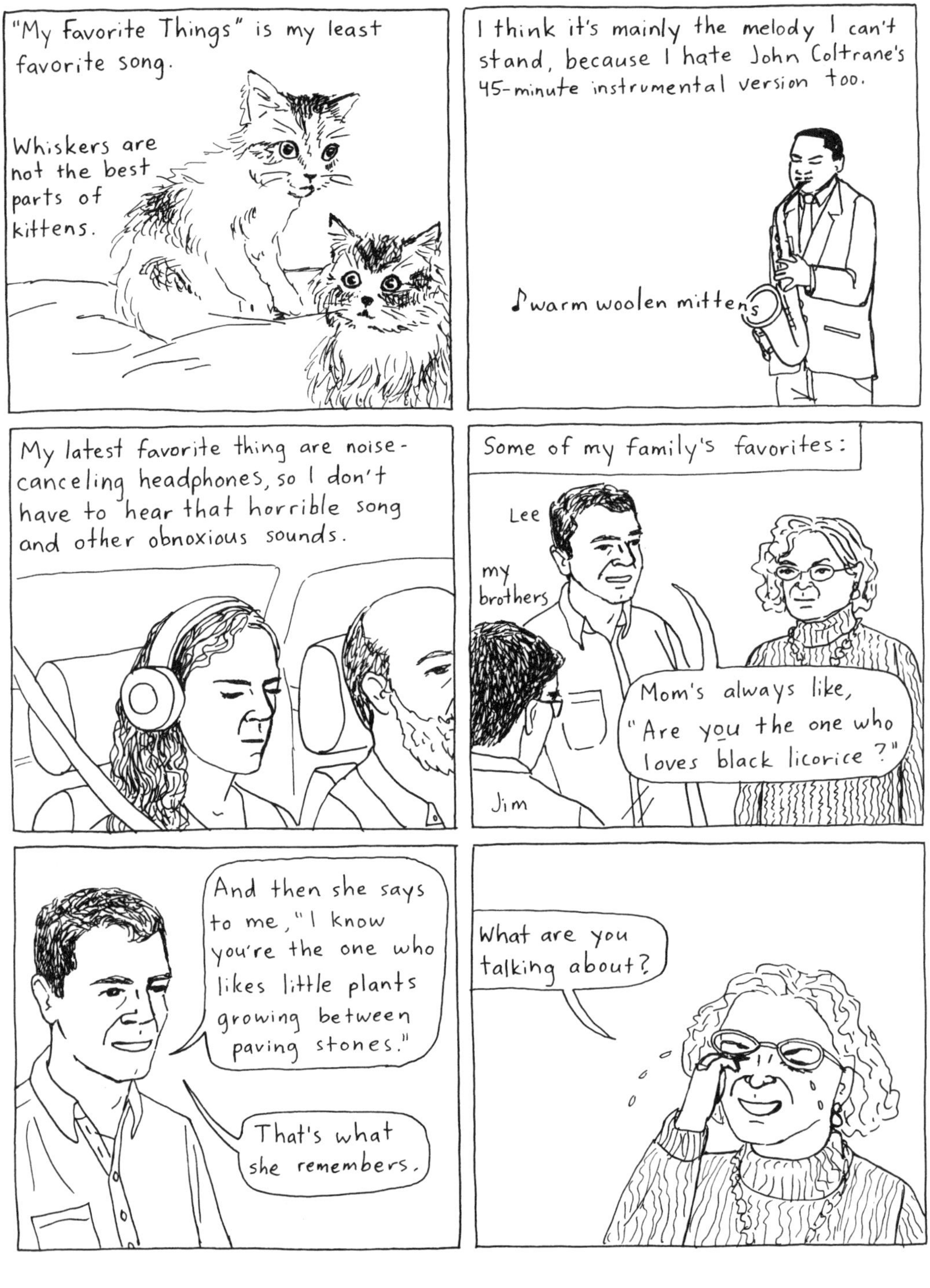

"My Favorite Things" is my least favorite song.
Whiskers are not the best parts of kittens.
I think it's mainly the melody I can't stand, because I hate John Coltrane's 45-minute instrumental version too.
♪warm woolen mittens
My latest favorite thing are noise-canceling headphones, so I don't have to hear that horrible song and other obnoxious sounds.
Some of my family's favorites:
Lee
my brothers
Jim
Mom's always like, "Are you the one who loves black licorice?"
And then she says to me, "I know you're the one who likes little plants growing between paving stones."
That's what she remembers.
What are you talking about?

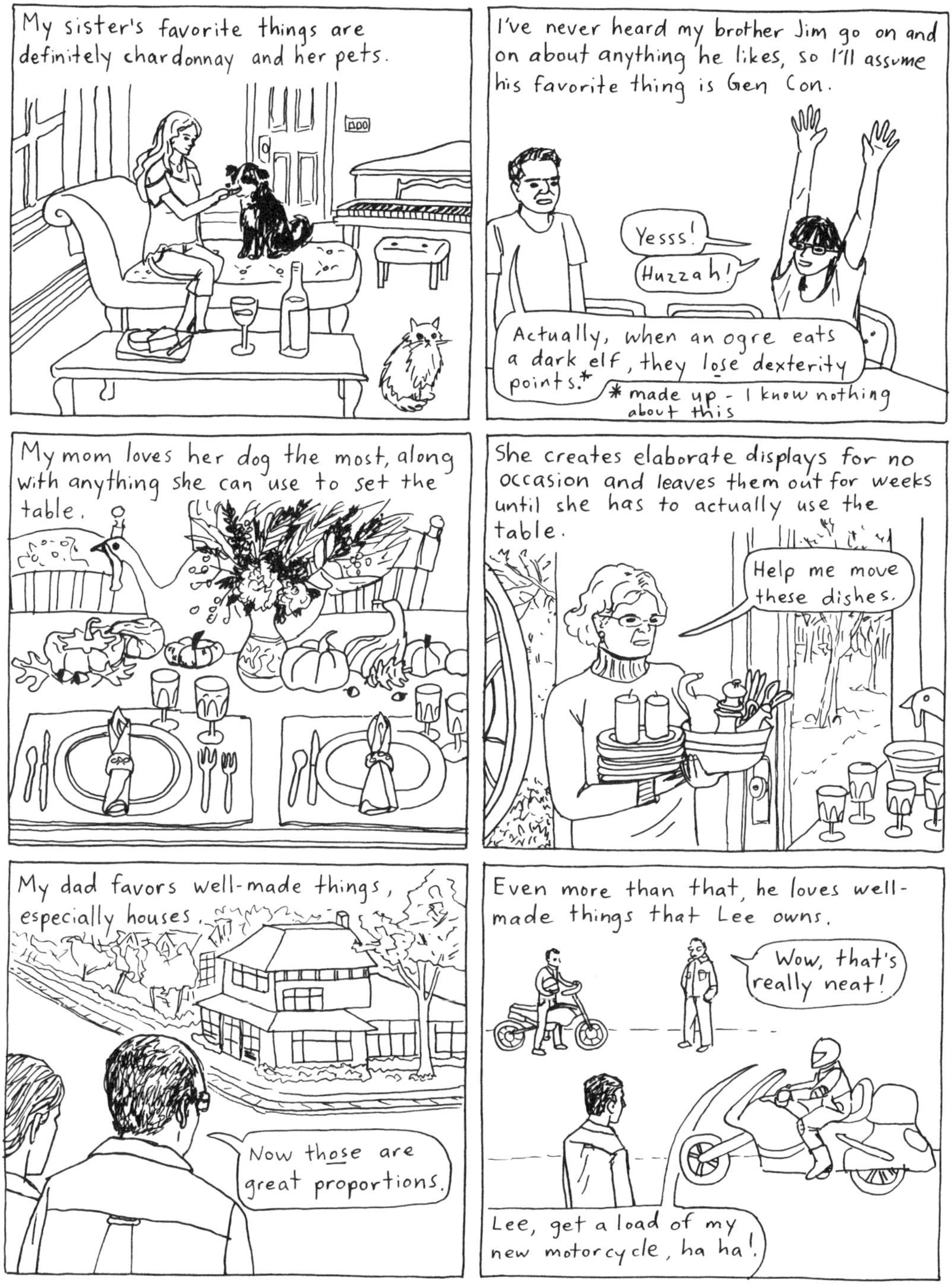
My sister's favorite things are definitely chardonnay and her pets.
I've never heard my brother Jim go on and on about anything he likes, so I'll assume his favorite thing is Gen Con.
Yesss!
Huzzah!
Actually, when an ogre eats a dark elf, they lose dexterity points.*
* made up - I know nothing about this
My mom loves her dog the most, along with anything she can use to set the table.
She creates elaborate displays for no occasion and leaves them out for weeks until she has to actually use the table.
Help me move these dishes.
My dad favors well-made things, especially houses.
Now those are great proportions.
Even more than that, he loves well-made things that Lee owns.
Wow, that's really neat!
Lee, get a load of my new motorcycle, ha ha!

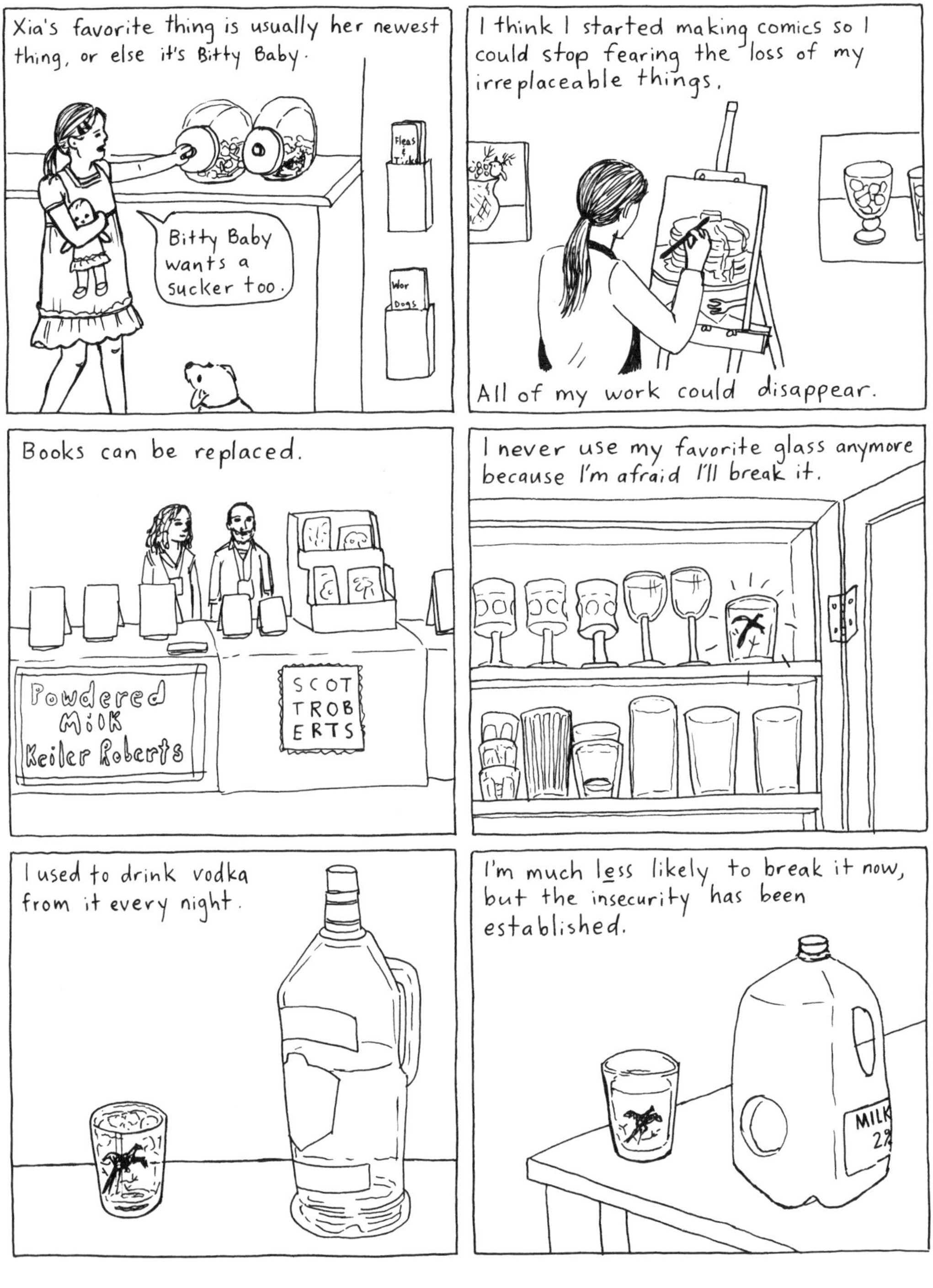
Xia's favorite thing is usually her newest thing, or else it's Bitty Baby.
Bitty Baby wants a sucker too.
I think I started making comics so I could stop fearing the loss of my irreplaceable things.
All of my work could disappear.
Books can be replaced.
Powdered Milk Keiler Roberts
SCOT TROB ERTS
I never use my favorite glass anymore because I'm afraid I'll break it.
I used to drink vodka from it every night.
I'm much less likely to break it now, but the insecurity has been established.

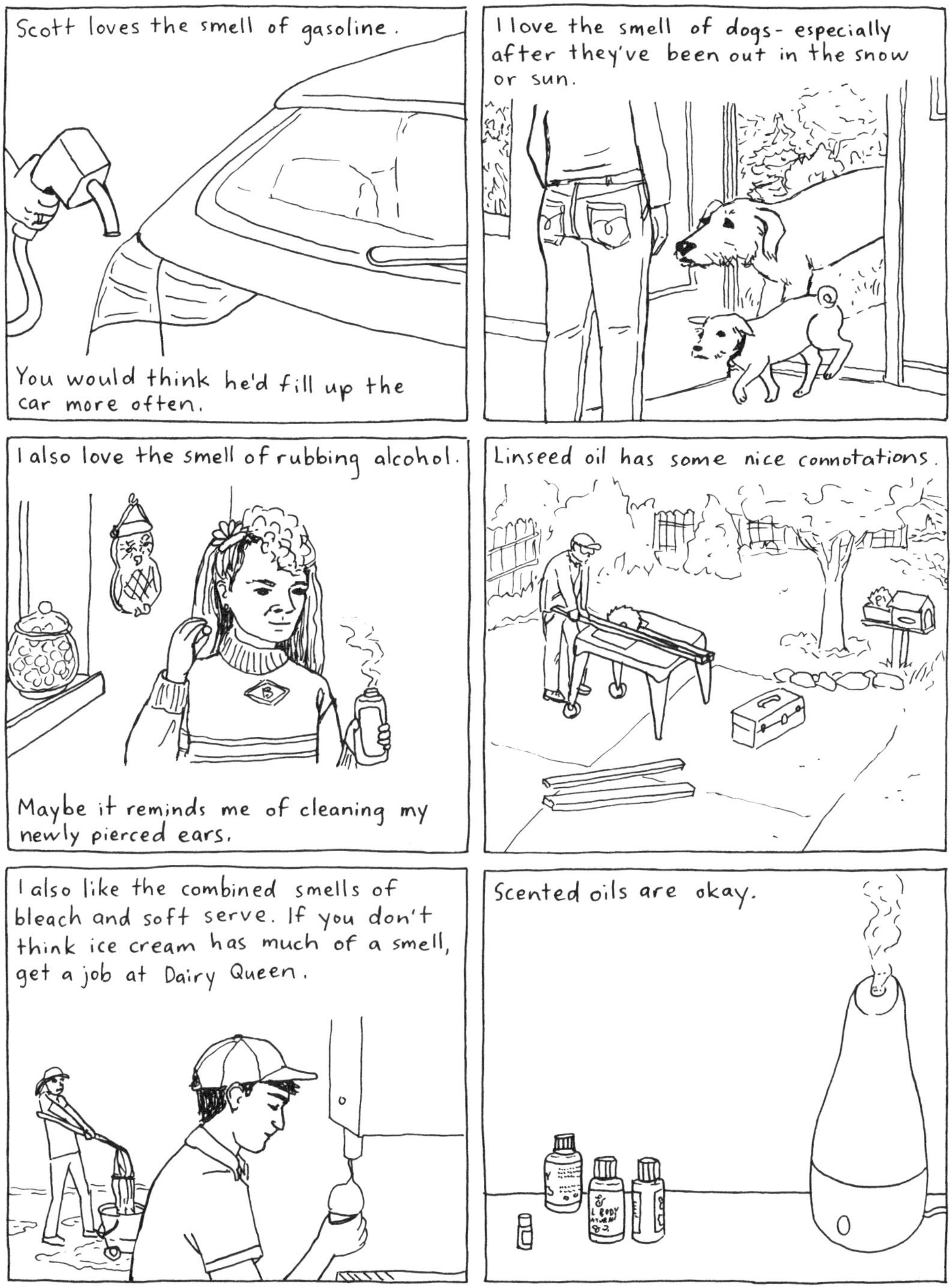
Scott loves the smell of gasoline.
You would think he'd fill up the car more often.
I love the smell of dogs- especially after they've been out in the snow or sun.
I also love the smell of rubbing alcohol.
Maybe it reminds me of cleaning my newly pierced ears.
Linseed oil has some nice connotations.
I also like the combined smells of bleach and soft serve. If you don't think ice cream has much of a smell, get a job at Dairy Queen.
Scented oils are okay.

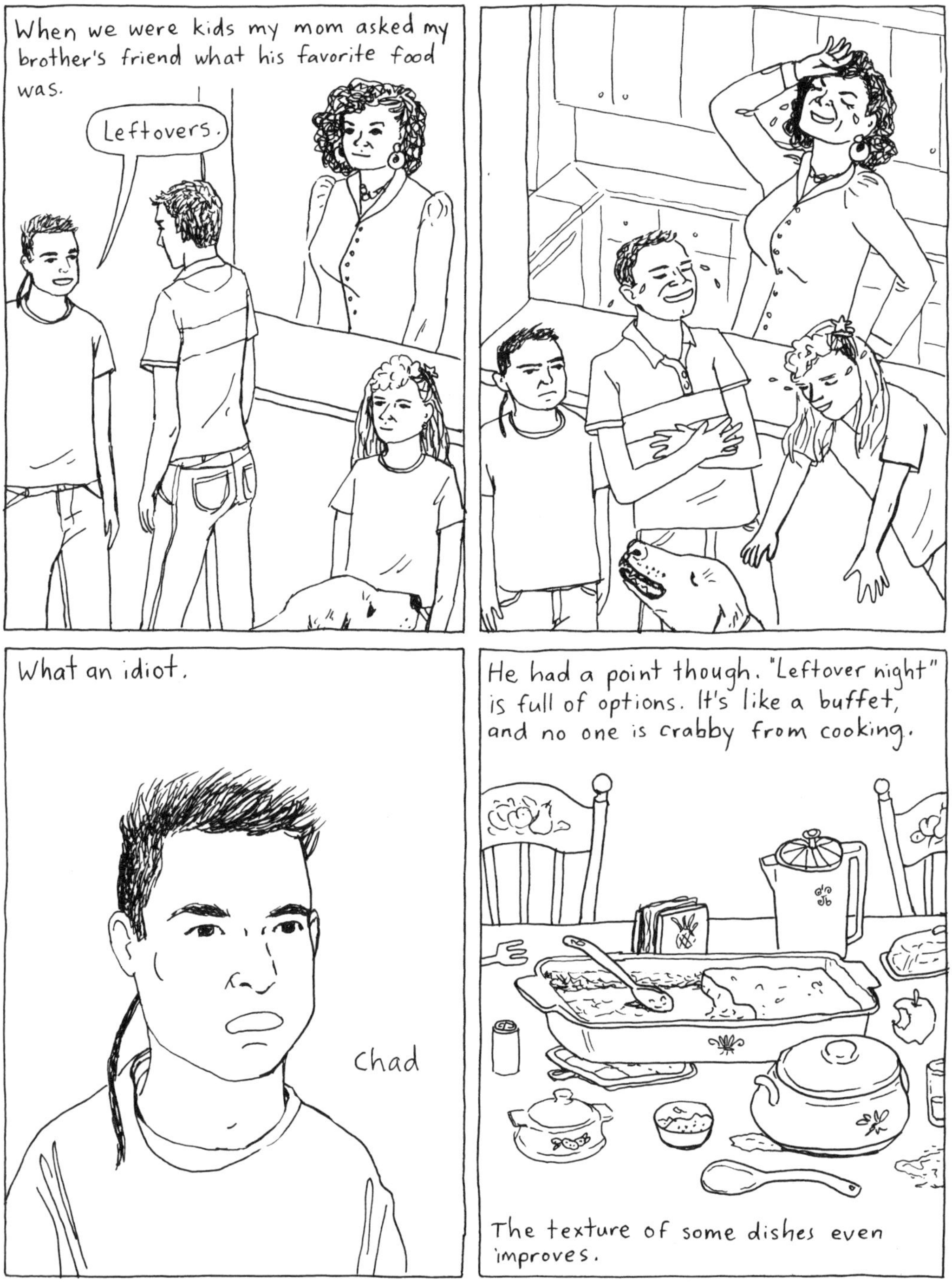
When we were kids my mom asked my brother's friend what his favorite food was.
Leftovers.
What an idiot.
Chad
He had a point though. "Leftover night" is full of options. It's like a buffet, and no one is crabby from cooking.
The texture of some dishes even improves.

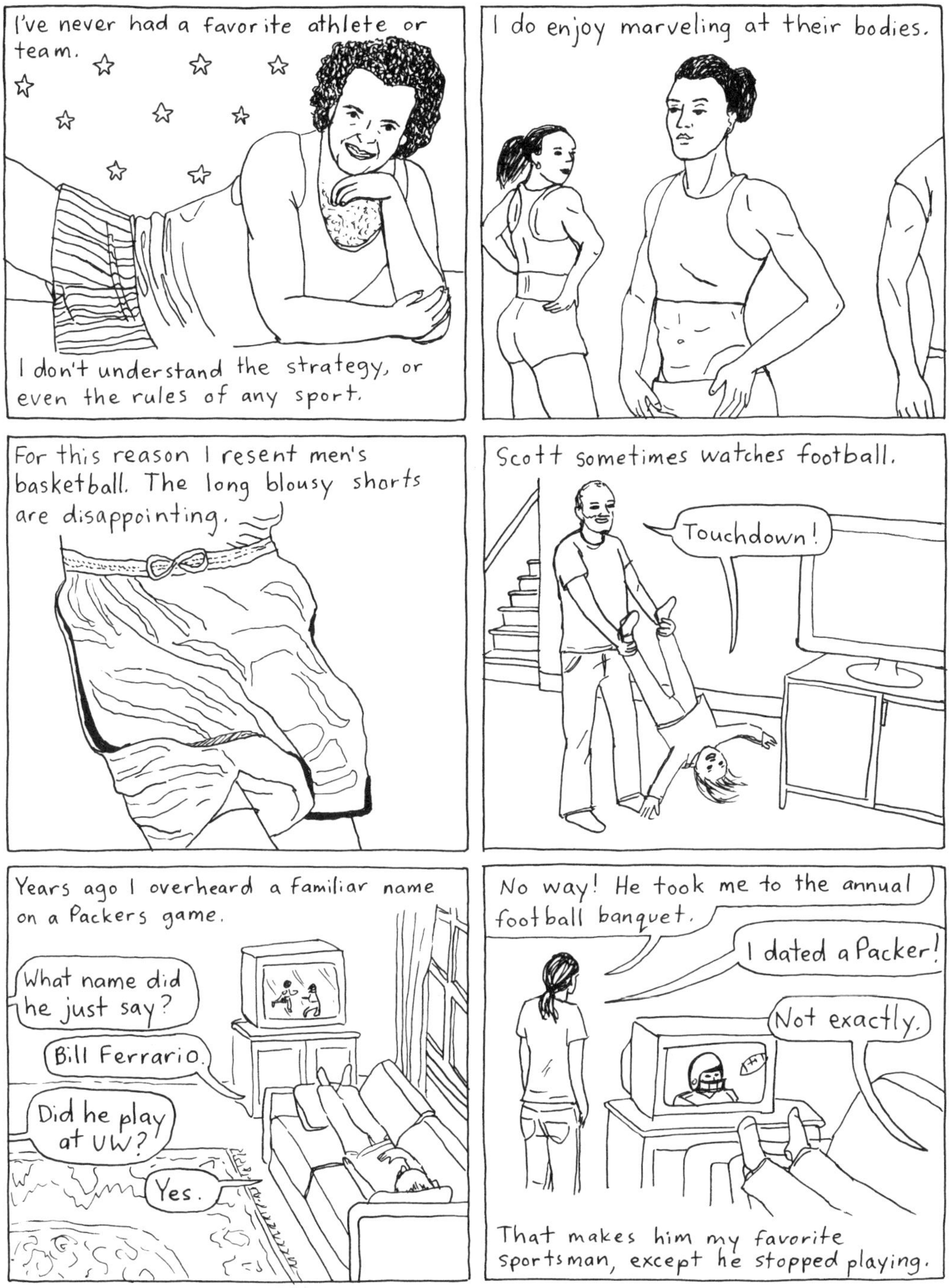
I've never had a favorite athlete or team.
I don't understand the strategy, or even the rules of any sport.
I do enjoy marveling at their bodies.
For this reason I resent men's basketball. The long blousy shorts are disappointing.
Scott sometimes watches football.
Touchdown!
Years ago I overheard a familiar name on a Packers game.
What name did he just say?
Bill Ferrario.
Did he play at UW?
Yes.
No way! He took me to the annual football banquet.
I dated a Packer!
Not exactly.
That makes him my favorite sportsman, except he stopped playing.

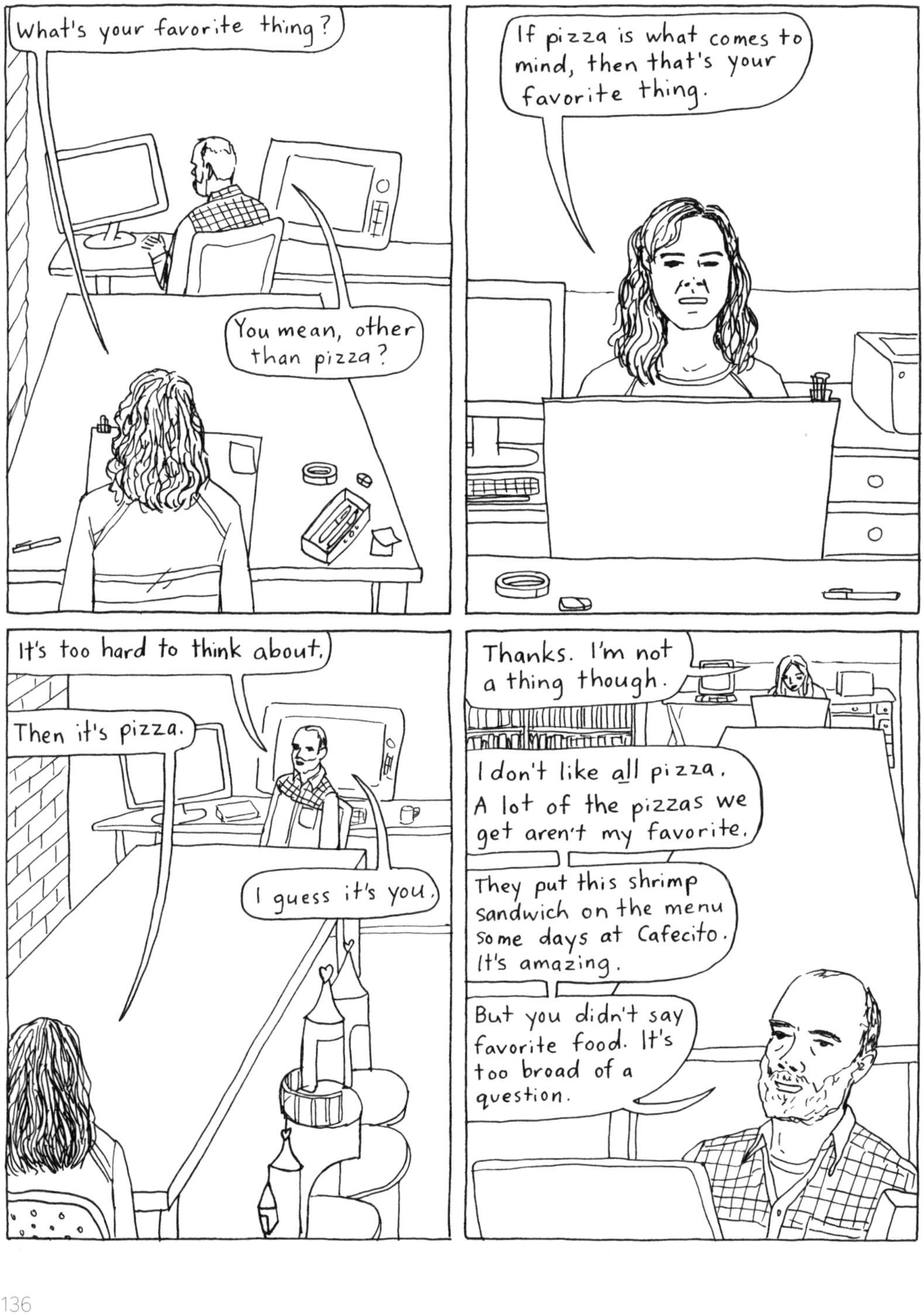

What's your favorite thing?
You mean, other than pizza?
If pizza is what comes to mind, then that's your favorite thing.
It's too hard to think about.
Then it's pizza.
I guess it's you.
Thanks. I'm not a thing though.
I don't like all pizza. A lot of the pizzas we get aren't my favorite.
They put this shrimp sandwich on the menu some days at Cafecito. It's amazing.
But you didn't say favorite food. It's too broad of a question.

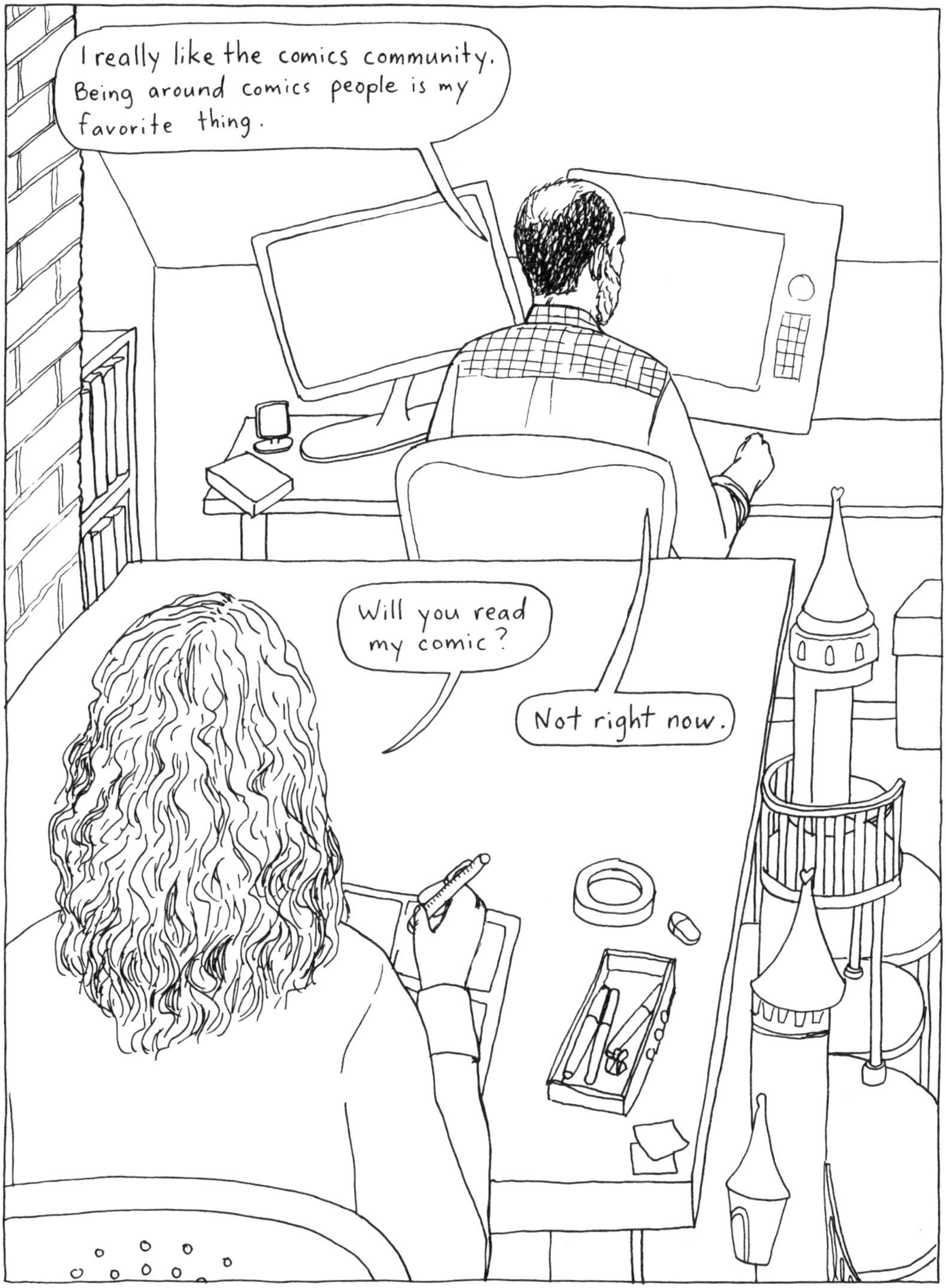
I really like the comics community. Being around comics people is my favorite thing.
Will you read my comic?
Not right now.

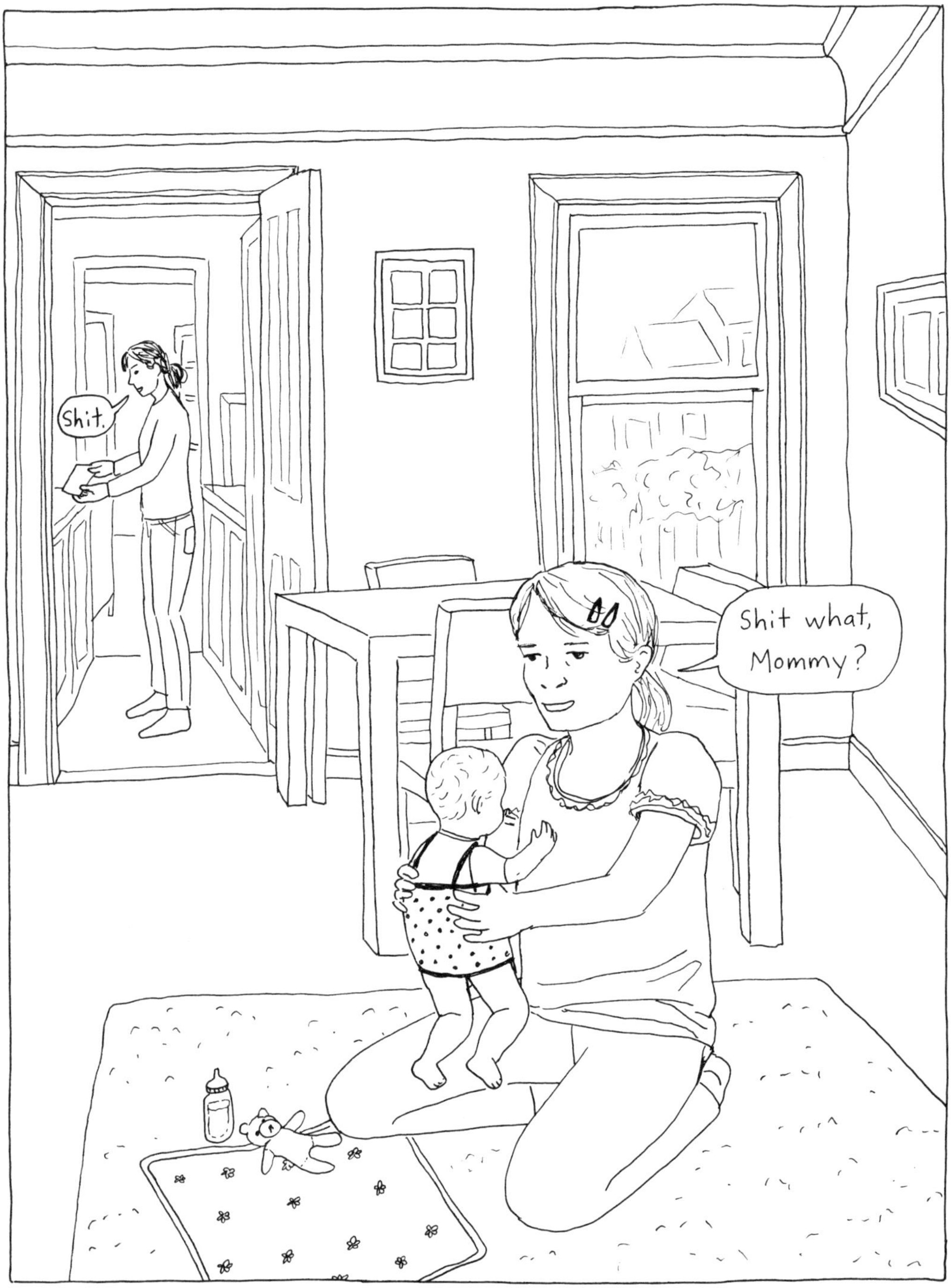
Shit.
Shit what, Mommy?

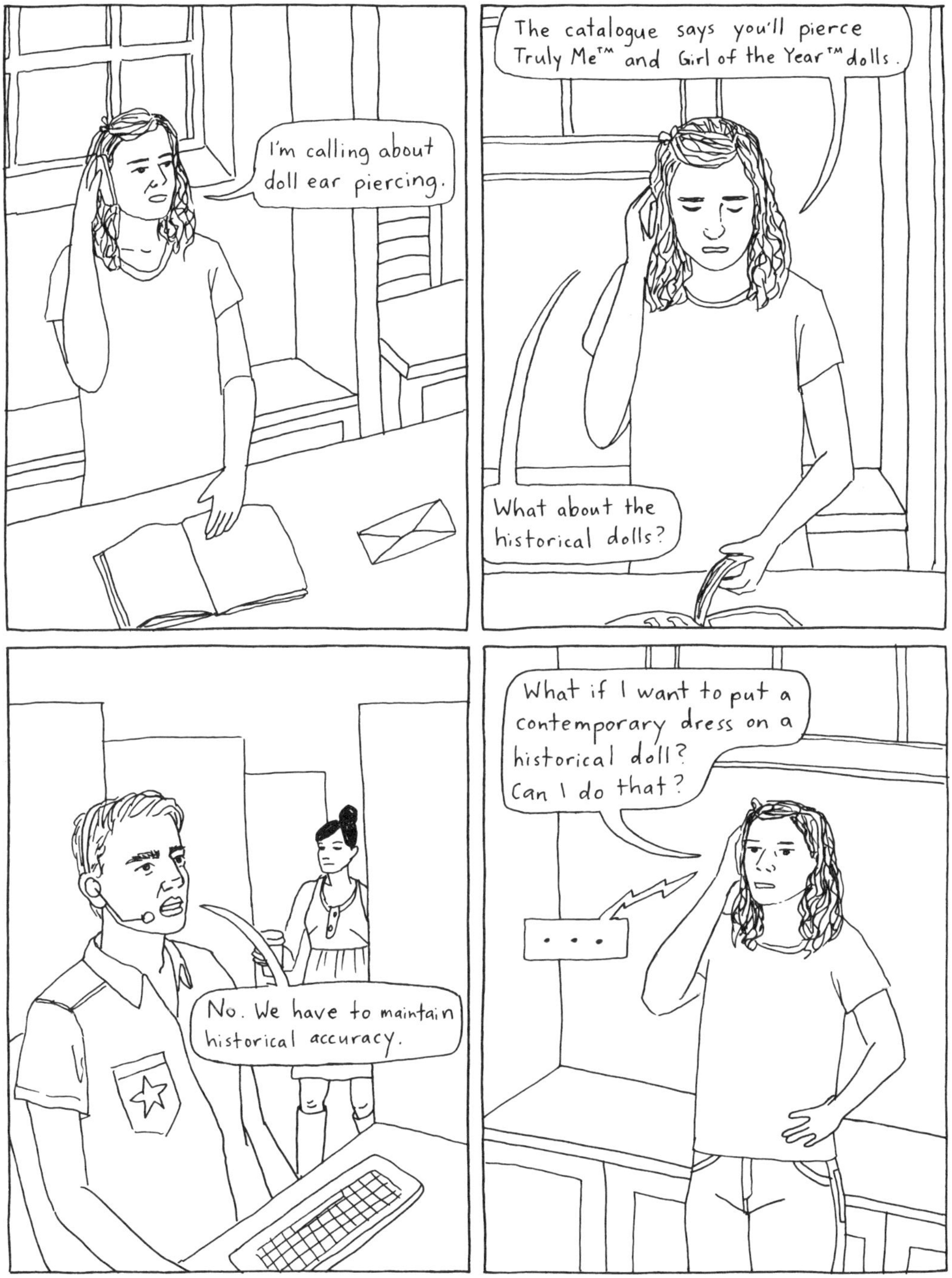
I'm calling about doll ear piercing.
The catalogue says you'll pierce Truly Me™ and Girl of the Year™ dolls.
What about the historical dolls?
No. We have to maintain historical accuracy.
What if I want to put a contemporary dress on a historical doll? Can I do that?
. . .

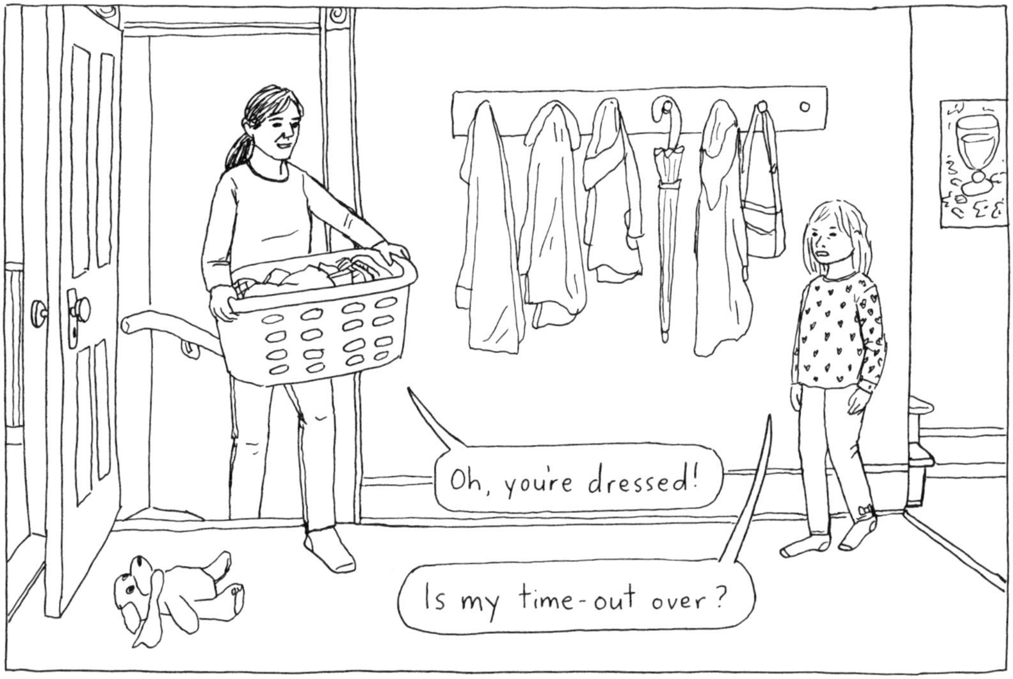
Oh, you're dressed!
Is my time-out over?

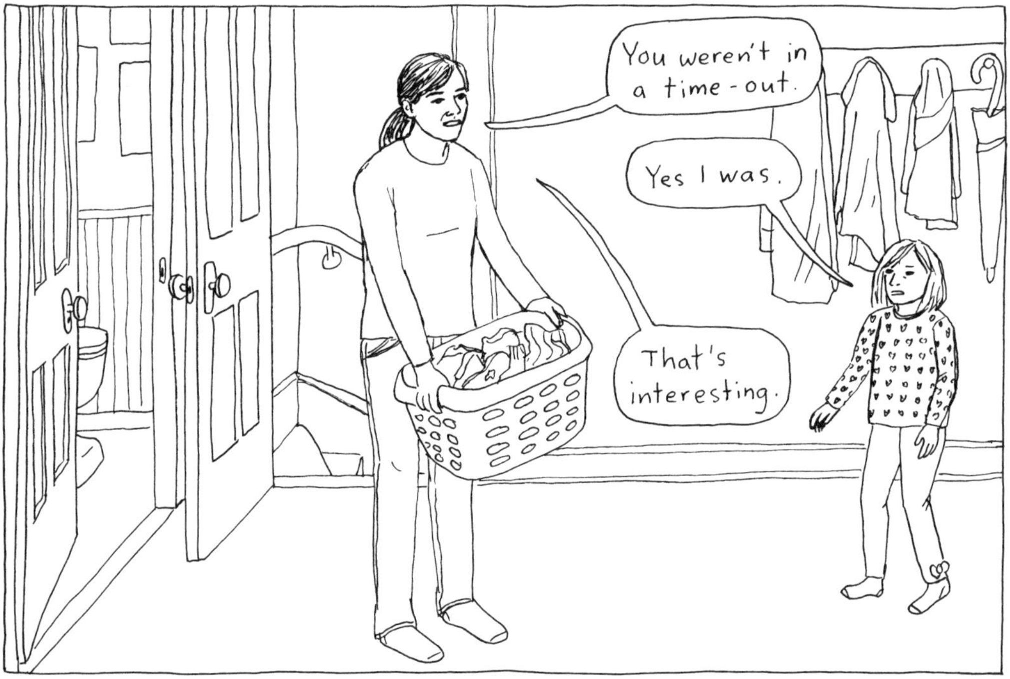
You weren't in a time-out.
Yes I was.
That's interesting.

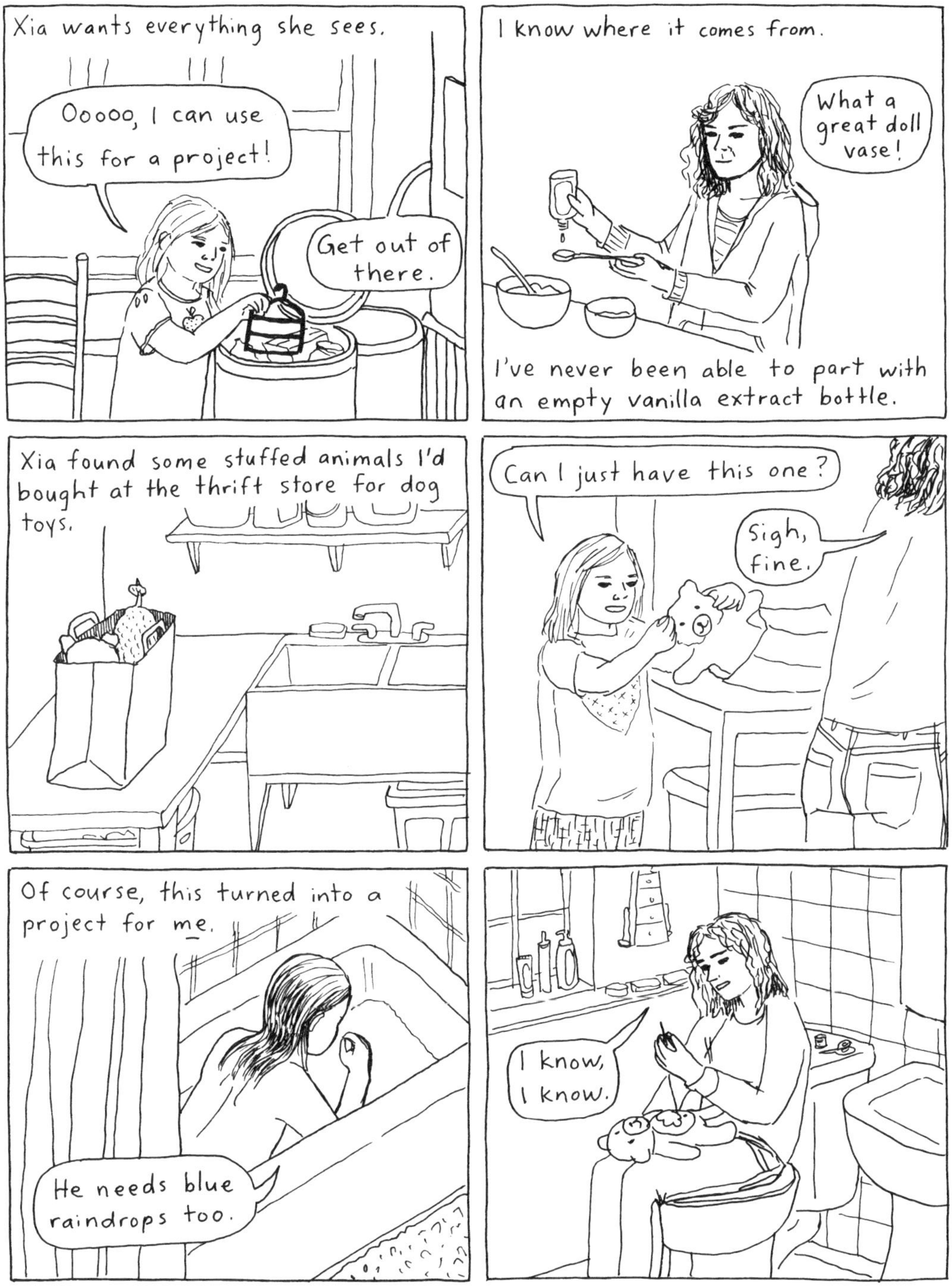
Xia wants everything she sees.
Ooooo, I can use this for a project!
Get out of there.
I know where it comes from.
What a great doll vase!
I've never been able to part with an empty vanilla extract bottle.
Xia found some stuffed animals I'd bought at the thrift store for dog toys.
Can I just have this one?
Sigh, fine.
Of course, this turned into a project for me.
He needs blue raindrops too.
I know, I know.

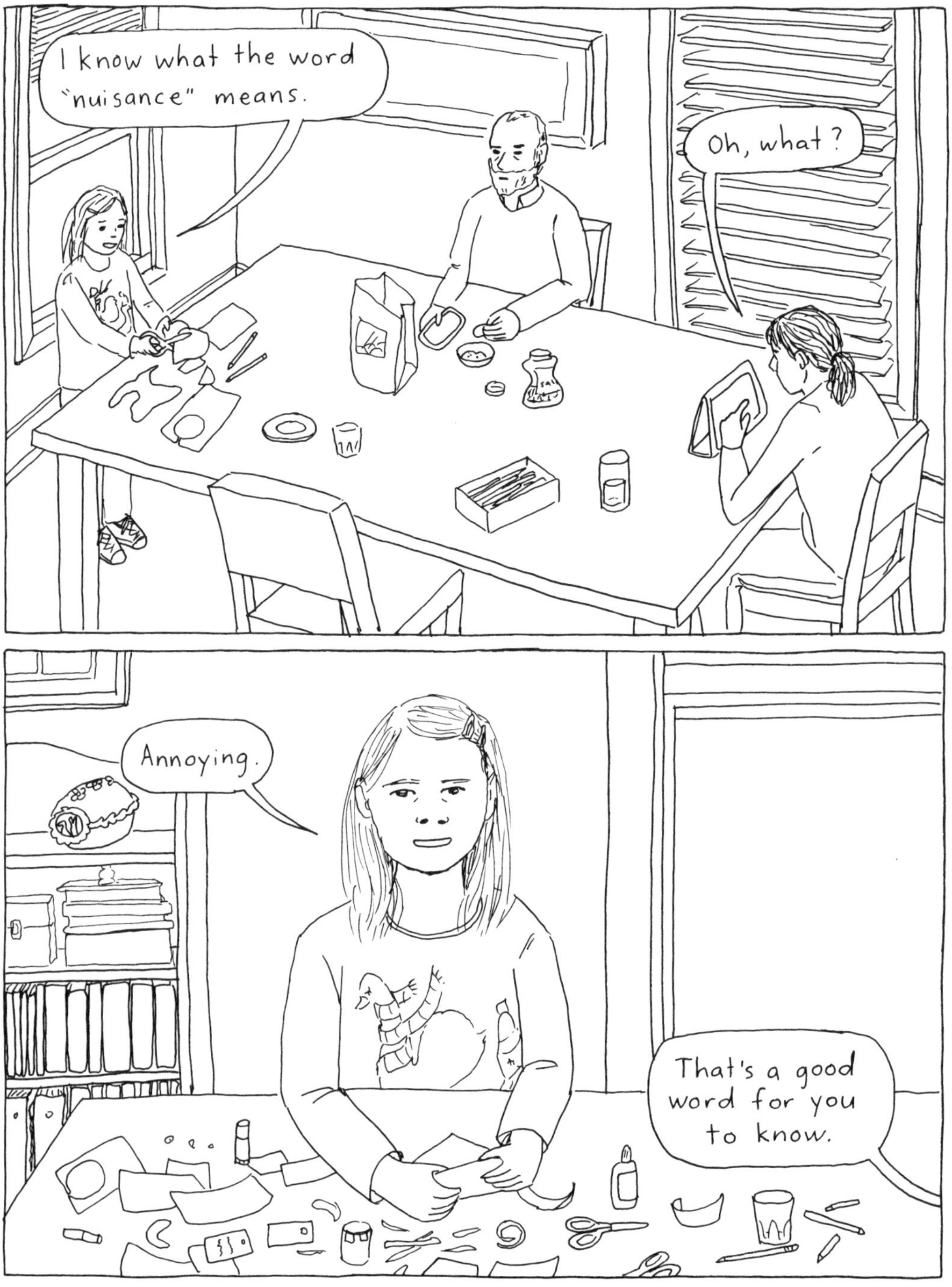
I know what the word "nuisance" means.
Oh, what?
Annoying.
That's a good word for you to know.

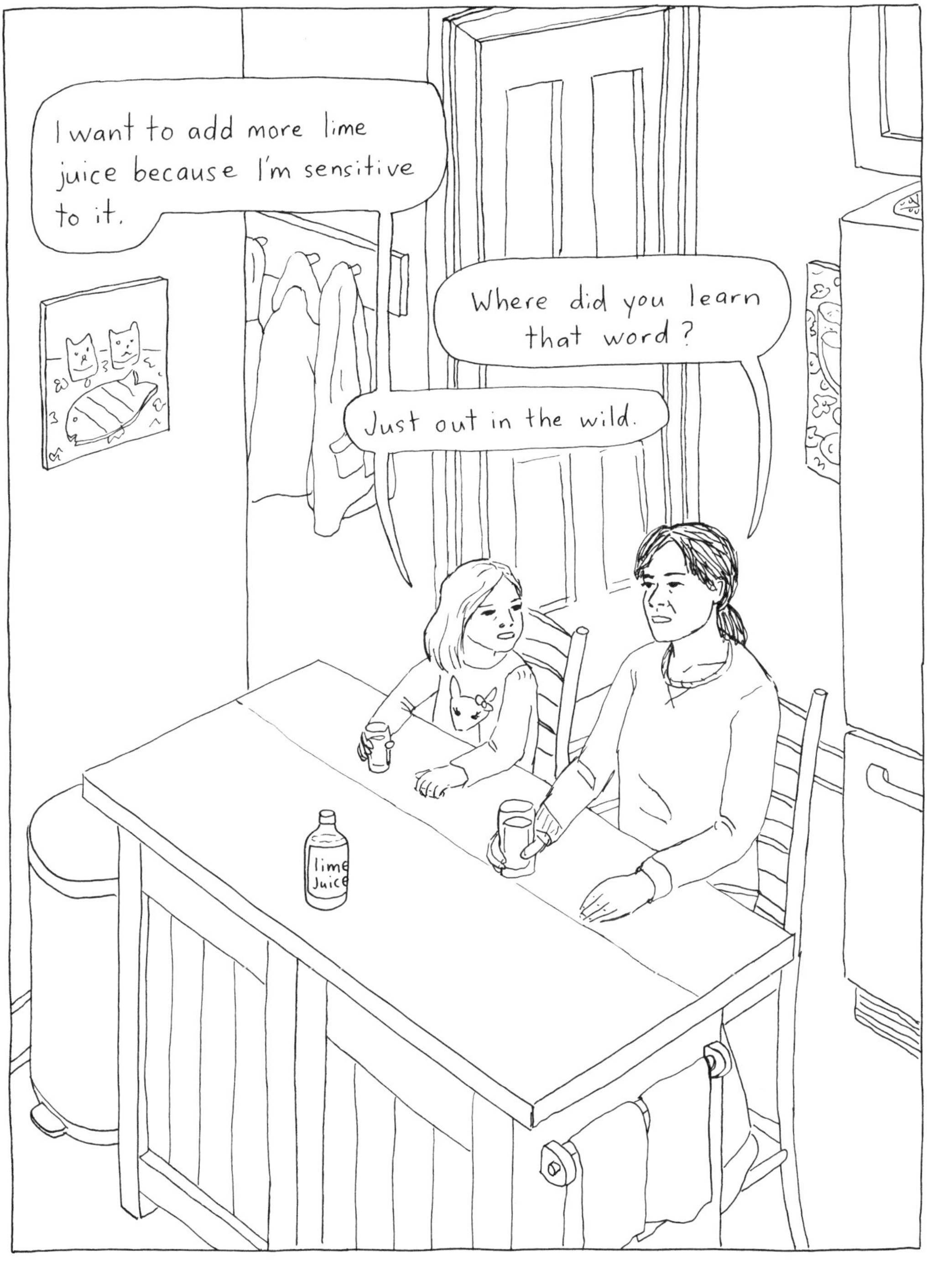
I want to add more lime juice because I'm sensitive to it.
Where did you learn that word?
Just out in the wild.
lime Juice

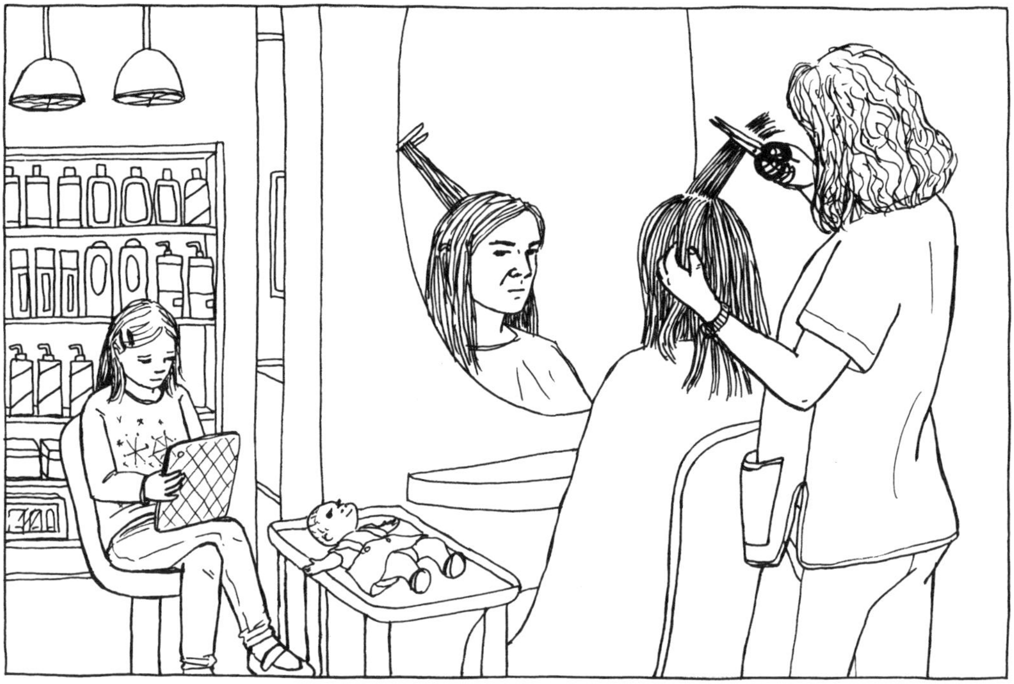

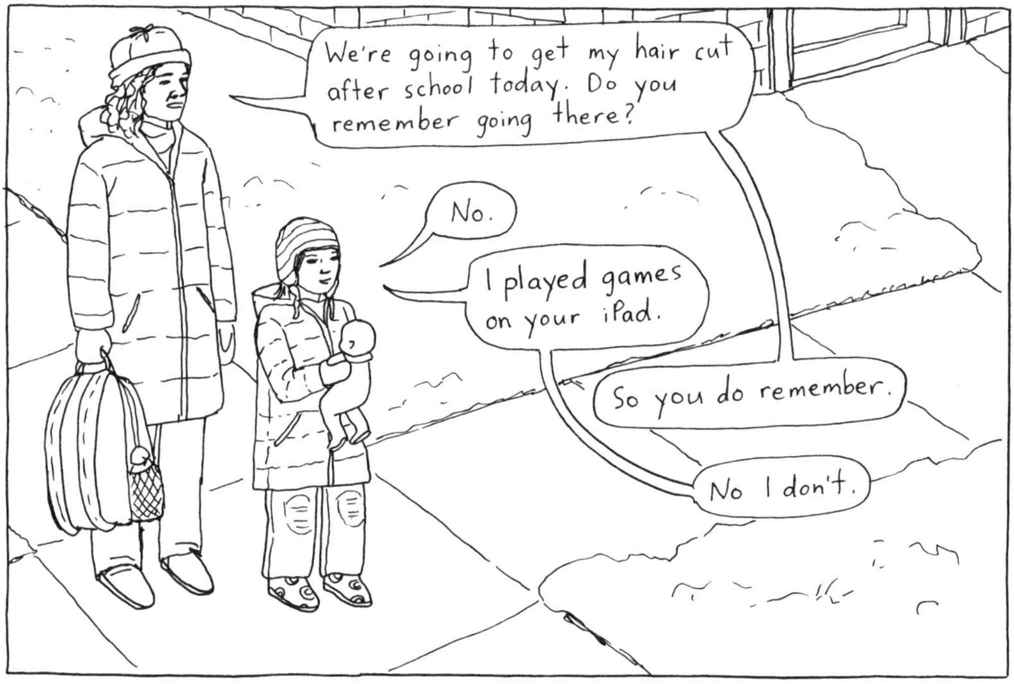
We're going to get my hair cut after school today. Do you remember going there?
No.
I played games on your iPad.
So you do remember.
No I don't.

I suspect the only way some people experience "too much of a good thing" is by eating or drinking excessively.

How many of us ever have too much love, money, health, or happiness?

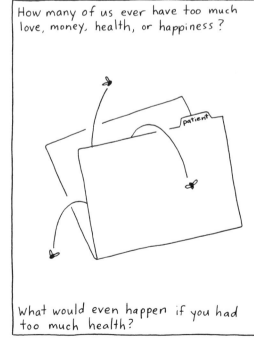

What would even happen if you had too much health?

I guess you'd miss out on a lot of interesting conversations with doctors.

That's why people who have affairs shouldn't own talking birds.

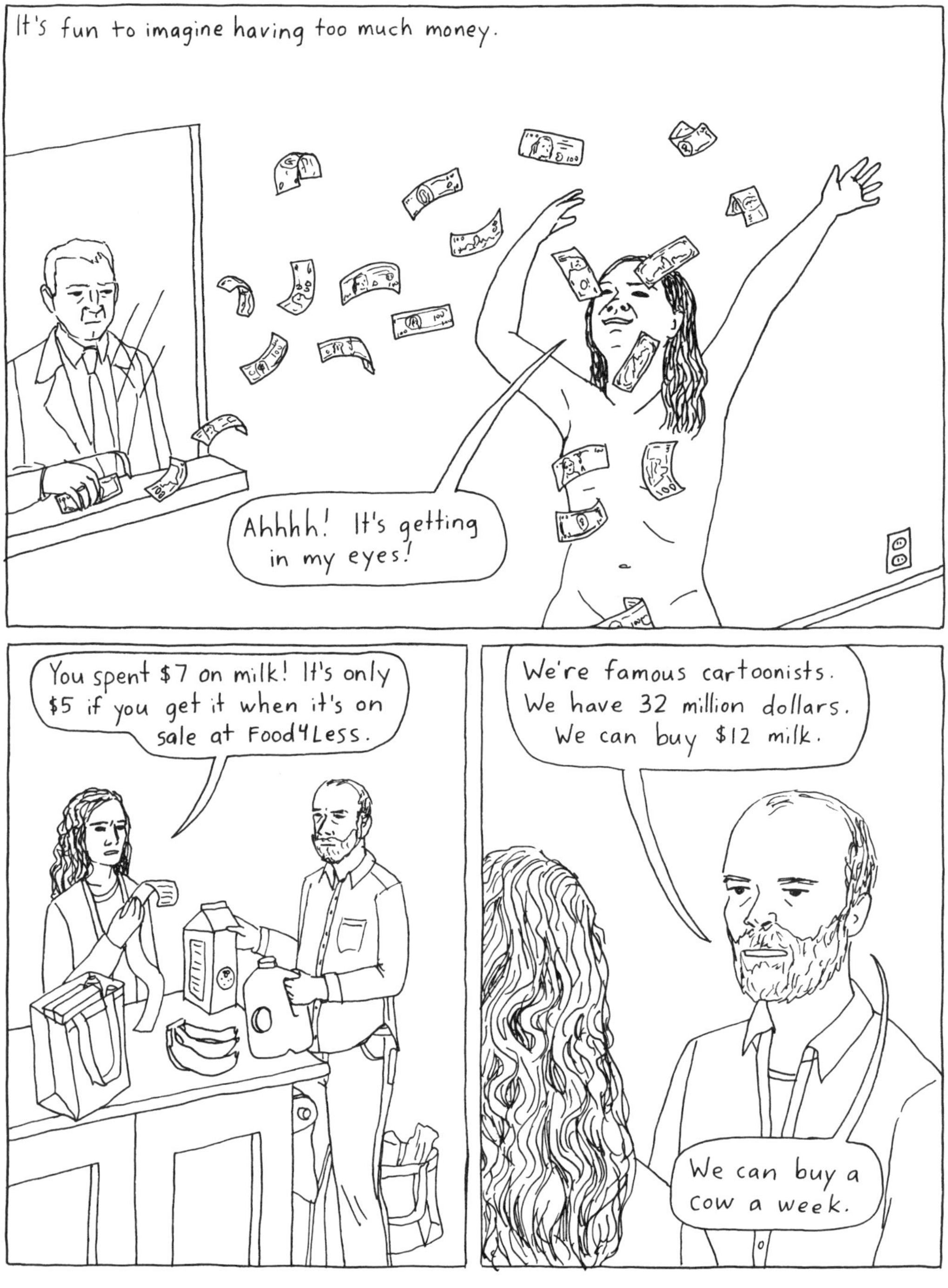
It's fun to imagine having too much money.
Ahhhh! It's getting in my eyes!
You spent $7 on milk! It's only $5 if you get it when it's on sale at Food4Less.
We're famous cartoonists. We have 32 million dollars. We can buy $12 milk.
We can buy a cow a week.

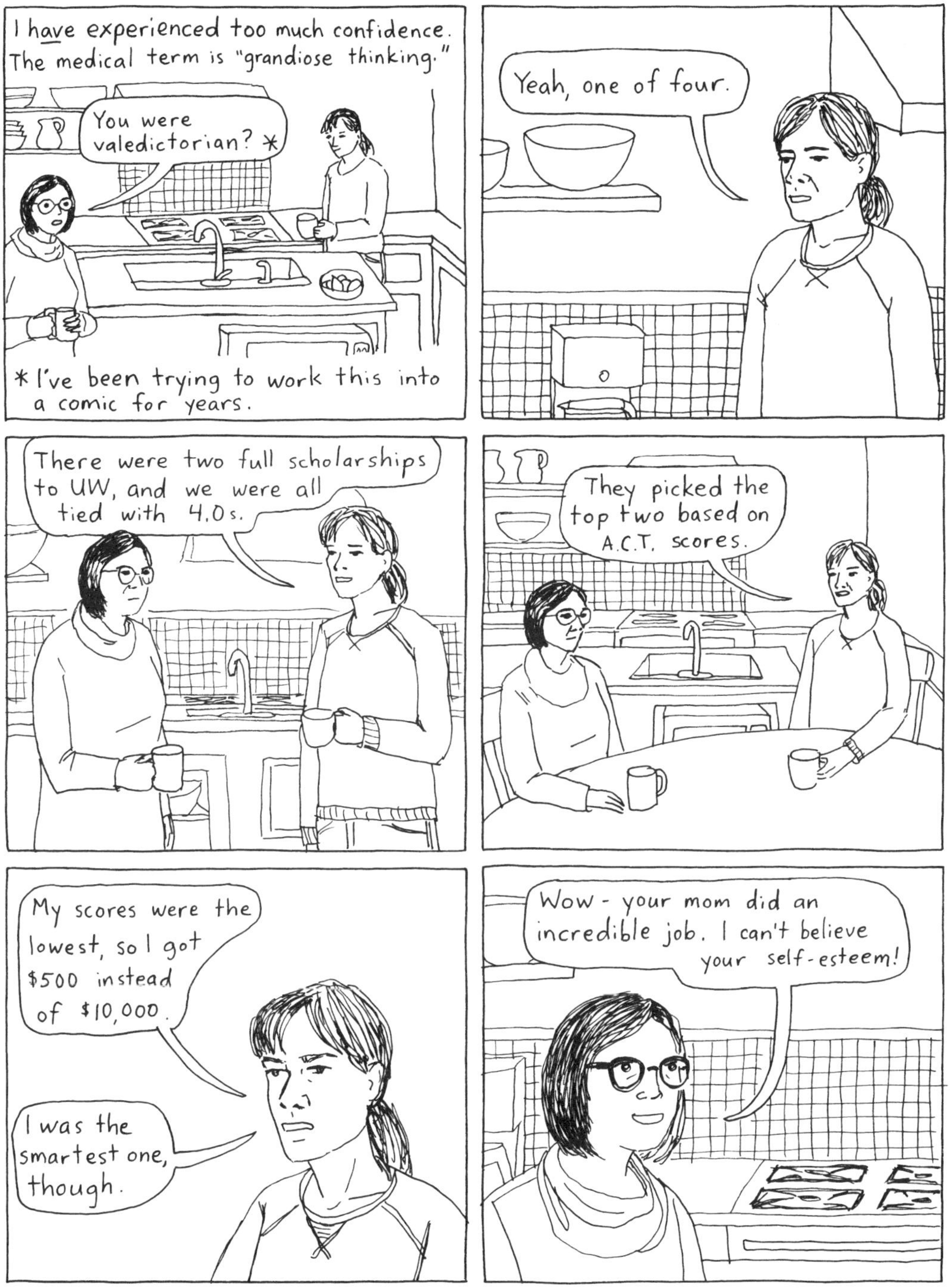

I have experienced too much confidence. The medical term is "grandiose thinking."
You were valedictorian? *
* I've been trying to work this into a comic for years.
Yeah, one of four.
There were two full scholarships to UW, and we were all tied with 4.0s.
They picked the top two based on A.C.T. scores.
My scores were the lowest, so I got $500 instead of $10,000.
I was the smartest one, though.
Wow - your mom did an incredible job. I can't believe your self-esteem!

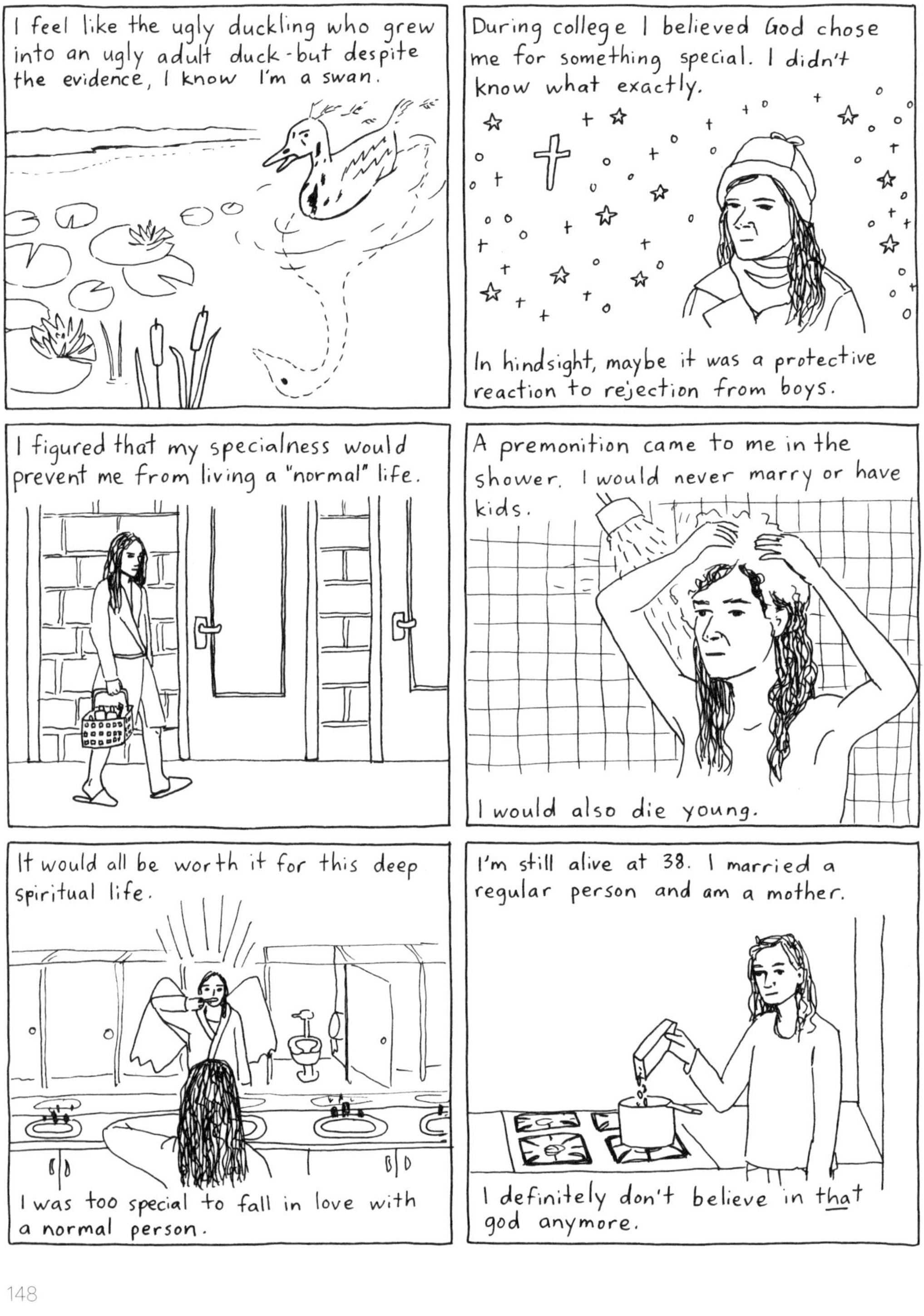

I feel like the ugly duckling who grew into an ugly adult duck-but despite the evidence, I know I'm a swan.
During college I believed God chose me for something special. I didn't know what exactly.
In hindsight, maybe it was a protective reaction to rejection from boys.
I figured that my specialness would prevent me from living a "normal" life.
A premonition came to me in the shower. I would never marry or have kids.
I would also die young.
It would all be worth it for this deep spiritual life.
I was too special to fall in love with a normal person.
I'm still alive at 38. I married a regular person and am a mother.
I definitely don't believe in that god anymore.

Occasionally I'm stifled by overabundant creativity.

Ordinarily I can look around myself with neutrality.

On some days, though, every object blooms with associated memories and feelings.

A box my grandpa made - his last project.

My Dad's favorite mug. He has the same one at his house.

Staedler Mars eraser - oh, German art supplies.

A stapler from a summer yard sale.

Nothing exists without meaning and sentimental value.

It's all connected in a way I believe I understand but can't explain.

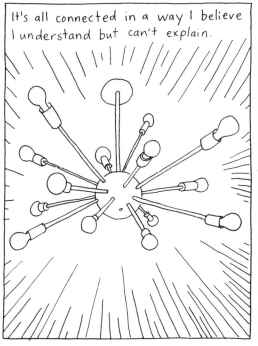

I have too many ideas to start anywhere. There's no way to actually make anything of it.

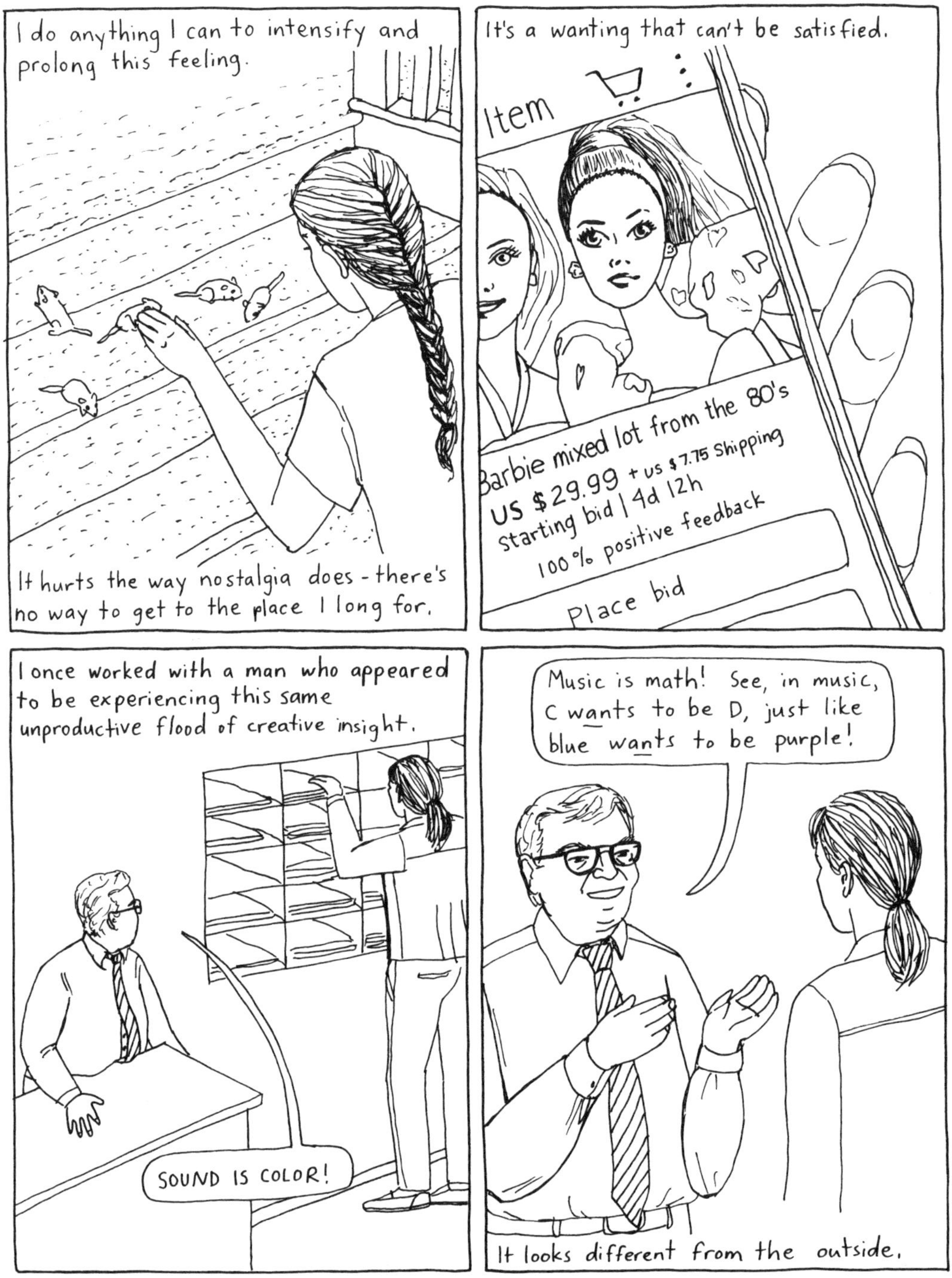
I do anything I can to intensify and prolong this feeling.
It hurts the way nostalgia does - there's no way to get to the place I long for.
It's a wanting that can't be satisfied.
Item
Barbie mixed lot from the 80's
US $29.99 + US $7.75 Shipping
Starting bid | 4d 12h
100% positive feedback
Place bid
I once worked with a man who appeared to be experiencing this same unproductive flood of creative insight.
SOUND IS COLOR!
Music is math! See, in music, C wants to be D, just like blue wants to be purple!
It looks different from the outside.

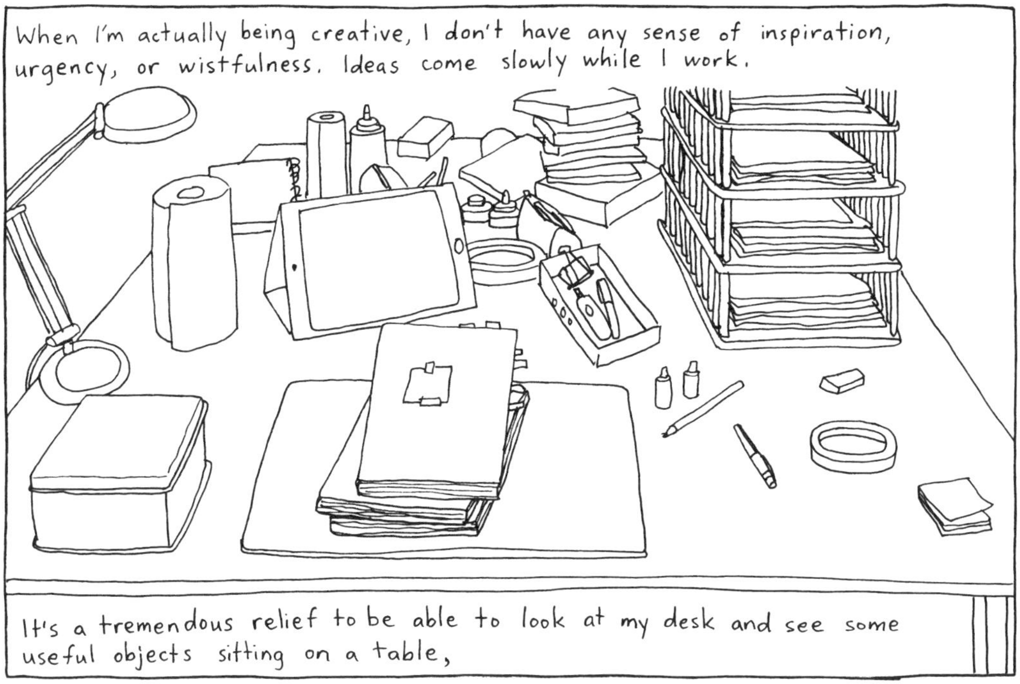
When I'm actually being creative, I don't have any sense of inspiration, urgency, or wistfulness. Ideas come slowly while I work.
It's a tremendous relief to be able to look at my desk and see some useful objects sitting on a table,

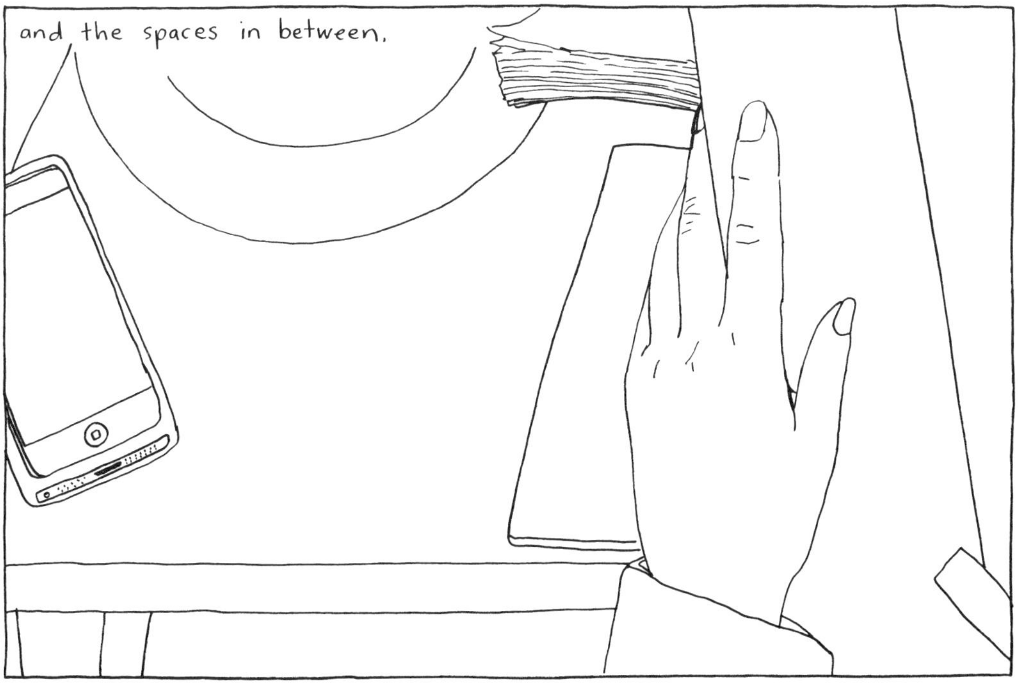
and the spaces in between.

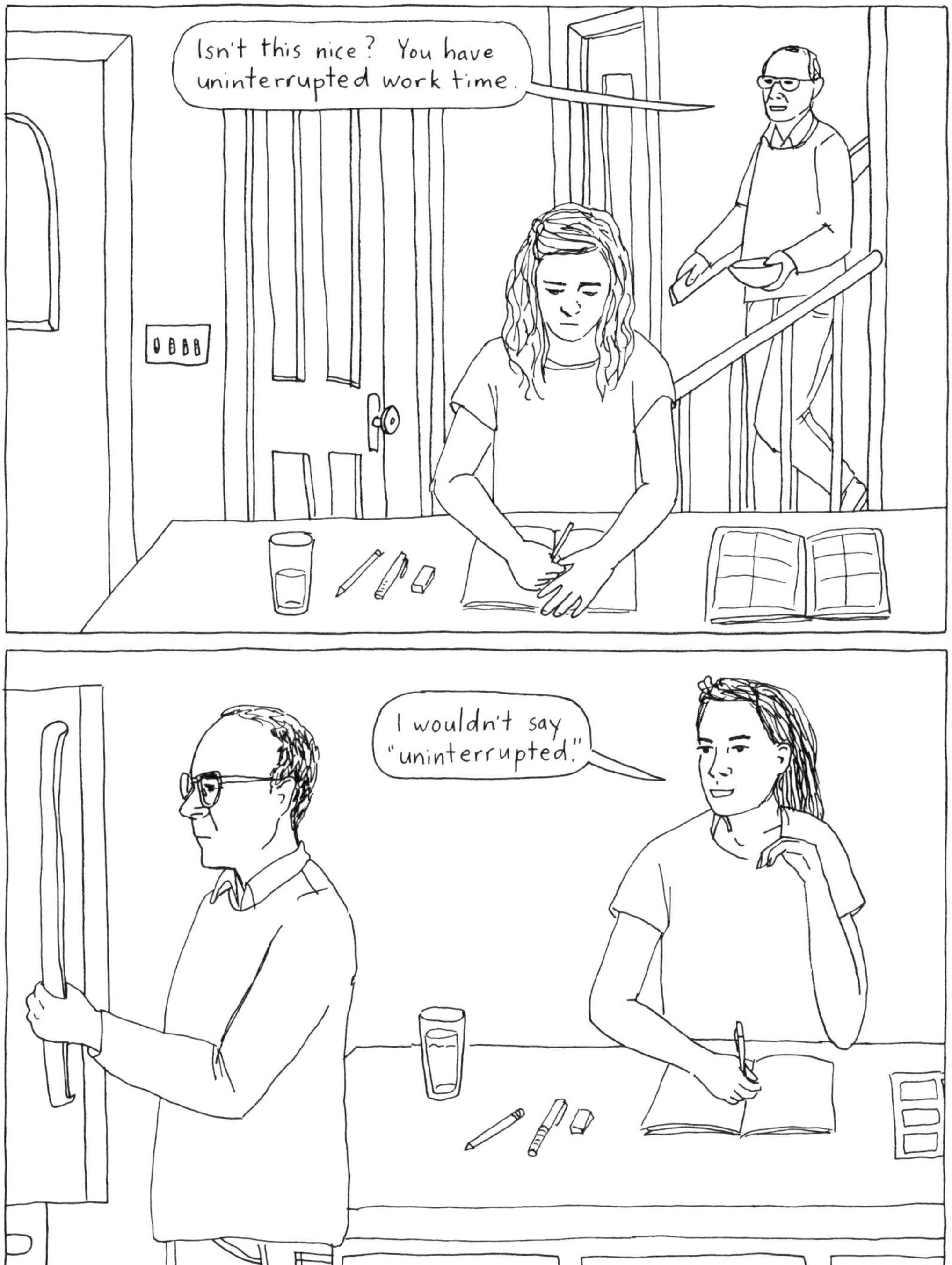
Isn't this nice? You have uninterrupted work time.
I wouldn't say "uninterrupted."

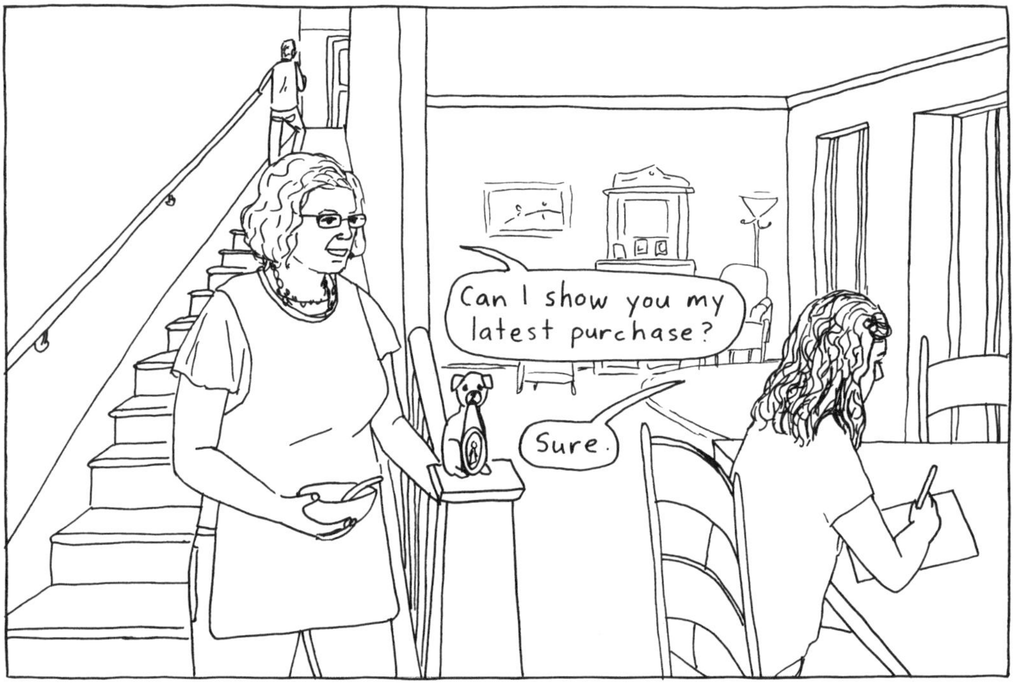
Can I show you my latest purchase?
Sure.

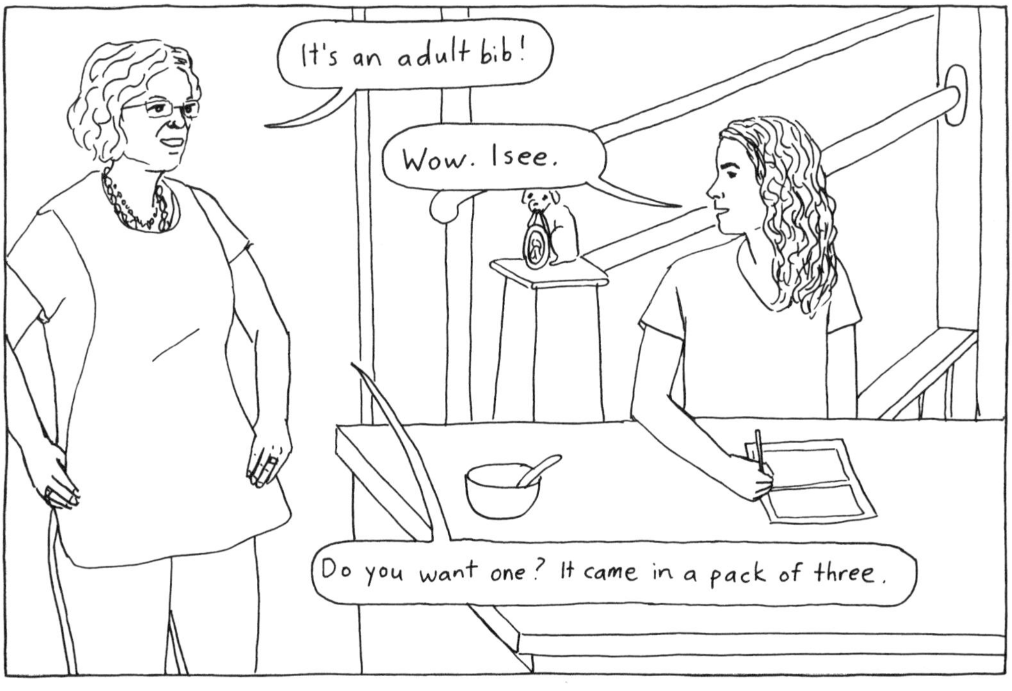
It's an adult bib!
Wow. I see.
Do you want one? It came in a pack of three.

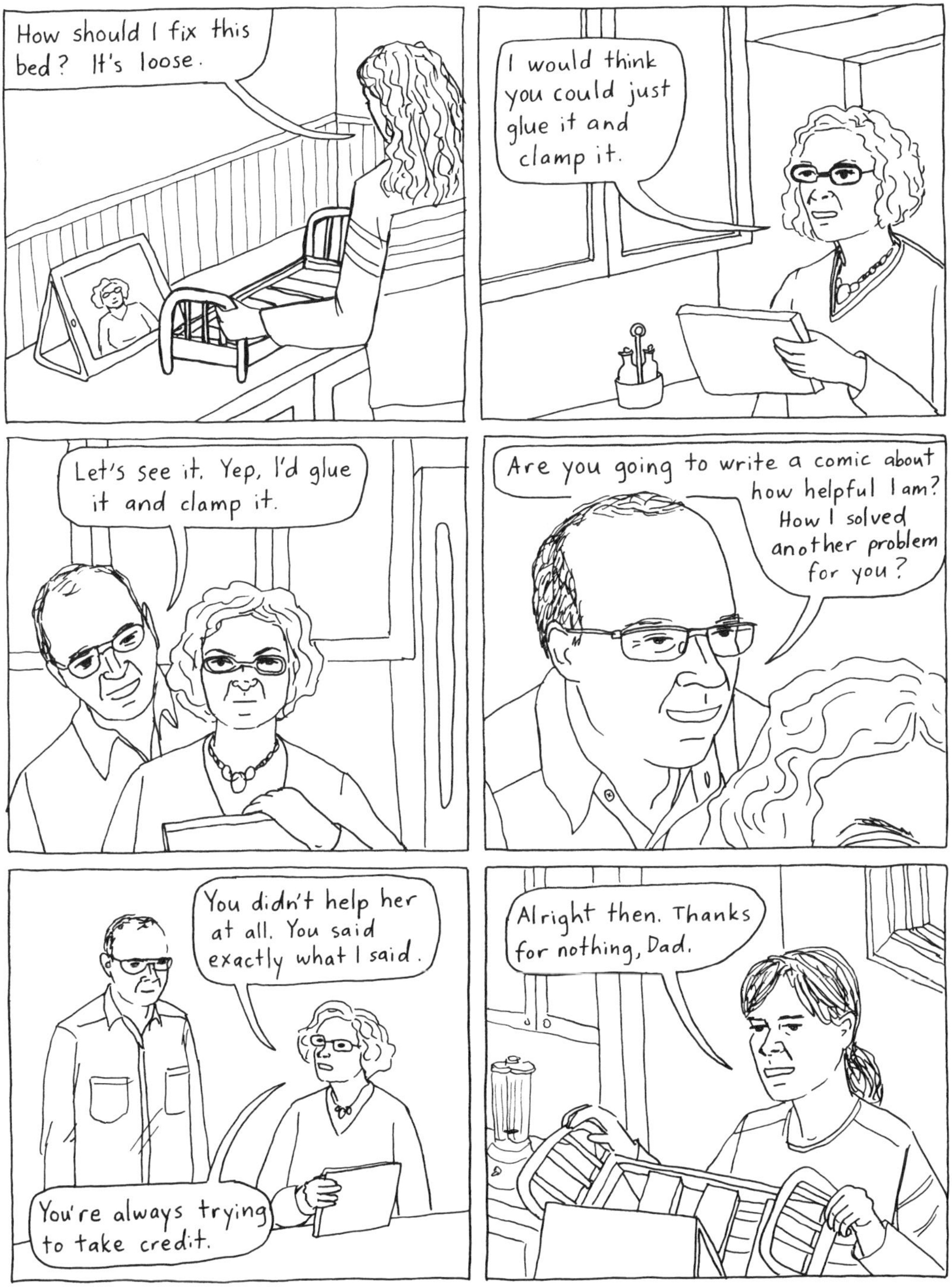
How should I fix this bed? It's loose.
I would think you could just glue it and clamp it.
Let's see it. Yep, I'd glue it and clamp it.
Are you going to write a comic about how helpful I am? How I solved another problem for you?
You didn't help her at all. You said exactly what I said.
You're always trying to take credit.
Alright then. Thanks for nothing, Dad.

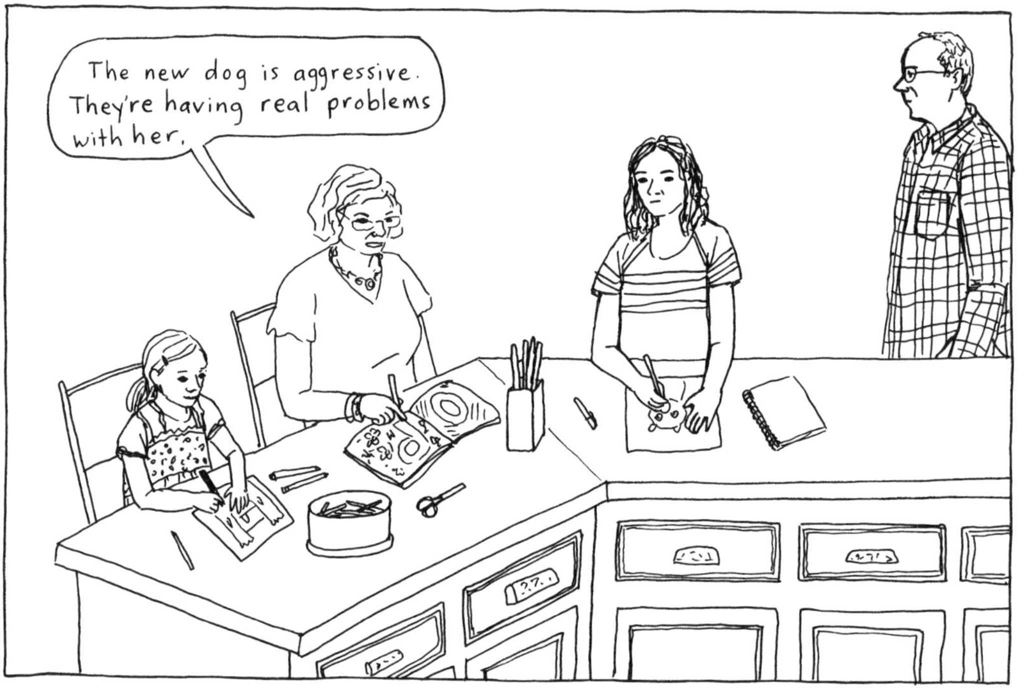
The new dog is aggressive. They're having real problems with her.

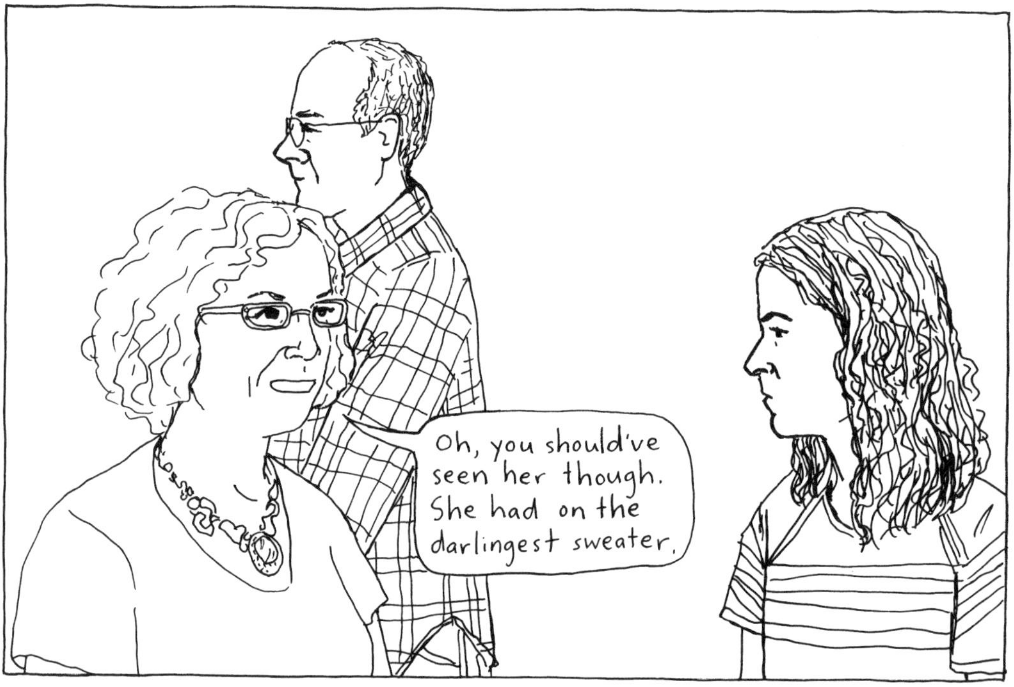
Oh, you should've seen her though. She had on the darlingest sweater.

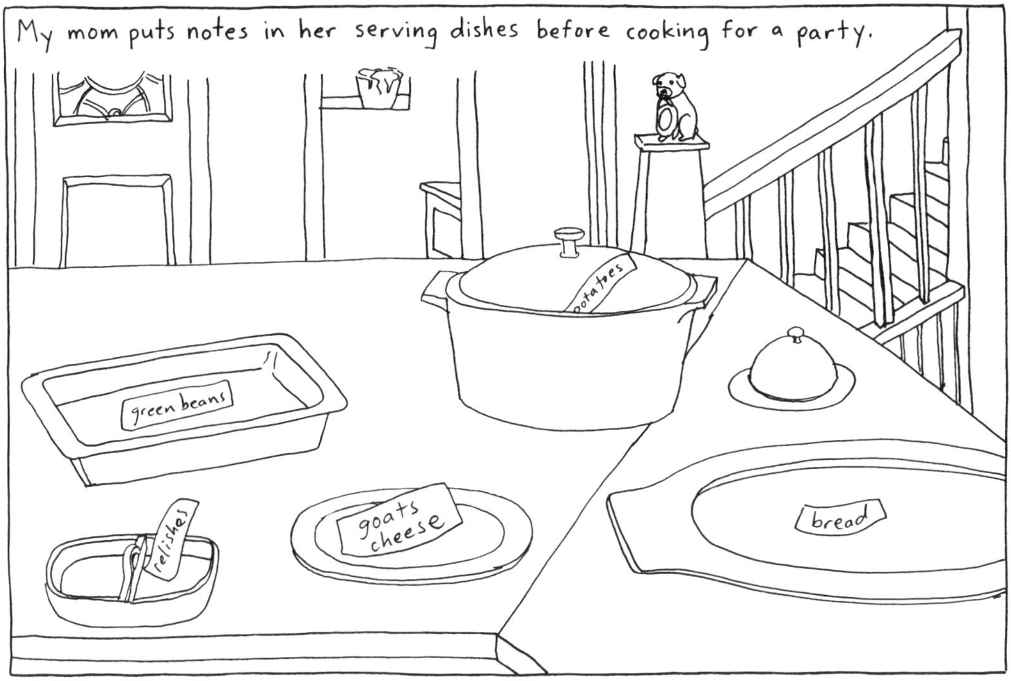
My mom puts notes in her serving dishes before cooking for a party.
potatoes
green beans
relishes
goats cheese
bread

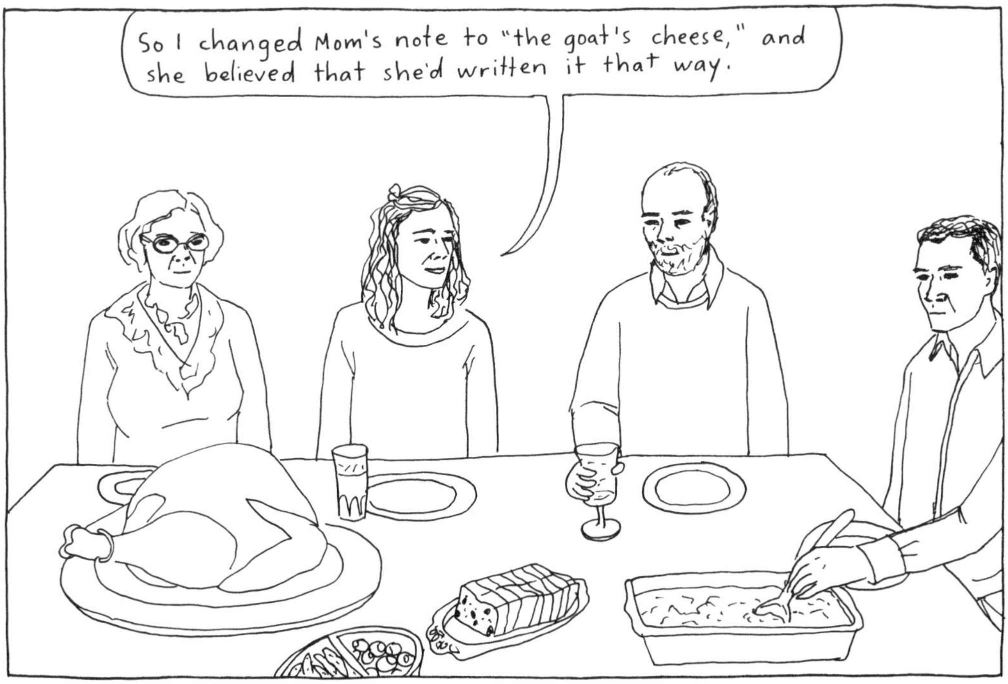
So I changed Mom's note to "the goat's cheese," and she believed that she'd written it that way.

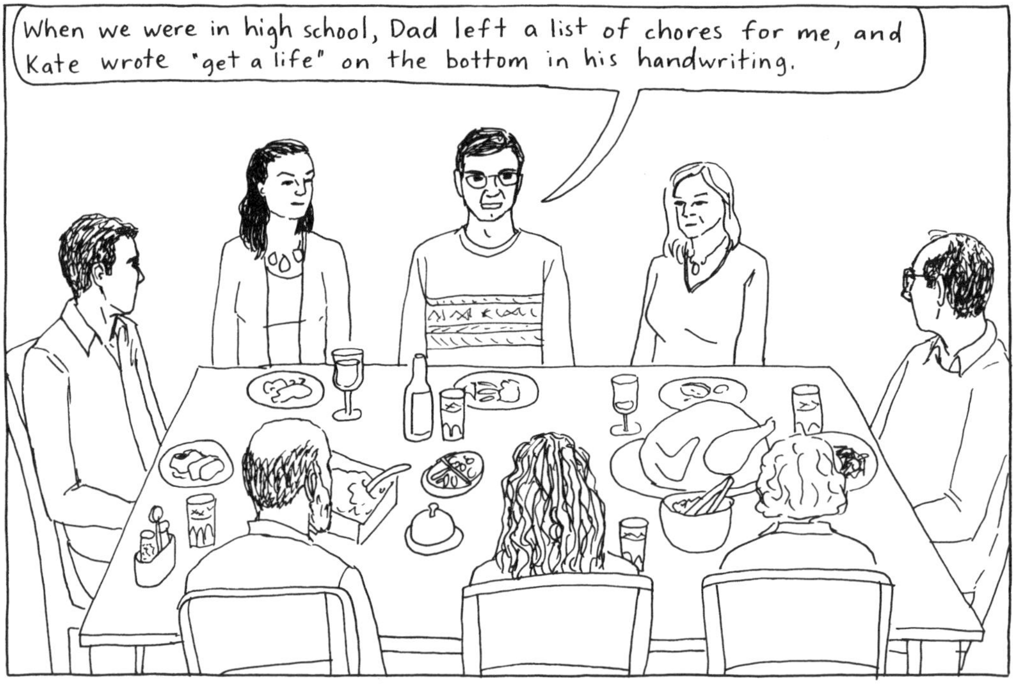
When we were in high school, Dad left a list of chores for me, and Kate wrote "get a life" on the bottom in his handwriting.

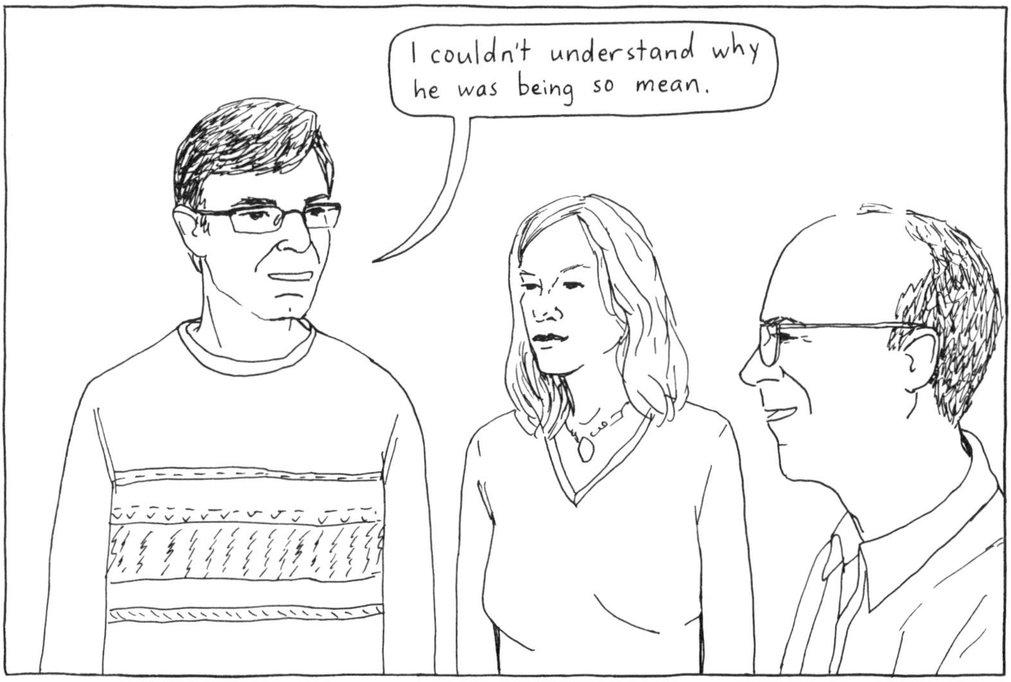
I couldn't understand why he was being so mean.

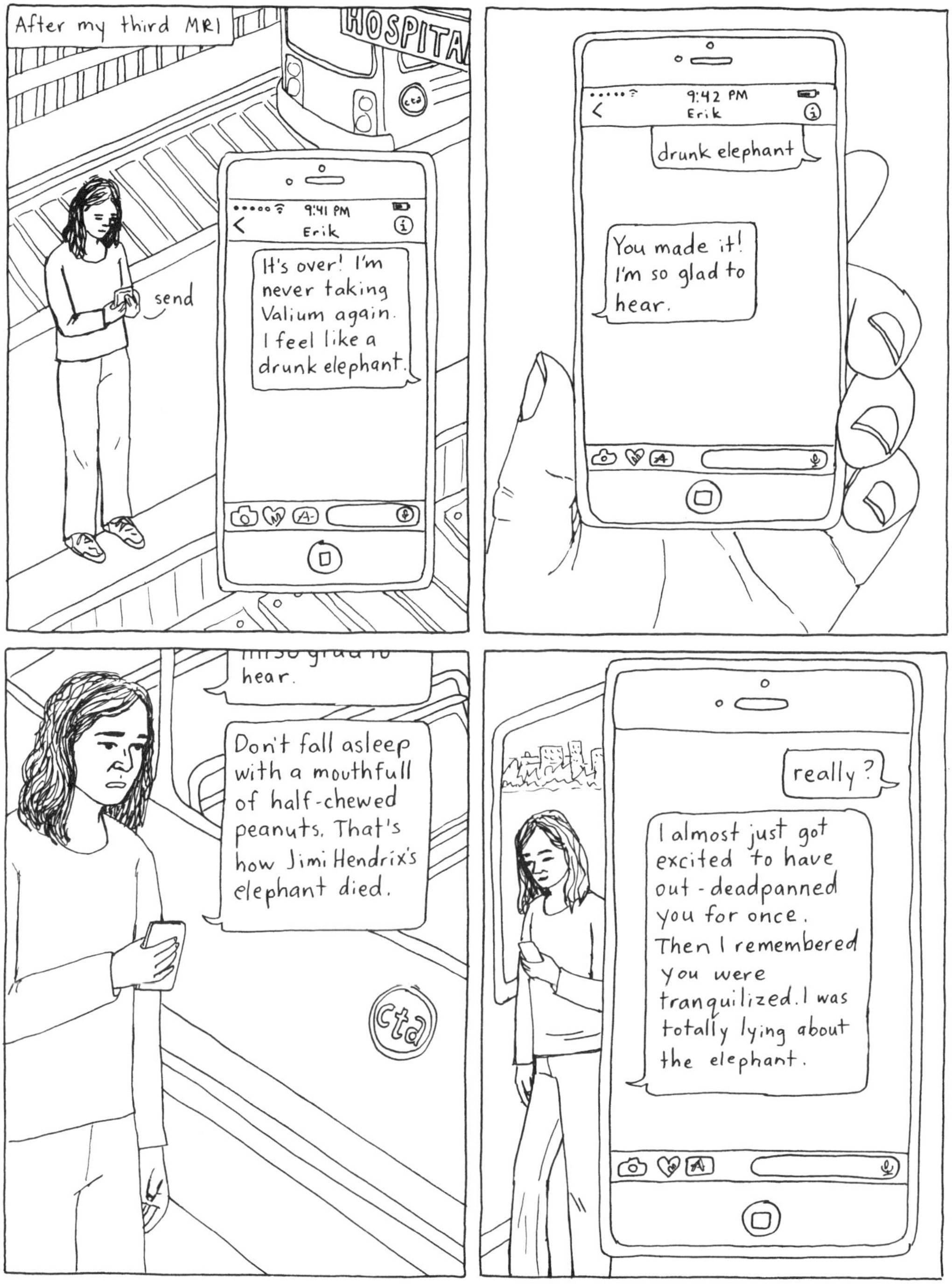
After my third MRI
HOSPITA
9:41 PM
Erik
It's over! I'm never taking Valium again. I feel like a drunk elephant.
send
9:42 PM
Erik
drunk elephant
You made it! I'm so glad to hear.
hear.
Don't fall asleep with a mouthfull of half-chewed peanuts. That's how Jimi Hendrix's elephant died.
cta
really?
I almost just got excited to have out-deadpanned you for once. Then I remembered you were tranquilized. I was totally lying about the elephant.

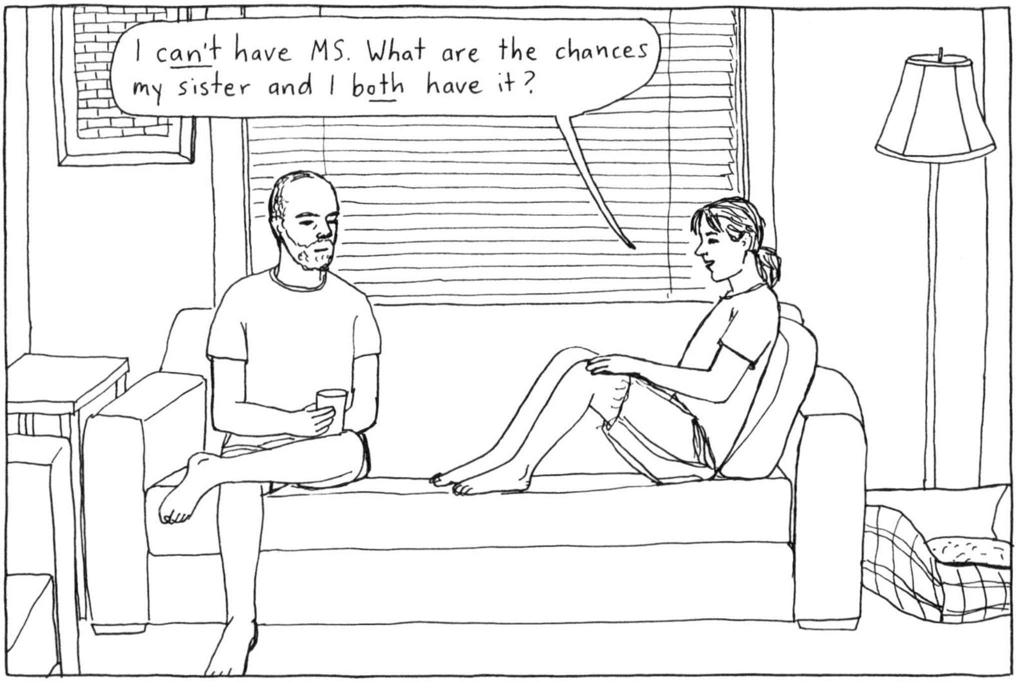
I can't have MS. What are the chances my sister and I both have it?

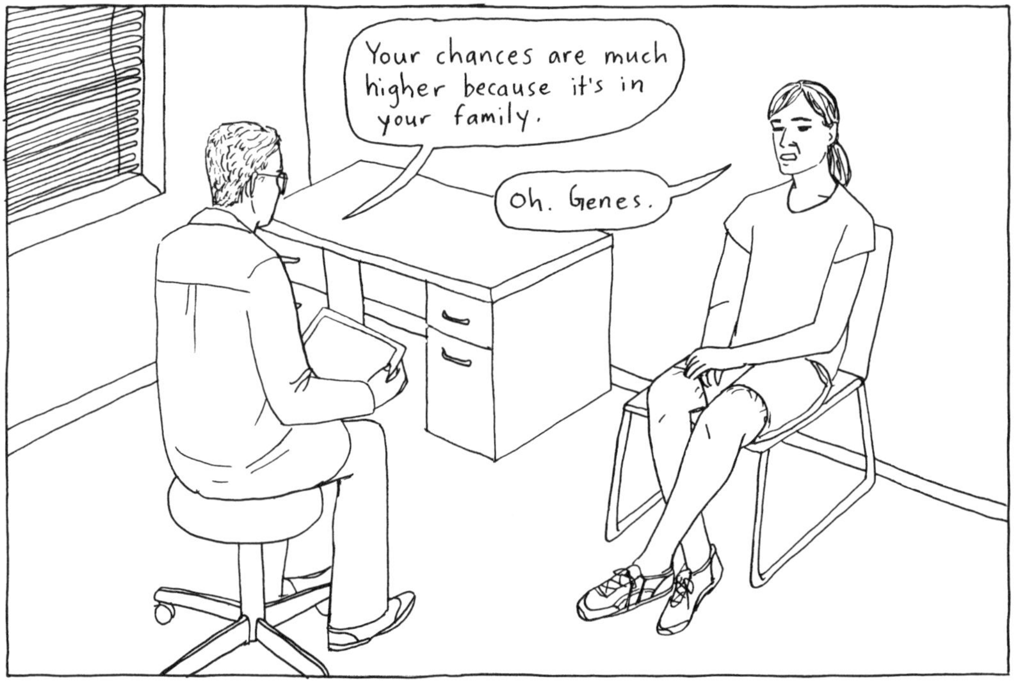
Your chances are much higher because it's in your family.
Oh. Genes.

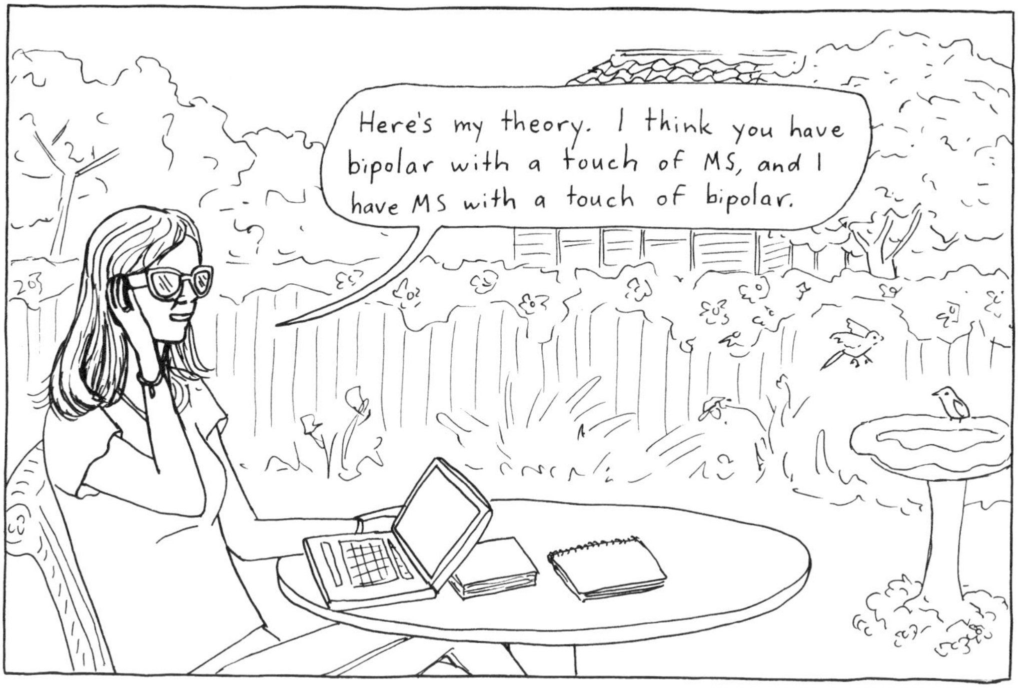
Here's my theory. I think you have bipolar with a touch of MS, and I have MS with a touch of bipolar.

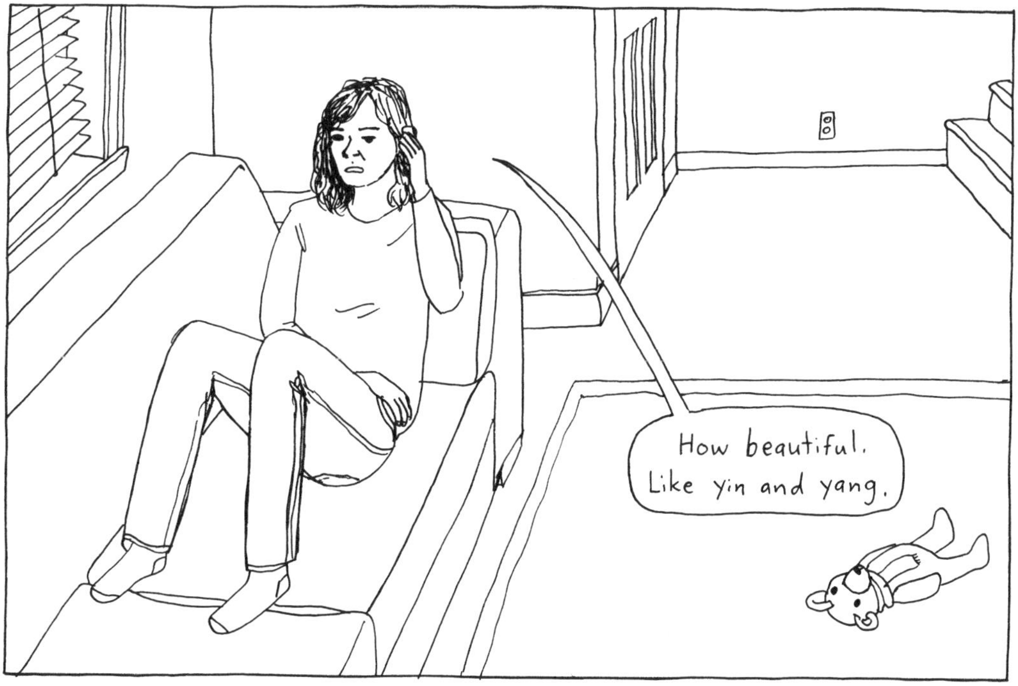
How beautiful. Like yin and yang.

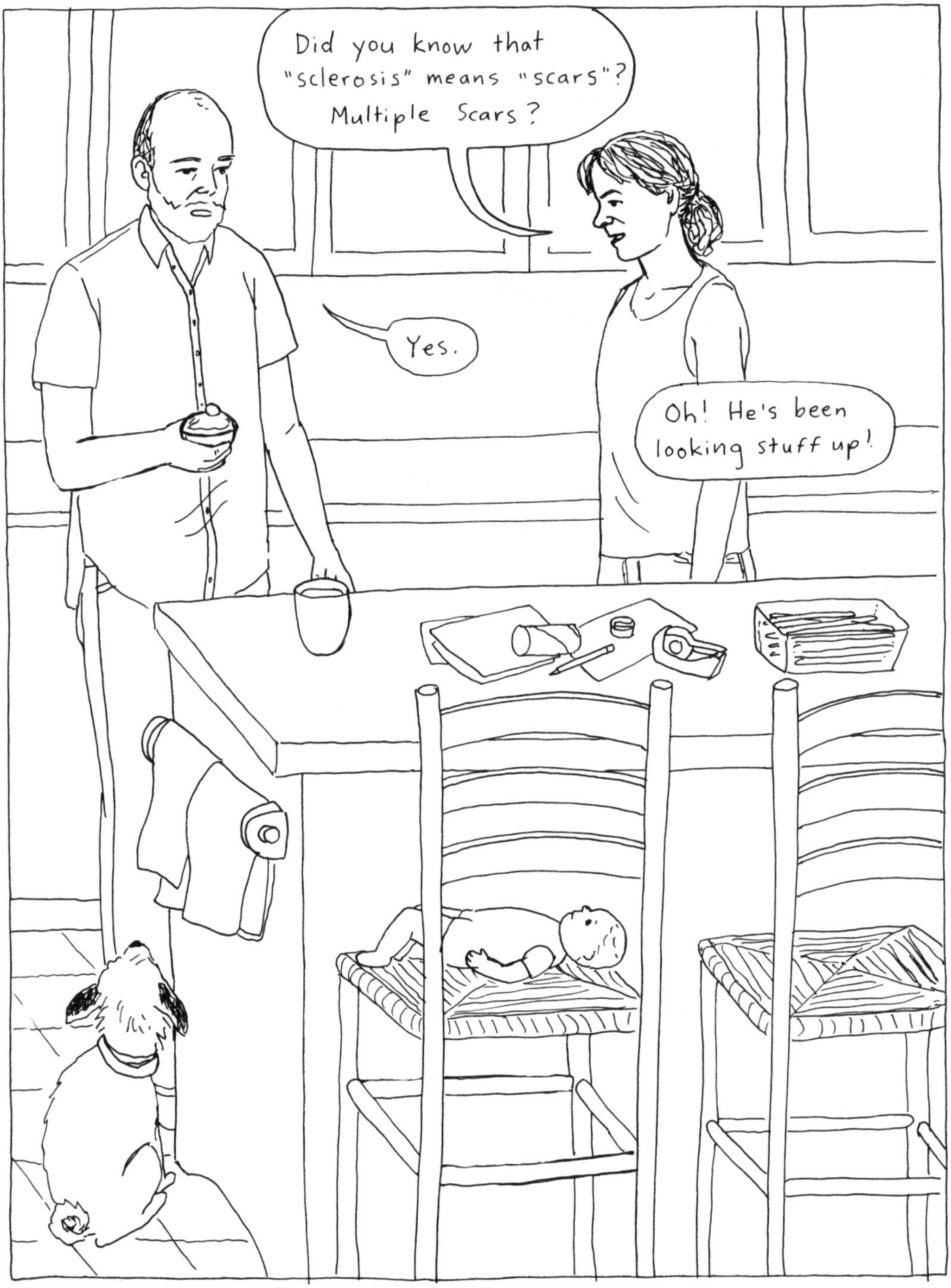
Did you know that "sclerosis" means "scars"? Multiple Scars?
Yes.
Oh! He's been looking stuff up!

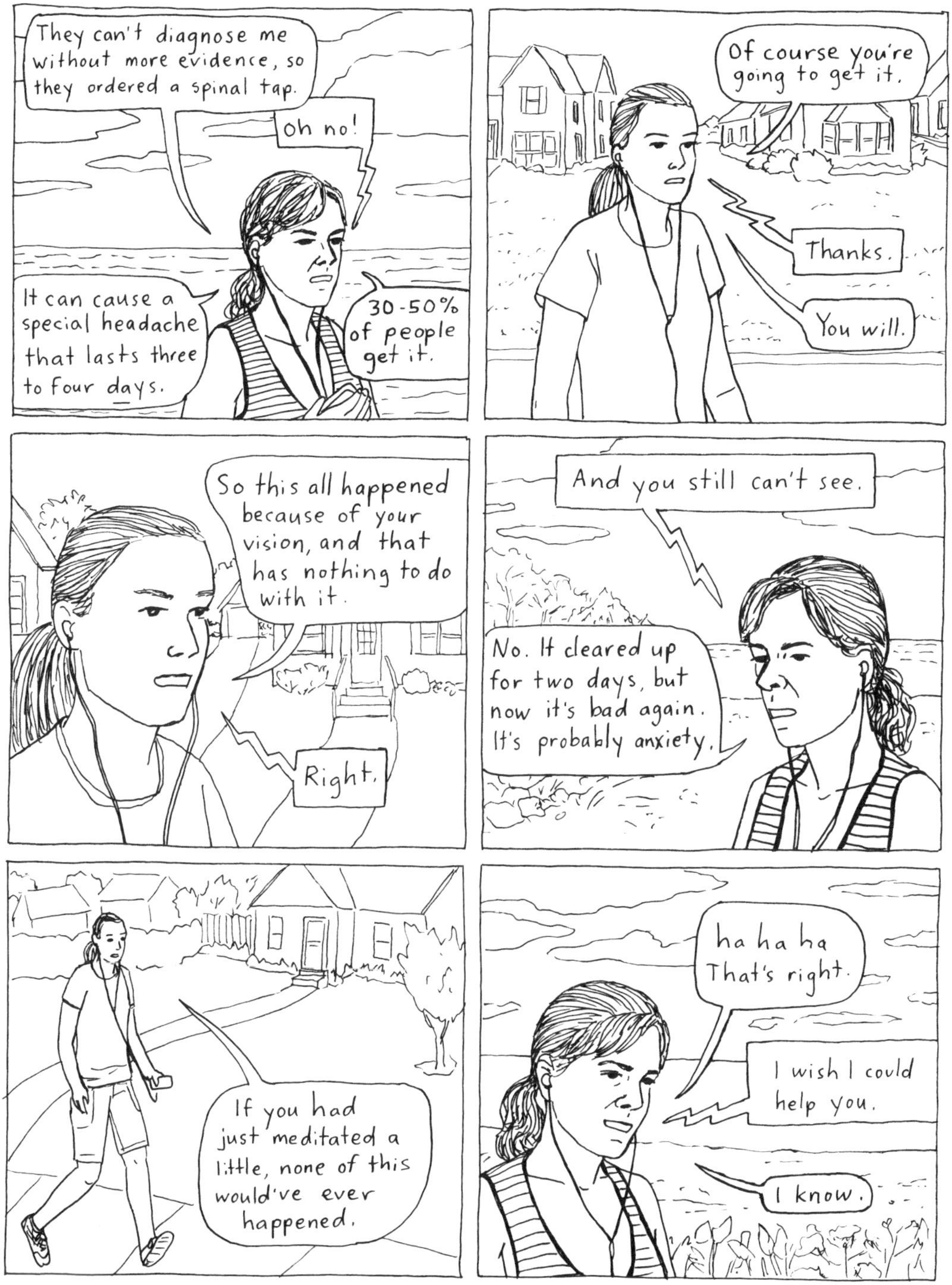
They can't diagnose me without more evidence, so they ordered a spinal tap.
Oh no!
It can cause a special headache that lasts three to four days.
30-50% of people get it.
Of course you're going to get it.
Thanks.
You will.
So this all happened because of your vision, and that has nothing to do with it.
Right.
And you still can't see.
No. It cleared up for two days, but now it's bad again. It's probably anxiety.
If you had just meditated a little, none of this would've ever happened.
ha ha ha
That's right.
I wish I could help you.
I know.

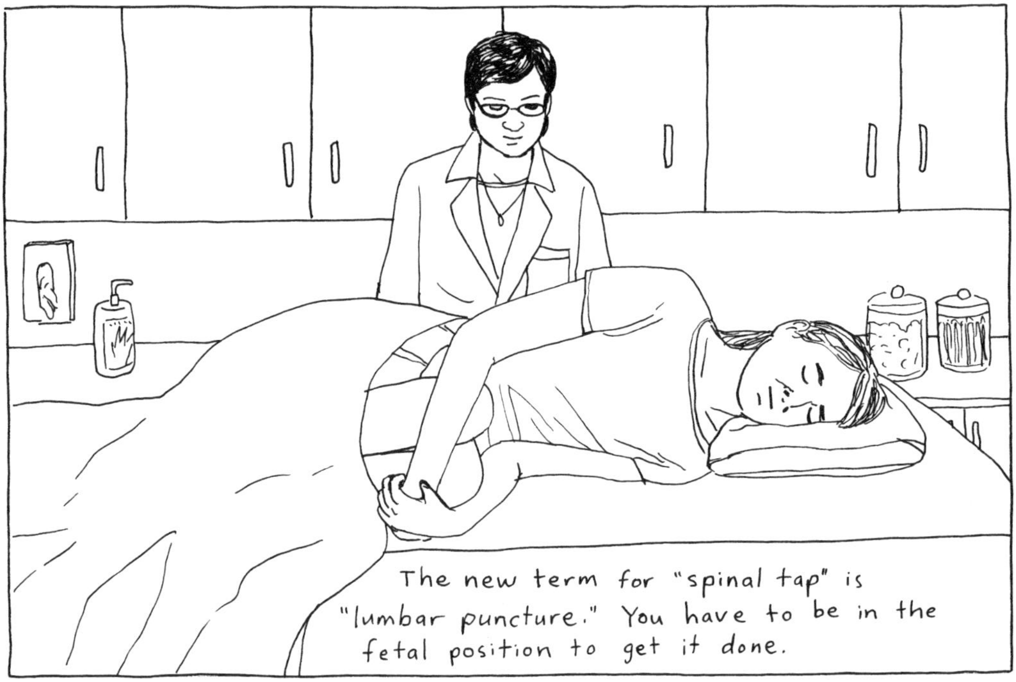
The new term for "spinal tap" is "lumbar puncture." You have to be in the fetal position to get it done.

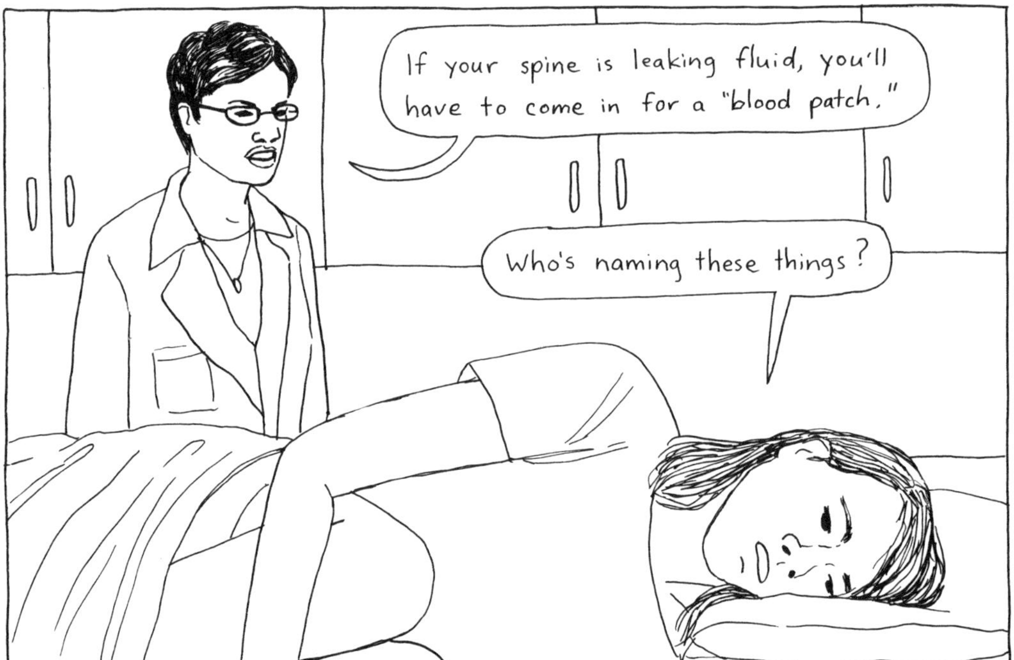
If your spine is leaking fluid, you'll have to come in for a "blood patch."
Who's naming these things?

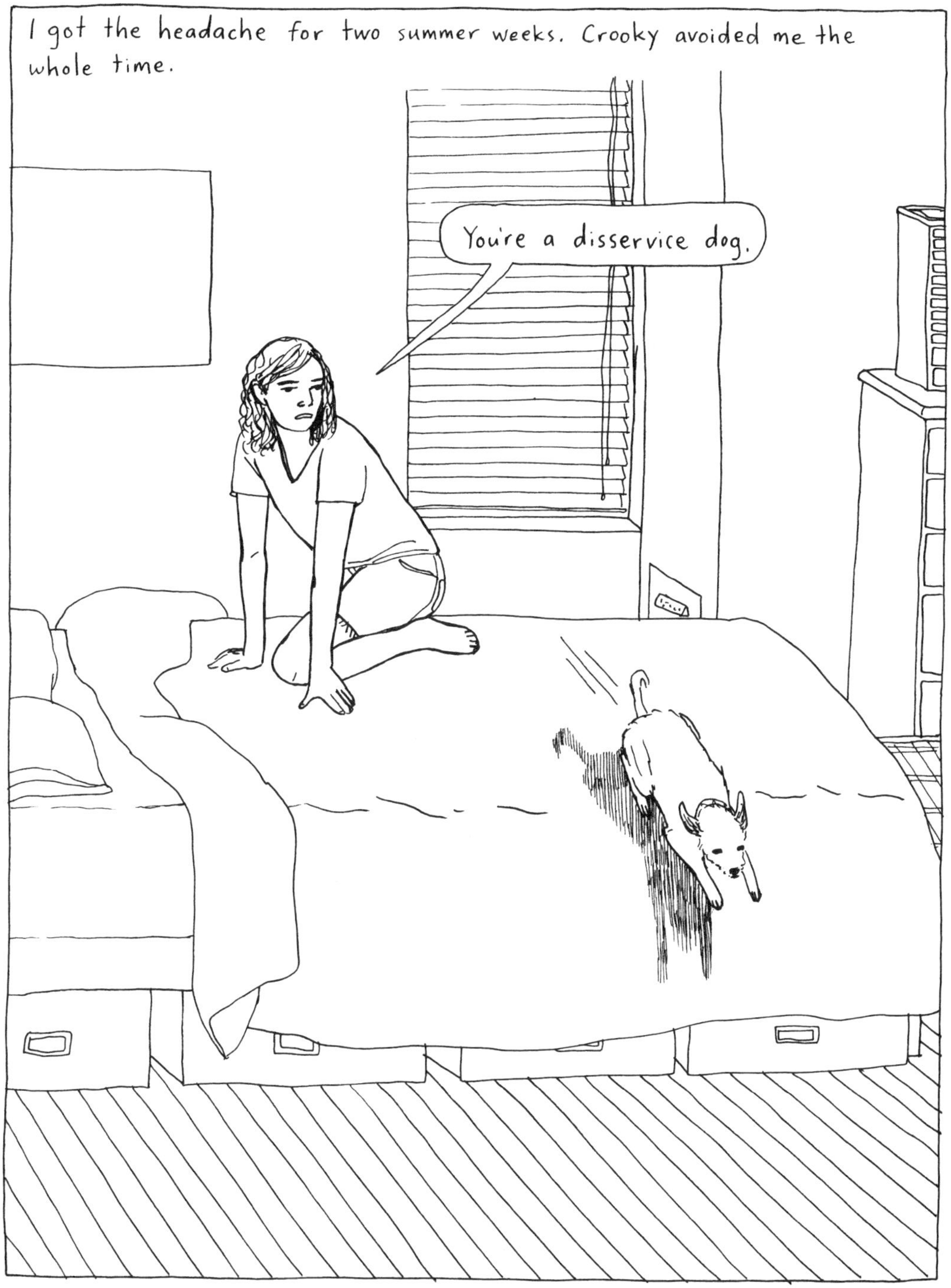
I got the headache for two summer weeks. Crooky avoided me the whole time.
You're a disservice dog.

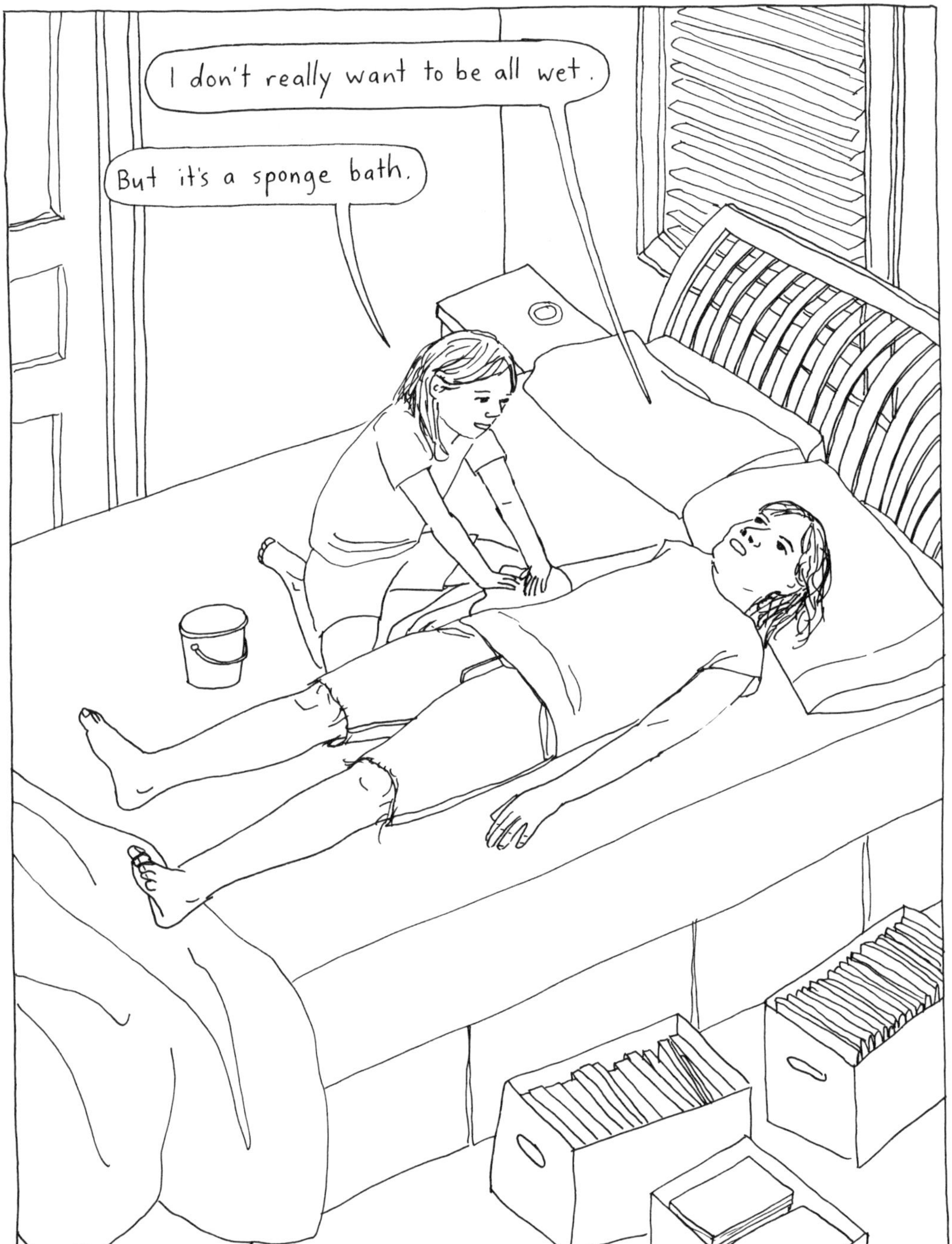
I don't really want to be all wet.
But it's a sponge bath.

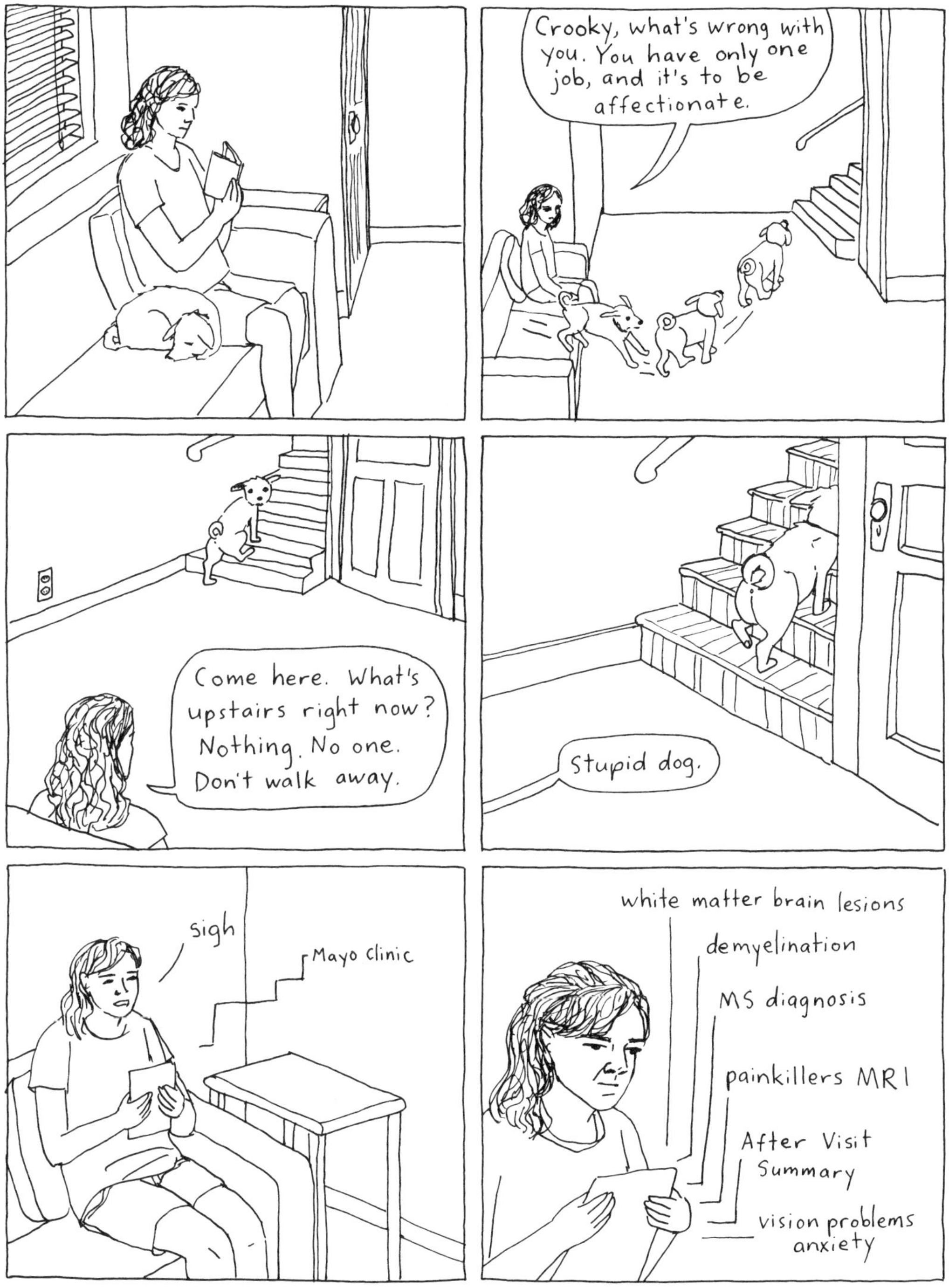
Crooky, what's wrong with you. You have only one job, and it's to be affectionate.
Come here. What's upstairs right now? Nothing. No one. Don't walk away.
Stupid dog.
sigh
Mayo Clinic
white matter brain lesions
demyelination
MS diagnosis
painkillers MRI
After Visit Summary
vision problems
anxiety

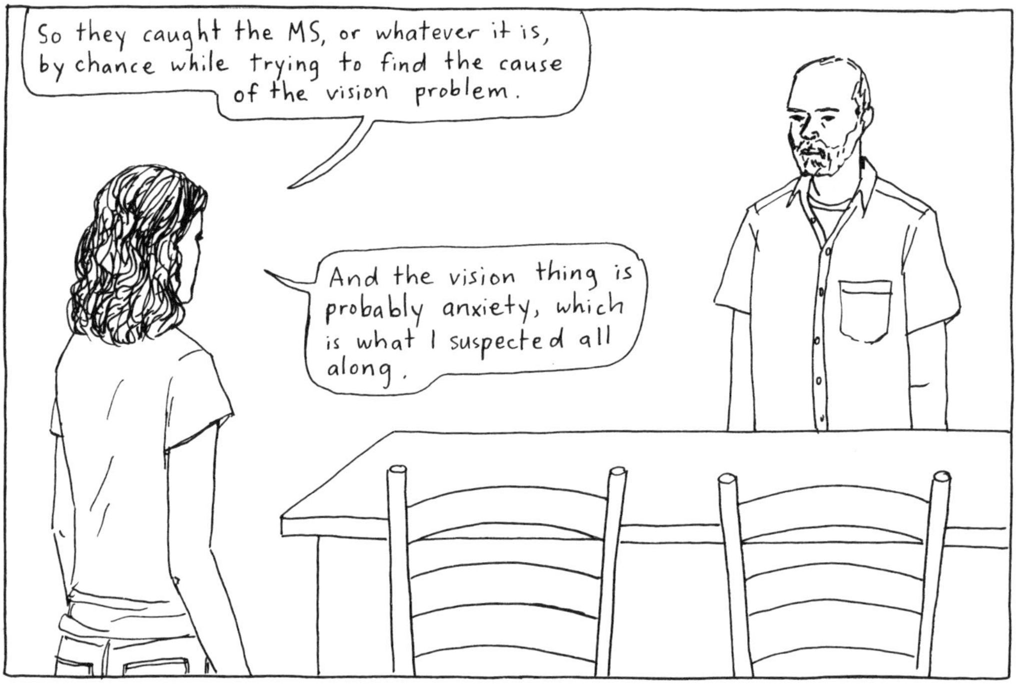
So they caught the MS, or whatever it is, by chance while trying to find the cause of the vision problem.
And the vision thing is probably anxiety, which is what I suspected all along.

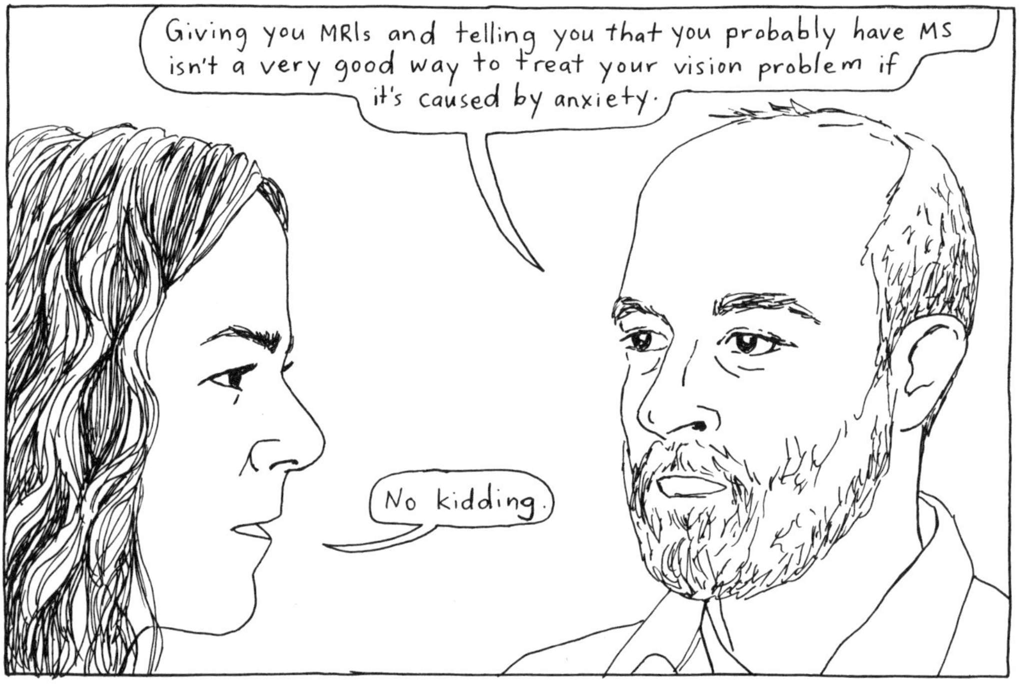
Giving you MRIs and telling you that you probably have MS isn't a very good way to treat your vision problem if it's caused by anxiety.
No kidding.

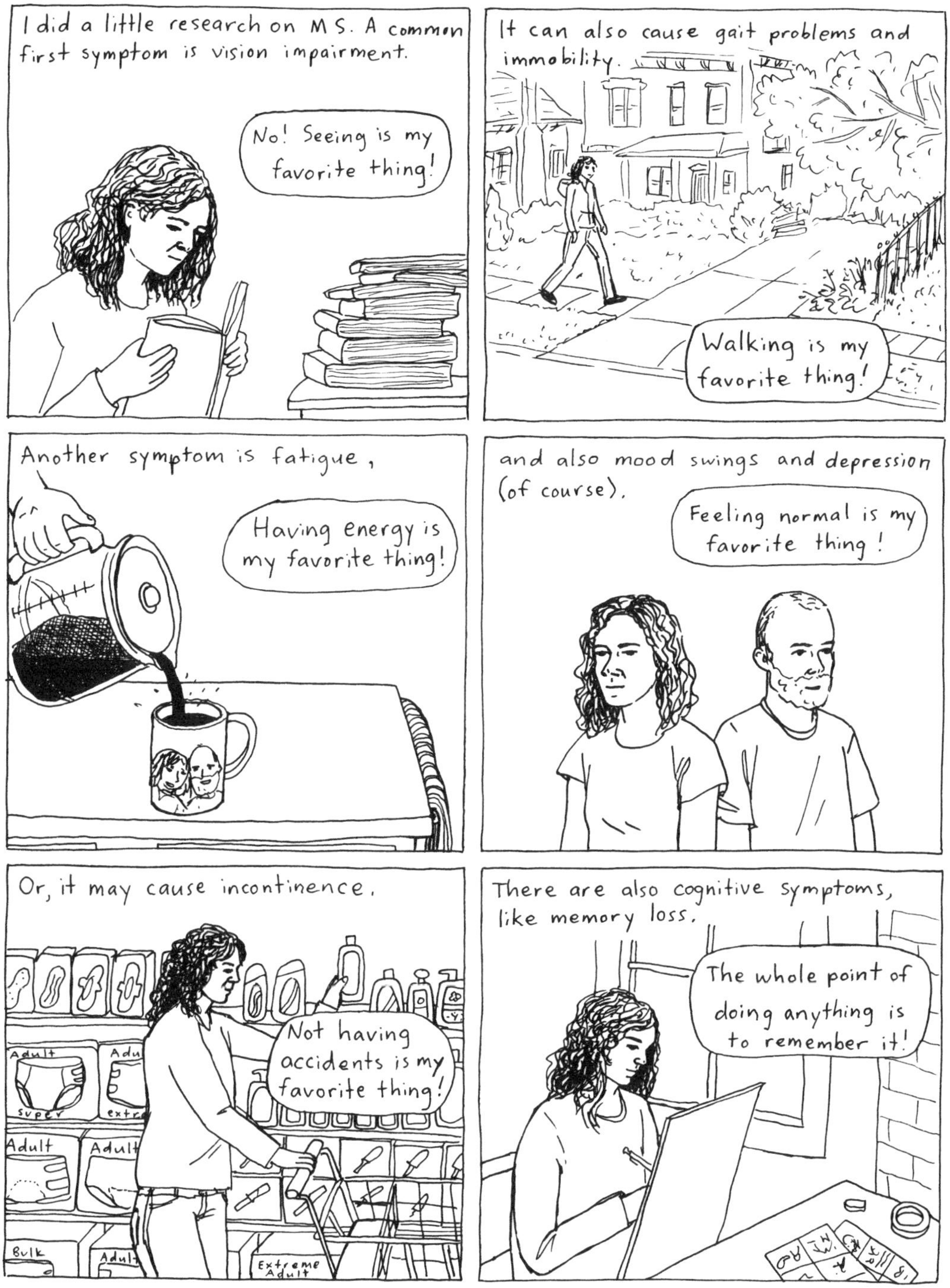
I did a little research on MS. A common first symptom is vision impairment.
No! Seeing is my favorite thing!
It can also cause gait problems and immobility.
Walking is my favorite thing!
Another symptom is fatigue,
Having energy is my favorite thing!
and also mood swings and depression (of course).
Feeling normal is my favorite thing!
Or, it may cause incontinence.
Not having accidents is my favorite thing!
Adult
super
Adult
Adult
Bulk
Adult
Extreme Adult
There are also cognitive symptoms, like memory loss.
The whole point of doing anything is to remember it!

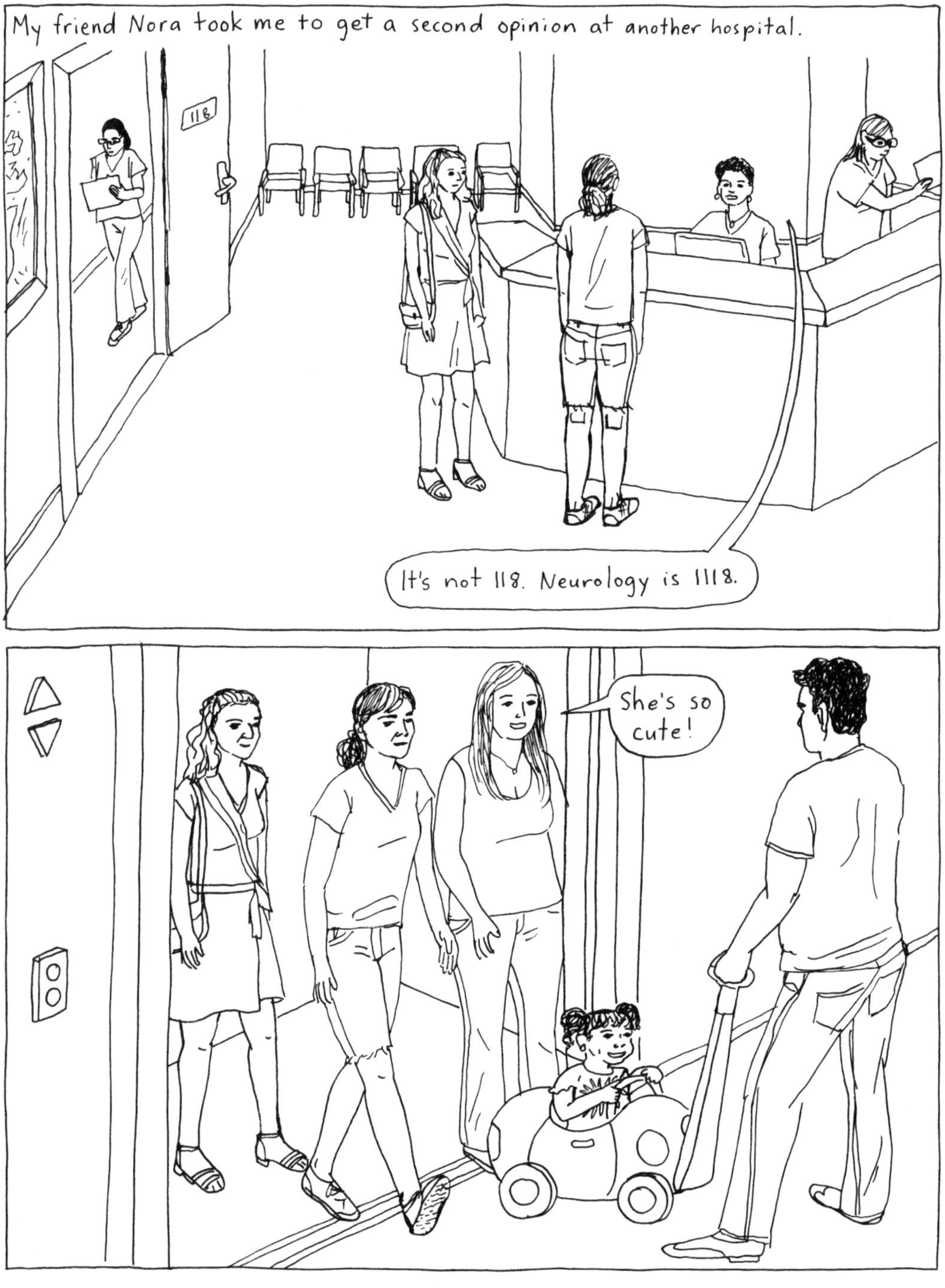
My friend Nora took me to get a second opinion at another hospital.
118
It's not 118. Neurology is 1118.
She's so cute!

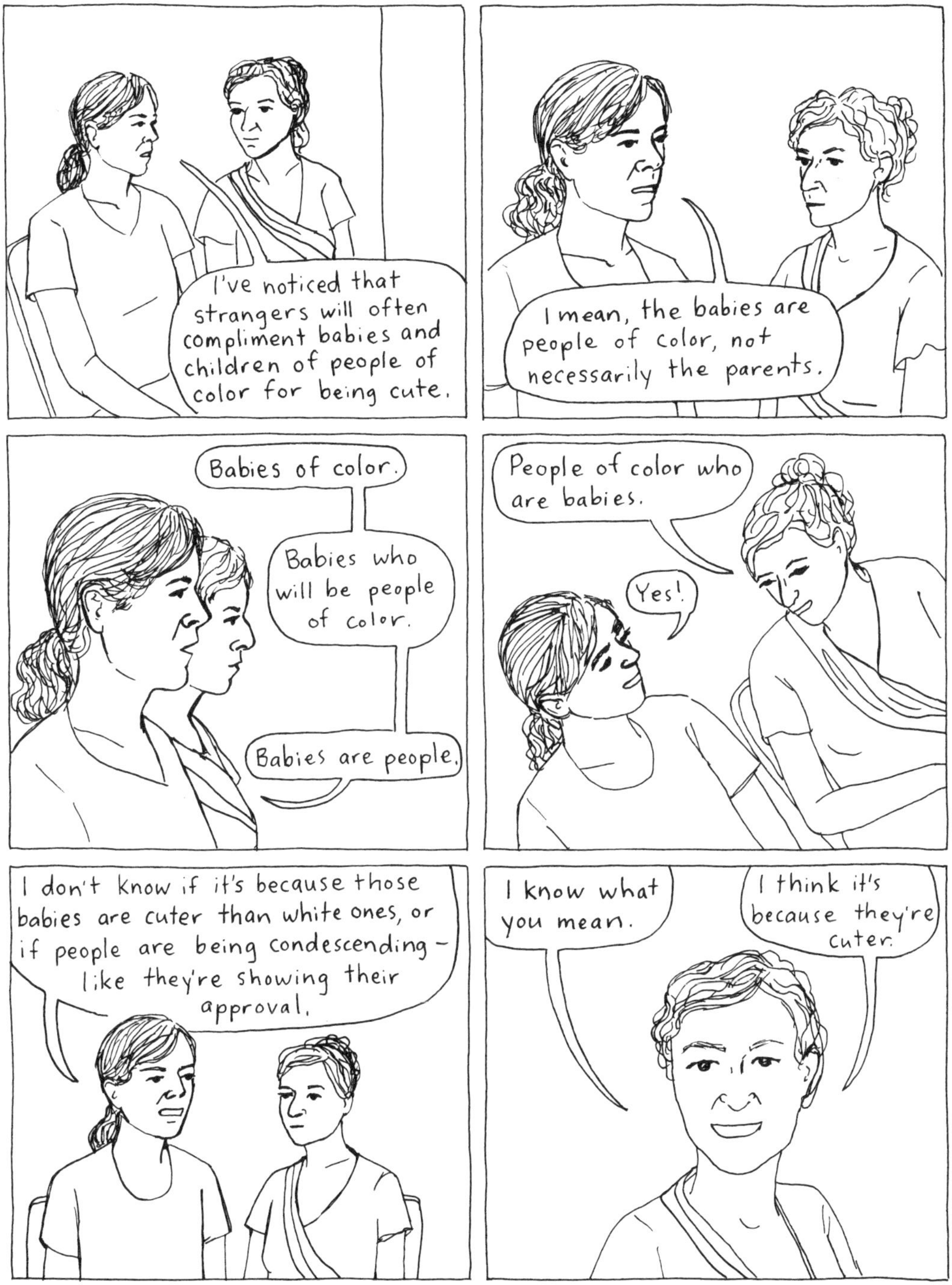

I've noticed that strangers will often compliment babies and children of people of color for being cute.
I mean, the babies are people of color, not necessarily the parents.
Babies of color.
Babies who will be people of color.
Babies are people.
People of color who are babies.
Yes!
I don't know if it's because those babies are cuter than white ones, or if people are being condescending - like they're showing their approval.
I know what you mean.
I think it's because they're cuter.

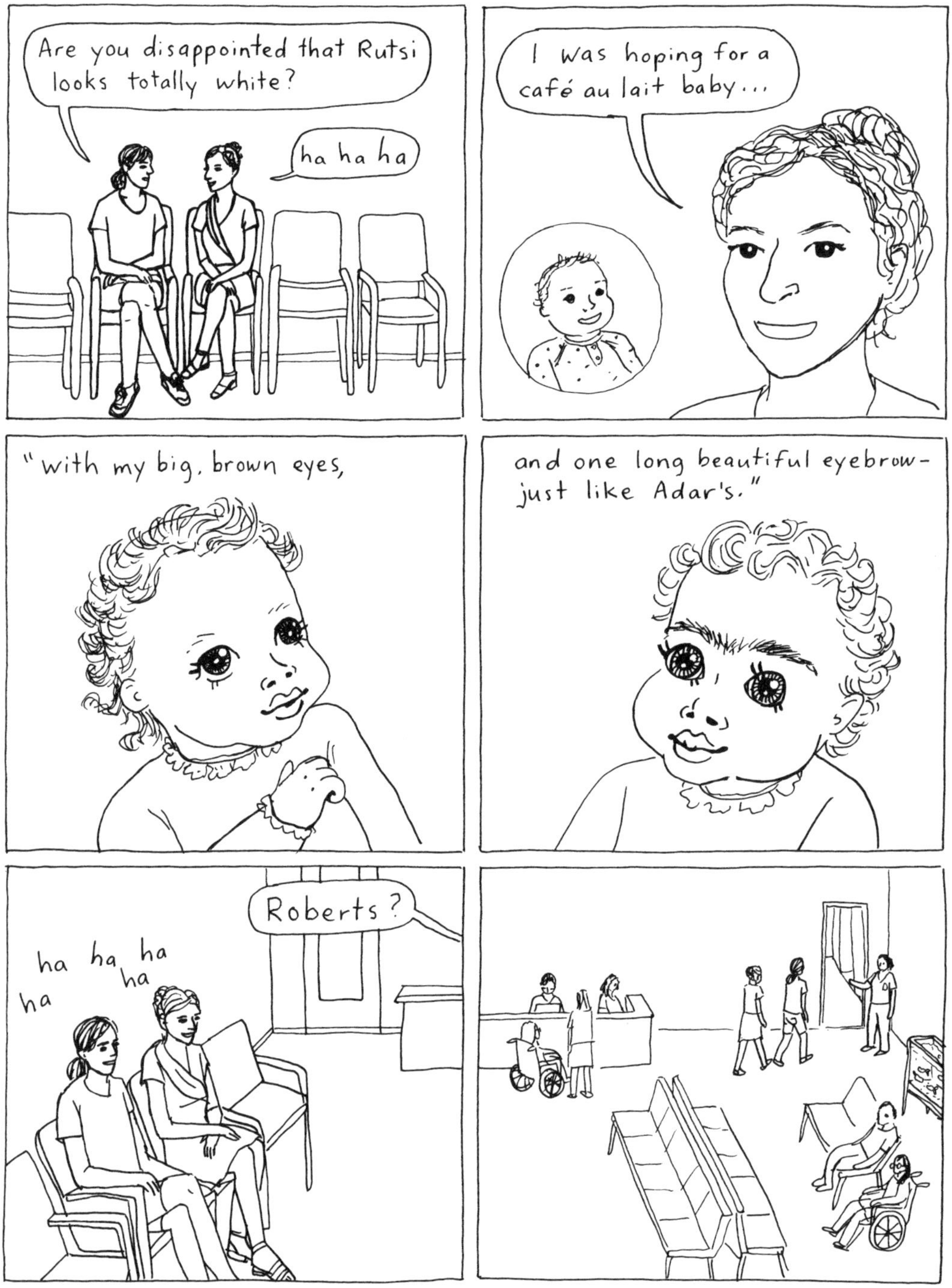
Are you disappointed that Rutsi looks totally white?
ha ha ha
I was hoping for a café au lait baby...
"with my big, brown eyes,
and one long beautiful eyebrow-just like Adar's."
Roberts?
ha ha ha ha ha

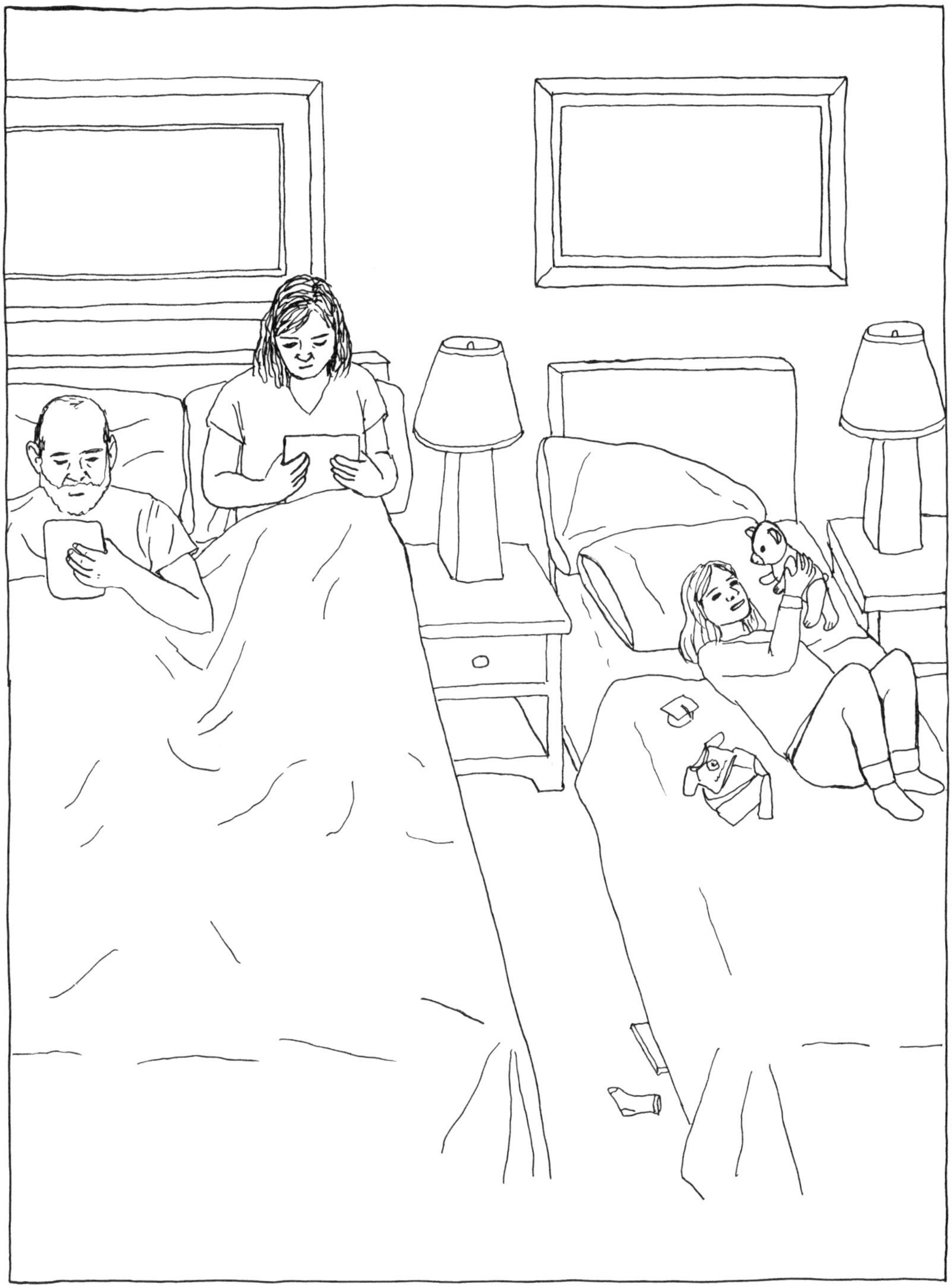

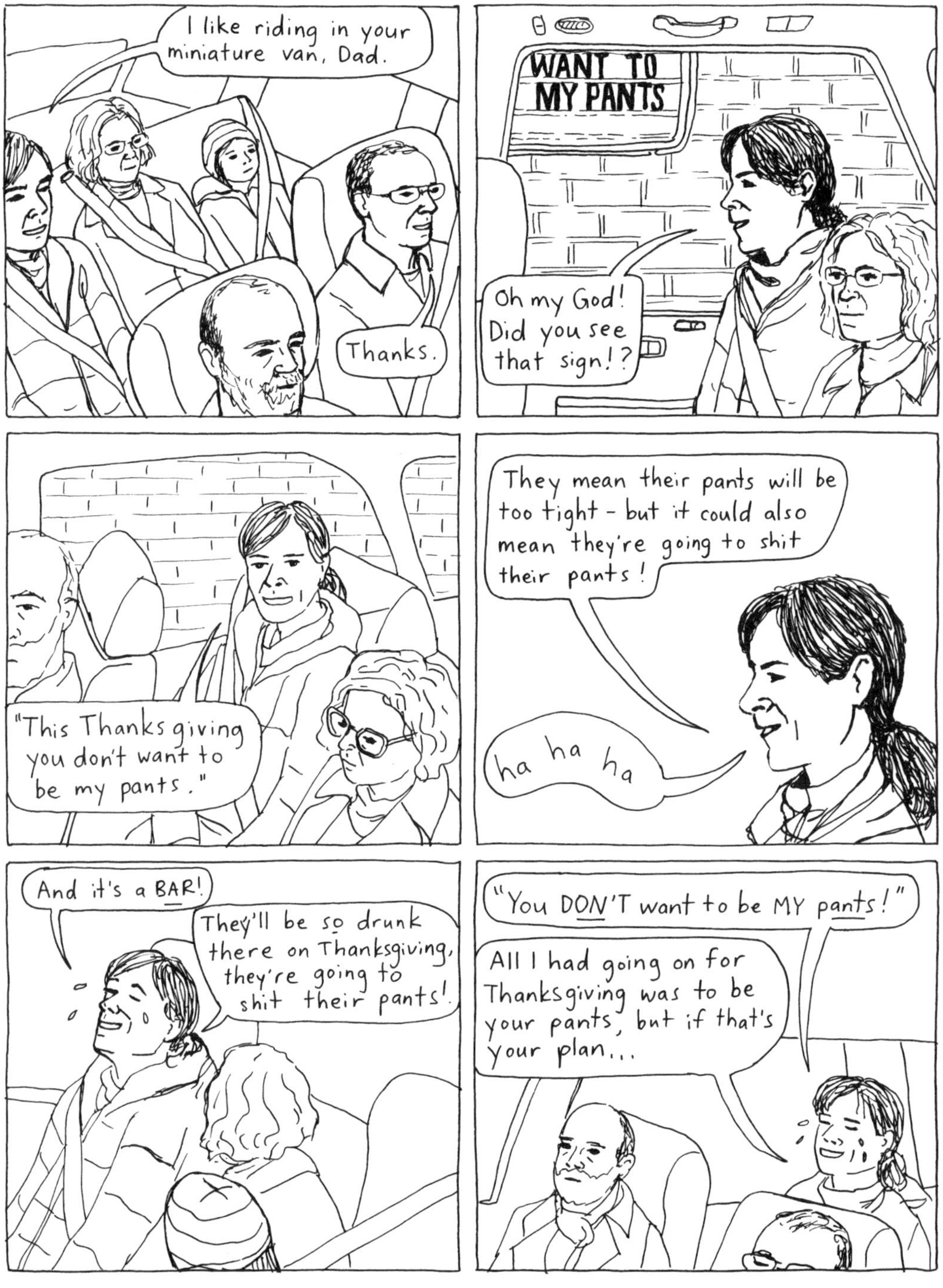
I like riding in your miniature van, Dad.
Thanks.
WANT TO MY PANTS
Oh my God! Did you see that sign!?
"This Thanksgiving you don't want to be my pants."
They mean their pants will be too tight - but it could also mean they're going to shit their pants!
ha ha ha
And it's a BAR!
They'll be so drunk there on Thanksgiving, they're going to shit their pants!
"You DON'T want to be MY pants!"
All I had going on for Thanksgiving was to be your pants, but if that's your plan...

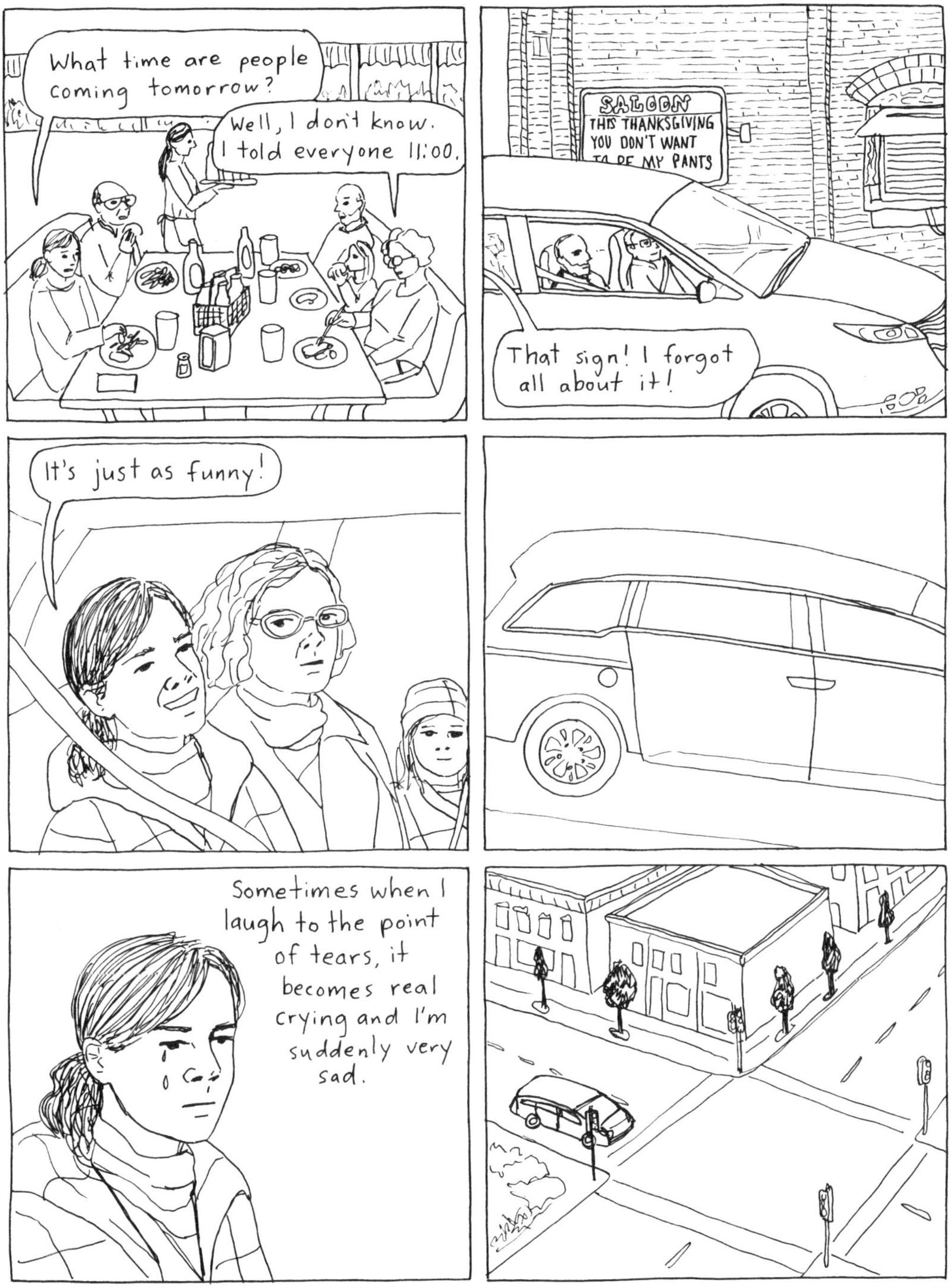
What time are people coming tomorrow?
Well, I don't know. I told everyone 11:00.
SALOON
THIS THANKSGIVING
YOU DON'T WANT
TO BE MY PANTS
That sign! I forgot all about it!
It's just as funny!
Sometimes when I laugh to the point of tears, it becomes real crying and I'm suddenly very sad.

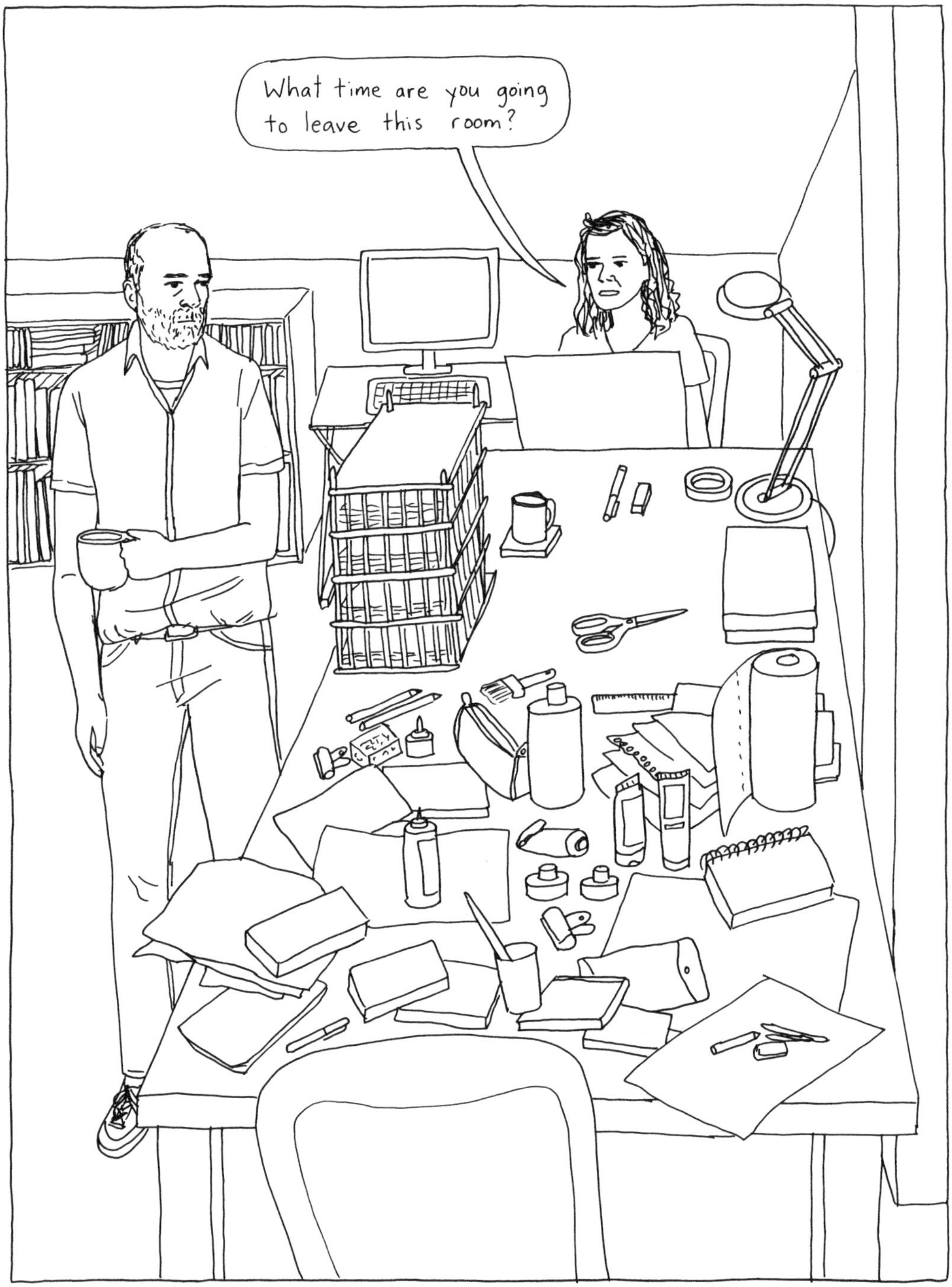
What time are you going to leave this room?

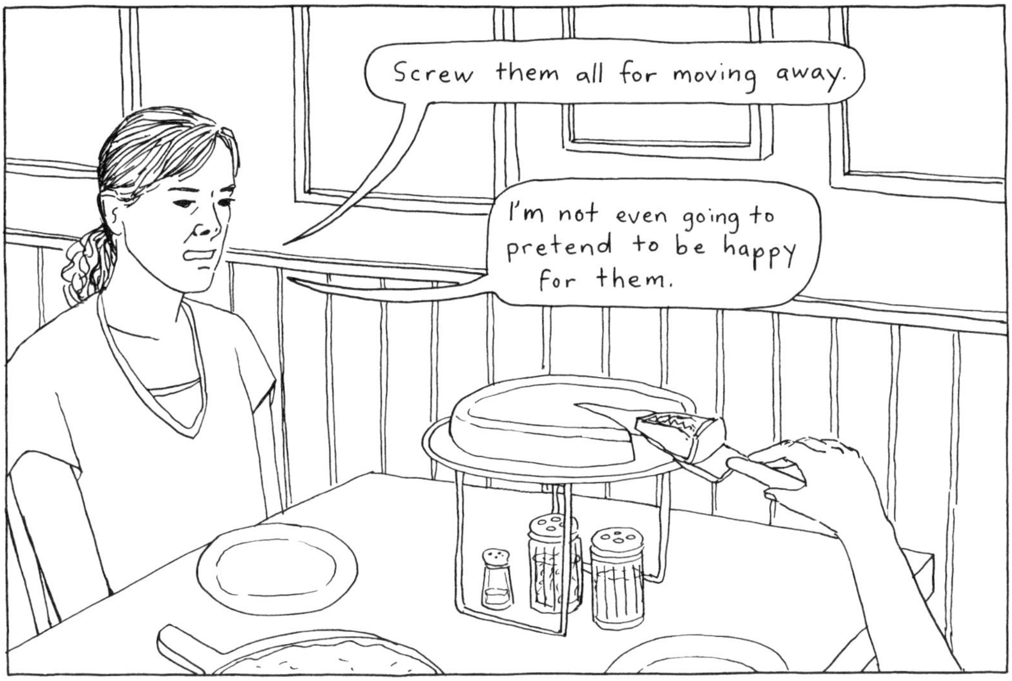
Screw them all for moving away.
I'm not even going to pretend to be happy for them.

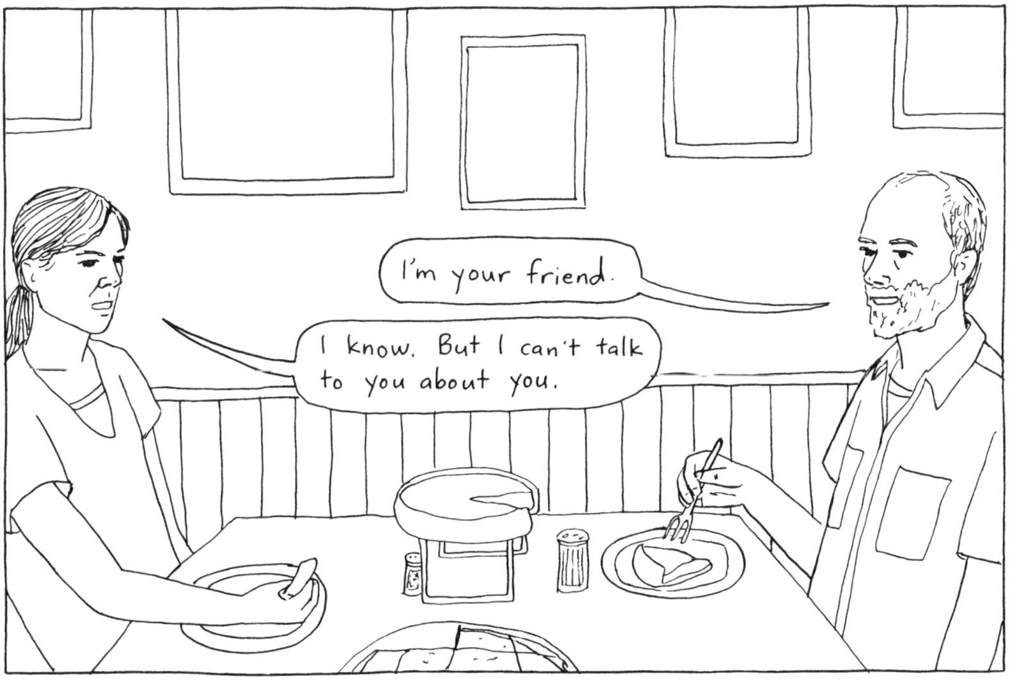
I'm your friend.
I know. But I can't talk to you about you.

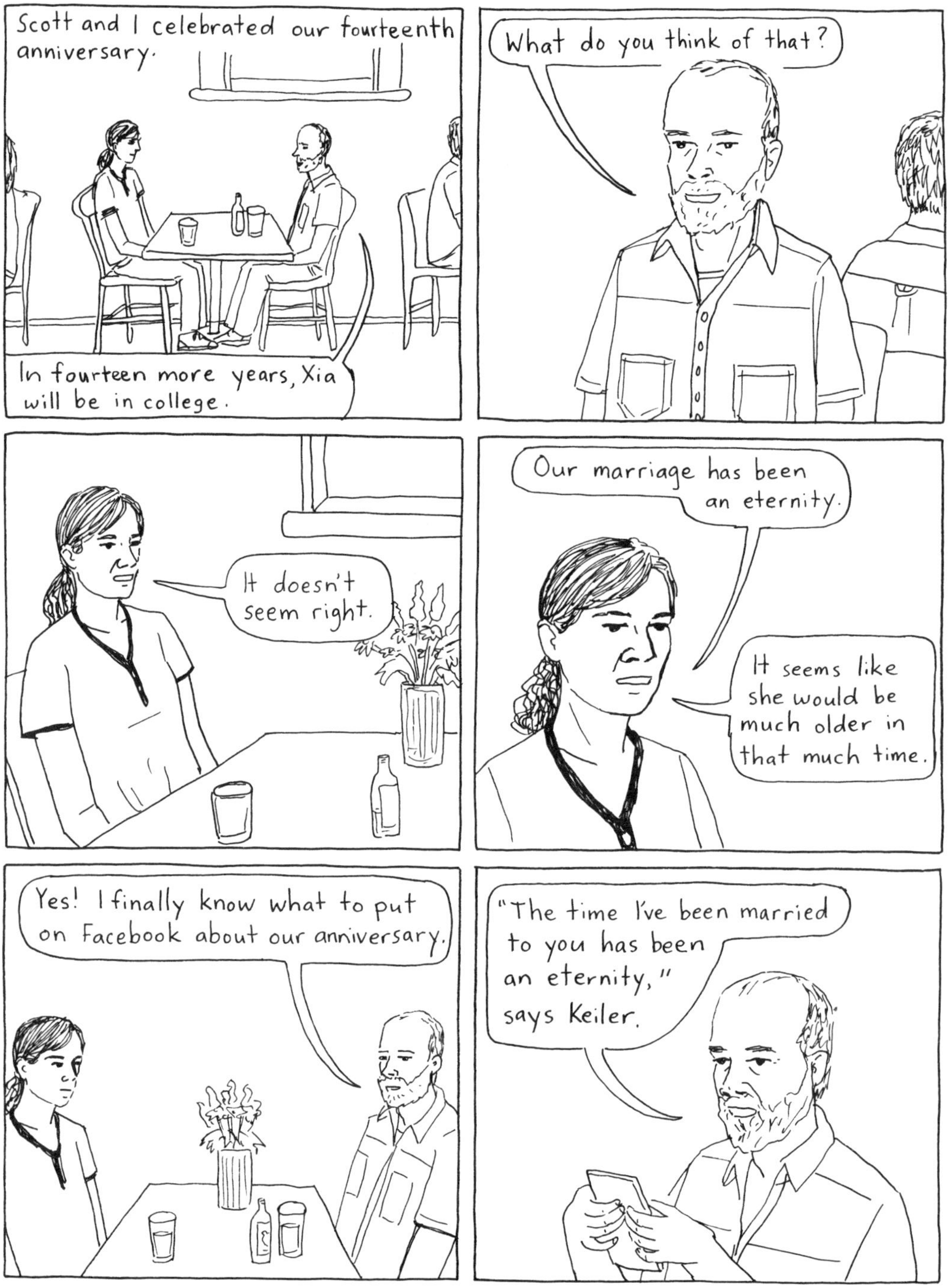
Scott and I celebrated our fourteenth anniversary.
In fourteen more years, Xia will be in college.
What do you think of that?
It doesn't seem right.
Our marriage has been an eternity.
It seems like she would be much older in that much time.
Yes! I finally know what to put on Facebook about our anniversary.
"The time I've been married to you has been an eternity," says Keiler.

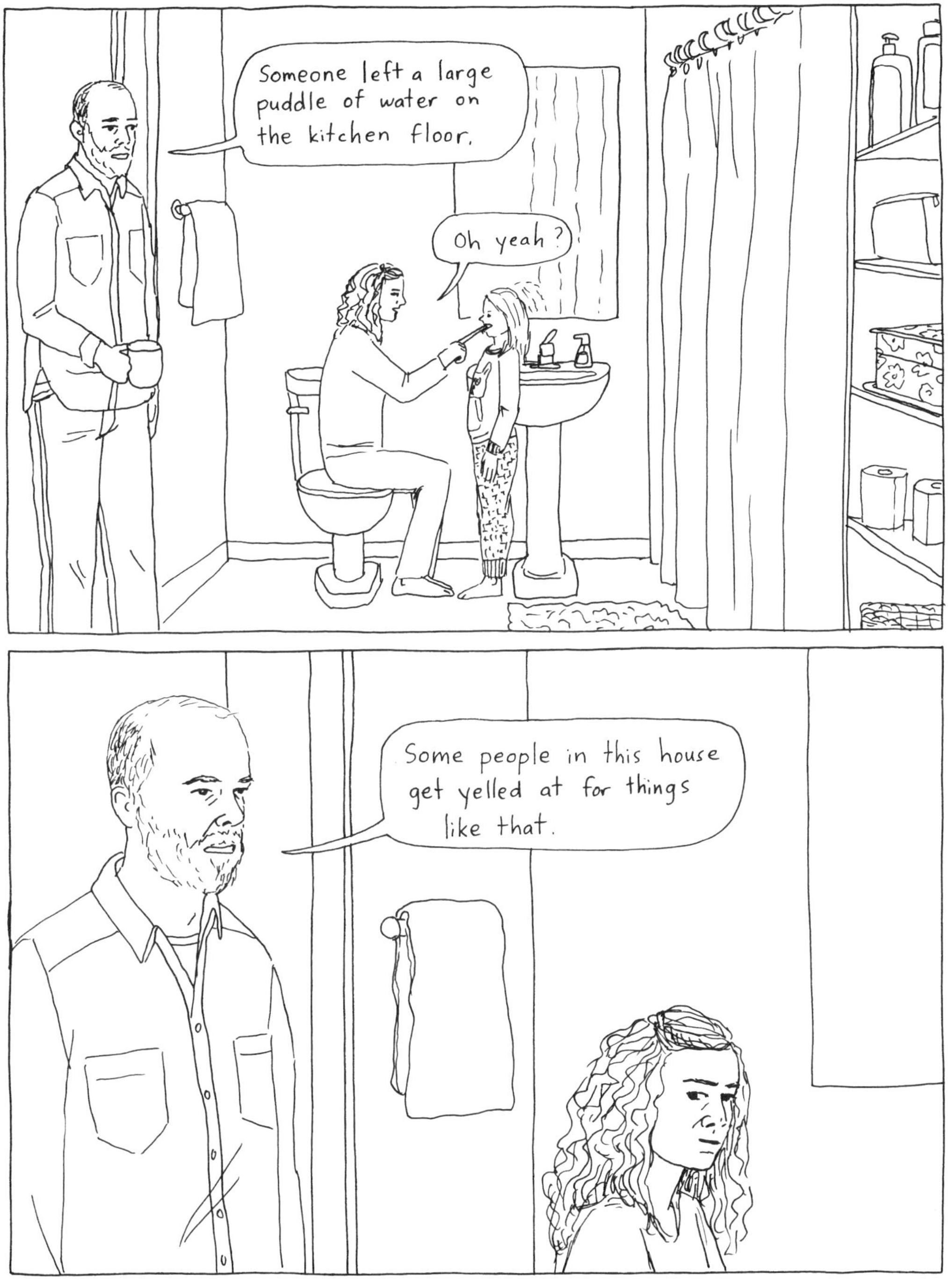
Someone left a large puddle of water on the kitchen floor.
Oh yeah?
Some people in this house get yelled at for things like that.

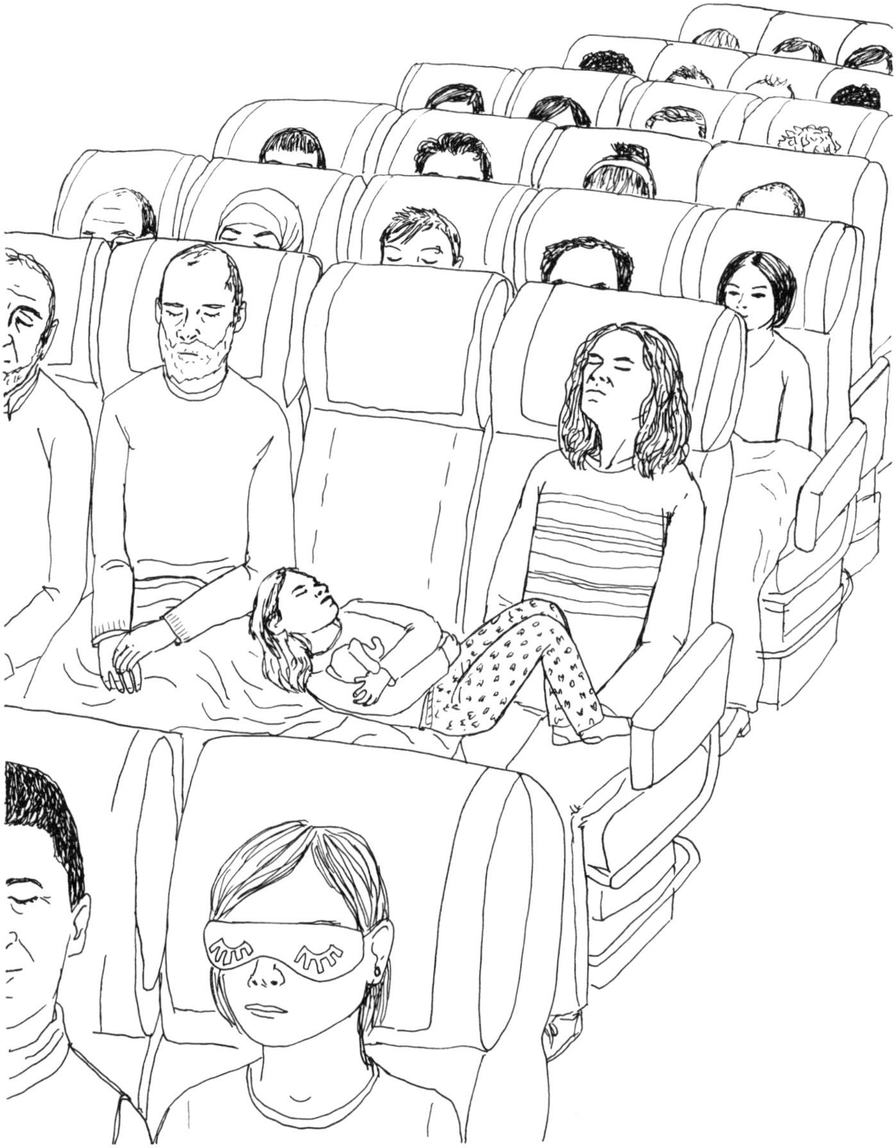

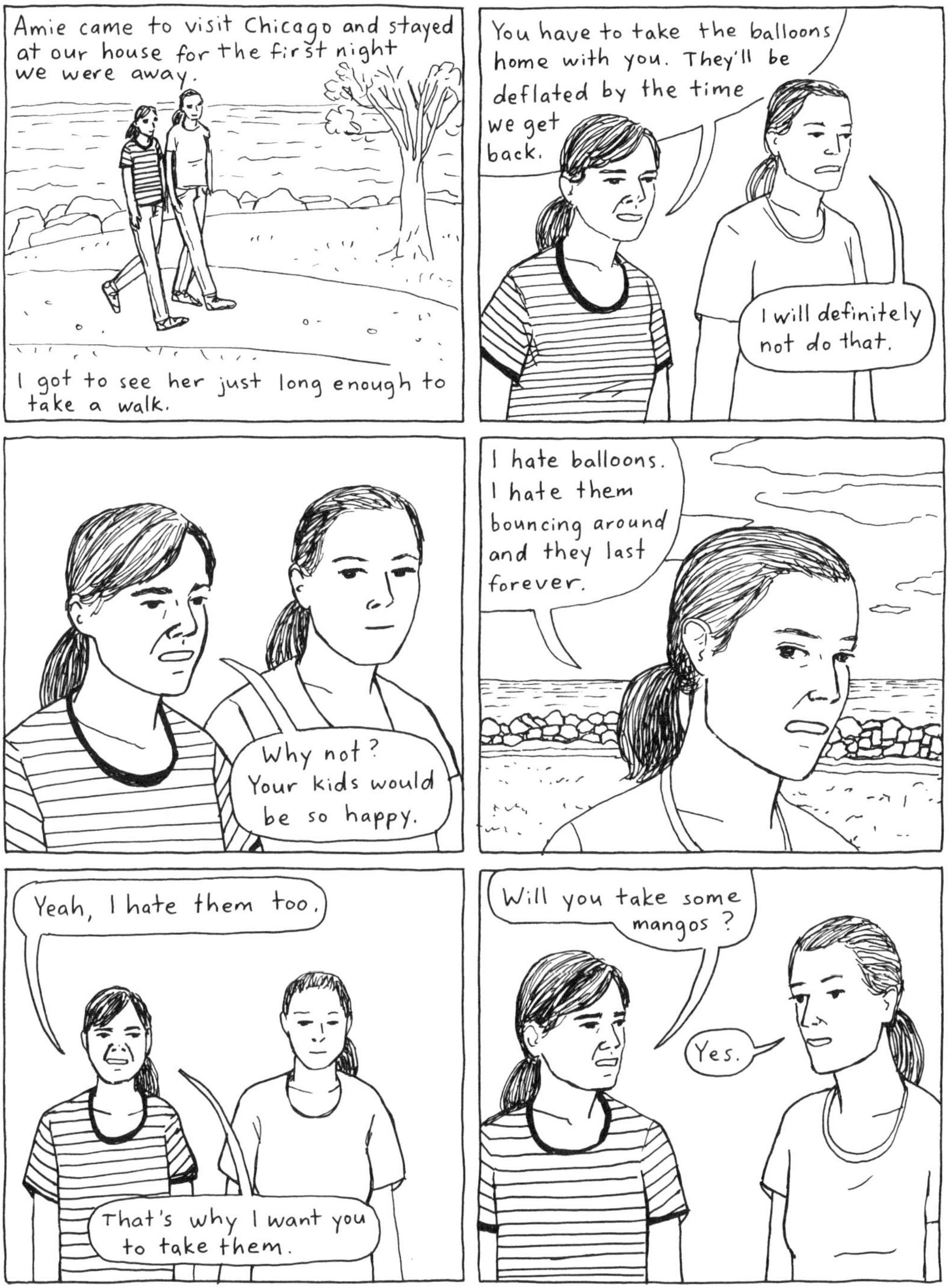
Amie came to visit Chicago and stayed at our house for the first night we were away.
I got to see her just long enough to take a walk.
You have to take the balloons home with you. They'll be deflated by the time we get back.
I will definitely not do that.
Why not? Your kids would be so happy.
I hate balloons. I hate them bouncing around and they last forever.
Yeah, I hate them too.
That's why I want you to take them.
Will you take some mangos?
Yes.

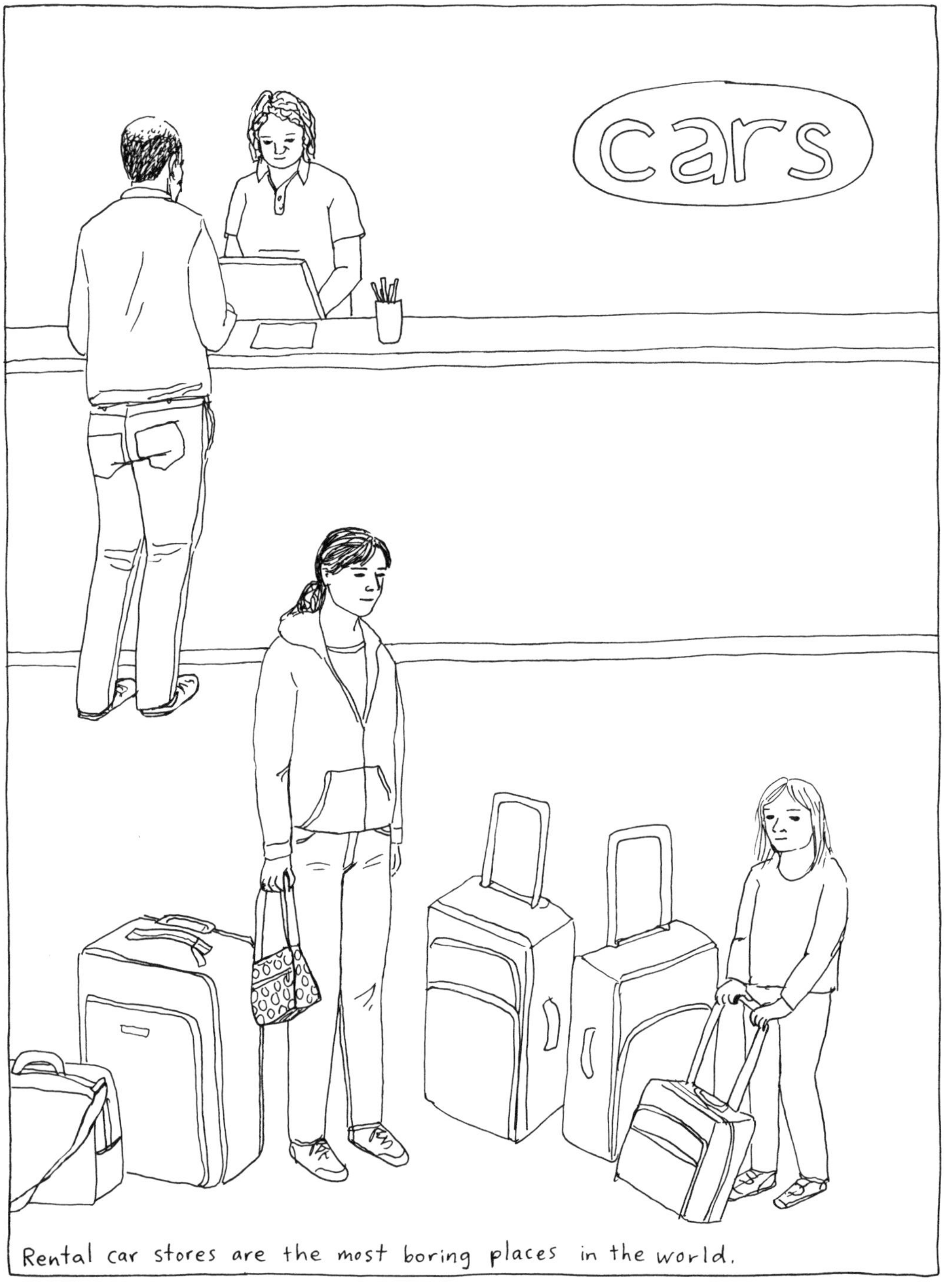
cars
Rental car stores are the most boring places in the world.

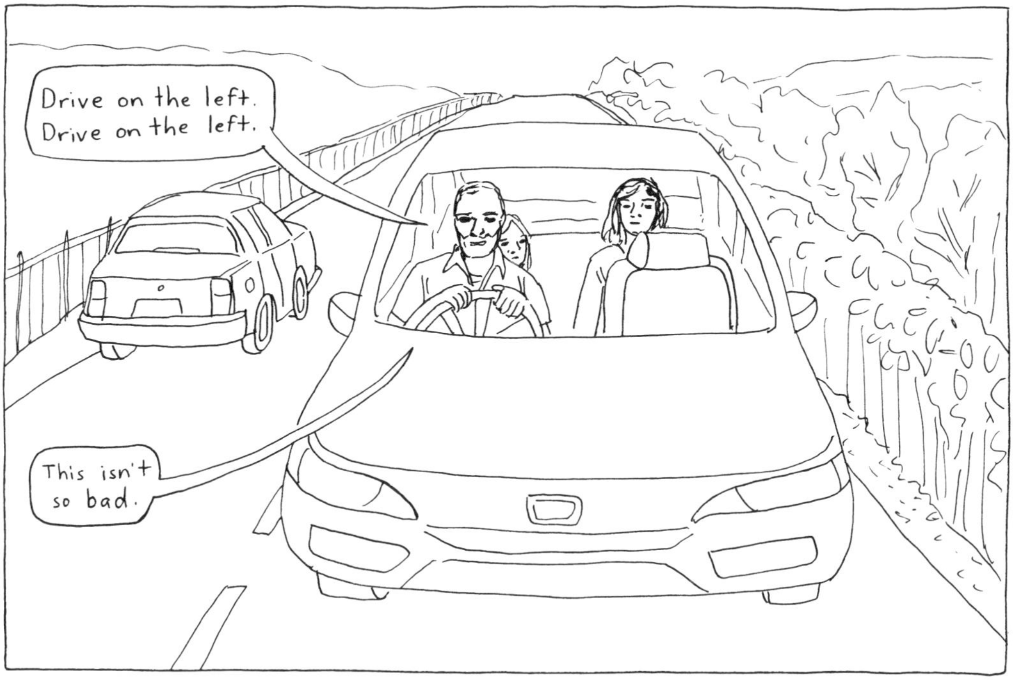
Drive on the left. Drive on the left.
This isn't so bad.

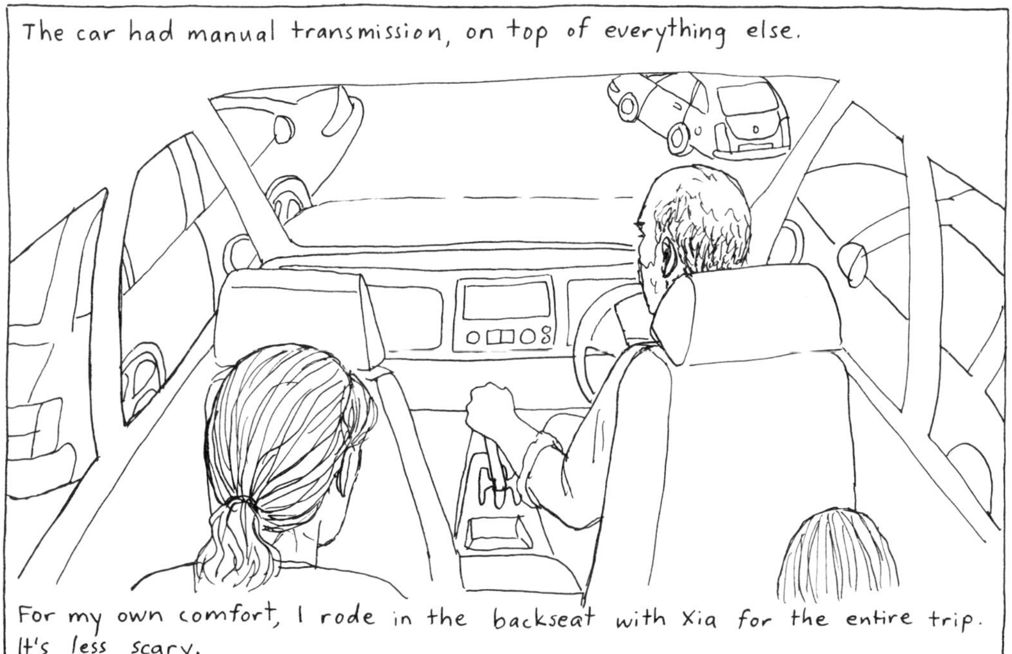
The car had manual transmission, on top of everything else.
For my own comfort, I rode in the backseat with Xia for the entire trip. It's less scary.

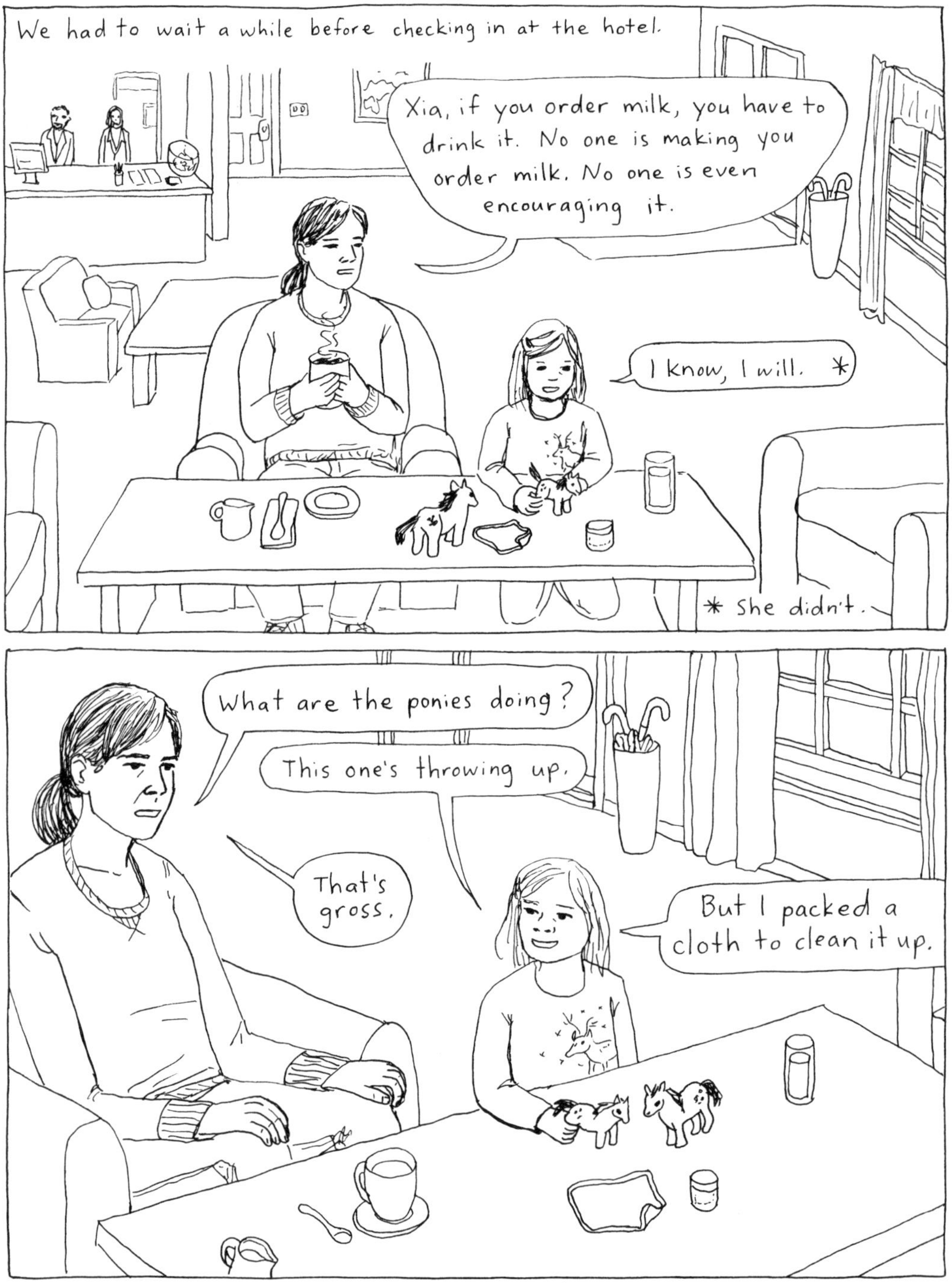
We had to wait a while before checking in at the hotel.
Xia, if you order milk, you have to drink it. No one is making you order milk. No one is even encouraging it.
I know, I will. *
* She didn't.
What are the ponies doing?
This one's throwing up.
That's gross.
But I packed a cloth to clean it up.

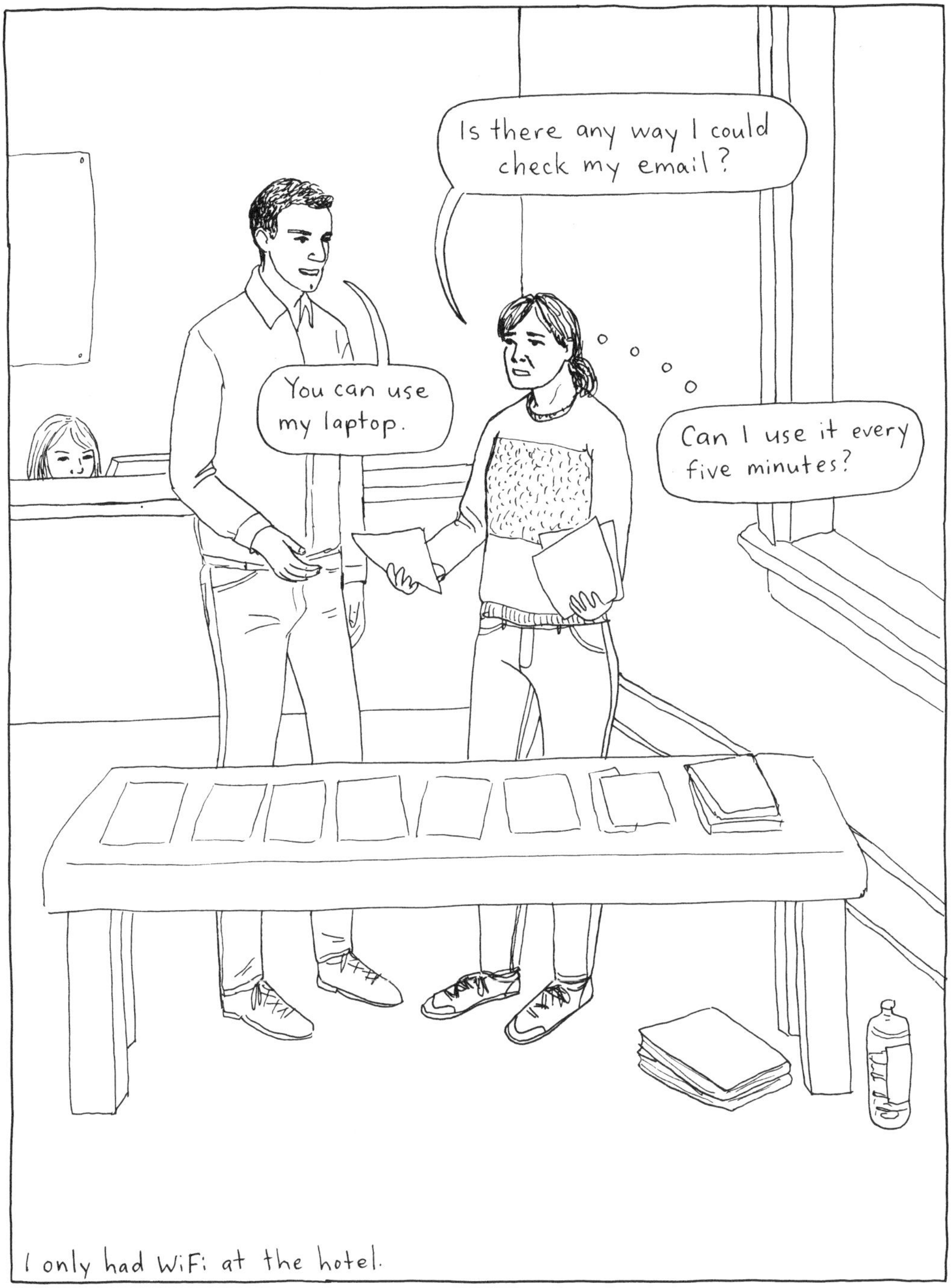
Is there any way I could check my email?
You can use my laptop.
Can I use it every five minutes?
I only had WiFi at the hotel.

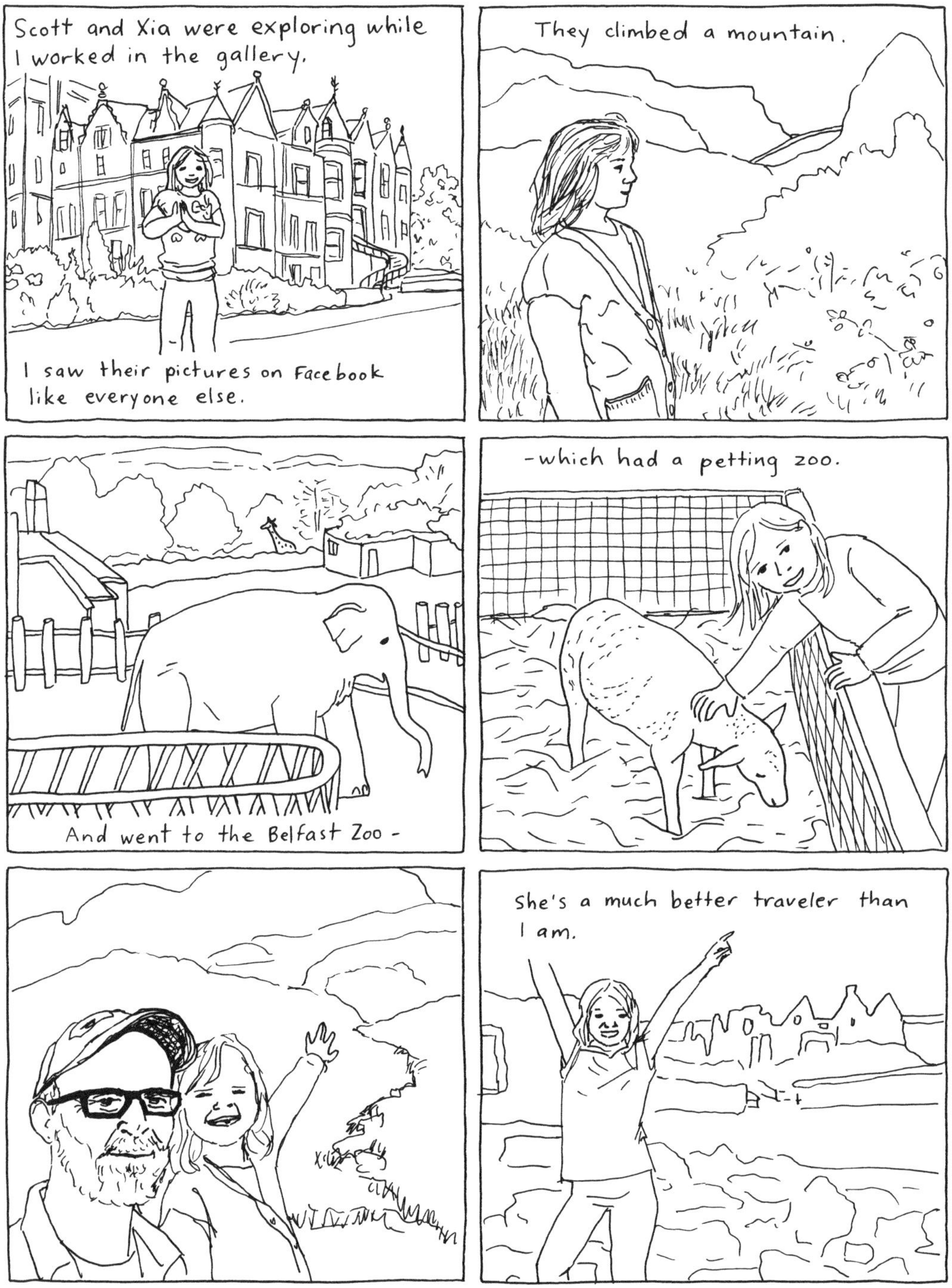
Scott and Xia were exploring while I worked in the gallery.
I saw their pictures on Facebook like everyone else.
They climbed a mountain.
And went to the Belfast Zoo -
-which had a petting zoo.
She's a much better traveler than I am.

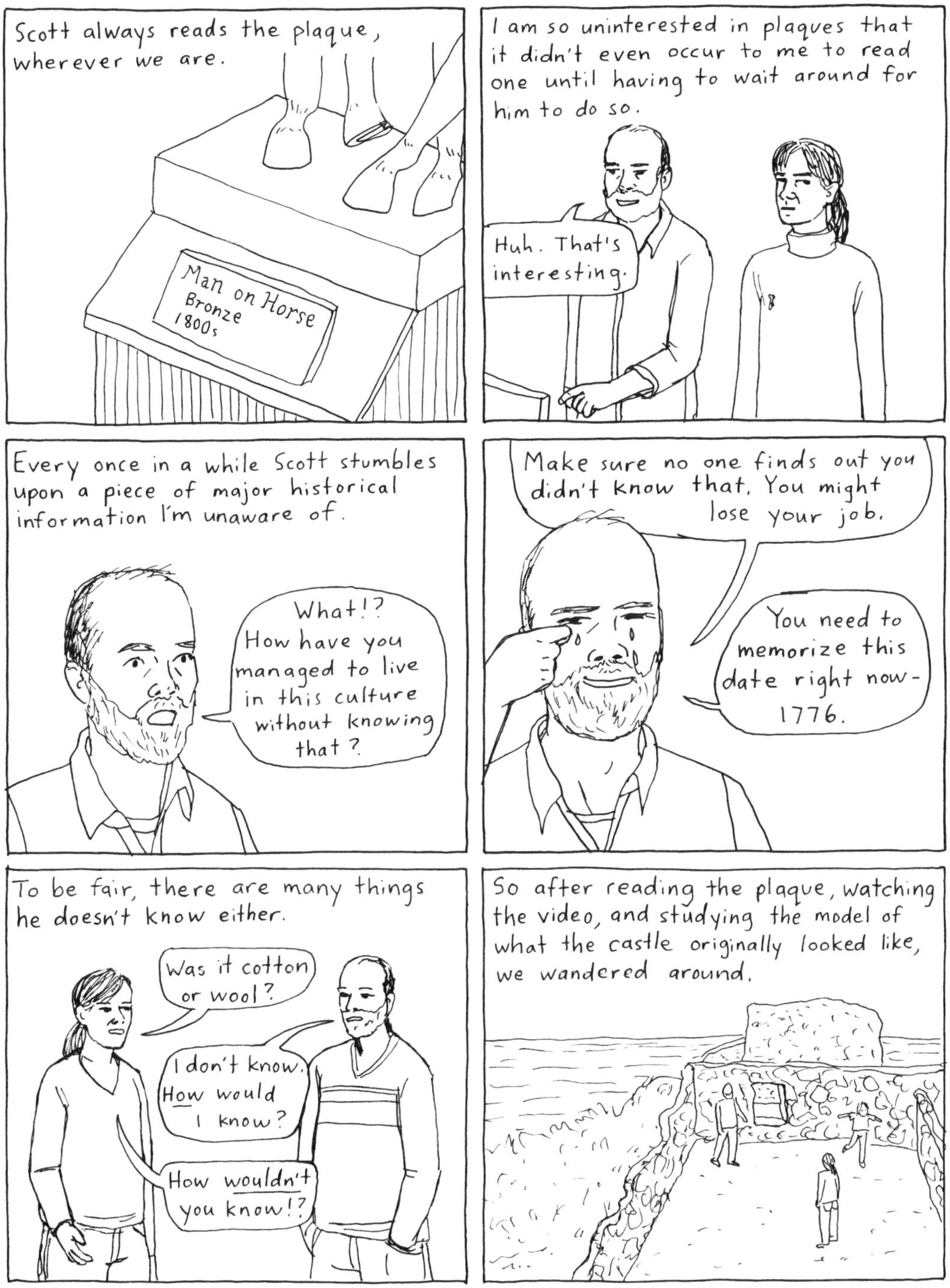
Scott always reads the plaque, wherever we are.
Man on Horse
Bronze
1800s
I am so uninterested in plaques that it didn't even occur to me to read one until having to wait around for him to do so.
Huh. That's interesting.
Every once in a while Scott stumbles upon a piece of major historical information I'm unaware of.
What!? How have you managed to live in this culture without knowing that?
Make sure no one finds out you didn't know that. You might lose your job.
You need to memorize this date right now- 1776.
To be fair, there are many things he doesn't know either.
Was it cotton or wool?
I don't know. How would I know?
How wouldn't you know!?
So after reading the plaque, watching the video, and studying the model of what the castle originally looked like, we wandered around.

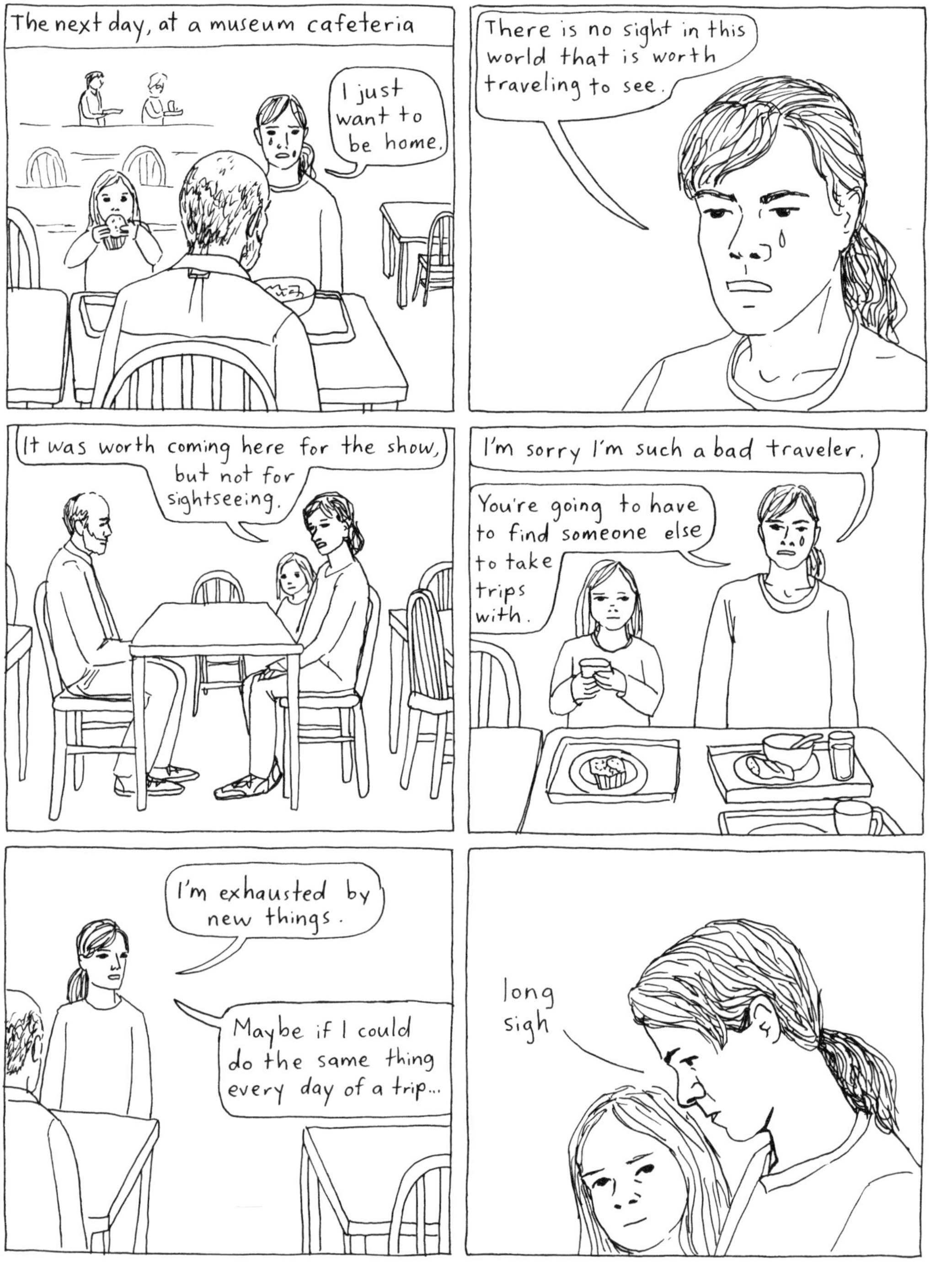
The next day, at a museum cafeteria
I just want to be home.
There is no sight in this world that is worth traveling to see.
It was worth coming here for the show, but not for sightseeing.
I'm sorry I'm such a bad traveler.
You're going to have to find someone else to take trips with.
I'm exhausted by new things.
Maybe if I could do the same thing every day of a trip...
long sigh

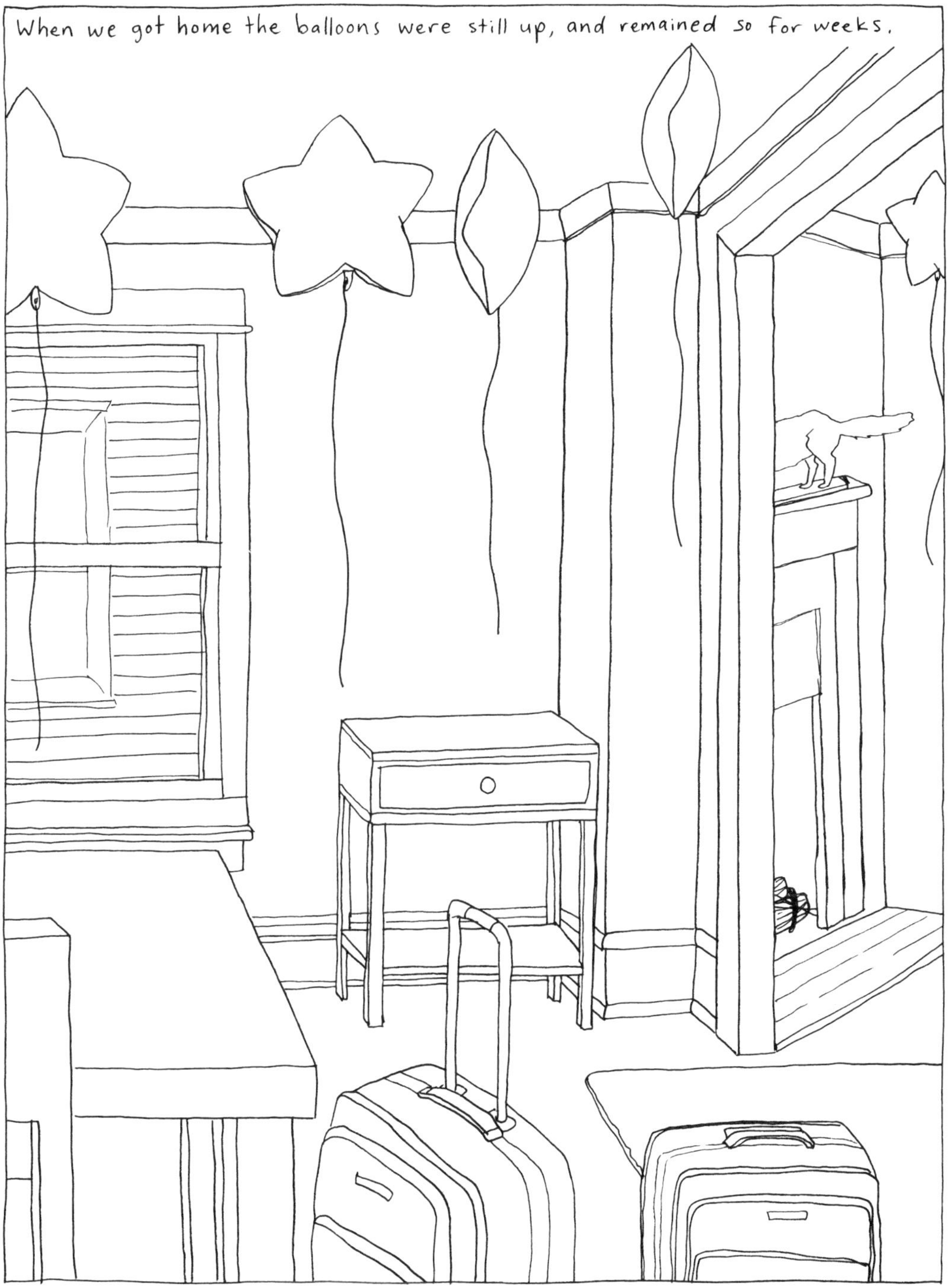
When we got home the balloons were still up, and remained so for weeks.

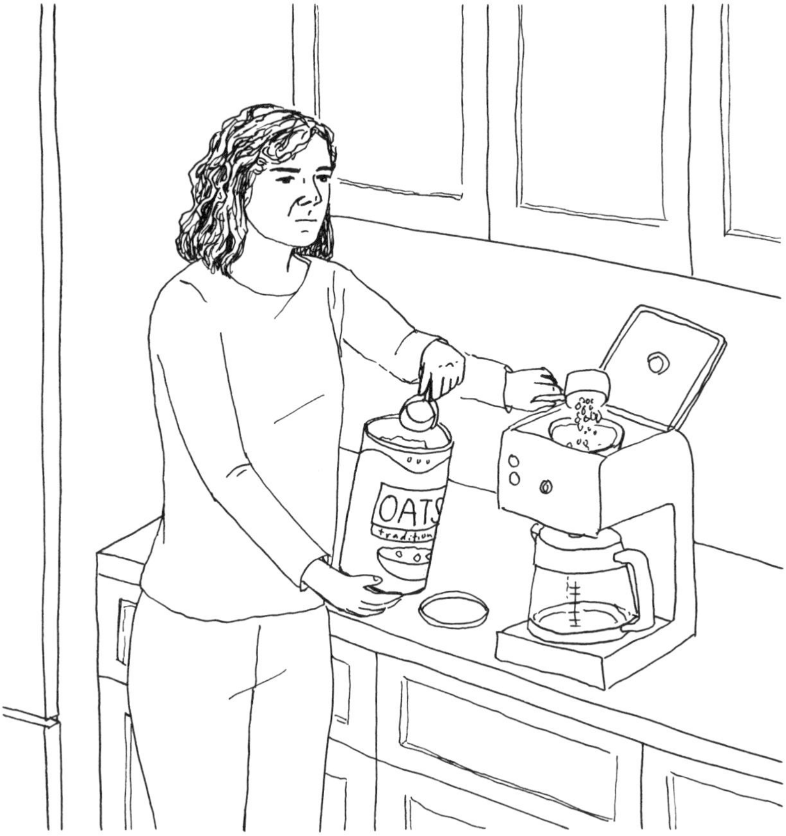
OATS

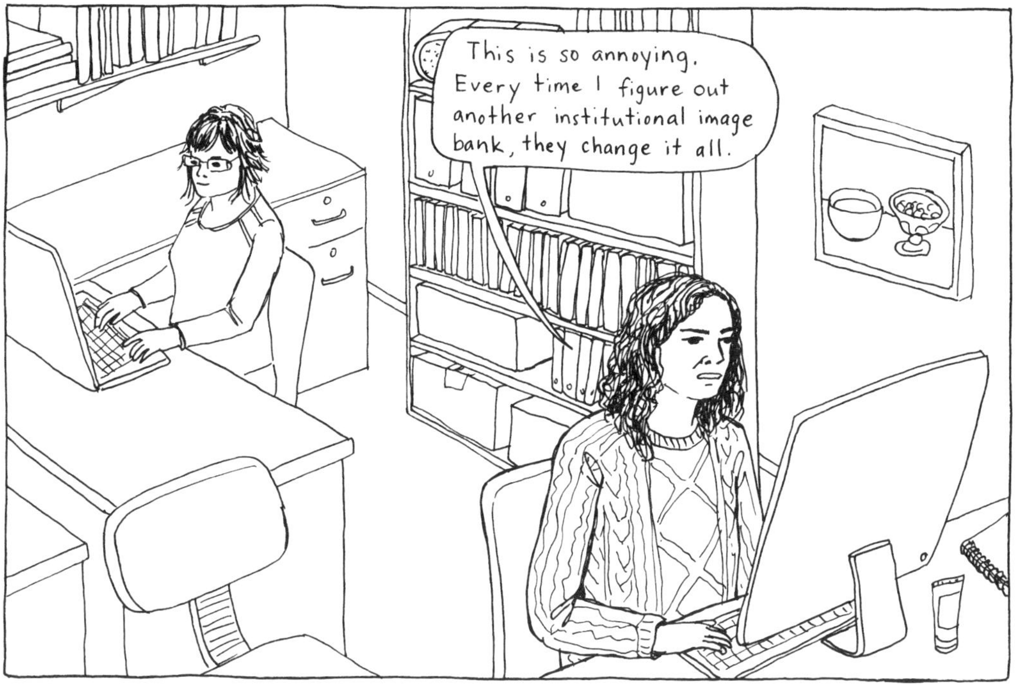
This is so annoying. Every time I figure out another institutional image bank, they change it all.

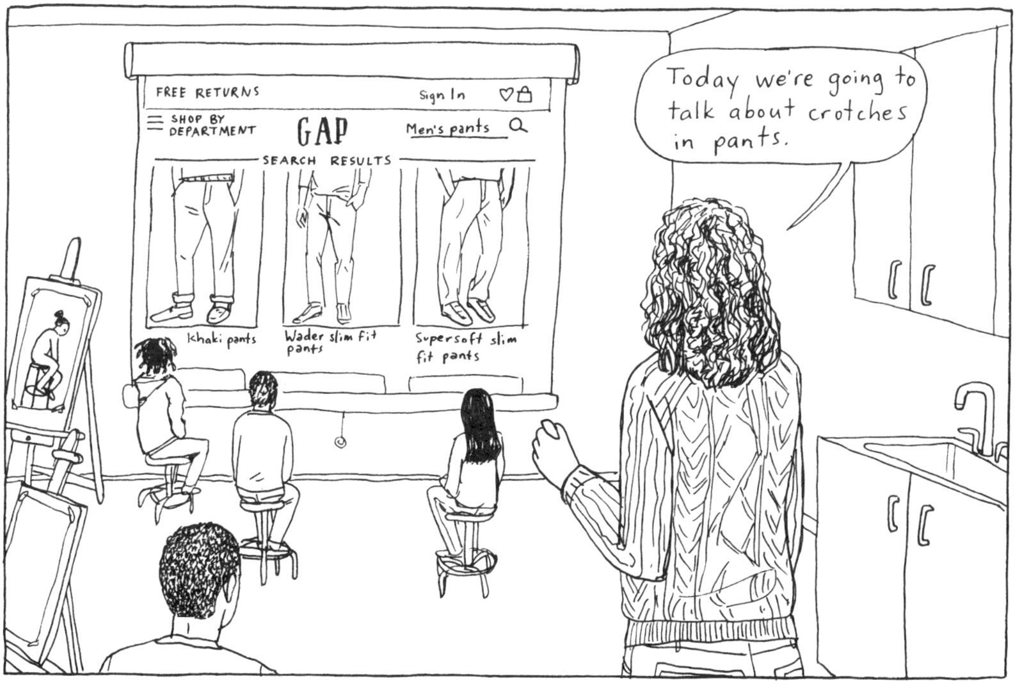
FREE RETURNS
Sign In
SHOP BY DEPARTMENT
GAP
Men's pants
SEARCH RESULTS
Khaki pants
Wader slim fit pants
Supersoft slim fit pants
Today we're going to talk about crotches in pants.

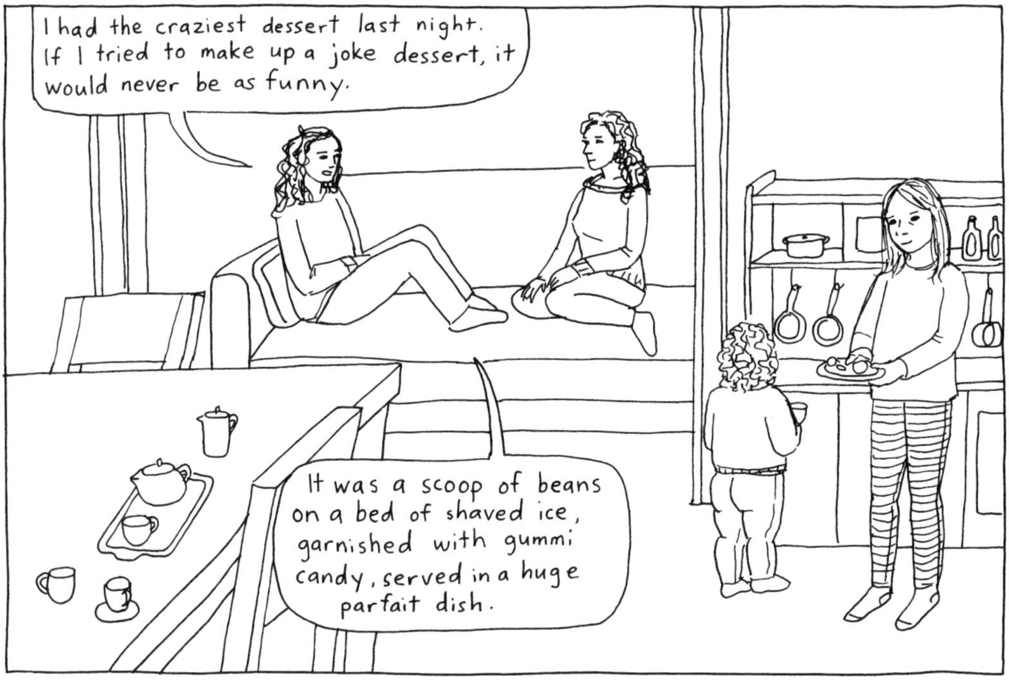
I had the craziest dessert last night. If I tried to make up a joke dessert, it would never be as funny.
It was a scoop of beans on a bed of shaved ice, garnished with gummi candy, served in a huge parfait dish.

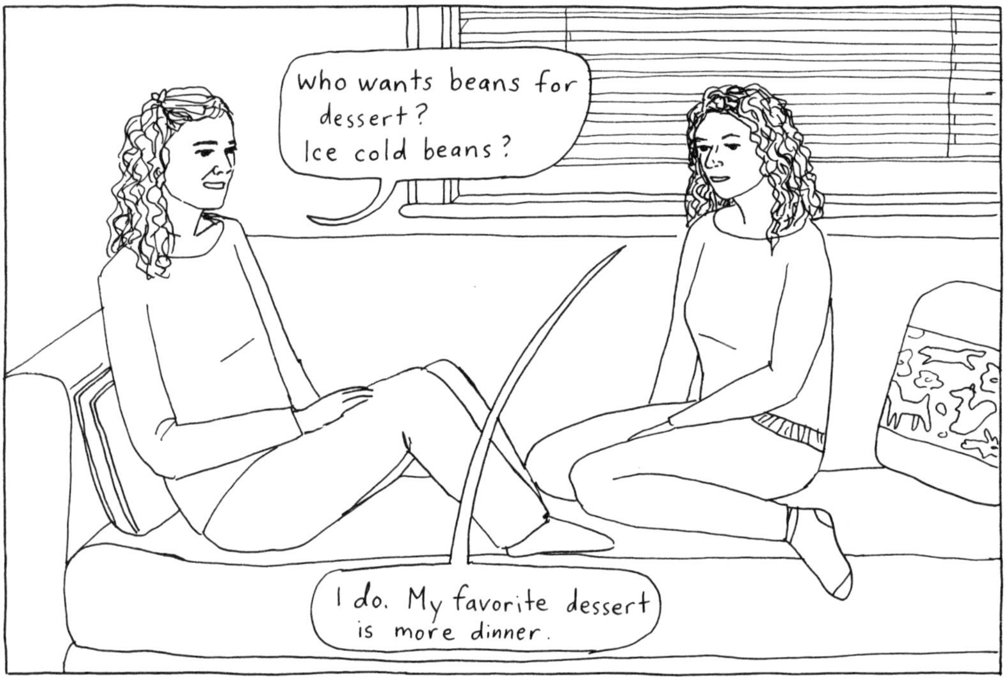
Who wants beans for dessert? Ice cold beans?
I do. My favorite dessert is more dinner.

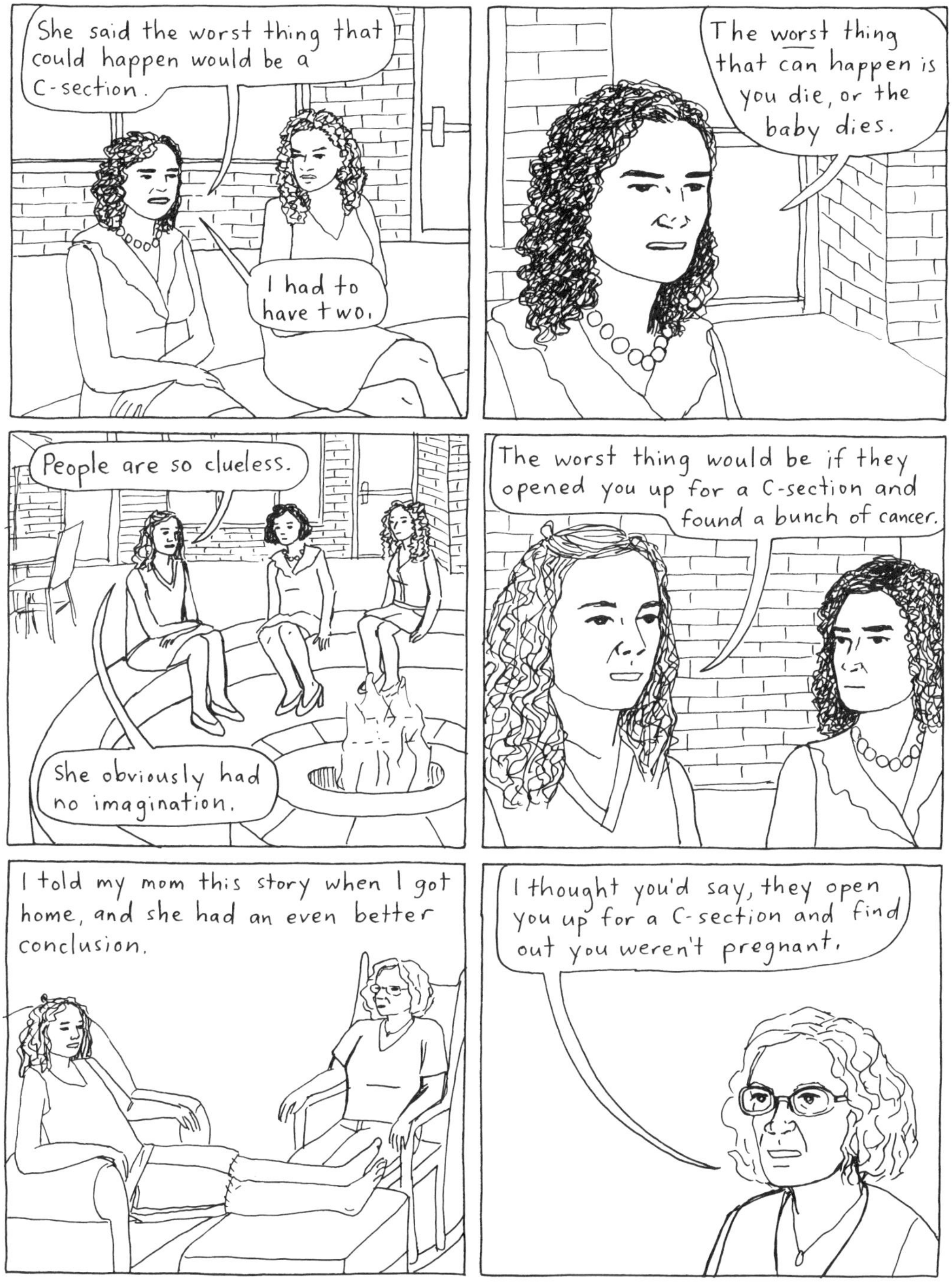
She said the worst thing that could happen would be a C-section.
I had to have two.
The worst thing that can happen is you die, or the baby dies.
People are so clueless.
She obviously had no imagination.
The worst thing would be if they opened you up for a C-section and found a bunch of cancer.
I told my mom this story when I got home, and she had an even better conclusion.
I thought you'd say, they open you up for a C-section and find out you weren't pregnant.

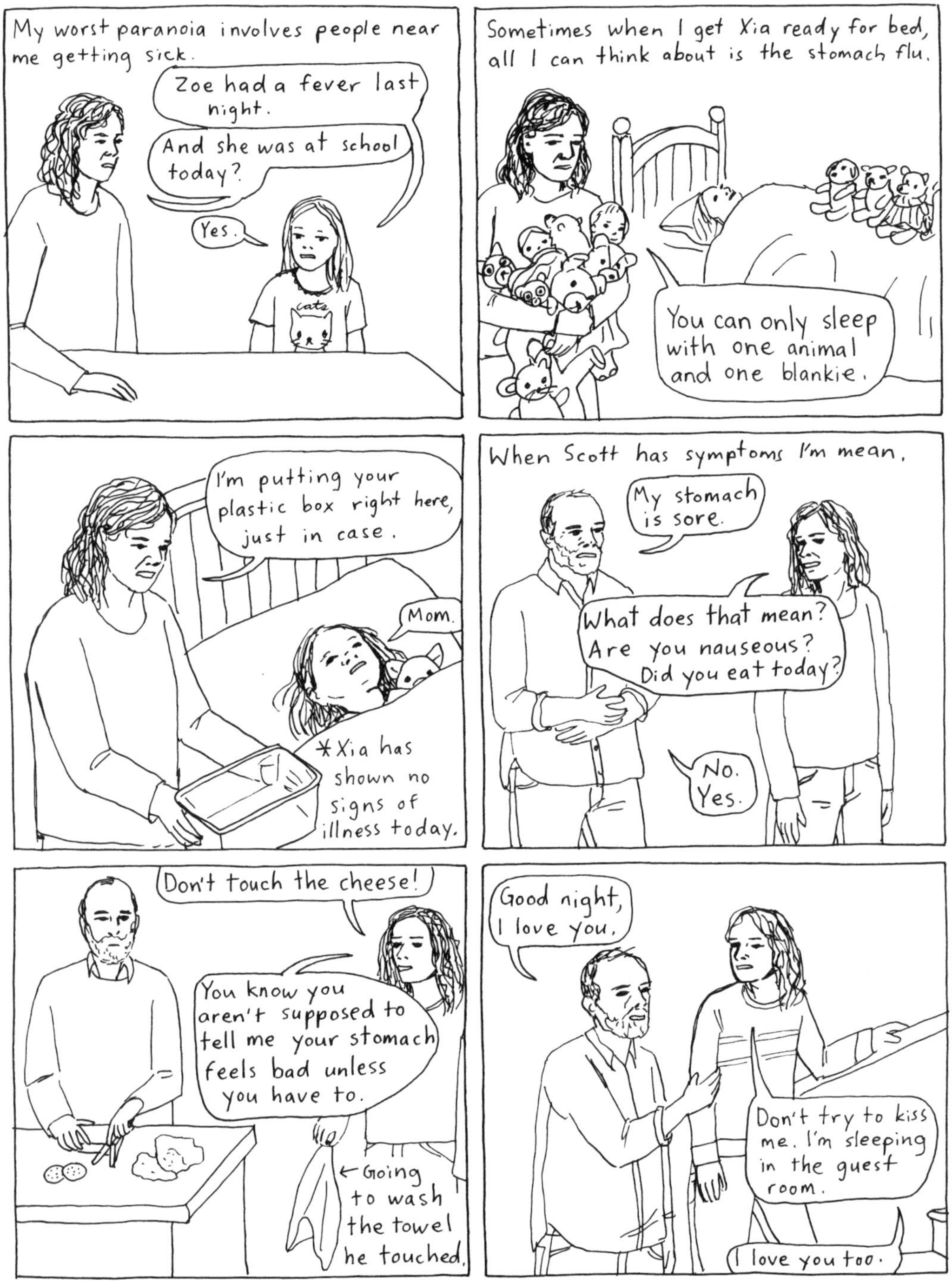
My worst paranoia involves people near me getting sick.
Zoe had a fever last night.
And she was at school today?
Yes.
Sometimes when I get Xia ready for bed, all I can think about is the stomach flu.
You can only sleep with one animal and one blankie.
I'm putting your plastic box right here, just in case.
Mom.
*Xia has shown no signs of illness today.
When Scott has symptoms I'm mean.
My stomach is sore.
What does that mean? Are you nauseous? Did you eat today?
No. Yes.
Don't touch the cheese!
You know you aren't supposed to tell me your stomach feels bad unless you have to.
← Going to wash the towel he touched.
Good night, I love you.
Don't try to kiss me. I'm sleeping in the guest room.
I love you too.

Seeing people nap depresses me.

I wish I weren't like this.

Supposedly, compassionate care-giving boosts your immune system.

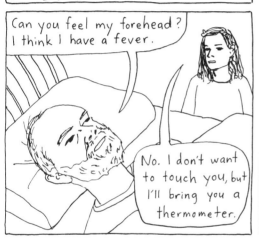

Can you feel my forehead? I think I have a fever.

No. I don't want to touch you, but I'll bring you a thermometer.

I'm feeling better. C'mere.

Did you shower yet?

I can't stand to imagine what it might be like to have a genuinely sick family member,

Clover has constipation.

That type of thinking, "It could be worse," only increases my anxiety. It never boosts my gratitude.

It could be worse.

No! I couldn't stand that!

195

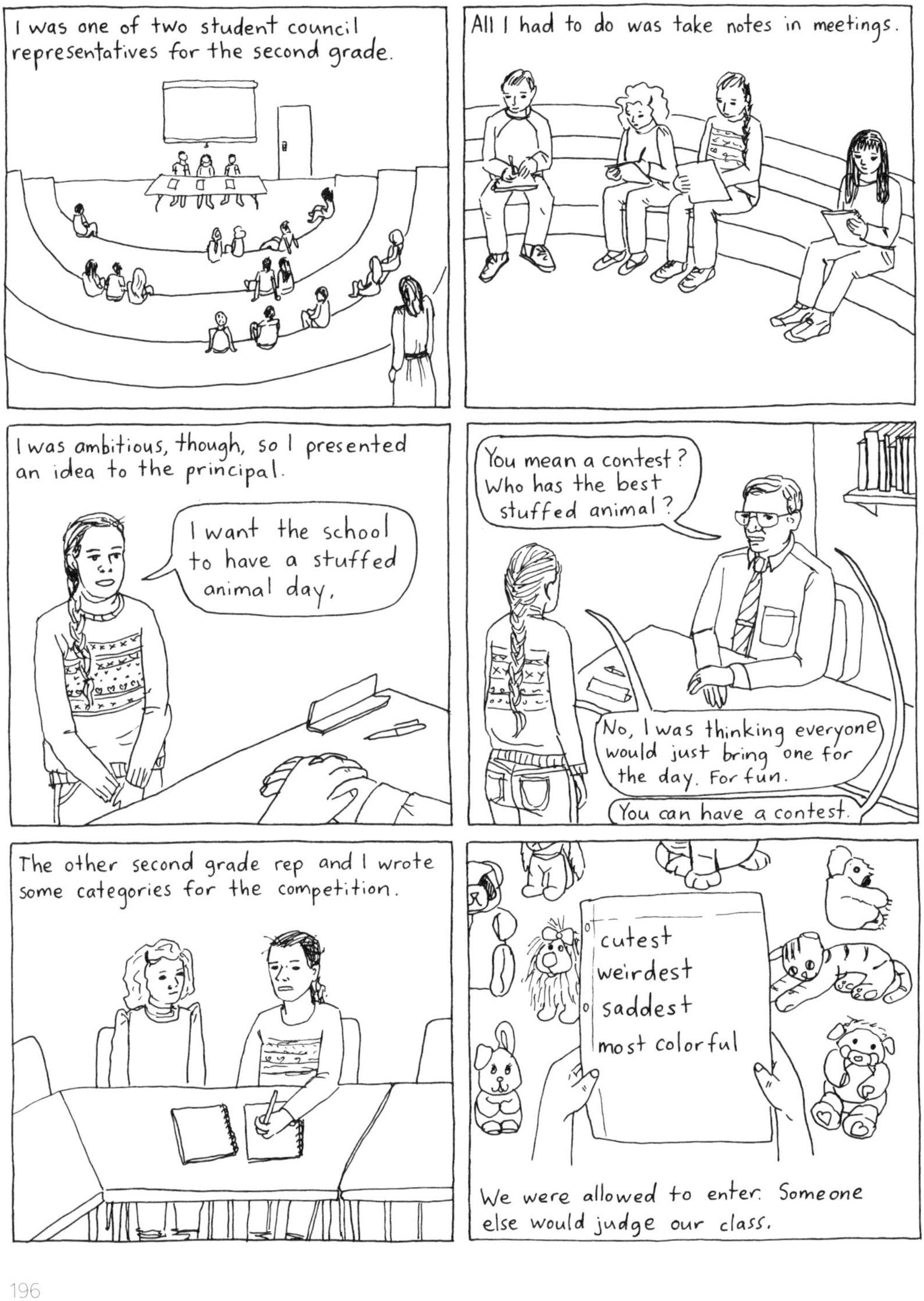

I was one of two student council representatives for the second grade.
All I had to do was take notes in meetings.
I was ambitious, though, so I presented an idea to the principal.
I want the school to have a stuffed animal day.
You mean a contest? Who has the best stuffed animal?
No, I was thinking everyone would just bring one for the day. For fun.
You can have a contest.
The other second grade rep and I wrote some categories for the competition.
cutest
weirdest
saddest
most colorful
We were allowed to enter. Someone else would judge our class.

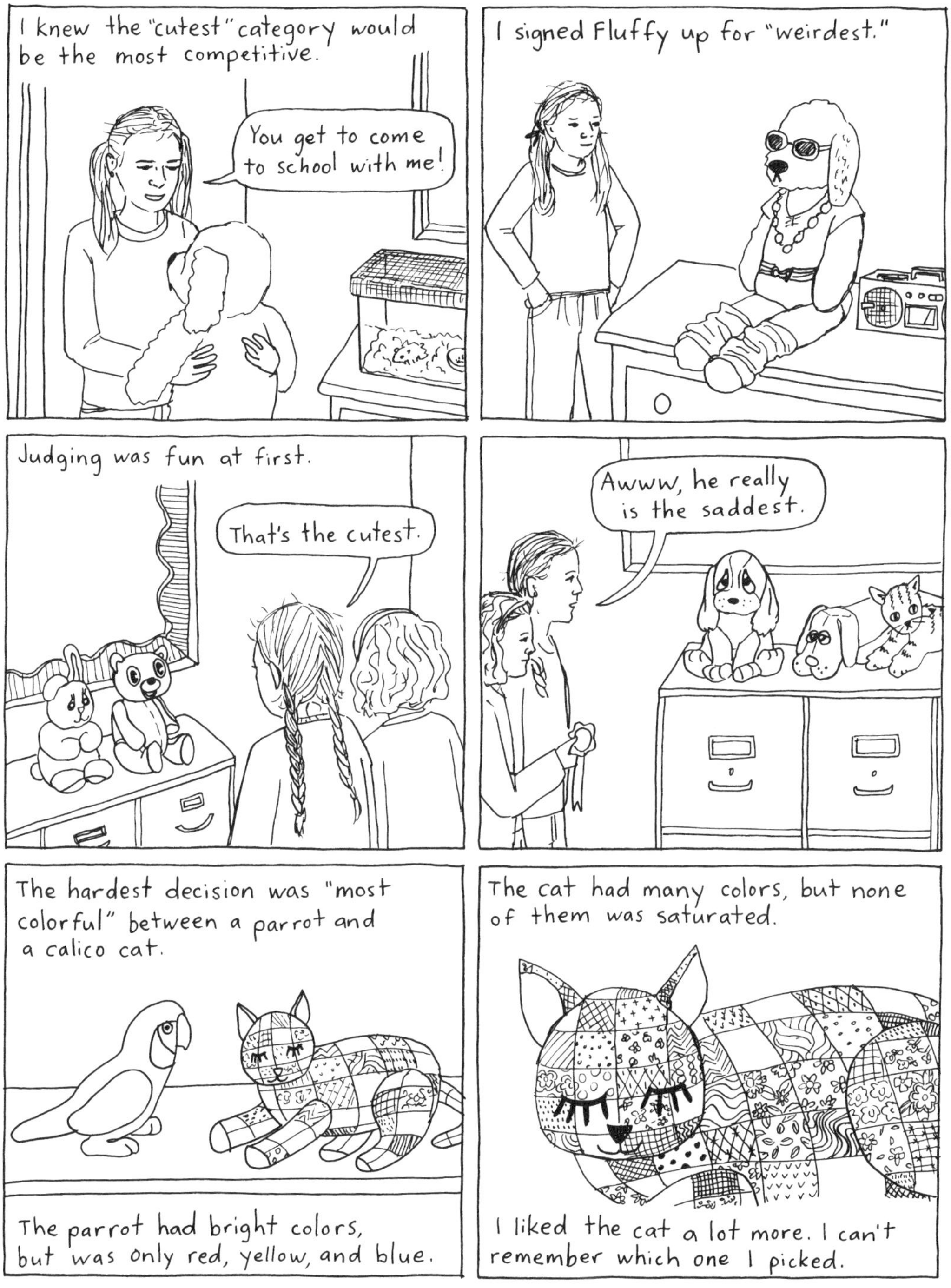

I knew the "cutest" category would be the most competitive.
You get to come to school with me!
I signed Fluffy up for "weirdest."
Judging was fun at first.
That's the cutest.
Awww, he really is the saddest.
The hardest decision was "most colorful" between a parrot and a calico cat.
The parrot had bright colors, but was only red, yellow, and blue.
The cat had many colors, but none of them was saturated.
I liked the cat a lot more. I can't remember which one I picked.

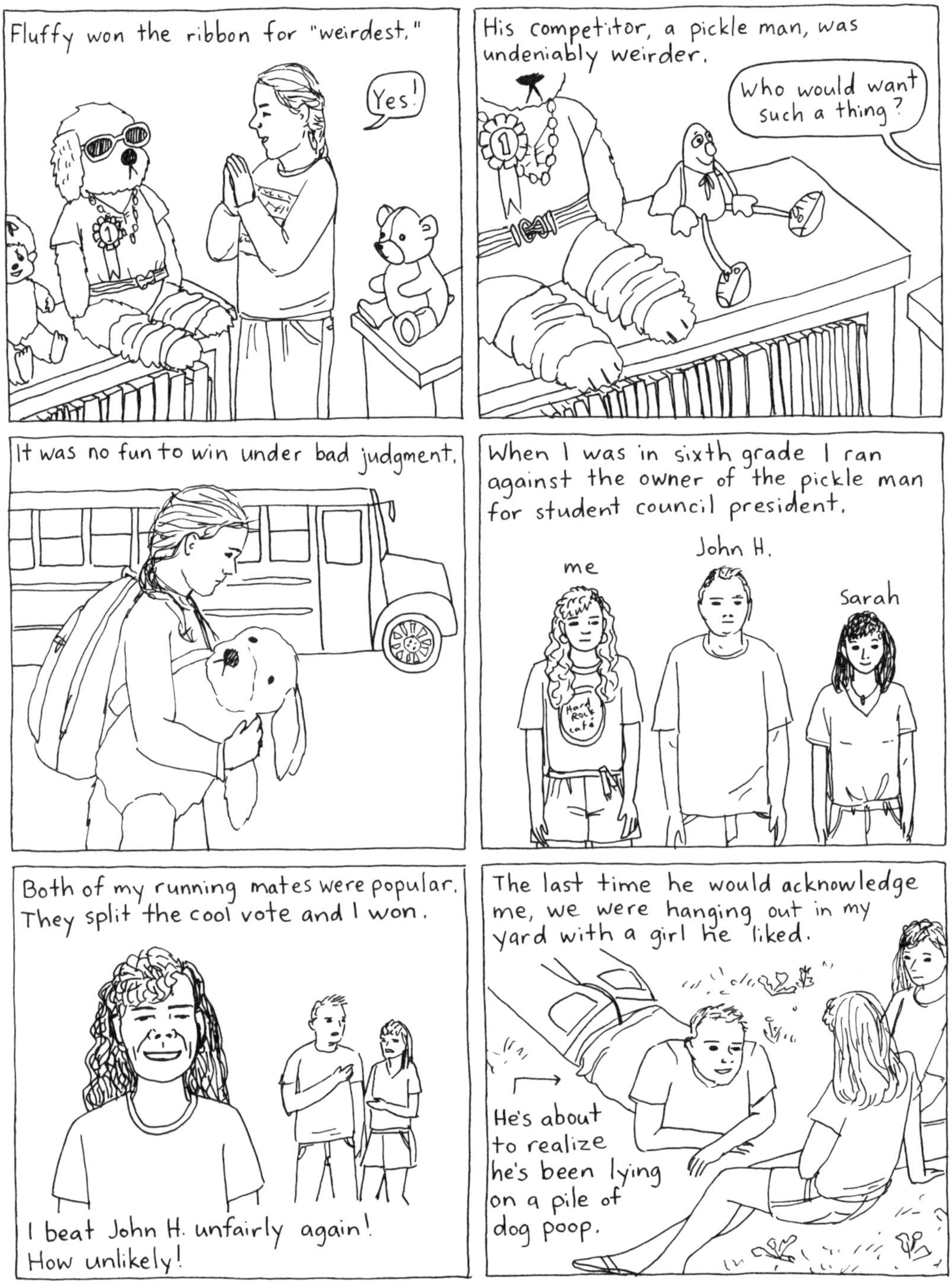
Fluffy won the ribbon for "weirdest."
Yes!
His competitor, a pickle man, was undeniably weirder.
Who would want such a thing?
It was no fun to win under bad judgment.
When I was in sixth grade I ran against the owner of the pickle man for student council president.
me
John H.
Sarah
Hard Rock café
Both of my running mates were popular. They split the cool vote and I won.
I beat John H. unfairly again! How unlikely!
The last time he would acknowledge me, we were hanging out in my yard with a girl he liked.
He's about to realize he's been lying on a pile of dog poop.

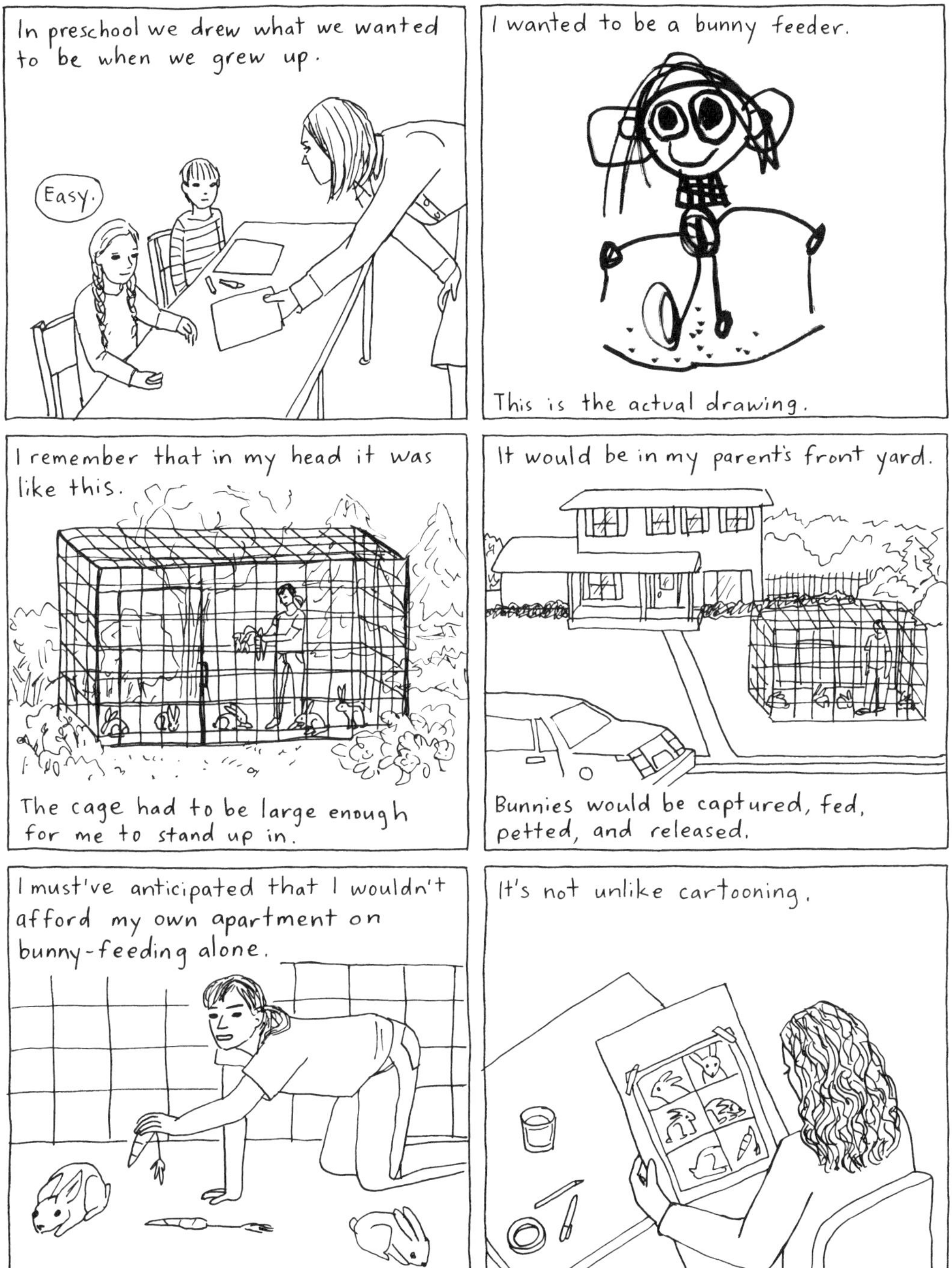
In preschool we drew what we wanted to be when we grew up.
Easy.
I wanted to be a bunny feeder.
This is the actual drawing.
I remember that in my head it was like this.
The cage had to be large enough for me to stand up in.
It would be in my parent's front yard.
Bunnies would be captured, fed, petted, and released.
I must've anticipated that I wouldn't afford my own apartment on bunny-feeding alone.
It's not unlike cartooning.

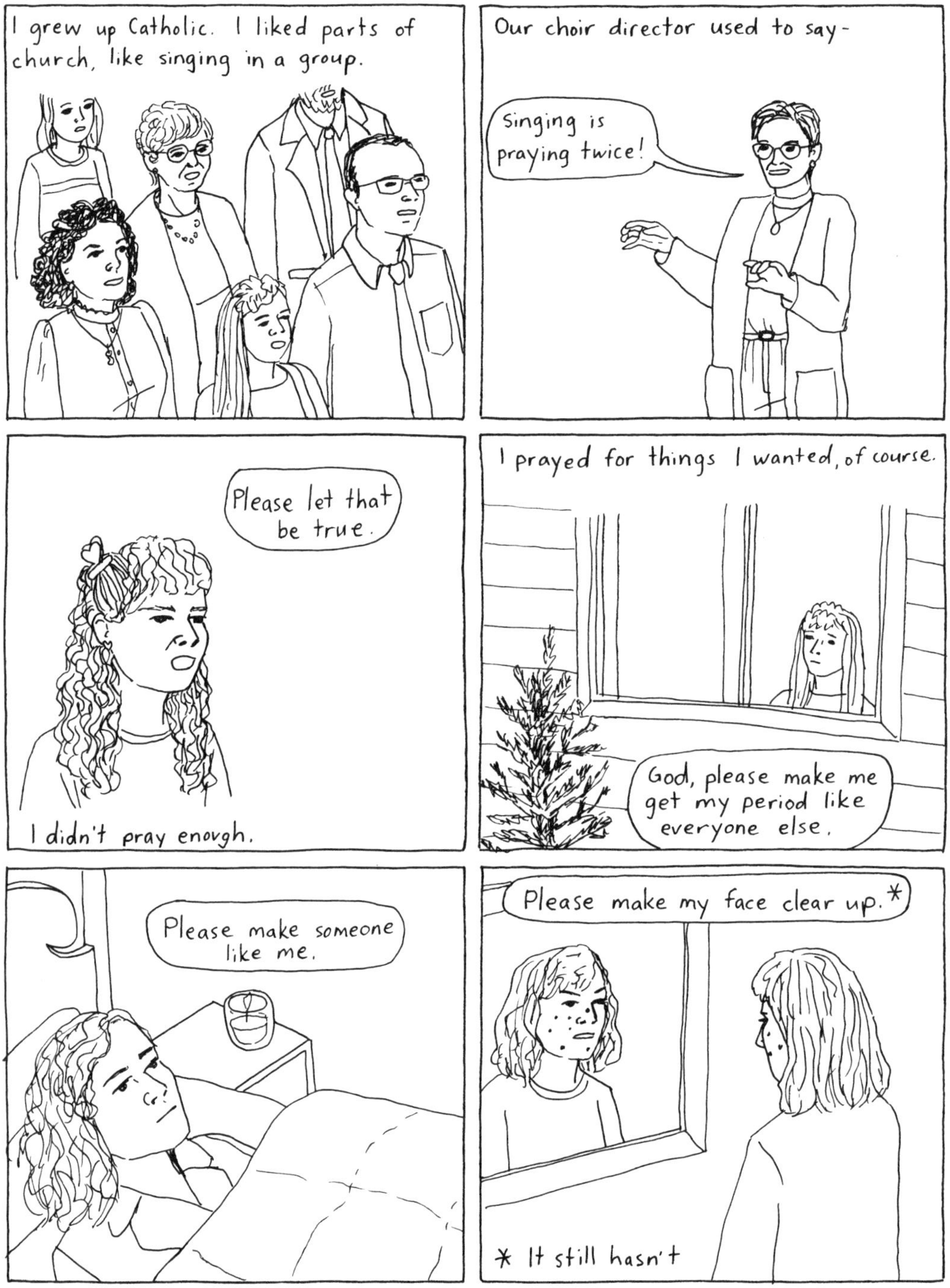
I grew up Catholic. I liked parts of church, like singing in a group.
Our choir director used to say-
Singing is praying twice!
Please let that be true.
I didn't pray enough.
I prayed for things I wanted, of course.
God, please make me get my period like everyone else.
Please make someone like me.
Please make my face clear up.*
* It still hasn't

I forgot about all the meaningful ways to pray.

Accept what is.

Don't judge.

Breathe.

The last time I recall praying to God was when I was in the hospital after my miscarriage.

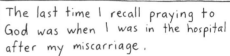

The only "decoration" on the wall was a crucifix.

I was too weak to walk across the room to the bathroom.

Don't look down.

A nurse helped me out of bed twice. Both times I fainted on the toilet instead of peeing.

Goddamn it.

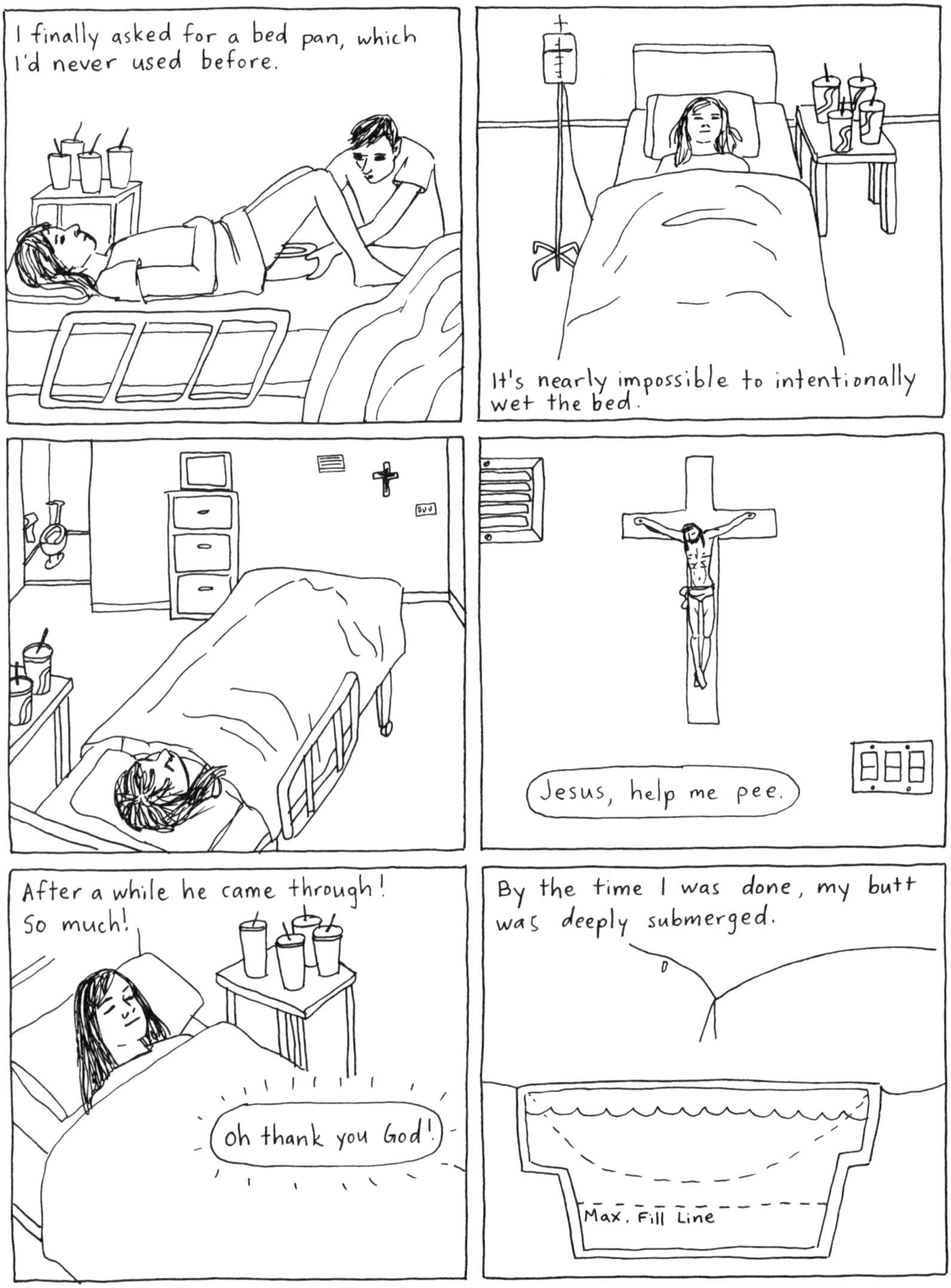
I finally asked for a bed pan, which I'd never used before.
It's nearly impossible to intentionally wet the bed.
Jesus, help me pee.
After a while he came through! So much!
Oh thank you God!
By the time I was done, my butt was deeply submerged.
Max. Fill Line

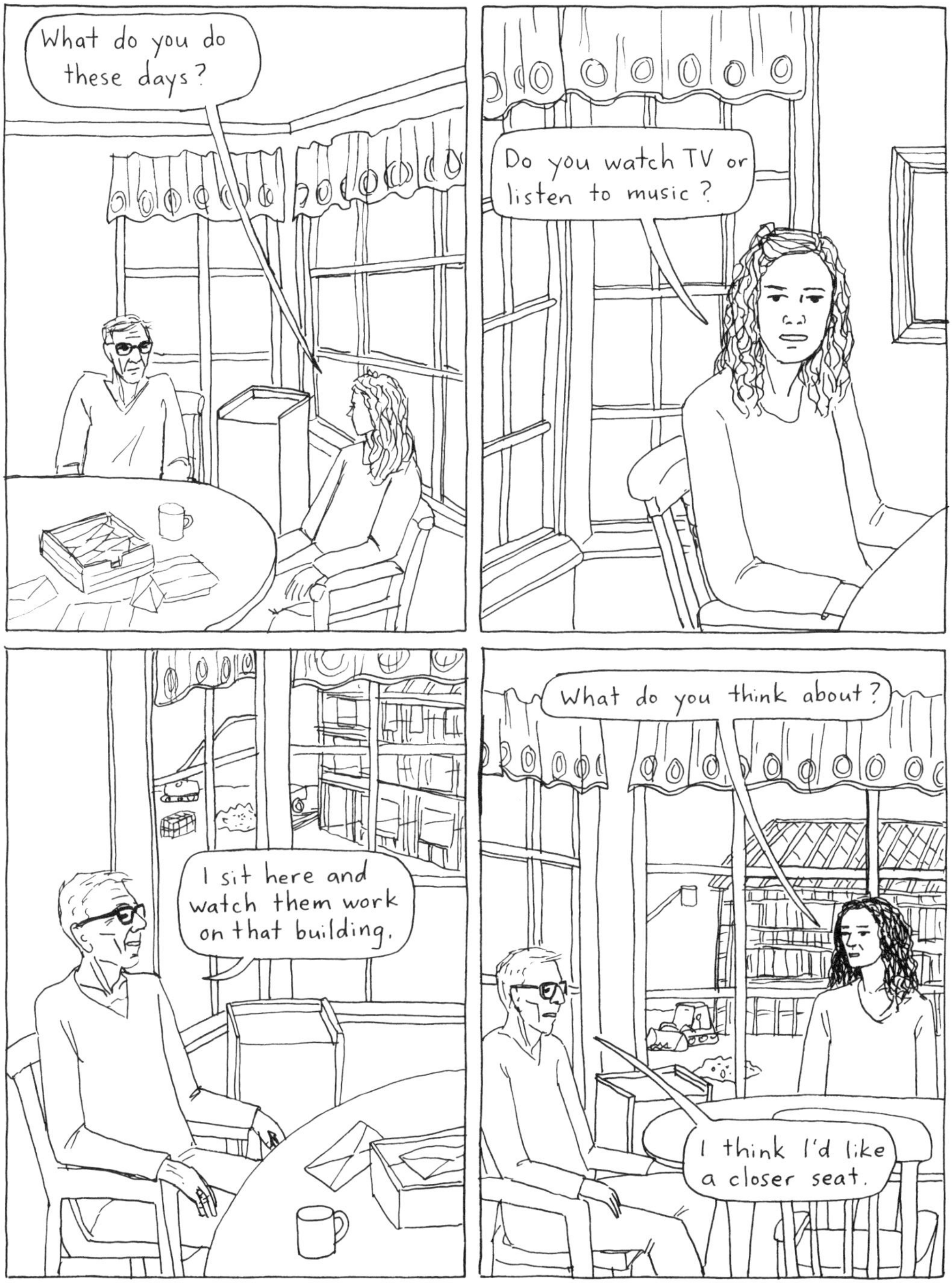
What do you do these days?
Do you watch TV or listen to music?
I sit here and watch them work on that building.
What do you think about?
I think I'd like a closer seat.

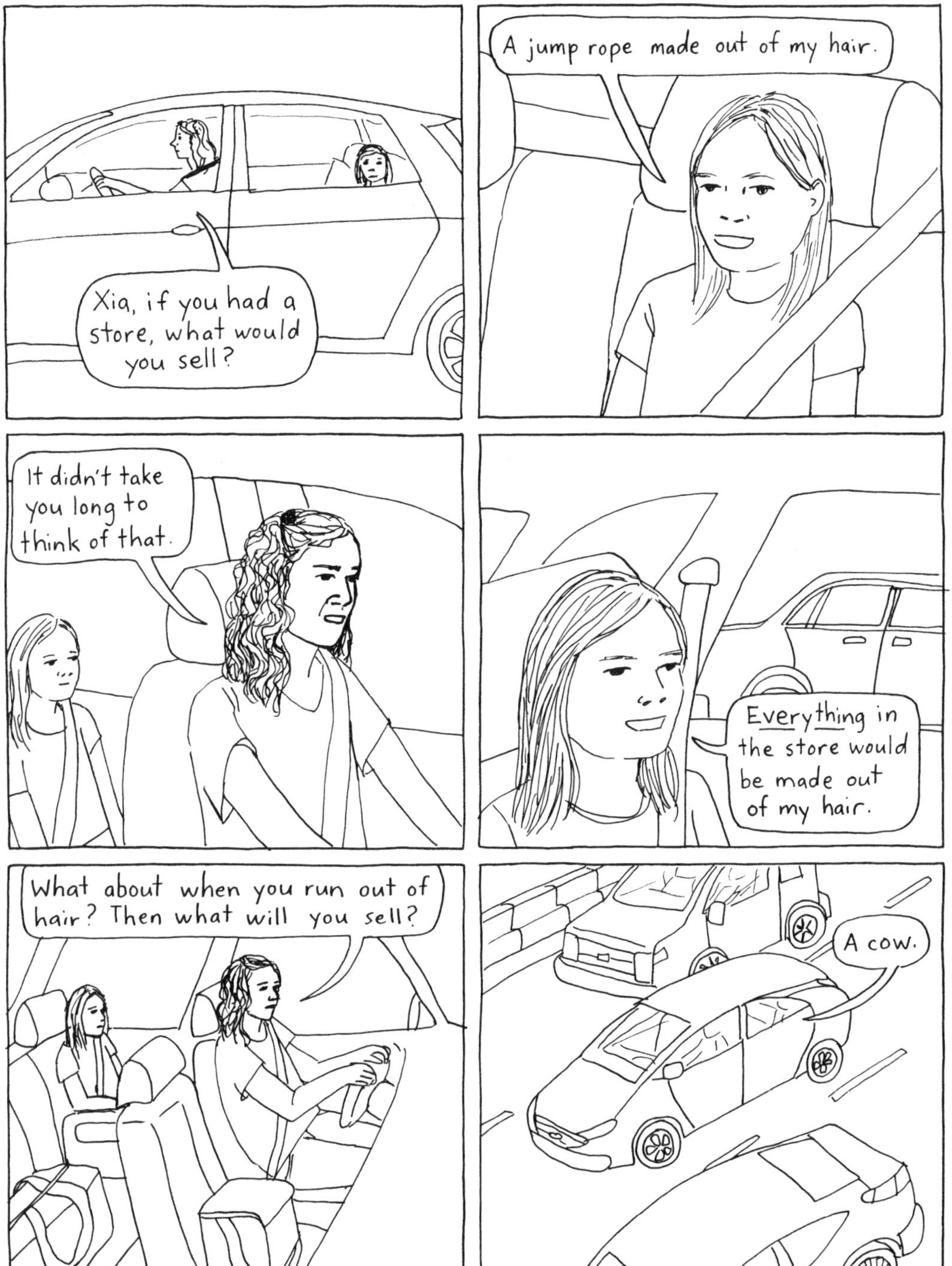
Xia, if you had a store, what would you sell?
A jump rope made out of my hair.
It didn't take you long to think of that.
Everything in the store would be made out of my hair.
What about when you run out of hair? Then what will you sell?
A cow.

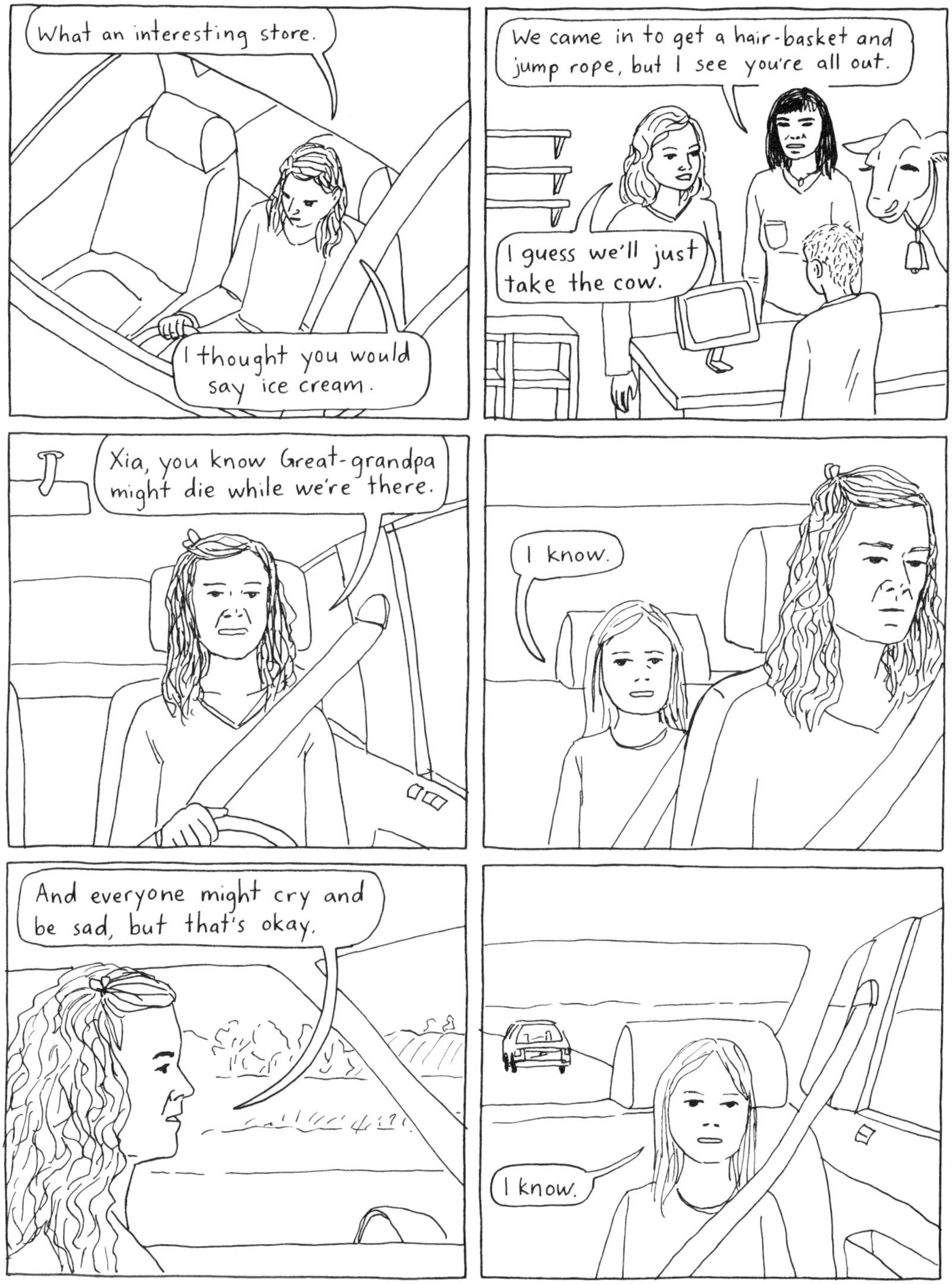
What an interesting store.
I thought you would say ice cream.
We came in to get a hair-basket and jump rope, but I see you're all out.
I guess we'll just take the cow.
Xia, you know Great-grandpa might die while we're there.
I know.
And everyone might cry and be sad, but that's okay.
I know.

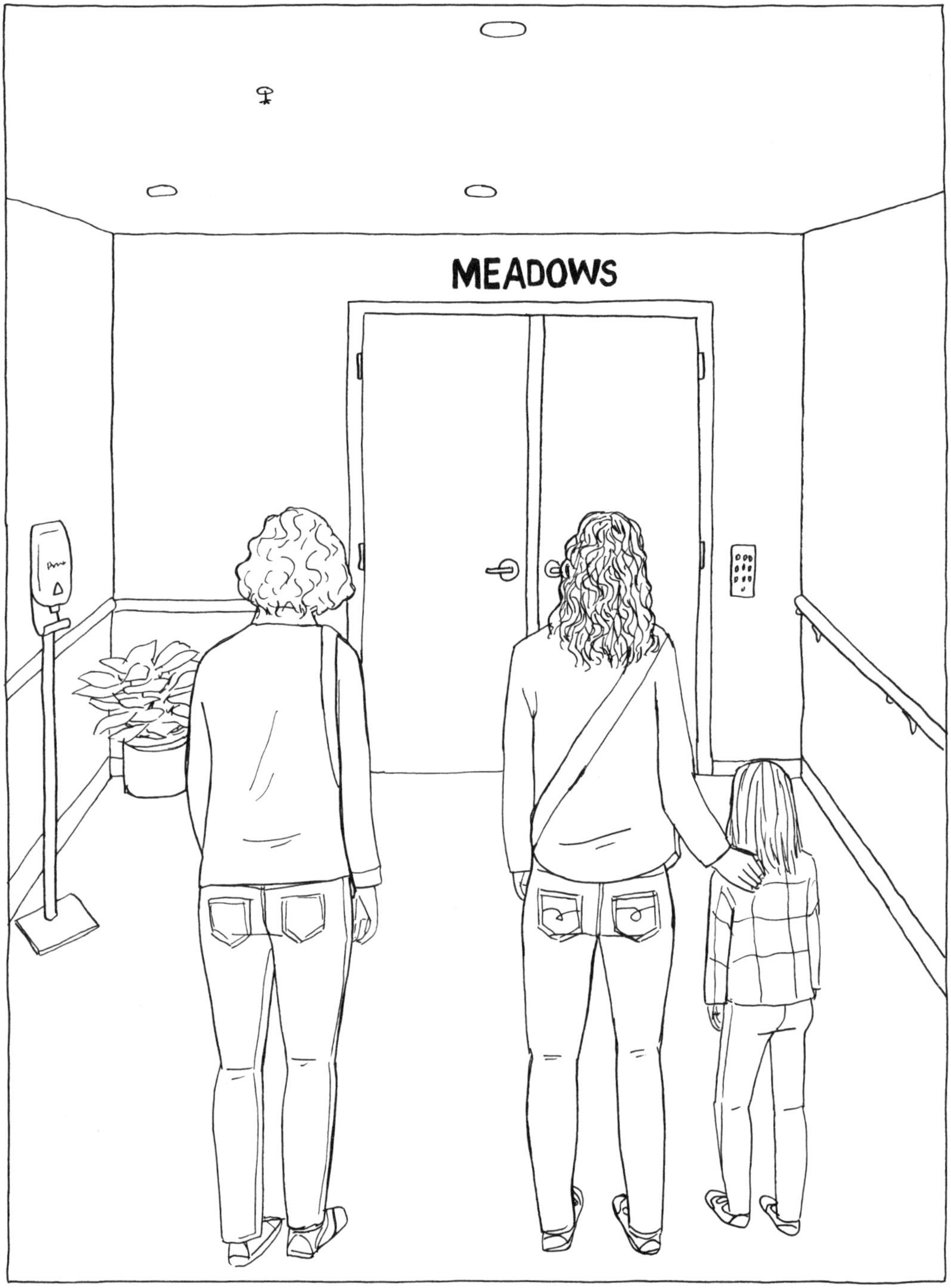
MEADOWS

Eight months ago my 98-year-old grandpa was still golfing.

Six months ago he was still driving.

Three months ago he gave a slide presentation of all the things he's made over his lifetime.

Monday he spoke a few times and responded to some questions.

Did he say "water?" Do you want some water, Dad?

I think he said "sweater."

Tuesday he was restless, moving his body without clear purpose.

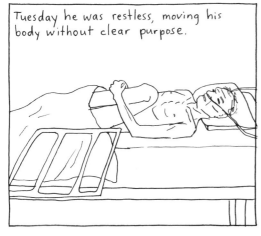

Wednesday he looked 1000 years old. His only movement was breathing, which stopped that afternoon.

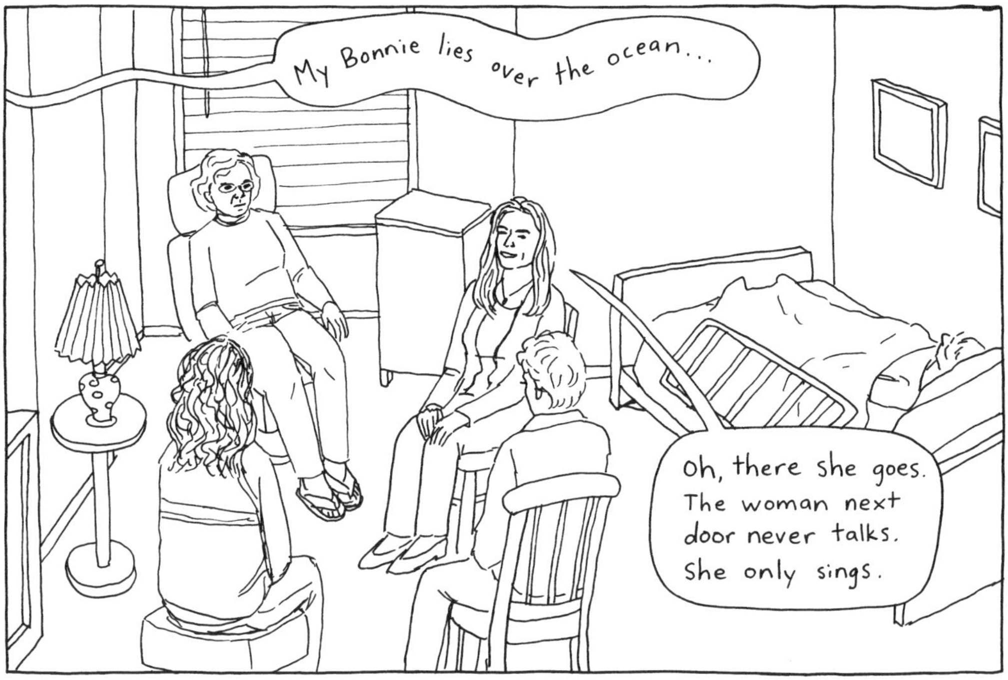
My Bonnie lies over the ocean...
Oh, there she goes. The woman next door never talks. She only sings.

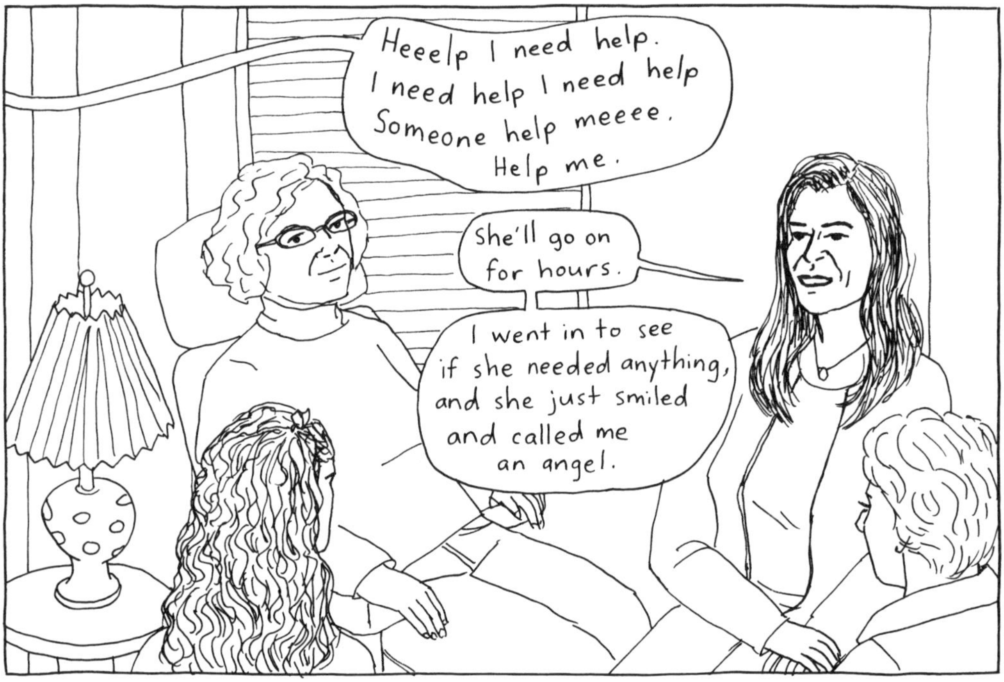
Heeelp I need help. I need help I need help Someone help meeee. Help me.
She'll go on for hours.
I went in to see if she needed anything, and she just smiled and called me an angel.

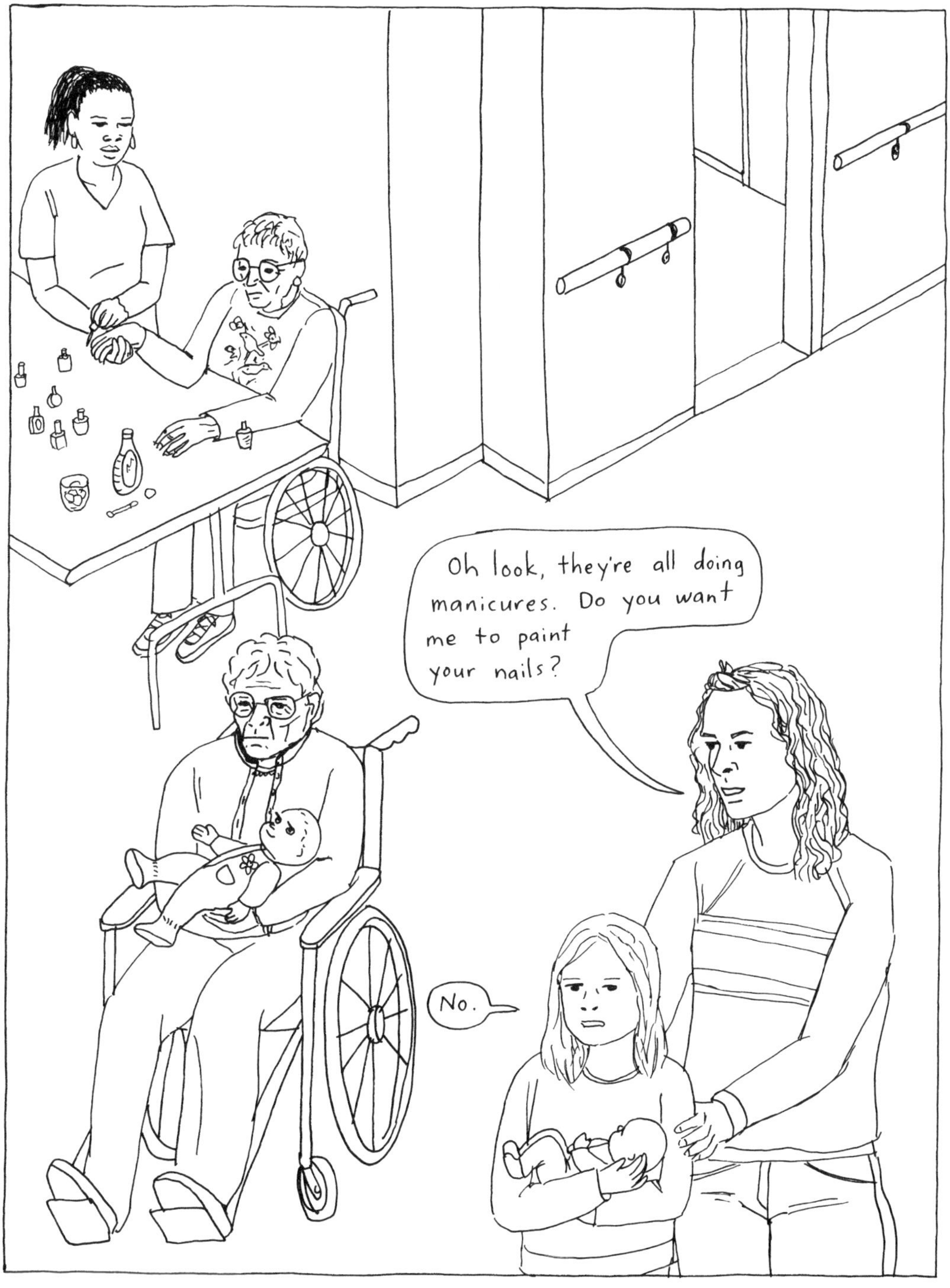
Oh look, they're all doing manicures. Do you want me to paint your nails?
No.

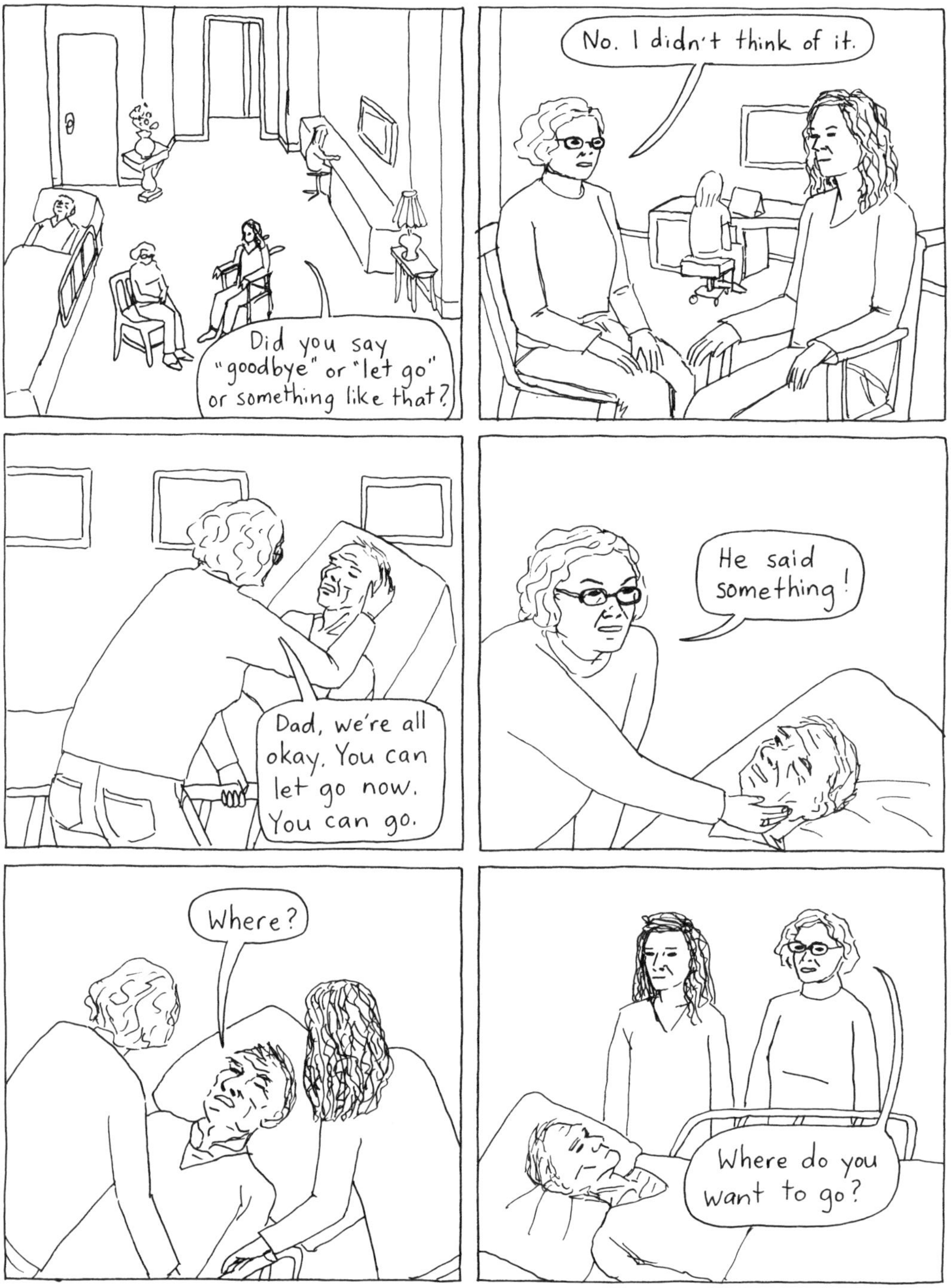
Did you say "goodbye" or "let go" or something like that?
No. I didn't think of it.
Dad, we're all okay. You can let go now. You can go.
He said something!
Where?
Where do you want to go?

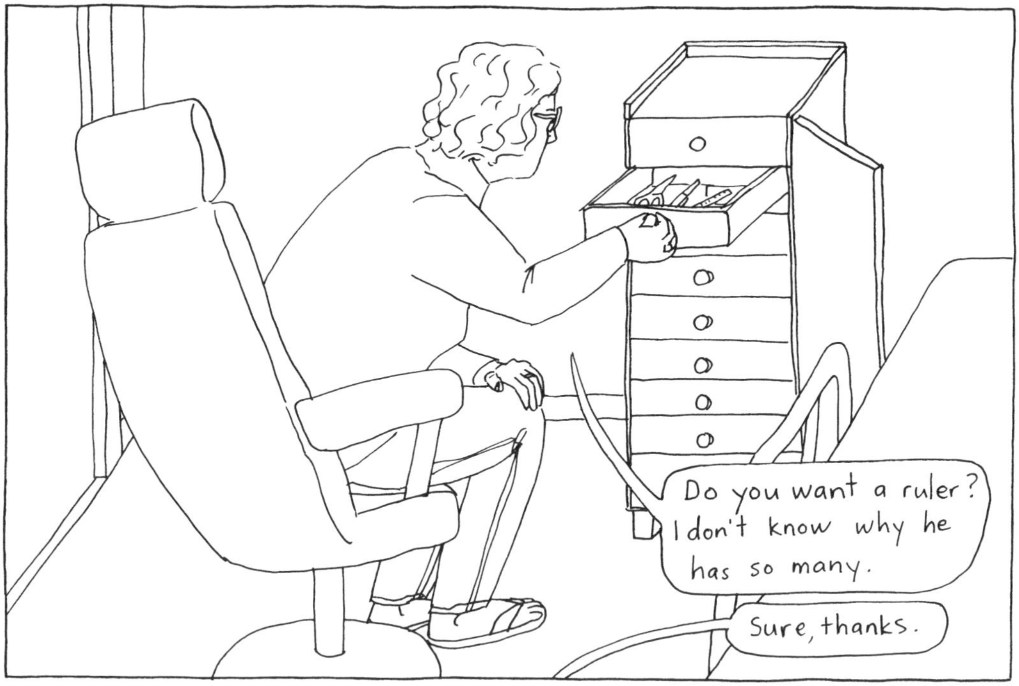
Do you want a ruler? I don't know why he has so many.
Sure, thanks.

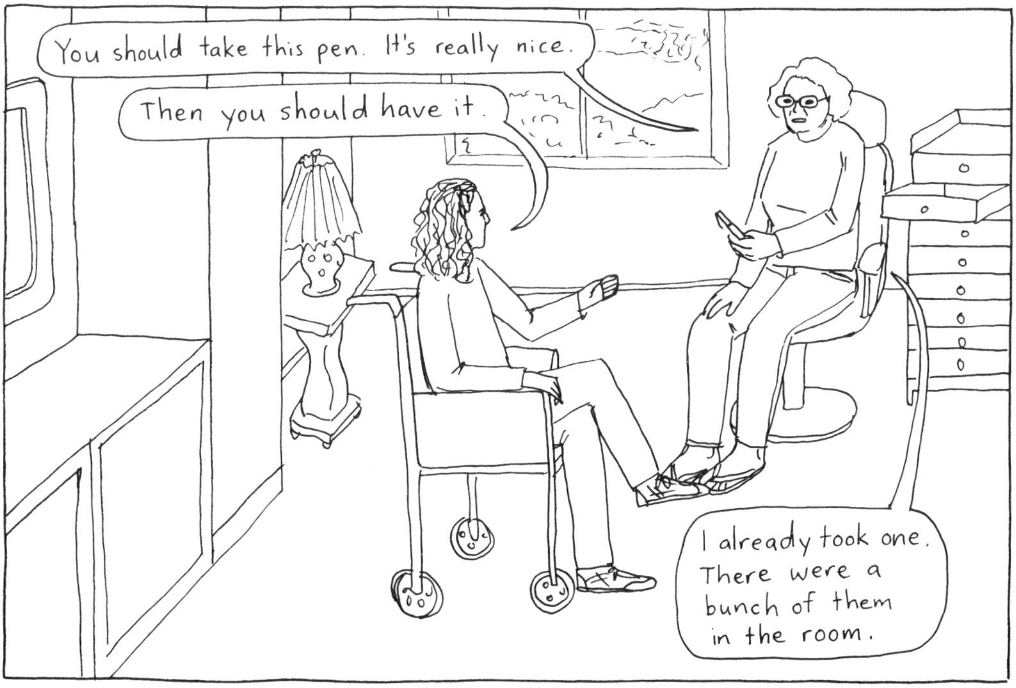
You should take this pen. It's really nice.
Then you should have it.
I already took one. There were a bunch of them in the room.

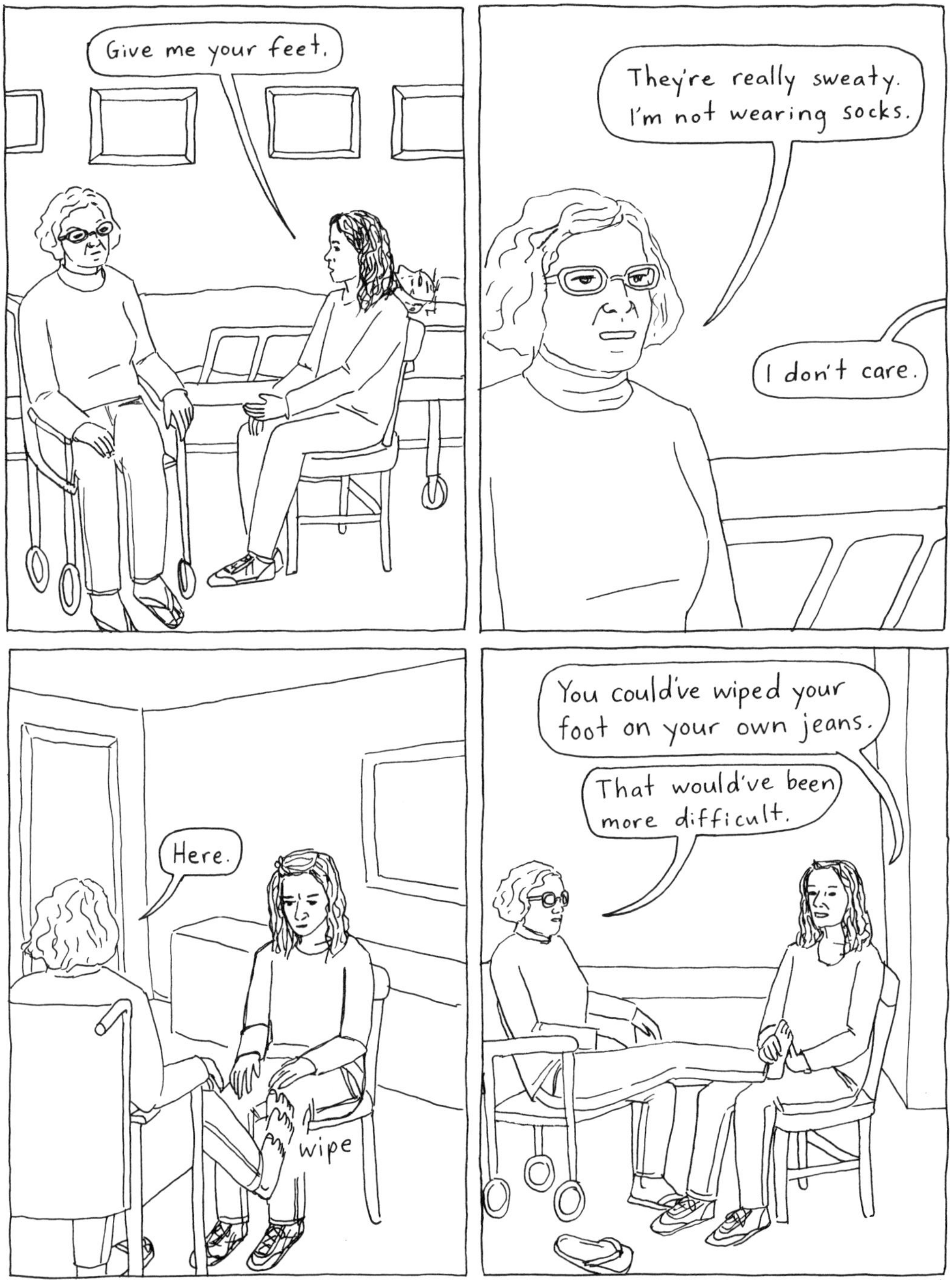

Give me your feet.
They're really sweaty. I'm not wearing socks.
I don't care.
Here.
wipe
You could've wiped your foot on your own jeans.
That would've been more difficult.

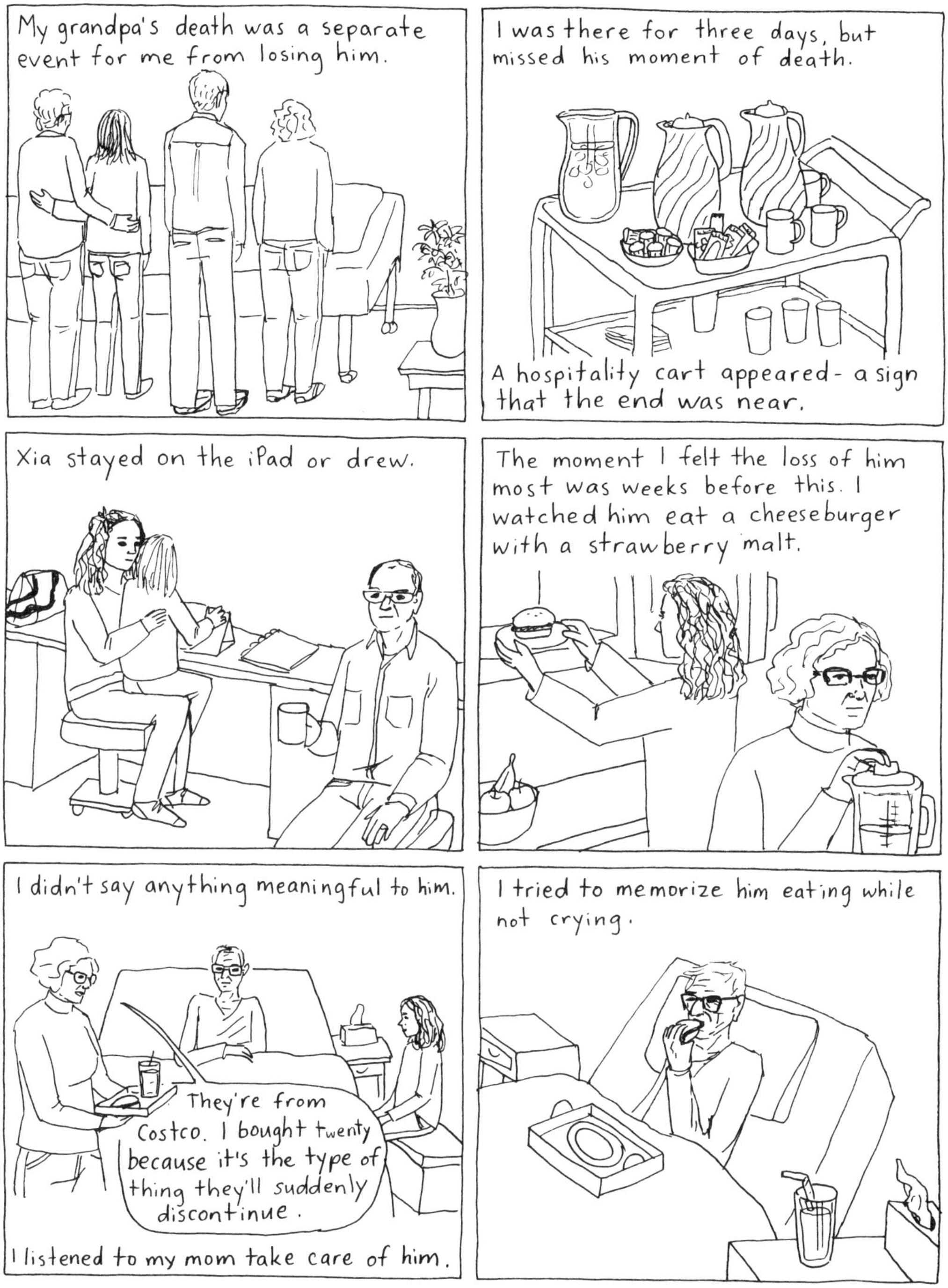
My grandpa's death was a separate event for me from losing him.
I was there for three days, but missed his moment of death.
A hospitality cart appeared - a sign that the end was near.
Xia stayed on the iPad or drew.
The moment I felt the loss of him most was weeks before this. I watched him eat a cheeseburger with a strawberry malt.
I didn't say anything meaningful to him.
They're from Costco. I bought twenty because it's the type of thing they'll suddenly discontinue.
I listened to my mom take care of him.
I tried to memorize him eating while not crying.

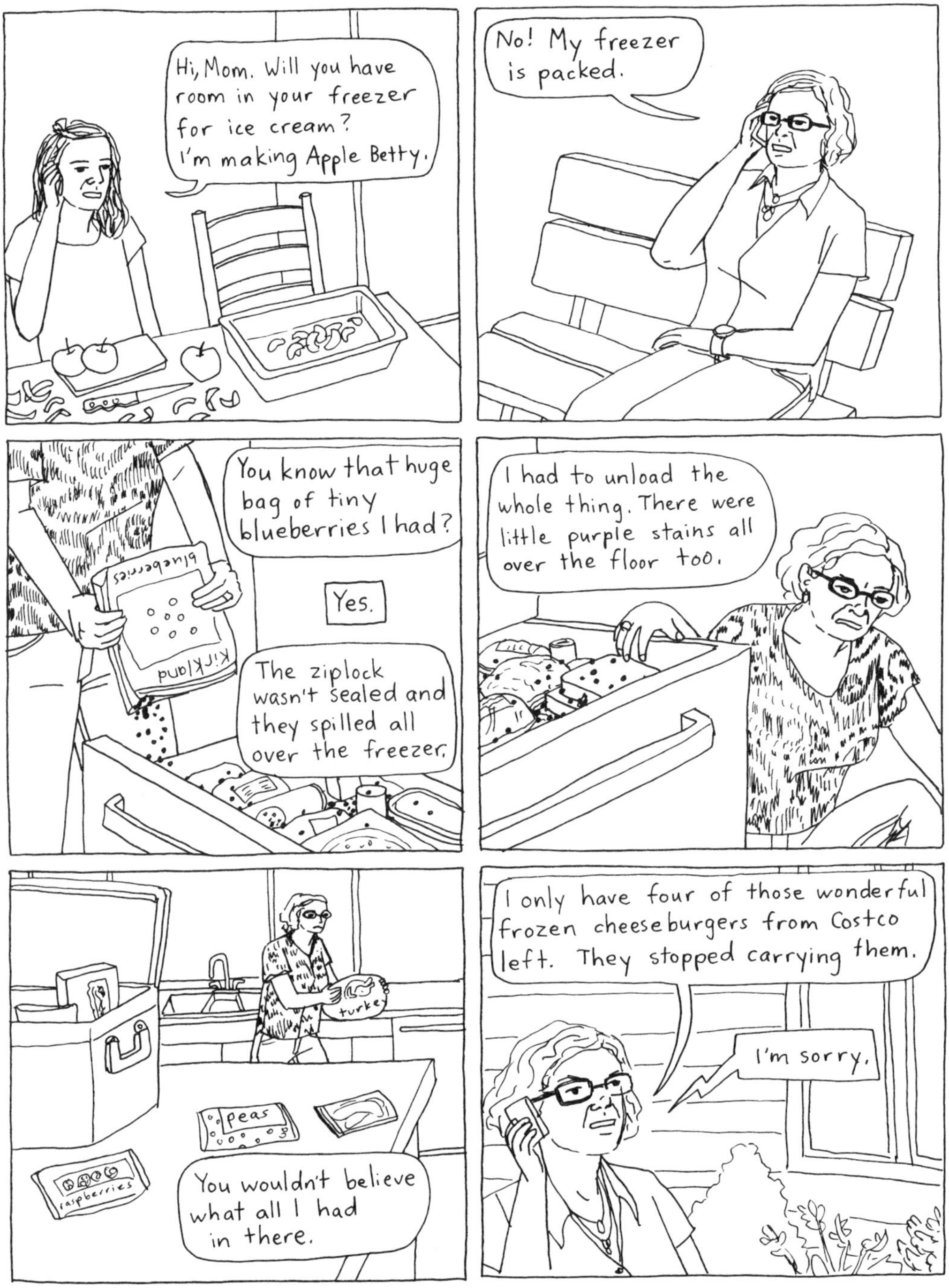
Hi, Mom. Will you have room in your freezer for ice cream? I'm making Apple Betty.
No! My freezer is packed.
You know that huge bag of tiny blueberries I had?
blueberries
Kirkland
Yes.
The ziplock wasn't sealed and they spilled all over the freezer.
I had to unload the whole thing. There were little purple stains all over the floor too.
turkey
peas
raspberries
You wouldn't believe what all I had in there.
I only have four of those wonderful frozen cheeseburgers from Costco left. They stopped carrying them.
I'm sorry.

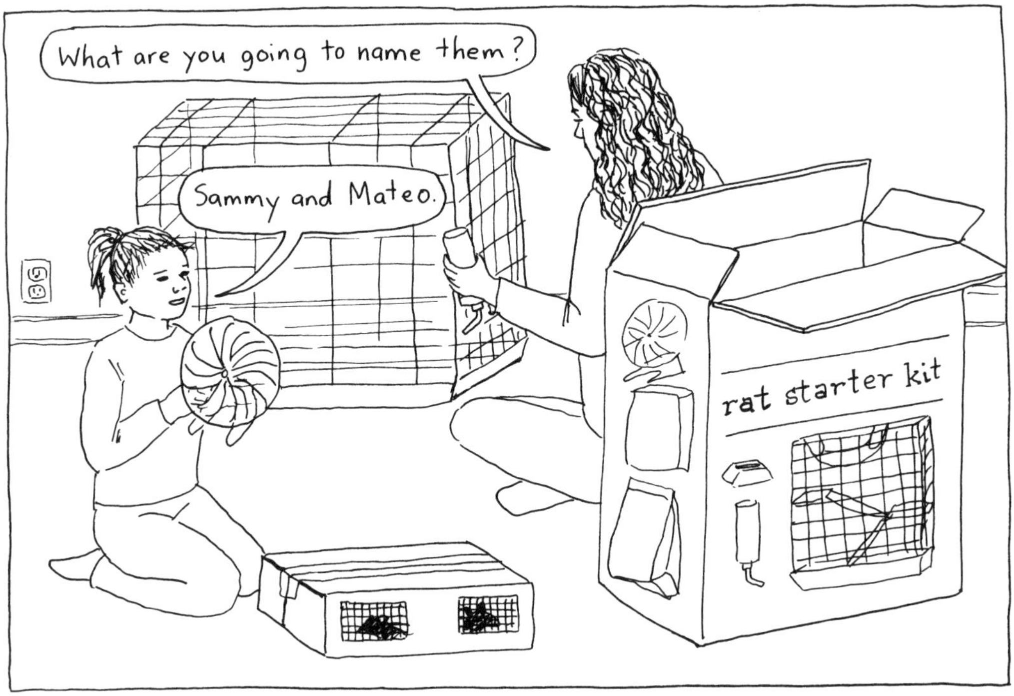
What are you going to name them?
Sammy and Mateo.
rat starter kit

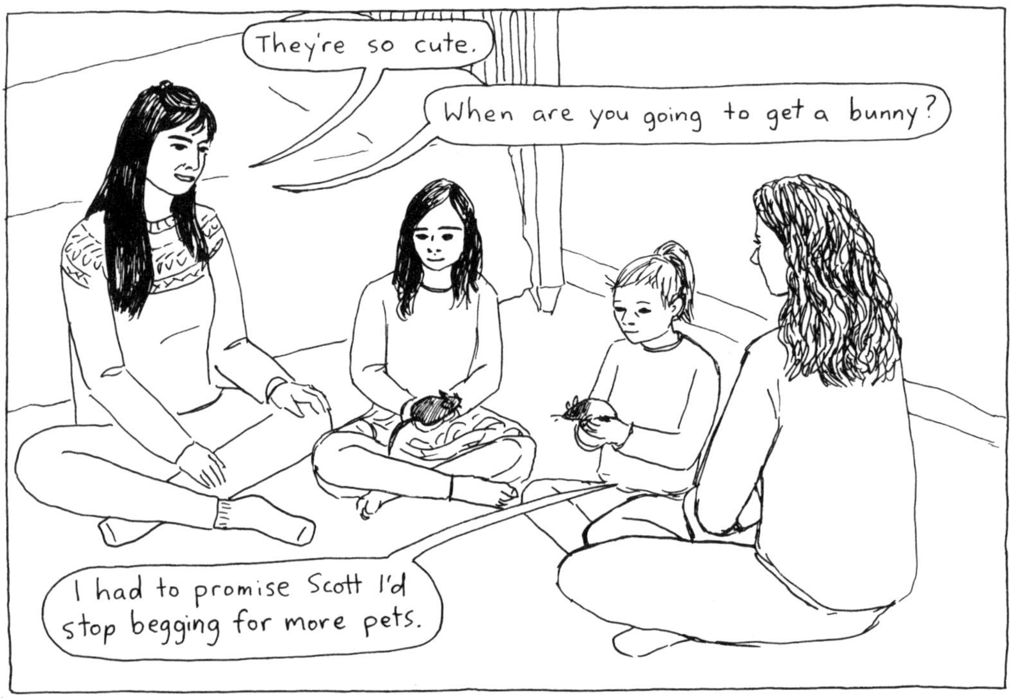
They're so cute.
When are you going to get a bunny?
I had to promise Scott I'd stop begging for more pets.

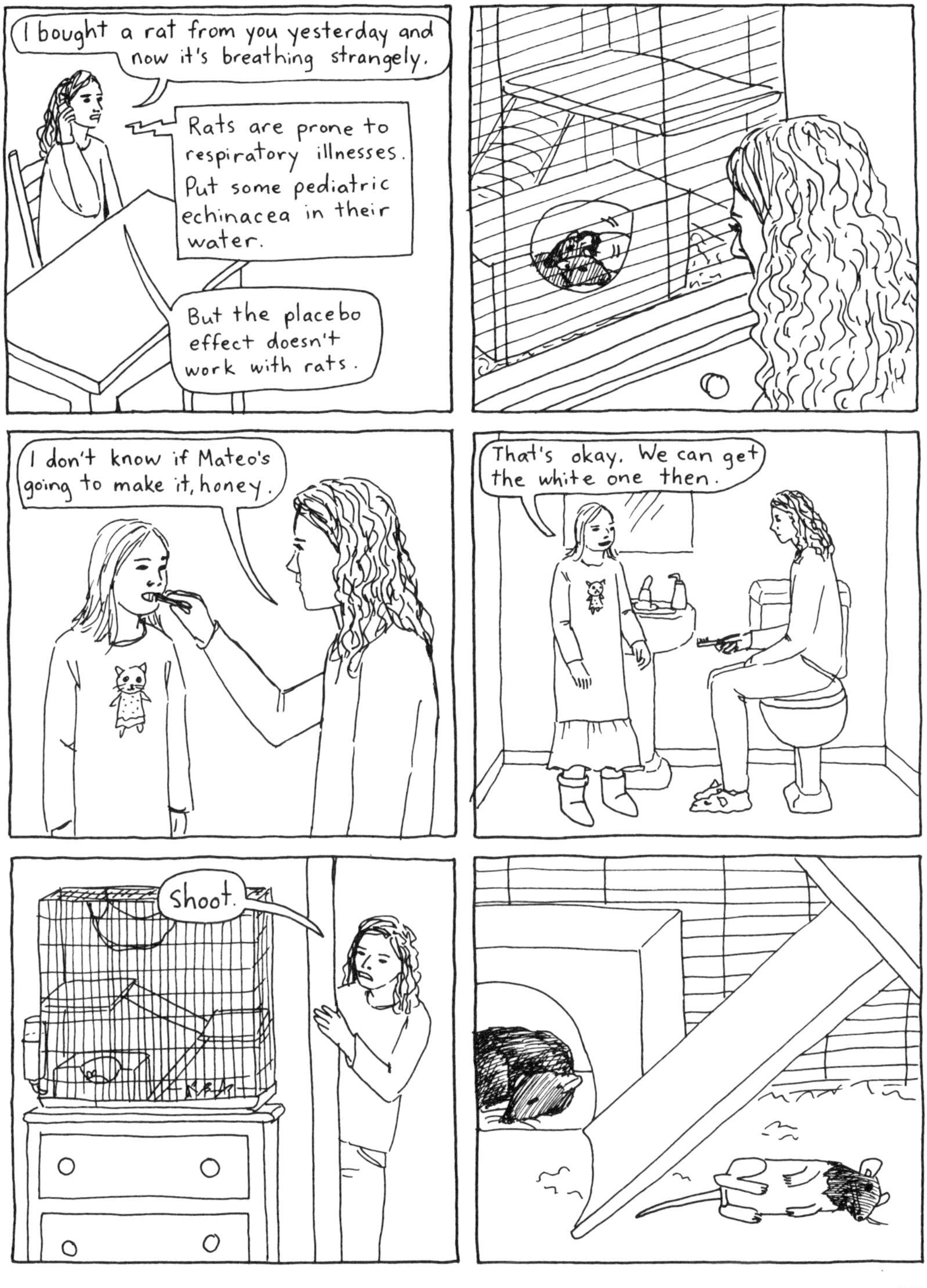
I bought a rat from you yesterday and now it's breathing strangely.
Rats are prone to respiratory illnesses. Put some pediatric echinacea in their water.
But the placebo effect doesn't work with rats.
I don't know if Mateo's going to make it, honey.
That's okay. We can get the white one then.
Shoot.

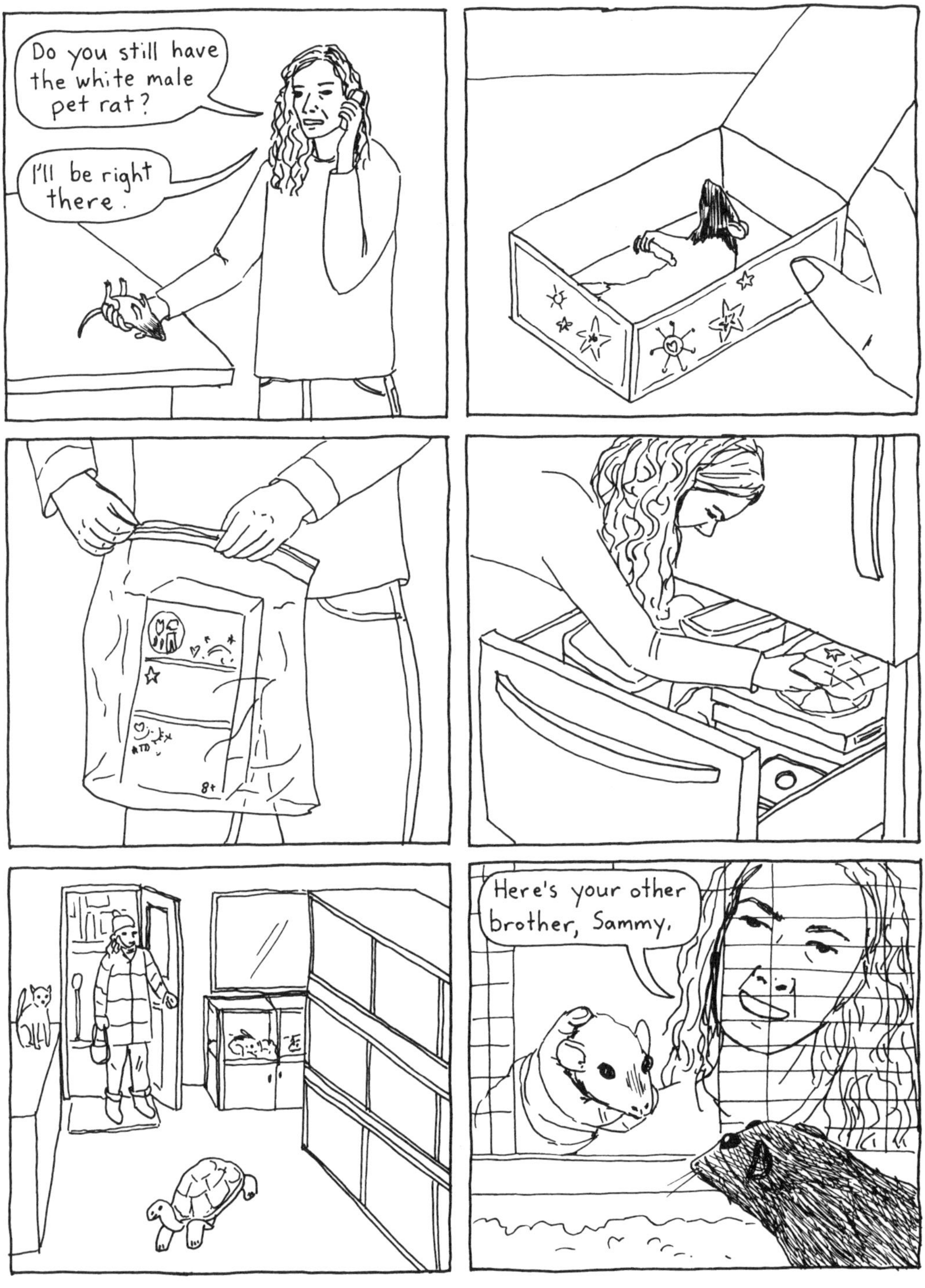
Do you still have the white male pet rat?
I'll be right there.
Here's your other brother, Sammy.

Xia, Mateo died. I'm sorry, honey.
I got the other rat for you.
Don't you want to go see your new rat yet?
In a while.
What are you going to name him?
Mateo Too. T-O-O.
Time for bed. What have you been making?
I ♥ rats!
mateo died!
come to funeral
monday after school
2018 Jan 29
mateo died!
come to funeral
monday after school
2018 Jan 29

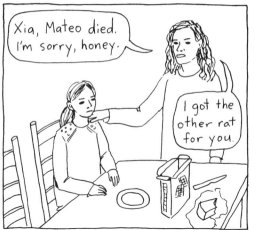

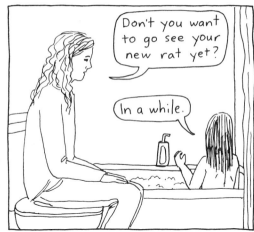

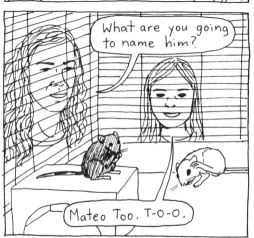

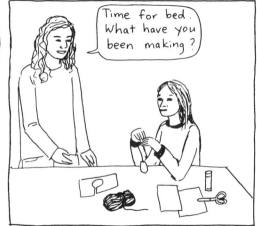

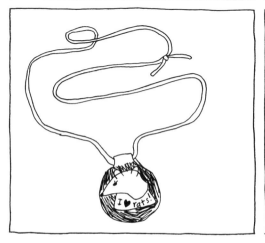

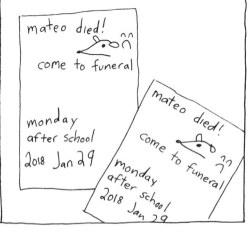

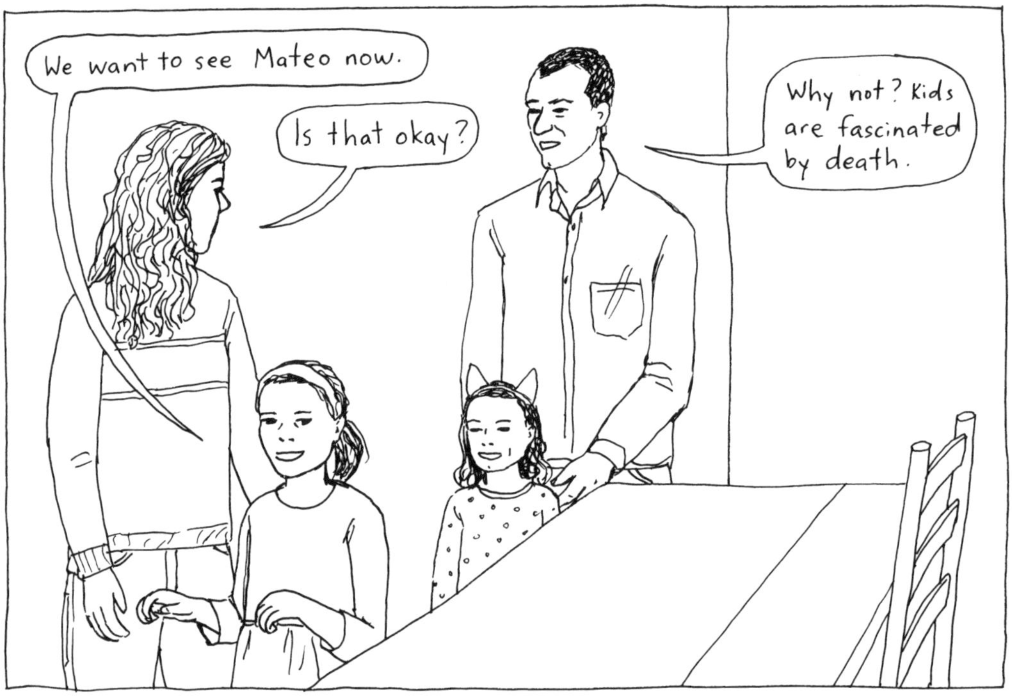
We want to see Mateo now.
Is that okay?
Why not? Kids are fascinated by death.

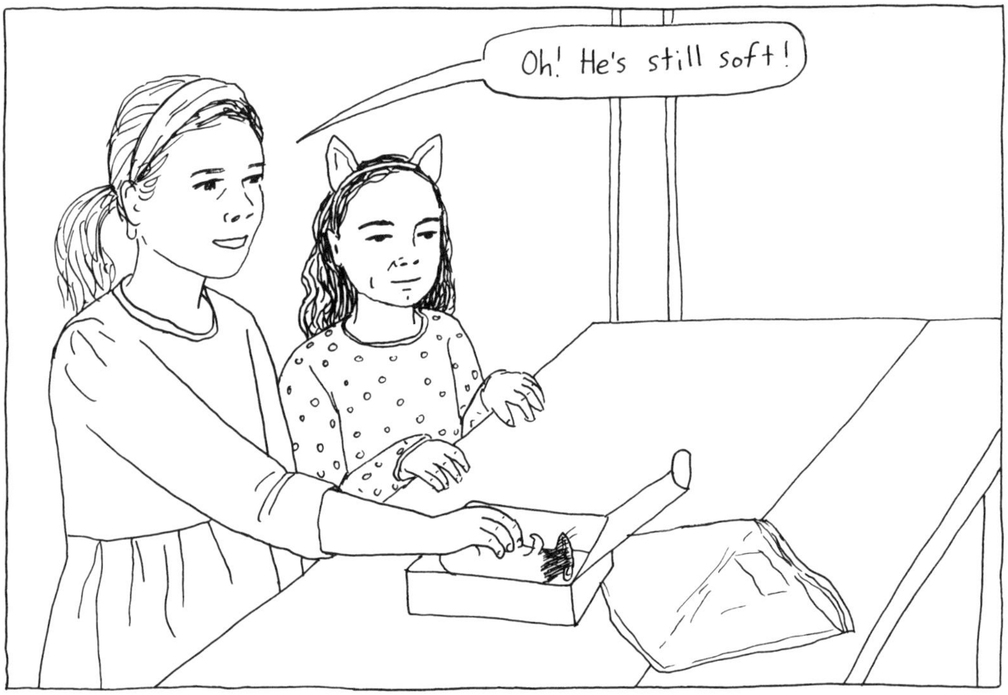
Oh! He's still soft!

Who was mateo?

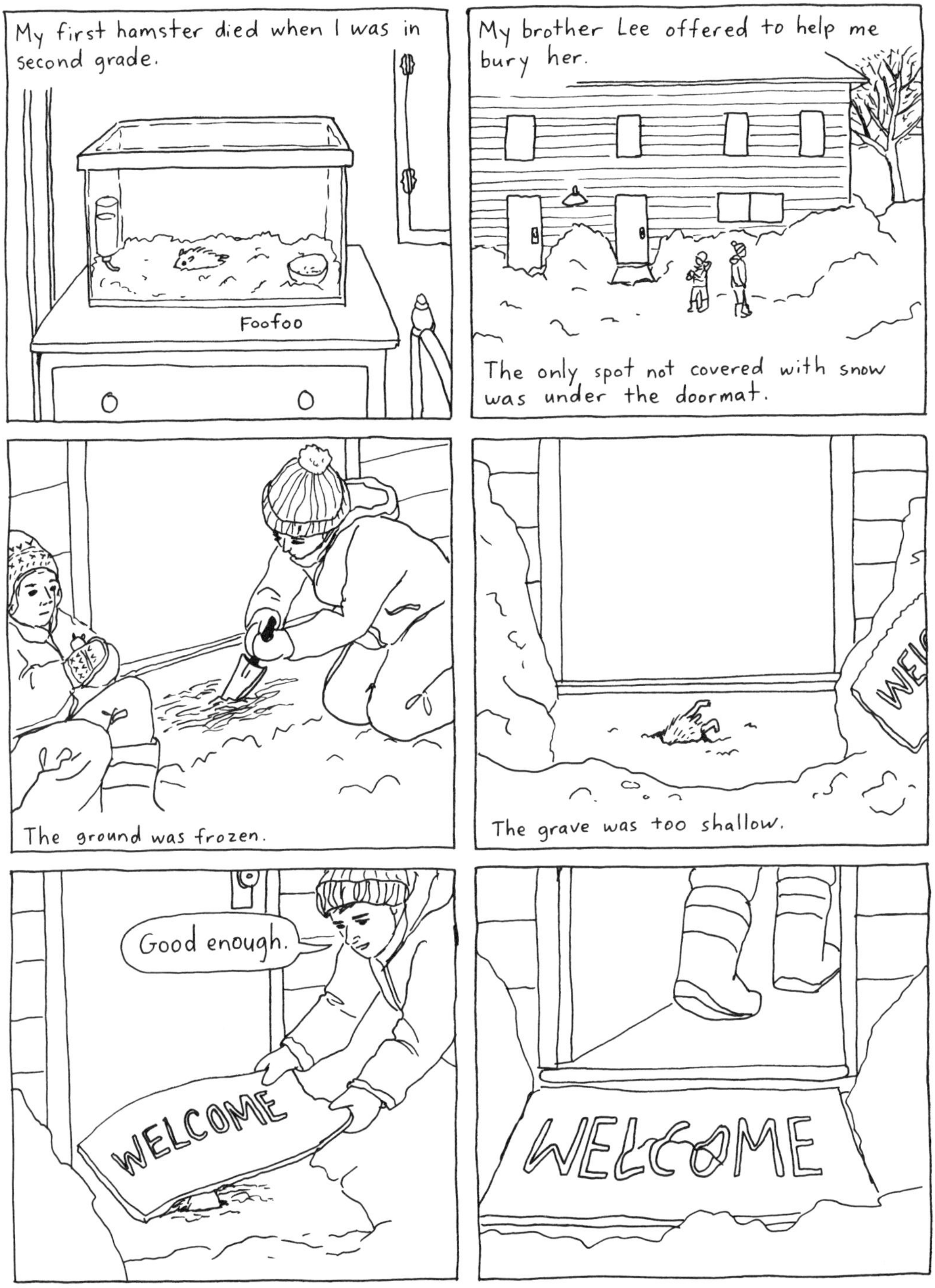
My first hamster died when I was in second grade.
Foofoo
My brother Lee offered to help me bury her.
The only spot not covered with snow was under the doormat.
The ground was frozen.
The grave was too shallow.
Good enough.
WELCOME
WELCOME

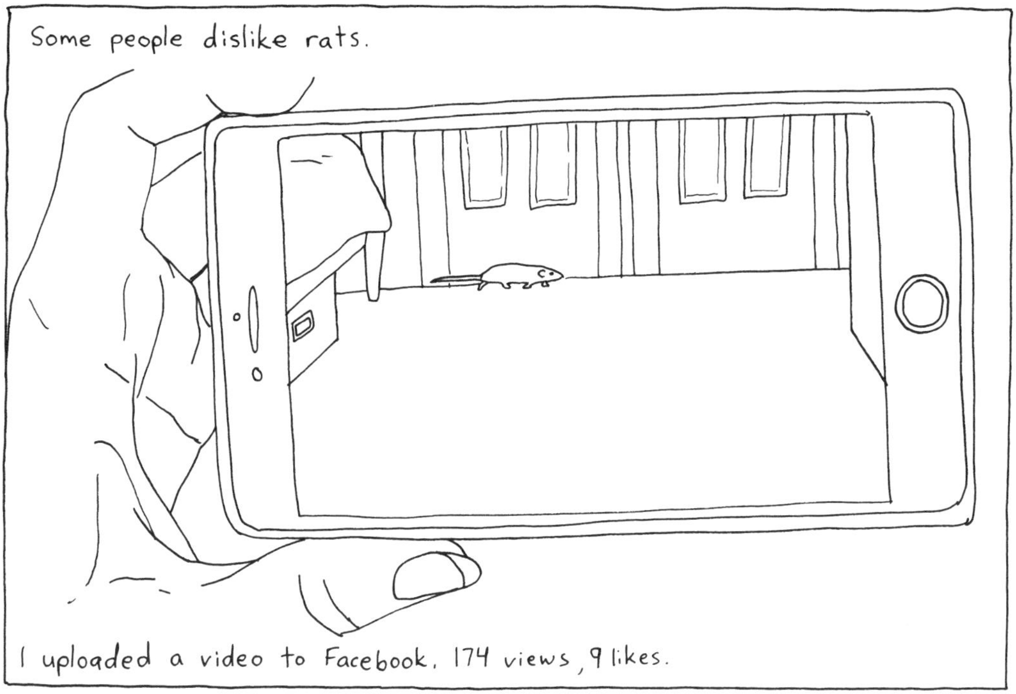
Some people dislike rats.
I uploaded a video to Facebook. 174 views, 9 likes.

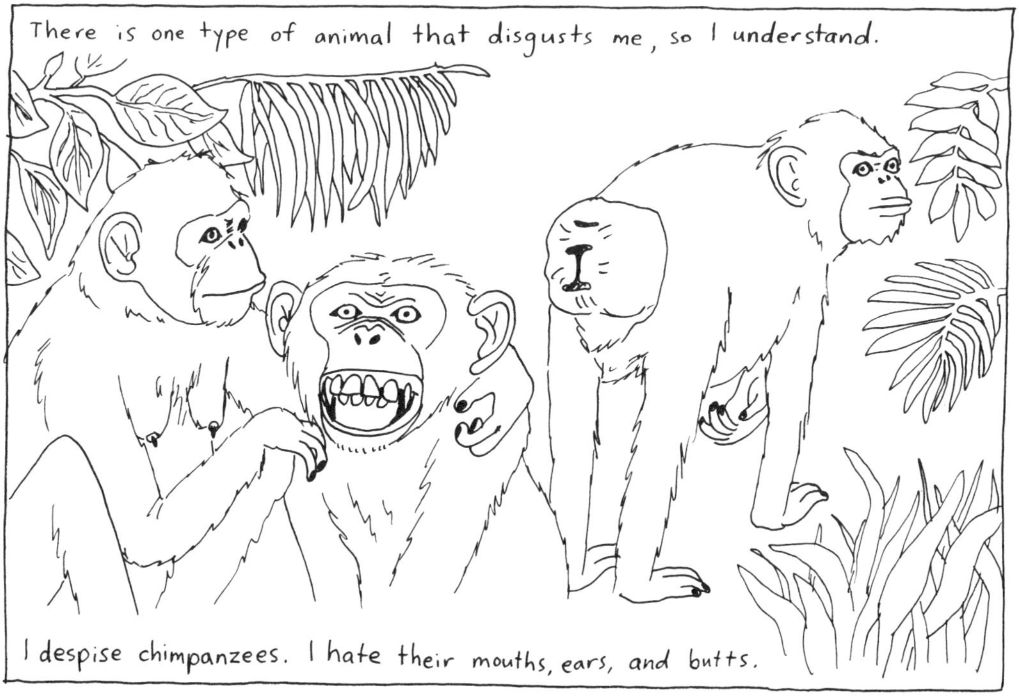
There is one type of animal that disgusts me, so I understand.
I despise chimpanzees. I hate their mouths, ears, and butts.

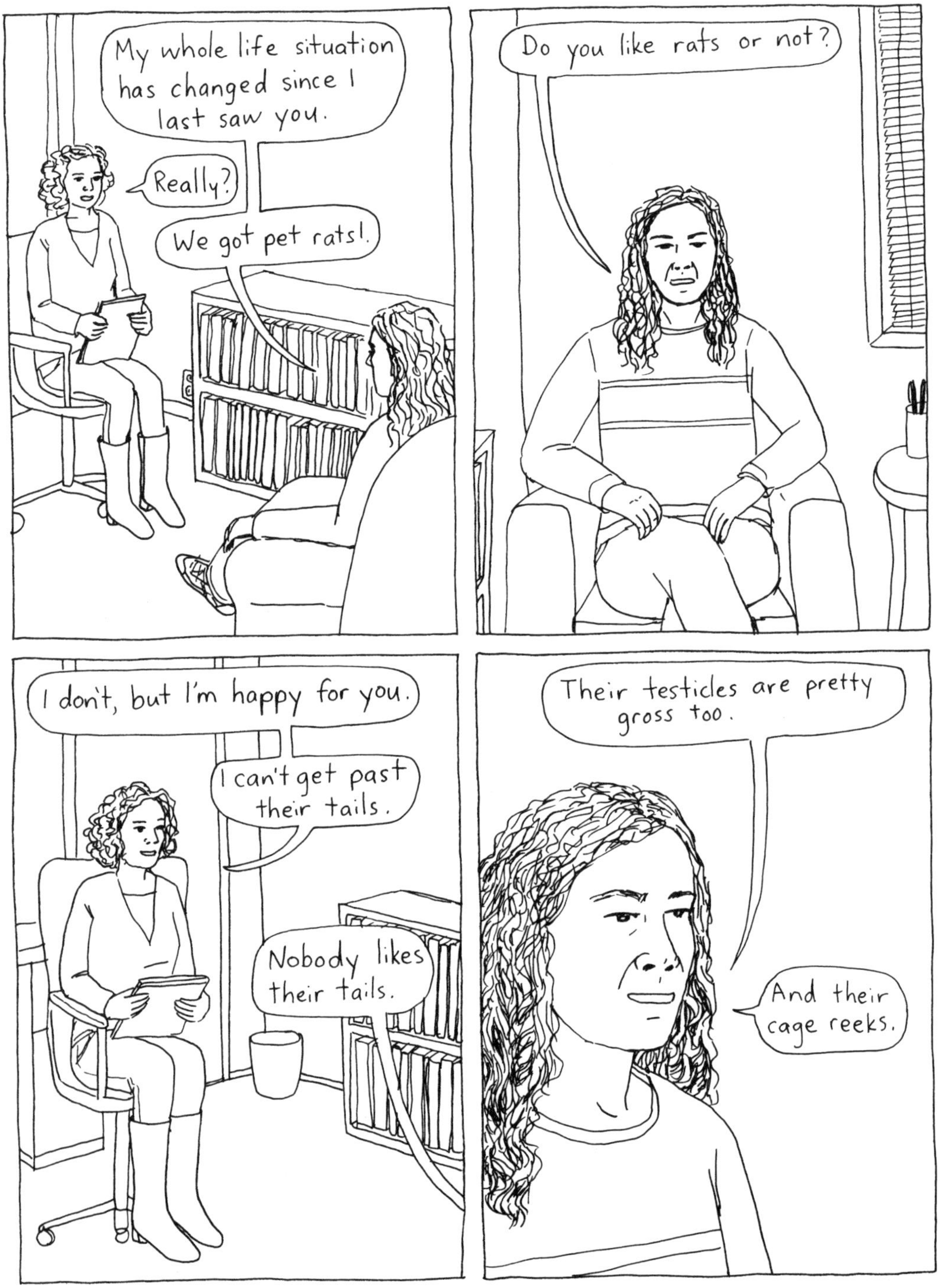
My whole life situation has changed since I last saw you.
Really?
We got pet rats!
Do you like rats or not?
I don't, but I'm happy for you.
I can't get past their tails.
Nobody likes their tails.
Their testicles are pretty gross too.
And their cage reeks.

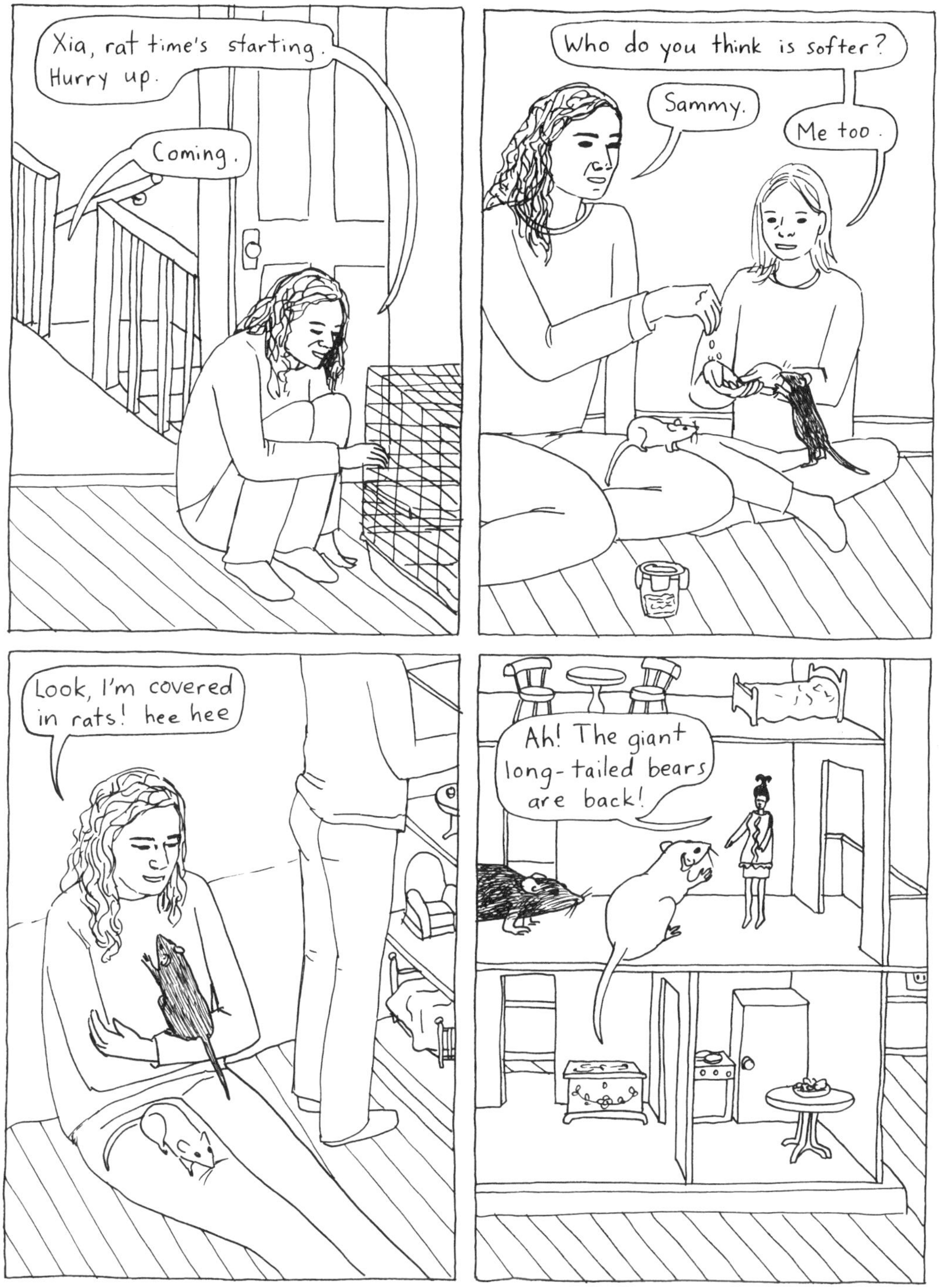
Xia, rat time's starting. Hurry up.
Coming.
Who do you think is softer?
Sammy.
Me too.
Look, I'm covered in rats! hee hee
Ah! The giant long-tailed bears are back!

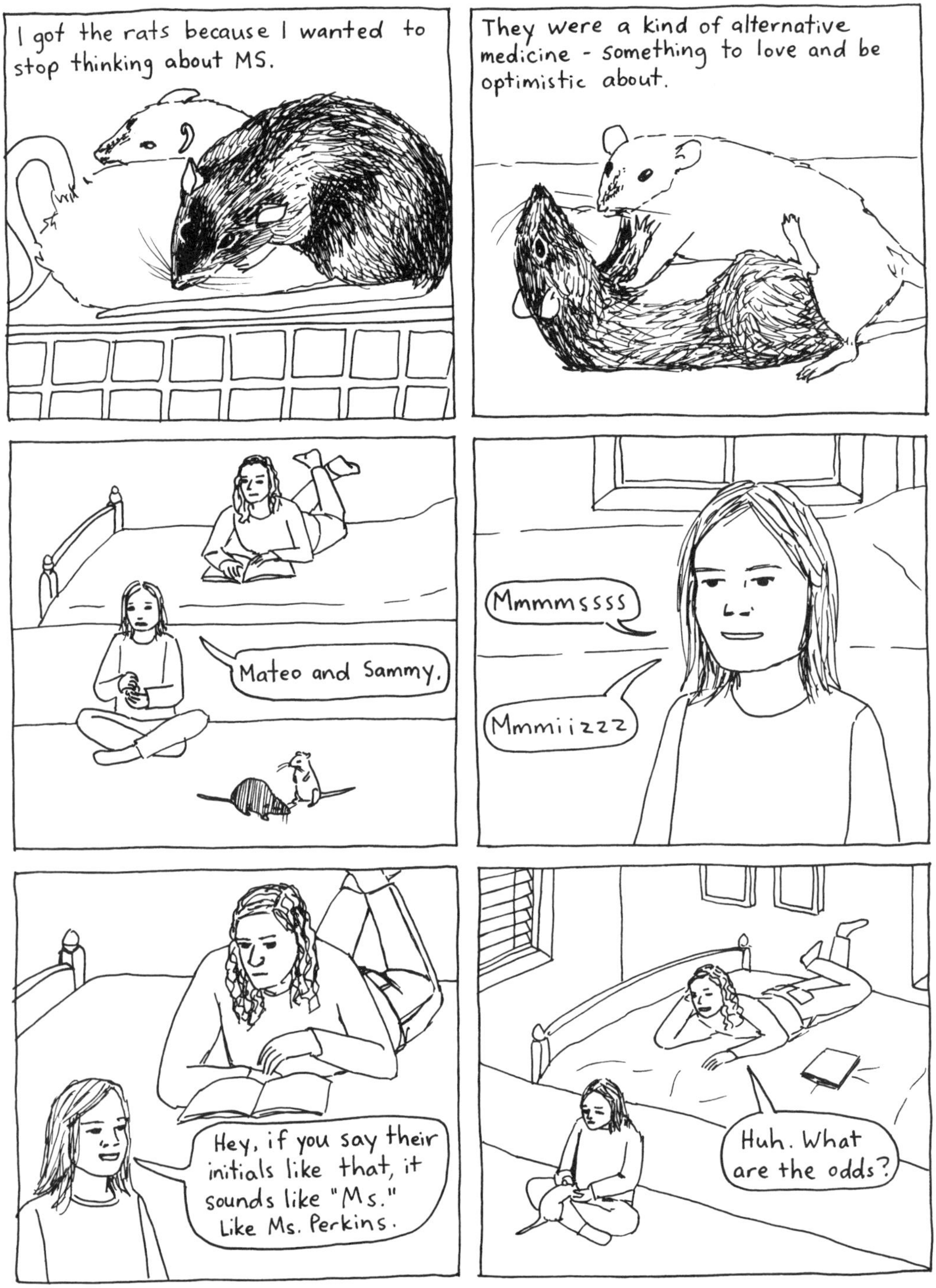
I got the rats because I wanted to stop thinking about MS.
They were a kind of alternative medicine - something to love and be optimistic about.
Mateo and Sammy.
Mmmmssss
Mmmiizzz
Hey, if you say their initials like that, it sounds like "Ms." Like Ms. Perkins.
Huh. What are the odds?

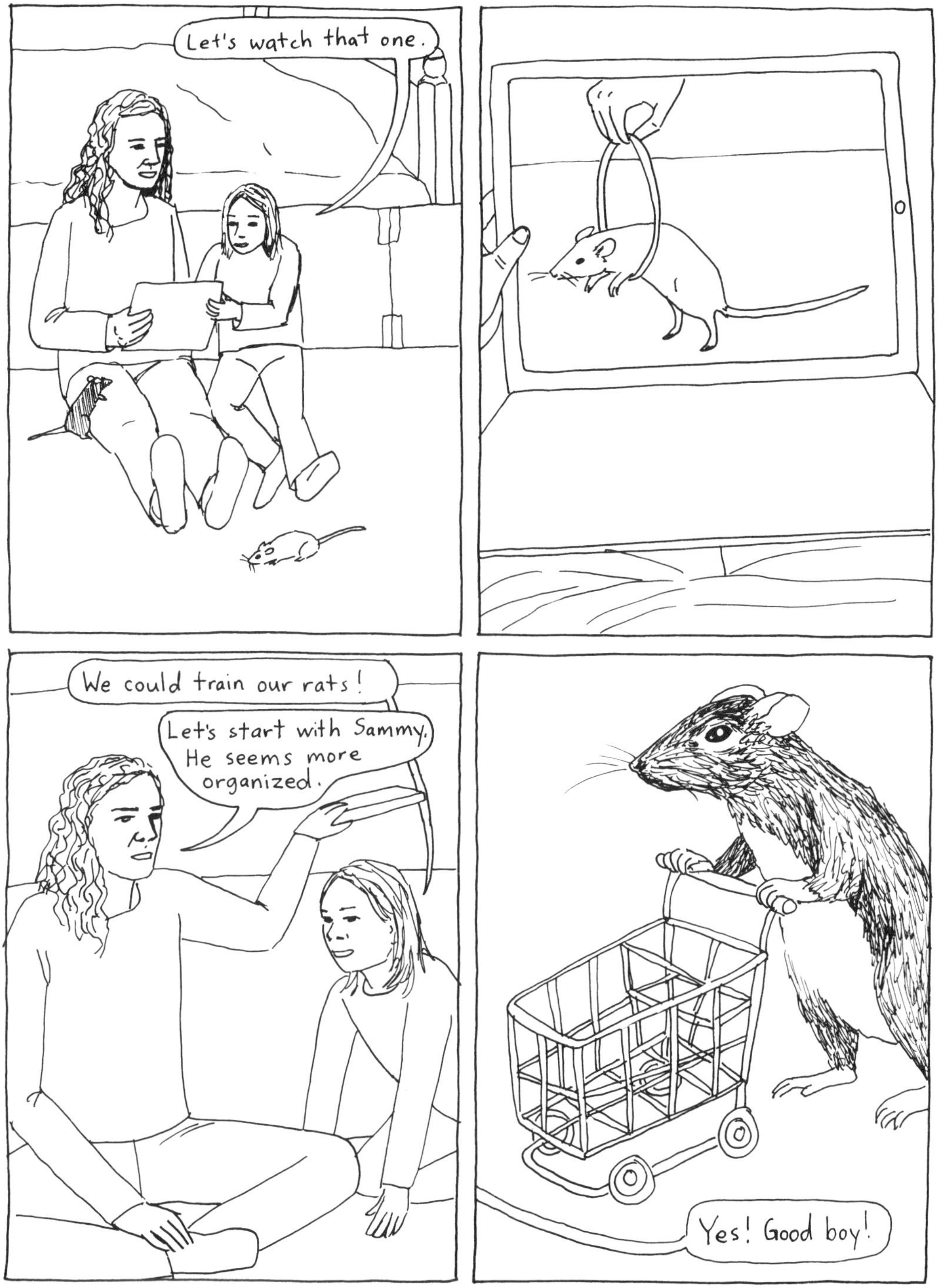
Let's watch that one.
We could train our rats!
Let's start with Sammy. He seems more organized.
Yes! Good boy!

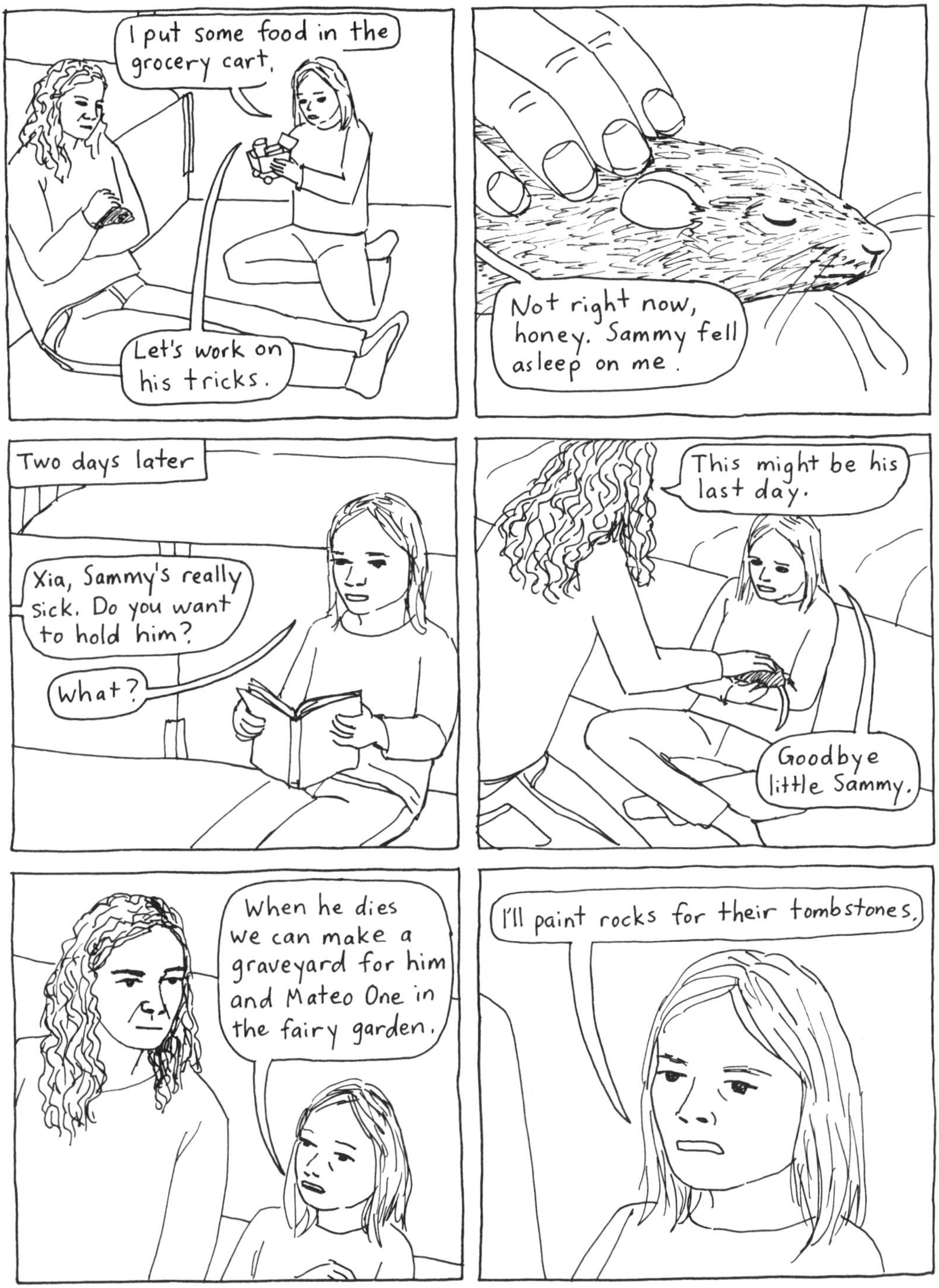
I put some food in the grocery cart.
Let's work on his tricks.
Not right now, honey. Sammy fell asleep on me.
Two days later
Xia, Sammy's really sick. Do you want to hold him?
What?
This might be his last day.
Goodbye little Sammy.
When he dies we can make a graveyard for him and Mateo One in the fairy garden.
I'll paint rocks for their tombstones.

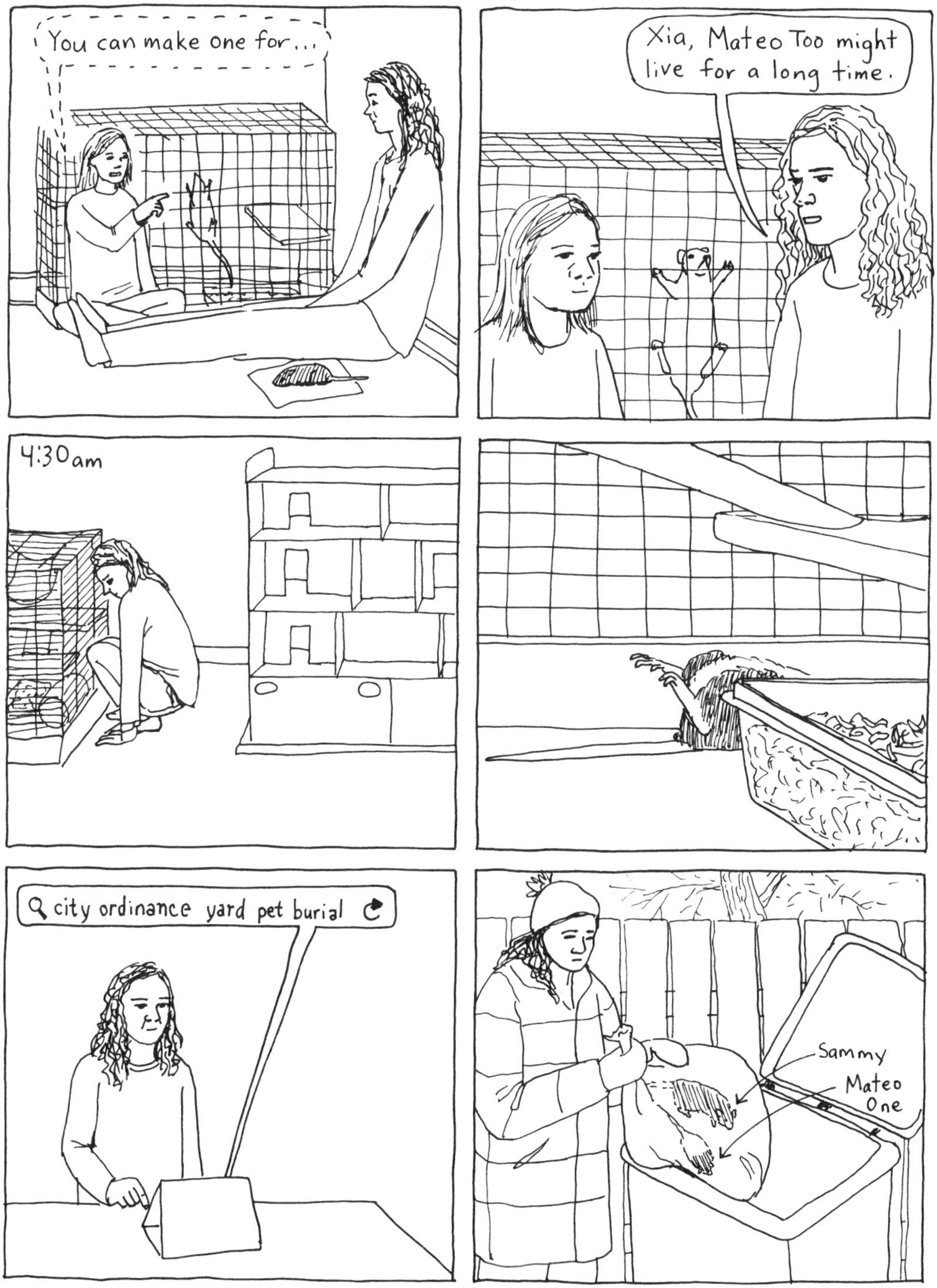
You can make one for...
Xia, Mateo Too might live for a long time.
4:30am
city ordinance yard pet burial
Sammy
Mateo One

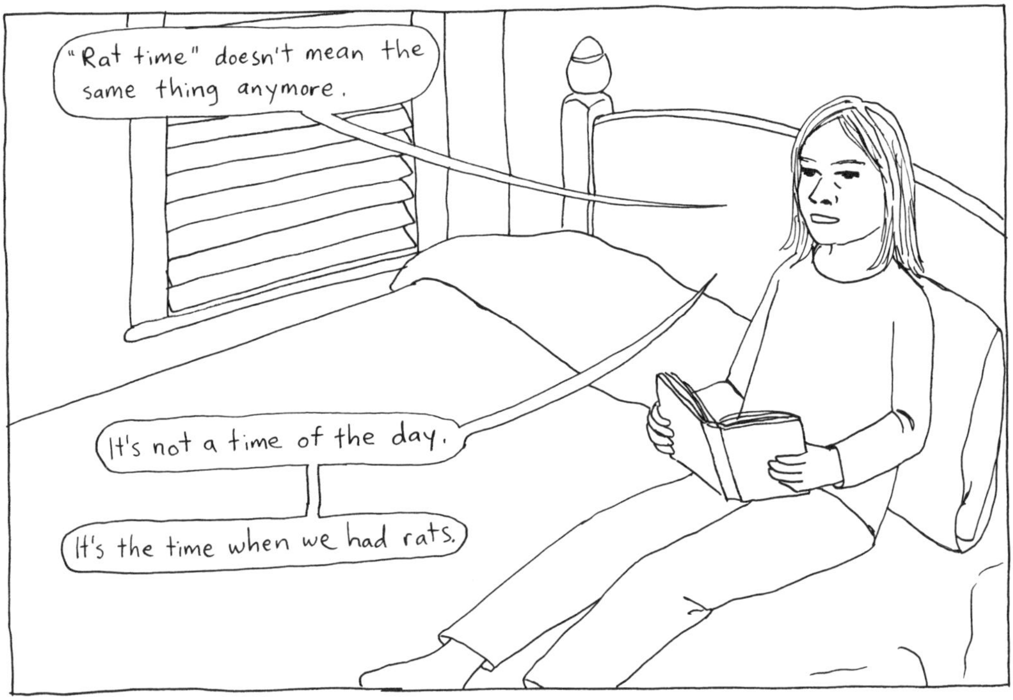
"Rat time" doesn't mean the same thing anymore.
It's not a time of the day.
It's the time when we had rats.

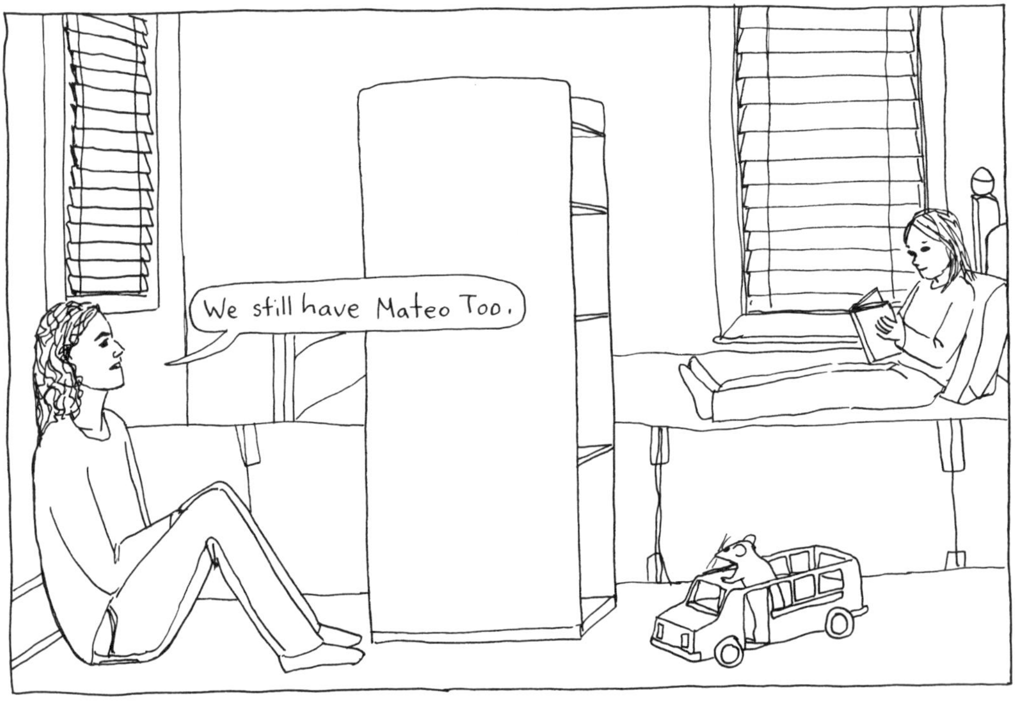
We still have Mateo Too.

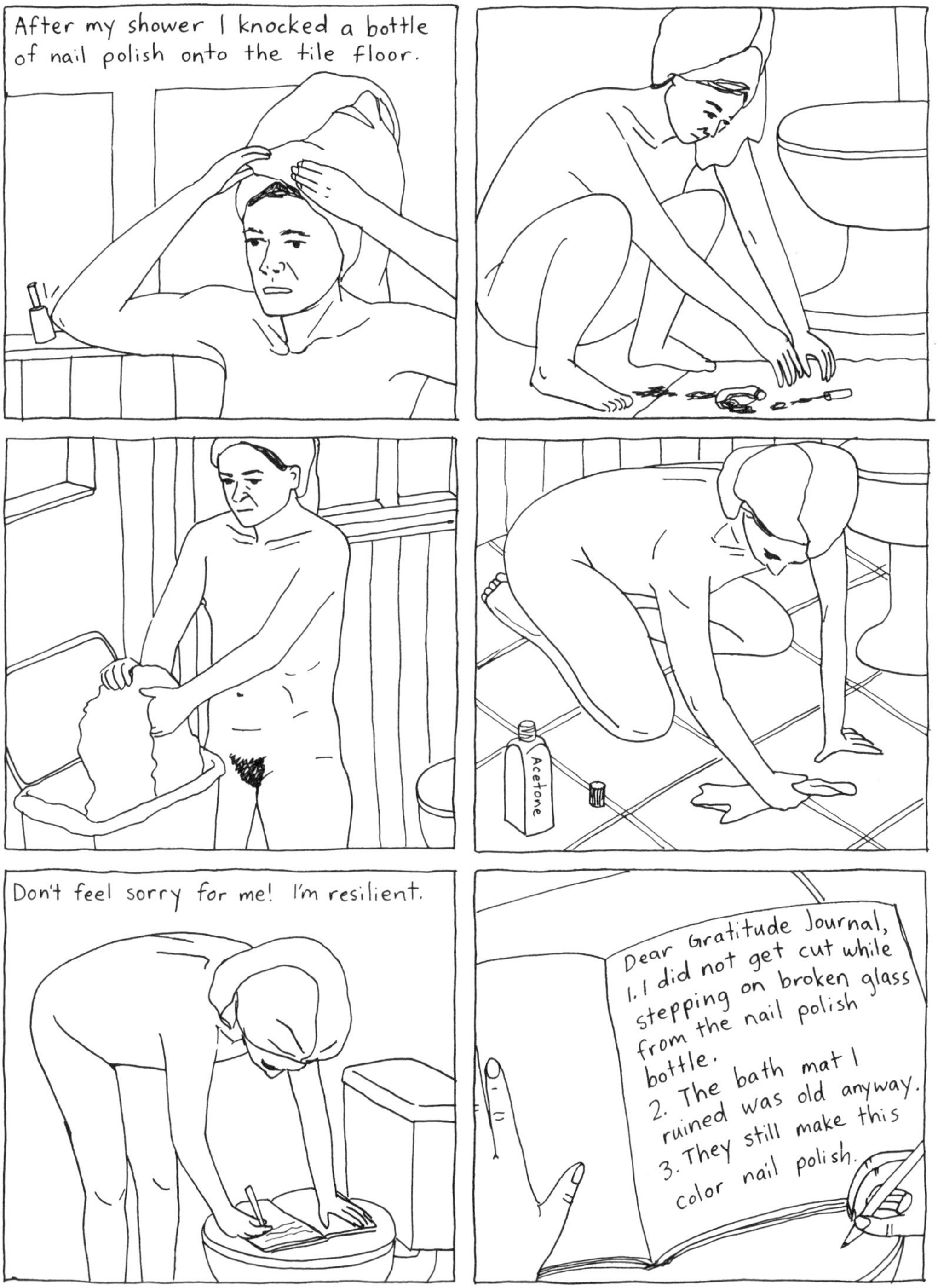
After my shower I knocked a bottle of nail polish onto the tile floor.
Acetone
Don't feel sorry for me! I'm resilient.
Dear Gratitude Journal,
1. I did not get cut while stepping on broken glass from the nail polish bottle.
2. The bath mat I ruined was old anyway.
3. They still make this color nail polish.

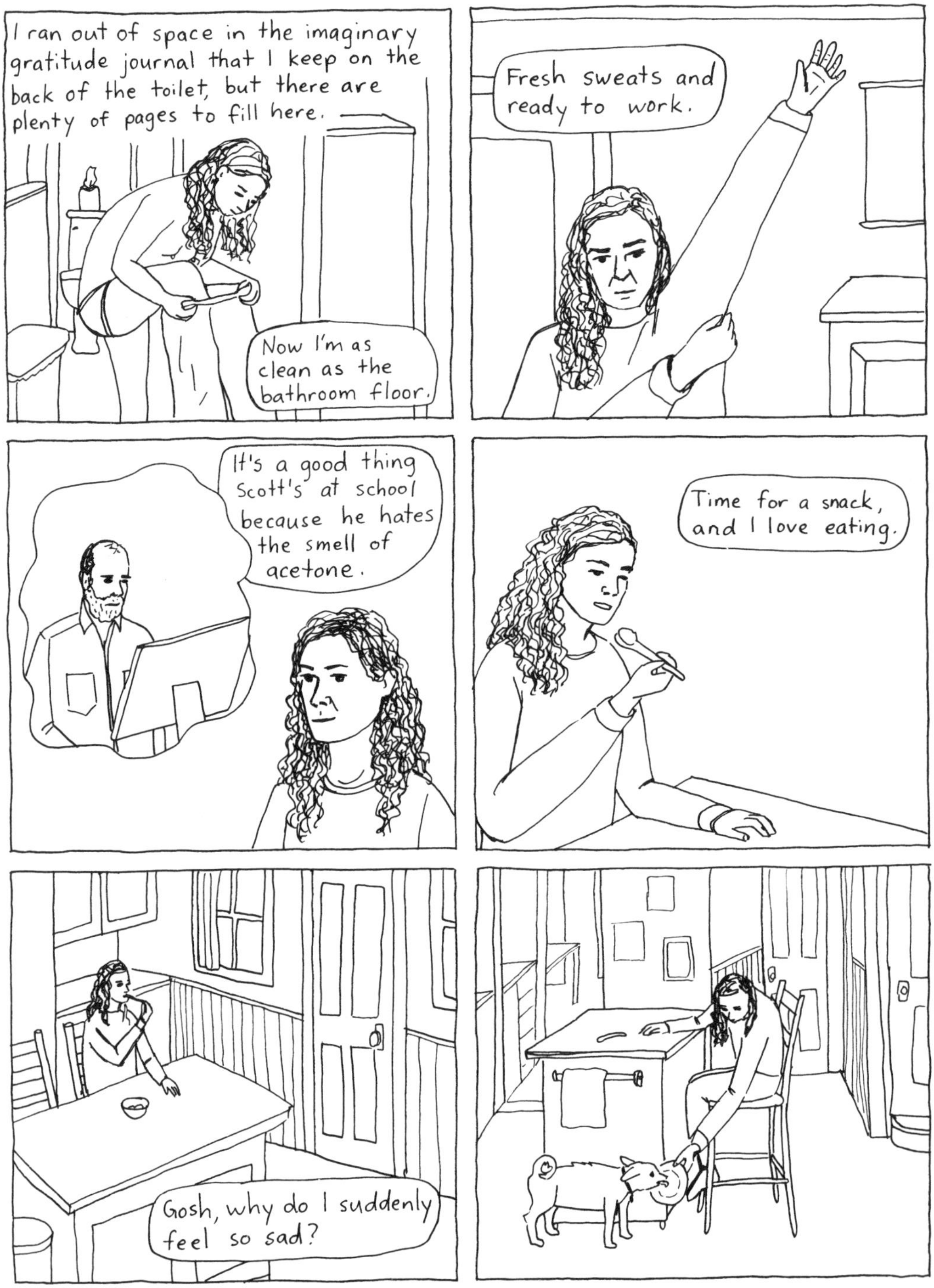
I ran out of space in the imaginary gratitude journal that I keep on the back of the toilet, but there are plenty of pages to fill here.
Now I'm as clean as the bathroom floor.
Fresh sweats and ready to work.
It's a good thing Scott's at school because he hates the smell of acetone.
Time for a snack, and I love eating.
Gosh, why do I suddenly feel so sad?

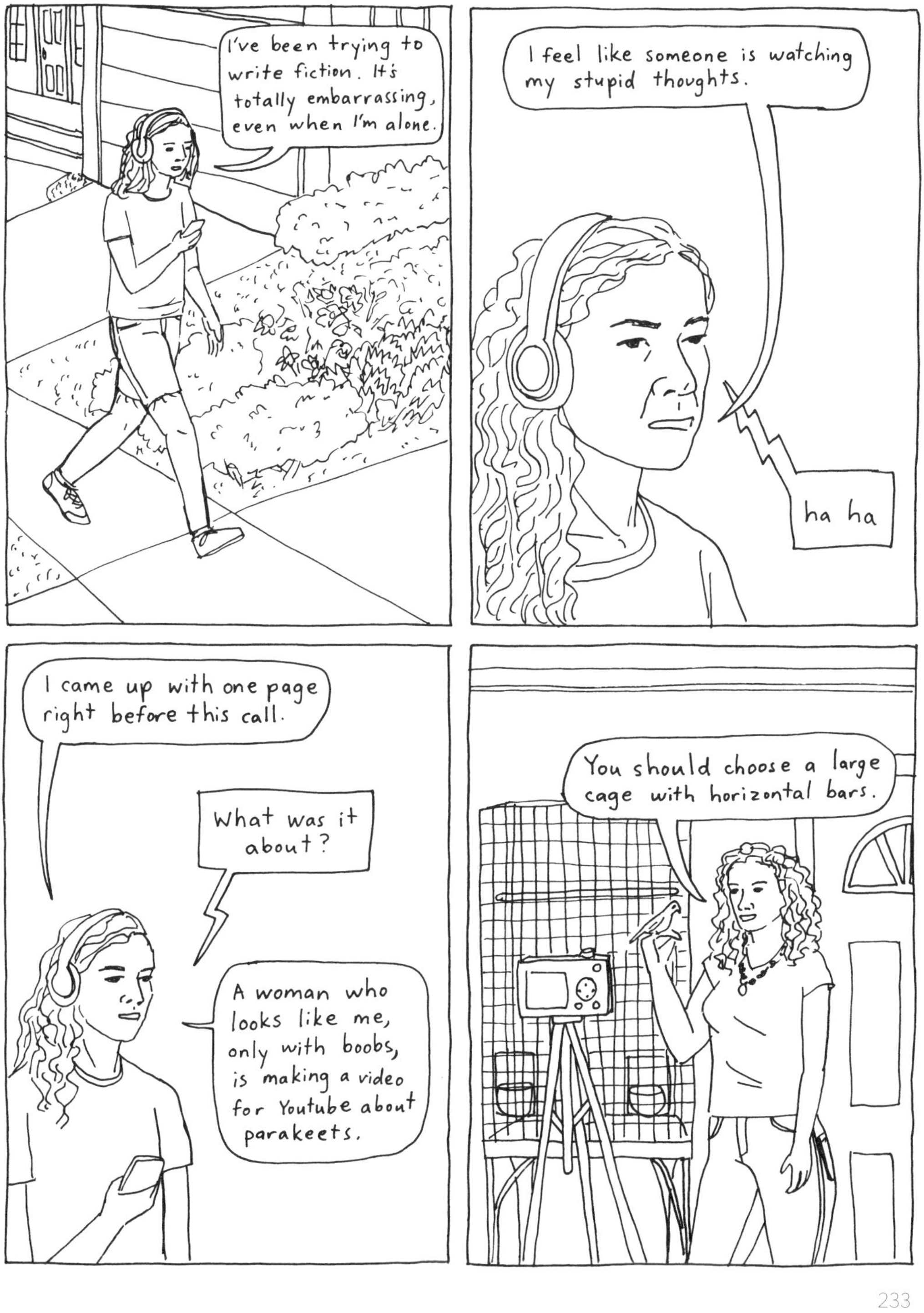
I've been trying to write fiction. It's totally embarrassing, even when I'm alone.
I feel like someone is watching my stupid thoughts.
ha ha
I came up with one page right before this call.
What was it about?
A woman who looks like me, only with boobs, is making a video for Youtube about parakeets.
You should choose a large cage with horizontal bars.

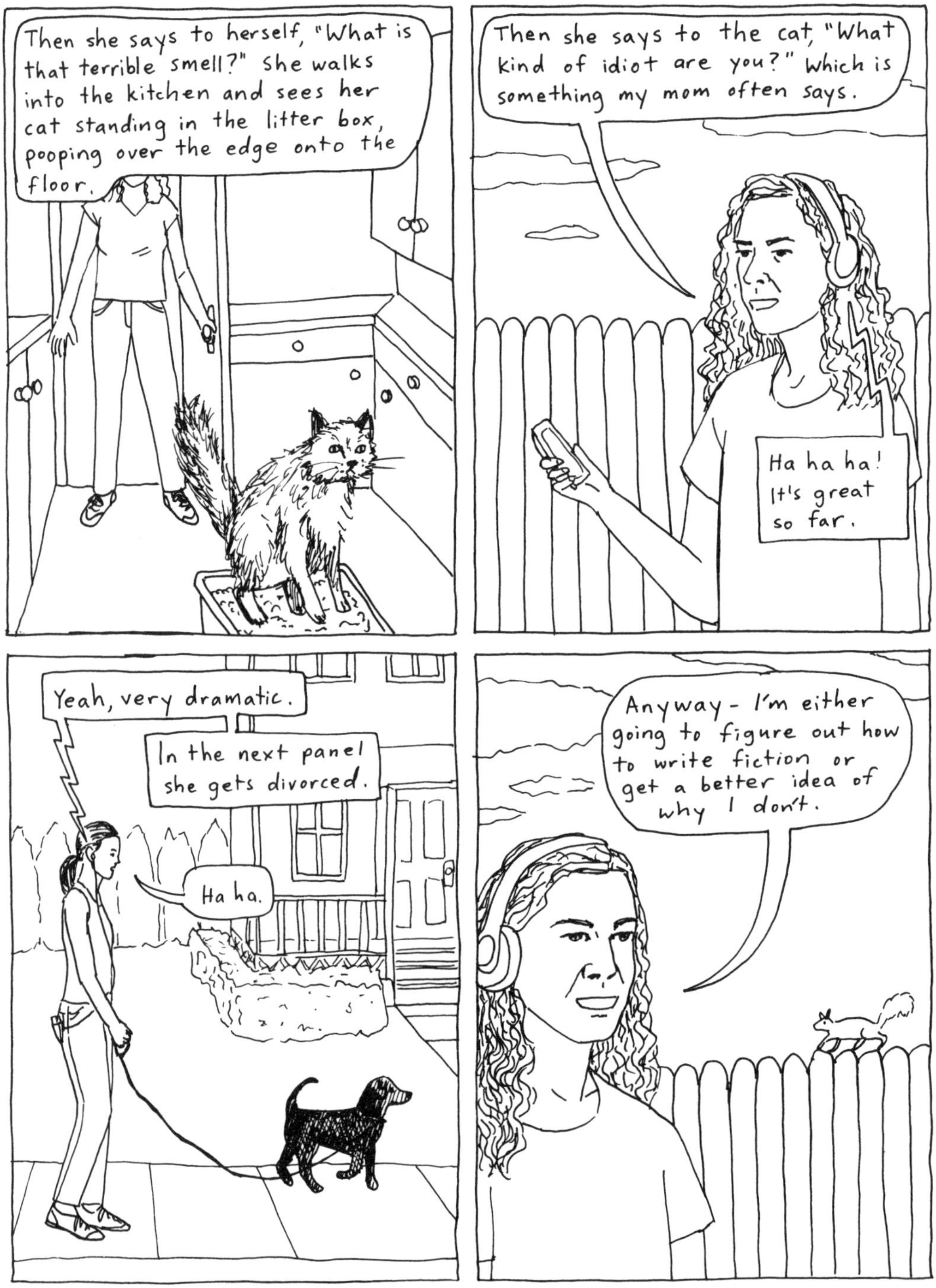

Then she says to herself, "What is that terrible smell?" She walks into the kitchen and sees her cat standing in the litter box, pooping over the edge onto the floor.
Then she says to the cat, "What kind of idiot are you?" Which is something my mom often says.
Ha ha ha! It's great so far.
Yeah, very dramatic.
In the next panel she gets divorced.
Ha ha.
Anyway - I'm either going to figure out how to write fiction or get a better idea of why I don't.

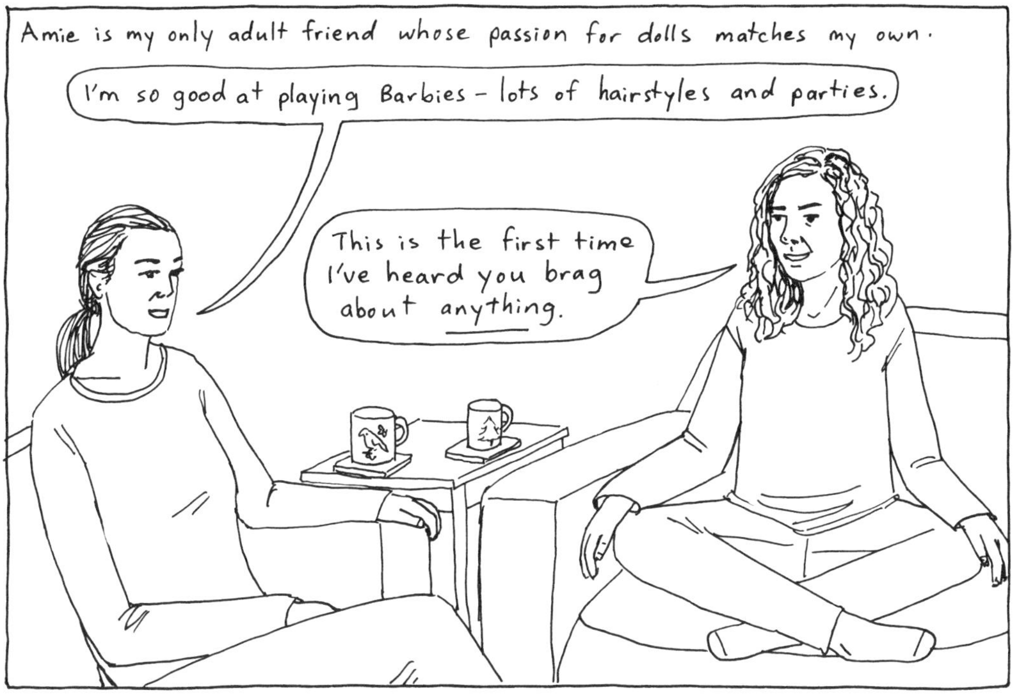
Amie is my only adult friend whose passion for dolls matches my own.
I'm so good at playing Barbies – lots of hairstyles and parties.
This is the first time I've heard you brag about anything.

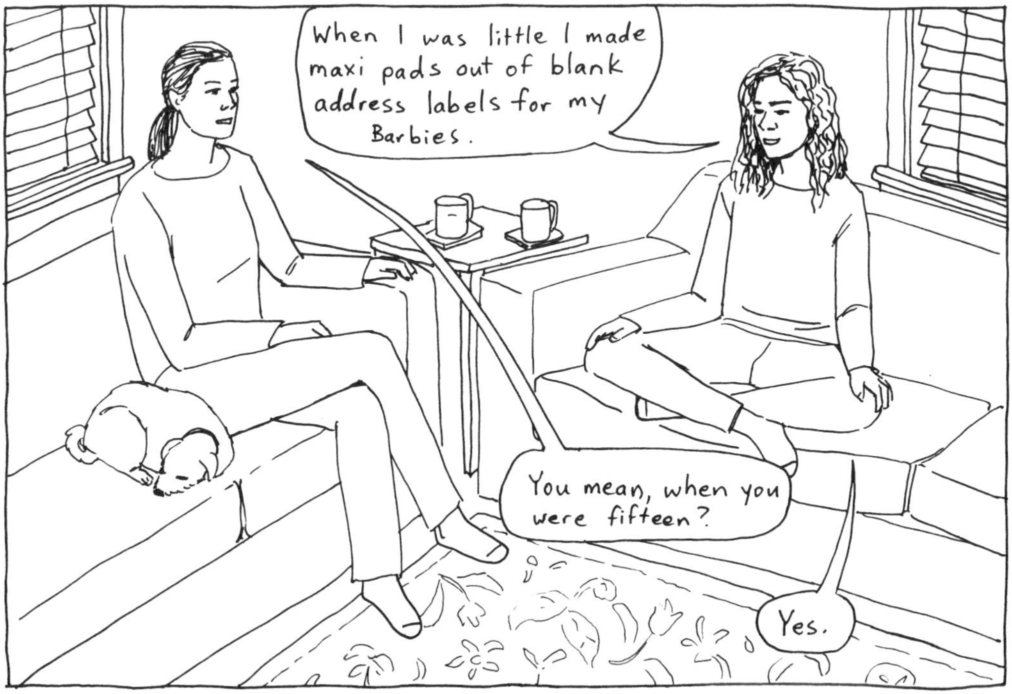
When I was little I made maxi pads out of blank address labels for my Barbies.
You mean, when you were fifteen?
Yes.

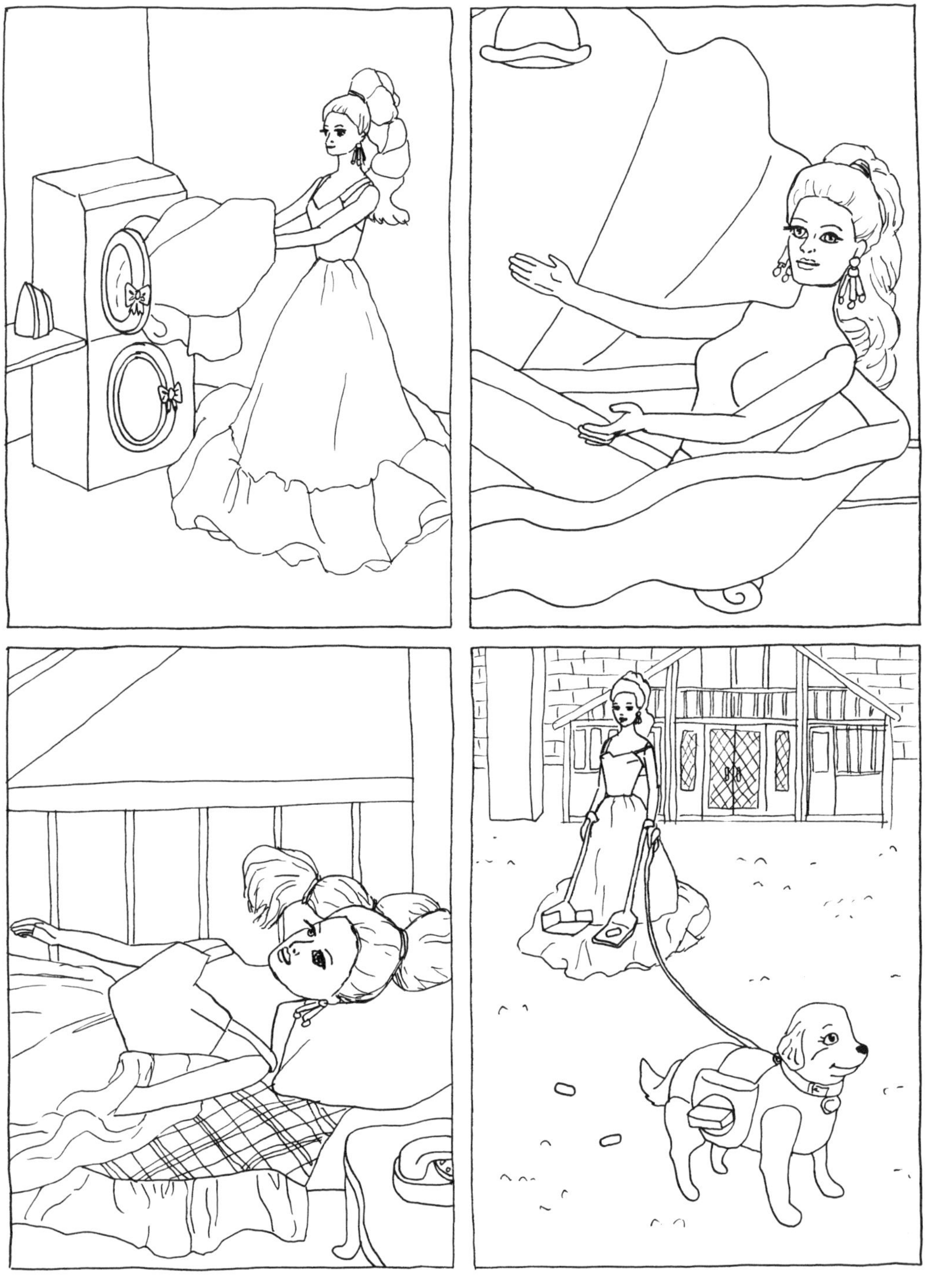

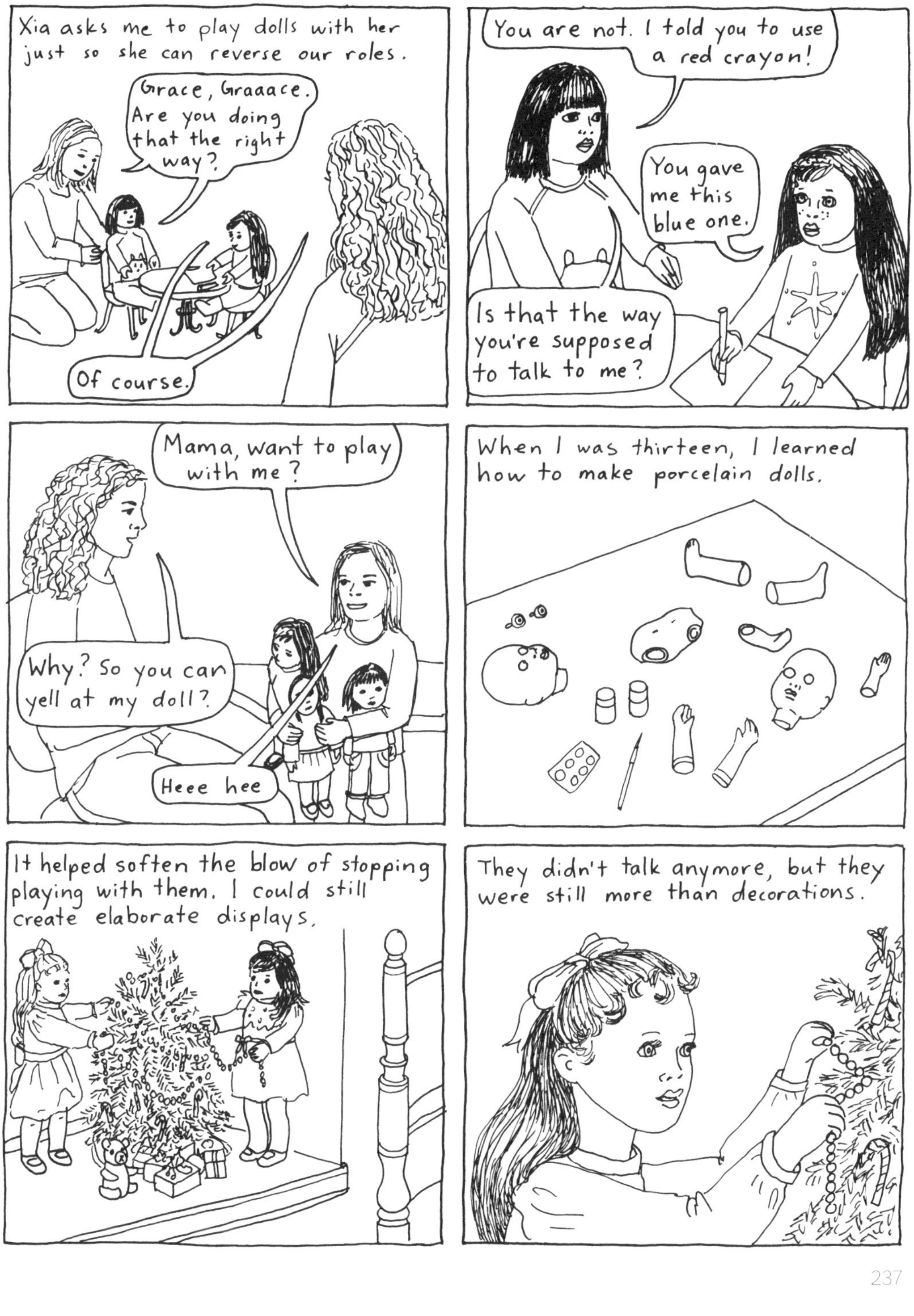
Xia asks me to play dolls with her just so she can reverse our roles.
Grace, Graaace. Are you doing that the right way?
Of course.
You are not. I told you to use a red crayon!
You gave me this blue one.
Is that the way you're supposed to talk to me?
Mama, want to play with me?
Why? So you can yell at my doll?
Heee hee
When I was thirteen, I learned how to make porcelain dolls.
It helped soften the blow of stopping playing with them. I could still create elaborate displays.
They didn't talk anymore, but they were still more than decorations.

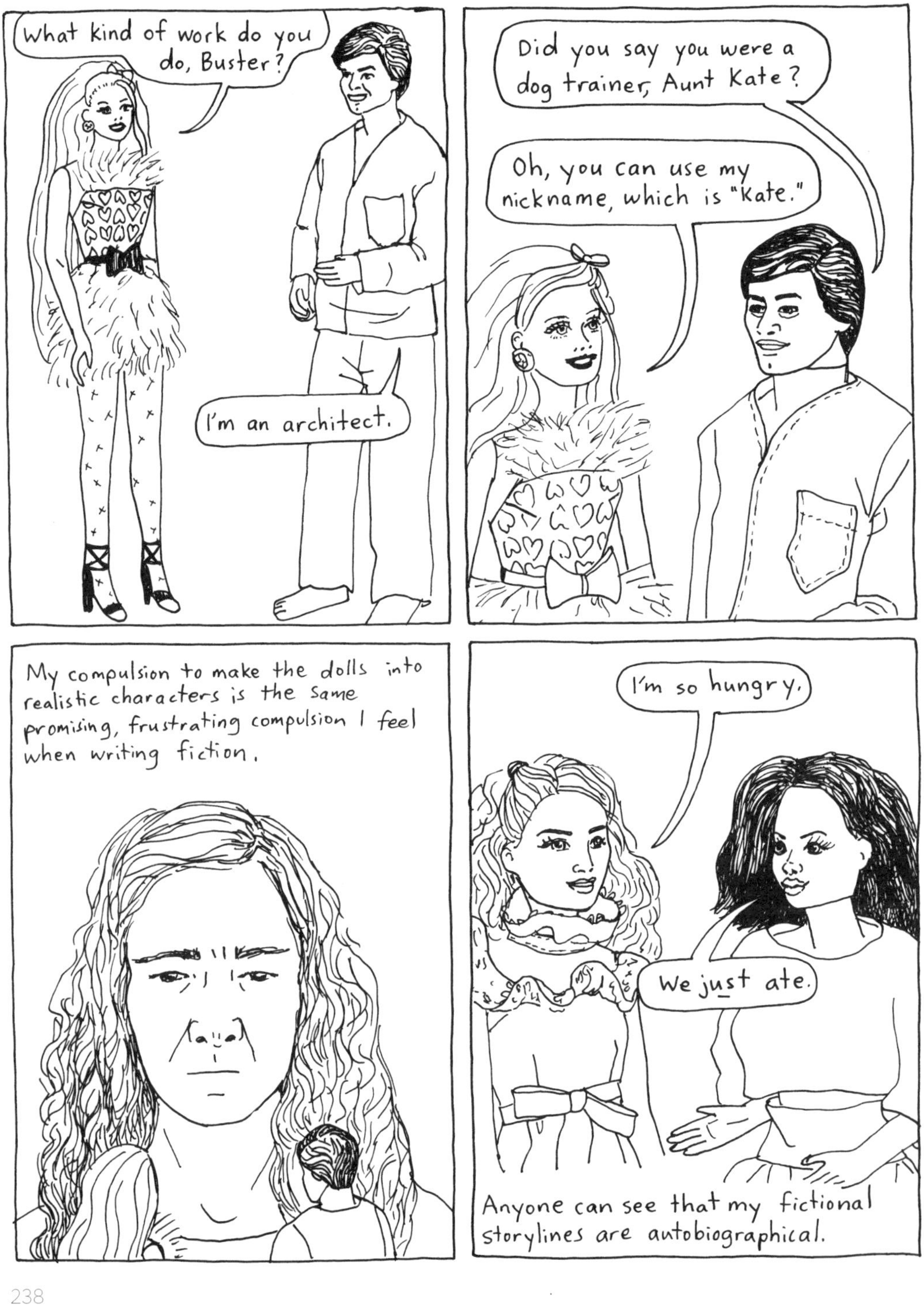
What kind of work do you do, Buster?
I'm an architect.
Did you say you were a dog trainer, Aunt Kate?
Oh, you can use my nickname, which is "Kate."
My compulsion to make the dolls into realistic characters is the same promising, frustrating compulsion I feel when writing fiction.
I'm so hungry.
We just ate.
Anyone can see that my fictional storylines are autobiographical.

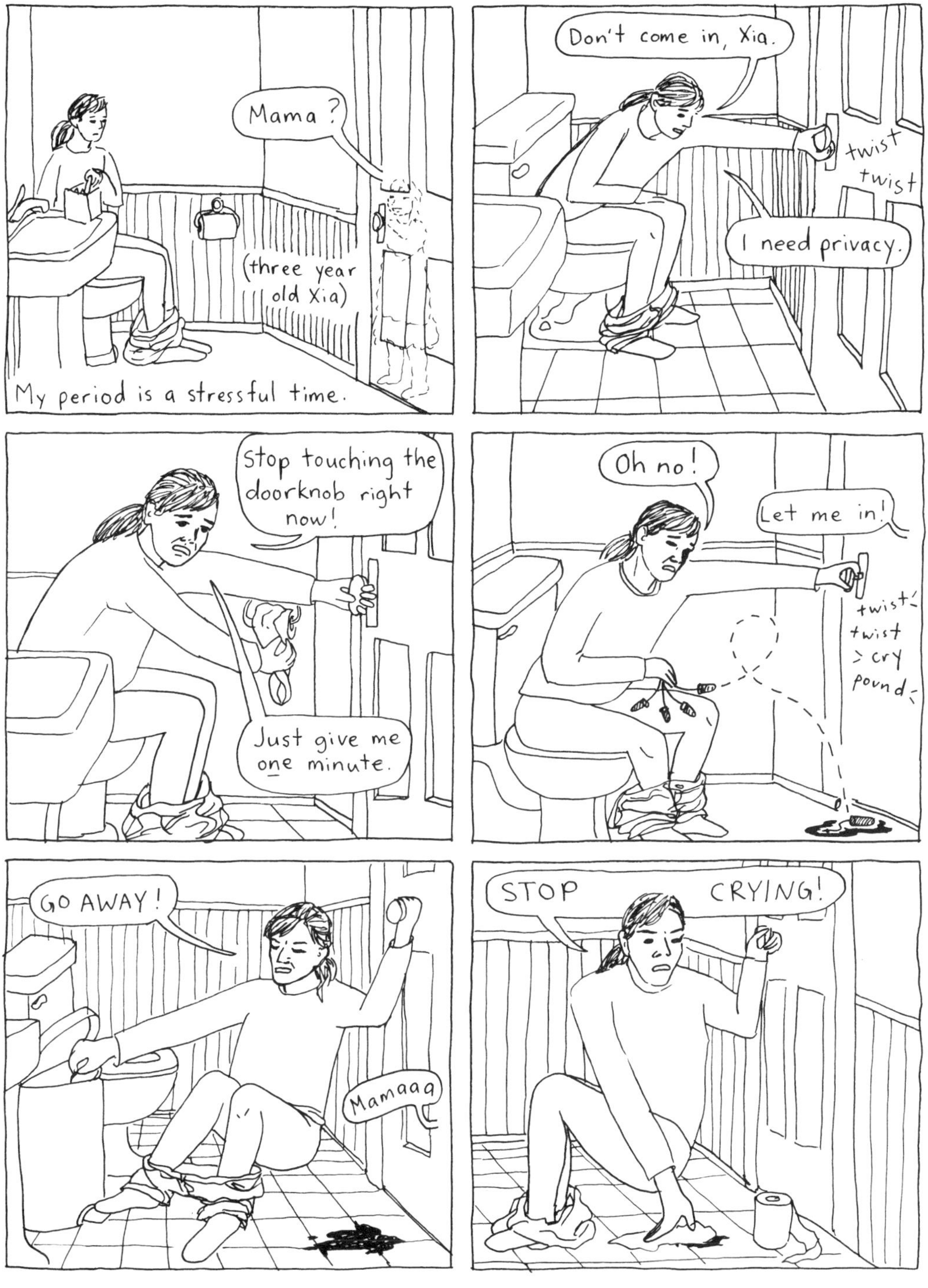
Mama?
(three year old Xia)
My period is a stressful time.
Don't come in, Xia.
twist twist
I need privacy.
Stop touching the doorknob right now!
Just give me one minute.
Oh no!
Let me in!
twist twist cry pound
GO AWAY!
Mamaaa
STOP CRYING!

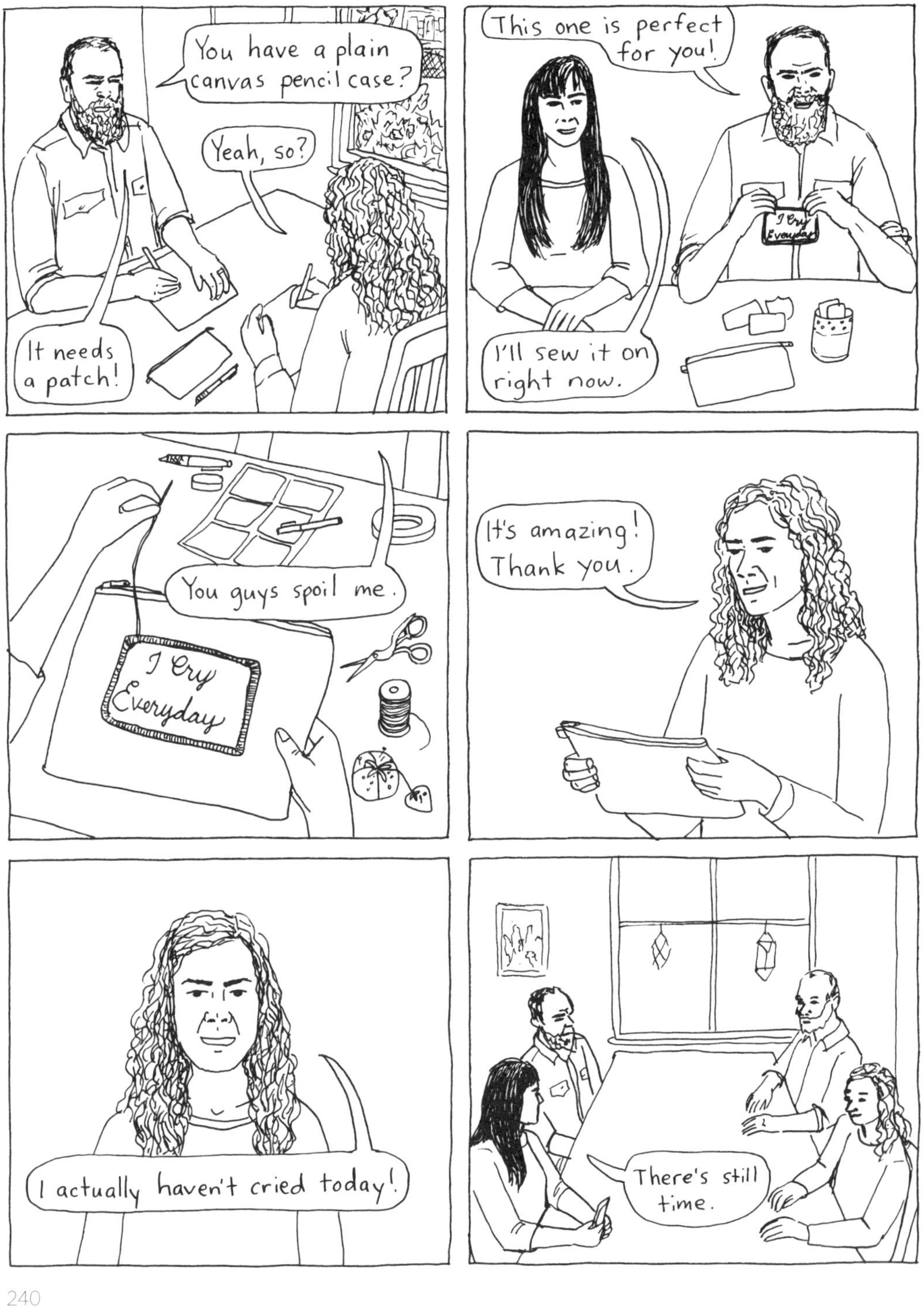

You have a plain canvas pencil case?
Yeah, so?
It needs a patch!
This one is perfect for you!
I Cry Everyday
I'll sew it on right now.
You guys spoil me.
I Cry Everyday
It's amazing! Thank you.
I actually haven't cried today!
There's still time.

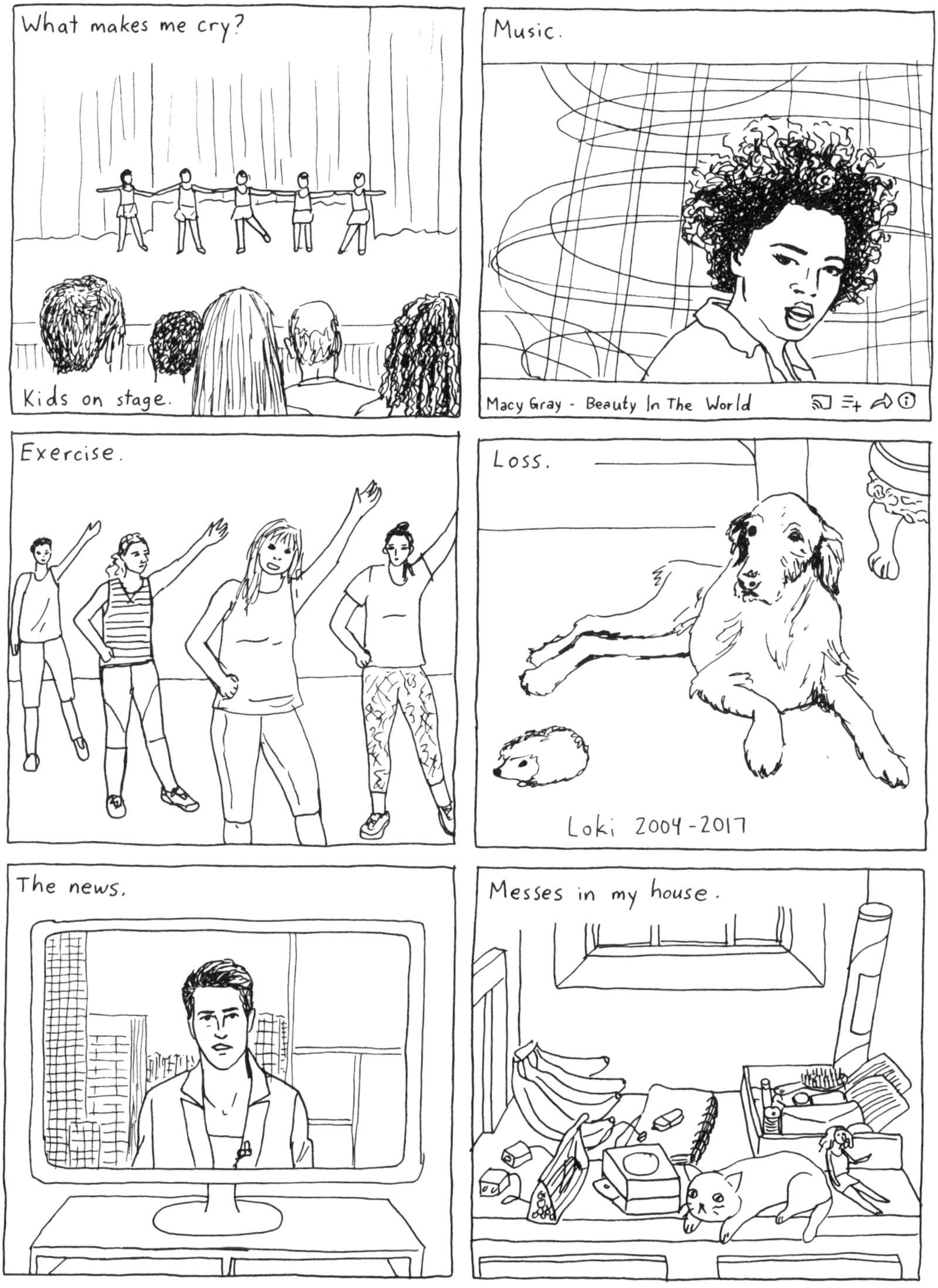
What makes me cry?
Kids on stage.
Music.
Macy Gray - Beauty In The World
Exercise.
Loss.
Loki 2004-2017
The news.
Messes in my house.

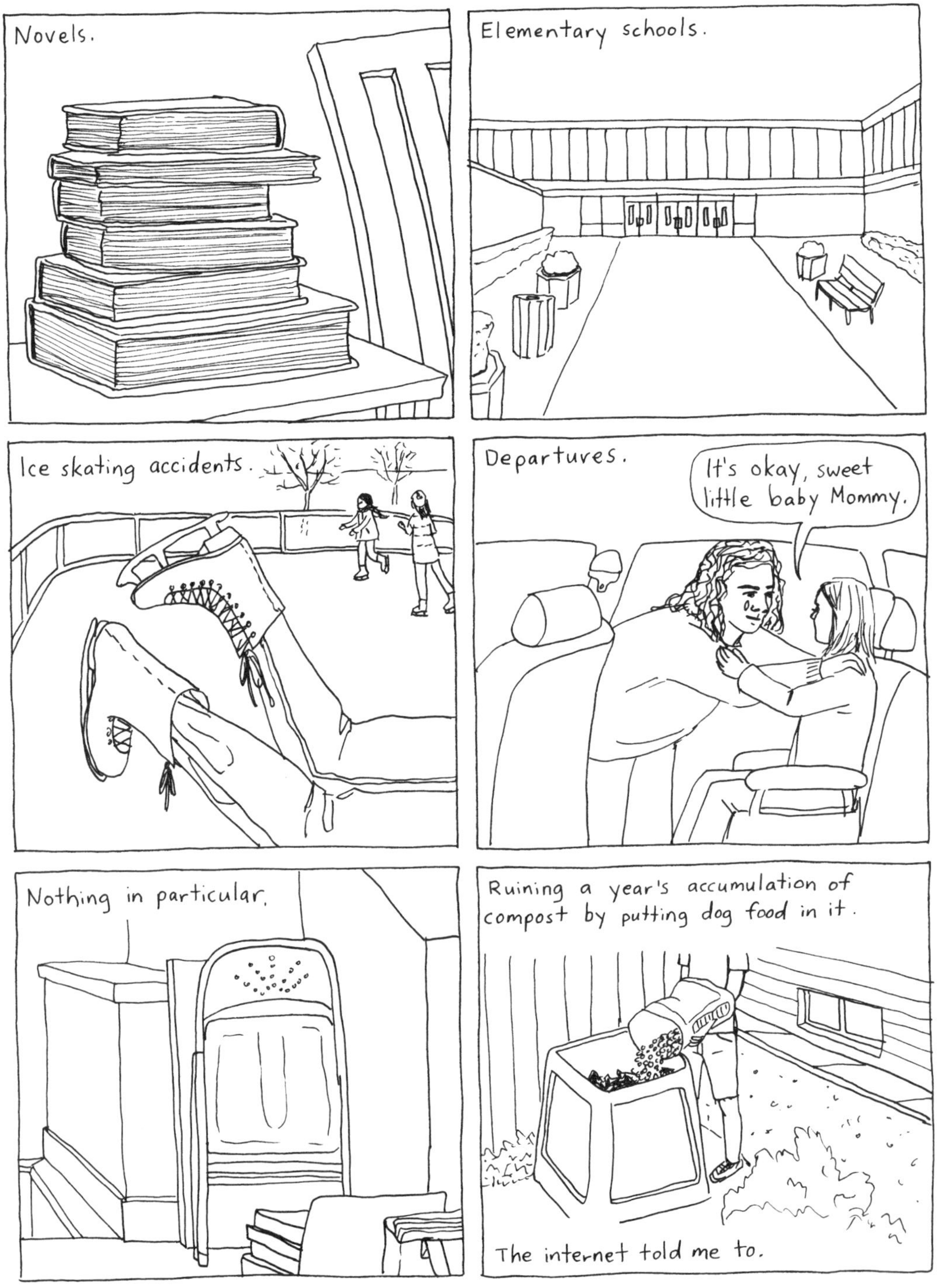
Novels.
Elementary schools.
Ice skating accidents.
Departures.
It's okay, sweet little baby Mommy.
Nothing in particular.
Ruining a year's accumulation of compost by putting dog food in it.
The internet told me to.

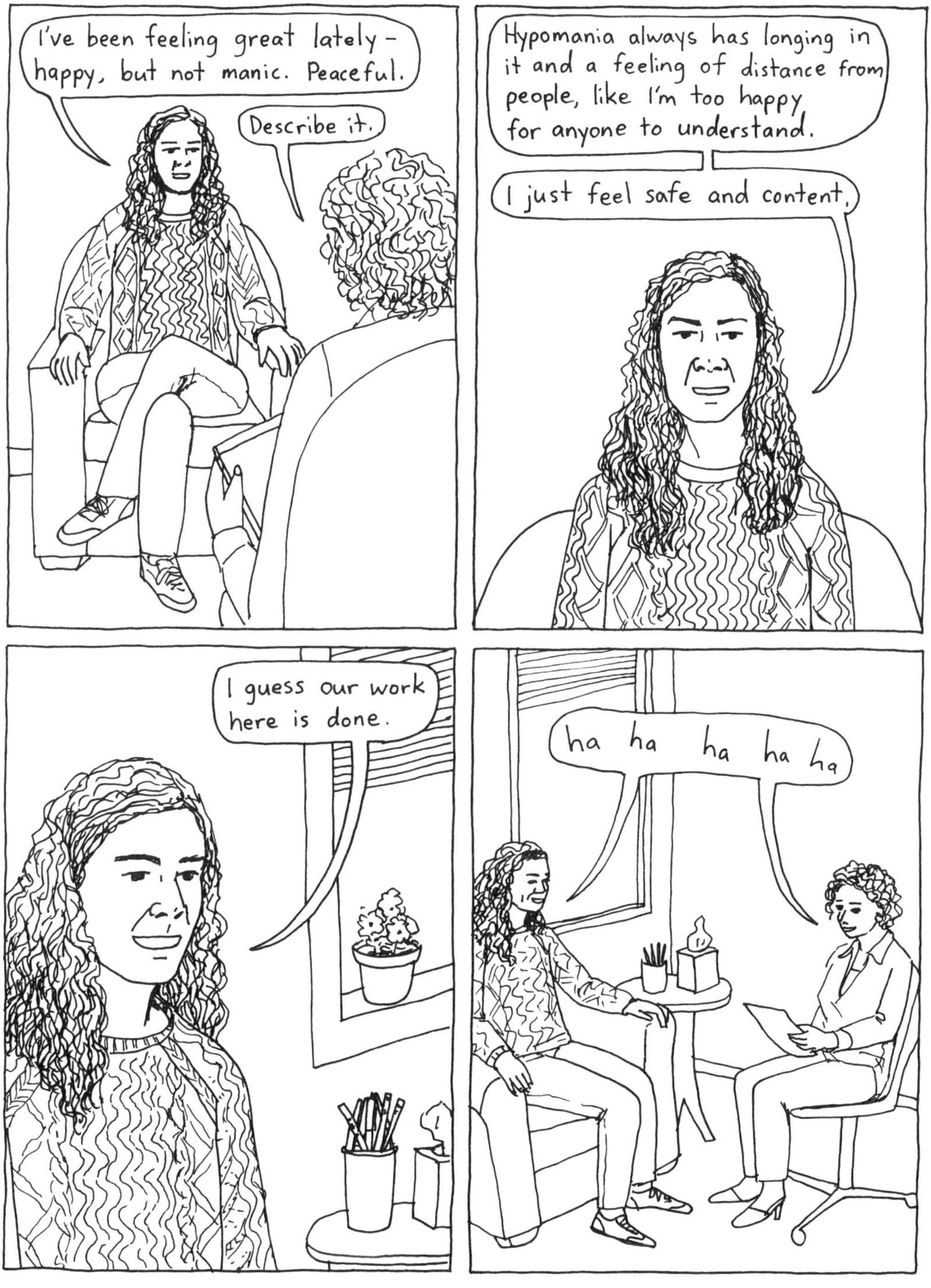
I've been feeling great lately – happy, but not manic. Peaceful.
Describe it.
Hypomania always has longing in it and a feeling of distance from people, like I'm too happy for anyone to understand.
I just feel safe and content.
I guess our work here is done.
ha ha ha ha ha

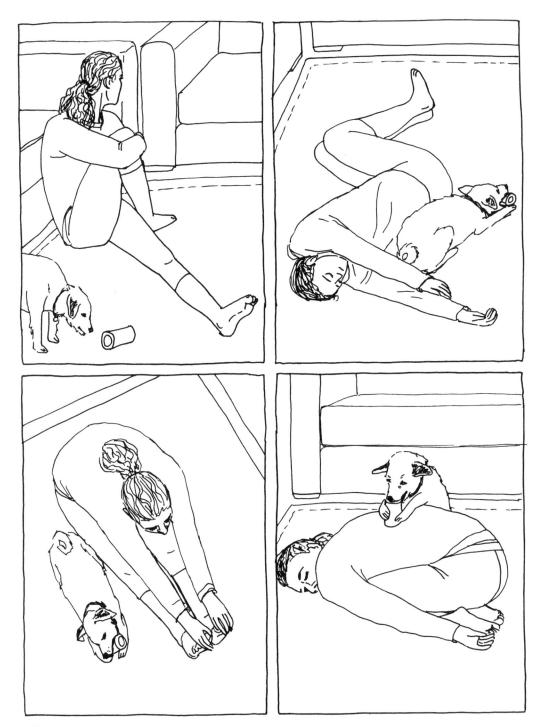

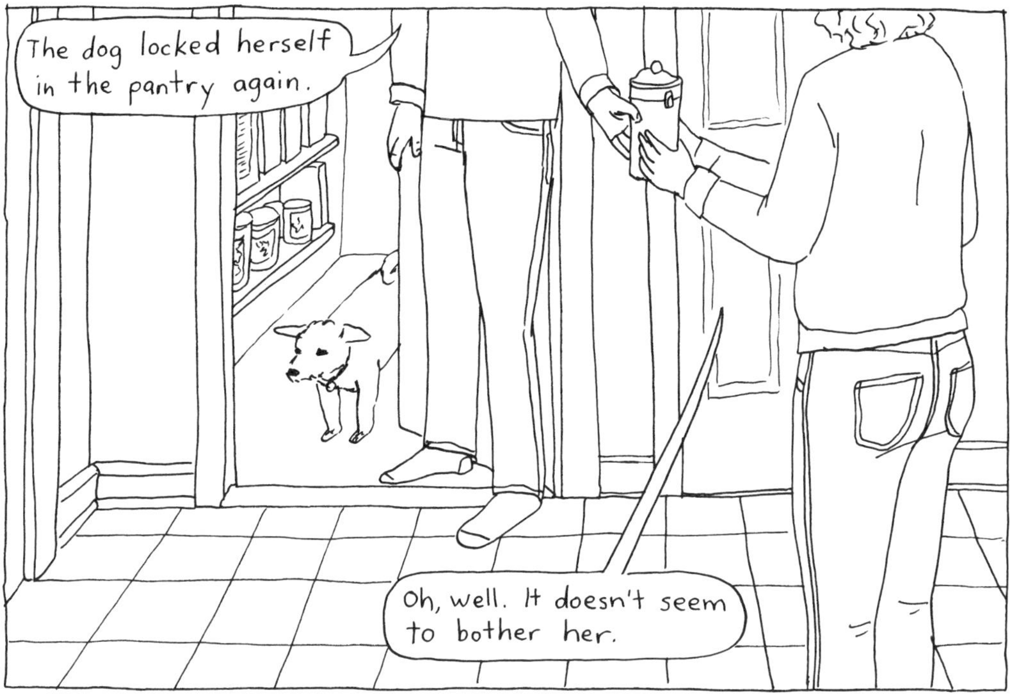
The dog locked herself in the pantry again.
Oh, well. It doesn't seem to bother her.

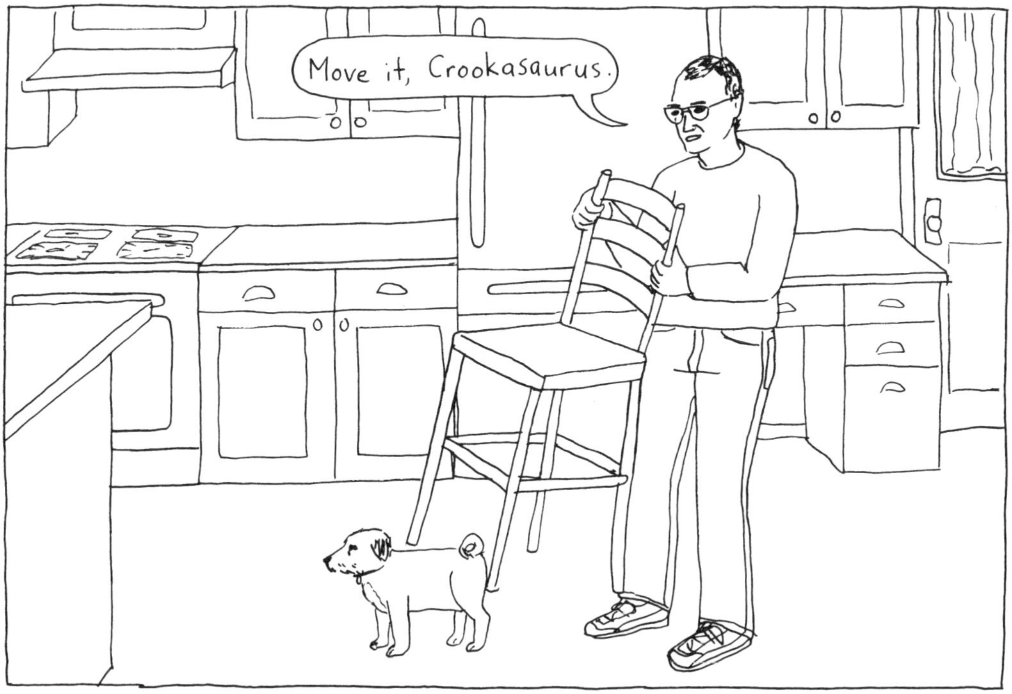
Move it, Crookasaurus.

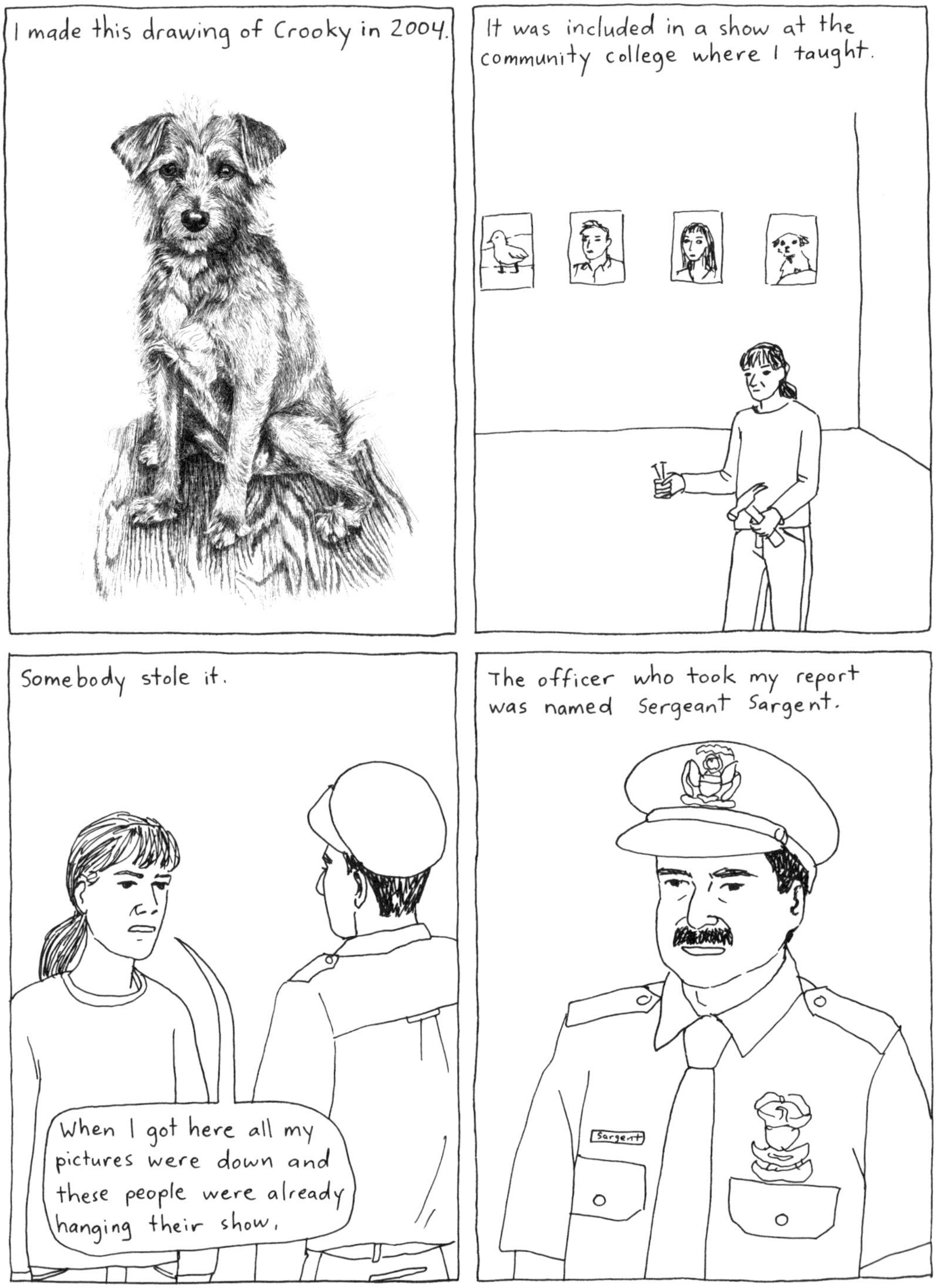
I made this drawing of Crooky in 2004.
It was included in a show at the community college where I taught.
Somebody stole it.
When I got here all my pictures were down and these people were already hanging their show.
The officer who took my report was named Sergeant Sargent.
Sargent

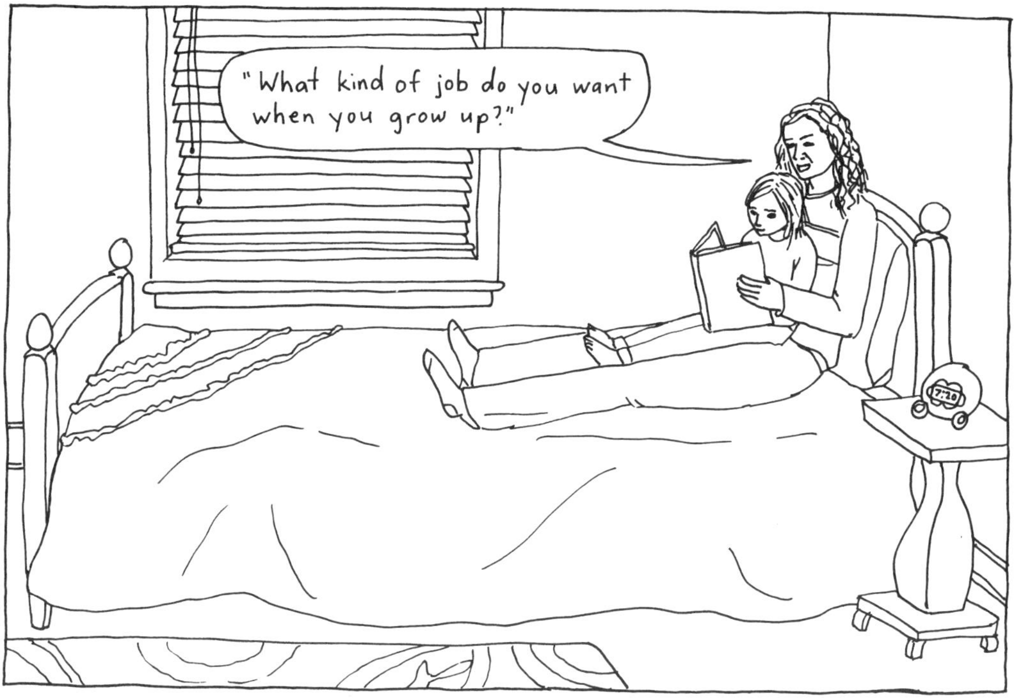
"What kind of job do you want when you grow up?"

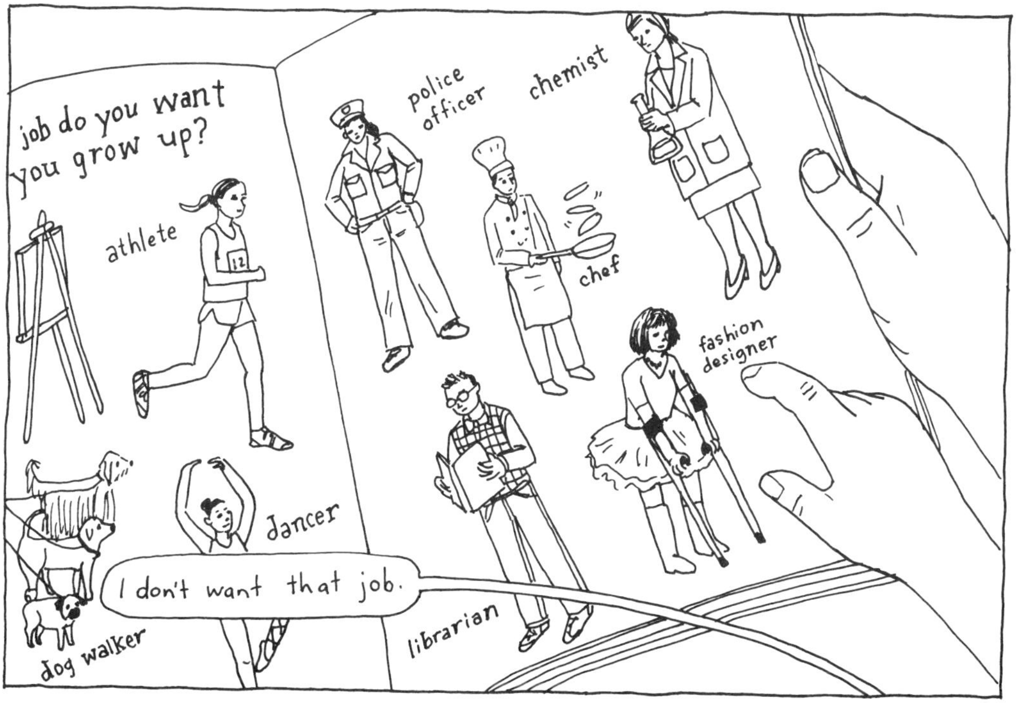
job do you want
you grow up?
athlete
police officer
chemist
chef
fashion designer
dancer
dog walker
librarian
I don't want that job.

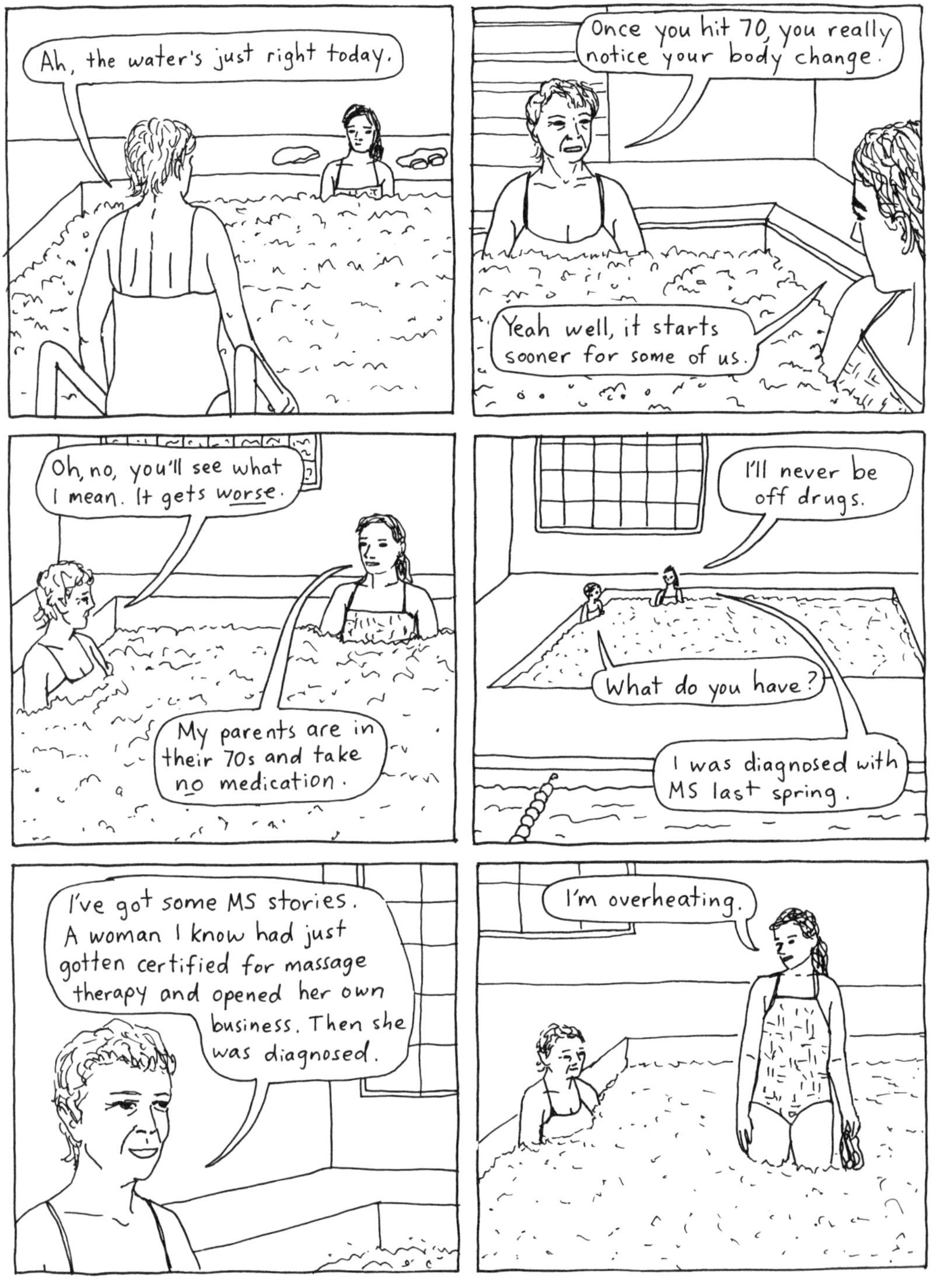

Ah, the water's just right today.
Once you hit 70, you really notice your body change.
Yeah well, it starts sooner for some of us.
Oh, no, you'll see what I mean. It gets worse.
My parents are in their 70s and take no medication.
I'll never be off drugs.
What do you have?
I was diagnosed with MS last spring.
I've got some MS stories. A woman I know had just gotten certified for massage therapy and opened her own business. Then she was diagnosed.
I'm overheating.

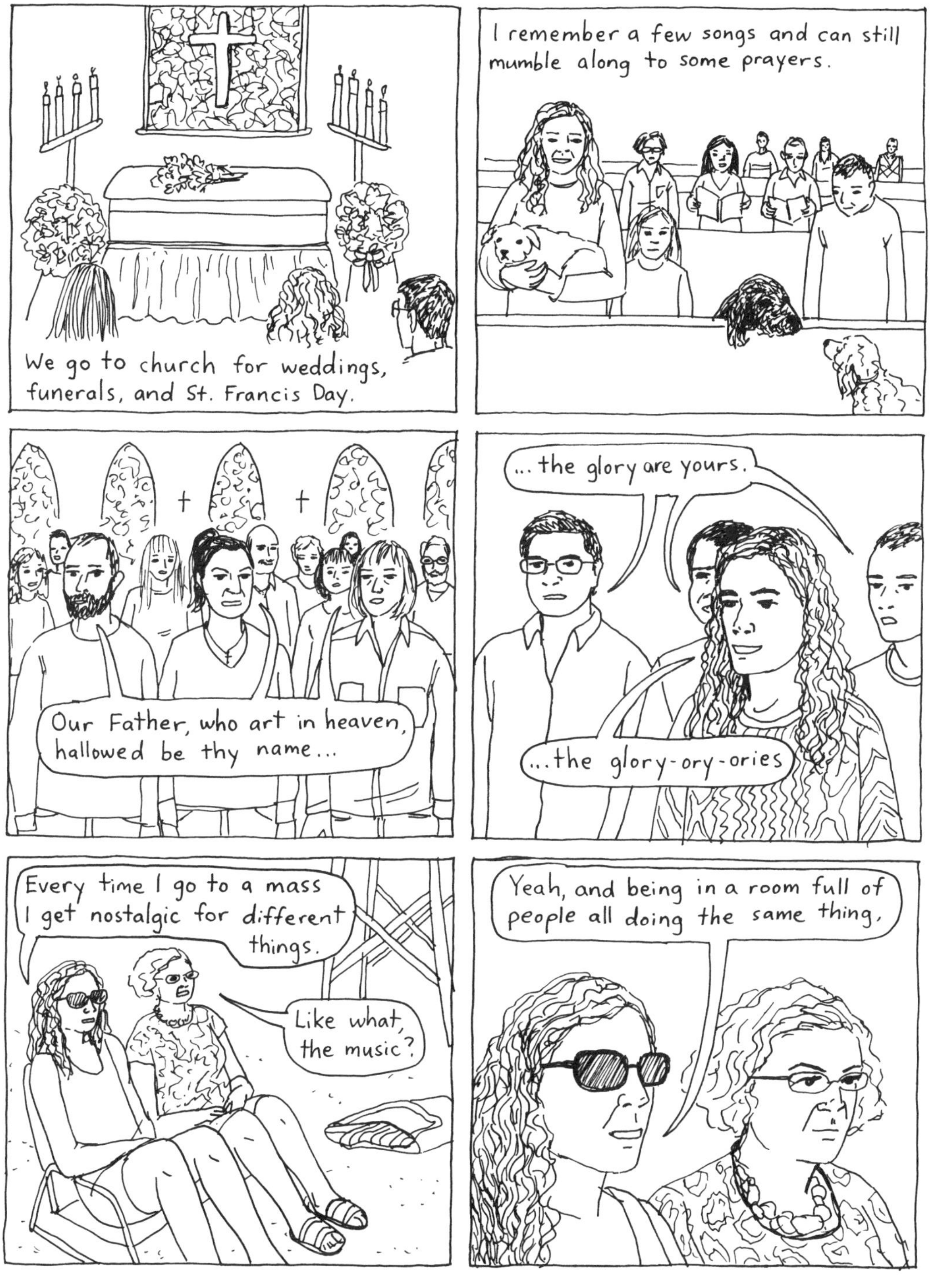

We go to church for weddings, funerals, and St. Francis Day.
I remember a few songs and can still mumble along to some prayers.
Our Father, who art in heaven, hallowed be thy name...
... the glory are yours.
...the glory-ory-ories
Every time I go to a mass I get nostalgic for different things.
Like what, the music?
Yeah, and being in a room full of people all doing the same thing.

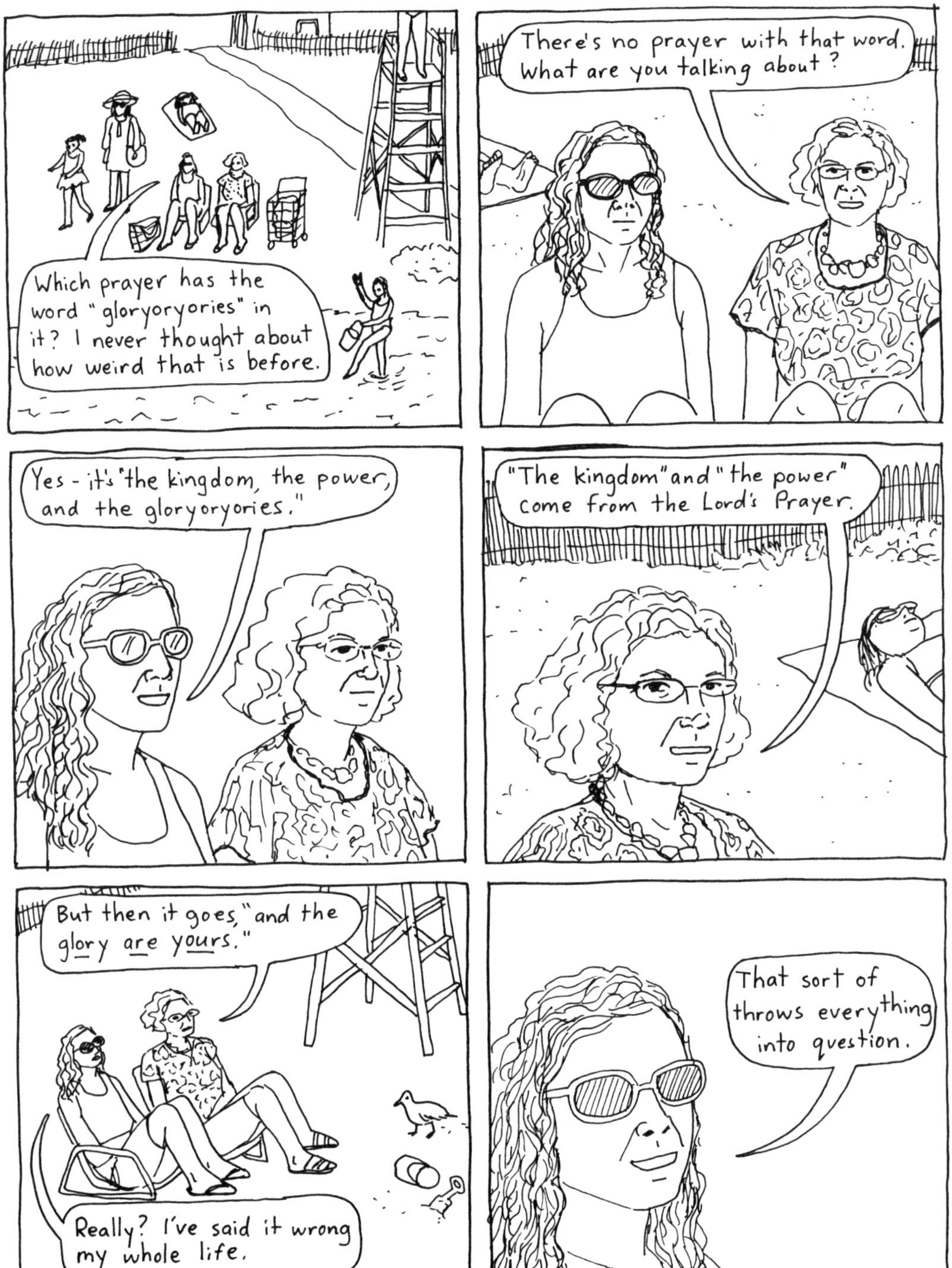
Which prayer has the word "gloryoryories" in it? I never thought about how weird that is before.
There's no prayer with that word. What are you talking about?
Yes - it's "the kingdom, the power, and the gloryoryories."
"The kingdom" and "the power" come from the Lord's Prayer.
But then it goes, "and the glory are yours."
Really? I've said it wrong my whole life.
That sort of throws everything into question.

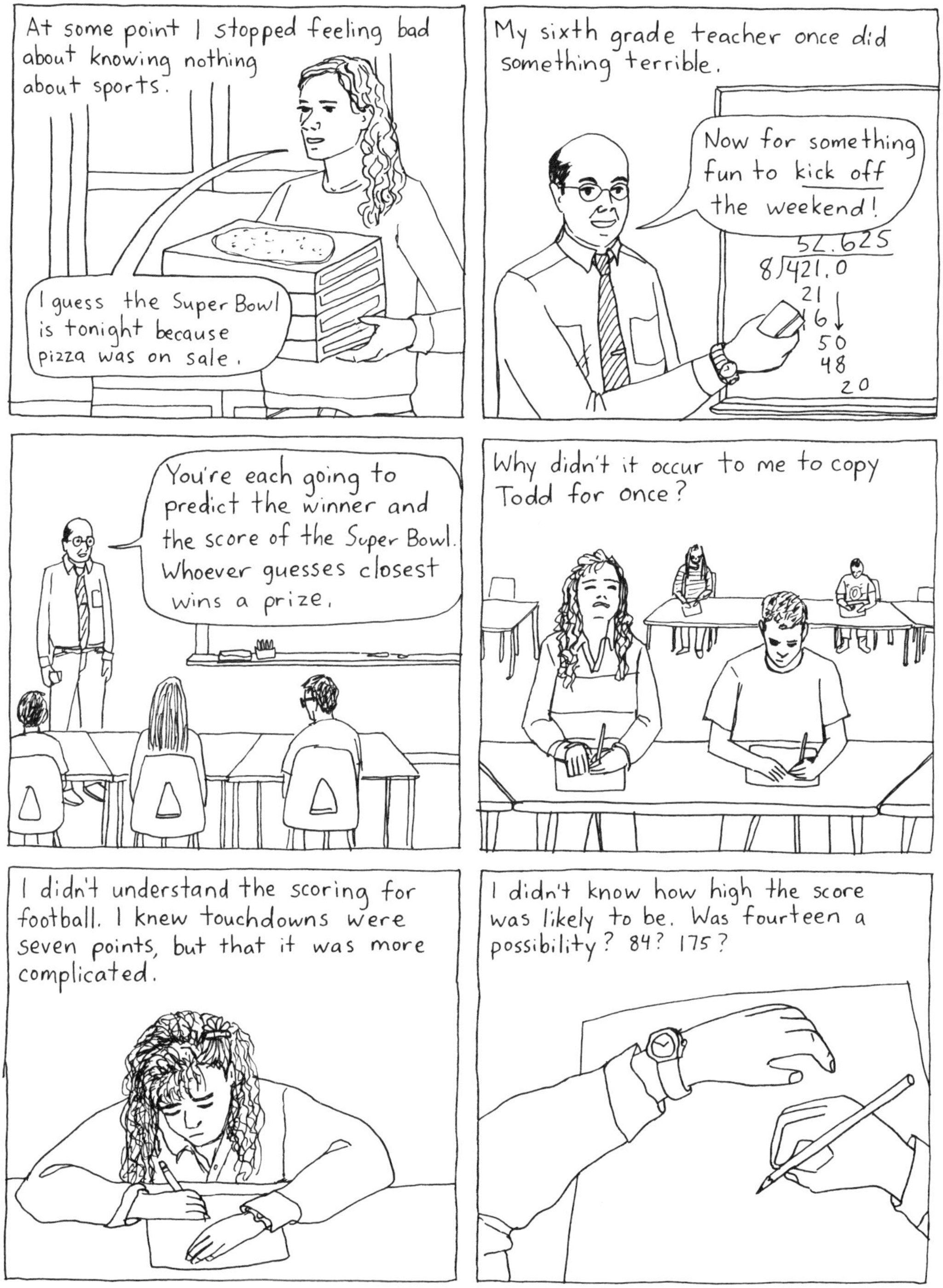
At some point I stopped feeling bad about knowing nothing about sports.
I guess the Super Bowl is tonight because pizza was on sale.
My sixth grade teacher once did something terrible.
Now for something fun to kick off the weekend!
52.625
8)421.0
21
16
50
48
20
You're each going to predict the winner and the score of the Super Bowl. Whoever guesses closest wins a prize.
Why didn't it occur to me to copy Todd for once?
I didn't understand the scoring for football. I knew touchdowns were seven points, but that it was more complicated.
I didn't know how high the score was likely to be. Was fourteen a possibility? 84? 175?

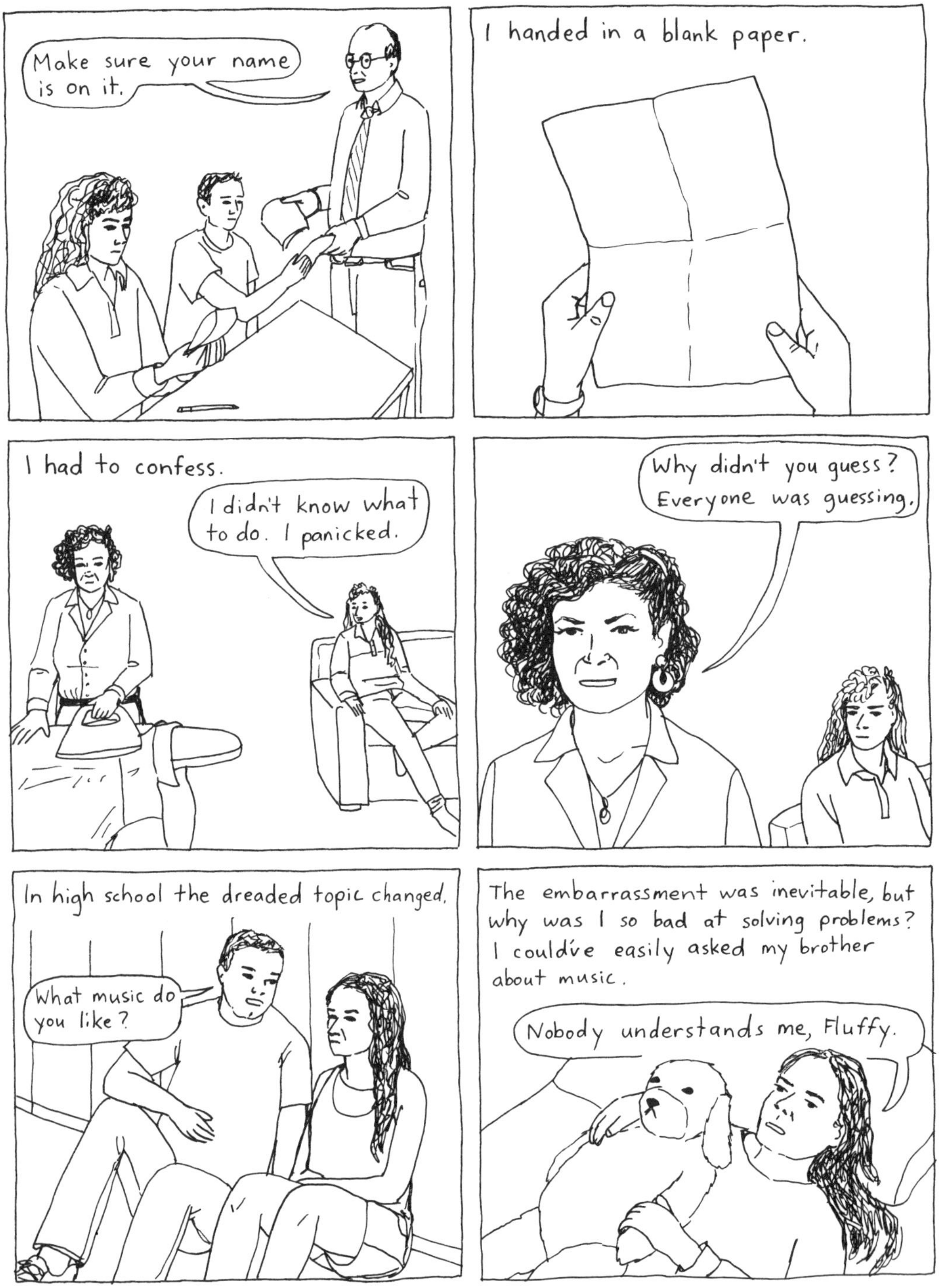
Make sure your name is on it.
I handed in a blank paper.
I had to confess.
I didn't know what to do. I panicked.
Why didn't you guess? Everyone was guessing.
In high school the dreaded topic changed.
What music do you like?
The embarrassment was inevitable, but why was I so bad at solving problems? I could've easily asked my brother about music.
Nobody understands me, Fluffy.

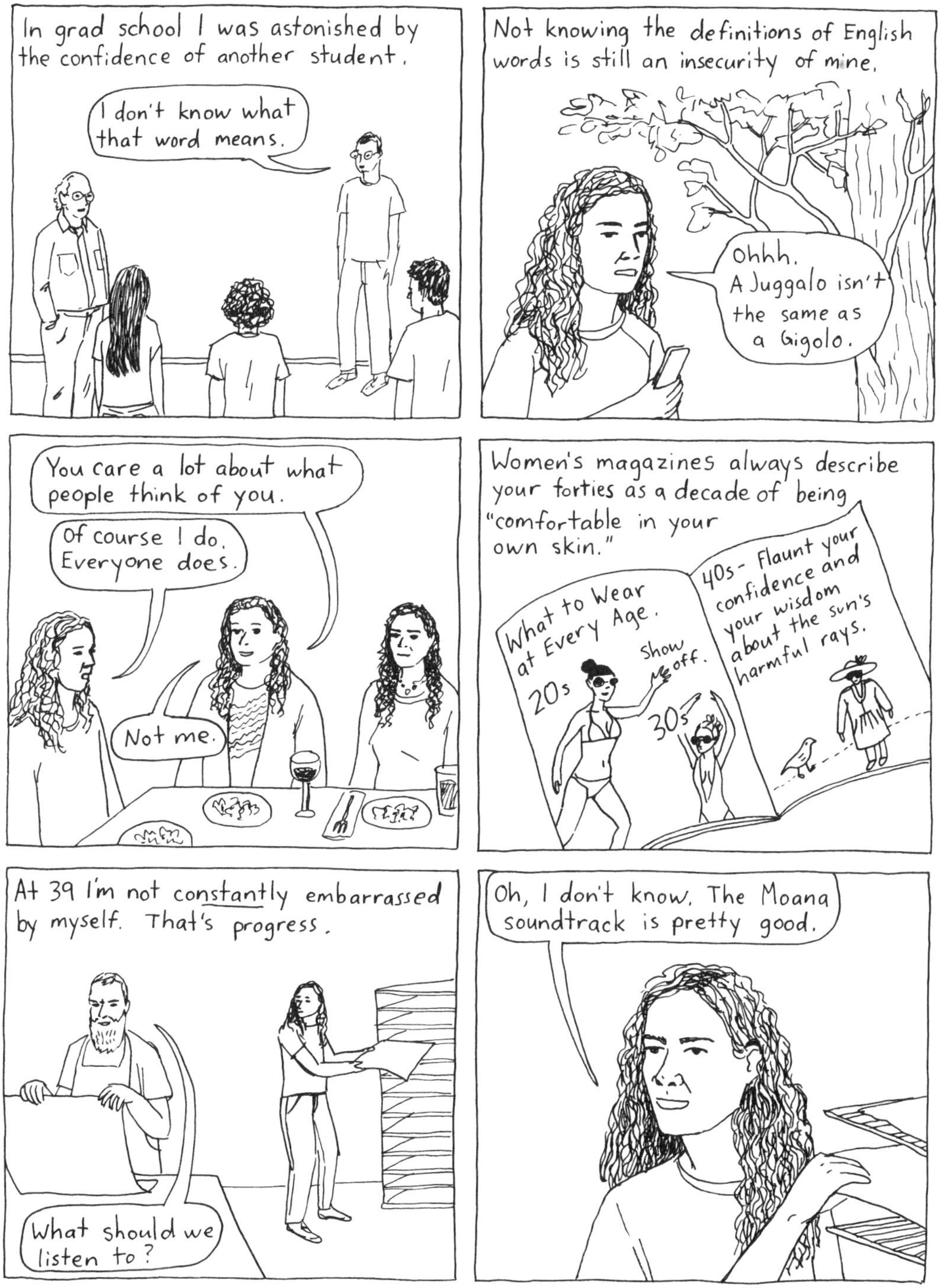
In grad school I was astonished by the confidence of another student.
I don't know what that word means.
Not knowing the definitions of English words is still an insecurity of mine.
Ohhh. A Juggalo isn't the same as a Gigolo.
You care a lot about what people think of you.
Of course I do. Everyone does.
Not me.
Women's magazines always describe your forties as a decade of being "comfortable in your own skin."
What to Wear at Every Age.
20s
Show off.
30s
40s - Flaunt your confidence and your wisdom about the sun's harmful rays.
At 39 I'm not constantly embarrassed by myself. That's progress.
What should we listen to?
Oh, I don't know. The Moana soundtrack is pretty good.

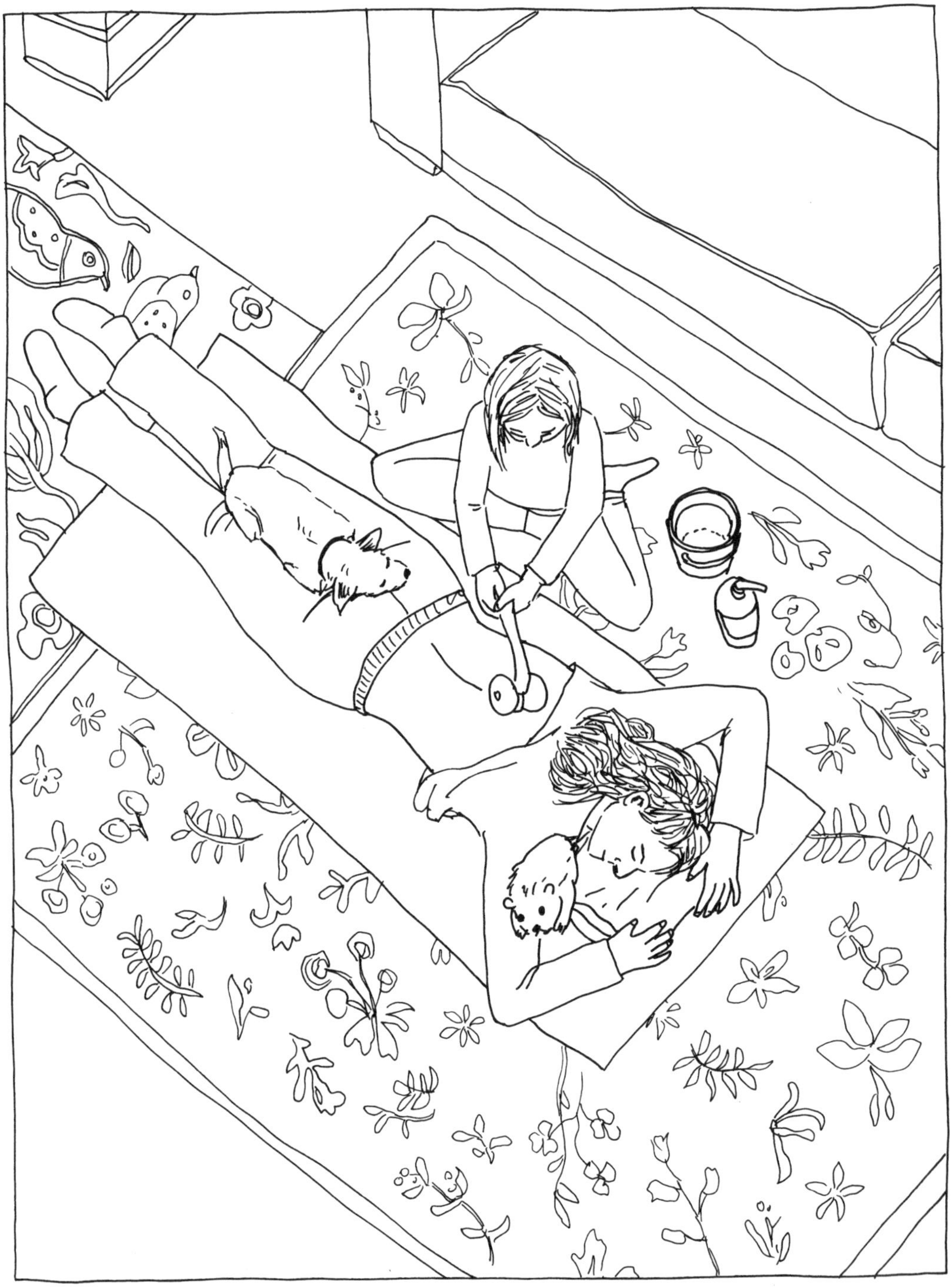

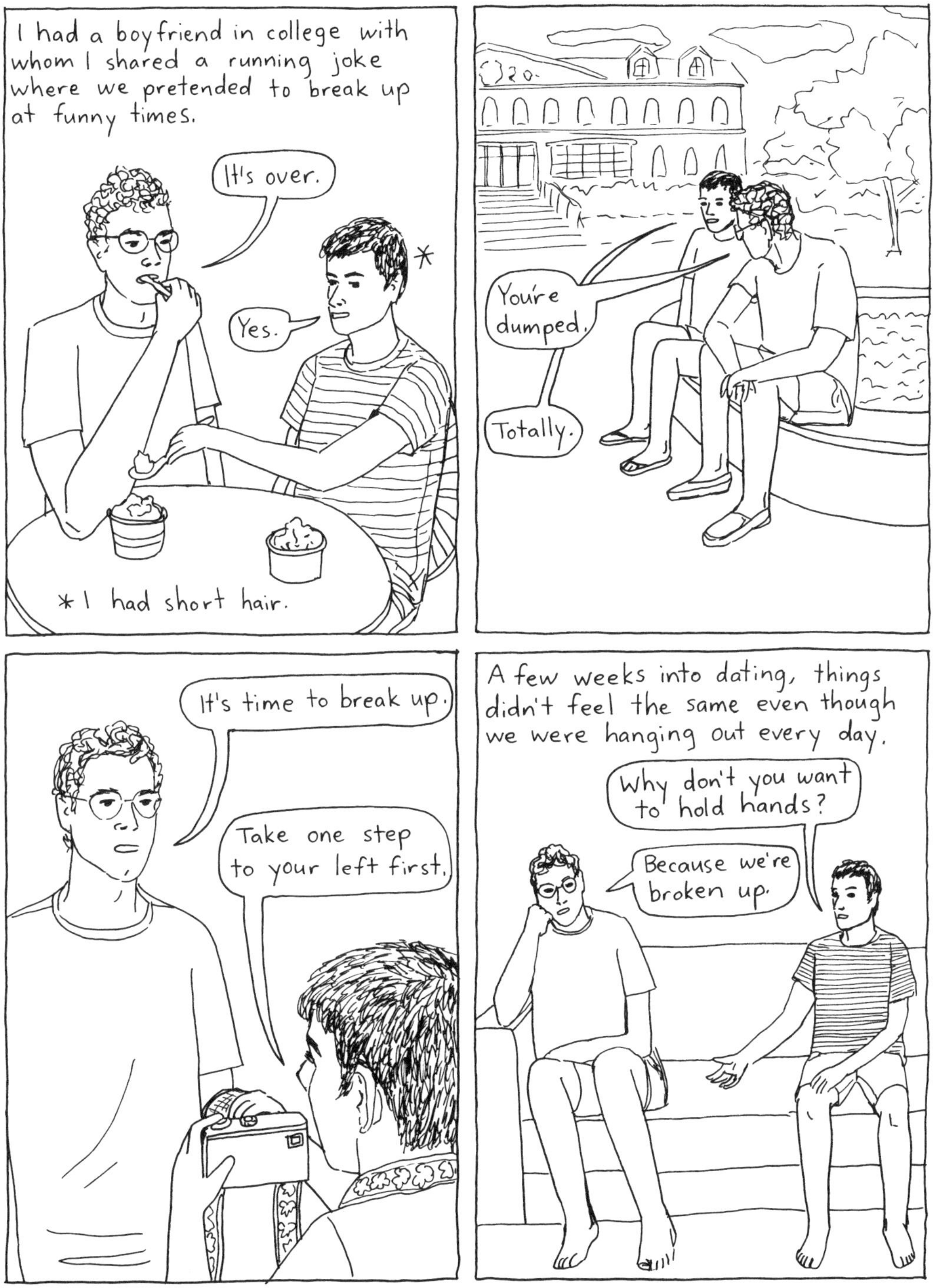
I had a boyfriend in college with whom I shared a running joke where we pretended to break up at funny times.
It's over.
Yes.
*
*I had short hair.
You're dumped.
Totally.
It's time to break up.
Take one step to your left first.
A few weeks into dating, things didn't feel the same even though we were hanging out every day.
Why don't you want to hold hands?
Because we're broken up.

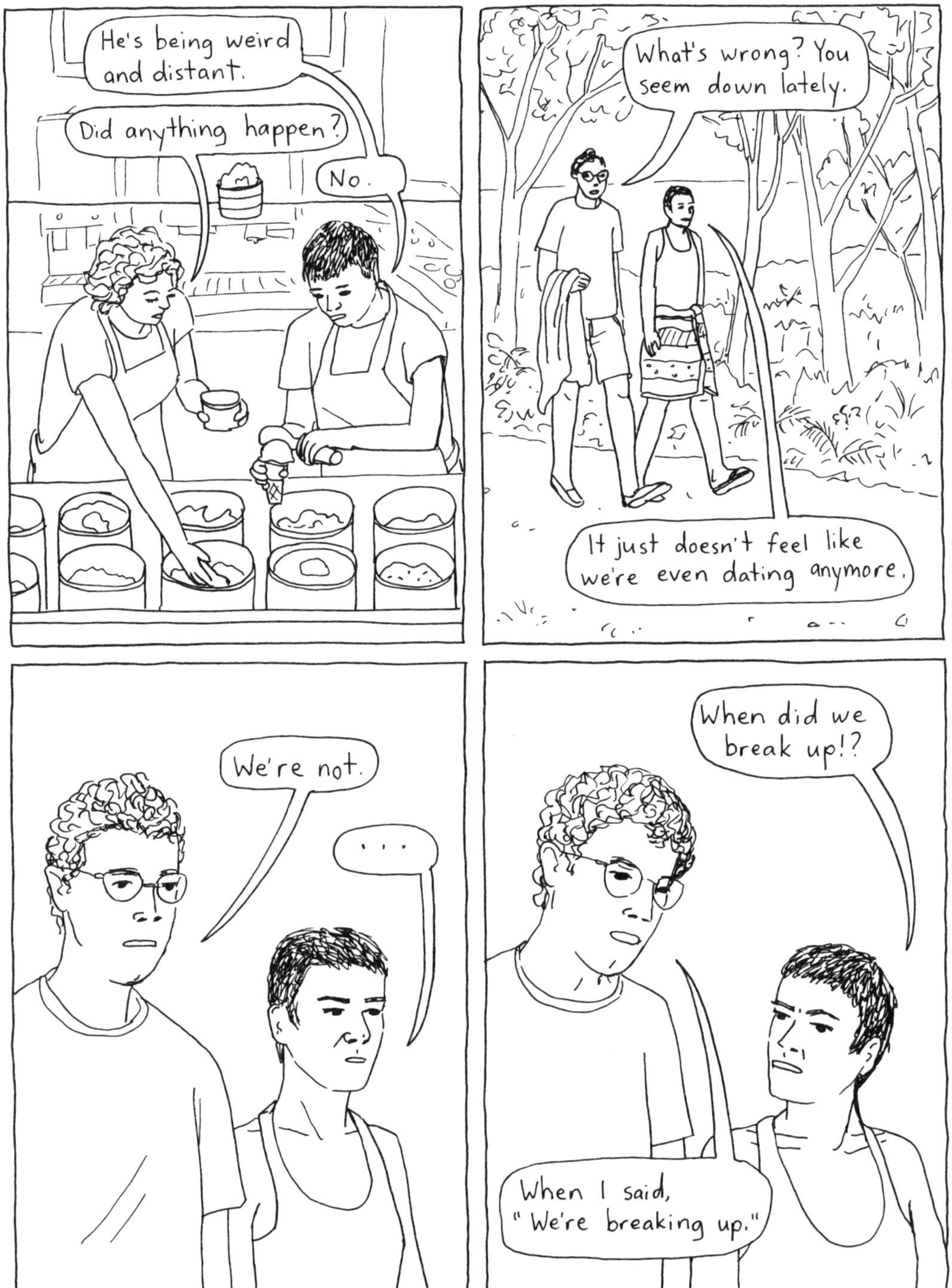
He's being weird and distant.
Did anything happen?
No.
What's wrong? You seem down lately.
It just doesn't feel like we're even dating anymore.
We're not.
...
When did we break up!?
When I said, "We're breaking up."

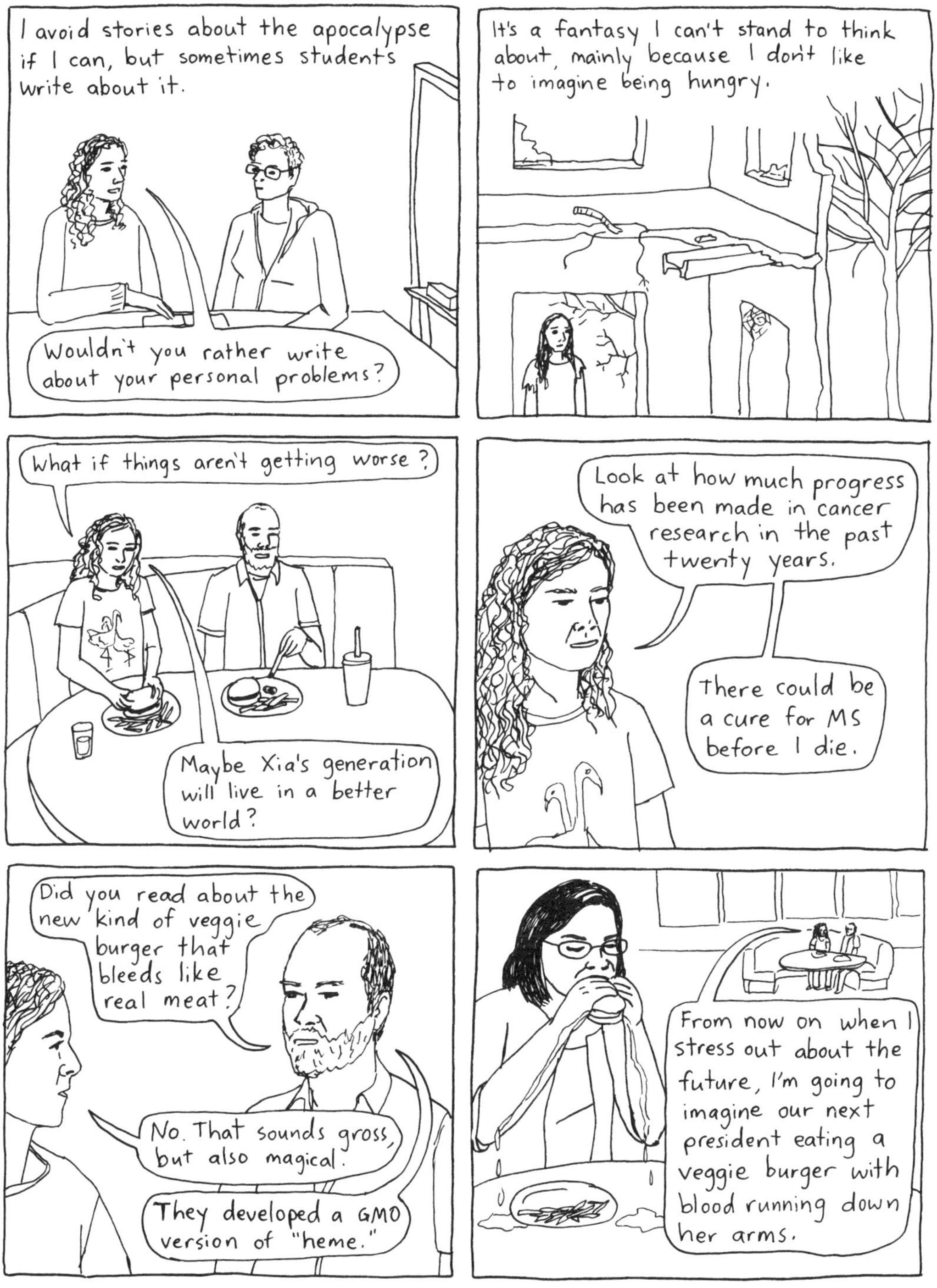
I avoid stories about the apocalypse if I can, but sometimes students write about it.
Wouldn't you rather write about your personal problems?
It's a fantasy I can't stand to think about, mainly because I don't like to imagine being hungry.
What if things aren't getting worse?
Maybe Xia's generation will live in a better world?
Look at how much progress has been made in cancer research in the past twenty years.
There could be a cure for MS before I die.
Did you read about the new kind of veggie burger that bleeds like real meat?
No. That sounds gross, but also magical.
They developed a GMO version of "heme."
From now on when I stress out about the future, I'm going to imagine our next president eating a veggie burger with blood running down her arms.

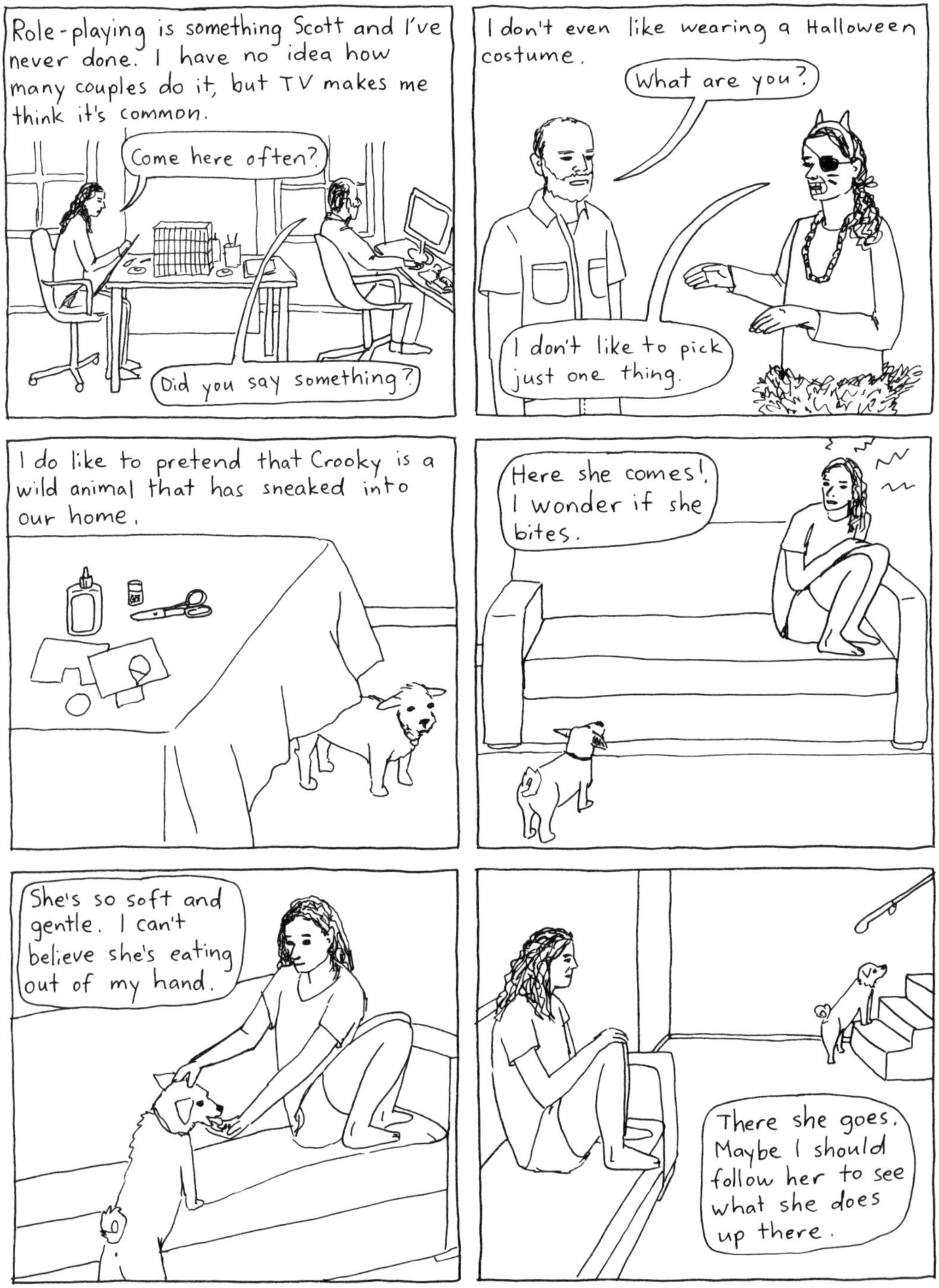
Role-playing is something Scott and I've never done. I have no idea how many couples do it, but TV makes me think it's common.
Come here often?
Did you say something?
I don't even like wearing a Halloween costume.
What are you?
I don't like to pick just one thing.
I do like to pretend that Crooky is a wild animal that has sneaked into our home.
Here she comes! I wonder if she bites.
She's so soft and gentle. I can't believe she's eating out of my hand.
There she goes. Maybe I should follow her to see what she does up there.

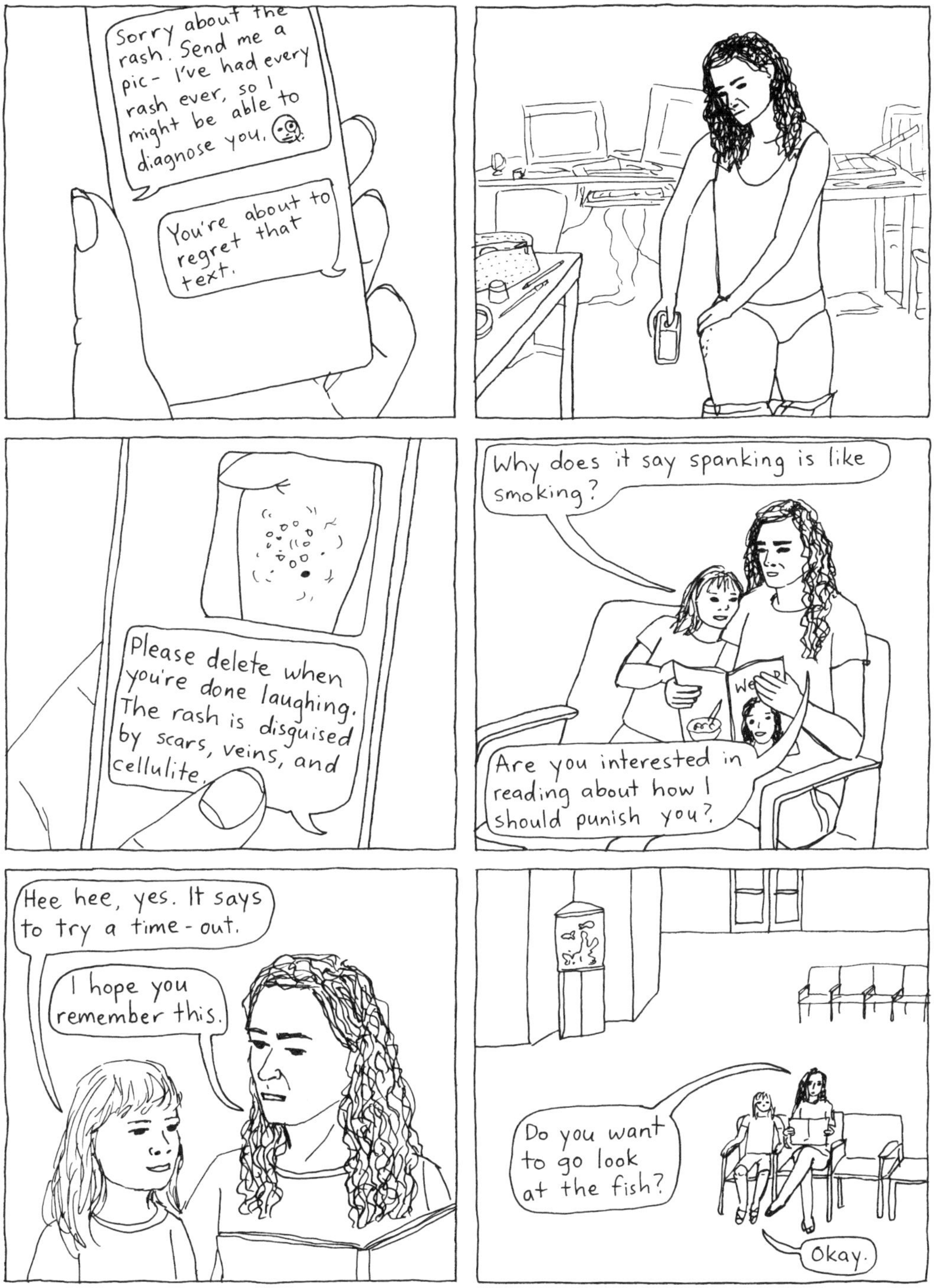
Sorry about the rash. Send me a pic- I've had every rash ever, so I might be able to diagnose you.
You're about to regret that text.
Please delete when you're done laughing. The rash is disguised by scars, veins, and cellulite.
Why does it say spanking is like smoking?
Are you interested in reading about how I should punish you?
Hee hee, yes. It says to try a time-out.
I hope you remember this.
Do you want to go look at the fish?
Okay.

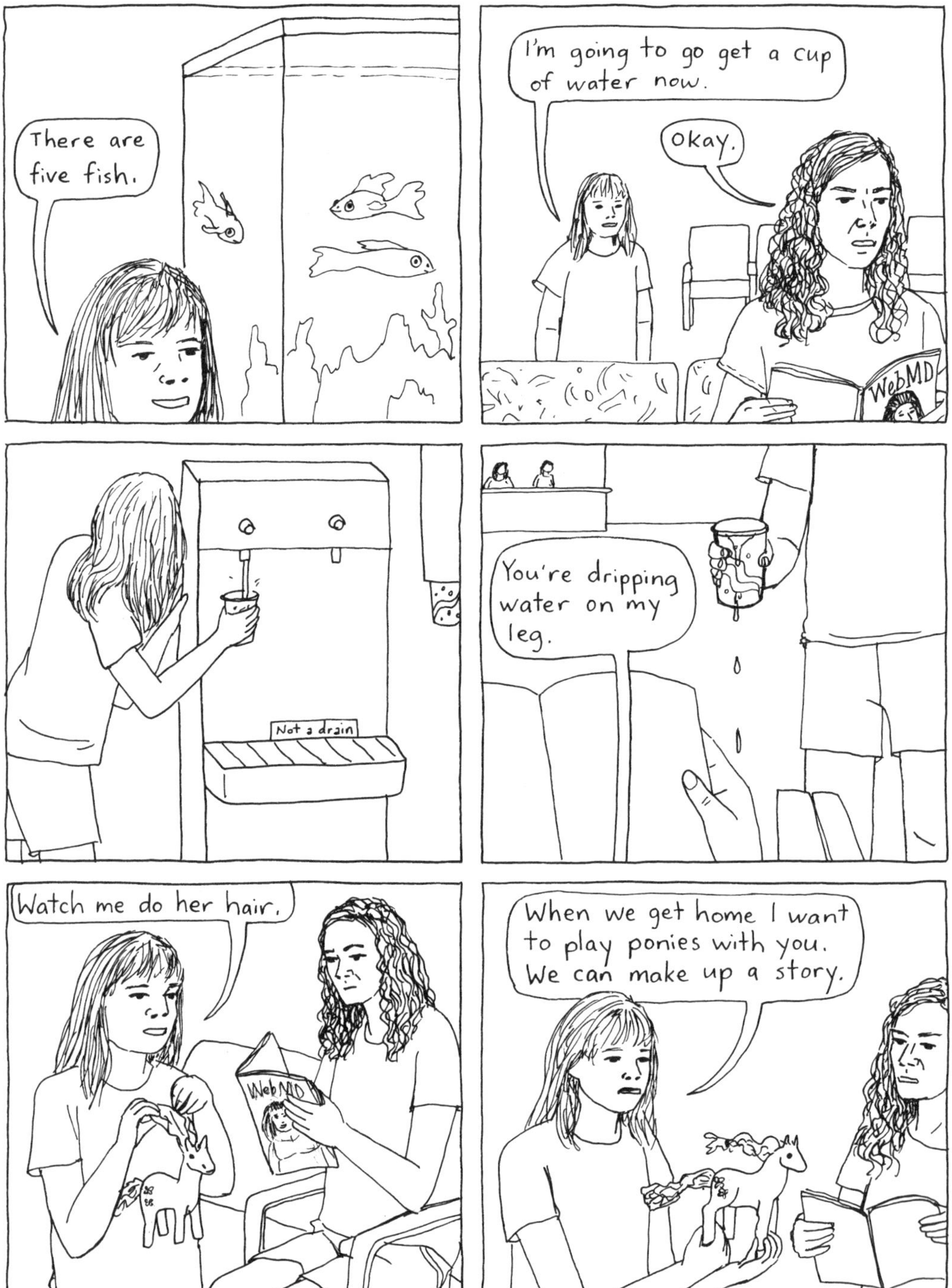
There are five fish.
I'm going to go get a cup of water now.
Okay.
Not a drain
You're dripping water on my leg.
Watch me do her hair.
WebMD
When we get home I want to play ponies with you. We can make up a story.

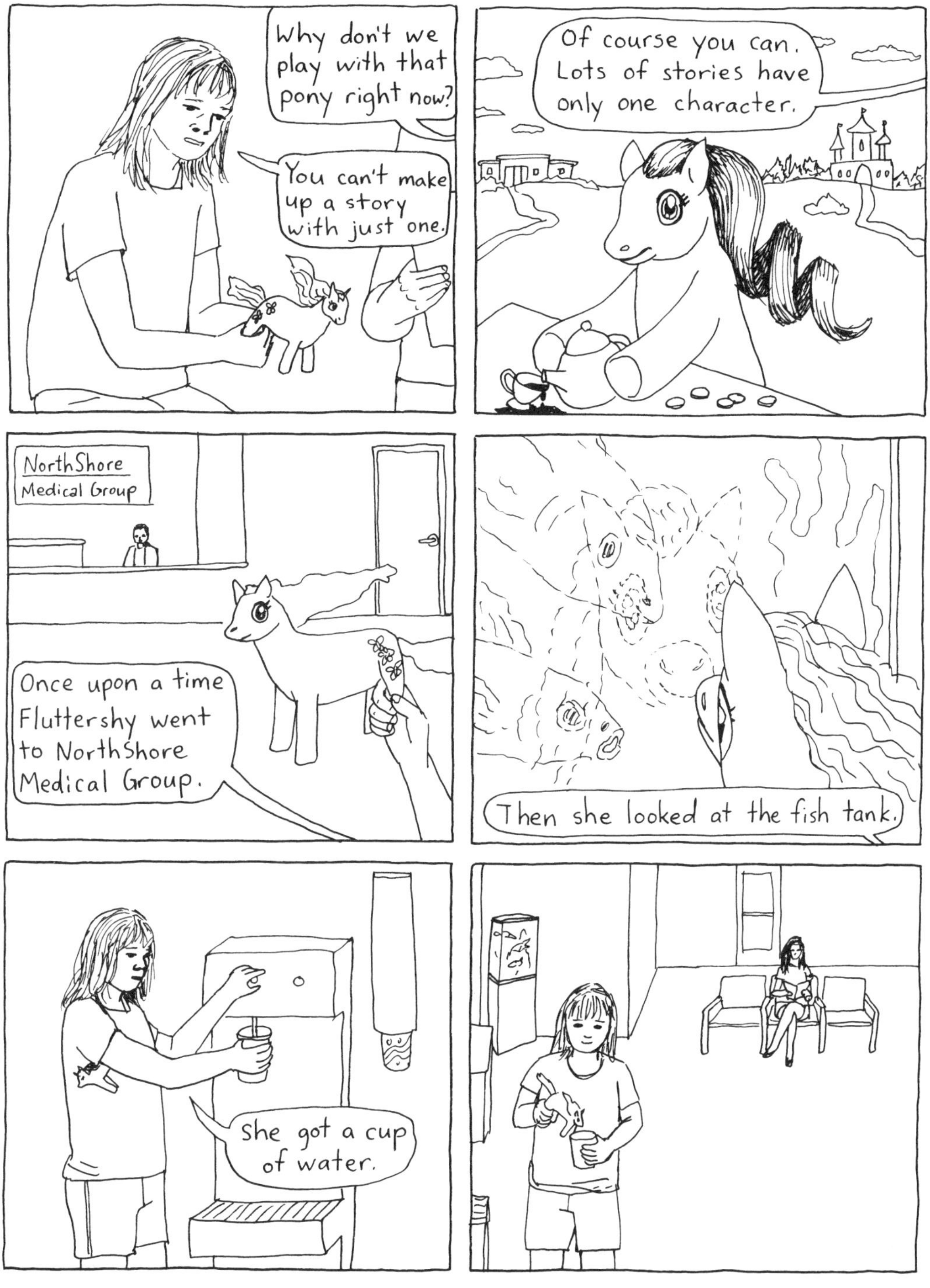
Why don't we play with that pony right now?
You can't make up a story with just one.
Of course you can. Lots of stories have only one character.
NorthShore Medical Group
Once upon a time Fluttershy went to NorthShore Medical Group.
Then she looked at the fish tank.
She got a cup of water.

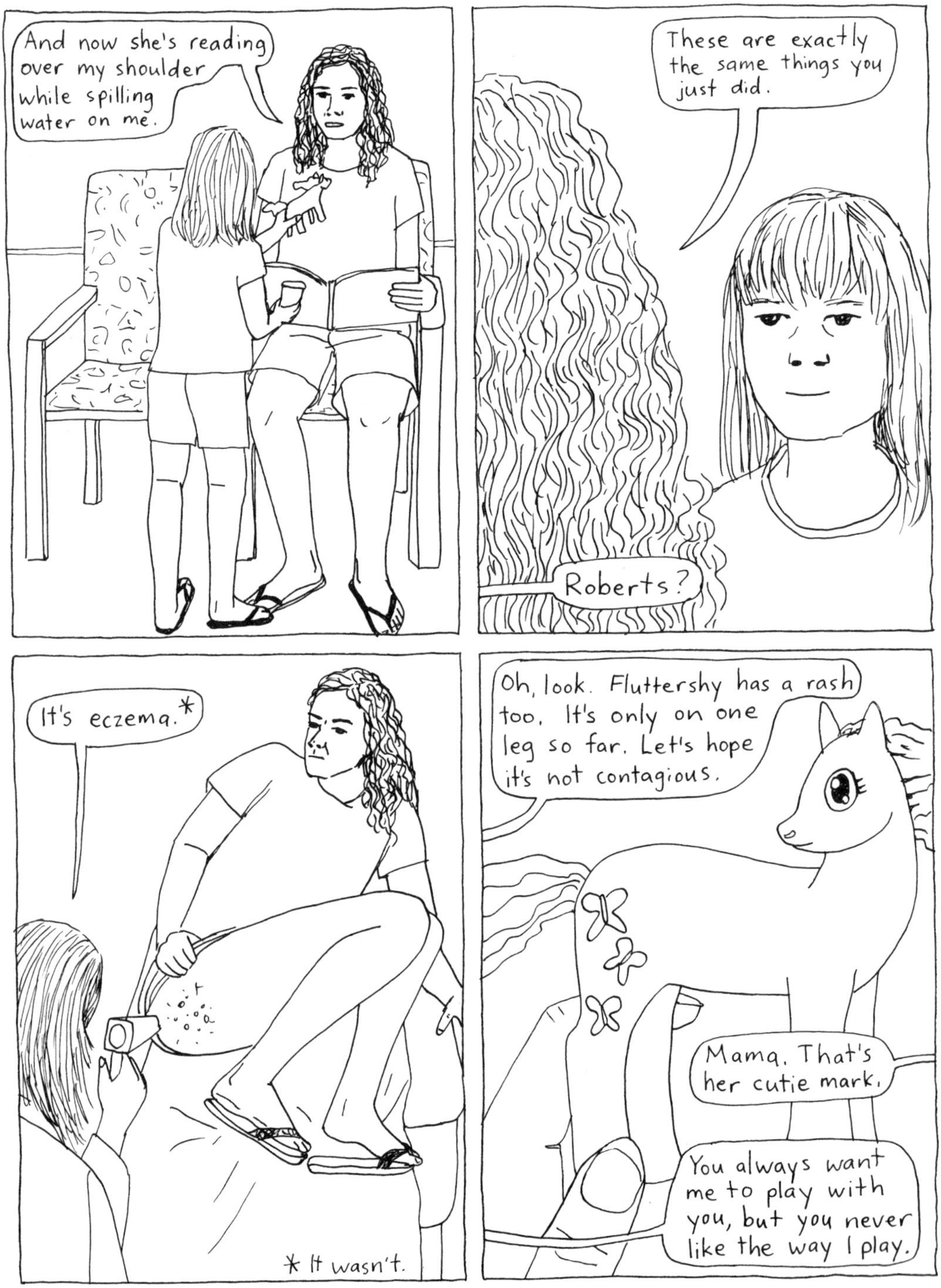
And now she's reading over my shoulder while spilling water on me.
These are exactly the same things you just did.
Roberts?
It's eczema.*
* It wasn't.
Oh, look. Fluttershy has a rash too. It's only on one leg so far. Let's hope it's not contagious.
Mama. That's her cutie mark.
You always want me to play with you, but you never like the way I play.

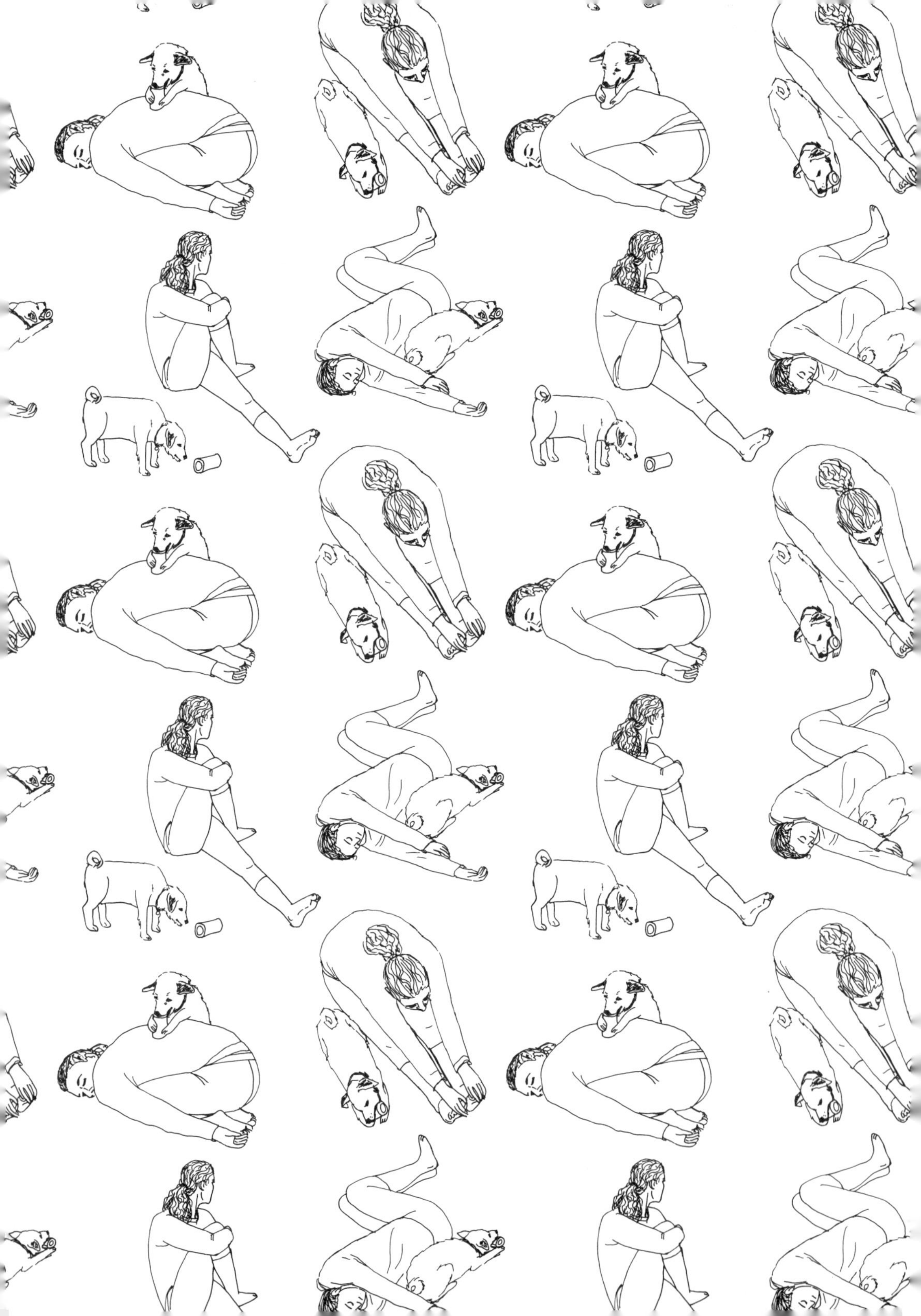